Mathematics in Context

BRITANNICA
Mathematics in Context

Level 1

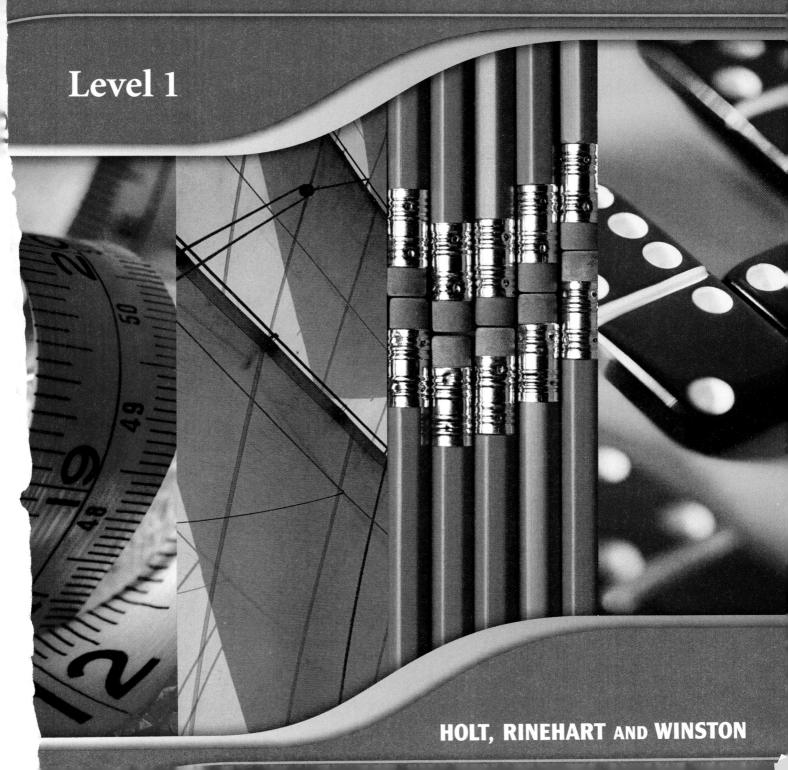

HOLT, RINEHART AND **WINSTON**

ISBN 0-03-040374-X

3 4 5 6 073 09 08 07 06

Picturing Numbers

Data Analysis and Probability

BRITANNICA
Mathematics in Context

HOLT, RINEHART AND WINSTON

Mathematics in Context is a comprehensive curriculum for the middle grades. It was developed in 1991 through 1997 in collaboration with the Wisconsin Center for Education Research, School of Education, University of Wisconsin-Madison and the Freudenthal Institute at the University of Utrecht, The Netherlands, with the support of the National Science Foundation Grant No. 9054928.

The revision of the curriculum was carried out in 2003 through 2005, with the support of the National Science Foundation Grant No. ESI 0137414.

 **National Science Foundation**
Opinions expressed are those of the authors
and not necessarily those of the Foundation.

Boswinkel, N., Niehaus, J., Gravemeijer, K., Wijers, M., Dekker, T., Middleton, J. A., Spence, M. S., Burrill, G., & Milinkovic, J. (2006). *Picturing numbers.* In Wisconsin Center for Education Research & Freudenthal Institute (Eds.), Mathematics in Context. Chicago: Encyclopædia Britannica, Inc.

ISBN 0-03-042402-X

1 2 3 4 5 6   073   09 08 07 06 05

The *Mathematics in Context* Development Team

Development 1991–1997

The initial version of *Picturing Numbers* was developed by Nina Boswinkel, Jansie Niehaus, and Koeno Gravemeijer. It was adapted for use in American schools by James A, Middleton, Mary S. Spence, Gail Burrill, and Jasmina Milinkovic.

Wisconsin Center for Education

Research Staff

Thomas A. Romberg
Director

Joan Daniels Pedro
Assistant to the Director

Gail Burrill
Coordinator

Margaret R. Meyer
Coordinator

Project Staff

Jonathan Brendefur
Laura Brinker
James Browne
Jack Burrill
Rose Byrd
Peter Christiansen
Barbara Clarke
Doug Clarke
Beth R. Cole
Fae Dremock
Mary Ann Fix

Sherian Foster
James A, Middleton
Jasmina Milinkovic
Margaret A. Pligge
Mary C. Shafer
Julia A. Shew
Aaron N. Simon
Marvin Smith
Stephanie Z. Smith
Mary S. Spence

Freudenthal Institute Staff

Jan de Lange
Director

Els Feijs
Coordinator

Martin van Reeuwijk
Coordinator

Mieke Abels
Nina Boswinkel
Frans van Galen
Koeno Gravemeijer
Marja van den Heuvel-Panhuizen
Jan Auke de Jong
Vincent Jonker
Ronald Keijzer
Martin Kindt

Jansie Niehaus
Nanda Querelle
Anton Roodhardt
Leen Streefland
Adri Treffers
Monica Wijers
Astrid de Wild

Revision 2003–2005

The revised version of *Picturing Numbers* was developed by Monica Wijers and Truus Dekker. It was adapted for use in American schools by Gail Burrill.

Wisconsin Center for Education

Research Staff

Thomas A. Romberg
Director

David C. Webb
Coordinator

Gail Burrill
Editorial Coordinator

Margaret A. Pligge
Editorial Coordinator

Project Staff

Sarah Ailts
Beth R. Cole
Erin Hazlett
Teri Hedges
Karen Hoiberg
Carrie Johnson
Jean Krusi
Elaine McGrath

Margaret R. Meyer
Anne Park
Bryna Rappaport
Kathleen A. Steele
Ana C. Stephens
Candace Ulmer
Jill Vettrus

Freudenthal Institute Staff

Jan de Lange
Director

Truus Dekker
Coordinator

Mieke Abels
Content Coordinator

Monica Wijers
Content Coordinator

Arthur Bakker
Peter Boon
Els Feijs
Dédé de Haan
Martin Kindt

Nathalie Kuijpers
Huub Nilwik
Sonia Palha
Nanda Querelle
Martin van Reeuwijk

Cover photo credits: (left, right) © Getty Images; (middle) © Corbis

Illustrations
v Christine McCabe/© Encyclopædia Britannica, Inc.; 1 Holly Cooper-Olds; 6 Christine McCabe/© Encyclopædia Britannica, Inc.; 26, 28, 37, 41 Holly Cooper-Olds

Photographs
1 © Corbis; 3 © Louis K. Meisel Gallery, Inc./Corbis; 4 Sam Dudgeon/HRW; 7 © Bettmann/Corbis; 10 Victoria Smith/HRW; 11 © Corbis; 12 Victoria Smith/HRW; 13 (left to right) © Corbis; Sam Dudgeon/HRW; 16 © Corbis; 17 (left to right) © Comstock, Inc.; Allan Munsie/Alamy; Jenny Thomas Photography/HRW Photo; 19 © Corel; 21 © Brand X Pictures; (left to right) © Corbis; © Joe McDonald/Corbis; 25 Fotosonline/Alamy; 29 © Corbis; 32 © Annie Griffiths Belt/Corbis; 35, 36 © Corbis; 38 Dennis MacDonald/Alamy; 39 © Corbis; 40 © PhotoDisc/Getty Images

◆ Contents

Letter to the Student   vi

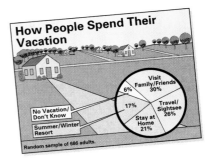

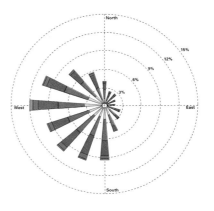

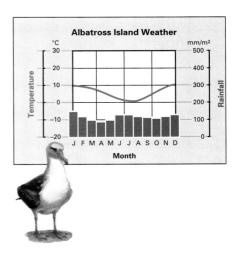

Dear Student,

Can you picture numbers? Sometimes a picture of the numbers in a problem makes things easier to understand.

In this unit, you will discover different ways to picture numbers. Pictures can help you tell a story about numbers and about what they represent such as fliers delivered, fuel in a tank gauges, and TV programs preferred.

You will look at bar graphs and number line plots. You will make a picture called a line graph to show how temperatures change from one time interval to the next.

You will create charts that look like pies to describe the results of your own surveys.

You will also begin to describe a distribution of data by some summary numbers—such as the maximum, the minimum, the mean, and the mode. You will learn how to think about the word *average* as the mean of a set of numbers.

In the end, you should understand something about how pictures can describe numbers and what types of pictures can help you understand different situations.

	Number of Babies in Litter								
Litter	1	2	3	4	5	6	7	8	9
A									
B									
C									
D									
E									
F									
G									
H									
I									
J									
K									
L									
M									
N									
O									
P									
Q									
R									

Sincerely,

The Mathematics in Context Development Team

Using Bar Graphs

Fliers

The number of whales in the world is decreasing rapidly. Peter, Carmenza, and Ann want to do something about the situation. They earn money by delivering advertising fliers to people's houses. For every flier they deliver, they get five cents, which they donate to the World Wildlife Fund.

Today, Peter delivered 100 fliers, Carmenza 200, and Ann 50.

1. How much money did the three of them earn?

Helen, Amber, John, and Diego also delivered fliers. In the table, you can see how many each of them delivered.

2. How many fliers were delivered in total?

Student	Peter	Carmenza	Ann	John	Amber	Helen	Diego
Number of Fliers Delivered	100	200	50	50	100	250	250

Peter showed the information about the number of fliers in the graph below. He called his display a *one-bar graph*.

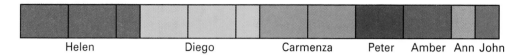

Helen   Diego   Carmenza   Peter   Amber Ann John

3. a. Name one advantage of Peter's one-bar graph compared to the table.

b. Name one disadvantage of Peter's one-bar graph compared to the table.

Number of Fliers Delivered

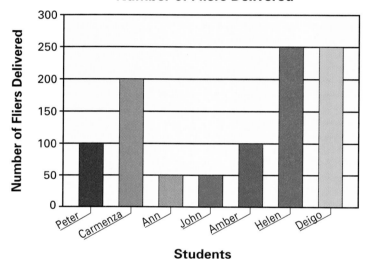

You can also present the data from the table in a **bar graph**, which uses a bar for each category rather than one bar as Peter did. In a bar graph, all bars have the same width.

4. a. Which way of presenting the number of fliers delivered do you prefer, the table or the bar graph? Why?

b. Reflect Think of another way to arrange the bars in the graph. What is one advantage of your new graph over the one above?

A bar graph has two **axes**, a **vertical axis** and a **horizontal axis**. In this graph, the vertical axis shows you how many fliers were delivered. The horizontal axis shows you who delivered them. A graph needs labels and a title in order to tell its story.

You could also make a bar graph showing how much money each student earned.

5. a. What would this graph look like?

b. How would it compare to the graph showing the number of fliers delivered?

Marbles

Bar graphs can be used to compare sizes or amounts of different things. On this graph, the horizontal axis identifies the things that are being compared (students). The vertical axis tells how many (marbles).

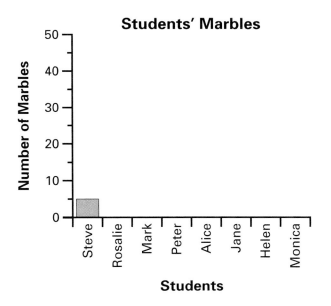

Here you can see that Steve has five marbles. Suppose you also know that:

- Rosalie has twice as many marbles as Steve.
- Mark has four times as many marbles as Rosalie.
- Peter has four marbles more than Steve.
- Alice has as many marbles as Steve.
- Jane has five fewer marbles than Rosalie.
- Helen lost all of the marbles she had.
- Monica has as many marbles as Rosalie.

6. Using the information on page 3, complete the bar graph on **Student Activity Sheet 1**.

7. **a.** Who has the most marbles? How many is that?

   b. Who has the fewest? How many is that?

   c. Explain how you got your answers.

Jose found another way to show how many marbles each person has. Look at his drawing called a picture graph.

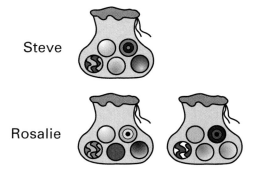

8. Make a graph to show how many marbles each student has. Make your graph different from José's graph and the one on **Student Activity Sheet 1**. Be sure to label everything on your graph.

How Long?

Elena is sure she can stand on one foot a really long time. She challenges Tomas, and he agrees to see who can stand longer. But he says they have to stand on one foot with their eyes shut!

9. **Reflect** Do you think it makes a difference whether their eyes are open or closed? Why or why not?

Have a classmate record how many seconds you can stand on one foot with your eyes shut. Write the number of seconds on a self-stick note. Then time how long a classmate can do this.

One way to picture data for your class is by recording the data on a **number line**. Your teacher has made a number line on the board. Tape your self-stick note at the appropriate spot on the number line. This way of picturing numbers is called a **number-line plot** or **dot plot**.

Use the number-line plot your class made on the board to answer questions 10–13.

10. a. Describe how long the students in your class can stand on one foot with their eyes closed.

b. What times seem to be the most common?

c. What is the *range* of times in your class?

11. a. What times seemed to be in the middle?

b. Was anyone able to stand for a really long time? How long? A really short time? How short?

The number-line plot is a graph of the length of times all of your classmates can stand on one foot with their eyes closed. Many of you probably have times that are pretty close together.

12. a. Group the times that are close together and tell what happens to the plot.

b. On **Student Activity Sheet 2**, complete the table using the data from your class. Are the groups in the table different from the ones chosen on the board?

13. Complete the graph on **Student Activity Sheet 2**, using the data from your table. Note that the bars in this graph should be drawn next to each other. The widths of all bars should be equal.

Your graph will look different from the graph made with the self-stick notes.

14. Reflect Explain how the new graph is different. What advantages does this graph have over the number-line plot?
What disadvantages?

Suppose you are a gymnastics coach and are looking for students who have very good balance.

15. Write a short report about the length of time students in your class can stand on one foot with their eyes closed.

Litter

Do you ever think about how long garbage lasts if left on its own to decay? Peter, Carmenza, and Ann found this information on the Internet.

Litter	Time to Decay
Newspaper	One year
Orange peel	Two years
Wool socks	Five years
Leather	50 years
Plastic bottle	450 years
Glass bottle	1 million years

"Let's draw a large bar graph for our classroom to make the students aware of this problem," Peter suggests.

16. Reflect Explain why Peter's idea is not a good one.

17. How would you make a poster to help your classmates think twice before they throw anything away? Use the information from the table.

18. Find two examples of data, not mentioned in this section, that can be presented in:

i. a bar graph;

ii. a number line graph.

Math History

Benjamin Banneker (1731-1806)

Benjamin Banneker was a self-educated scientist, astronomer, inventor, and writer. He was one of the first African-Americans to gain distinction in science, and he used this distinction to campaign against slavery.

When Banneker was 21 years old, he took apart a neighbor's pocket watch, drew all its pieces, and put it back together. He then carved a large wooden replica of each piece and made a clock. The clock worked, striking each hour for more than 40 years.

In 1773, Banneker began making astronomical calculations that enabled him to successfully forecast a 1789 solar eclipse.

In 1791, Banneker was hired by President George Washington to assist Andrew Ellicott with surveying the 10-mile square Federal Territory (now Washington, D.C.) to lay out the new capital of the United States.

Banneker is best known for his six annual Farmer's Almanacs published between 1792 and 1797. The almanacs included information on medicine and medical treatment, and listed tides, astronomical information, and eclipses. Banneker did all of the calculations in the almanacs himself.

Summary

Tables and graphs can be used to describe a wide variety of situations. Graphs take information and summarize it in a way that is easy to read. They can show the number of marbles a person has, the length of time students in your class can stand on one foot, or almost anything you want. They can also help you see which things are alike, which things are most common, which things fall in the middle, and how far apart things are. To make a graph readable, label it carefully. Label the axes and give the graph a title.

In this section you learned about bar graphs, picture graphs, and number-line plots. Bar graphs are for data that you can put into categories, but the categories can be put on the graph in any order. The bars in a bar graph are all equal in width.

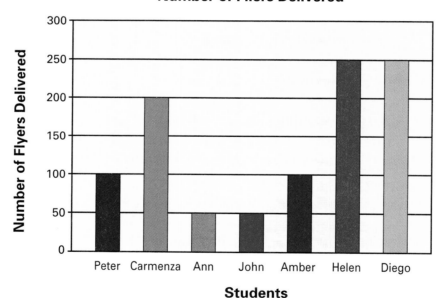

Number of Fliers Delivered

A number-line plot shows data that can be quantified or described by numbers on a number line. A mark for each data point is made on a number line.

1. **a.** Find a bar graph in a newspaper or magazine and describe what it shows.

   b. Can the data you found be presented in a different way? How?

Neville and Sonia created this number-line plot.

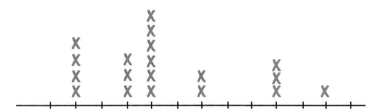

They forgot to label the axes and give it a title.

2. **a.** What does this graph tell you about the data Neville and Sonia gathered?

   b. Copy and label the graph so that it fits a situation that makes sense for the data.

Favorite Sport	Number of Sixth Grade Students	Number of Seventh Grade Students
Football	4	8
Basketball	6	6
Tennis	8	3
Swimming	3	2
Other	4	6

3. Use the data presented in the table to create bar graphs that compare the favorite sports of sixth graders and seventh graders.

 For Further Reflection

Why do newspapers often use graphs to present information?

A Piece of the Pie

Fuel Gauges

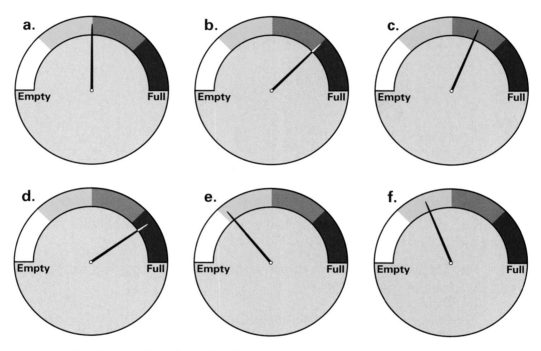

1. Gas tank **a** is half full. How full is each of the other tanks?

2. If a full tank contains 40 liters of gasoline, how much gas is there when the gauge has each of the readings shown? (Hint: The first tank has 20 liters of gasoline.)

Catherine lives in Nashville, Tennessee. Her friend Monica moved to Atlanta, Georgia. One day Catherine drove to Georgia to visit Monica. Unfortunately, she forgot how expensive gas is and spent all of her money filling up her gas tank! Catherine wondered if she would make it to Atlanta from Nashville on one tank of gas. And if she could make it back home again without having to buy gas!

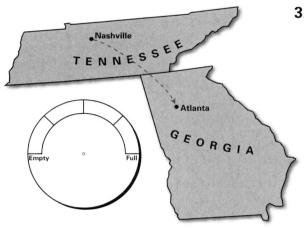

3. On **Student Activity Sheet 3**, mark the fuel gauges as indicated in the statements below.

   a. As Catherine drove away from home, the tank was almost full.

   b. After 110 kilometers, about a quarter of the gas had been used up.

   c. Halfway to Atlanta, the tank was more than half empty.

   d. Fifty-five kilometers later, there was only three-eighths of a tank left.

   e. What do you think happened? Complete the story.

How People Spend Their Vacation

No Vacation/
Don't Know

6%

Summer/
Winter
Resort
17%

Visit
Family/Friends
30%

Stay at
Home
21%

Travel/
Sightsee
26%

Random sample of 686 adults.

Magazines and newspapers present information in different ways. The pie chart to the left shows a typical example using percents. People often use percents to show fractions or parts of something. The whole amount is 100%.

4. a. What number represents 100% in this survey?

   b. How many people would 50% represent?

5. What does this graph tell you?

6. About what fraction of people in the survey travel and sightsee?

7. About how many people surveyed said they visit friends or family while on vacation?

8. **Reflect** Graphs like the one shown on this page are called **pie charts**. Why do you think they are called pie charts?

Data Collection

The data expressed in graphs are often gathered by means of a **survey**. In a survey, people are asked questions about an issue, and their answers are tallied. A pie chart may be used to present the results of a survey.

Students at Lakeside Middle School surveyed a **random** group of 60 students.

Here are some results.

Question I
How Do You Get to School?

Answers	
Bus	30 people
Foot	14 people
Bike	8 people
Car	8 people

Question II
What Is Your Favorite Drink?

Answers	
Cola	$\frac{1}{3}$ of the group
Lemonade	$\frac{1}{6}$ of the group
Grape Drink	$\frac{1}{4}$ of the group
Root Beer	$\frac{1}{6}$ of the group
Other	$\frac{1}{12}$ of the group

9. What do you think the word *random* means?

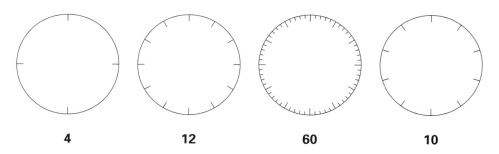

| 4 | 12 | 60 | 10 |

10. **a.** Choose a circle on **Student Activity Sheet 4** that will help you make a pie chart for question I. Use the circle to make a pie chart for question 1.

   b. Do the same for question II.

   c. Describe the results of the survey.

Like the students at Lakeside Middle School, you are going to collect data. The data you collect in this activity will be used throughout the rest of the unit.

Instructions

For each category on **Student Activity Sheet 5**, circle the word or phrase that fits you best.

When everyone in the class has finished, cut out all of the squares and place them in ballot boxes—one ballot box for each question. When you come to appropriate places in the unit, you can then use the data from each question.

Ways of Traveling to School

Mr. Ramirez's class at San Juan Middle School is studying transportation. They had a discussion about how students travel to school.

Angela:

Too many students have their parents drive them to school. The extra traffic makes it dangerous. All of the cars also cause pollution.

Brian:

Plenty of students ride the bus, and buses cause pollution, too.

Mr. Ramirez decided to survey the students to find out how they get to school. He wants to know what part of the student body comes to school in a car and what part takes the bus. Here are the responses to his survey question.

Student	Transportation	Student	Transportation
Peter	Bus	John	Foot
Jean	Bicycle	Steve	Car
Shu Yi	Car	Martin	Car
Paulo	Car	George	Foot
Susan	Car	Julia	Foot
Hiroko	Foot	Roberto	Car
Brian	Bus	Arden	Car
Harry	Car	Bill	Foot
Joe	Bus	Dominik	Car
Esther	Foot	Cathy	Bicycle
Angela	Foot	Jill	Bicycle

11. Organize the data that Mr. Ramirez collected in a new table that makes it easier to understand.

Another way to organize the data is to make a bar graph.

12. Create a bar graph to make this data easier to understand. Don't forget to label the axes and add a title to the graph.

Transportation to School

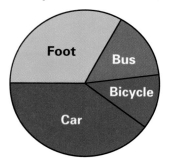

The pie chart displays the information from the table in another way.

13. Look at the pie chart. Does it tell you the same thing the table does? Why or why not?

14. a. Compare the bar graph you made to the pie chart. Which would you use to settle the disagreement between Brian and Angela? Why?

   b. Could you use a number-line plot to show the data? Why or why not?

The bus company has decided to change its school route unless at least 25% of the students ride a bus to school.

15. Does Mr. Ramirez's class meet the 25% rule of the bus company? Why or why not?

After the discussion in Mr. Ramirez's class, Arden, Susan, Steve, and Martin decide to take the bus to school.

16. a. What percentage of the class will now ride the bus to school? Will the bus company change the school route?

 b. Reflect The bus company wants to increase the number of students riding the bus. What are some reasons for riding the bus that the company could give to students and families?

Take out the data you collected about the ways in which students in your class get to school.

17. a. Does your class data meet the 25% rule of the bus company?

b. Do you think you have enough information to provide a picture of how many students in your whole school ride the bus? Explain.

18. a. What number represents 25% of your class?

b. Is that number equivalent to 25% of Mr. Ramirez's class? Explain.

Television Programs

A television network wants to know what kinds of programs people like to watch the most. To find out, they hired a company who took a survey of about 1,000 people. People chose the kinds of programs shown on this page.

Television Viewer Preferences

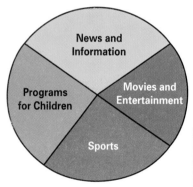

The pie chart shows the survey results.

19. a. Estimate the fraction of people who prefer programs for children.

 b. About how many people is this?

 c. In your notebook, copy and complete the table below. Use the pie chart to help you.

Type of Show	Estimated Fraction	Number of People
News and Information		
Movies and Entertainment		
Sports		
Programs for Children		

20. Compare the network's survey results to your class results. What are the similarities and differences?

Graphs Tell a Story

Stacked bar graphs and pie charts can be used to tell the same story in different ways. Every year, Monroe Middle School organizes a sports day. Students can choose from six different sports: soccer, basketball, bicycling, softball, skating, and volleyball. The stacked bar graphs and the pie charts show the results of a survey of four classes.

21. In your own words, explain what a stacked bar graph is.

22. Match each stacked bar graph with the pie chart that tells the same story. Be ready to explain your choices.

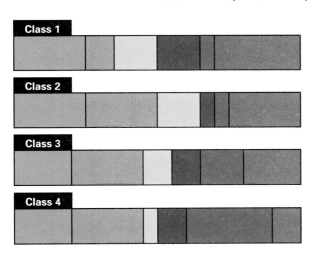

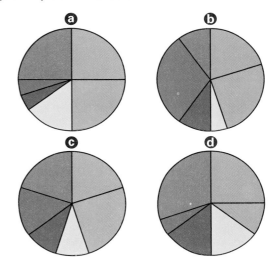

Favorite Sports

- Soccer
- Basketball
- Bicycling
- Softball
- Skating
- Volleyball

23. Examine the data you collected in class about favorite sports. Make a pie chart, a bar graph, or a stacked bar graph of your data.

24. Reflect What are the advantages and disadvantages of each of these three kinds of graphs? Which graph did you use? Why?

25. Tell the story that is presented in the graphs for class 2.

26. Reflect Based on your data, which sports would you include if you were organizing a sports day for your class?

Summary

In this section, you studied pie charts, bar graphs, and stacked bar graphs. A pie chart is a circle divided into sections or "pieces of pie." Each piece represents a category of data. The size of the piece shows the fraction or percent that category is of the whole pie. Each piece of the pie chart is labeled, or a legend next to it shows what is meant by each piece. Don't forget the title!

New Eastland Students' Favorite Performers

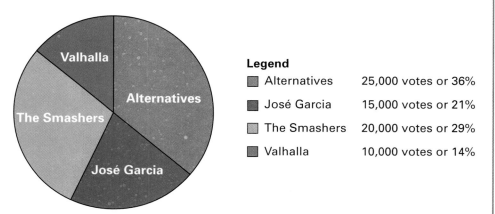

Legend
- Alternatives — 25,000 votes or 36%
- José Garcia — 15,000 votes or 21%
- The Smashers — 20,000 votes or 29%
- Valhalla — 10,000 votes or 14%

A stacked bar graph is a bar that represents the entire amount. The bar is divided into parts showing the fraction or part for the different categories making up the total amount.

New Eastland Students' Favorite Performers

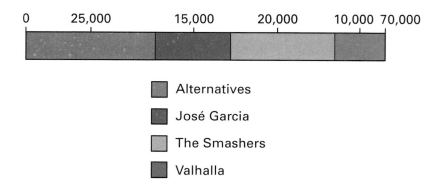

- Alternatives
- José Garcia
- The Smashers
- Valhalla

Graphs tell a story about the data they represent. Different graphs represent data in different ways, so they tell different stories. The type of graph you use depends on what you want to say about a situation.

The two graphs represent the results of a survey on the kinds of pets people prefer.

Favorite Pets

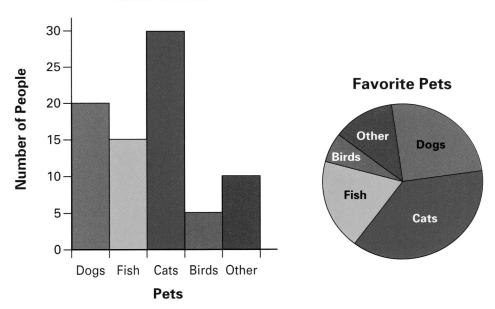

1. **Reflect** Can the two graphs represent the same data? Explain why or why not.

2. **a.** Think of a question about the data that can best be answered using the bar graph.

   b. Think of a question about the data that can best be answered using the pie chart.

A Piece of the Pie

Here is a table showing the results of a survey on computer games given to students at Western Middle School.

Computer Games		
Favorite Computer Game	Number of Students	Percentage of Students
Book of Magic	129	20
Hit the Safe	33	5
Tic Tac Go	190	30
Tilings	98	15
Island	73	11
Falling Problems	119	19
Total	642	100

3. a. Create a graph that tells the story of these data. Explain why you used the graph you did.

   b. Which computer game is the most popular one? How is this shown in your graph?

 For Further Reflection

Start making an overview of the different types of graphs in the unit and complete it while working through the rest of the unit. Name the characteristics of each graph as you enter it in your overview.

A Picture is Worth a Thousand Words

Your Profession

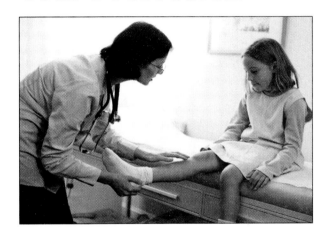

Raisa thinks about growing up to be a doctor. She wonders what the other students in her class want to be.

Raisa surveyed her classmates. Based on the survey results, she drew this **pictograph**.

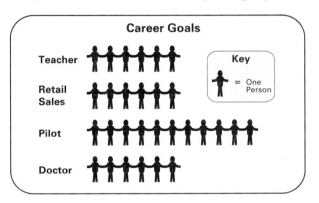

1. Why do you think this graph is called a pictograph?

2. How many students in Raisa's class want to be teachers?

3. How many students are there in each of the other categories?

Student Survey Results	
Teacher	63
Retail Sales	47
Pilot	40
Doctor	33
Other	73

Raisa's class decided to collect data from all the students at school. The results are in the table.

4. Make a pictograph to represent the data.

5. a. Make a pictograph of the data on professions that you collected as a class.

   b. How many of your classmates want to be teachers?

6. Compare the graphs you made in problems 4 and 5. How are they alike? How are they different? Explain.

In the previous sections you studied bar graphs.

7. a. Why would someone choose to use a pictograph instead of a bar graph?

b. Reflect Which graph do you prefer—a bar graph or a pictograph? Explain.

Cat and Mouse

Which animal has more babies per litter, a mouse or a cat? Grace and Huong wanted to find out. First, they collected data. They asked all the people in their school who have mice or cats whether or not their pets have ever had a litter and if so, how many babies were in the litter. Grace and Huong collected the following data about 18 mice and 12 cats.

Mouse	A	B	C	D	E	F	G	H	I	J	K	L	M	N	O	P	Q	R
Number of Babies in Litter	4	8	9	3	7	6	9	8	5	5	8	9	8	3	9	5	4	7

Cat	A	B	C	D	E	F	G	H	I	J	K	L
Number of Babies in Litter	4	6	3	5	5	3	8	3	7	5	4	10

To understand this situation better, Grace and Huong made pictographs.

Litter	Number of Babies in Litter								
	1	2	3	4	5	6	7	8	9
A	🐭	🐭	🐭	🐭	🐭				
B	🐭	🐭	🐭	🐭	🐭	🐭	🐭	🐭	
C	🐭	🐭	🐭	🐭	🐭	🐭	🐭	🐭	🐭
D	🐭	🐭	🐭	🐭					
E	🐭	🐭	🐭	🐭	🐭	🐭	🐭		
F	🐭	🐭	🐭	🐭	🐭	🐭			
G	🐭	🐭	🐭	🐭	🐭	🐭	🐭	🐭	🐭
H	🐭	🐭	🐭	🐭	🐭	🐭			
I	🐭	🐭	🐭	🐭	🐭				
J	🐭	🐭	🐭	🐭	🐭				
K	🐭	🐭	🐭	🐭	🐭	🐭	🐭	🐭	
L	🐭	🐭	🐭	🐭	🐭	🐭	🐭	🐭	🐭
M	🐭	🐭	🐭	🐭	🐭	🐭	🐭		
N	🐭	🐭	🐭						
O	🐭	🐭	🐭	🐭	🐭	🐭	🐭	🐭	
P	🐭	🐭	🐭	🐭	🐭	🐭			
Q	🐭	🐭	🐭	🐭	🐭				
R	🐭	🐭	🐭	🐭	🐭	🐭	🐭		

Litter	Number of Babies in Litter									
	1	2	3	4	5	6	7	8	9	10
A	🐱	🐱	🐱	🐱	🐱					
B	🐱	🐱	🐱	🐱	🐱	🐱	🐱			
C	🐱	🐱	🐱	🐱						
D	🐱	🐱	🐱	🐱	🐱					
E	🐱	🐱	🐱	🐱	🐱	🐱				
F	🐱	🐱	🐱	🐱						
G	🐱	🐱	🐱	🐱	🐱	🐱	🐱	🐱		
H	🐱	🐱	🐱	🐱						
I	🐱	🐱	🐱	🐱	🐱	🐱	🐱			
J	🐱	🐱	🐱	🐱	🐱	🐱				
K	🐱	🐱	🐱	🐱	🐱					
L	🐱	🐱	🐱	🐱	🐱	🐱	🐱	🐱	🐱	🐱

Grace:

I think cats have more babies on average. There's even a cat that had 10 babies. It's definitely the cat.

Huong:

I disagree. I think it's mice because they didn't have as many litters with three or four babies.

8. **Reflect** What do you think? Which animal typically has more babies?

Grace:

I want to see how many babies each mouse has on average. Let's redraw the graphs.

Litter	Number of Babies in Litter								
	1	2	3	4	5	6	7	8	9
A									
B									
C									
D									
E									
F									
G									
H									
I									
J									
K									
L									
M									
N									
O									
P									
Q									
R									

9. What did Grace do? Do the same for the cats using **Student Activity Sheet 6**.

Grace concluded that the mice have about six babies each, and the cats have about five.

10. Do you agree with Grace?

11. Try to be more precise than "about six babies" or "about five babies." Explain your reasoning.

12. **Reflect** For some species of animals to survive, they need many offspring. Why do you think mice might need to have more babies than cats?

Mean and Mode

The **mean** is a one-number summary for a group of data that shows how much each would have if the total amount was balanced over everyone. Look at the litters of ten dogs from a breed known as Jack Russell terriers.

Dog	Fifi	Queenie	Domino	Chiquita	Kasey	Ginger	Belle	Truly	Cookie	Lady
Number of Puppies	4	3	3	4	2	2	3	2	4	3

Huong: If the puppies were divided equally among the ten litters, how many puppies would each dog have?

Grace: Three! It's called the mean, or **average**.

13. Is it true that the mean is three pups per litter? Explain how you checked it.

Youri used another way to find the mean.

Youri: I added all the puppies. Then I took the total number of puppies and divided that number by the total number of mother dogs. There are 30 puppies and 10 mother dogs, so the mean is $30 \div 10 = 3$.

14. Reflect Do you think Youri's strategy always works? Why or why not?

15. a. Use the data collected in your class to make a graph titled "Our Favorite Kind of Music." Choose your own type of graph and explain your choice.

b. Reflect Can you find the mean kind of music preferred in your class? Why or why not?

Another one-number summary for a group of data is the **mode**, the most frequent observation. In the data set you used for problem 15, this is the most frequently chosen kind of music.

16. Which kind of music was chosen most frequently in you class?

Throwing Darts

DeKalb Middle School has a dart-throwing contest. Each grade selects a team for the school playoffs. These are the rules for selecting team members.

- You must throw at least three times.
- You may not throw more than ten times.
- All throws must be recorded.
- To be considered for the team, the mean of all of your throws must be at least 35 points.

The school uses a special dartboard. The bull's-eye is worth 45 points. Each section is worth the number of points shown. The outer ring is worth zero points.

17. If you throw a dart and get 34 points, what does your next throw have to be to **compensate** so that your mean for the two throws is at least 35?

18. If, instead, your next throw is worth 32 points, how many points would you have to make on your third throw?

19. Jamal's first throw was worth 30 points. After two more throws, he qualified. What could his points for the next two throws have been?

Here are Michelle's throws.

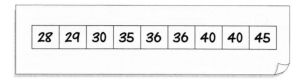

20. Will Michelle qualify?

These are Tirza's throws.

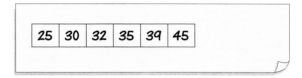

21. If Tirza wants to qualify on her next throw, how many points does she have to make?

By the end of the qualifying period, three sixth-graders had qualified for the school playoffs.

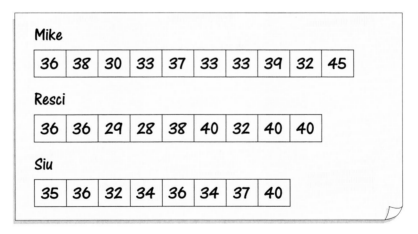

Each grade can have at most two contestants.

22. Who would you pick? Make a number-line plot for each student to help you make a decision.

In the final competition, the winner averages 43 points in five throws.

23. Give two possibilities for the points the winner got for each of the five throws.

Going on Vacation

In summer, many people go on vacation. Some want to go to a sunny place where they can swim and surf. To help people decide where to go, travel agencies make brochures with information about temperature, rainfall, and the amount of sun in different countries.

Suppose a bar graph shows the noontime temperatures during one September in Paradise, a popular tourist resort.

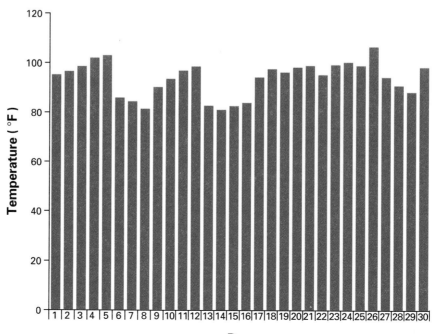

24. Reflect If you worked for a travel agency and you wanted to find one number to describe the temperature in September in Paradise, what number would you choose?

25. What do you think the mean temperature in September was? (You do not have to be exact.)

26. Draw a horizontal line on the graph on **Student Activity Sheet 7** to mark the mean temperature in September.

    a. Compare the number of days above the mean temperature to the number of days below the mean temperature.

    b. Reflect Would you expect the number of days above the mean temperature to be the same as the number of days below the mean temperature. Why or why not?

27. Reflect Explain how compensation can be used to find the average temperature in September.

Summary

Pictographs use pictures to represent numbers. When making a pictograph, you have to decide how many of something each picture represents.

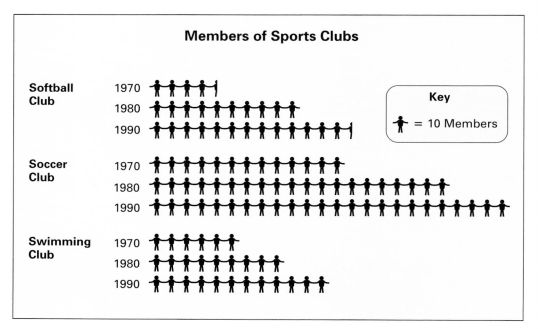

The data represented in pictographs can also be represented with other types of graphs, such as bar graphs, pie charts, or number-line plots.

The *mean*, or *average*, is a one-number summary for a set of data that "balances" the total among all the parts involved. You can find the mean by using a compensation strategy or by finding the total and dividing.

The *mode* is another one-number summary for a set of data. The mode is the value that appears most frequently in the data set.

Check Your Work

Kay, a stickler for accuracy, opened ten boxes of pushpins and counted the number of pins in each box. She found the following numbers of pins in the 10 boxes.

104, 100, 98, 99, 103, 97, 100, 102, 98, 103

1. a. What would a number-line plot show you about the number of pushpins in each of the boxes that Kay counted?

   b. Find the mean number of pushpins. Explain your reasoning.

   c. Kay thinks the mean number of pushpins cannot be a decimal number. Explain why Kay is wrong.

2. Kay had to describe the number of pushpins per box to her teacher. What could her description have been?

Tamesha, Randi, Suoko, Valerie, and Tim decided to pool their money to see how much each could spend on a comic book. The table shows how much money each one had to start.

	Amount of Money
Tamesha	$1.40
Randi	$0.75
Suoko	$2.15
Valerie	$1.65
Tim	$3.30

3. a. How would you suggest they divide up their money to see how much each one could spend if they were going to spend equal amounts?

   b. How does this problem relate to finding the mean or average amount of money they have?

 For Further Reflection

Suppose a newspaper article describes the average number of points a basketball player earns per game. What do you think the article means by the word *average*?

Bars or Lines— Get the Picture?

Temperature

February 15, 1936: In North Dakota, the temperature was a record low of 60 degrees below zero!

1. **a.** In your notebook, make a drawing of a thermometer that shows this temperature.

   b. What is today's temperature outside of your classroom right now? Draw a new thermometer to show this temperature.

Some sixth-grade students placed a thermometer outside the school in a shady place. They recorded the temperature every hour during the school day. The table shows the data they collected.

Temperatures During School Time	
Time	**Temperature (°F)**
9:00 A.M.	75°
10:00 A.M.	78°
11:30 A.M.	83°
12:00 P.M.	88°
1:00 P.M.	93°
2:00 P.M.	94°
3:00 P.M.	90°

This is how the students represented their data in a graph.

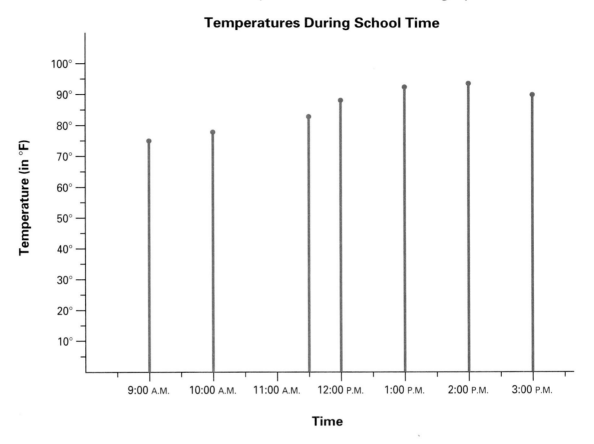

Temperatures During School Time

2. a. The students forgot to record the temperature at 11:00. They measured at 11:30 instead. On **Student Activity Sheet 8**, add the temperature you think would have been recorded at 11:00 A.M.

b. On **Student Activity Sheet 8**, connect the end points of each temperature in the graph by straight **line segments**.

The new graph you created is called a **line graph** or **plot-over-time graph**. This graph shows how the temperature changed during the day. A line graph is often used to show how things (like temperatures) change over time.

3. If the students had measured the temperature every half hour, how would the line graph change? If the students measured every quarter of an hour?

For the graph below, the temperature was measured every minute over one day.

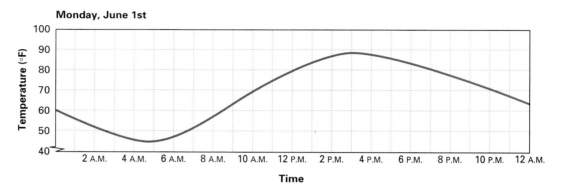

Monday, June 1st

4. What was the highest temperature on this Monday? What was the lowest temperature?

The highest temperature is called the **maximum** temperature.
The lowest temperature is called the **minimum** temperature.

5. Did the temperature vary much on this Monday? What was the difference between the maximum and the minimum temperatures?

6. What do you know about the maximum temperature for Tuesday? What do you know about the minimum temperature?

This graph shows the daily January temperatures for one particular year in Madison, Wisconsin.

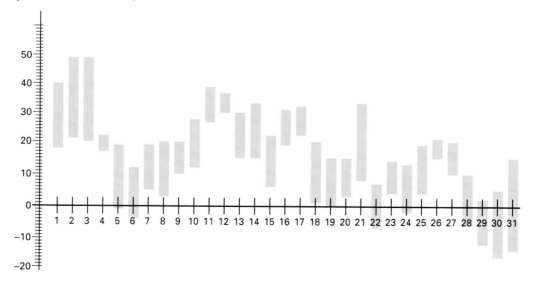

7. What can you tell about the temperatures in January from the graph?

The top of each bar represents the maximum temperature measured that day. The bottom of each bar represents the minimum temperature measured that day.

8. What were the minimum and maximum temperatures on January 22?

A newspaper article said:

> The temperature in Madison dipped below zero eight times last month.

9. What are the dates referred to in the article?

10. Estimate the number of days when the minimum temperature was above the freezing point in January that year.

11. On what day did the greatest change in temperature occur? The least change? How can you tell from the graph?

12. Write a short newspaper article that describes the graph. Use your answers from the previous questions and consider the following.

- When was the daily maximum temperature the highest?
- When was the daily maximum temperature the lowest?
- When was the daily minimum temperature the highest?
- When was the daily minimum temperature the lowest?

This table shows the typical average temperatures for each month in 15 vacation spots.

Typical Average Temperatures (°F)

Vacation Spot	J	F	M	A	M	J	J	A	S	O	N	D
Acapulco	88	88	88	88	89	90	91	91	90	90	90	89
Antigua	80	80	80	82	90	90	90	90	89	89	89	83
Aruba	83	84	84	86	88	88	88	91	91	90	89	86
Cancún	84	85	88	91	94	92	92	91	90	88	86	82
Cozumel	84	85	88	91	94	92	92	91	90	88	86	82
Grand Cayman	88	87	86	88	88	89	90	91	91	89	88	88
Ixtapa	89	90	92	93	89	88	89	90	91	91	90	89
Jamaica	86	87	87	88	90	90	90	90	89	89	89	87
Los Cabos	73	74	79	83	88	93	95	93	92	89	82	74
Manzanillo	77	78	82	86	83	88	93	95	93	92	89	74
Mazatlán	73	74	79	83	84	92	94	92	92	90	85	71
Nassau	76	76	78	80	84	88	89	90	88	84	81	79
Puerto Vallarta	76	77	81	85	83	88	93	95	93	92	89	75
St. Martin/St. Kitts	80	81	82	83	86	86	86	87	87	86	85	84
U.S. Virgin Islands	80	81	82	83	88	88	90	90	88	87	86	86

13. Based on the temperatures in the table above, where would you prefer to go on a vacation in January? Why?

14. **a.** Use the table to make separate number-line plots for the temperatures of Los Cabos and Ixtapa.

   b. Compare the two plots. Explain the differences in the temperatures at these two resorts.

15. Was it important to use the same scale to create the number-line plots in problem 14a? Why or why not?

16. **a.** In the title of the table, you see the words *typical average temperatures*. How do you think the average temperature for a month is calculated?

   b. How do the mean yearly temperatures in Los Cabos and Ixtapa compare?

You could plot the typical mean temperatures for each month in a graph. Since separate dots could be confusing if more than one resort is presented in the graph, the dots are connected by straight lines and different kinds of dots are used.

The graph shown here is a line graph of the temperatures in three of the resort areas from the table on page 36.

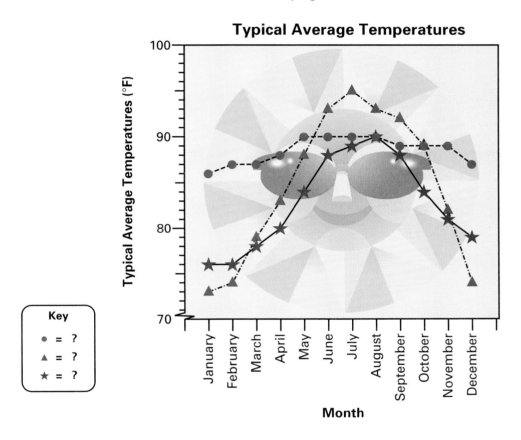

Typical Average Temperatures

Key

● = ?
▲ = ?
★ = ?

Month

17. The key on this graph is incomplete. Figure out which resort areas these lines represent. Write them in your notebook.

18. Which of these three resort areas has the best climate? Why do you think so? Describe the temperature changes over one year for that area.

19. Look in an almanac or check with your local weather bureau to find the typical temperatures for your city. Describe the temperature changes over one year for your city.

Three Sports Clubs

Bar graphs and pictographs can give a quick overview of the data, but they are not very helpful if you want to answer questions such as "Which grew the most over the years?"

Newville has a number of sports clubs. The table shows the numbers of members in three sports clubs for different years.

Number of Club Members Per Year

Year	Sports Club		
	Softball	Soccer	Swimming
1970	45	130	60
1980	100	200	90
1990	135	240	120
2000	150	250	130

On **Student Activity Sheet 9**, you see the beginning of a line graph.

20. a. What do you think the three dots on the graph represent?

   b. Plot the other points for the club represented here. Connect the dots with line segments.

21. Plot the data for the other clubs on **Student Activity Sheet 9** and draw the connecting line segments. You may want to use different colors for each graph or use different types of dots.

22. Does the graph help you decide which club grew the fastest?

23. If you look at how many new members joined a club in this 30-year period, which club grew the most?

24. If you look at how many times larger the total number of members in 2000 is than the total in 1970, which club grew the most?

25. a. Based on your answers to problems 22, 23, and 24, which club do you think grew the most?

   b. Reflect Why was a plot-over-time chosen to represent the information?

Combining Graphs

Sometimes different types of graphs are combined to represent information. This may also help you to see a relationship between different data sets.

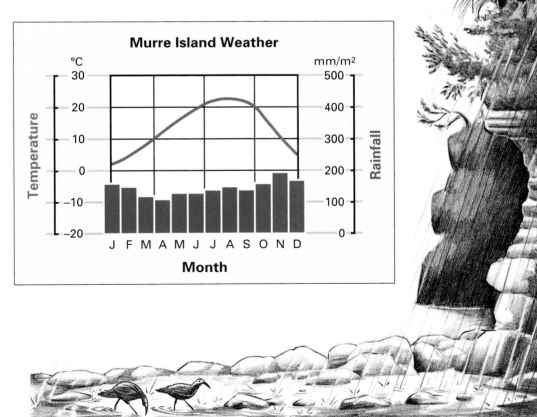

This graph shows the mean temperature and amount of rainfall for each month of the year on Murre Island, situated in the Pacific Northwest. The curve represents temperature in degrees Celsius. The bars indicate rainfall in millimeters per square meter (mm/m^2).

Murre Island Weather

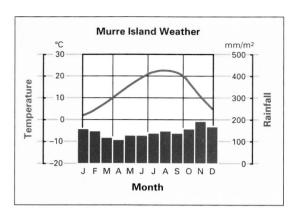

Murre Island Weather

Month

26. **a.** Do you see a relationship between the temperature and rainfall on Murre Island? Explain.

b. Do graphs made with double vertical axes have the potential to be confusing? Explain your thinking.

27. Write a short description of the weather on Murre Island. Give reasons to support your description.

28. What time of the year would you advise tourists to visit Murre Island if you knew they wanted to hike around the island?

Another island, Albatross Island, is rocky and wind-swept. It is covered in tussock grass that can grow up to nine feet high. The island is home to a large breeding colony of Black-browed albatross, as well as a number of Rockhopper penguins.

The graph shows the mean temperature and amount of rainfall for each month of the year on Albatross Island. The curve represents temperature in degrees Celsius. The bars indicate rainfall in millimeters per square meter.

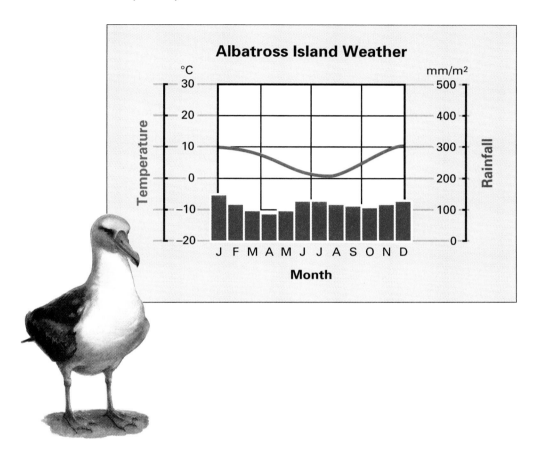

29. Compare the weather on Albatross Island with the weather on Murre Island.

30. Based on weather conditions, which island do you think would attract more tourists as a nature refuge, Murre Island or Albatross Island? Explain.

Summary

In this section, you learned how to make a line graph to show change over time. A line graph or plot-over-time graph shows how numbers change in different circumstances. When a line in a graph goes down as the time advances, something else (like the temperature or the number of people) is getting smaller; when a line in a graph goes up as the time advances, something else is getting larger. Graphs can help you see patterns and trends and are useful in making decisions.

The smallest number in a set of data is called the *minimum*. The largest number is called the *maximum*.

Sometimes different types of graphs are combined, which may help you see a relationship between different data about the same situation.

Check Your Work

1. What are some differences between a line graph or plot-over-time and a bar graph?

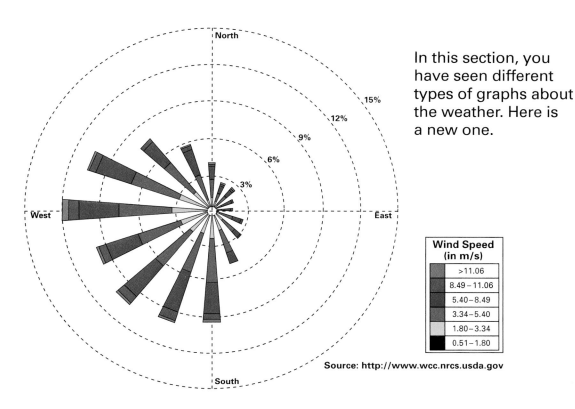

In this section, you have seen different types of graphs about the weather. Here is a new one.

Wind Speed (in m/s)	
	>11.06
	8.49 – 11.06
	5.40 – 8.49
	3.34 – 5.40
	1.80 – 3.34
	0.51 – 1.80

Source: http://www.wcc.nrcs.usda.gov

The wind rose shows how often the wind comes from a certain direction. The longer a bar, the more often the wind comes from the corresponding direction.

2. **a.** During the 31-day period shown in the graph, what percent of the time did the wind come from the north?

The color of the bars gives an indication of the wind speed. Wind speed is expressed in the legend in meters per second (m/s).

b. What direction did the strongest winds come from during this period—North (N), East (E), South (S), or West (W)? What was the wind speed of the strongest winds?

c. Find some other information based on the graph.

 For Further Reflection

Think of an advantage of using a line graph instead of another representation. Give an example.

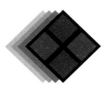

Additional Practice

Section Ⓐ Using Bar Graphs

1. Students at Roosevelt Middle School are raising money by selling raffle tickets for $5 each.

Students	Number of Raffle Tickets Sold
Juan	12
Suzanne	27
Briana	18
David	35

   a. Describe what the table shows.

   b. Make a bar graph showing how much money each student raised. Make sure that your bar graph is clearly labeled.

2. Use the following information to create a bar graph.

   • Daren has started a coin collection. He has two foreign coins.
   • Hector has six coins more than Daren
   • Elory has half as many coins as Hector
   • Gina has three fewer coins than Elory.
   • Loritz has as many coins as Elory and Gina put together.

Section Ⓑ A Piece of the Pie

Favorite Amusement Park Rides

Tea Cup 18%

Tilt-a-Whirl 26%

Flying Swings 10%

Octopus 10%

Roller Coaster 36%

The graph represents the results of a survey of 150 students.

1. a. What does this graph tell you?

   b. How many students prefer to ride on the Octopus?

   c. About what fraction of the students prefer the Tilt-a-Whirl?

2. Create a stacked bar graph that tells the same story as the pie chart.

Section C A Picture is Worth a Thousand Words

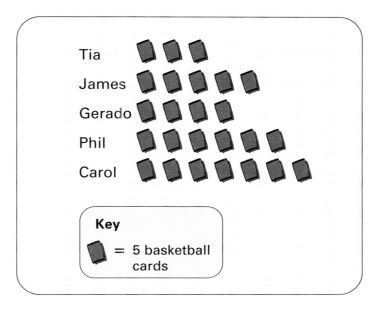

1. Write an appropriate title for the pictograph.

2. a. What is the largest number of basketball cards any student has?

   b. How many more cards does Gerado have than Tia?

3. a. If Jody is 23, Mary is 31, and LaShanda is 27, what is their mean age?

   b. If Jody is 2, Mary is 31, and LaShanda is 57, why is it not a good idea to compute the mean age?

Section D Bars or Lines—Get the Picture?

The table shows the typical average temperatures each day for one week in six cities.

City	S	M	T	W	T	F	S
Dallas	101	96	101	102	101	103	101
Springfield	86	80	90	89	91	93	92
Orlando	99	88	95	96	99	97	98
Chicago	100	99	102	103	102	104	103
Aspen	80	80	79	82	83	81	82
Boston	94	91	92	94	95	92	93

1. **a.** Which city had the highest average temperature on Thursday? The lowest?

   b. What is the difference between the maximum average temperature and the minimum average temperature on Thursday?

2. **a.** What was the mean temperature in Dallas for the week?

   b. Which city had the highest average temperature for the week?

3. **a.** Create a graph that shows two line graphs: one for the average daily temperatures of Boston, the other for the average daily temperatures of Springfield.

   b. Compare the two graphs. Explain the differences in the temperatures.

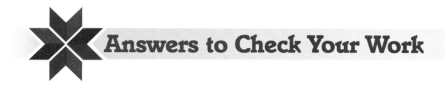

Answers to Check Your Work

Section A Using Bar Graphs

1. a. Have a classmate look at your bar graph and the description to see if they make sense.

b. The data you found can probably be presented in a table as well. Whether or not the data can be presented in a different type of graph depends on the example you found. You might want to discuss your answers with a classmate.

2. a. You can tell that there are 19 pieces of data, but without labels on the axes and without a title on the graph, it is almost impossible to tell something about the data Neville and Sonia gathered.

b. Your answer will be different from the ones shown here. Sample responses:

The number line graph represents the number of baseball hats owned by each student in the sixth grade.

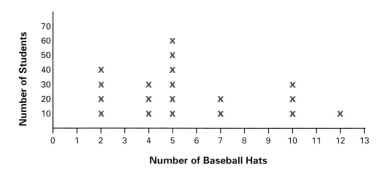

The number line plot represents the shoes sizes of 19 students.

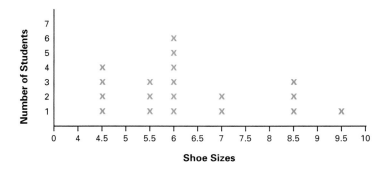

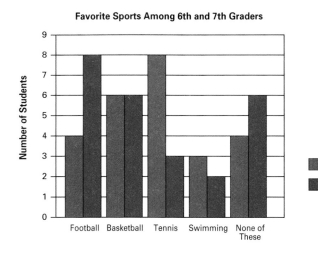

Favorite Sports Among 6th and 7th Graders

3. You might have different graphs to show the comparison. One example is below. Share your answer with a classmate.

Section Ⓑ A Piece of the Pie

1. Yes. You might say that each bar in the bar graph matches the part with the same label in the pie graph. For example, 20 dogs is one-fourth of the total of 80 animals, and in the pie chart, the dogs' part is one-fourth of the pie.

2. Sample questions:

   a. How many more people chose dogs than fish as their favorite pet?

   b. Do more than half the people surveyed prefer cats?

3. **a.** Here are two sample graphs that tell the story of the data. Your graph may be different.

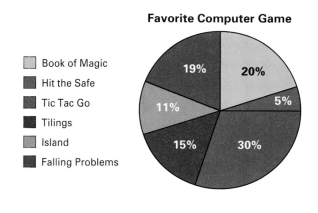

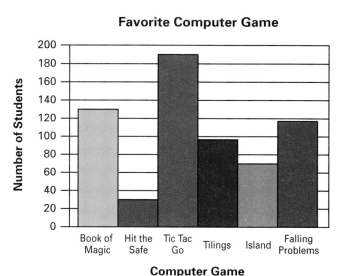

You might say you chose the pie chart because you wanted to show how the parts were related to the whole thing. You might say you chose the bar graph because you wanted to show the numbers as close as possible.

Or you could say:

b. The pie chart shows the that Tic Tac Go is the most popular because it is the largest slice of the pie.

The bar graph shows that Tic Tac Go is the most popular because it is the tallest bar.

Section **C** A Picture is Worth a Thousand Words

1. a. A number-line plot shows exactly how many pushpins were in each box and how the numbers varied from box to box.

b. 100.4 is the mean. You can calculate the mean by adding up the number of pushpins in each box and dividing the total by 10.

104 + 100 + 98 + 99 + 103 + 97 + 100 + 102 + 98 + 103 = 1,004; 1004 ÷ 10 = 100.4 pins per box

You can also use the compensation method:

97 + 103 → 100 + 100
98 + 102 → 100 + 100
98 + 99 + 103 → 100 + 100 + 100, which makes a sum of 700 pins.
100 + 100 + 700 = 900; 900 + 104 = 1,004;
since 1,004 is 4 pins away from an even 1,000 pins (which divided by 10 boxes is 100 pins per box), that leaves 4 pins to be distributed among the 10 boxes.

c. Even if numbers of pins are whole numbers, the mean can be a decimal number. Sample explanations:

A mean of 100.4 means that on average, ten boxes have 100 pins each, and four of them have one pin extra.

A mean of 100.4 means that there are 1004 pins divided over 10 boxes.

2. Since the mean or average number of pushpins for the boxes Kay looked at is a little more than 100, but not 101 (100.4), she could have said that there were about 100 pushpins per box.

3. a. You can figure out different ways to divide up the money. For example, you might start by having everyone with $0.75 (the smallest amount to start) and then have them pool the rest to make $2.55 + $0.65 + $0.90 + $1.40, or $5.50, which would give everyone another $1 and another $0.10, so each would have $1.00 + $0.10 + $0.75, or $1.85.

b. The amount they would each spend if they spent the same amount would be the mean, $1.85.

Section D Bars or Lines—Get the Picture?

1. You may have noted that a bar graph is used to present categories of data—like the number of brochures each student has delivered—in a visual way. A line graph gives a picture of how something like temperature changes over time.

Even though there is no data for the intervals between the times the temperature was measured, the change is continuous. Therefore, the temperature in between measurements lies on the connecting line. A bar graph describes data for separate categories, and it does not make sense to connect them because there is no data in between the bars representing people and how many brochures they delivered.

2. a. A little less than 4% of the time.

b. From the four directions mentioned, the strongest winds came from the West. The speed was greater than 11.06 m/s. However, the strongest winds of all came from a direction West by Southwest.

c. Sample information you may have found from the graph:

Winds more often come from West to East and less often from North or South.

The most common speeds were from 3.34 m/s to 8.49 m/s.

Models You Can Count On

Number

BRITANNICA
Mathematics
in
Context

HOLT, RINEHART AND WINSTON

Mathematics in Context is a comprehensive curriculum for the middle grades. It was developed in 1991 through 1997 in collaboration with the Wisconsin Center for Education Research, School of Education, University of Wisconsin-Madison and the Freudenthal Institute at the University of Utrecht, The Netherlands, with the support of the National Science Foundation Grant No. 9054928.

This unit is a new unit prepared as a part of the revision of the curriculum carried out in 2003 through 2005, with the support of the National Science Foundation Grant No. ESI 0137414.

National Science Foundation

Opinions expressed are those of the authors
and not necessarily those of the Foundation.

Abels, M., Wijers, M., Pligge, M., and Hedges, T. (2006). *Models You Can Count On.* In Wisconsin Center for Education Research & Freudenthal Institute (Eds.), Mathematics in Context. Chicago: Encyclopædia Britannica, Inc.

ISBN 0-03-038578-4

2 3 4 5 6 073 09 08 07 06 05

The *Mathematics in Context* Development Team

Development 2003–2005

Models You Can Count On was developed by Mieke Abels and Monica Wijers.
It was adapted for use in American schools by Margaret A. Pligge and Teri Hedges.

Wisconsin Center for Education
Research Staff

Thomas A. Romberg
Director

David C. Webb
Coordinator

Gail Burrill
Editorial Coordinator

Margaret A. Pligge
Editorial Coordinator

Freudenthal Institute Staff

Jan de Lange
Director

Truus Dekker
Coordinator

Mieke Abels
Content Coordinator

Monica Wijers
Content Coordinator

Project Staff

Sarah Ailts
Beth R. Cole
Erin Hazlett
Teri Hedges
Karen Hoiberg
Carrie Johnson
Jean Krusi
Elaine McGrath

Margaret R. Meyer
Anne Park
Bryna Rappaport
Kathleen A. Steele
Ana C. Stephens
Candace Ulmer
Jill Vettrus

Arthur Bakker
Peter Boon
Els Feijs
Dédé de Haan
Martin Kindt

Nathalie Kuijpers
Huub Nilwik
Sonia Palha
Nanda Querelle
Martin van Reeuwijk

Cover photo credits: (left to right) © Comstock Images; © Corbis; © Getty Images

Illustrations
1, 3, 8, 12, 13, 16, 18, 19, 26 Christine McCabe/ © Encyclopædia Britannica, Inc.; **28** Holly Cooper-Olds; **29** (top) Christine McCabe/ © Encyclopædia Britannica, Inc. (bottom) Holly Cooper-Olds; **30, 34, 35** Holly Cooper-Olds; **37** (bottom) Christine McCabe/ © Encyclopædia Britannica, Inc.; **40** © Encyclopædia Britannica, Inc.; **45, 46, 49, 52, 55, 56, 60,** Christine McCabe/© Encyclopædia Britannica, Inc.

Photographs
1–5, 7, 11 Victoria Smith/HRW; **20** Don Couch/HRW Photo; **23** Sam Dudgeon/HRW Photo; **27** © Corbis; **42** © Paul A. Souders/Corbis; **43** © Corbis; **44** Image 100/Alamy; **46** PhotoDisc/Getty Images; **47** (top) Photo courtesy of the State Historical Society of Iowa, Des Moines; (bottom) ©SSPL / The Image Works; **50** Sam Dudgeon/HRW; **51** © Index Stock; **54** Mike Powell/Getty Images

◆ Contents

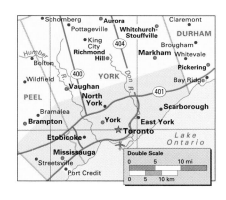

Dear Student,

Welcome to the unit *Models You Can Count On*.

Math students today can no longer be comfortable merely doing pencil and paper computations. Advances in technology make it more important for you to do more than perform accurate computations. Today, it is important for you to make sense of number operations. You need to be able solve problems with the use of a calculator, confident that your result is accurate. When shopping in a store, you need to be able to estimate on the spot to make sure you are getting the best deal and that the cash register is working properly.

In this unit, you will look at different number models to help you improve your understanding of how numbers work. You will examine various recipes that could be used to feed large groups of people. You will consider how students can share garden plots. You will observe computer screens during a program installation. You will make sense of signs along a highway or bike trail. In each situation, a special model will help you make sense of the situation. You will learn to use these models and count on them to solve any problem!

We hope you enjoy this unit.

Sincerely,

The Mathematics in Context Development Team

The Ratio Table

Recipe

Today, both men and women prepare food in the kitchen. Have you ever worked in the kitchen? Think about your favorite recipe.

1. Make a list of the ingredients you need for this recipe. What else do you need to prepare your recipe?

Ms. Freeman wants to make a treat for her class. This is her favorite recipe. It makes 50 Cheese Puffles.

Cheese Puffles (makes 50)

Ingredients: 2 cups wheat flour
1 cup unsalted butter
2 cups grated cheese
4 cups rice cereal

Directions: Preheat the oven to 400°F. Cream the flour, butter, and cheese together in a large bowl. Add rice cereal and mix into a dough. Shape Puffles into small balls, using your hands. Bake until golden, about 10-15 minutes. Let cool.

There are 25 students in Ms. Freeman's class.

2. a. How many Cheese Puffles will each student get if Ms. Freeman uses the amounts in the recipe?

   b. If she wants each student to have four Cheese Puffles, how can you find out how much of each ingredient she needs?

Ms. Freeman invites her colleague, Ms. Anderson, to help her make the Cheese Puffles. They decide to make enough Puffles to treat the entire sixth grade. There are four sixth-grade classes with about 25 students in each class.

3. How much of each ingredient should they use? Explain.

School Supplies

Jason manages the school store at Springfield Middle School. Students and teachers often purchase various school items from this store.

One of Jason's responsibilities is to order additional supplies from the Office Supply Store.

Today Jason has to make an order sheet and calculate the costs.

Use **Student Activity Sheet 1** to record your answers to questions 4–6.

Item	Cost
6 boxes of rulers	$_____
25 packs of notebooks	$_____
9 boxes of protractors	$_____
5 boxes of red pens	$_____
8 boxes of blue pens	$_____
Total Cost	$_____

Jason starts with 6 boxes of rulers. He uses a previous bill to find the cost. The last bill shows:

3 boxes of rulers	$150

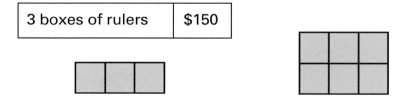

4. Find the price for 6 boxes of rulers. Explain how you found the price.

Jason's last order was for 10 packs of notebooks.

10 packs of notebooks	$124

5. Calculate the price for 25 packs of notebooks. Show your calculations.

Here is the rest of the bill.

10 boxes of protractors	$420
20 boxes of red pens	$240
10 boxes of blue pens	$120

6. a. Use the information from this bill to calculate the price for nine boxes of protractors. Show your work.

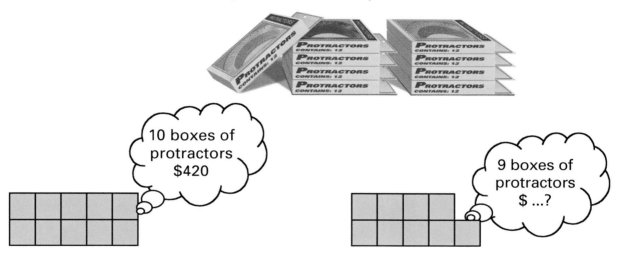

10 boxes of protractors $420

9 boxes of protractors $ ...?

b. Complete the order sheet on **Student Activity Sheet 1.**

Jason uses a **ratio table** to make calculations like the ones in the previous problems. Here is his reasoning and work.

"I know that the price of 20 boxes of red pens is $240. I use this information to set up the labels and the first column of the ratio table. Now I can calculate the price of five boxes of red pens."

Number of Boxes of Red Pens	20	10	5
Price (in Dollars)	240	120	60

7. **a.** Explain how Jason found the numbers in the second and third columns.

   b. Use the information in Jason's ratio table to calculate the price of 15 boxes of red pens. Explain how you found your price.

   c. Use the ratio table below to calculate the price for 29 boxes of red pens. (You may add more columns if you need them.) Explain how you found the numbers in your columns.

Number of Boxes of Red Pens	20				
Price (in dollars)	240				

When using a ratio table, there are many different operations you can use to make the new columns.

8. Name some operations you can use to make new columns in a ratio table. You may want to look back to problem 7.

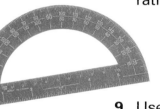

Packages shipped to the school store contain different amounts of items; for example, one box of protractors contains one dozen protractors.

9. Use **Student Activity Sheet 2** to find the number of protractors in 8, 5, and 9 boxes.

   a. 8 boxes:

Number of Boxes	1	2	4	8
Number of Protractors	12			

   How did you find the number of protractors in the last column?

   b. 5 boxes:

Number of Boxes	1	10	5
Number of Protractors	12		

   How did you find the number of protractors in the last column?

   c. 9 boxes:

Number of Boxes	1	10	9
Number of Protractors	12		

   How did you find the number of protractors in the last column?

10. Jason ordered a supply of 132 protractors. How many boxes will be shipped? You can use the ratio table on **Student Activity Sheet 2**.

Number of Boxes	1		
Number of Protractors	12		

A math teacher at Springfield Middle School would like to have calculators for her class. The school store offers calculators for $7 each. She asked her sixth-grade students to calculate the total price for 32 calculators. Here are strategies from three of her students.

Romero

Number of Calculators	1	2	4	8	16	32
Price (in dollars)	7	14	28	56	112	224

11. Describe the steps Romero used.

Cindy

Oops!!

Number of Calculators	1	10	30	32
Price (in dollars)	7	70	210	212

Cindy did something wrong when she filled in the last column.

12. a. Explain how Cindy found the numbers in the last column. Explain why this is not correct.

b. What should the numbers in the last column be?

Sondra

Number of Calculators	1	10	20	30	2	32
Price (in dollars)	7	70	140	210	14	224

13. Describe the steps Sondra used for her ratio table.

A ratio table is a convenient tool you can use to solve problems. You start with two numbers that are related to each other as a ratio. Then you can use an operation to create a column with new numbers in the table so that they have the same ratio. Using arrows, you can keep track of the operations you used.

Here are operations you can use.

Doubling or Multiplying by Two

packages	1	2	4
pencils	15	30	60

×2, ×2

Halving or Dividing by Two

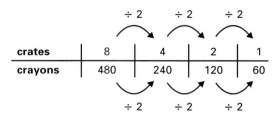

crates	8	4	2	1
crayons	480	240	120	60

÷2, ÷2, ÷2

Times Ten

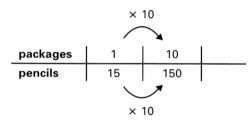

packages	1	10
pencils	15	150

× 10

Multiplying

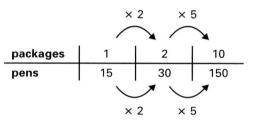

packages	1	2	10
pens	15	30	150

×2, ×5

Dividing

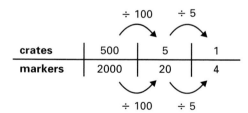

crates	500	5	1
markers	2000	20	4

÷100, ÷5

For the two operations below, you would choose two columns in the ratio table and add them together or find the difference.

Adding Columns

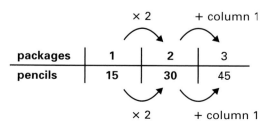

packages	1	2	3
pencils	15	30	45

×2, + column 1

Subtracting Columns

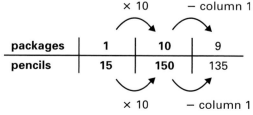

packages	1	10	9
pencils	15	150	135

× 10, − column 1

You can use more than one operation in one ratio table. For example, here is Walter's solution for the problem "How many pencils are in 90 packages?"

Walter

Packages	1	2	4	8	9	90
Pencils	15	30	60	120	135	1,350

14. What operations did Walter use? How will he answer the question?

The Office Supply Store where Jason buys the supplies for the school store displays a poster of some products sold.

Office Supply Store			
Item	Number in Box	Price per Box	Notes
Bottle of Glue	5	$6.25	
Calculator	4	$26	
Notebook, lined	10	$17.50	
Pen: blue, black, or red	48	$12	
Gel Pen	20	$7	
Pencil with eraser	15	$2.25	Special offer: $1.50 per box
Protractor	12	$42	
Ruler (30 cm)	25	$50	
Tape	8	$7.20	

Jason ordered 720 pens and received 15 boxes. He wants to know how many pens are in each box. He sets up the following ratio table.

Boxes	15	......	......
Pens	720	......	......

15. How many pens are in one box? You may copy and use Jason's ratio table to find the answer.

Number of Gel Pens	20	10	1
Price (in dollars)	7	3.50	0.35

For the school store Jason wants to create notes for single-priced items. He uses a ratio table to calculate the price for one gel pen.

16. a. What operations did Jason use in his ratio table?

    b. Ahmed buys 3 gel pens. How much does he have to pay for them?

Ms. Anderson wants all of her students in sixth grade to have a lined notebook. She buys the notebooks from the school store and sells them to her students. There are 23 students in her class.

17. Create and use a ratio table to calculate how much Ms. Anderson has to pay for 23 lined notebooks.

Recipe

Play Dough **(1 portion)**

Ingredients: $2\frac{1}{2}$ cups flour   2 cups water
                $\frac{1}{2}$ cup salt   2 tablespoons salad oil
                1 tablespoon   food coloring
                  powdered alum

Directions: In a large bowl, mix flour, salt, and alum together; set aside.
             In a medium saucepan, bring water and oil to a boil. Remove from heat and pour over flour mixture. Knead the dough. Color dough by adding a few drops of food coloring. Store in covered container.

Ms. Anderson plans to make play dough for her class. She finds the recipe above on the Internet.

18. a. Copy and use the ratio table below to find out how many cups of flour Ms. Anderson needs in order to make two portions of play dough.

Number of Portions	1	2		
Cups Flour	$2\frac{1}{2}$			

b. How many cups of flour does Ms. Anderson need for 11 portions?

Ms. Anderson has a 5-pound bag of flour. She wonders how many cups of flour are in the bag. She looks in a cookbook and finds that one cup of flour weighs 4 ounces (oz). Her bag of flour weighs 80 oz.

19. How many cups of flour are in Ms. Anderson's bag of flour? You may use the following ratio table.

Cups Flour				
Weight (in ounces)				

Suppose Ms. Anderson uses the entire bag of flour to make play dough.

20. a. How many portions can she make? You may want to use the ratio tables from problems 18 and 19.

b. How much of each ingredient will she need for this number of portions? You may want to use an extended ratio table like this one. Note that *tbsp* means "tablespoon" and *tsp* means "teaspoon."

Number of Portions				
Cups Flour				
Cup Salt				
Tbsp Alum				
Cups Water				
Tbsp Salad Oil				

A The Ratio Table

Summary ⟫

A ratio table is a useful tool to organize and solve problems. To set up a ratio table, label each row and set up the first-column ratio.

You can use several operations to make a column with new numbers.

Here are some examples of operations you can use.

Multiplying   **Adding Columns**

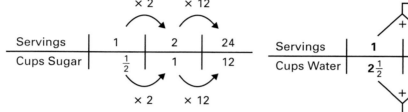

When using ratio tables, you often use a combination of operations to get the desired result. The examples below show different possibilities using combinations of operations that have the same result.

Combination of Operations

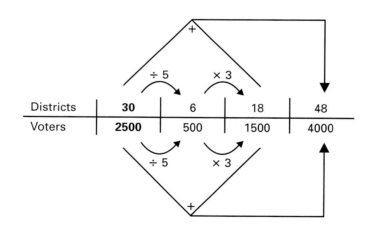

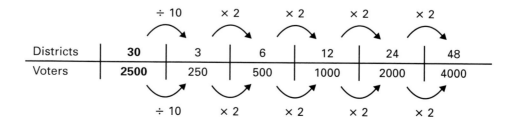

Check Your Work

Notebooks are shipped with 25 notebooks in one package.

1. How many notebooks are in 16 packages? Show your solution in a ratio table.

Number of Packages			
Number of Notebooks			

2. Jason ordered 575 notebooks for Springfield Middle School. How many packages will he receive?

3. a. Refer to the Office Supply Store price list on page 8 and write down the prices for black pens, protractors, and rulers.

   b. Use ratio tables to calculate the price of these items: one black pen, one protractor, one ruler.

   c. Calculate the cost for seven of each item.

Kim and Jamila plan to make a special snack for their class of 20 students. They found this recipe.

Banana Pops (8 servings)

Ingredients: 4 just-ripe bananas
1 cup topping, such as ground toasted almonds, toasted coconut, or candy sprinkles
8 wooden craft sticks
$\frac{1}{2}$ cup honey

Directions:  Spread toppings of your choice on a plate or plates. Peel bananas and cut in half crosswise. Insert a craft stick into each cut end. Pour honey onto a paper plate. Roll the banana in honey until it is fully coated. Roll banana in topping of choice until coated on all sides, pressing with fingers to help topping adhere. Place pops on waxed paper-lined cookie sheet. Serve at once.

4. How much of each ingredient do they need if they make 20 servings?

 For Further Reflection

 Explain why this problem cannot be solved with a ratio table.

Usually Stefanie boils an egg in six minutes. How many minutes does she need to boil four eggs?

Make up a problem that can be solved with a ratio table.

The Bar Model

School Garden

Every spring, Springfield Middle School allows groups of students to sign up and maintain garden plots. All garden plots are the same size. Below is a portion of the school garden with seven plots in it. Each group divides a plot into equal pieces for each student.

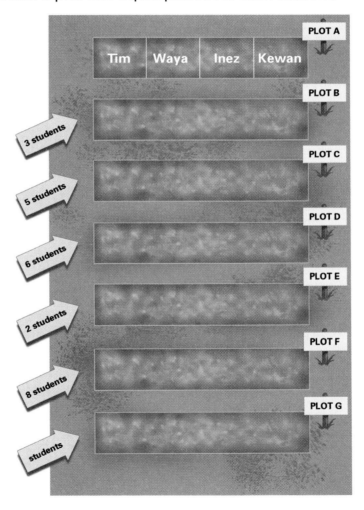

Inez, Kewan, Tim, and Waya maintain Plot A. They used string to divide their garden plot into four equal pieces.

1. a. Explain how they used string to equally divide Plot A.

   b. Use a fraction to describe what part of the plot each student claims.

Marc, Melinda, and Joyce maintain Plot B. They also want to divide their plot into equal pieces using strips of tape.

Use **Student Activity Sheet 3** for problems 2–4.

2. **a.** Cut out one length of the paper strip. Use the strip to divide Plot B into three equal parts.

   b. Label each part of Plot B with a fraction.

The other plots will be divided among groups of 5, 6, 2, and 8 students. One plot is unclaimed.

3. **a.** Use the paper strip to divide Plots C–F into the number of equal pieces indicated.

   b. Label each part with a fraction. Be prepared to explain how you used the strip to divide the plots.

4. Choose a different number of students to share the last garden plot, Plot G. Divide Plot G accordingly.

In problems 2–4 above, you used a paper strip as a kind of measuring strip to make equal parts. You used fractions to describe each part; for example:

Tim, Waya, and Inez share three-fourths of Plot A. A fraction relationship to describe this situation is $\frac{1}{4} + \frac{1}{4} + \frac{1}{4} = \frac{3}{4}$.

5. Use garden Plots B–G to describe five other fraction relationships.

Measuring strips can be used to find parts of a whole.

If you have three parts out of four, you can express this as the fraction $\frac{3}{4}$ on a **fraction bar**.

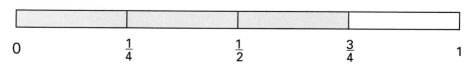

6. **Reflect** How are a measuring strip and a fraction bar the same? How are they different?

Water Tanks

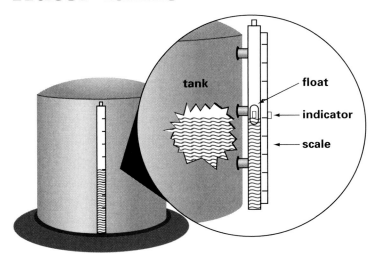

tank
float
indicator
scale

Students use a supply of rainwater, stored in tanks, to water the garden plots.

The largest tank in the garden holds 400 liters (L) of water. However, during a dry spell, it usually has less than 400 L of water.

The outside of the tank has a gauge that shows the level of the water in the tank.

You can use a gauge like a fraction bar.

7. Here is a drawing of the water gauge on four different days.

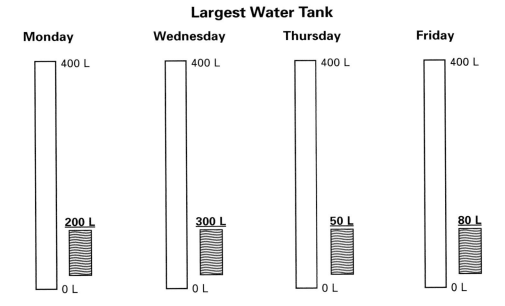

Largest Water Tank

| Monday | Wednesday | Thursday | Friday |

On **Student Activity Sheet 4**, shade each gauge to show the water level indicated for that day.

8. Next to your shading, write the fraction that best describes the water level on each day.

9. Make your own drawing of the gauge on Tuesday. You will need to select the amount of water (in liters) in the tank, shade the part on the gauge, and describe this part with a fraction.

There are different-sized water tanks available at the school garden. By looking at the gauge on a tank, the students can see how much water is inside the tank.

Here are two tanks, one with a water capacity of 50 L and the other 300 L.

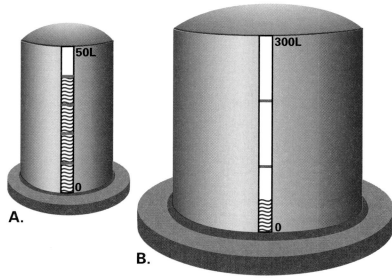

A.

B.

10. **a.** Explain which of these two water tanks has more water. How did you find out?

b. What fraction of the tank contains water? In your notebook, write the fraction for the shaded area of each gauge.

c. How many liters of water are there in each tank? Write the number of liters in each tank next to the shaded part.

Below are the gauges of three other tanks in the school garden. The maximum capacity of each tank is indicated on top of each gauge.

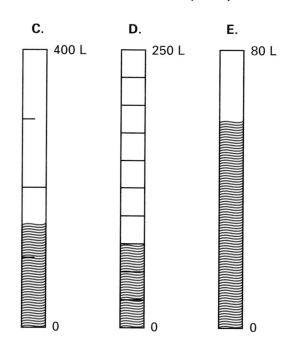

C. 400 L

D. 250 L

E. 80 L

11. **a.** What part of each tank is filled? Write each answer as a fraction on **Student Activity Sheet 4** next to the shaded area of the gauge.

b. How many liters of water are in each tank now? Write the number of liters in each tank next to the shaded part.

This week, Tim and Waya have to take care of watering all of the plots. They will connect a hose to one of the water tanks. They want to use the tank that has the most water.

12. Describe how Tim and Waya might determine which tank they will use.

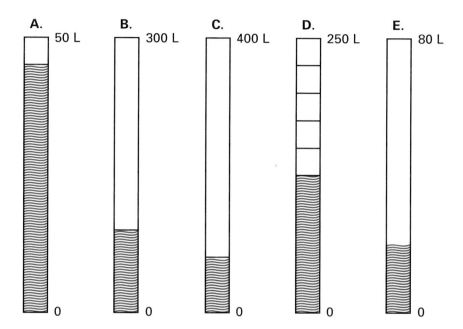

13. What part of each tank is filled? Write your answer as a fraction next to the shaded part of each tank on **Student Activity Sheet** 5.

14. How many liters of water are in each tank? Write your answer next to the shaded part of each tank.

15. Reflect   Which tank would you suggest Tim and Waya use?

Percents on the Computer

Manita found a program on a website, and she wants to install the program on her computer. First she starts to download the file. After a while, she sees this window on her screen.

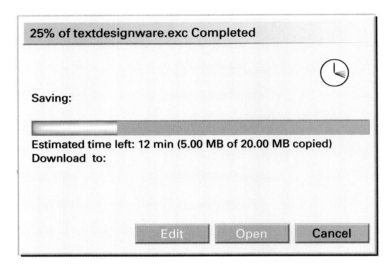

16. **a.** Describe the information given in this window.

    b. Describe how to find the total time it will take Manita to download the file.

When the program is downloaded, Manita starts to install it. A new window appears with a bar.

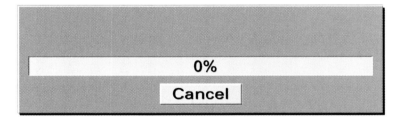

Then the bar changes into:

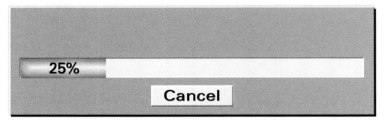

17. What does this bar tell you?

Eight minutes after she started to install the program, the bar shows:

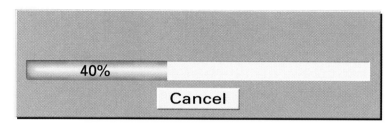

18. Estimate how many more minutes Manita has to wait until the program is installed.

Manita wonders how she can make an exact calculation for the total installation time. She starts to draw the following **percent bar**.

19. Copy the bar in your notebook and show how you can use this model to find the total installation time.

Manita installs a second program. After 3 minutes, the window shows:

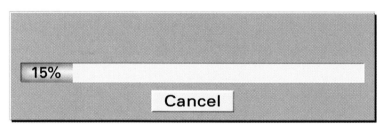

20. a. Estimate how many more minutes it will take Manita to install the program.

To make an accurate calculation, you can set up a percent bar like this one.

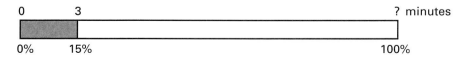

b. Copy the percent bar in your notebook and calculate the total time it will take Manita to install this program.

Percent bars can be used to find parts of a whole, expressed in a percentage. A fully shaded strip or bar represents the whole, or 100%. Half of the bar represents 50%, and $\frac{1}{4}$ of the bar represents 25%.

0%   25%   50%   100%

Percent bars can be used to solve problems using estimations or exact calculations.

21. **Reflect** Make up your own story of downloading or installing a program. Create a percent bar to illustrate the situation.

A Final Tip

22. If the bill for your lunch were $6.99, what would you leave as a tip for the waiter in each of these situations?

    a. The food and service were excellent.

    b. The food and service were average.

    c. The food was good, but the service was poor.

Most waiters depend on tips for their income. Most waiters are paid less than minimum wage, so the standard tip for good service is usually 15% to 20% of the total bill before the sales tax is added. Of course, leaving a tip is optional, and customers often leave more or less than 15% to 20%, depending on the quality of the food and service.

23. a. Copy the percent bar below and write each of your tips from problem 22 in an appropriate position.

0%   100%

   b. Which of your three tips from problem 22 was between 10% and 15%? Use the percent bar to help you to figure this out.

24. Estimate tips of 10%, 15%, and 20% for the following bills: $39.90, $80.10, and $14.50.

Use **Student Activity Sheet 6** to answer the following question.

25. a. Based on the service and tip indicated, fill in the tip for each bill on **Student Activity Sheet 6**.

Tip Tables			
Bill	Excellent Service = 20%	Average Service = 15%	Disappointing to Poor Service = 10%
$6.25			
$12.50			
$25.00			
$100.00			
$1.00			
$8.00			

   b. Extend each table with two additional bills and tips of your own.

   c. Reflect Look at your table entries in the blue columns. Describe anything extraordinary about these tip amounts.

Summary

Fraction Bar

If you have three parts out of four, you can express this as a fraction on a fraction bar. The parts are expressed as fractions.

Percent Bar

A fraction bar with percentages instead of fractions is called a percent bar. A percent bar can be used to find parts of a whole. The parts are expressed as percentages.

You can use a percent bar to solve problems using estimations or exact calculations. Here are two examples.

Example 1

After five minutes, 20% of the time has elapsed. What is the total time?

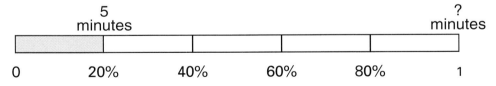

Here are three different solution strategies.

- Calculate 10% (2.5 minutes) and then 100% (25 minutes).

- Calculate 40% (10 minutes), then 80% (20 minutes), and finally, 100% (25 minutes).

- Use fractions: The shaded part is $\frac{1}{5}$ of the whole, so you need 5 parts (5 × 5 minutes). The total time is 25 minutes.

Example 2

The bill is $32.00. Calculate a 15% tip.

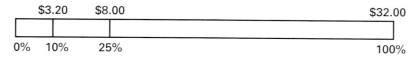

Here are two different solution strategies.

- Calculate 10% ($3.20), then 5% ($1.60), adding for 15% ($4.80).
- Calculate 25% ($8.00), then 10% ($3.20), subtracting for 15% ($4.80).

Check Your Work

Two coffee pots are used for Family Night at Springfield Middle School. Each coffee pot has a gauge that shows how much coffee is in each pot.

Use **Student Activity Sheet 7** for problems 1 and 2.

1. One coffee pot holds 60 cups of coffee.

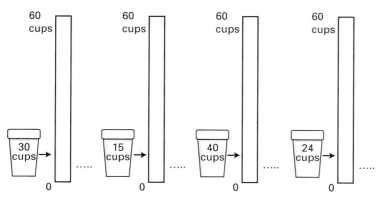

a. Shade each gauge to show the coffee level for the number of cups of coffee indicated.

b. Next to your shading, write the fraction that best describes the coffee level.

2. The second coffee pot holds 80 cups of coffee. These drawings show the gauge at four different times during the evening.

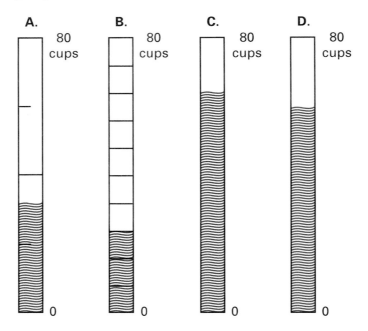

   A.   B.   C.   D.

a. For each drawing, what fraction of the coffee pot is filled with coffee? Write your answer as a fraction and as a percent next to each shaded part on **Student Activity Sheet 7**.

b. For each drawing, how many cups of coffee remain in the coffee pot? Write your answer next to each shaded part.

3. Copy these bars in your notebook. The shaded part of each bar is the time elapsed during a download. For each bar, make an accurate calculation of the total time.

a.

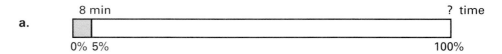

b.

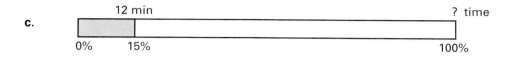

c.

12 min   ? time

0%   15%   100%

d.

1 hour   ? time

0%   80%   100%

4. Estimate tips of 10%, 15%, and 20% for the following bills: $20.10 and $11.95.

For Further Reflection

Juan went out to dinner on Friday night and left a 20% tip. Marisa went out for breakfast on Sunday morning and left a 15% tip. Marisa claims that she gave a larger tip than Juan. Is this possible? Explain.

The Number Line

Distances

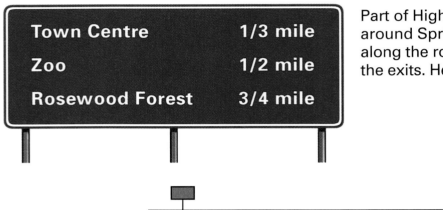

Part of Highway 22 is the beltway around Springfield. Signs posted along the road show the distances to the exits. Here is one of these signs.

Town Centre	1/3 mile
Zoo	1/2 mile
Rosewood Forest	3/4 mile

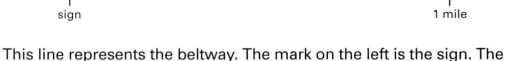

sign   1 mile

This line represents the beltway. The mark on the left is the sign. The mark on the right is 1 mile (mi) down the road from the sign.

1. a. Copy the drawing above. Use the information on the sign to position each of the three exits onto the line.

b. Which of these two pairs of exits are farther apart?

i. the exit from Town Centre to the Zoo

ii. the exit from the Zoo to Rosewood Forest

Show how you found your answer.

The next sign along the beltway is posted at the Zoo exit. Some information is missing in the sign on the right.

Rosewood Forest	____ mile
Airport	____ mile

2. a. Copy this sign and fill in the missing distances. To fill in the airport distance, you need to know that the Rosewood Forest exit is exactly halfway between the Zoo exit and the Airport exit.

b. How far is the Airport exit from the first sign?

c. Place your Airport exit on the line you drew for problem 1a.

You can use what you know about fraction strips to order different fractions on a **number line.**

Fraction strips

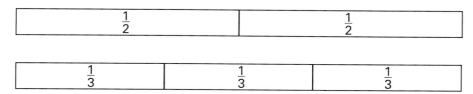

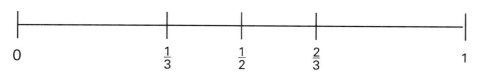

Number Line

0	$\frac{1}{3}$	$\frac{1}{2}$	$\frac{2}{3}$	1

Biking Trail

Rosewood Forest is a nature preserve that is open for recreation. Most famous is a bike trail that is 30 kilometers (30 km) long. Along the trail there are rest areas and special places for wildlife viewing. Here is a list of the places along this trail.

- restrooms (R1): $\frac{1}{3}$ of the way
- restrooms (R2): $\frac{3}{4}$ of the way.
- bee colony (BC): $\frac{1}{2}$ of the way.
- picnic area (P): $\frac{2}{3}$ of the way.
- wilderness campground (W): $\frac{5}{6}$ of the way.
- bird-viewing hut (H): $\frac{1}{5}$ of the way
- grazing cattle (C): $\frac{3}{5}$ of the way

Visitors can obtain a leaflet with information about the trail and the locations of the special places along it. This line represents the trail.

```
├──────────────────────────────────────────────────────────────┤
```
Start   **End**

3. **a.** Draw your own line representing the trail.

   b. Correctly position each special place along this trail. To save space, write only the corresponding letter of each special place.

Sam and Nicole take a rest at the bird-viewing hut (H).

4. What part of the trail do they still have to bike?

An additional picnic area is being built closer to the start of the trail. It will be located between the bird-viewing hut (H) and the first restrooms (R1).

5. Correctly position the new picnic area (P2) on your trail line. Describe the location using a fraction.

Signposts

Sam and Nicole are biking the Henson Creek Trail in Maryland. They are not sure where they are right now. When they see a signpost, they stop and look at their map of the trail.

Using the information on the signpost and the map, they start to figure out where they are. A map of the Henson Creek Trail is on **Student Activity Sheet 8**.

6. **a.** Why are there two arrows on the signpost pointing in two different directions?

   b. According to the signpost, how far are Sam and Nicole from Oxon Hill Road?

   c. Which road are they closer to—Tucker Road or Bock Road?

7. Use **Student Activity Sheet 8** to estimate where Sam and Nicole are now. Mark that spot on the map.

Map of Henson Creek Trail

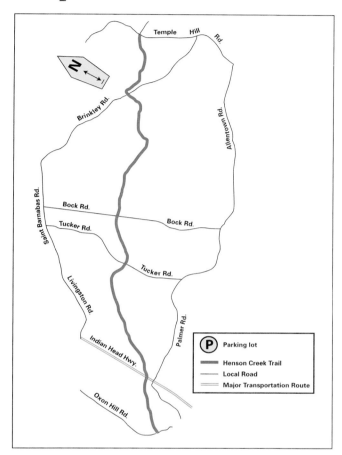

The distances on this type of signpost are written with one decimal, so tenths of a mile are used.

You can use the **bar model** to make a number line.

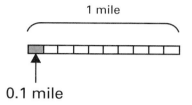

1 mile

0.1 mile

Each mile is divided into ten parts, so each part is one-tenth of a mile.

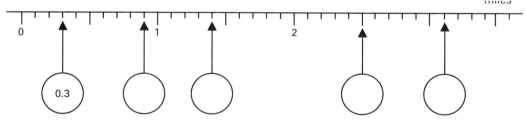

0.3

8. a. Explain why 0.3 is placed correctly on this number line.

b. On **Student Activity Sheet 8**, fill in each of the empty circles with an appropriate decimal number.

c. Place the following decimal numbers on this number line: 0.7, 2.1, and 3.4.

HENSON CREEK TRAIL

OXON HILL Rd 0.5mi

TUCKER ROAD 2.1mi
BOCK ROAD 2.8mi

The signpost from problem 6 shows the distance to Tucker Road and the distance to Bock Road.

9. What is the distance from Tucker Road to Bock Road?

Sam and Nicole continue their bike trip along the trail. After a while, they see this signpost.

10. How do you know that this signpost is where Brinkley Road crosses the trail? Indicate the location of this signpost on the map of **Student Activity Sheet 8.**

The bike trail crosses Bock Road, Tucker Road, and Oxon Hill Road. To get a better picture of all of the distances, you can use a number line representing the trail. The signpost from problem 10 is placed at zero (0) location.

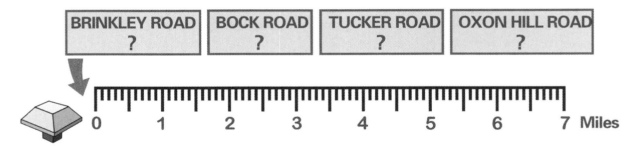

Use Student Activity Sheet 9 to answer problems 11–13.

11. Locate where the trail crosses each of the following roads: Bock Road, Tucker Road, and Oxon Hill Road. To save space, use arrows to connect each road to its location on the number line.

12. How many miles did Sam and Nicole bike from the first signpost to the signpost at Brinkley Road?

13. On the number line in problem 11, indicate where the bike trail crosses Temple Hill Road.

A new signpost will be placed where the bike trail crosses Tucker Road. What distances will this signpost show? You can use the number line on page 30 to help you calculate the distances.

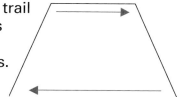

14. Copy the drawing and write the distances on the signpost.

The Jump Jump Game

Objective of the game: Use a number line to "jump" from one number to another in as few jumps as possible.

How to play: To get to a number, players can make jumps of three different lengths: 0.1, 1, and 10. Players can jump forward or backward.

Example: Jump from 0 to 0.9

If you make jumps of 0.1, then you need nine jumps to go from 0 to 0.9.

However, you can go from 0 to 0.9 in two jumps.

15. Use **Student Activity Sheet 9** to show how you can jump from 0 to 0.9 in two jumps.

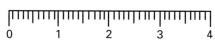

If you don't have a picture of a numbered number line, you can draw your own empty number line. You can show your jumps by drawing curves of different lengths—a small curve for a jump length of 0.1, a medium curve for a jump length of 1, and a large curve for a jump length of 10.

Here is one example: Jump from 1.6 to 2.5.

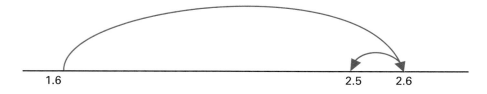

16. Describe the moves shown above. How many total jumps were made?

Here is the beginning of another round: Jump from 0 to 22.9.

You can make two jumps of 10, then one jump of 1, another jump of 1, and then…?

17. Describe the different ways you can jump to the final destination of 22.9.

18. Use **Student Activity Sheet 10** to complete the ten rounds as described on the next pages.

Complete Rounds 1 and 2 individually. After each round, write the total number of jumps you made in the box at the right.

Round 1: Go from 0 to 5.3 in the fewest jumps.

Round 2: Go from 0 to 6.9 in the fewest jumps.

Compare your results with a classmate. Score two points for a win and one point for a tie.

Do the following problems individually.

Round 3: Go from 0 to 29.8 in the fewest jumps.

Round 4: Go from 0 to 28.1 in the fewest jumps.

Round 5: Go from 0 to 51.6 in the fewest jumps.

Compare your results with a classmate. Score two points for a win and one point for a tie. Keep track of your total score.

The next few problems are a little different. Do the problems individually.

Round 6: Go from 5.0 to 26.8 in the fewest jumps.

Round 7: Go from 32.4 to 54.6 in the fewest jumps.

Compare your results with a classmate. Score two points for a win and one point for a tie. Keep track of your total score.

Round 8: Go from 4.5 to 8.4 in the fewest jumps.

Round 9: Go from 5.6 to 17.3 in the fewest jumps.

Round 10: Go from 44.4 to 51.6 in the fewest jumps.

Compare your results with a classmate. Score two points for a win and one point for a tie. Write your total score in the star on **Student Activity Sheet 10** or draw your own star.

19. Make up three additional Jump Jump Game problems.

Guess the Price

On the television show "Guess the Price," contestants attempt to guess the actual prices of various items. The person who guesses the closest to the actual price wins that item and is eligible for the Big Wheel Finale. People watching at home can see a number line that shows the correct price and the guesses of each contestant.

Nathalie, Leo, Maria, and Ben are today's contestants. Their first task is to guess the price of a new release DVD. The actual price is $11.95.

The home viewers see this number line.

$11.95

Nathalie guesses $11.50. The number line now shows:

$11.50 $11.95

The guesses of the three other contestants are:

Maria: $12.00   Leo: $12.50   Ben: $11.75

20. a. Create the number line for this scenario. Who won the DVD?

b. Whose guess is the farthest from the actual price? How far is it?

The next scenario involves a pair of jogging shoes.

The actual price is $98.75. The line shows:

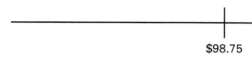

$98.75

Here are the contestants' guesses.

Nathalie: $100   Maria: $96.20   Leo: $91.99   Ben: $99.25

21. a. Create the number line for this scenario.

b. Whose guess is the closest to the actual price? Whose is the farthest from it?

The next scenario involves a DVD player whose actual price is $165.30.

Here are the contestants' guesses.

Nathalie: $150.80   Maria: $170   Leo: $160.99   Ben: $171.25

22. a. Create the number line for this scenario.

b. Whose guess is the closest to the actual price? Whose is the farthest from it?

⬥ The Number Line

Summary ✕✕

In this section, you ordered fractions and decimals on a **number line**.

To position fractions on a number line, you can use what you know about fraction bars and the order of fractions.

Fraction Bar

One-third is less than one-half.

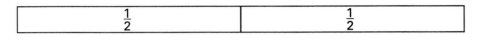

$$\frac{1}{2} \quad \frac{1}{2}$$

$$\frac{1}{3} \quad \frac{1}{3} \quad \frac{1}{3}$$

Number Line

On a number line, one-third is located to the left of one-half

$$0 \quad \frac{1}{3} \quad \frac{1}{2} \quad \frac{2}{3} \quad 1$$

You can use a number line to find how far apart two decimal numbers are positioned. This can help you if you need to add or subtract decimal numbers.

Example 1

1   1.8 2   2.7   3

Calculate 2.7 − 1.8.
On the number line, 1.8 and 2.7 are 0.9 apart, so 2.7 − 1.8 = 0.9.

Example 2

You can draw your own empty number line.
Find 2.8 − 1.6. Or how far apart are 1.6 and 2.8?
A jump of 1 and two jumps of 0.1 total 1.2.
So 1.6 and 2.8 are 1.2 units away from each other.
2.8 − 1.6 = 1.2

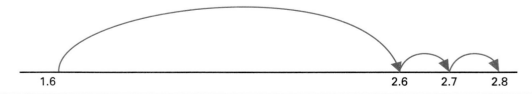

1.6   2.6   2.7   2.8

The line below represents the beltway. Two locations are indicated: the location of the sign and a distance of one mile down the road from the sign.

Sign   1 mile

1. **a.** Copy the drawing above. Use the information on the sign to correctly position each of the three exits onto the line.

   b. Which of these two pairs of exits are farther apart?

      i. The South Street exit and the Main Street exit

      ii. The Main Street exit and the Harbor exit

   Show how you found your answer.

South Street $\frac{1}{3}$ mile

Main Street $\frac{3}{4}$ mile

Harbor $1\frac{1}{4}$ mile

The next sign along the beltway is posted at the Main Street exit. Some information is missing in the sign on the right.

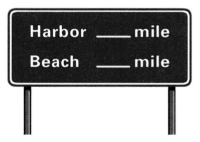

Harbor ____ mile

Beach ____ mile

2. The distance from the harbor to the beach is is twice as far as the distance from Main Street to the harbor.

   a. Copy this sign and fill in the missing distances.

   b. How far is the beach from the first sign?

   c. Place the Beach exit on the line in your drawing from problem 1a.

Here is another signpost on the Henson Creek Trail. The mileage information on the signpost is missing. The signpost is located where the bike trail crosses Bock Road.

3. How far away is this signpost from all the other roads that cross the bike trail? Add the missing mileage information to the signpost on **Student Activity Sheet 9**. (Hint: Use the number line from problem 10 or **Student Activity Sheet 9** to help you).

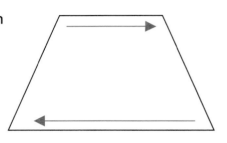

Play the Jump Jump Game using your own paper. Remember that players can make jumps of three different lengths: 0.1, 1, and 10. Players can jump forward and backward. Write down your best score.

4. Go from 0 to 48.1 in the fewest jumps possible.

0 ───────────────────────────────► ☐

5. Go from 6.8 to 10.7 in the fewest jumps possible.

◄───────────────────────────────► ☐

In this scenario of the Price Guessing Game, contestants guess the price of a baseball cap whose actual price is $6.89. The line shows the price.

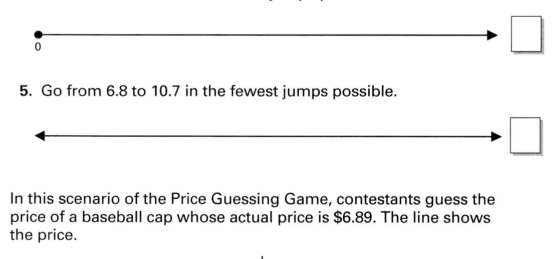

$6.89

These are the contestants' guesses.

Nathalie: $9.99   Maria: $8.50

Leo: $5.00   Ben: $7.75

6. a. Show the actual price and the guesses on the number line.

   b. Whose guess is the closest to the actual price? Whose guess is the farthest from it?

   c. What are the differences between each guess and the actual price?

 ## For Further Reflection

Complete each number sentence so that the distance between the pair of decimal numbers on the left side is the same as the distance between the pair on the right side. Try to reason about the numbers before you calculate distances. You might not need to do any distance calculations to make these number sentences true.

   a. $9.3 - 4.1 = 8.3 - \ldots.$

   b. $6.8 - 2.5 = \ldots. - 3.5$

   c. $7.5 - \ldots. = 9.5 - 2.7$

   d. $\ldots. - 1.4 = \ldots. - 5.8$

   e. make up your own problem

   $\ldots. - \ldots. = \ldots. - \ldots.$

Which problems were the easiest for you to do? Why? Write about anything new you may have discovered about subtraction problems.

The Double Number Line

Double Scale Line

In many countries, distances are expressed in kilometers. In the United States, distances are represented in miles. Today, many maps use a **double scale line**, using both kilometers and miles. This map of Toronto, Canada, has a double scale line.

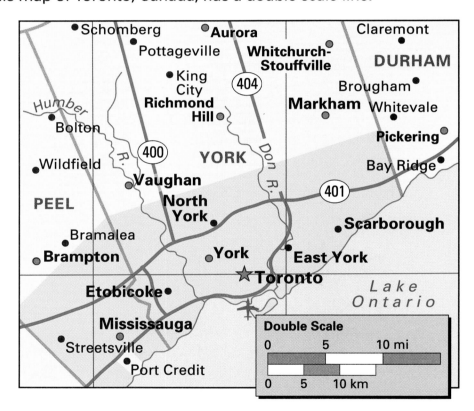

1. **a.** Describe how you might use the double scale line.

   b. Use the double scale line to find three relationships between miles and kilometers. Write your relationships like this.

   …. miles equal about …. kilometers

   …. kilometers equal about …. miles

The Toronto City Centre Airport is located on an island close to the coast. The distance from downtown Toronto to the airport is about 4 km.

2. **a.** Estimate this distance using miles.

   b. About how many kilometers equals 5 mi? Show how you found your answer.

You can measure distance two different ways: as the crow flies (in a straight line) or as Taxi Cab distance (along the ground from place to place). The distance as the crow flies is shorter (except for cases in which the two distances are the same).

The distance from downtown Toronto to Vaughan as the crow flies is about 15 mi.

3. About how many kilometers is this distance? Show how you found your answer.

This is part of a distance table. You can read the distances between Toronto and other large cities. Distances are given in both kilometers and miles. Some information is missing.

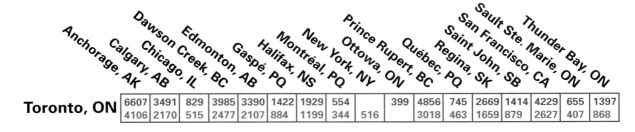

	Anchorage, AK	Calgary, AB	Chicago, IL	Dawson Creek, BC	Edmonton, AB	Gaspé, PQ	Halifax, NS	Montréal, PQ	New York, NY	Ottowa, ON	Prince Rupert, BC	Québec, PQ	Regina, SK	Saint John, SB	San Francisco, CA	Sault Ste. Marie, ON	Thunder Bay, ON
Toronto, ON	6607	3491	829	3985	3390	1422	1929	554		399	4856	745	2669	1414	4229	655	1397
	4106	2170	515	2477	2107	884	1199	344	516		3018	463	1659	879	2627	407	868

4. How far is the distance between Toronto and Chicago in kilometers? What is this distance in miles? How can you be sure which is which?

5. Find the missing information. You do not have to be precise.

City Blocks

Springfield city blocks are made up of streets and avenues, that are very regular and look much like a grid. Each city block in Springfield is usually $\frac{1}{8}$ mile long.

Springfield

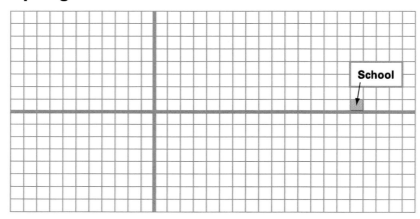

Gary lives $\frac{1}{2}$ mi from school. He walks to school every morning.

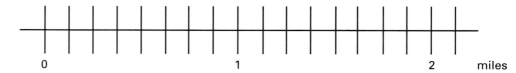

6. How many city blocks does Gary walk to school? How did you figure this out?

Sharon lives $1\frac{1}{4}$ mi from school. She bikes to school every morning.

7. How many city blocks does she bike to school? How did you figure this out?

8. Use the city map on **Student Activity Sheet 11** to locate where Gary and Sharon could live.

Rene travels 11 blocks from home to school.

9. a. How many miles is this? How did you find out?

    b. Would you advise Rene to use her bike or to walk to school? Give reasons to support your answer.

Marcus wants to find out how far Ms. Anderson lives from school. He knows she travels 19 city blocks to school. He draws a **double number line** like this.

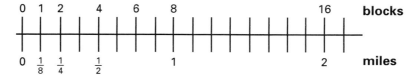

This double number line is drawn to scale, with numbers on top as well as on the bottom. Learning how to use a double number line will help you make precise calculations effortlessly.

10. a. On **Student Activity Sheet 11**, use this double number line to find out how far Ms. Anderson lives from school.

    b. Use the double number line to find out how many city blocks there are in $1\frac{3}{4}$ mi.

Every morning, Gary takes about 10 minutes to walk $\frac{1}{2}$ mi to school. Sharon's bike is broken, so she is making plans to walk $1\frac{1}{4}$ mi to school. She asks Gary how long this might take her.

11. a. Copy the double number line below in your notebook. Using a grid helps to partition the spaces evenly.

    b. Use the double number line to calculate how long it will take Sharon to walk to school. State any assumptions you are making in finding your answer.

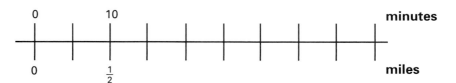

Gary and Sharon like to hike. This weekend they plan to walk a $4\frac{3}{4}$-mi lake trail. They estimate how long they will hike. Gary uses a double number line like the one on page 43.

12. Draw a double number line and use it to find the time needed for the hike.

Sharon uses a ratio table to make the same calculation.

Minutes	10	20	80	5	15	....
Miles	$\frac{1}{2}$	1	4	$\frac{1}{4}$	$\frac{3}{4}$	$4\frac{3}{4}$

13. a. Explain how Sharon decided on the numbers in each new column in the table.

b. Which model do you prefer, the double number line or the ratio table? Explain your preference.

Weights and Prices

Jack's Delicatessen sells many different kinds of food. Jack is the shop owner. He imports fresh deli meats and more than 80 kinds of cheese. Workers slice the food items, weigh them, and calculate the prices.

Susan weighs a piece of pepper salami at 0.2 kilograms (kg).

14. Explain how Susan will calculate the price for this piece. What information does she need?

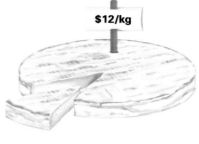

Ahmed is shopping for some brie, a kind of French cheese. He wants the piece to weigh about $\frac{1}{4}$ kg. Susan cuts off a piece and puts it on the scale. The scale shows:

15. a. Does Ahmed have the amount of brie he wants?

b. Calculate how much Ahmed has to pay for this piece of brie.

Ahmed often buys brie at Jack's Delicatessen. Lately he has been thinking about a clever way to estimate the price. The scale reminds him of a double number line. He creates the following double number line including both weight and price on it.

16. Show how Ahmed can use this double number line to estimate the price for 0.7 kg of brie.

This week, brie is on sale for $9.00 per kilogram.

17. What is the sale price of 0.7 kg of brie? Show how you found your answer.

18. a. Select three different pieces of brie to purchase and write down the weight of each piece.

b. Draw a scale pointer to mark each weight on a different number line. (You may want to exchange your notebook with a classmate after both of you have drawn your pointers.)

c. Estimate the regular price and the sale price of the three pieces of brie.

$9/kg

Jack's Delicatessen also sells fruit. This week, California grapes are on sale for $1.89 per kilogram.

Grapes $1.89/kg

Madeleine places her grapes on the scale. This is what she sees.

```
|TT|TT|TT|TTT|TTT|TTT|
0       0.5      1    ↑        2kg
```

19. a. How much do Madeleine's grapes weigh?

   b. Estimate how much Madeleine has to pay for the grapes. You may want to use a double number line for your estimation and explanation.

Ahmed decides to use the money he has left to buy some grapes. He counts his money and realizes he has $1.25.

20. Estimate what weight of grapes Ahmed can buy for $1.25. Show how you found your answer.

Susan weighed fruit for 5 customers. She wrote the prices on small price tags, but, unfortunately, the tags got mixed up.

21. Match the information written below to the corresponding price tags. Find out which note belongs to each customer. Show your work.

Mounim	0.5 kg grapes for $1.50/kg
Claire	1.8 kg apples for $1.25/kg
Frank	2.5 kg oranges for $1.90/kg
Nadine	1.1 kg bananas for $2.50/kg
Gail	0.9 kg kiwis for $2.40/kg

$4.75 $0.75 $2.75

$2.25 $2.16

Math History

Edmund Gunter (1581-1626), an English mathematician, invented a measurement tool for surveying. It came into common usage around 1700 and was the standard unit for measuring distances for more than 150 years.

Gunter's Chain is 66 ft long. Its usefulness comes from its connection to decimals; it is divided into 100 links.

From 1832 to 1859, the General Land Office conducted the original public land survey of Iowa.

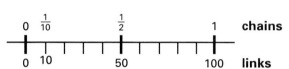

22. How many chains make one mile?

Because Gunter's chain was used to measure America, the United States did not use the metric system (developed in France in 1790).

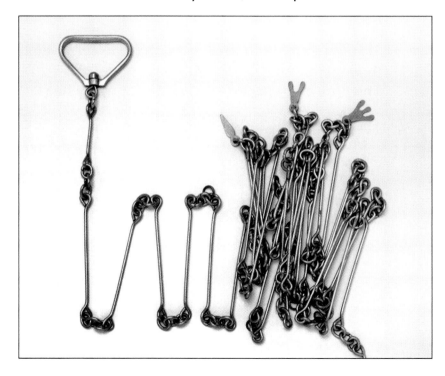

The Double Number Line

Summary

Double Number Line

A **double number line** is a number line with a scale on top and a different scale on the bottom so that you can organize and compare items that change regularly according to a rule or pattern.

Example 1

The price changes $12 for every kilogram purchased.

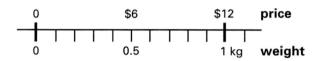

Example 2

The time changes by 10 minutes for every half-mile walked.

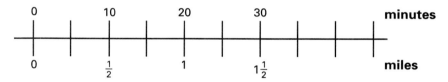

You can use a double number line to solve problems with fractions, decimals, and ratios.

Ratio Table Model

You can use a ratio table to solve these same problems.

Example 3

The time changes by 10 minutes for every half-mile walked.

Minutes	10	20	80	5	15	....
Miles	$\frac{1}{2}$	1	4	$\frac{1}{4}$	$\frac{3}{4}$	$4\frac{3}{4}$

On a double number line, as on a single number line, the numbers always appear in order.

Many American cities have a street plan that looks like a grid. Philip read the following on the Internet.

A lot of American cities are laid out with grids of $\frac{1}{16}$ mi by $\frac{1}{8}$ mi (metric equivalents: 100 m by 200 m). Major streets are usually at $\frac{1}{4}$-, $\frac{1}{2}$-, or 1-mi intervals.

Philip uses this information to set up the following relationships between miles and meters.

1. Help Philip use the double number line to find the distance between major U.S. streets. Write your answers using the metric system.

Near the end of the week, Jack sells a basket of mixed fruit for $1.25 per kilogram.

2. **a.** How much mixed fruit can you purchase for $5.00?

   b. The scale indicates 3.2 kg. What is the price for this fruit?

Sharon's bike is fixed so she and Gary plan a $7\frac{1}{2}$-mi bike ride. They want to estimate how long they will bike.

Sharon knows that it takes $7\frac{1}{2}$ minutes to bike the $1\frac{1}{4}$ mi to school.

3. Use a double number line or a ratio table to find the amount of time they will bike.

 For Further Reflection

How are double number lines and ratio tables alike? How are they different? Which do you find easier to use?

E

Choose Your Model

In Sections A through D, you used different models. These models help you to solve problems involving ratios, fractions, decimals, and percents, and they often make calculations easier.

These are the models you used.

ratio table   percent bar   double number line

fraction bar   number line

In this section, you can choose the model you like best to represent and solve each problem. Sometimes you will need only a simple calculation instead of a model.

School Camp

Around April of every year, all seventh- and eighth-grade students at Springfield Middle School go on an overnight camping trip. To make preparations, Mrs. Ferrero prepares the following list for this year's trip.

Class 7A	27 students
Class 7B	31 students
Class 8A	23 students
Class 8B	24 students

1. Students travel to the camp in small buses. Each bus can hold 15 students. How many buses are needed to send all of the students to camp?

The campsite is located at Rosewood Forest, which is 150 mi from school. Jared wonders how long it will take to travel to the campsite. He estimates that the buses will drive about 45 mi per hour on average.

2. Choose a model to estimate the time needed to travel to the campsite.

During the trip, a canoe trip is organized. The canoes can be rented at the campsite's office. There are canoes available for rent for 2, 3, 4, or 5 people each.

3. Mrs. Ferrero prefers to rent all the same size canoes. How many canoes of what size should Mrs. Ferrero rent for the students? Explain how you found your answer.

Many team-building activities are planned for the campers. On Tuesday, an Olympic competition is held. Campers compete in a 200-m run and the long jump.

Faiza and Pablo wonder what the long jump Olympic record is. They found the following information.

In 1996, at the Olympic Games in Atlanta, Carl Lewis (USA) jumped a distance of 8.5 m in the long jump.

Faiza and Pablo looked for a meter stick and a yardstick.

4. a. Which one is longer—a meter stick or a yardstick?

　　b. About how many yards are there in 8.5 m?

　　c. About how many feet are there in 8.5 m?

Activity

Meter Spotting

For this activity, you will need a meter stick or a measuring tape at least one meter long.

First, estimate a distance by pacing off a distance of about one meter. Measure your distance after each attempt to monitor your progress.

- Using one-meter steps, pace off the distance of Carl Lewis's 1996 Olympic winning long jump.

- Use a meter stick or a measuring tape to measure (as precisely as possible) the distance that Carl Lewis jumped.

- Compare the distance you estimated and the distance you measured. Was your estimation too short? Too long? How much is the difference?

A meter can be divided into 10 smaller units, called **decimeters** (dm).

- Use your meter stick to measure the length of 1 dm.

In the distance of Carl Lewis's jump, fit eight whole meters. The part that remains is smaller than one meter.

- How many decimeters fit in the remaining part?

Here is a part of a meter stick in its actual size. The meter stick is divided into decimeters.

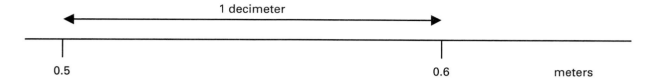

1 decimeter

0.5   0.6   meters

5. a. How many jumps of 1 dm do you have to make if you jump from 0 to 0.5 m?

b. How many jumps of 1 dm do you have to make if you jump from 0.6 m to 1 m?

6. Copy the following sentences and fill the blanks.

a. One meter is _____ decimeters

b. Two meters is _____ decimeters.

c. One decimeter is _____ meter.

d. Five decimeters is _____ meter.

A meter can be divided into 100 smaller units, called **centimeters** (cm).

Here is the same part of the meter stick from problem 5, but now the meter stick is divided into centimeters.

0.50   0.60   meters

7. a. How many jumps of 1 cm do you have to make if you jump from 0 to 0.50 m?

b. How many jumps of 1 cm do you have to make if you jump from 0.60 m to 1 m?

8. Write four statements similar to the ones in problem 6, but now use meters and centimeters.

9. Copy and complete each sentence.

   a. 8.50 meters is 8 meters and _____ decimeters.

   b. 8.50 meters is 8 meters and _____ centimeters.

Carl Lewis won his fourth Olympic medal in 1996. At that time, the world record holder was Mike Powell (USA). He made a jump of 8.95 m in 1991.

10. How much longer was Mike Powell's World Record jump compared to Carl Lewis's Olympic jump?

11. How many centimeters is the record of Mike Powell away from the magic barrier of 9 m?

Faiza, Juanita, Zinzi, and Margie are competing in the long jump. The results before Margie jumped are:

   Faiza 3.03 m   Juanita 3.10 m   Zinzi 2.95 m

Margie jumped a little under 3 m, but she did better than Zinzi.

12. a. Name 3 possible jump lengths for Margie.

    b. Order this group's results.

    c. Place all possible results on a number line and find out the differences in centimeters among the jumps of the 4 girls.

Here are the times for the six boys running the 200-m event.

Peter	27.05 seconds	Mustafa	27.93 seconds
Pablo	28.01 seconds	Jesse	27.15 seconds
Sam	26.84 seconds	Igor	28.60 seconds

13. **a.** Which two boys finished the closest to each other? What was the time difference?

   b. What was the time difference between the finish of the first and the last-place finishers?

Every day, six groups prepare dinner for 20 people. Each small group consists of five campers. Each group does all of the shopping and the cooking.

One group makes muffins for breakfast. This is the recipe they use.

Honey Make My Morning Muffins
(10 to 12 muffins)

Ingredients: $\frac{1}{2}$ cup milk

$\frac{1}{4}$ cup honey

1 egg, beaten

$2\frac{1}{2}$ cups buttermilk baking mix
(sometimes called biscuit mix)

Directions: In a medium bowl, combine milk, honey, and beaten egg; mix well. Add baking mix and stir until moistened. Spoon into greased muffin tins. Bake at 400°F for 18–20 minutes.

---

14. This group decides to make 30 muffins. Calculate how much of each ingredient the group needs.

15. What would you put on your shopping list for this group?

Another group decides to make pancakes. This is their recipe.

Buttermilk Pancakes
(about 14 pancakes)

Ingredients:

2 cups all-purpose flour

2 tablespoons sugar

2 teaspoons baking powder

$\frac{3}{4}$ teaspoon baking soda

$\frac{1}{2}$ teaspoon salt

2 cups buttermilk

$\frac{1}{3}$ cup milk

2 large eggs

$\frac{1}{4}$ cup butter or margarine, melted

3–4 tablespoons butter, vegetable oil, or shortening, for frying

$\frac{1}{2} - \frac{3}{4}$ cups pure maple syrup and additional butter (optional)

Directions:

1. Heat oven to 200°F. Combine flour, sugar, baking powder, baking soda, and salt in a large bowl. Whisk until blended. Combine buttermilk, milk, eggs and melted butter in a medium bowl. Whisk until blended.

2. Heat a large nonstick griddle. When griddle is hot, add buttermilk mixture to dry ingredients; mix batter with a wooden spoon just until blended. Lumps are okay.

3. Reduce heat to medium and grease griddle with butter, oil or shortening. Using a ladle or a $\frac{1}{3}$-cup dry measure, pour spoonfuls of batter a few inches apart onto the hot greased griddle. Cook until small bubbles begin to form on the top and some pop, 2 to 3 minutes. Carefully turn pancakes with a flexible spatula, then cook 1 to 2 minutes more, until golden brown. Serve immediately with maple syrup and additional butter, if desired, or keep pancakes warm in oven. Repeat process with remaining batter.

16. How many pancakes and how much of each ingredient do they need to prepare breakfast for 20 people?

While three students of this group prepare the pancakes, the two others make spaghetti sauce for dinner tonight.

When the sauce is ready, they have 2 liters (L) of sauce. They want to put the sauce in the refrigerator. They find three plastic containers; each can hold $\frac{3}{4}$ L.

17. Will they be able to store all of the sauce in these three containers? Show your work.

On the last night, students perform a talent show. Some students sing, some do a short skit, and others form a band. Isabel, Larry, and Warda organize the evening program. Mr. De Felko is willing to go to the next town to have copies made. At Plinko's, the cost of 10 copies is $1.15. Xelox charges $1.70 for 15 copies.

18. a. Where would you recommend that Isabel, Larry, and Warda send Mr. De Felko? Show how you found your answer.

    b. If tax in the local area is 4%, calculate the total bill for your recommendation.

Summary

Deci- and *centi-*

The prefix *deci-* is used with the metric system. It stands for 0.1, or $\frac{1}{10}$.

So if you divide 1 m into 10 equal parts, the size of each part is 1 decimeter (dm); 1 dm is $\frac{1}{10}$ of a meter.

The prefix *centi-* is used with the metric system. It stands for 0.01, or $\frac{1}{100}$.

So if you divide 1 m into 100 equal parts, the size of each part is 1 centimeter (cm); 1 cm is $\frac{1}{100}$ of a meter.

A distance of 3.25 m can mean:

- $3\frac{1}{4}$ m
- 3 m and 25 cm
- 3 m $2\frac{1}{2}$ dm
- 3 m 2 dm and 5 cm

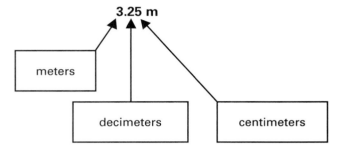

Models

These are the models that you have used in this unit.

ratio table	number line
fraction bar	empty number line
percent bar	double number line

For examples of these models, look at the summaries of the previous sections in this unit.

1. Tamara jumped 4.37 m and Janet jumped 4.49 m. Explain how much farther Janet jumped.

2. Karen received a photo from her pen pal in Europe. The photo has dimensions of 15 cm by 10 cm. Karen looks on the Internet for photo frames. There are different-sized frames available. Which of the following frames can she use without cutting the photo?

   a. 5 by 3.5 inches

   b. 6 by 4 inches

   c. 8 by 6 inches

3. A piece of pepperoni weighs 2,400 grams.

   Where would you make a cut to make one of the pieces weigh about 1,800 grams?

4. What will this dinner cost you in Iowa, where the sales tax is 5%? Remember to calculate the sales tax and the tip separately on the cost of the dinner.

Check	
Dinner	$7.99
Includes Buffet	
& Sundae Bar	
Thank You	

5. For dinner, one group makes pizza for 20 people. They use this recipe.

Honey Chicken Pizza
(6 servings)

Ingredients:

$\frac{3}{4}$ cup + 2 tablespoons prepared tomato-based pizza sauce

$\frac{1}{4}$ cup honey

$\frac{1}{2}$ teaspoon hot pepper sauce, or to taste

1 cup diced or shredded, cooked chicken breast

1 tube (10 oz.) refrigerated pizza dough

1 tablespoon olive oil

3 oz. blue cheese, finely crumbled ($\frac{3}{4}$ cup)

$\frac{1}{2}$ cup finely diced celery

Directions:

Heat pizza sauce and honey; remove from heat. Stir in hot pepper sauce. Mix 2 tablespoons sauce with chicken; reserve. Shape pizza dough according to package directions for thin-crusted pizza. Brush pizza shell with 1 tablespoon olive oil. Spread remaining $\frac{3}{4}$ cup sauce over dough. Scatter reserved chicken over sauce. Bake at 500°F until lightly browned, about 10 minutes. Remove from oven. Sprinkle pizza with cheese, then celery. Cut pizza into 6 wedges.

Pick a number of slices they will make. Calculate how much they need of each ingredient. Finally, make a shopping list. You may need to look up some information about the packaging of certain products.

For Further Reflection

In this unit, you have used several different tools (ratio tables, percent bars, fraction bars, number lines, and double number lines). Explain how each is different and how they are similar to one another. Choose your favorite and tell why it is your favorite.

Additional Practice

Section A The Ratio Table

1. **a.** Marty takes six steps for every 4 m. How many steps does Marty take for 100 m? One kilometer?

    b. For every three steps Marty takes, his father takes only two. How many steps does Marty's father take for 100 m?

2. At the school store at Springfield Middle School, Jason ordered erasers. A package containing 25 erasers costs $3. What is the price of a single eraser? Show your work.

    Here is a recipe for Scottish Pancakes.

Scottish Pancakes (makes about 16 pancakes)	
Ingredients:	
1 cup all-purpose flour	$\frac{3}{4}$–1 cup milk
2 tablespoons sugar	1 egg, lightly beaten
1 teaspoon baking powder	2 tablespoons butter, melted
$\frac{1}{4}$ teaspoon baking soda	extra melted butter
$\frac{1}{2}$ teaspoon lemon juice or vinegar	
Directions:	
Sift flour, sugar, baking powder, and soda into a medium-size mixing bowl. Add juice or vinegar to the milk to sour it; allow to stand for 5 minutes.	
Make a well in the center of the dry ingredients and add the egg, $\frac{3}{4}$ cup milk, and the butter; mix to form a smooth batter. If the batter is too thick to pour from the spoon, add remaining milk.	
Brush base of frying pan lightly with melted butter. Drop 1-2 tablespoons of mixture onto base of pan, about $\frac{3}{4}$ inch apart. Cook over medium heat for 1 minute, or until underside is golden. Turn pancakes over and cook the other side. Remove from pan; repeat with remaining mixture.	

Ms. Anderson wants to try out the recipe in her family. However, she thinks eight pancakes will be enough.

3. **a.** How much of each ingredient does she need?

    b. Ms. Anderson wants to use the recipe to make pancakes at a school fair. How much of each ingredient does she need for 80 pancakes?

Section B The Bar Model

1. Which fraction best describes the shaded part of each measuring strip?

450 L   100%

2. Susan and Hielko had solar collectors installed for their hot water system. The tank can hold 450 L of water. On the left is a model of the gauge that is fixed to the tank.

Last week, $\frac{2}{5}$ of the water tank was filled with water.

   a. Copy the gauge in your notebook and color the part of the gauge that represents $\frac{2}{5}$.

   b. What percentage of the tank was filled?

   c. How many liters were in the tank when it was $\frac{2}{5}$ full?

   d. It is best to keep the water tank filled up to at least 80%. In your drawing for part **a**, write this percentage next to the gauge in its proper place.

   e. Write 80% as a fraction and simplify.

3. For his birthday party, Paul took his friends to a hamburger restaurant. The total bill was $24.78. Paul wants to add about 15% to the bill as a tip. Make an accurate estimate of the amount Paul will pay.

4. Copy the table below and fill in the blanks.

Fraction	Percentage
$\frac{1}{2}$	50
$\frac{1}{4}$	
	10
$\frac{15}{100}$	
$\frac{3}{5}$	
1	100

Section ◆ The Bar Model

1.

The distance of 1 mi is represented on this number line.

    a. What fraction can replace the question mark?

    b. Use arrows to indicate a distance of $\frac{1}{2}$ mi, $\frac{1}{4}$ mi, and $\frac{2}{3}$ mi.

2. This part of a number line is exactly 12 cm.

    a. Copy this picture in your notebook. Use a ruler.

    b. Use arrows to indicate the following fractions as accurately as possible: $\frac{1}{6}$, $1\frac{5}{6}$, $\frac{9}{12}$, $\frac{3}{4}$, and $1\frac{2}{3}$.

3. **a.** Use a number line to go from 3.9 to 5.8 in the fewest number of jumps. You may make jumps of 0.1, 1, and 10.

    b. How far apart are 3.9 and 5.8?

4. Mr. Henderson's class is playing a game in which students have to estimate distances in meters and centimeters. The estimates are shown on a number line, and whoever is the closest to the real distance wins. Note that 10 cm is 0.1 m.

Here are the estimates from four students for the length of the classroom.

Anouk	9 meters	Ilse	8.75 meters
Barry	7.8 meters	Henry	9.2 meters

Mr. Henderson measured the length of the classroom and found it was 8 m and 90 cm.

    a. Draw a number line indicating the positions of the four estimates and the actual length.

    b. Who won this game?

5. At the world swimming championships in Barcelona, Spain, on July 25, 2003, Michael Phelps swam the finals of the 200-m race in a new world record time of 1 minute and 56.04 seconds. In the semifinals, he finished 1.48 seconds earlier. Calculate Michael Phelps's time in the semifinals.

Section ◆D◆ The Double Number Line

1. Five miles is the equivalent of exactly 8 km.

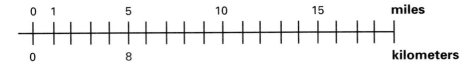

   a. How many miles equal 12 km?

   b. In cities in The Netherlands, the speed limit for driving is 50 kilometers per hour (km/h). About how many miles per hour is that?

2. If Norman bikes to school, it takes him about a quarter of an hour to cover the 3 mi.

   a. At the same average speed, how many miles can Norman bike in $1\frac{1}{2}$ hours?

   b. How long would a 15-mi trip take at the same average speed?

3. Ahmed buys a piece of cheese at Jack's Delicatessen. This is what the scale shows.

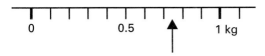

   a. What is the amount in kilograms shown on the scale?

   b. Find out how much Ahmed has to pay if the price of 1 kg of the cheese is $9. You may use a double number line.

   c. The piece is too expensive for Ahmed. Jack shows him another piece and says, "This will cost you $5.40." What is the weight of this piece of cheese?

4. Kendra has a pen pal in Europe named Richard. "How tall are you?" she asked in an e-mail to him. "I am 1.85 meters tall. How tall are you?" Richard writes. "I'm 5 feet 6 inches tall," Kendra answers.

Who is the taller of the two? You may use the general rule that there is a little less than 3 feet (ft) in 1 m and there are 12 inches (in) in 1 ft. Show your work.

Section E Choose Your Model

1. Michelle walks about 5 km/hr. At the same average speed, how many kilometers does she walk in $2\frac{1}{4}$ hours?

2. Order the following numbers from small to large:

   $2\frac{1}{3}$, 2.7, 2.09, 1.98, $2\frac{3}{4}$, 0.634

3. Outdoor Living is selling a backpack for $27.95. How many backpacks can the school purchase with $500? (Schools are exempt from paying sales tax.)

Name	Country	Result (in meters)	Date
Beamon	USA	8.90	10-18-1968
Boston	USA	8.27	10-17-1968
Boston	USA	8.12	09-02-1960
Owens	USA	8.06	08-04-1936
Hamm	USA	7.73	07-31-1928
Gutterson	USA	7.60	07-12-1912
Irons	USA	7.48	07-22-1908
Prinstein	USA	7.34	09-01-1904
Kraenzlein	USA	7.18	07-15-1900
Prinstein	USA	7.17	07-14-1900
Clark	USA	6.35	04-07-1896

Here is a table of the Olympic Record holders for the long jump through August 2004.

4. a. Since 1896, how much has the Olympic long jump record increased?

   b. Which person held the Olympic long jump record for the longest time period? For the shortest time period?

   c. Which person increased the Olympic long jump record the most?

Section A ▸ The Ratio Table

1. You may have used different operations. However, your answer should be 400 notebooks, as shown in this ratio table, where the number of packages is doubled each time.

Number of Packages	1	2	4	8	16
Number of Notebooks	25	50	100	200	**400**

2. You may have used the results of problem 1 or a different strategy, but your answer should be 23 packages as shown in this ratio table.

Number of Packages	16	4	2	1	**23**
Number of Notebooks	400	100	50	25	575

Pens (Numbers)	48	24	4	1
Price (in dollars)	12	6	1	0.25

Protractors	12	6	2	1
Price (in dollars)	42	21	7	3.50

Rulers (Numbers)	25	1
Price (in dollars)	50	2

3. **a.** 48 pens for $12
   12 protractors for $42
   25 rulers for $50

   b. $0.25 per pen
   $3.50 per protractor
   $2.00 per ruler

   c. $1.75 for 7 pens $7 \times \$0.25 = \$1.75$
   $24.50 for 7 protractors $7 \times \$3.50 = \$24.50$
   $14.00 for 7 rulers $7 \times \$2.00 = \$14.00$

4. There are different ways to find the answers.

   For example, to find the number of bananas, you could have reasoned that for eight servings, you need four bananas. Thus for 16 servings, you need 8 bananas, and for 4 servings, you need 2 bananas. Thus, for 20 servings, you need 10 bananas.

   The number of craft sticks is the same as the number of servings, so 20 craft sticks.

   They need $2\frac{1}{2}$ cups of topping and $1\frac{1}{4}$ cups of honey.

Section B The Bar Model

1. a., b.

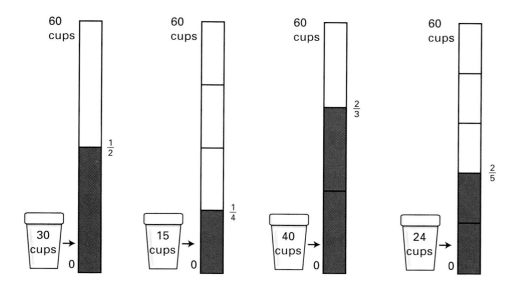

2. a. A ($\frac{3}{8}$ or 37.5%), B ($\frac{3}{10}$ or 30%), C ($\frac{8}{10}$ or 80%), D ($\frac{3}{4}$ or 75%)

b. A (30 cups), B (24 cups), C (64 cups), D (60 cups)

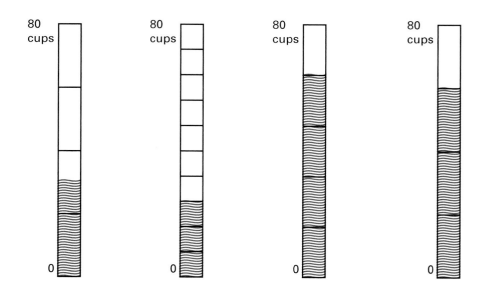

3. You may have used different strategies, but your answers should be the same as these.

a. Answer: 160 minutes

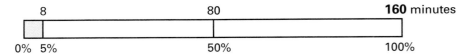

Sample strategy: Calculate 50% (times ten) and then calculate 100% (double).

b. Answer: 25 minutes

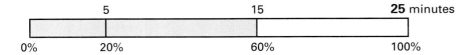

Sample strategy: Calculate 20% (divide by 3) and then calculate 100% (times 5).

c. Answer: 80 minutes

Sample strategy: Calculate 5% (divided by 3), then calculate 50% (times ten), and then calculate 100% (double).

d. Answer: $1\frac{1}{4}$ hours or 75 minutes. Different strategies are possible.

Example 1:

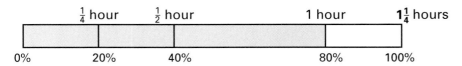

Calculate 40% (halving), and then calculate 20% (halving) and then 100% (times 5).

Example 2:
Using minutes:

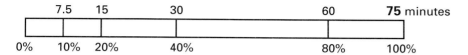

Strategy:

Calculate 40% (halving), then calculate 20% (halving), then 10% (halving), and then 100% (times 10).

4. A percent bar using estimates $20 ($20.10) and $12 ($11.95) may support your estimations.

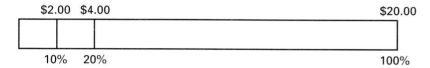

10% of $20.10 is about $2.00.

15% of $20.10 is about $2.00 + $1.00 = $3.00.

20% of $20.10 is about $4.00.

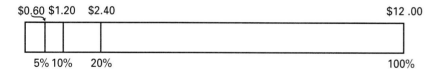

10% of $11.95 is about $1.20.

15% of $11.95 is about $1.20 + $0.60 = $1.80.

20% of $11.95 is about $2.40.

Section ◆C◆ The Number Line

1. a.

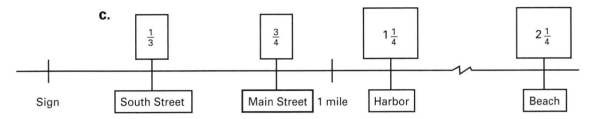

b. The Main Street exit and the Harbor exit. You may divide the line in 12 equal pieces to find the differences.

2. a. Harbor $\frac{1}{2}$ mile

Beach $1\frac{1}{2}$ mile

b. $2\frac{1}{4}$ mile (1 mile further down from Harbor).

c.

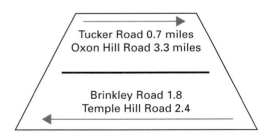

3. Your sign should contain this same mileage information.

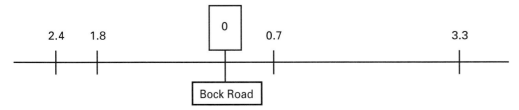

Tucker Road 0.7 miles
Oxon Hill Road 3.3 miles

Brinkley Road 1.8
Temple Hill Road 2.4

Strategy:

The sign is located at Bock Road. You should create a number line showing Bock road at the zero location.

4. From 0, make five jumps of 10 to the right, and then you arrive at 50.

From 50, you make two jumps of 1 to the left, and then you arrive at 48. The final jump is one of 0.1 to the right.

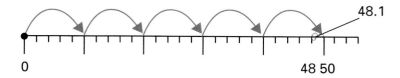

A total of 8 jumps

5. Four jumps of 1 and one jump of 0.1 are five jumps total.

6. a.

b. Ben's guess was the closest. Nathalie's guess was the farthest off.

c. Nathalie: $3.10 (too high)
Leo: $1.89 (too low)
Maria: $1.61 (too high)
Ben: $0.86 (too high)

Section D The Double Number Line

1. Major streets are usually 400, 800, or 1,600 m apart.
Sample explanation:

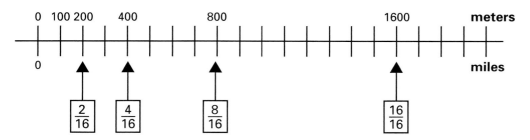

2. a. 4 kg. Sample strategy using a double number line:

b. The price for 3.2 kg of apples is $4.00.

To get 3.2 kg, you can add 0.2 to 3.

The price for 3.2 kg of apples is $3.75 + $0.25 = $4.00.

3. 45 minutes are needed.
Sample strategy using a double number line:

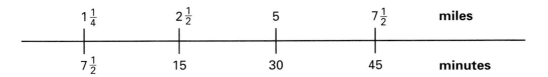

Calculations: First double, and then times 3.

The same calculations can be made using a ratio table.

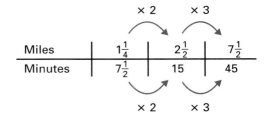

Section E Choose Your Model

1. You can draw a number line and then use jumps to find the difference.

   The answer: Janet jumped 0.12 m (or 12 cm) farther.

   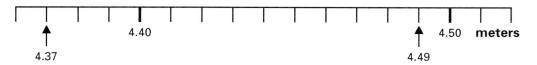

2. A way to solve this problem is using a ruler with centimeters and inches. The 8 in. by 6 in. frame is best.

   a. The length is 5 inches, which is about 12.5 cm; that is too small, because the length of the photo is 15 cm.

   b. Both 6 inches and 4 inches are a little larger than 15 cm and 10 cm.

   c. This frame is large enough: 8 inches is more than 16 cm, and 6 inches is more than 12 cm.

3. You can think of a double number line to find the solution.

   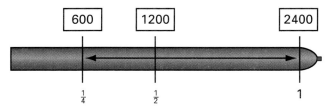

   You have to cut at $\frac{3}{4}$, because $\frac{1}{4}$ is 600 grams, and the rest is $\frac{3}{4}$, which is 1,800 grams.

4. Assuming a 15% tip, the cost of the dinner with tax and tip will be: $7.99 + $1.20 + $0.40 = $9.59

   To find the tax and the tip, you can use a percent bar.

   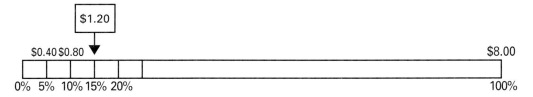

5. You can use an extended ratio table to organize your work.

Number of Pizzas	1	2	4
Cups pizza sauce	$\frac{3}{4}$	$1\frac{1}{2}$	3
Tbsp pizza sauce	2	4	8
Cups of honey	$\frac{1}{4}$	$\frac{1}{2}$	1
Tsp hot pepper sauce	$\frac{1}{2}$	1	1
Cups chicken breast	1	2	4
Tubes pizza dough	1	2	4
Tbsp olive oil	1	2	4
Cups blue cheese	$\frac{3}{4}$	$1\frac{1}{2}$	3
Cups diced celery	$\frac{1}{2}$	1	2

Here is a shopping list for making 4 pizzas.

Possible shopping list:
One jar of honey (12-ounce container)
Four cups of sauce, or 48-ounce container
Two chicken breasts
Four tubes of pizza dough
A small bottle of hot pepper sauce
One small bottle of olive oil (4 tablespoons)
12 ounces of blue cheese
One head of celery

Expressions and Formulas

BRITANNICA
Mathematics in Context

Algebra

HOLT, RINEHART AND WINSTON

Mathematics in Context is a comprehensive curriculum for the middle grades.
It was developed in 1991 through 1997 in collaboration with the Wisconsin Center
for Education Research, School of Education, University of Wisconsin-Madison and
the Freudenthal Institute at the University of Utrecht, The Netherlands, with the
support of the National Science Foundation Grant No. 9054928.

The revision of the curriculum was carried out in 2003 through 2005, with the
support of the National Science Foundation Grant No. ESI 0137414.

National Science Foundation

Opinions expressed are those of the authors
and not necessarily those of the Foundation.

Gravemeijer, K., Roodhardt, A., Wijers, M., Kindt, M., Cole, B. R., & Burrill, G. (2006)
Expressions and formulas. In Wisconsin Center for Education Research & Freudenthal
Institute (Eds.), Mathematics in Context. Chicago: Encyclopædia Britannica.

ISBN 0-03-039617-4

2 3 4 5 6 073 08 07 06 05

The *Mathematics in Context* Development Team

Development 1991–1997

The initial version of *Expressions and Formulas* was developed by Koeno Gravemeijer, Anton Roodhardt, and Monica Wijers. It was adapted for use in American schools by Beth R. Cole and Gail Burrill.

Wisconsin Center for Education

Research Staff

Thomas A. Romberg
Director

Joan Daniels Pedro
Assistant to the Director

Gail Burrill
Coordinator

Margaret R. Meyer
Coordinator

Project Staff

Jonathan Brendefur
Laura Brinker
James Browne
Jack Burrill
Rose Byrd
Peter Christiansen
Barbara Clarke
Doug Clarke
Beth R. Cole
Fae Dremock
Mary Ann Fix

Sherian Foster
James A, Middleton
Jasmina Milinkovic
Margaret A. Pligge
Mary C. Shafer
Julia A. Shew
Aaron N. Simon
Marvin Smith
Stephanie Z. Smith
Mary S. Spence

Freudenthal Institute Staff

Jan de Lange
Director

Els Feijs
Coordinator

Martin van Reeuwijk
Coordinator

Mieke Abels
Nina Boswinkel
Frans van Galen
Koeno Gravemeijer
Marja van den Heuvel-Panhuizen
Jan Auke de Jong
Vincent Jonker
Ronald Keijzer
Martin Kindt

Jansie Niehaus
Nanda Querelle
Anton Roodhardt
Leen Streefland
Adri Treffers
Monica Wijers
Astrid de Wild

Revision 2003–2005

The revised version of *Expressions and Formulas* was developed by Monica Wijers and Martin Kindt. It was adapted for use in American schools by Gail Burrill.

Wisconsin Center for Education

Research Staff

Thomas A. Romberg
Director

David C. Webb
Coordinator

Gail Burrill
Editorial Coordinator

Margaret A. Pligge
Editorial Coordinator

Project Staff

Sarah Ailts
Beth R. Cole
Erin Hazlett
Teri Hedges
Karen Hoiberg
Carrie Johnson
Jean Krusi
Elaine McGrath

Margaret R. Meyer
Anne Park
Bryna Rappaport
Kathleen A. Steele
Ana C. Stephens
Candace Ulmer
Jill Vettrus

Freudenthal Institute Staff

Jan de Lange
Director

Truus Dekker
Coordinator

Mieke Abels
Content Coordinator

Monica Wijers
Content Coordinator

Arthur Bakker
Peter Boon
Els Feijs
Dédé de Haan
Martin Kindt

Nathalie Kuijpers
Huub Nilwik
Sonia Palha
Nanda Querelle
Martin van Reeuwijk

Cover photo credits: (left to right) © PhotoDisc/Getty Images; © Corbis;
© Getty Images

Illustrations
1, 6 Holly Cooper-Olds; **7** Thomas Spanos/© Encyclopædia Britannica,
Inc.; **8** Christine McCabe/© Encyclopædia Britannica, Inc.; **13** (top)
16 (bottom) Christine McCabe/© Encyclopædia Britannica, Inc.;
25 (top right) Thomas Spanos/© Encyclopædia Britannica, Inc.;
29 Holly Cooper-Olds; **32, 36, 40, 41** Christine McCabe/© Encyclopædia
Britannica, Inc.

Photographs
3 © PhotoDisc/Getty Images; **14** © Corbis; 15 John Foxx/Alamy;
26, 32, 33 © PhotoDisc/Getty Images; **34** SuperStock/Alamy;
43 © PhotoDisc/Getty Images

◆ Contents

Dear Student,

Welcome to *Expressions and Formulas*.

Imagine you are shopping for a new bike. How do you determine the size frame that fits your body best? Bicycle manufacturers have a formula that uses leg length to find the right size bike for each rider. In this unit, you will use this formula as well as many others. You will devise your own formulas by studying the data and processes in the story. Then you will apply your own formula to solve new problems.

In this unit, you will also learn new forms of mathematical writing. You will use arrow strings, arithmetic trees, and parentheses. These new tools will help you interpret problems as well as apply formulas to find problem solutions.

As you study this unit, look for additional formulas in your daily life outside the mathematics classroom, such as the formula for sales tax or cab rates. Formulas are all around us!

Sincerely,

The Mathematics in Context Development Team

Arrow Language

Bus Riddle

Imagine you are a bus driver. Early one morning you start the empty bus and leave the garage to drive your route. At the first stop, 10 people get on the bus. At the second stop, six more people get on. At the third stop, four people get off the bus and seven more get on. At the fourth stop, five people get on and two people get off. At the sixth stop, four people get off the bus.

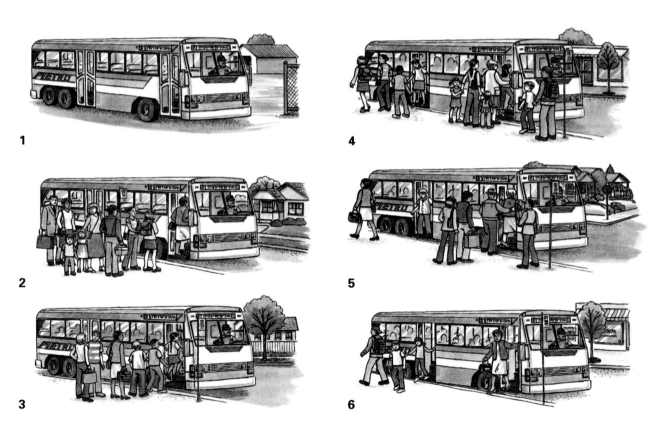

1. How old is the bus driver?

2. Did you expect the first question to ask about the number of passengers on the bus after the sixth stop?

3. How could you determine the number of passengers on the bus after the sixth stop?

When four people get off the bus and seven get on, the number of people on the bus changes. There are three more people on the bus than there were before the bus stopped.

4. Here is a record of people getting on and off the bus at six bus stops. Copy the table into your notebook. Then complete the table.

Number of Passengers Getting off the Bus	Number of Passengers Getting on the Bus	Change
5	8	3 more
9	13	
16	16	
15	8	
9	3	
		5 fewer

5. Study the last row in the table. What can you say about the number of passengers getting on and off the bus when you know that there are five fewer people on the bus?

For the story on page 1, you might have kept track of the number of passengers on the bus by writing:

$$10 + 6 = 16 + 3 = 19 + 3 = 22 - 4 = 18$$

6. Reflect Do you think that representing the numbers in this format is acceptable mathematically? Why or why not?

To avoid using the equal sign to compare amounts that are not equal, you can represent the calculation using an arrow symbol.

$$10 \xrightarrow{+6} 16 \xrightarrow{+3} 19 \xrightarrow{+3} 22 \xrightarrow{-4} 18$$

Each change is represented by an arrow. This way of writing a string of calculations is called *arrow language*. You can use **arrow language** to describe any sequence of additions and subtractions, whether it is about passengers, money, or any other quantities that change.

7. Why is arrow language a good way to keep track of a changing total?

Ms. Moss has $1,235 in her bank account. She withdraws $357. Two days later, she withdraws $275 from the account.

8. Use arrow language to represent the changes in Ms. Moss's account. Include the amount of money she has in her account at the end of the story.

Kate has $37. She earns $10 delivering newspapers on Monday. She spends $2.00 for a cup of frozen yogurt. On Tuesday, she visits her grandmother and earns $5.00 washing her car. On Wednesday, she earns $5.00 for baby-sitting. On Friday, she buys a sandwich for $2.75 and spends $3.00 for a magazine.

9. a. Use arrow language to show how much money Kate has left.

b. Suppose Kate wants to buy a radio that costs $53. Does she have enough money to buy the radio at any time during the week? If so, which day?

Monday	It snowed 20.25 inches.
Tuesday	It warmed up, and 18.5 inches of snow melted.
Wednesday	Two inches of snow melted.
Thursday	It snowed 14.5 inches.
Friday	It snowed 11.5 inches in the morning and then stopped.

Ski Spectacular had 42 inches of snow on the ground on Sunday. This table records the weather during the week.

10. How deep was the snow on Friday afternoon? Explain your answer.

Wandering Island

Wandering Island constantly changes shape. On one side of the island, the sand washes away. On the other side, sand washes onto shore. The islanders wonder whether their island is actually getting larger or smaller. In 1998, the area of the island was 210 square kilometers (km^2). Since then, the islanders have recorded the area that washes away and the area that is added to the island.

Year	Area Washed Away (in km^2)	Area Added (in km^2)
1999	5.5	6.0
2000	6.0	3.5
2001	4.0	5.0
2002	6.5	7.5
2003	7.0	6.0

11. What was the area of the island at the end of 2001?

12. a. Was the island larger or smaller at the end of 2003 than it was in 1998?

b. Explain or show how you got your answer.

Summary ✄

Arrow language can be helpful to represent calculations.

Each calculation can be described with an arrow.

$$\text{starting number} \xrightarrow{\text{action}} \text{resulting number}$$

A series of calculations can be described by an **arrow string**.

$$10 \xrightarrow{+6} 16 \xrightarrow{+3} 19 \xrightarrow{+3} 22 \xrightarrow{-4} 18$$

Check Your Work ⟩⟩

Airline Reservations

There are 375 seats on a flight to Atlanta, Georgia, that departs on March 16. By March 11, 233 of the seats were reserved. The airline continues to take reservations and cancellations until the plane departs. If the number of reserved seats is higher than the number of actual seats on the plane, the airline places the passenger names on a waiting list.

The table shows the changes over the five days before the flight.

Date	Seats Requested	Cancellations	Total Seats Reserved
3/11			233
3/12	47	0	
3/13	51	1	
3/14	53	0	
3/15	5	12	
3/16	16	2	

1. Copy and complete the table.

2. Write an arrow string to represent the calculations you made to complete the table.

3. On which date does the airline need to form a waiting list?

4. To find the total number of reserved seats, Toni, a reservations agent, suggests adding all of the new reservations and then subtracting all of the cancellations at one time instead of using arrow strings. What are the advantages and disadvantages of her suggestion?

5. **a.** Find the result of this arrow string.

   $$12.30 \xrightarrow{\ +\ 1.40\ } \underline{\hphantom{xxx}} \xrightarrow{\ -\ 0.62\ } \underline{\hphantom{xxx}} \xrightarrow{\ +\ 5.83\ } \underline{\hphantom{xxx}} \xrightarrow{\ -\ 1.40\ } \underline{\hphantom{xxx}}$$

   b. Write a story that could be represented by the arrow string.

6. Write a problem that you can solve using arrow language. Then solve the problem.

7. Why is arrow language useful?

 ## For Further Reflection

Juan says that it is easier to write 15 + 3 = 18 − 6 = 12 + 2 =14 than to make an arrow string. Tell what is wrong with the string that Juan wrote and show the arrow string he has tried to represent.

Smart Calculations

Making Change

At most stores today, making change is easy. The clerk just enters the amount of the purchase and the amount received. Then the computerized register shows the amount of change due. Before computerized registers, however, making change was not quite so simple. People invented strategies for making change using mental calculation. These strategies are still useful to make sure you get the right change.

1. a. When you make a purchase, how do you know if you are given the correct change?

b. Reflect How might you make change without using a calculator or computerized register?

A customer's purchase is $3.70. The customer gives the clerk a $20 bill.

2. Explain how to calculate the correct change without using a pencil and paper or a calculator.

It is useful to have strategies that work in any situation, with or without a calculator. Rachel suggests that estimating is a good way to begin. "In the example," she explains, "it is easy to tell that the change will be more than $15." She says that the first step is to give the customer $15.

Rachel explains that once the $15 is given as change to the customer, you can work as though the customer has paid only the remaining $5. "Now the difference between $5.00 and $3.70 must be found. The difference is $1.30—or one dollar, one quarter, and one nickel."

3. Do you think that Rachel has proposed a good strategy? Why or why not?

Many people use a different strategy that gives small coins and bills first. Remember, the total cost is $3.70, and the customer pays with a $20 bill.

The clerk first gives the customer a nickel and says, "$3.75."

Next, the clerk gives the customer a quarter and says, "That's $4."

Then the clerk gives the customer a dollar and says, "That's $5."

The clerk then gives the customer a $5 bill and says, "That makes $10."

Finally, the clerk gives the customer a $10 bill and says, "That makes $20."

This method could be called "making change to twenty dollars."

This method could also be called **"the small-coins-and-bills-first method."**

4. **a.** Does this method give the fewest possible coins and bills in change? Explain.

   b. Why do you think it might also be called the small-coins-and-bills-first method?

These methods illustrate strategies to make change without a computer or calculator. They are strategies for mental calculations, and they can be illustrated with arrow strings.

Another customer's bill totals $7.17, and the customer pays with a $10 bill.

5. **a.** Describe how you would make change using the small-coins-and-bills-first method.

   b. Does your solution give the customer the fewest coins and bills possible?

Arrow language can be used to illustrate the small-coins-and-bills-first method. This arrow string shows the change for the $3.70 purchase.

$$\$3.70 \xrightarrow{+\,\$0.05} \$3.75 \xrightarrow{+\,\$0.25} \$4.00 \xrightarrow{+\,\$1.00} \$5.00 \xrightarrow{+\,\$5.00} \$10.00 \xrightarrow{+\,\$10.00} \$20.00$$

6. a. What might the clerk say to the customer when giving the customer the amount in the third arrow?

   b. What is the total amount of change?

   c. Write a new arrow string with the same beginning and end but with only one arrow. Explain your reasoning.

Now try some shopping problems. For each problem, write an arrow string using the small-coins-and-bills-first method. Then write another arrow string with only one arrow to show the total change.

7. a. You give $10.00 for a $5.85 purchase of some cat food.

   b. You give $20.00 for a $7.89 purchase of a desk fan.

   c. You give $10.00 for a $6.86 purchase of a bottle of car polish.

   d. You give $5.00 for a $1.76 purchase of pencils.

A customer gives a clerk $2.00 for a $1.85 purchase. The clerk is about to give the customer change, but she realizes she does not have a nickel. So the clerk asks the customer for a dime.

8. Reflect What does the clerk give as change? Explain your strategy.

Skillful Computations

In problem 7, you wrote two arrow strings for the same problem. One arrow string had several arrows and the other had only one arrow.

9. Shorten the following arrow strings so each has only one arrow.

a. $375 \xrightarrow{+\,50} \underline{} \xrightarrow{+\,50} \underline{}$ is the same as $375 \xrightarrow{?} \underline{}$

b. $158 \xrightarrow{-\,1} \underline{} \xrightarrow{+\,100} \underline{}$ is the same as $158 \xrightarrow{?} \underline{}$

c. $1{,}274 \xrightarrow{-\,1{,}000} \underline{} \xrightarrow{+\,2} \underline{}$ is the same as $1{,}274 \xrightarrow{?} \underline{}$

You can use arrow strings to represent your thought processes when making change using mental calculations. Some arrow strings, such as the one in problem 9a, are easier to calculate when they have fewer steps. You can make some arrow strings easier to use by making them shorter or longer.

10. For each of the arrow strings, make a longer string that is easier to use to do the calculation. Then use the new arrow string to find the result.

a. $527 \xrightarrow{+99} \underline{\ ?\ }$ **b.** $274 \xrightarrow{-98} \underline{\ ?\ }$

Change each of the following calculations into an arrow string with one arrow. Then make a longer arrow string that is simpler to solve using mental calculation.

11. a. $1{,}003 - 999$ **b.** $423 + 104$ **c.** $1{,}793 - 1{,}010$

12. a. Guess the result of this arrow string and then copy and complete it in your notebook.

$$273 \xrightarrow{-100} \underline{\ ?\ } \xrightarrow{+99} \underline{\ ?\ }$$

b. If the 273 in part **a** is replaced by 500, what is the new result?

c. What if 1,453 is substituted for 273?

d. What if 76 is substituted for 273?

e. What if 112 is substituted for 273?

f. Use one arrow to show the result for any first number.

Numbers can be written using different combinations of sums and differences. Some of the ways make it easier to perform mental calculations. To calculate 129 + 521, you can write 521 as 500 + 21 and use an arrow string.

$$129 \xrightarrow{+21} 150 \xrightarrow{+500} 650$$

Sarah computed 129 + 521 as follows:

$$129 \xrightarrow{+500} \underline{\ \ } \xrightarrow{+20} \underline{\ \ } \xrightarrow{+1} \underline{\ \ }$$

13. Is Sarah's method correct?

14. How could you rewrite 267 – 28 to make it easier to calculate using mental computation?

Summary ❯❯

Sometimes an arrow string can be replaced by a shorter string that is easier to calculate mentally.

$$\underline{\quad} \xrightarrow{+\ 64} \underline{\quad} \xrightarrow{+\ 36} \underline{\quad} \text{ becomes } \underline{\quad} \xrightarrow{+\ 100} \underline{\quad}$$

Sometimes an arrow string can be replaced by a longer string that makes the calculation easier to calculate mentally without changing the result.

$$\underline{\quad} \xrightarrow{-\ 99} \underline{\quad} \text{ becomes } \underline{\quad} \xrightarrow{+\ 1} \underline{\quad} \xrightarrow{-\ 100} $$

or

$$\underline{\quad} \xrightarrow{-\ 99} \underline{\quad} \text{ becomes } \underline{\quad} \xrightarrow{-\ 100} \underline{\quad} \xrightarrow{+\ 1} $$

The small-coins-and-bills-first method is an easy way to make change.

Check Your Work ❯❯

Complete each of the following arrow strings.

1. a. $20 \xrightarrow{+\ 15} \underline{\quad} \xrightarrow{-\ 8} \underline{\quad} \xrightarrow{+\ \frac{1}{2}} \underline{\quad}$

   b. $6.77 \xrightarrow{+\ 0.03} \underline{\quad} \xrightarrow{+\ 0.20} \underline{\quad} \xrightarrow{+\ 13} 20$

   c. $12.10 \xrightarrow{+\ 0.20} \underline{\quad} \xrightarrow{+\ 0.70} \underline{\quad} \xrightarrow{+\ 7} 20$

2. For each of these arrow strings, either write a new string that will make the computation easier to calculate and explain why it is easier, or explain why the string is already as easy to calculate as possible.

a. $423 \xrightarrow{+\ 237}$ ____

b. $544 \xrightarrow{-\ 24}$ ____

c. $29 \xrightarrow{+\ 54}$ ____ $\xrightarrow{-\ 25}$ ____

d. $998 \xrightarrow{+\ 34}$ ____

3. Write two examples in which a shorter string is easier to calculate mentally. Include both the short and long strings for each example.

4. Write two examples in which a longer string would be easier to calculate mentally. Show both the short and long strings for each example.

5. Explain why knowing how to shorten an arrow string can be useful in making change.

 For Further Reflection

Write an arrow string that shows how to make change for a $4.15 purchase if you handed the clerk a $20.00 bill. Show how you would alter this string if the clerk had no quarters or dimes to use in making change.

C

Formulas

Supermarket

Tomatoes cost $1.50 a pound. Carl buys 2 pounds (lb) of tomatoes.

1. a. Find the total price of Carl's tomatoes.

b. Write an arrow string that shows how you found the price.

At Veggies-R-Us, you can weigh fruits and vegetables yourself and find out how much your purchase costs. You select the button on the scale that **corresponds** to the fruit or vegetable you are weighing.

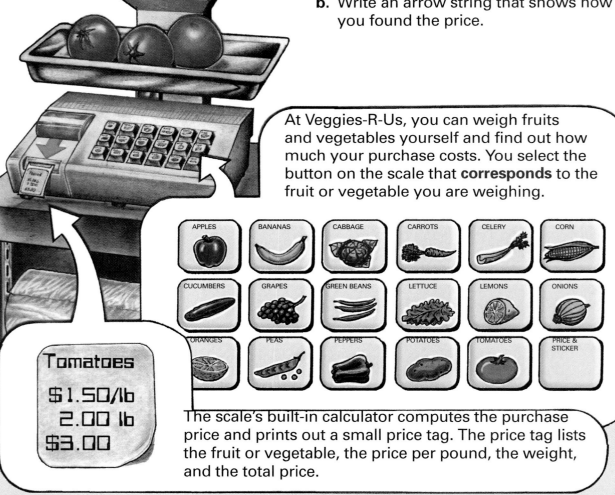

The scale's built-in calculator computes the purchase price and prints out a small price tag. The price tag lists the fruit or vegetable, the price per pound, the weight, and the total price.

weight $\longrightarrow$ [ ] $\longrightarrow$ price

The scale, like an arrow string, takes the weight as an **input** and gives the price as an **output**.

2. Find the price for each of the following weights of tomatoes, using this arrow string:

$$\text{weight} \xrightarrow{\times \$1.50} \text{price}$$

a. 4 lb $\xrightarrow{\times \$1.50}$ ___?___

b. 3 lb $\xrightarrow{\times \$1.50}$ ___?___

c. 0.5 lb $\xrightarrow{\times \$1.50}$ ___?___

The prices for other fruits and vegetables are calculated in the same way. Green beans cost $0.90 per pound.

3. **a.** Write an arrow string to show the calculation for green beans.

   b. Calculate the price for 3 lb of green beans.

The Corner Store does not have a calculating scale. The price of tomatoes at the Corner Store is $1.20 per pound. Siu bought tomatoes, and her bill was $6.

4. What was the weight of Siu's tomatoes? How did you find your answer?

Formulas

Taxi Fares

In some cabs, the fare for the ride is shown on a meter. At the Rainbow Cab Company, the fare increases during the ride depending on the distance traveled. You pay a base amount no matter how far you go, as well as a price for each mile you ride. The Rainbow Cab Company charges these rates.

$ 09.50

The base price is $2.00.

The price per mile is $1.50.

5. What is the price for each of these rides?

   a. stadium to the railroad station: 4 miles

   b. suburb to the center of the city: 7 miles

   c. convention center to the airport: 20 miles

The meter has a built-in calculator to find the fare. The meter calculation can be described by an arrow string.

6. Which of these strings shows the correct price? Explain your answer.

number of miles $\xrightarrow{\times\ \$1.50}$ _____ $\xrightarrow{+\ \$2.00}$ total price

$2.00 $\xrightarrow{+\ \text{number of miles}}$ _____ $\xrightarrow{\times\ \$1.50}$ total price

number of miles $\xrightarrow{\times\ \$2.00}$ _____ $\xrightarrow{\times\ \$1.50}$ total price

The Rainbow Cab Company changed its fares. The new prices can be found using an arrow string.

number of miles $\xrightarrow{\times \$1.30}$ _____ $\xrightarrow{+ \$3.00}$ total price

7. Is a cab ride now more or less expensive than it was before?

8. Use the new rate to find the fare for each trip.

    a. from the stadium to the railroad station: 4 miles

    b. from a suburb to the center of the city: 7 miles

    c. from a convention center to the airport: 20 miles

9. Compare your answers before the rate change (from problem 5) to those after the rate change.

After the company changed its rates, George slept through his alarm and had to take a cab to work. He was surprised at the cost: $18.60!

10. a. Use the new rate to calculate the distance from George's home to work.

    b. Write an arrow string to show your calculations.

The arrow string for the price of a taxi ride shows how to find the price for any number of miles.

number of miles $\xrightarrow{\times \$1.30}$ _____ $\xrightarrow{+ \$3.00}$ total price

Stacking Cups

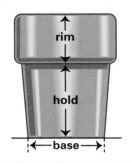

Materials:

Each group will need a centimeter ruler and at least four cups of the same size. Plastic cups from sporting events or fast-food restaurants work well.

Measure and record the following:

- the total height of a cup
- the height of the rim
- the height of the hold

(Note: The hold is the distance from the bottom of the cup to the bottom of the rim.)

- Stack two cups. Measure the height of the stack.
- Without measuring, guess the height of a stack of four cups.
- Write down how you made your guess. With a partner, share your guess and the strategy you used.

Make a stack of four cups and measure it. Was your guess correct?

11. Calculate the height of a stack of 17 cups. Describe your calculation with an arrow string.

12. a. There is a space under a counter where cups will be stored. The space is 50 centimeters (cm) high. How many cups can be stacked to fit under the counter? Show your work.

   b. Use arrow language to explain how you found your answer.

Sometimes a **formula** can help you solve a problem. You can write a formula to find the height of a stack of cups if you know the number of cups.

13. Complete the following arrow string for a formula using the number of cups as the input and the height of the stack as the output.

   number of cups $\xrightarrow{\ ?\ }$? $\xrightarrow{\ ?\ }$ height of stack

Suppose another class has cups of different sizes. The students use a formula for finding the height of a stack of their cups.

   number of cups $\xrightarrow{\ -\ 1\ }$ ___ $\xrightarrow{\ \times\ 3\ }$ ___ $\xrightarrow{\ +\ 15\ }$ height of stack

14. a. How tall is a stack of 10 of these cups?

   b. How tall is a stack of 5 of these cups?

   c. Sketch one of the cups. Label your drawing with the correct height.

   d. Explain what each of the numbers in the formula represents.

Now consider this arrow string.

   number of cups $\xrightarrow{\ \times\ 3\ }$ ___ $\xrightarrow{\ +\ 12\ }$ height

15. Could this arrow string be used for the same cup from problem 14? Explain.

We can write the arrow string as a formula, like this.

   number of cups $\times$ 3 + 12 = height

16. Could the formula in problem 13 also be used to solve the problem?

17. These cups will be stored in a space 50 cm high. How many cups can be placed in a stack? Explain how you found your answer.

Bike Sizes

You have discovered some formulas written as arrow strings. On the next pages, you will use formulas that other people have developed.

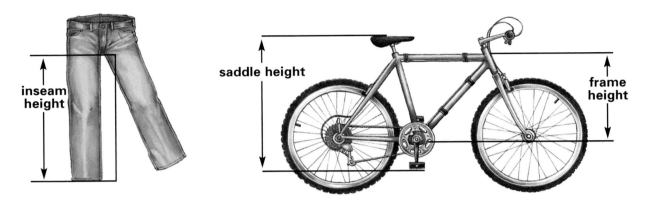

Bike shops use formulas to find the best saddle and frame height for each customer. One number used in these formulas is the **inseam** of the cyclist. This is the length of the cyclist's leg, measured in centimeters along the inside seam of the pants.

The saddle height is calculated with this formula.

inseam (in cm) × 1.08 = saddle height (in cm)

18. a. Do you think you can use any numbers at all for *inseam length*? Why or why not?

b. Write an arrow string for the formula.

c. Use the arrow string to complete this table.

Inseam (cm)	50	60	70	80
Saddle Height (cm)	....	64.8	....	....

d. How much does the saddle height change for every 10-cm change in the inseam? How much for every 1-cm change?

To get a quick overview of the relationship between inseam length and saddle height, you can make a graph of the data in the table. In this graph, the point labeled A shows an inseam length of 60 cm with the corresponding saddle height of 64.8 cm. For **plotting** this point, 64.8 is rounded to 65.

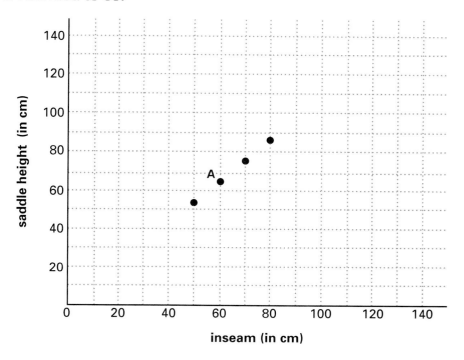

19. **a.** Go to **Student Activity Sheet 1**. Label the point for the inseam of 80 cm with a B. What is the corresponding saddle height in whole centimeters?

    b. Choose three more lengths for the inseam. Calculate the saddle heights, round to whole centimeters, and plot the points in the graph on **Student Activity Sheet 1**.

    c. Why is it reasonable to round the values for saddle height to whole centimeters before you plot the points?

If you complete the calculations accurately, the points in the graph can be connected by a straight line.

20. **a.** Go to **Student Activity Sheet 1**. Connect all points in the graph with a line.

    b. If you extend your line, would it intersect the point (0, 0) in the bottom left corner? Why or why not?

    c. A line goes through an **infinite** number of points. Does every point you can locate on the line you drew provide a reasonable solution to the bike height problem? Explain your reasoning.

21. Write a question you can solve using this graph. Record the answer to your own question. Exchange questions with a classmate. Then answer the question and discuss with your classmate.

Look at the formula for the frame height of a bicycle.

inseam (in cm) × 0.66 + 2 = frame height (in cm)

22. **a.** Write an arrow string for the formula.

b. Complete the table (round the frame height to a whole number) and draw the graph for this formula on **Student Activity Sheet 2**.

Inseam (cm)	50	60	70	80	....	....
Frame Height Calculated (cm)	....	....	....	....		
Frame Height Rounded (cm)						

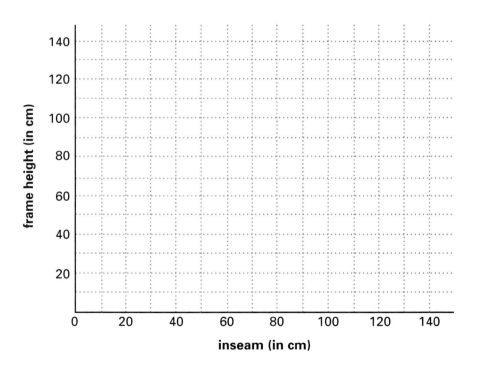

Margit used the formula to find the first two frame heights in the table. She did not round the heights. Then she used the first two values to calculate the third value.

23. a. Explain how Margit may have used the first two values to find the third.

b. Check to see if her method also works to find the next frame heights.

c. How might Margit find the frame height for an inseam of 65 cm?

24. a. If you connect all points in this graph and extend your line, does the line you drew intersect the origin (0, 0)? Why or why not?

b. Find the frame height for Ben, whose inseam length is 75 cm.

Formulas are often written with the result at the beginning of the formula.

saddle height (in cm) = inseam (in cm) × 1.08
frame height (in cm) = inseam (in cm) × 0.66 + 2

25. Study this bike.

a. What is the frame height?

b. What is the saddle height?

c. Do both of these numbers correspond to the same inseam length? How did you find your answer?

Formulas

Summary

A formula shows a procedure that can be applied over and over again for different numbers in the same situation.

Bike shops use formulas to fit bicycles to their riders.

inseam (in cm) × 0.66 + 2 = frame height (in cm)

Written with the result first:

frame height (in cm) = inseam (in cm) × 0.66 + 2

Many formulas can be described with arrow strings; for example:

$$\text{inseam} \xrightarrow{\times\,0.66} \underline{} \xrightarrow{+\,2} \text{frame height}$$

You can use the string to make a table for the formula. From the data in the table, you can draw a graph. Some problems are easier to solve with a graph, some are easier to solve using a formula, some with an arrow string, and some are easier to solve using a table. You have studied many strategies to solve problems.

Check Your Work

1. a. Write the following formula about taxi costs as an arrow string.

total price = number of miles × $1.40 + $1.90

b. Why is it useful to write a formula as an arrow string?

The manager of the Corner Store wants to help customers estimate the total cost of their purchases. She posts a table next to a scale.

2. Help the manager by copying and completing this table.

Weight	Tomatoes $1.20/lb	Green Beans $0.80/lb	Grapes $1.90/lb
0.5 lb			
1.0 lb			
2.0 lb			
3.0 lb			

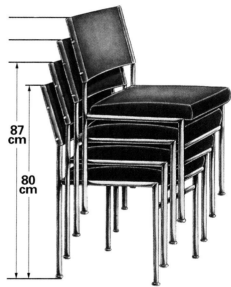

87 cm

80 cm

This picture shows a stack of chairs. Notice that the height of one chair is 80 cm and a stack of two chairs is 87 cm high.

Damian suggests that the following arrow string can be used to find the height of a stack of these chairs.

number of chairs $\xrightarrow{-1}$ ____ $\xrightarrow{\times 7}$ ____ $\xrightarrow{+80}$ height

3. a. Explain the meaning of each of the numbers in the arrow string.

b. Alba thinks a different arrow string could also solve the problem.

number of chairs $\xrightarrow{\times}$ ____ $\xrightarrow{+}$ height

What numbers should Alba use in her arrow string? Explain your answer.

This graph represents the height of stacks of chairs. The number of chairs in the stack is on the **horizontal axis**, and the height of the stack is on the **vertical axis**.

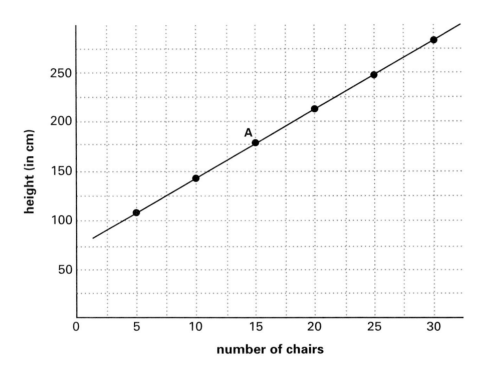

4. **a.** What does the point labeled A represent?

   b. Does each point on the line that is drawn have a meaning? Explain your reasoning.

   c. Explain why the graph will not intersect the point (0, 0).

   d. Use the graph to determine the number of chairs that can be put in a stack that will fit in a storage space of 116 cm high.

   e. Check your answer using an arrow string.

 For Further Reflection

State your preferences for using a graph or an arrow string to display the saddle height for a bicycle. Explain why you think this is the better way to describe the data.

D

Reverse Operations

Distances

Marty is going to visit Europe. He wants to prepare himself to use the different forms of currencies and different units of measure. He knows distances in Europe are expressed only in kilometers and never in miles. He looks on the Internet for a way to convert miles to kilometers. The computer uses an estimate for the relationship between miles and kilometers.

1. **Reflect** Think of a problem that Marty can do using the converter while he is traveling.

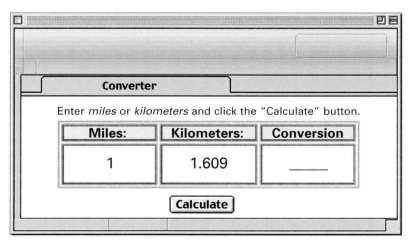

Converter

Enter *miles* or *kilometers* and click the "Calculate" button.

Miles:	Kilometers:	Conversion
1	1.609	_____

[Calculate]

Marty wants to practice converting miles to kilometers. He decides to use an arrow string to make calculations.

number of miles $\xrightarrow{\times \ 1.6}$ *number of kilometers*

2. **a.** Marty lives 30 miles from his office. About how many kilometers is that?

   b. Marty's parents live about 200 miles away. About how many kilometers is that?

   c. About how many kilometers is a distance of 10,000 miles?

3. **a.** Copy and complete this table.

Miles	10	20	30	40	50	60	70	80	90	100
Kilometers										

   b. Use the table to estimate how many kilometers are in 35 miles. Explain your reasoning.

In Europe, Marty travels 70 km from the airport to his hotel.

4. Use the table to estimate the distance in miles. Show your work.

While traveling in Europe, Marty wants to estimate the distances in miles. He uses the fact that 80 kilometers is about 50 miles and thinks of this rule.

number of kilometers $\xrightarrow{\div \ 80}$ ____ $\xrightarrow{\times \ 50}$ *number of miles*

5. Will this new rule give the same results? Explain.

Marty thinks the rule is a bit difficult to use with large numbers. He wonders if he can change the numbers and use this rule instead.

number of kilometers $\xrightarrow{\div 8}$ _____ $\xrightarrow{\times 5}$ *number of miles*

6. Will this new rule result in reasonable estimates? Explain.

Marty uses the rule to convert the distances he will travel from kilometers to miles.

7. Copy the table with Marty's travel plans. Convert the distances into miles and record them in your table.

Amsterdam–Paris	514 kilometers	.... miles
Paris–Barcelona	839 kilometers	.... miles
Barcelona–Rome	879 kilometers	.... miles
Rome–Berlin	1185 kilometers	.... miles
Berlin–Amsterdam	576 kilometers	.... miles

Marty's friend Pascale from Paris will be visiting Marty in the United States next summer. She wants to be able to convert miles into kilometers when she is traveling in the United States.

8. a. How can Marty's rule be changed to convert miles into kilometers? Write the new rule as an arrow string.

b. Is the result using this rule the same as the result using the Internet converter? Explain.

Pascale wants to tour the United States. She wants to visit some interesting places, such as national parks, theme parks, and major cities.

9. Reflect Make a list of five interesting places Pascale might like to visit. Find the distances in miles between them (use the Internet or an atlas) and convert them to kilometers.

Going Backwards

Pat and Kris are playing a game. One player writes down an arrow string and the output (answer) but not the input (starting number). The other player has to determine the input.

Here are Pat's arrow string and output.

$$? \xrightarrow{+4} \underline{} \xrightarrow{\times 10} \underline{} \xrightarrow{-2} \underline{} \xrightarrow{\div 2} 29$$

10. a. What should Kris give as the input? Explain how you found this number.

b. One student found an answer for Kris by using a **reverse arrow string**. What number should go above each of the reversed arrows?

$$\underline{} \xleftarrow{} \underline{} \xleftarrow{} \underline{} \xleftarrow{} \underline{} \xleftarrow{} 29$$

When it was her turn, Kris wrote:

$$? \xrightarrow{+3} \underline{} \xrightarrow{\div 6} \underline{} \xrightarrow{+5} \underline{} \xrightarrow{-2} 6$$

11. a. What will Pat give as the input? Explain how you found this number.

b. Write the reverse arrow string that can be used to find the input.

Beech Trees

The park near Jessica's house is full of beech trees. Some botanists observed that a tree grows fairly evenly when it is between 20 and 80 years old. They developed two formulas that describe the growth of beech trees if the age is known. They are written as arrow strings.

$$\text{age} \xrightarrow{\times 0.4} \underline{\quad} \xrightarrow{-2.5} \text{thickness} \qquad \text{age} \xrightarrow{\times 0.4} \underline{\quad} \xrightarrow{+1} \text{height}$$

In these arrow strings, age is in years and height is in meters; thickness is in centimeters and is measured 1 meter (m) from the ground.

12. Find the heights and thicknesses of trees that are 20, 30, and 40 years old.

13. Jessica wants to know the age of a tree. How can she find it?

Jessica uses some straight sticks to help her measure the thickness (diameter) of a tree. She finds that the tree is 25.5 cm thick.

14. About how old is the tree?

Jessica estimates the height of another beech tree as about 20 m.

15. Use this estimate of the height to find the age of the tree.

Jessica realizes that she can make a new formula. Her new formula gives the height of a tree if the thickness is known.

16. Write Jessica's formula as an arrow string.

D Reverse Operations

Summary

Every arrow has a reverse arrow. A reverse arrow represents the **opposite operation**.

For example, the reverse of $\xrightarrow{\div\,4}$ is $\xleftarrow{\times\,4}$.

Reverse arrows can be used to make reverse arrow strings.

For example, $\underline{\quad}\xrightarrow{\div\,4}\underline{\quad}\xrightarrow{\times\,3}\underline{\quad}$ reverses to

$\underline{\quad}\xleftarrow{\times\,4}\underline{\quad}\xleftarrow{\div\,3}\underline{\quad}$, which is the same as

$\underline{\quad}\xrightarrow{\div\,3}\underline{\quad}\xrightarrow{\times\,4}\underline{\quad}$.

Check Your Work

You may want to use a calculator.

From Amsterdam in The Netherlands to Chicago, Illinois, the distance is 4,090 miles.

1. **a.** If Marty uses the Internet conversion utility, how many kilometers will he find for the distance?

   b. How many kilometers will Marty find if he applies the arrow string strategy from problem 2 on page 26?

   c. The difference you found between the answers using the Internet conversion utility and the arrow string should be 37 km. Show how you can find this difference. Why is the difference not really important?

Carmen and Andy are at the store buying ham and cheese for sandwiches. Carmen is buying Swiss cheese that costs $4.40 per pound. She decides to buy 0.75 lb. She wants to know what the cost will be before she orders the cheese.

2. Write an arrow string to show the cost.

Carmen wrote this arrow string.

$$\$4.40 \xrightarrow{\div 4} \$1.10 \xrightarrow{\times 3} \$3.30$$

3. Is Carmen's arrow string correct? Why or why not?

4. Write the reverse arrow string for each of these strings.

    a. input $\xrightarrow{+2}$ ____ $\xrightarrow{\times 3}$ ____ $\xrightarrow{-4}$ output

    b. input $\xrightarrow{\div 2}$ ____ $\xrightarrow{-5}$ ____ $\xrightarrow{+7}$ output

5. Try sample numbers to find out if your reverse arrow strings are correct. Show your work.

 For Further Reflection

Explain when it may be important to have exact calculations and when a reasonable estimate is acceptable.

Order of Operations

Home Repairs

Jim is a contractor specializing in small household repairs that require less than a day to complete. For most jobs, he uses a team of three people. For each of the three people, Jim charges the customer $25 in travel expenses and $37 per hour. Jim uses a calculator to calculate the bills. He uses a standard form for each bill.

Jim MacIntosh Total Repairs
147 Franklin Rd., Wakeshire

Customer:_____$_____
Labor_____ hours at $37/hour....................$25.00
Travel costs:......................................$_____
                                                   $_____
Total cost per worker..............................
Total bill = total cost per worker X3.............$_____
(3 workers)

1. Use the forms on **Student Activity Sheet 3** to show the charge for each of these plumbing repair jobs.

   a. Replacing pipes for Mr. Ashton: 3 hours

   b. Cleaning out the pipes at Rodriguez and Partners: $2\frac{1}{2}$ hours

   c. Replacing faucets at the Vander house: $\frac{3}{4}$ hour

People often call Jim to ask for a price estimate for a particular job. Because Jim is experienced, he can estimate how long a job will take. He then uses the table to estimate the cost of the job.

Hours	Labor Cost per Worker (in dollars)	Travel Cost per Worker (in dollars)	Cost per Worker (in dollars)	Total for Three Workers (in dollars)
1	37	25	62	186
2	74	25	99	297
3	111	25	136	408
4	148	25	173	519
5				
6				
7				

2. a. What do the **entries** in the first row of the table represent?

b. Add the next row for five hours to the table.

3. a. Reflect Explain the regularity in the column for the labor cost per worker.

b. Study the table. Make a list of all of the regularities you can find. Explain the regularities.

4. a. Draw an arrow string that Jim could use to make more rows for the table.

b. Use your arrow string to make two more rows (for 6 and 7 hours) for the table.

Arithmetic Trees

While working on the home repair cost problems, Enrique wrote this arrow string to find the cost of having three workers for two hours of repairs.

$$2 \xrightarrow{\times\ 37} \underline{\hspace{1cm}} \xrightarrow{+\ 25} \underline{\hspace{1cm}} \xrightarrow{\times\ 3} \underline{\hspace{1cm}}$$

Karlene was working with Enrique, and she wrote this expression.

$$2 \times 37 + 25 \times 3$$

Karlene found an answer of 149. Enrique is very surprised.

5. a. How did Karlene find 149 as her answer?

   b. Why is Enrique surprised?

Karlene and Enrique decide that the number sentence $2 \times 37 + 25 \times 3$ is not necessarily the same as the arrow string.

$$2 \xrightarrow{\times\ 37} \underline{\hspace{1cm}} \xrightarrow{+\ 25} \underline{\hspace{1cm}} \xrightarrow{\times\ 3} \underline{\hspace{1cm}}$$

There is more than one way to interpret the number sentence. The calculations can be completed in different orders.

6. Solve each of the problems below. Compare your answers to those of other students in your class.

   a. $1 + 11 \times 11$

   b. $10 \times 10 + 1$

   c. $10 \xrightarrow{\times\ 10} \underline{\hspace{1cm}} \xrightarrow{+\ 2} \underline{\hspace{1cm}}$

   d. How can you be sure that everyone will get the same answer?

Sometimes the context of a problem helps you understand how to calculate it. For instance, in the home repair problem, Karlene and Enrique knew that the 3 represents the number of workers. So it makes sense to first calculate the subtotal of 2 × 37 + 25 and then multiply the result by three. Sometimes people are not careful how they write the calculations for a problem.

$$2 \times 37 = 74 + 25 = 99 \times 3 = 297$$

7. Why is this not a good way to write the calculations?

So that everyone gets the same answer to a string of calculations with different operations, mathematicians have agreed that multiplication and division should be completed before addition and subtraction in an expression.

8. Use the mathematicians' rule to find the value for each expression.

    a. 32 + 5 × 20

    b. 18 ÷ 3 + 2 × 5

    c. 47 − 11 + 6 × 8

Calculators and computers nearly always follow the mathematicians' rule. Some old or very simple calculators, however, do not use the rule.

9. a. Use the mathematicians' rule to find 5 × 5 + 6 × 6 and 6 × 6 + 5 × 5.

    b. Does your calculator use the mathematicians' rule? How did you decide?

    c. **Reflect** Why do you think calculators have built-in rules?

To make sure that everyone agrees on the value of an expression, it is important to have a way to write expressions so that it is clear which calculation to do first, which next, and so on.

This is a very simple map, not drawn to scale. Suppose the distance from A to D is 15 miles. You can see in the drawing that the distance from A to B is 6 miles, and the distance from B to C is 4 miles.

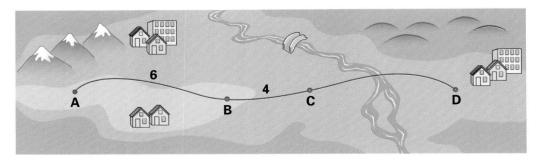

10. What is the distance from C to D? Write down your calculations.

Telly found the distance from C to D by adding 6 and 4. Then she subtracted the result from 15. She could have used an **arithmetic tree** to record this calculation.

- To make an arithmetic tree, begin by writing down all of the numbers.

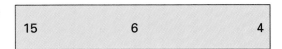

- Then pick two numbers. Telly picked 6 and 4.

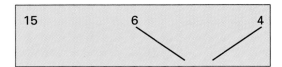

- Telly added the numbers and found the sum of 10.

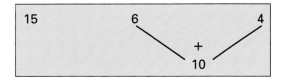

- Telly selected the 15 and the new 10.

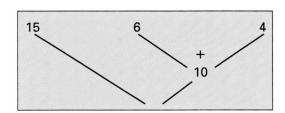

- She subtracted to find a difference of 5.

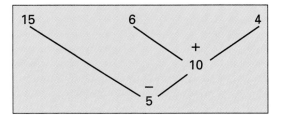

11. Complete **Student Activity Sheet 4**.

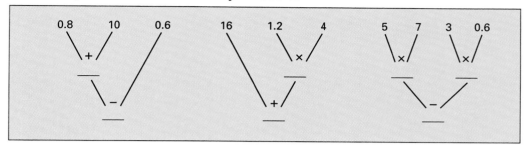

Remember, you should multiply first and then add the products.

12. Which of the following trees shows the accurate result of the expression 1 × 2 + 3 × 4?

    a.   **b.**   **c.**

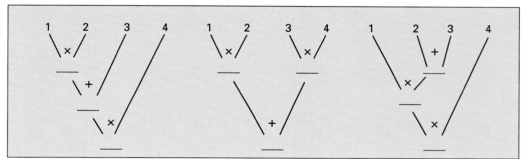

13. Which of the trees from problem 12 shows the same calculation as this arrow string?

$$1 \xrightarrow{\times 2} \underline{\quad} \xrightarrow{+3} \underline{\quad} \xrightarrow{\times 4} \underline{\quad}$$

Alex feels that the calculation for repair bills should begin with the travel costs. The travel cost is part of the base rate; the customer always has to pay them. Flo thinks that it is impossible to begin an arrow string with the travel cost.

14. Is it impossible to begin an arrow string with the travel cost? Explain.

This is an arithmetic tree for calculating the bill for a two-hour home repair job expressing the travel costs first.

15. Does this arithmetic tree give the costs (as shown in the table for problem 2 on page 33)?

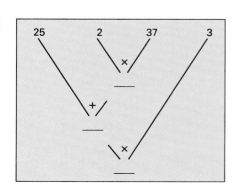

It is possible to build an arithmetic tree using words instead of numbers. In the left column of the table, a word tree has been built to describe the repair bill. In the right column, numbers represent the words.

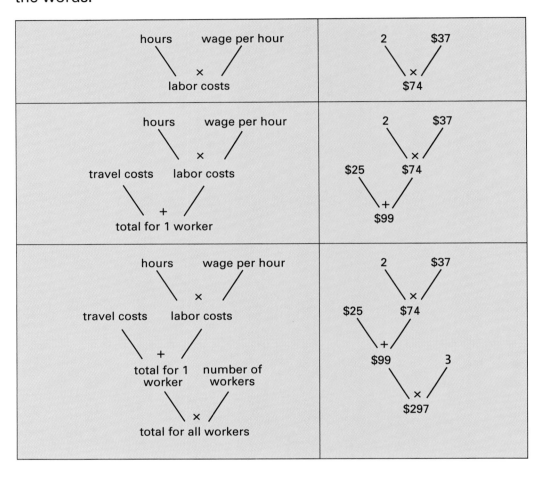

When some of the branches are extended, the tree looks like the one from problem 15.

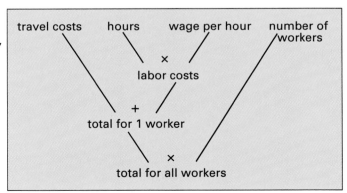

16. Make a word tree that shows how to find the height of a stack of cups.

Flexible Computation

Arithmetic trees are another strategy to make calculating some addition and subtraction problems easier.

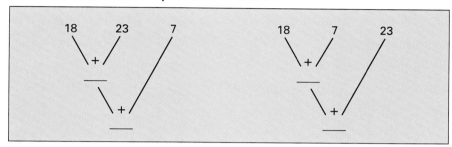

17. **a.** Compare the two trees.

b. Design a tree that makes adding the three numbers easier to do.

Addition problems with more numbers have many possible arithmetic trees. Here are two trees for $\frac{1}{2} + \frac{1}{4} + \frac{3}{4} + \frac{3}{2}$.

18. **a.** Copy the trees and find the sum.

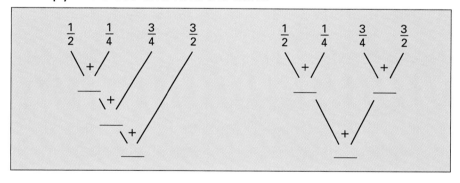

b. Design two other arithmetic trees for the same problem and find the answers.

c. Which arithmetic tree makes $\frac{1}{2} + \frac{1}{4} + \frac{3}{4} + \frac{3}{2}$ easiest to calculate? Why?

19. Design an arithmetic tree that makes each of the following problems easy to calculate.

a. $7 + 3 + 6 + 4$ **b.** $4.5 + 8.9 + 5.5 + 1.1$ **c.** $\frac{4}{10} + \frac{1}{2} + \frac{1}{10} + \frac{3}{4}$

20. How are different arithmetic trees for the same problem the same? How might they differ?

You may have noticed that if a problem has only addition, the answer is the same no matter how you draw the arithmetic tree. You may wonder if this is true for subtraction.

21. Do the following trees give the same result?

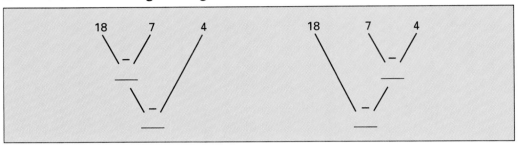

Return to the Supermarket

The automatic calculating scale at Veggies-R-Us is not working. Ms. Prince buys 0.5 lb of grapes and 2 lb of tomatoes.

22. What is the total cost for the grapes and tomatoes?

23. Can you write an arrow string to show how to calculate Ms. Prince's bill? Why or why not?

24. Can Ms. Prince's bill be calculated with an arithmetic tree? If so, make the tree. If not, explain why.

Dr. Keppler buys 2 lb of tomatoes, 0.5 lb of grapes, and $\frac{1}{2}$ lb of green beans.

25. Make an arithmetic tree for the total bill for the tomatoes, grapes, and beans.

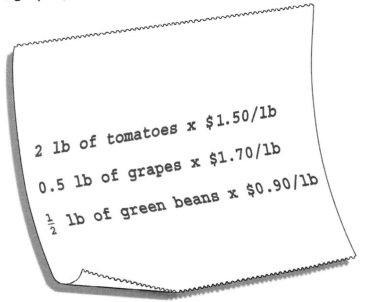

2 lb of tomatoes x $1.50/lb

0.5 lb of grapes x $1.70/lb

$\frac{1}{2}$ lb of green beans x $0.90/lb

The store manager provides calculators for each of the clerks. The calculators use the rule that multiplication is calculated before addition. Then the store manager wrote these directions.

amount of tomatoes × 1.50 + amount of grapes × 1.70 + amount of green beans × 0.90 =
(in pounds)   (in pounds)   (in pounds)

26. If the clerks punch in a calculation using these directions, will they find the correct total for the bill?

What Comes First?

Arithmetic trees are useful because they resolve any question about the order of the calculation. The problem is that they require a lot of room on your paper. Copy the first tree below.

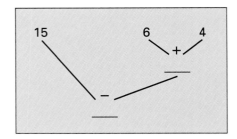

Since the 6 + 4 is simplified first, circle it on your copy.

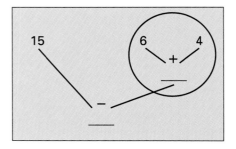

The tree can then be simplified.

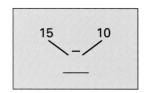

Instead of the second arithmetic tree, you could write:

$$15 - \overline{6 + 4}$$

27. What does the circle represent?

The whole circle is not necessary. People often write 15 − (6 + 4). This does not require as much space, but the **parentheses** show how the numbers are grouped together.

28. a. Rewrite the tree using parentheses to indicate which numbers are associated.

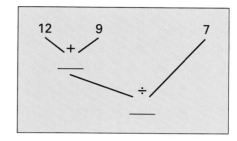

b. Make a tree for 3 × (6 + 4).

c. What is the value of 5 × (84 − 79)?

d. Rewrite the tree using parentheses.

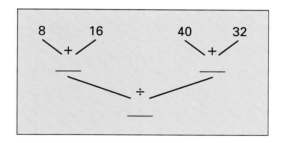

29. Use parentheses to find the correct total bill for Karlene's problem in the Home Repair section.

2 × 37 + 25 × 3

E ▸ Order of Operations

Summary ▶◀

The beginning of this unit introduced **arrow language** to represent formulas. There are several ways to write formulas.

You can express formulas with words.

cost = tomatoes × $1.50 + grapes × $1.70 + green beans × $0.90
    (in lb)   *(in lb)*   *(in lb)*

You can express formulas with **arithmetic trees**.

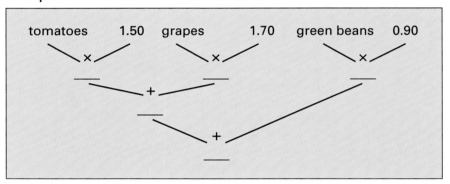

Arithmetic trees show the order of calculation. If a problem is not in an arithmetic tree and does not have parentheses, there is a rule for the **order of operations**: Complete multiplication and division before addition and subtraction.

$1 \times 2 + 3 \div 4 - 5$ is represented in this tree.

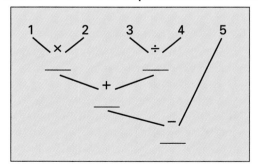

You can use parentheses to convert an arithmetic tree to an expression that shows which operations to do first.

$$(5 \times 4) + (3 \div 2) - 1 = 20.5$$

1. **a.** Use the mathematicians' rule to simplify this expression.

$$24 \div 3 + 5 \times 8 - 10$$

You may use an arithmetic tree if you wish.

   b. Write $24 \div 3 + 5 \times 8 - 10 = $ _____ using parentheses so that the expression reflects the mathematicians' rule for order of operations.

2. Design an arithmetic tree that makes each of the following problems easier to solve using mental calculation.

   a. $17 + 6 + 3 + 7 + 4$ **c.** $\frac{3}{10} + \frac{1}{2} + \frac{1}{10} + \frac{3}{4} + \frac{1}{10}$

   b. $4.5 + 8.9 + 5.5 + 1.1$

You can estimate your ideal weight using the following rule:

$$weight \text{ (in kilograms)} = \frac{height \text{ (in cm)} - 100 + (4 \times circumference \text{ of wrist in cm)}}{2}$$

This general rule applies for adult men. For women, the rule is slightly different: Replace 100 with 110.

3. **a.** Write an arithmetic tree to represent the general rule for women.

Matthew is 175 cm tall. The circumference of his wrist is 17 cm.

   b. Use the rule to estimate Matthew's ideal weight.

Andrew is 162 cm tall. The circumference of his wrist is 16 cm. His weight is 54 kilograms (kg).

   c. Does Andrew weigh too much or too little, according to the general rule?

 For Further Reflection

How might you modify the mathematician's rule for the order of operations to calculate $(3 \times 5 - 2 + 7) \div 4$?

Additional Practice

Section Ⓐ Arrow Language

1. Here is a record for Mr. Kamarov's bank account.

Date	Deposit	Withdrawal	Total
10/15			$210.24
10/22	$523.65	$140.00	
10/29	$75.00	$40.00	

   a. Find the totals for October 22 and October 29.

   b. Write arrow strings to show how you found the totals.

   c. When does Mr. Kamarov first have a minimum of $600 in his account?

2. Find the results for these arrow strings.

   a. $15 \xrightarrow{\ -\ 3\ } \underline{\quad} \xrightarrow{\ +\ 11\ } \underline{\quad}$

   b. $3.7 \xrightarrow{\ +\ 1.9\ } \underline{\quad} \xrightarrow{\ +\ 8.8\ } \underline{\quad} \xrightarrow{\ -\ 1.6\ } \underline{\quad}$

   c. $3{,}000 \xrightarrow{\ -\ 1{,}520\ } \underline{\quad} \xrightarrow{\ -\ 600\ } \underline{\quad} \xrightarrow{\ +\ 5{,}200\ } \underline{\quad}$

Section Ⓑ Smart Calculations

1. For each shopping problem, write an arrow string to show the change the clerk should give the customer. Be sure to use the small-coins-and-bills-first method. Then write another arrow string that has only one arrow to show the total change.

   a. A customer gives $20.00 for a $9.59 purchase.

   b. A customer gives $5.00 for a $2.26 purchase.

   c. A customer gives $16.00 for a $15.64 purchase.

2. Rewrite these arrow strings so that each has only one arrow.

    a. $750 \xrightarrow{+35} \underline{\quad} \xrightarrow{+40} \underline{\quad}$

    b. $63 \xrightarrow{-3} \underline{\quad} \xrightarrow{+50} \underline{\quad}$

    c. $439 \xrightarrow{+1} \underline{\quad} \xrightarrow{-20} \underline{\quad}$

3. Rewrite each arrow string with a new string that will make the computation easier to calculate. Explain why your new string makes the computation easier, or why it is not possible to simplify the string.

    a. $74 \xrightarrow{+66} \underline{\quad}$ b. $231 \xrightarrow{-58} \underline{\quad}$ c. $459 \xrightarrow{+27} \underline{\quad}$

Section C Formulas

If Clarinda is connected to the Internet for a total of three hours one month, she pays $15 plus three times $2, or $21, for the month.

1. Which string shows the cost for Clarinda's Internet service through Tech Net? Explain your answer.

    a. $\$15 \xrightarrow{+\$2} \underline{\quad} \xrightarrow{\times \text{number of hours}} \text{total cost}$

    b. $\text{number of hours} \xrightarrow{+\$15} \underline{\quad} \xrightarrow{\times \$2} \text{total cost}$

    c. $\text{number of hours} \xrightarrow{\times \$2} \underline{\quad} \xrightarrow{+\$15} \text{total cost}$

2. How much does it cost Clarinda for these monthly usage amounts?

    a. 5 hours   b. 20 hours   c. $6\frac{1}{2}$ hours

Another Internet access company, Online Time, charges only $10 per month, but $3 per hour.

3. Write an arrow string that finds the cost of Internet access through Online Time.

4. If Clarinda uses the Internet approximately 10 hours a month, which company should she use—Tech Net or Online Time?

Carlos works at a plant nursery that sells flower pots. One type of flower pot has a rim height of 4 cm and a hold height of 16 cm.

5. How tall is a stack of two pots? Three pots?

6. Write a formula using arrow language that can be used to find the height of any stack if you know the number of pots.

7. Carlos has to stack these pots on a shelf that is 45 cm high. How many pots can he place in a stack this high? Explain your answer.

8. Compare the following pairs of arrow strings and determine whether they provide the same results.

   a. input $\xrightarrow{\times 8}$ _____ $\xrightarrow{\div 2}$ output

      input $\xrightarrow{\div 2}$ _____ $\xrightarrow{\times 8}$ output

   b. input $\xrightarrow{+ 5}$ _____ $\xrightarrow{\times 3}$ output

      input $\xrightarrow{\times 3}$ _____ $\xrightarrow{+ 5}$ output

   c. input $\xrightarrow{\div 2}$ _____ $\xrightarrow{+ 1}$ _____ $\xrightarrow{+ 6}$ output

      input $\xrightarrow{\div 2}$ _____ $\xrightarrow{+ 6}$ _____ $\xrightarrow{+ 1}$ output

Section Ⓓ Reverse Operations

Ravi lives in Bellingham, Washington. He travels to Vancouver, Canada, frequently. When Ravi was in Canada, he used this rule to estimate prices in U.S. dollars.

number of Canadian dollars $\xrightarrow{\div 4}$ _____ $\xrightarrow{\times 3}$ number of U.S. dollars

1. Using Ravi's formula, estimate U.S. prices for these Canadian prices.

   a. a hamburger for $2 Canadian

   b. a T-shirt for $18 Canadian

   c. a movie for $8 Canadian

   d. a pair of shoes for $45 Canadian

2. Write a formula that Ravi can use to convert U.S. dollars to Canadian dollars.

3. Write the reverse string for each of these strings.

   a. input $\xrightarrow{\;-1\;}$ ____ $\xrightarrow{\;\times\,2.5\;}$ ____ $\xrightarrow{\;+\,4\;}$ output
   b. input $\xrightarrow{\;+\,6\;}$ ____ $\xrightarrow{\;-\,2\;}$ ____ $\xrightarrow{\;\div\,5\;}$ output

4. Find the input for each string.

   a. input $\xrightarrow{\;+\,10\;}$ ____ $\xrightarrow{\;\div\,2\;}$ ____ $\xrightarrow{\;-\,3\;}$ 9
   b. input $\xrightarrow{\;\times\,4\;}$ ____ $\xrightarrow{\;-\,5\;}$ ____ $\xrightarrow{\;\div\,3\;}$ ____ $\xrightarrow{\;+\,1\;}$ 10

Section E ▶ Order of Operations

1. In your notebook, copy and complete the arithmetic trees.

   a.   **b.**   **c.**

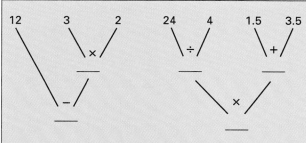
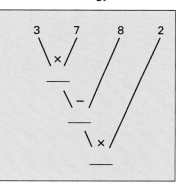

2. Make or design an arithmetic tree and find the answer.

   a. $10 + 1.5 \times 6$ b. $(10 + 1.5) \times 6$ c. $15 \div (2 \times 2 + 1)$

Suzanne took her cat to the veterinarian for dental surgery. (Her cat had never brushed his teeth!) Before the surgery, the veterinarian gave Suzanne an estimate for the cost: $55 for anesthesia, $30 total for teeth cleaning, $18 per tooth pulled, $75 per hour of surgery, and the cost of medicine.

3. Draw an arithmetic tree to represent the total cost of Suzanne's bill from the veterinarian. Use words in your arithmetic tree when necessary.

Answers to Check Your Work

Section Ⓐ Arrow Language

1.

Date	Seats Requested	Cancellations	Total Seats Reserved
3/11			233
3/12	47	0	**280**
3/13	51	1	**330**
3/14	53	0	**383**
3/15	5	12	**376**
3/16	16	2	**390**

2. Arrow strings will vary. Sample response:

   3/12 $233 \xrightarrow{+47} 280 \xrightarrow{-0} 280$

   3/13 $280 \xrightarrow{+51} 331 \xrightarrow{-1} 330$

   3/14 $330 \xrightarrow{+53} 383 \xrightarrow{-0} 383$

   3/15 $383 \xrightarrow{+5} 388 \xrightarrow{-12} 376$

   3/16 $376 \xrightarrow{+16} 392 \xrightarrow{-2} 390$

3. The airline needs to begin a waiting list on March 14.

4. Answers will vary. Sample response:

   One advantage is that it quickly tells you how many people are booked for the flight on the 16th. One disadvantage is that you do not know on what day the waiting list was started.

5. **a.** $12.30 \xrightarrow{+1.40} 13.70 \xrightarrow{-0.62} 13.08 \xrightarrow{+5.83} 18.91 \xrightarrow{-1.40} 17.51$

   b. Discuss your answer with a classmate. Sample response:

   Vic had $12.30 in his pocket. His mom gave him $1.40 for bus fare. On the way to the bus stop, he bought a pen for $0.62. Then he sold his lunch to Joy for $5.83. He paid the bus driver $1.40. How much did Vic have left?

6. Discuss your answer with a classmate. Sample response:

Fourteen people got on the empty bus at the first stop. At the second stop, two got off and eight got on. How many were still on the bus? [20 people, or 21 people if you count the driver]

$$14 \xrightarrow{-2} 12 \xrightarrow{+8} 20$$

7. Sample response:

Arrow language shows all the steps in order so that you can find answers that are in the middle of a series of calculations.

Section **B** Smart Calculations

1. a. $20 \xrightarrow{+15} 35 \xrightarrow{-8} 27 \xrightarrow{+\frac{1}{2}} 27.5$

b. $6.77 \xrightarrow{+0.03} 6.80 \xrightarrow{+0.20} 7 \xrightarrow{+13} 20$

c. $12.10 \xrightarrow{+0.20} 12.30 \xrightarrow{+0.70} 13 \xrightarrow{+7} 20$

2. a. Sample response:

$$423 \xrightarrow{+7} 430 \xrightarrow{+30} 460 \xrightarrow{+200} 660$$

This string is easier because you can add the numbers in the ones place, then add the numbers in the tens place, and finally add the numbers in the hundreds place.

b. Sample response:

This string is already easy because you can easily subtract 20 from 40 to get 20, and then subtract 4, so the answer is 520.

c. Sample response:

$$29 \xrightarrow{-25} 4 \xrightarrow{+54} 58$$

This string is easier because when you subtract 25 first, it leaves an easy number to work with.

d. Sample response:

$$998 \xrightarrow{+2} 1{,}000 \xrightarrow{+32} 1{,}032$$

This string is easier because when you add 2 to 998, you get lots of zeros that are easy to work with. It's easy to add numbers to 1,000.

3. Check your answer with a classmate. Sample response:

(long) $232 \xrightarrow{+31} 263 \xrightarrow{+19} 282$

(short) $232 \xrightarrow{+50} 282$

Short strings are easier when the total of the numbers over the arrows is a multiple of 10 or a number between 1 and 10.

4. Check your answer with a classmate. Sample response:

(short) $232 \xrightarrow{+98} 330$

(long) $232 \xrightarrow{+100} 332 \xrightarrow{-2} 330$

Longer strings are easier when the total of the numbers over the arrows is not a multiple of 10 or a number between 1 and 10.

5. Sample explanation:

The shortened arrow string shows the total amount of change.

Section C Formulas

1. a. number of miles $\xrightarrow{\times 1.40}$ _____ $\xrightarrow{+1.90}$ total price

b. Using an arrow string makes calculations easier.

2.

Weight	Tomatoes $1.20/lb	Green Beans $0.80/lb	Grapes $1.90/lb
0.5 lb	$0.60	$0.40	$0.95
1.0 lb	$1.20	$0.80	$1.90
2.0 lb	$2.40	$1.60	$3.80
3.0 lb	$3.60	$2.40	$5.70

3. a. The − 1 means that one chair is subtracted from the total number of chairs in the stack; × 7 means that for each chair that is added, the height of the stack will grow 7 cm. The + 80 represents the height of the first chair in the stack.

b. Alba should use × 7 and + 73 above the arrows. She wrote × 7 because each chair adds 7 cm to the height of the stack. Next, + 73 is added for the height of the first chair minus the 7 cm that was already added in the first step.

4. a. The point on the graph labeled A represents a stack of 15 chairs with a total height of about 175 cm.

b. Not every point on the graph has a meaning. For example, you cannot add "half a chair," or the total height of the stack cannot be 100 cm.

c. The arrow strings can be used to find the height of one or more of these chairs. Zero chairs makes no sense. Also, if 0 is used for the number of chairs in Damian's arrow string, the result is:

$$0 \xrightarrow{-1} -1 \xrightarrow{\times 7} -7 \xrightarrow{+80} 73 \text{ cm}$$

d. About six chairs.

e. $5 \xrightarrow{\times 7} 35 \xrightarrow{+73} 108 \text{ cm}$

A stack of five chairs requires 108 cm of space.

$6 \xrightarrow{\times 7} 42 \xrightarrow{+73} 115 \text{ cm}$

So six chairs will fit.

$7 \xrightarrow{\times 7} 49 \xrightarrow{+73} 122 \text{ cm}$

Seven will not.

Section **D** Reverse Operations

1. a. 4,090 × 1.609 ≈ 6,581 km. Your answer should not contain decimals because the original measurement is rounded to the nearest mile.

b. 4,090 × 1.6 ≈ 6,544 km

c. 6,581 − 6,544 ≈ 37

Discuss your answer with a classmate. Sample responses:
- You do not know how 4,090 miles was measured. As an airplane flies? Making computations using a model of the earth? Using and converting sea miles? They will all result in different outcomes.
- 37 km compared to 6,500 (or 6,581 or 6,544) is less than 1%. That is not a very big difference.
- If you are traveling that far, 37 km is not a very big difference.

2. $4.40 $\xrightarrow{\times 0.75}$ $3.30

3. Carmen's string is correct because 0.75 is the same as $\frac{3}{4}$.
By dividing by 4, she found one-fourth of the price. Next she multiplied by three, which results in three-fourths of the price.

4. a. output $\xrightarrow{+4}$ ____ $\xrightarrow{÷3}$ ____ $\xrightarrow{-2}$ input
(divided by)

b. output $\xrightarrow{-7}$ ____ $\xrightarrow{+5}$ ____ $\xrightarrow{-2}$ input

5. Check your answers with a classmate. You should have used several numbers to check if your arrow string works.

Section **E** Order of Operations

1. a. 38

b. (24 ÷ 3) + (5 × 8) − 10 = ____

2. Sample answers:

a.

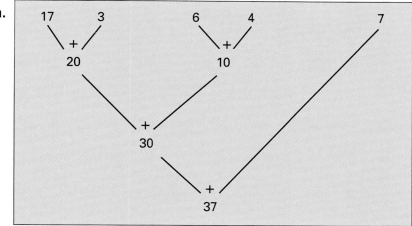

b.

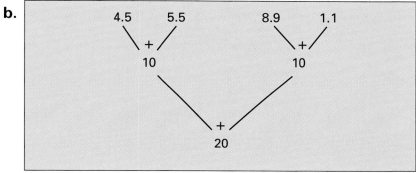

c.

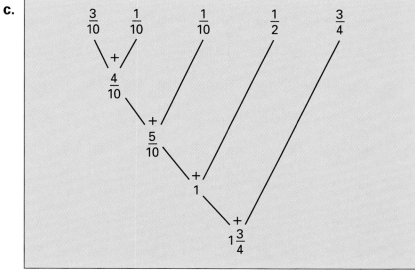

3. a.

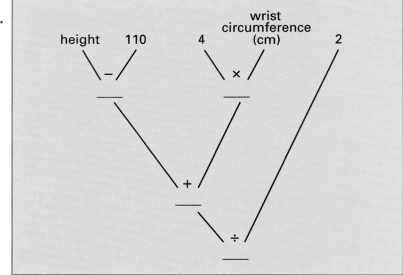

b. Matthew should weigh 71.5 (or 72) kg.

c. Andrew's ideal weight is 63 kg according to the general rule. So he does not weigh enough.

Take a Chance

Data Analysis and Probability

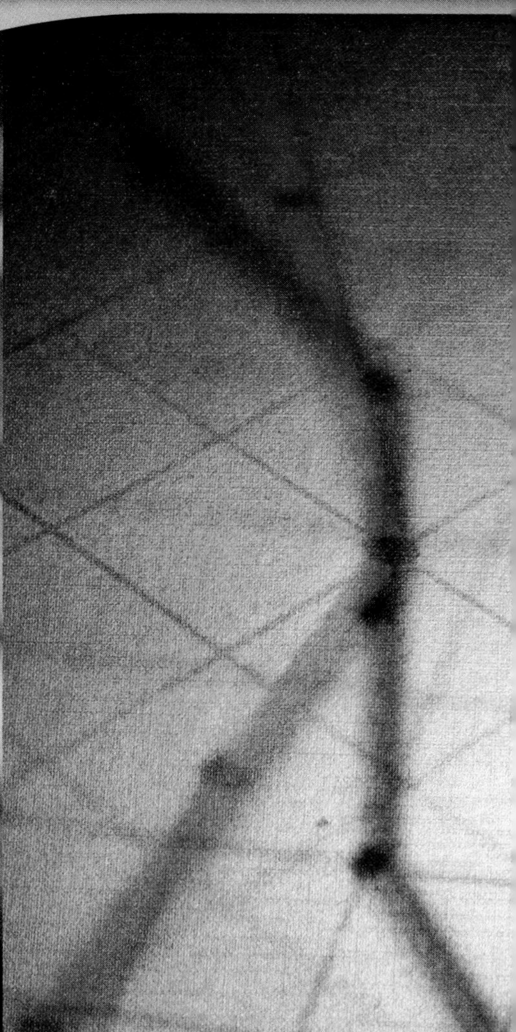

BRITANNICA
Mathematics
in
Context

HOLT, RINEHART AND WINSTON

Mathematics in Context is a comprehensive curriculum for the middle grades.
It was developed in 1991 through 1997 in collaboration with the Wisconsin Center
for Education Research, School of Education, University of Wisconsin-Madison and
the Freudenthal Institute at the University of Utrecht, The Netherlands, with the
support of the National Science Foundation Grant No. 9054928.

The revision of the curriculum was carried out in 2003 through 2005, with the
support of the National Science Foundation Grant No. ESI 0137414.

National Science Foundation
Opinions expressed are those of the authors
and not necessarily those of the Foundation.

Jonker, V., van Galen, F., Boswinkel, N., Wijers, M., Bakker, A., Simon, A. N.,
Burrill, G., & Middleton, J. A. (2005). *Take a chance.* In Wisconsin Center for
Education Research & Freudenthal Institute (Eds.), Mathematics in Context.
Chicago: Encyclopædia Britannica.

ISBN 0-03-039613-1

2 3 4 5 6 073 09 08 07 06 05

The *Mathematics in Context* Development Team

Development 1991–1997

The initial version of *Take a Chance* was developed by Vincent Jonker, Frans van Galen, Nina Boswinkel, and Monica Wijers. It was adapted for use in American schools by Aaron N. Simon, Gail Burrill, and James A. Middleton.

Wisconsin Center for Education

Research Staff

Thomas A. Romberg
Director

Joan Daniels Pedro
Assistant to the Director

Gail Burrill
Coordinator

Margaret R. Meyer
Coordinator

Project Staff

Jonathan Brendefur	Sherian Foster	
Laura Brinker	James A, Middleton	
James Browne	Jasmina Milinkovic	
Jack Burrill	Margaret A. Pligge	
Rose Byrd	Mary C. Shafer	
Peter Christiansen	Julia A. Shew	
Barbara Clarke	Aaron N. Simon	
Doug Clarke	Marvin Smith	
Beth R. Cole	Stephanie Z. Smith	
Fae Dremock	Mary S. Spence	
Mary Ann Fix		

Freudenthal Institute Staff

Jan de Lange
Director

Els Feijs
Coordinator

Martin van Reeuwijk
Coordinator

Mieke Abels	Jansie Niehaus
Nina Boswinkel	Nanda Querelle
Frans van Galen	Anton Roodhardt
Koeno Gravemeijer	Leen Streefland
Marja van den Heuvel-Panhuizen	
Jan Auke de Jong	Adri Treffers
Vincent Jonker	Monica Wijers
Ronald Keijzer	Astrid de Wild
Martin Kindt	

Revision 2003–2005

The revised version of *Take a Chance* was developed by Arthur Bakker and Monica Wijers. It was adapted for use in American schools by Gail Burrill.

Wisconsin Center for Education

Research Staff

Thomas A. Romberg
Director

David C. Webb
Coordinator

Gail Burrill
Editorial Coordinator

Margaret A. Pligge
Editorial Coordinator

Project Staff

Sarah Ailts	Margaret R. Meyer
Beth R. Cole	Anne Park
Erin Hazlett	Bryna Rappaport
Teri Hedges	Kathleen A. Steele
Karen Hoiberg	Ana C. Stephens
Carrie Johnson	Candace Ulmer
Jean Krusi	Jill Vettrus
Elaine McGrath	

Freudenthal Institute Staff

Jan de Lange
Director

Truus Dekker
Coordinator

Mieke Abels
Content Coordinator

Monica Wijers
Content Coordinator

Arthur Bakker	Nathalie Kuijpers
Peter Boon	Huub Nilwik
Els Feijs	Sonia Palha
Dédé de Haan	Nanda Querelle
Martin Kindt	Martin van Reeuwijk

Cover photo credits: (left, right) © Getty Images; (middle) © Corbis

Illustrations
4 (bottom) Jason Millet; **6** (top left and right) Mona Daily; (bottom) Jason Millet; **13** (top, bottom left and middle), **15** (top and bottom) Jason Millet; **23** (top) Holly Cooper-Olds; (bottom left) Mona Daily; **27** (all) **31** (left) Jason Millet

Photographs
1 (all) Mary Stone Photography/HRW; **2, 3** (left) Victoria Smith/HRW; (middle) Mary Stone Photography/HRW; (right) © PhotoDisc/Getty Images; **7** (top left) © PhotoDisc/Getty Images; (top right) Mary Stone Photography/HRW; (bottom) John Langford/HRW; **23, 26** © PhotoDisc/Getty Images; **27** (all) Mary Stone/HRW; **29** (top) Mary Stone/HRW; (bottom) Peter Van Steen/HRW Photo; **30** Peter Van Steen/HRW Photo

◆ Contents

Dear Student,

You are about to begin the study of the *Mathematics in Context* unit *Take a Chance*. Think about the following words and what they mean to you: *fair, sure, uncertain, unlikely*, and *impossible*. In this unit, you will see how these words are used in mathematics.

You will toss coins and roll number cubes and record the outcomes. Do you think you can predict how many times a coin will come up heads if you toss it a certain number of times? Is the chance of getting heads greater than the chance of getting tails? As you investigate these ideas, you are beginning the study of probability.

When several different things can happen, you will learn how to count all of the possibilities in a smart way. During the next few weeks, keep alert for statements about chance you may read or hear, such as "The chance of rain is 50%." You might even keep a record of such statements and bring them to share with the class.

We hope you enjoy learning about chance!

Sincerely,

The Mathematics in Context Development Team

Fair

Hillary and Robert

This unit follows Hillary and Robert, students at Eagle Middle School in Maine, as they experiment with using chance to make decisions.

Hillary

Robert

You probably already know some things about **chance**.

1. **Reflect** What do you think of when someone says the word *chance*?

Choosing

During lunch, Hillary and Robert both want to play Super Math Whiz III, a computer game. The game is installed on one computer in the classroom. Since only one person can play at a time, Hillary and Robert have to decide who will play the game first.

2. How could you solve this problem in a **fair** way?

3. What do you think it means for something to be fair?

There are many situations in which you have to find a fair way to make a decision.

Robert says to Hillary, "If you throw a 6 with this number cube, you can play; otherwise, I'll play."

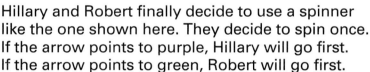

4. Do you think this is fair? Why or why not?

5. Can you come up with a better way to decide?

Hillary and Robert finally decide to use a spinner like the one shown here. They decide to spin once. If the arrow points to purple, Hillary will go first. If the arrow points to green, Robert will go first.

6. Is this a fair method? Why or why not?

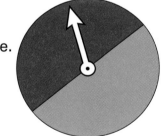

By now, everyone in Hillary and Robert's class has heard about the computer game and wants to play. Hillary says, "Okay, okay! Let's put all of our names in a hat, and the person whose name is drawn gets to play."

7. Is this fair? Why or why not?

A method for choosing is *fair* if it gives everyone the same chance of being chosen.

8. Think of two other situations in which it is important to be fair.

Fair Again

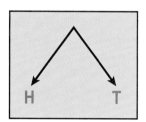

Hillary and Robert both want to play the computer game again the next day. They decide to toss a coin to see who will play first. Since there is an equal chance (sometimes called a 50-50 chance) of getting either heads or tails, this is a fair method.

You can draw a diagram with branches like a tree to show the two possibilities. The path you take on the **tree diagram** depends on the side of the coin that comes up.

9. a. What do the **H** and the **T** stand for?

   b. Robert says, "You know, the diagram shows there's a 50-50 chance of getting heads or tails." Explain what Robert means.

Look at a number cube.

10. a. How many different numbers can you roll on a number cube?

   b. Draw a diagram to show the different possibilities.

11. How could Robert and Hillary use a number cube to decide in a fair way who will play the game first?

12. Hillary and Robert have a black-and-white cube. Hillary wins if it comes up white, and Robert wins if it comes up black. How can you tell if the cube has been colored in a fair way?

Hillary's class is studying dinosaurs. The teacher, Mr. Lotto, would like the students to report on dinosaur bones found in different parts of the world.

Mr. Lotto decides to divide the world into three regions (see the map on page 5):

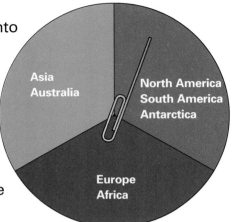

- North America, South America, and Antarctica;
- Europe and Africa; and
- Asia and Australia.

The students in the class think it will be fair if they use a spinner to assign one of these regions to each of them.

Activity

Making a Spinner

You can make your own spinner that looks like this one. You will need a sheet of paper, a paper clip, and a compass.

- Draw a circle on a blank sheet of paper with the compass. Mark the point in the middle.
- Take a paper clip and straighten one end.
- Use a pencil to hold the paper clip over the center of the circle.
- Divide the spinner into three equal parts as shown. Write the name of one of the regions in each part.

Spin the spinner 15 times. Record the results.

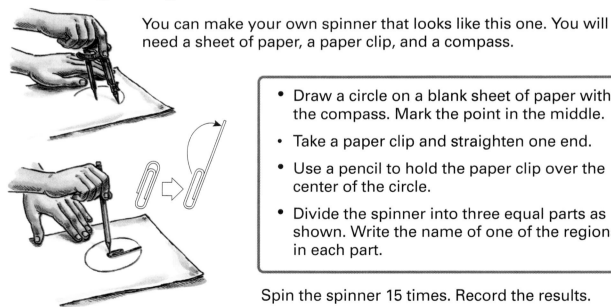

13. Can you tell from your results whether your spinner can be used to make fair decisions? Explain.

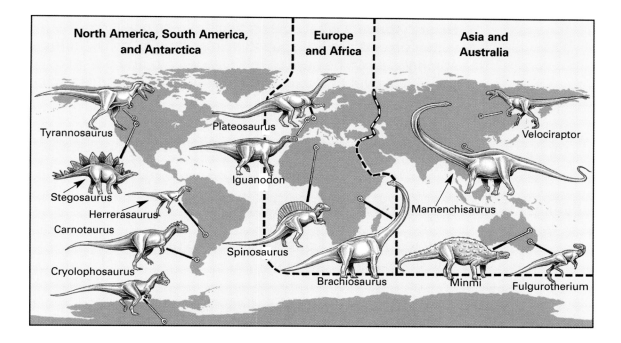

Shanna wonders whether a spinner made out of a triangle can be used to make fair decisions.

14. a. Draw a triangle on a sheet of paper. Can you make the triangle into a fair spinner?

    b. How can you tell whether it is fair?

    c. Can any triangle be made into a fair spinner? Support your answer with some examples.

Jonathan wonders if he can use a number cube to choose regions in a fair way.

15. a. Can he? If so, how?

    b. Kara wonders if she can use a coin. Can she?

16. How can you tell whether a particular method will be fair? Explain your answer.

Since many bones were recently found in Europe and Africa, Mr. Lotto thinks more students should be reporting on this region than on each of the other regions.

17. a. How could you make a spinner so the region Europe and Africa is picked more often than each of the others?

    b. Would this spinner be fair?

Hillary wonders what other objects can be used to make fair decisions. When objects are not shaped as regularly as coins, number cubes, or spinners, it can be hard to tell. One way to find out is to flip or spin the object over and over again to see what happens each time.

Activity

Different Chance Objects

Your teacher will divide the class into groups. Each group will get one of the items listed below:

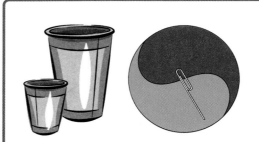

- A large paper cup
- A small paper cup
- A chalkboard eraser
- A bottle cap
- A spinner like the one on the left

Your job is to find out whether you can use your item in any way to make a fair decision.

18. Toss or spin your item 30 times. Make a table of your results. When you are done, decide whether you can use your item to make a fair decision. Report your results to the class. Keep these results because you will use them again later in the unit.

The Concert

Compass Rose, a rock band Hillary likes, is coming to play in Eagle next week. Hillary's mother got four tickets to the concert. She will take Hillary and two of Hillary's friends.

Unfortunately, Hillary has three friends she wants to bring, and she has to find a fair way to decide who will go with her.

19. Find a fair way to decide which two friends will go with Hillary. You may use coins, number cubes, spinners, or anything else you think may be fair.

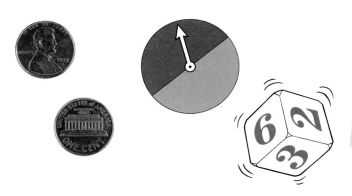

Oh no! Another of Hillary's friends wants to go too!

20. Come up with a fair way to decide which two of the four will go with Hillary now.

21. Give your opinion about the fairness of each of the following situations:

   a. A referee tosses a coin before a game to see which of two soccer teams gets to choose a goal.

   b. In Mr. Ryan's class, there are 10 boys and 15 girls. To decide who will be hall monitors each day, Mr. Ryan draws the name of one girl from a box holding all of the girls' names and then draws the name of one boy from a box holding all of the boys' names.

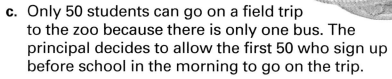

   c. Only 50 students can go on a field trip to the zoo because there is only one bus. The principal decides to allow the first 50 who sign up before school in the morning to go on the trip.

   d. In the United States, all people 18 years old or older are eligible to vote for a presidential candidate.

A Fair

Summary ⧓

There are many situations in daily life that involve **chance** or require you to make **fair** decisions. *Fair* means that every possibility has the same chance of occurring.

In order to make fair decisions, you should use a fair method. Things that can help you make fair decisions are coins, number cubes, and spinners. Many other objects can also help you make fair decisions.

Check Your Work ▶▶

1. **a.** Can you toss a pencil to make a fair decision? Explain your answer.

   b. Can you toss a thumbtack to make a fair decision? Explain your answer.

Hillary is riding her bike. She is on her way to visit one of her friends. She has not yet decided if she will visit Laura or Asja. Hillary decides, "If the next traffic light is green, I will visit Asja; otherwise, I will visit Laura."

2. Is this a fair way to decide? Explain.

Three students from Hillary's class want to play a game. They need to decide who will go first in the game.

3. Describe how they can make a fair decision in each of the following ways:

   a. using a number cube

   b. using a spinner (Also draw a spinner they can use.)

   c. using one coin (This is not easy!)

   d. using another way (Decide on this way yourself.)

Every week, a quiz show on television features two competing teams from local schools. A participating school may send 40 students to sit in the audience. The principal of Eagle Middle School has decided that each of the eight classes in the school should hold a drawing to select five students who will go to the studio.

Here is a list of the eight classes at Eagle School.

Class	Number of Students	Number Selected
Mr. Johnson	75	5
Mr. Geist	77	5
Ms. Lanie	50	5
Ms. McCall	51	5
Mr. Ford	74	5
Ms. Durden	75	5
Mr. Shore	70	5
Mr. Luxe	52	5

The principal says her method is fair.

4. **a.** Is the principal's method fair?

   b. If you were a student at Eagle Middle School, in which class would you want to be?

   c. Hillary and Robert have decided to design a different method that will be fair for the principal to use. What method do you think they might design?

 For Further Reflection

You have been asked to choose a method for making a fair decision. Think of a situation that would require a fair decision and describe at least three methods you could use.

What's the Chance?

Up and Down Events

Sometimes it is difficult to predict whether an event will take place. Other times you know for sure.

1. Use **Student Activity Sheet 1**. Put a check in the column that best describes your confidence that each event will take place.

	Statement	Sure It Won't	Not Sure	Sure It Will
A	You will have a test in math sometime this year.			
B	It will rain in your town sometime in the next four days.			
C	The number of students in your class who can roll their tongues will equal the number of students who cannot.			
D	You will roll a 7 with a normal number cube.			
E	In a room of 367 people, two people will have the same birthday.			
F	New Year's Day will come on the third Monday in January.			
G	When you toss a coin once, heads will come up.			
H	If you enter "2 + 2 =" on your calculator, the result will be 4.			

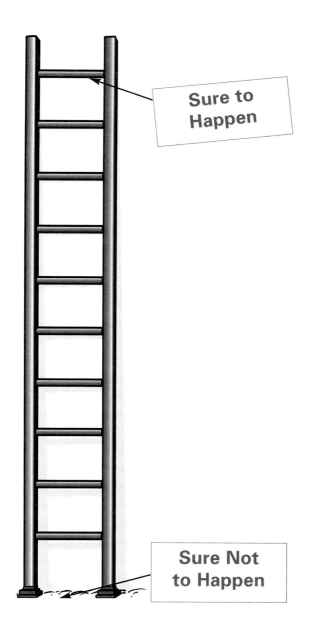

Sure to Happen

Sure Not to Happen

If you are wondering about the chance a particular event will happen, thinking about a ladder may help.

If you are pretty sure something will occur, you can think of it as being near the top of the ladder.

If you are pretty sure something will not occur, you can think of it as being near the bottom of the ladder.

If you are sure something will not happen, you can think of it as being on the ground!

You can mark on a drawing of a ladder how great the chance is a particular event will occur.

2. Draw a ladder like the one on the left. Put the three statements below on your ladder.

   a. The next car you see on the road will have been built in the United States.

   b. A gorilla will visit your school tomorrow.

   c. Your fingernails will grow today.

3. Now go back to the table on page 10 and put the statements from the table on one ladder. Explain why you put the statements where you did.

4. Put the following statements about chance on a ladder:

   "I'm sure it will happen."   "There's a 50-50 chance."

   "That's unlikely."   "It's very likely to happen."

   "It probably will."   "There's no way it will occur."

   "There's a 100% chance."   "It seems very unlikely."

   "There's a 0% chance."   "It could happen."

Match 'Em Up

Dan is doing an experiment. He has a bag containing pieces of paper of equal size, numbered 1 to 20. He is going to pick a number from the bag. Here are some possible outcomes for the number he will pick.

   a. It will be even.

   b. It will be divisible by 5.

   c. It will be a 1 or a 2.

   d. The digits in the number will add up to 12.

   e. It will be less than 16.

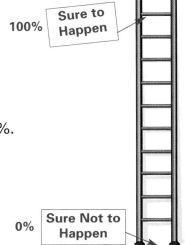

5. Put the five statements on a ladder like the one on the right and explain why you put them where you did.

The ladder shows that the chance of an event occurring is between 0% and 100%.

- Events you are sure are going to happen will be at the top.

- Events you are sure will not happen will be at the bottom.

- Events you are not sure about will be somewhere in between.

Frog Newton

Hillary is walking to the science lab carrying her pet bullfrog, Newton.

Newton, in fear for his life...

...jumps out of his aquarium and hops off as fast as his little feet can carry him.

Hillary finally finds Newton. He is sitting on a tile in the hall.

Hall

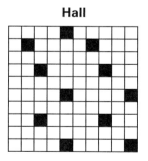

6. Look at the floor in the hall. Do you think Hillary found Newton sitting on a black tile or a white tile? Explain.

Cafeteria

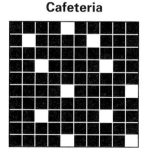

7. What if, instead, Newton was found on a tile in the cafeteria: Is it likely he was on the same color tile?

Here is another tile floor.

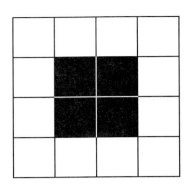

8. Suppose Newton made another dash for freedom on this floor. Draw a scale like the one here. Mark the chance Newton will end up on a black tile. Explain why you marked the scale where you did.

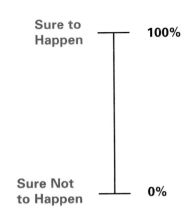

Now look at another floor.

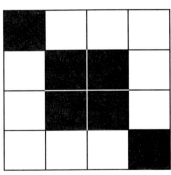

9. a. On the same scale that you used for problem 8, mark the chance Newton will end up on a black tile on this floor.

b. Is it greater or less than the chance in problem 8? Explain.

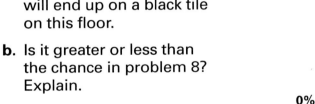

10. a. On **Student Activity Sheet 2**, color the first floor so Newton will have a 50% chance of landing on a black tile.

b. Mark the 50% chance on the scale on **Student Activity Sheet 2**.

c. What is another way of saying "The chance is 50%"?

11. a. For the floor in problem 8, you can say the chance Newton will end up on a black tile is 4 out of 16. Explain.

b. Jim says, "That's the same as 1 out of 4." Do you agree? Explain.

c. What fraction can be used to express this chance? And what percent?

d. Look at the floor from problem 9. What is the chance Newton will end up on a black tile on this floor?

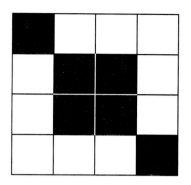

12. a. Color the second floor on **Student Activity Sheet 2** so Newton's chance of ending up on a black tile will be **1 out of 5**.

b. Now color the third floor on **Student Activity Sheet 2** with any pattern of black and white tiles. What is the chance Newton will end up on a black tile on the floor you made?

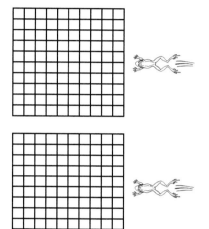

13. Reflect If you had a black-and-white tile floor, explain how you could find the chance a frog hopping around on it will stop on a black tile.

It turns out that Newton didn't have to worry. He is only part of an experiment at the science fair on the number of flies frogs eat.

Spinners

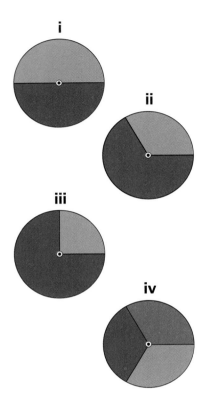

i

ii

iii

iv

14. Study the spinners on the left.

   a. Can you use spinner **i** to make fair decisions? Explain your answer.

   b. Can you use spinner **ii**, **iii**, or **iv** to make fair decisions?

   c. Draw a new spinner—different from **i**, **ii**, **iii**, and **iv**—that can be used to make fair decisions.

15. **a.** Draw a chance ladder in your notebook. For each spinner on the left, mark the ladder to show the chance of landing in the purple part.

   b. Use a method other than a ladder to express the chance of landing in the purple part of each spinner.

Jim made this spinner and colored this floor. Jim says, "The spinner and the floor give the same chance of landing in the purple part."

16. Do you agree with Jim? Explain.

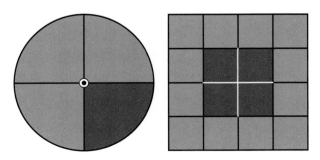

17. Look in the newspaper for statements about chance. Put your statements on a chance ladder. Bring the ladder to school and explain why you decided to place statements where you did.

Here are some examples to help you.

Baseball Update

Chances for a Run at Division Title Slim

By Mel Bergman
of The Reporter staff

It was no surprise that the Cal-away CooCoos' manager Regg Loopendorf refused to give a statement regarding his team's

even though the seri led to a new definitio Future chances for a can only hope that it

Dry Spell May End Soon

...der world will end all to bring
and that world that we can all be
...will return the focus that

UPL
Reports that a new attempts to br
ival f

Home Buyer's Guide

THIS MAY BE YOUR LAST CHANCE TO BUY A NEW HOME ON SILVER LAKE

Site rating guide
★★★★

LATEST LUXURIOUS LISTINGS

The last 20 homes will go on sale this weekend.

The size and number of families wanting to settle in this spectacular area has increased dramatically over the last few weeks. The few

the range of views and the availability of easy access to many of the recreational outlets bring a new meaning to the term "Land of Dreams"

B ▸ What's the Chance?

Summary ⪡

In this section, you saw different ways of expressing chances. You have seen that the chances on a ladder can be expressed with percents. If it is certain something will happen, you can say the chance is 100%. If it is certain it will not happen, the chance is 0%. Chances can also be expressed with fractions. You can make a chance ladder and label it with fractions instead of percents.

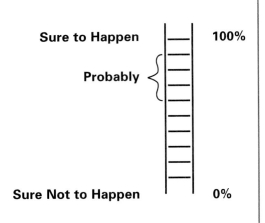

Check Your Work ▸▸

1. **a.** What fraction will you use to represent a 50-50 chance?

   b. Put some other fractions where they belong on a chance ladder.

   c. Where will you put a chance of $\frac{1}{6}$ on a chance ladder?

2. Here are some statements about chances. Some of them belong together; they are just different ways of saying the same thing.

   On **Student Activity Sheet 3**, connect all statements that say the same thing. One example has already been done.

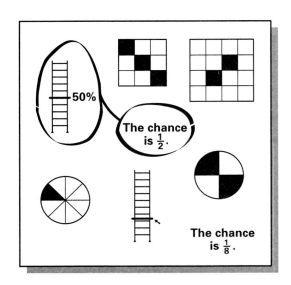

3. Draw a spinner and a tile pattern, each with a black part that represents a chance of 20%.

4. **a.** If your teacher chooses a student's paper to be read in class, what is the chance your paper will be chosen?

   b. How can your teacher do this in a fair way? If your teacher chooses fairly, what is the chance your teacher will choose your paper?

 ## For Further Reflection

One of your classmates was absent this week. In writing and using drawings, try to explain to the classmate the mathematics that he or she missed this week. Use drawings with your explanation. Make sure to include percents, fractions, and chance ladders.

C
Let the Good Times Roll

Chancy Business

If you roll a number cube one time, the chance you will roll a 6 is the same as the chance you will roll 5, 4, 3, 2, or 1.

1. If you roll a number cube 30 times, about how many times do you think you will roll a 6?

Activity

2. Make a table like the one shown below. Roll a number cube 30 times. **Tally** the number that comes up for each roll.

Number Rolled	Number of Times It Came Up
1	
2	
3	
4	
5	
6	

3. Did what happen differ from what you expected to happen? How?

4. What do you think will happen if you increase the number of rolls to 60?

Nina rolled a number cube. She recorded the results in a table.

Number Rolled	Number of Times It Came Up
1	///
2	THL THL /
3	THL THL
4	THL THL /
5	THL ///
6	THL THL ///

5. a. How many times did Nina roll the number cube?

   b. Nina says, "The chance of rolling 1 on the next roll is greater than the chance of rolling 6." Do you think she is right?

6. a. Robert rolled a number cube six times. Do you think he rolled a 4? Explain.

   b. Then Robert rolled the number cube 20 times more. Do you think he rolled a 4 this time?

Now We're Rolling!

Hillary rolled a number cube many times as part of an experiment.

7. Unfortunately, Hillary's pen leaked and covered up the number of times 6 came up. What do you think is written under the spill? Explain.

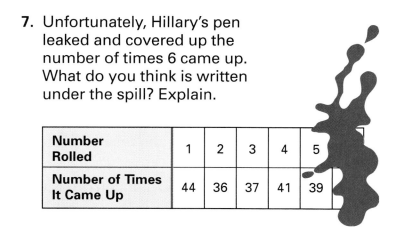

Number Rolled	1	2	3	4	5	
Number of Times It Came Up	44	36	37	41	39	

Tossing and Turning

During World War II, English mathematician John Kerrich was locked in a cell. He had a coin with him and decided to do an experiment to pass the time. While in the cell, he tossed the coin 10,000 times and recorded the results.

Here is the start of a chart he might have made.

Number of Tosses	Total Number of Heads
1	0
2	0
3	1
4	1
5	2
6	2
7	3
8	3
9	4

8. a. Did the first toss come up heads?

   b. On which toss did the mathematician get heads for the first time?

   c. How many tosses did it take to get three heads?

   d. How many tails had come up after eight tosses?

9. About how many heads do you think had come up after 10,000 tosses?

10. **Reflect** How does the percent of heads change as the number of coin tosses increases?

Activity

11. a. If you toss a coin 30 times, how many times do you expect heads to come up?

    Toss a coin 30 times. Tally the results in a table like the one on the right.

    b. Did your results match what you predicted?

    c. Combine your results with those of everyone in the class. How do the class results compare to your individual results?

H	T

As you toss a coin many times, the percent of heads approaches 50%, or $\frac{1}{2}$. We say the chance of getting heads is $\frac{1}{2}$.

On any single toss, though, you cannot tell whether heads or tails will come up. Although you cannot predict a single event with certainty, if you repeat an experiment many times, a pattern may appear.

Think B4 You Act

Pick a number from 1 to 4 and write it on a piece of paper.

12. **a.** If every student in the class writes down one number, how many times do you expect each number to be picked?

b. Count all the 1s, 2s, 3s, and 4s selected and put the information in a table. Study the results. Is this what you expected? Why or why not?

13. **Reflect** If you were a game show host and were putting a prize behind one of four doors, where would you put the prize? Give a reason for your choice.

Find the Chance

In problem 18 on page 6, you experimented with these objects:

- A large paper cup
- A small paper cup
- A chalkboard eraser
- A bottle cap
- A spinner like the one on the left

14. Look again at problem 18 on page 6. Based on the 30 tosses or spins for your object, estimate the chance of each outcome.

Let the Good Times Roll

Summary

You can find the chance of an event by experimenting with many, many trials. In the short run, what happens may not be what you expect. But in the long run, your results will get closer and closer to what you expect.

When you are tossing a coin or rolling a number cube, each new **trial** will offer the same chances as the previous one. A coin or number cube cannot "remember" what side it landed on last.

Check Your Work

1. **a.** If you toss a coin 10 times and get heads every time, what is the chance of getting heads on the 11th toss?

   b. If you roll a number cube over and over again, what do you think will happen to the percent of even numbers that come up?

Suppose you were to toss a fair coin 100 times.

2. **a.** About how many heads would you expect to get?

   b. Would it be reasonable to get 46 heads? Why or why not?

Robert and his classmates are going to roll a number cube 500 times and record their results in a table.

3. Predict their results by filling in the second row of the table with numbers you think are likely for Robert's class. Then explain why you filled in the numbers the way you did.

Number Rolled	1	2	3	4	5	6
Number of Times It Came Up						

4. **a.** Design a three-color spinner that is not fair. Spin it 30 times and record the results.

   b. Based on the 30 spins, estimate the chance for each color.

Robert made a four-color spinner. After 50 spins, he recorded the following results.

Red	12
Blue	24
Green	6
Purple	8

5. **a.** Draw what his spinner may have looked like.

   b. If you used the spinner you drew 50 times, would the results be exactly the same as in the table? Why or why not?

 For Further Reflection

"If you toss a coin 6 times and you get heads every time, then it is more likely that tails will come up on the next roll." Is this statement true or false? Why or why not?

Let Me Count the Ways

Families

There are many different types of families.

Some families have one adult.

Some families have two adults, and some families have more.

Some families have children, and some do not.

1. a. Suppose you look at 20 families with two children. How many of these families do you think will have one boy and one girl?

b. Other students in your class may not agree with your answer to part **a**. Explain why you think your answer is the most likely. Drawing a diagram may be helpful.

2. You can simulate a study of two-child families by tossing two pennies. Heads will represent a girl, and tails will represent a boy. Toss the two pennies 20 times. See how many families with one boy and one girl you get. Was the result the same as your guess for problem 1a?

 girl

 boy

Robert's Clothes

Here are Robert's clothes.

Here are the pants and T-shirts Robert wears to school most often.

3. Find a way to show all of the outfits Robert can wear to school. How many possible outfits are there?

4. Hillary bought Robert a new T-shirt when she went to the Compass Rose concert. How many outfits can Robert wear now? Explain.

5. How many outfits could Robert wear if he had four shirts and three pairs of pants?

Hillary's Clothes

One day, Hillary chooses her shirt and pants with her eyes closed.

6. What outfit do you expect to see Hillary wearing?

7. How could Hillary have used number cubes to help her choose her clothes?

8. Hillary says, "The chance I will pick my star shirt and plaid pants is 1 out of 36." Is Hillary right? Explain.

Two Children Again

Tree diagrams can be useful for smart counting and solving problems about chance.

Consider families with children once more.

A tree diagram can show the two possibilities for one child.

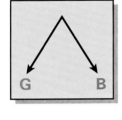

9. Each path on this tree diagram represents an equal chance. What is the chance of having a girl?

If a family has a second child, you can extend the tree diagram like this one.

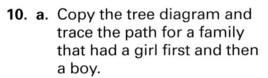

10. a. Copy the tree diagram and trace the path for a family that had a girl first and then a boy.

b. What are all the possible **combinations** for a family with two children?

c. If there were 20 families with two children in Hillary's class, about how many would you expect to have two girls? What is the chance a family would have two girls?

d. Is the chance greater of having two girls or of having a boy and a girl? Explain.

Now consider families that have three children.

11. a. Extend the tree diagram to show a third child.

b. List all of the different possibilities for a family with three children.

c. Robert says, "It's less likely for a family to have three girls than to have two girls and a boy." Explain this statement.

d. Use the tree diagram from part **a** to make some other statements.

Open or Closed?

For a group of three people, here is a way of choosing one person.

Stand in a circle, facing one another. One of you (or everyone at once) says, "One, two, three...go!" At "Go," each person puts out either an open hand or a closed fist.

Hillary, Robert, and Kevin played the game. Each winner is shown on the right in the table below.

Hillary	Robert	Kevin	Winner
			Robert
			Hillary
			No Winner

12. Name another situation in which there is no winner with this method.

13. How many combinations of open and closed hands are possible in the game? List as many as you can. You can use a tree diagram.

14. Do you think this is a fair way to decide something? Explain.

Activity

Sum It Up

15. Roll two different-color number cubes. Using all of the pairs of numbers that can come up, what are the different sums you can get?

    Hillary and Robert sometimes play Sum It Up during lunch.

They each pick one of the possible sums of two number cubes. Then they roll the number cubes, and the first person to roll his or her sum four times wins. The loser has to clean up the winner's lunch table.

16. Which sum do you think will be best to pick?

Play the game with another person. If you both want the same number, come up with a fair way to decide who gets the number. Record the sums.

17. What was the winning sum in your game?

Play the game five or six times. Change numbers if you want.

18. Now what do you think is the best sum to choose?

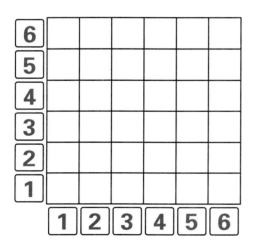

19. Student Activity Sheet 4 has a grid showing the possible numbers for each of two number cubes.

  a. For each square, fill in the sum of the numbers.

  b. How many different pairs are possible when you roll two number cubes?

  c. How many ways can you get a sum of 10 with two number cubes?

  d. What is the best number to pick if you are playing Sum It Up? Is your answer different from your choice in problem 18 above?

20. a. Draw a tree diagram to show all of the possible combinations for rolling two number cubes. It might be messy!

  b. Color the squares in the grid from problem 19 and the paths in the tree diagram from part **a** that give the sum of 10.

  c. What is the chance of rolling the sum of 10?

21. a. What is the chance of rolling two 1s? What is the chance of rolling doubles?

  b. What is the chance of rolling 7?

22. What do you think is the chance of *not* getting 10? *Not* getting 7?

Treasure

During a hike along the shoreline at low tide, Hillary and Robert find a big chessboard on the sand.

On a nearby rock, they find this inscription:

Start in the lower left, Matey,
And toss a coin four times;
If ye have come to get the treasure here,
Then follow these instructions o' mine;
Go north with heads
And east with tails;
Dig in the place ye find;
Unless ye dig where most end up,
Ye won't have cents of mine!

23. Hillary and Robert could have tossed the coin four times and gotten HHHT.

    a. What route fits this result? On which square would they end?

    b. Other routes lead to the same square. How many different outcomes would lead to this square? Explain your reasoning.

24. Hillary and Robert toss the coin four times and follow the instructions from the inscription. Color all possible squares on the chessboard where they could end.

25. **Reflect** Hillary and Robert have time to dig only one hole before the tide comes back. Where will you tell them to dig for the treasure? Explain how you decide where to dig the hole.

D Let Me Count the Ways

Summary ➤

In this section, you learned that counting the number of ways an event can occur can help you find the chances of the event.

You can write all of the possible ways something can occur, or you can draw pictures. Tree diagrams are one type of helpful picture.

A tree diagram can give information about:

- all possible outcomes; and
- the chance any single outcome will occur.

Check Your Work ➤➤

Here is a tree diagram of problem 3 (Robert's clothes) from page 27.

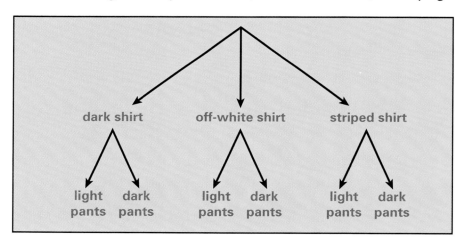

1. If Robert picks his clothes at random, what is the chance he will pick a striped shirt and light pants?

2. Draw a tree diagram that ends with eight branches. Write a story that fits your diagram.

3. Robert has to choose his meal in a restaurant. For an appetizer, he can choose soup or salad. For the main course, he can choose vegetarian, fish, or beef. The desserts are ice cream and fruit salad. Make a tree diagram and count all of the possible three-course meals.

4. Robert and Hillary want to make a secret language with dots and dashes (· and –). They decide every letter of the alphabet should be an arrangement of four signs (dots or dashes). For instance, A will be ···· (4 dots), and B will be ··· – (dot, dot, dot, dash). Do they have enough combinations to make their secret language? You may use a tree diagram.

5. Invent a chance game that is not fair. Explain why it is not fair.

 For Further Reflection

Tree diagrams are very useful for solving certain types of problems. Describe when you might use a tree diagram. Give at least one problem as an example.

Additional Practice

Section A Fair

1. In your own words, define each of the following.

   a. chance   b. fair

2. Give an example that shows how a coin could be used to do the following.

   a. make a fair decision

   b. make an unfair decision

3. Troy says, "There is a 70% chance we will win the game tonight." Explain what this means.

4. The teacher announces, "Everyone with brown eyes can leave school early today!" Is this a fair decision or not? Explain.

5. Decide whether each event listed below is fair. Explain your decision.

   a. All boys get five pieces of candy each, and all girls get four.

   b. All students with brown hair get an A.

   c. A bag is filled with 10 white marbles and 10 red ones. Without looking, you reach in the bag and grab a marble. If you grab a white one, your team goes first in the game.

   d. A bag is filled with 20 white marbles and 10 green ones. Without looking, you reach in the bag and grab a marble. If you grab a green one, your team goes first in the game.

Section B What's the Chance

1. Draw a ladder like the one on the left. Then put these statements about chance on the ladder.

   a. It will definitely happen.

   b. There is a 25% chance it will happen.

   c. It will not happen.

   d. There is a 0% chance it will happen.

   e. There is a 100% chance it will happen.

2. What number could you use to represent an event that is sure to happen?

3. What number could you use to represent an event that definitely will not happen?

4. What fraction could you use to represent each of the following chances?

   a. a 50% chance

   b. a 25% chance

   c. a 75% chance

5. a. Draw a spinner that can be used to make a fair decision.

   b. Explain why the spinner you drew in part **a** can be used to make a fair decision.

6. Put each of the following percents on a chance ladder.

a. 10%	d. 75%
b. 25%	e. 100%
c. 50%	

Section ◆C◆ Let the Good Times Roll

1. In 100 coin tosses, about how many times would you expect heads to come up? Explain.

2. In 36 rolls of a number cube, about how many times would you expect to roll a 6?

3. a. Roll a number cube 36 times and record the results of each roll.

   b. How many times did you roll a 6?

   c. Compare your results for problem 3a with the predictions you made for problem 2.

   d. Compare your results for problem 3a with those of at least two other classmates. Did you get the same results? Is this reasonable or not?

4. If you roll a number cube three times and get a 3 every time, what is the chance of getting a 3 on the next roll?

5. If you win the lottery once, will the first win improve your chances of winning again? Explain.

Section ◆D◆ Let Me Count the Ways

1. In your own words, explain what a tree diagram is and how it can be used.

2. If you have three shirts and three pairs of pants, how many different outfits can you make? Support your answer with a diagram.

3. If you roll two number cubes, what is the chance of rolling each of the following?

   a. doubles

   b. two even numbers

   c. two odd numbers

   d. two numbers that add up to 6

   e. two numbers that add up to 8

4. Suppose you have a bag of jellybeans that contains:

     10 red jellybeans
     20 green jellybeans
     15 yellow jellybeans
      5 purple jellybeans

   a. If you pull one jellybean out of the bag without looking, what color jellybean will you expect to get? Why?

   b. If you pull a jellybean out of the bag without looking, what is your chance of getting a purple one? Explain how you found your answer.

5. Make up a problem in which the chance of one outcome is twice as great as the chance of the other.

Section Ⓐ Fair

1. **a.** Yes, a pencil can be used for fair decisions if:
    1) the pencil has regularly shaped sides;
    2) the chance of landing on the eraser is very small; and
    3) you number the sides.

    You might find out by flipping a pencil 100 times, or just by looking at its sides.

    b. No. A thumbtack is too irregularly shaped to be predictable. You will have to toss it many times to determine whether it can be used to make a fair decision.

2. This is hard to determine. It is fair only if the traffic light is green for the same amount of time it is not green, which is not likely.

3. **a.** A number cube can be used to decide who goes first if each student is assigned two numbers. For instance, student A is assigned 1 and 2; student B, 3 and 4; and student C, 5 and 6. A number cube can also be used if each student is assigned only one number. If an unassigned number comes up, the cube is rolled again.

    b. A spinner can be used if it is divided into three equal parts and each student is assigned one of the parts.

    c. It is possible to use one coin, but you will have to design a clever way to make decisions. For instance:

    Round 1: Toss the coin three times, once for each student. If it comes up heads, the student has lost and will not go first. If it comes up tails, the student is still in the running. If all three tosses come up heads, start over. If more than one student is still in, go to round 2. Round 2: Repeat round 1. Toss the coin once for each remaining student. Continue until only one student remains. He or she will go first in the game.

    d. Different answers are possible. One might be to write each student's name on a piece of paper, put the names in a hat or a box, and draw one name.

4. a. No, because students in different classes do not have the same chance of being chosen because different numbers of students are in each class.

   b. Ms. Lanie's class. A student in the class with the fewest total students has the best chance of being chosen.

   c. Answers will vary. One fair method would be to put the names of all of the students in the school in one hat, mix up the names, and pick 40 names from the hat without looking.

Section **B** What's the Chance

1. a. $\frac{1}{2}$, or any fraction that is equivalent to it, such as $\frac{5}{10}$ or $\frac{50}{100}$.

   b. You may have different answers. Here is one example. Discuss your answer with a classmate and see if you agree with the placement on the ladder.

c.

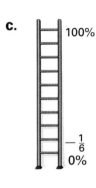

2.

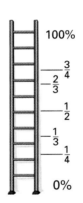

3. Spinner: $\frac{1}{5}$ should be black and the other $\frac{4}{5}$ another color (you may estimate the $\frac{1}{5}$). For the tile floor, $\frac{1}{5}$ of the tiles should be black and the rest should be another color (for instance, white). It is easy if the floor has a number of tiles that can be divided by 5. So you can make a floor of 25 tiles, 5 of which are black.

4. **a.** If the teacher chooses fairly, the chance will be 1 out of the number of students in the class. If not, all kinds of other factors could be involved in the chance. For instance, a teacher may choose from only the papers that received an A grade.

   b. The teacher can put all of the students' names in a box and pick one. Then the chance your paper will be chosen is 1 out of the number of students in your class.

Section ◆G◆ Let the Good Times Roll

1. **a.** 50% or $\frac{1}{2}$. Each flip of the coin is independent of the flips before.

   b. The percent of even numbers will probably get closer to 50%.

2. **a.** You would expect to get heads about half the time, or 50 heads.

   b. It would be reasonable, because you don't always get exactly what you expect. Your results should be close to your expectations, though, and 46 is pretty close to 50.

3. Different answers are possible. The number of times each number is rolled should be about the same because each number has the same chance of coming up. In the long run, each number should come up in about $\frac{1}{6}$ of the rolls. So the results for each number should be close to $\frac{500}{6}$, which is about 83. Use 500 as the total number of rolls in your calculations. A possible answer follows.

Number Rolled	1	2	3	4	5	6
Number of Times It Came Up	80	78	90	85	76	91

4. **a.** Discuss your answers with a classmate. The colored sections must be different in size. If the difference is great enough, it will affect the results of the spins.

   b. Use the number of times out of 30 spins the spinner landed on each color to estimate the chance for that color. You may write this as a percent. If this is difficult for you, look at problem 14.

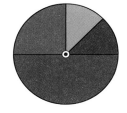

5. **a.** Spinner must be about $\frac{1}{2}$ blue, $\frac{1}{4}$ red, $\frac{1}{8}$ green, and $\frac{1}{8}$ purple.

   b. The results would probably be similar. Since 50 spins is not many, the results may differ a little from what you expect. If you do not feel sure, make the spinner and spin it 50 times.

Answers to Check Your Work

Section D Let Me Count the Ways

1. The chance is $\frac{1}{6}$, or one out of six.

2. Show your story to a classmate to see if he or she agrees with your work. You may have different stories that start with different numbers of outcomes, but be sure your diagram ends in eight branches.

3. The tree diagram can help you count.

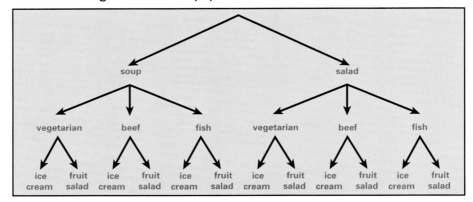

You may also reason that there are 2 × 3 × 2 = 12 possibilities.

4.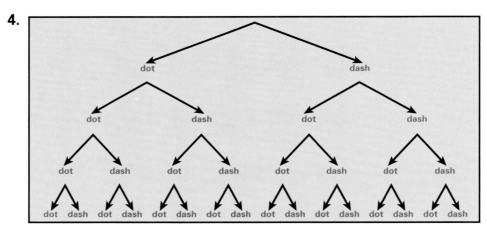

No; there are only 16 possibilities. For each of the four positions in each combination of symbols, you can use either a dot or a dash. So there are 2 × 2 × 2 × 2 = 16 different arrangements possible, but there are 26 letters in the alphabet. If arrangements with 1, 2, or 3 symbols were also allowed, there would be enough to make all 26 letters. This is how it is in Morse code.

5. There are many possibilities. You can, for instance, make spinners with unequal parts. Discuss with a classmate whether your game is unfair.

40 Take a Chance

Fraction Times

BRITANNICA
Mathematics
in
Context

Number

HOLT, RINEHART AND WINSTON

Mathematics in Context is a comprehensive curriculum for the middle grades.
It was developed in 1991 through 1997 in collaboration with the Wisconsin Center
for Education Research, School of Education, University of Wisconsin-Madison and
the Freudenthal Institute at the University of Utrecht, The Netherlands, with the
support of the National Science Foundation Grant No. 9054928.

The revision of the curriculum was carried out in 2003 through 2005, with the
support of the National Science Foundation Grant No. ESI 0137414.

National Science Foundation
Opinions expressed are those of the authors
and not necessarily those of the Foundation.

Keijzer, R., van Galen, F., Gravemeijer, K., Abels, M., Dekker, T., Shew, J. A., Cole,
B. R., Brendeful, J. & Pligge, M. A. (2006). *Fraction times.* In Wisconsin Center for
Education Research & Freudenthal Institute (Eds.), Mathematics in Context.
Chicago: Encyclopædia Britannica, Inc.

ISBN 0-03-039619-0

2 3 4 5 6 073 09 08 07 06 05

The *Mathematics in Context* Development Team

Development 1991–1997

The initial version of *Fraction Times* was developed by Ronald Keijzer, Frans van Galen, and Koeno Gravemeijer. It was adapted for use in American schools by Julia A. Shew, Beth R. Cole, and Jonathan Brendefur.

Wisconsin Center for Education Research Staff

Thomas A. Romberg
Director

Joan Daniels Pedro
Assistant to the Director

Gail Burrill
Coordinator

Margaret R. Meyer
Coordinator

Freudenthal Institute Staff

Jan de Lange
Director

Els Feijs
Coordinator

Martin van Reeuwijk
Coordinator

Project Staff

Jonathan Brendefur
Laura Brinker
James Browne
Jack Burrill
Rose Byrd
Peter Christiansen
Barbara Clarke
Doug Clarke
Beth R. Cole
Fae Dremock
Mary Ann Fix

Sherian Foster
James A. Middleton
Jasmina Milinkovic
Margaret A. Pligge
Mary C. Shafer
Julia A. Shew
Aaron N. Simon
Marvin Smith
Stephanie Z. Smith
Mary S. Spence

Mieke Abels
Nina Boswinkel
Frans van Galen
Koeno Gravemeijer
Marja van den Heuvel-Panhuizen
Jan Auke de Jong
Vincent Jonker
Ronald Keijzer
Martin Kindt

Jansie Niehaus
Nanda Querelle
Anton Roodhardt
Leen Streefland
Adri Treffers
Monica Wijers
Astrid de Wild

Revision 2003–2005

The revised version of *Fraction Times* was developed by Mieke Abels and Truus Dekker. It was adapted for use in American schools by Margaret A. Pligge.

Wisconsin Center for Education Research Staff

Thomas A. Romberg
Director

David C. Webb
Coordinator

Gail Burrill
Editorial Coordinator

Margaret A. Pligge
Editorial Coordinator

Freudenthal Institute Staff

Jan de Lange
Director

Truus Dekker
Coordinator

Mieke Abels
Content Coordinator

Monica Wijers
Content Coordinator

Project Staff

Sarah Ailts
Beth R. Cole
Erin Hazlett
Teri Hedges
Karen Hoiberg
Carrie Johnson
Jean Krusi
Elaine McGrath

Margaret R. Meyer
Anne Park
Bryna Rappaport
Kathleen A. Steele
Ana C. Stephens
Candace Ulmer
Jill Vettrus

Arthur Bakker
Peter Boon
Els Feijs
Dédé de Haan
Martin Kindt

Nathalie Kuijpers
Huub Nilwik
Sonia Palha
Nanda Querelle
Martin van Reeuwijk

Cover photo credits: (left to right) © Comstock Images; © Corbis; © Getty Images

Illustrations
35, 39 Holly Cooper-Olds

Photographs
1 (left to right) © Corbis; Don Couch/HRW Photo; HRW Photo/Marty Granger/Edge Productions; **4** HRW Photo/Marty Granger/Edge Productions; **7** © Corbis; **8** (left to right) HRW Photo/Marty Granger/Edge Productions; © Brand X Pictures; © John A. Rizzo/PhotoDisc/Getty Images; **9** © Bettmann/Corbis; **14** © Corbis; **15** (top) © ImageState; (middle) © G. K. & Vikki Hart/Getty Images/PhotoDisc; (bottom) © Corbis; **16** HRW Photo/Marty Granger/Edge Productions; **18** Don Couch/HRW Photo; **19** HRW Photo/Marty Granger/Edge Productions; **24** (top right) HRW Photo/Marty Granger/Edge Productions; (left) © PhotoDisc/Getty Images; **25** © Corbis; **26** Thomas Spanos/Encyclopædia Britannica, Inc.; **28** © PhotoDisc/Getty Images; **33** (top) © BananaStock Ltd.; (bottom) Don Couch/HRW Photo; **35** HRW Photo/Marty Granger/Edge Productions; **37** © Corbis; **38, 39** Don Couch/HRW Photo; **43, 44** © PhotoDisc/Getty Images

◆ Contents

Dear Student,

Have you ever noticed all the numbers and graphs in the newspaper? Reporters use numbers and graphs to highlight important information in a story. Take a look at today's newspaper headlines and you'll see what we mean.

In this unit, you will learn how to use numbers and graphs to describe important events and information. You will learn how to convert among ratios, decimals, fractions, and percents, and you will discover when it is better to choose one type of number over another.

You will also learn how to add and subtract fractions. Knowing this, you will be able to conduct surveys and compare the results using fractions, percents, ratios, bar charts, and pie charts.

We hope you enjoy investigating the *Fraction Times* news clippings and other articles from your local newspapers.

Sincerely,

The Mathematics in Context Development Team

Survey Results

The Newspaper

Reporters for the newspaper *Fraction Times* use charts and graphs with their articles to help readers understand the information. Here is the front page of *Fraction Times*.

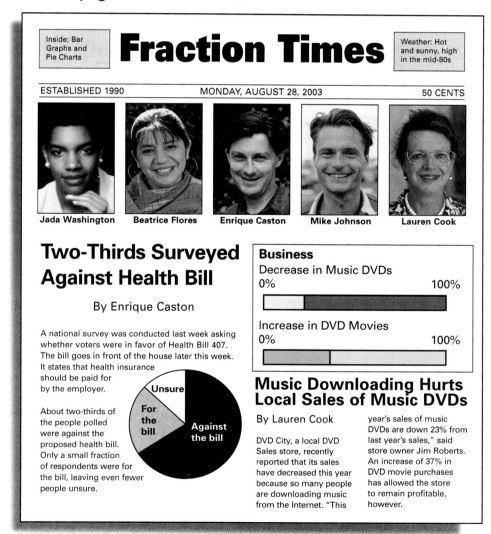

1. **a.** What types of charts do you see on the front page of *Fraction Times?*

   b. Without reading the articles, summarize the information in each chart.

Activity

Favorite Colors—From Bar Charts to Pie Charts

For this activity, you need:

> - **Student Activity Sheet 1**
> - markers or crayons
> - scissors
> - tape

Select your favorite color.

Red 卌 II

Ask everyone in your class to choose a favorite color. List the favorite colors chosen in your class and tally the number of students who choose that color. Don't forget to include yourself!

To represent the results, cut out one complete bar from **Student Activity Sheet 1**. Each segment of the bar can represent a classmate participating in the **survey**.

Color the bar to show the number of students who like each color. For example, if seven students chose red as their favorite color, color seven consecutive segments of the bar red. Do this for all of the colors chosen by the students in your class.

- How many students participated in the survey?
- How many students chose each color? Write the fraction for each color.

Now you can use the **bar chart** to make a **pie chart**.

Cut off the segments you didn't color.

Form a ring with the colors facing inside. Tape both ends of the bar together to form the ring.

Place the ring on a sheet of paper and draw a circle by tracing around the ring's inside edge.

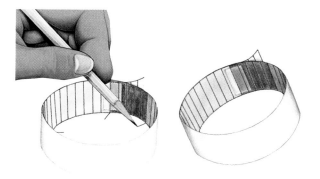

On your paper, mark inside the circle where the different colors begin and end.

Finally, remove the ring to complete the pie chart.

Now mark the color sections in the circle.

Estimate the location of the center of the circle.

Connect the marks you made on the edge of the circle with the center of the circle.
Each "pie piece" is a section of the circle.

Color each section to correspond to the color on the tape.

Ms. Green's class did the same Favorite Color Activity on the computer. Here are the results.

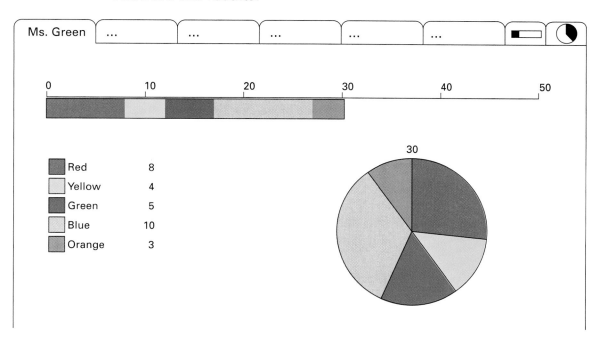

	Red	8
	Yellow	4
	Green	5
	Blue	10
	Orange	3

2. Look at the survey results from Ms. Green's class and the survey results from your class. How do the results compare? Write four conclusions. For each conclusion, write what you used as a source: the numbers, the pie chart, or the bar chart.

Just for Teens

Fraction Times plans to launch a new section called "Just for Teens." Each Saturday, *Fraction Times* will feature an article on young people's books, movies, music, and food. Surveys will be used to investigate what teens are most interested in.

Enrique Caston
Fraction Times **Reporter**

Enrique Caston is the book reviewer. He asked two teachers to conduct surveys about students' favorite types of books. Here is what he found.

Mr. Jackson's class (20 students)
Mystery............................0
Adventure 10
Science Fiction 5
Biography..........................0
Humor 5

Ms. Lee's class (40 students)
Mystery............................5
Adventure 15
Science Fiction 4
Biography..........................0
Humor............................16

3. **a.** Use two bars from **Student Activity Sheet 1** to show each class's results.

   b. Whose class prefers adventure books?

   c. Explain why it will be easier for Enrique to compare the data if the bars have the same number of segments.

   d. Use two new bars from **Student Activity Sheet 1** to show each class's results so that both bars have the same number of colored segments. Do not paste the bar charts in your notebook yet. You will need them in problem 9.

   e. Compare the survey results.

Enrique wants to see how pie charts show the same survey information as the color bars. He begins with Mr. Jackson's class.

He thinks, "A pie chart for these results is easy to make, because 10 out of 20 is half the class, and 5 out of 20... ."

4. **a.** Complete Enrique's thoughts.

   b. In your notebook, draw a circle and use this drawing to make a pie chart for Mr. Jackson's class. Be sure to include a chart key.

5. a. Make a pie chart for Ms. Lee's class results using the bar chart you made in problem 3d.

   b. On your paper, show a bar chart and pie chart for each class. Write the fraction of the class choosing each category.

   c. What is obvious in a pie chart that is not as obvious from a bar chart?

The "Just for Teens" staff is writing a weekly education column. They ask several classes, "What is your favorite school subject?" The survey results from two sixth-grade classes are shown here.

Ms. Byrd's class (20 students)
Social Studies 0
Math 15
English 5
Science 0
Physical Education 0

Mr. Chaparro's class (30 students)
Social Studies 3
Math 15
English 0
Science 2
Physical Education 10

Mr. Chaparro's class is larger than Ms. Byrd's class. This makes it more difficult to compare the results than it would be if the classes were the same size.

6. a. Use **Student Activity Sheet 2** to cut out two bars. Even though the class sizes differ, be creative and show the data using bars that have the same number of segments. Keep these bars handy because you will use them again in problem 7.

   b. Write a fraction to represent the number of students in each class who prefer each subject.

Peter works in the design department of *Fraction Times*. He uses a computer applet to create pie charts. The pie charts created from the Favorite Subject survey are shown here.

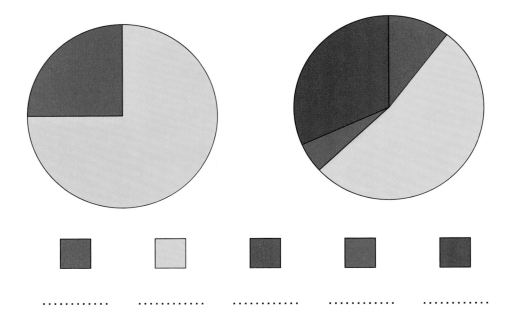

....

7. a. Peter's screen is shown on **Student Activity Sheet 3**. Use the results of the Favorite Subject survey in problem 6 to complete the missing details.

    b. Use the bar charts you created for problem 6 to form two new rings.

    c. Compare your rings to Peter's pie charts on **Student Activity Sheet 3**. How closely do the section categories match up?

    d. Write a fraction to represent the number of students in each class who prefer each subject.

8. Reflect Help the staff of "Just for Teens" by writing a short article about the Favorite Subject survey. Use fractions to compare the two classes.

You can use two bars with the same number of segments to compare two groups of different sizes. **Ratio tables** can help you determine the number of segments to include in the bar. For example, if you want to compare a class of 25 students to a class of 20 students:

Number of Segments per Student	1	2	3	4		4 segments for each student
Total Number of Segments	25	50	75	100		

Number of Segments per Student	1	2	3	4	5	5 segments for each student
Total Number of Segments	20	40	60	80	100	

The number 100 is a **common multiple** of 25 and 20.

Note that 200, 300, 400, … are also common multiples of 25 and 20.

In Joshua's class, 7 out of 30 students each has a cat. In Marlene's class, 11 out of 45 students each has a cat. To compare these data, you can create bar charts that have the same number of segments.

9. a. Find three numbers that are common multiples of 30 and 45.

  b. If you use the same size bars, how many segments would you use for the students in Joshua's and Marlene's classes?

  c. For each class, how many segments would you color to show the number of students who owned cats? Explain how you determined this number.

  d. Which class owns more cats? Explain.

  e. Which is more: 7 out of 30 or 11 out of 45? Explain.

Survey Results

Lauren Cook is the food critic for "Just for Teens." She wants to know teens' favorite foods. Here are survey results from two classrooms.

Lauren Cook
Fraction Times Reporter

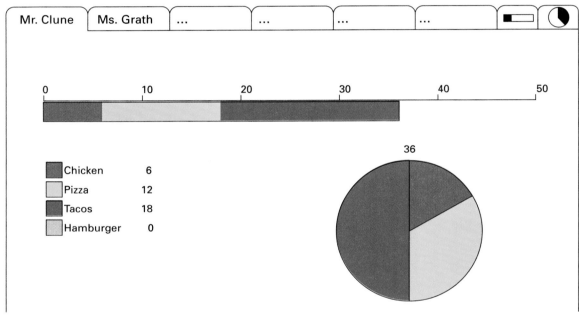

Mr. Clune | Ms. Grath | ... | ... | ... | ...

	Chicken	6
	Pizza	12
	Tacos	18
	Hamburger	0

36

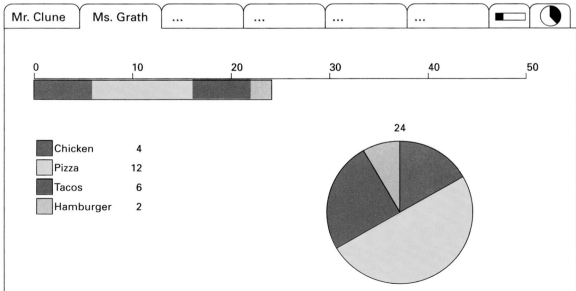

Mr. Clune | Ms. Grath | ... | ... | ... | ...

	Chicken	4
	Pizza	12
	Tacos	6
	Hamburger	2

24

Lauren draws conclusions from the data. She notices, "More students in Mr. Clune's class prefer chicken than in Ms. Grath's class."

10. **a.** Explain how this conclusion can be correct.

   b. Explain how this conclusion can be wrong.

11. Summarize the food data from both classes. Include your most interesting findings about the data.

Math History

Florence Nightingale (1820–1910)

Nursing pioneer Florence Nightingale was not the first person to use diagrams for presenting statistical data. However, she was the first to use them for convincing people of the need for change.

With this diagram, she showed that injured soldiers were more likely to die from diseases in a hospital (indicated by the blue outer wedges) than from wounds on the battlefield (indicated by the red wedges in the center).

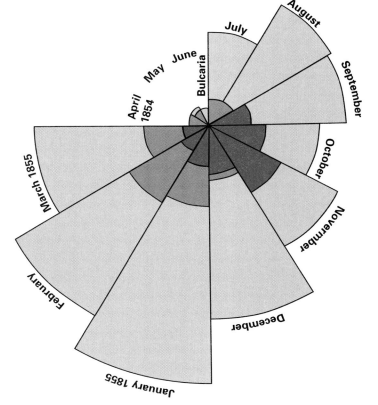

A Survey Results

Summary

Data from two classes with different numbers of students can be represented in several ways. For example, you can compare 3 out of 10 students to 4 out of 15:

- using two bars of different sizes that have the same number of segments as the number of people in that group:

A bar of 10 segments   A bar of 15 segments

- using bars that have the same number of segments:

  Ratio tables can help you to find the number of segments to include in the bar.

Number of Segments per Student	1	2	3
Total Number of Segments	10	20	30

1 out of 10 is the same as 3 out of 30

Number of Segments per Student	1	2
Total Number of Segments	15	30

1 out of 15 is the same as 2 out of 30

30 is a common multiple of 10 and 15.

Two bars of 30 segments

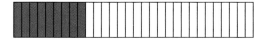 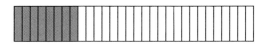

- Using fractions:

  3 out of 10 is $\frac{3}{10}$.

  3 out of 10 is the same as
  9 out of 30, which is $\frac{9}{30}$.

  4 out of 15 is $\frac{4}{15}$.

  4 out of 15 is the same as
  8 out of 30, which is $\frac{8}{30}$.

- Using pie charts:

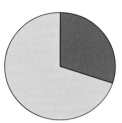 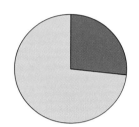

Check Your Work

Ms. Garbett wonders what sports her students watch on TV. To make it interesting, she surveys students and their parents. Here are results for each group that was asked, "What is your favorite sport to watch on TV?"

Students (20)	
Football	8
Basketball	5
Hockey	2
Tennis	1
Baseball	4

Parents (30)	
Football	10
Basketball	5
Hockey	3
Tennis	6
Baseball	6

1. a. Use **Student Activity Sheet 2** to create a bar chart that summarizes the data from each group. Include labels to show how the colors correspond to the sports.

   b. Create a pie chart for each group, Students and Parents. Include chart keys.

   c. For each group, write the fraction that corresponds to each sport category.

   d. Which group prefers to watch basketball?

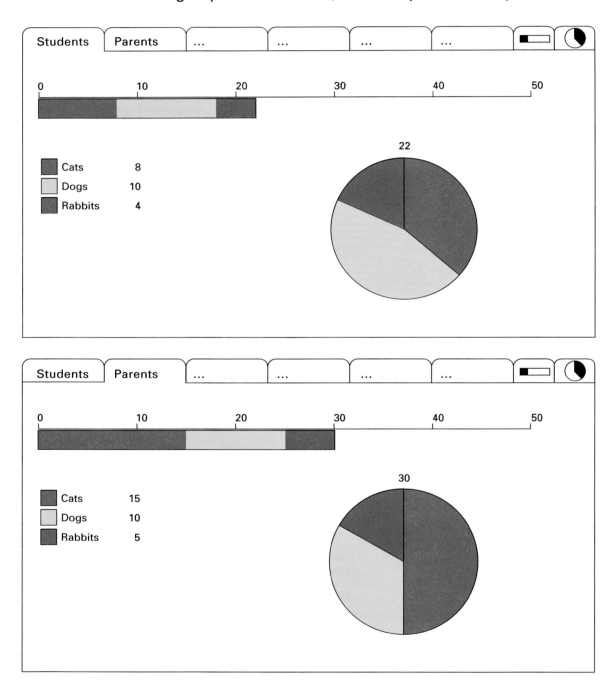

Survey Results

Ms. Garbett and her class enjoy discussing the students' and parents' preferences. They decide to conduct more surveys. Here are computer results from each group that was asked, "What is your favorite pet?"

Students | Parents | ... | ... | ... | ...

| 0 | 10 | 20 | 30 | 40 | 50 |

	Cats	8
	Dogs	10
	Rabbits	4

22

Students | **Parents** | ... | ... | ... | ...

| 0 | 10 | 20 | 30 | 40 | 50 |

	Cats	15
	Dogs	10
	Rabbits	5

30

2. **a.** For each group, write the fraction that corresponds to each category.

   b. Summarize the pet data from both groups. Include your most interesting findings from the data.

3. Conduct your own survey and summarize the results. You might survey your classmates' favorite TV shows, hobbies, or bands. Provide the category choices for your question. Asking a few students your questions before conducting the survey can help you identify the categories. Include a bar chart and pie chart in your summary. Use **Student Activity Sheet 1** to display your findings.

 For Further Reflection

Do you think it is easier to read a bar chart or a pie chart? Explain why you think so.

B> It Adds Up

Pet Survey

Jada Washington
Fraction Times **Reporter**

Jada Washington writes the "At Home" section of *Fraction Times*. While researching an article on dog ownership, she found this summary of a survey.

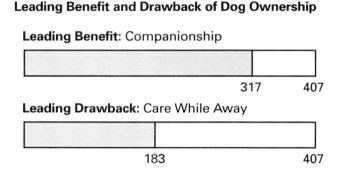

Leading Benefit and Drawback of Dog Ownership

Leading Benefit: Companionship

317   407

Leading Drawback: Care While Away

183   407

In her article, Jada uses simple fractions to describe the survey results.

1. a. Explain why the **benchmark fraction** $\frac{3}{4}$ is a good estimate to represent the number of people who named "companionship" as the major benefit of owning a dog.

   b. Which benchmark fraction can be used as an estimate to represent the number of people who named "care while away" as a major drawback of owning a dog?

Jada gave the graphs to the art department and asked an artist to sketch pie charts that show the same information. The graphic artist sketched the following pie charts.

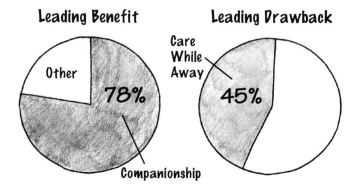

Leading Benefit   Leading Drawback

Other   Care While Away
        78%   45%
   Companionship

2. **a.** **Reflect** Compare the bar charts and pie charts. Which do you prefer?

   b. Do the percentages in the pie charts seem reasonable? Explain.

Jada wants to know how many pets people own. For her survey, she randomly called 30 people and used fractions to summarize the survey results.

- $\frac{1}{6}$ have no pets.
- $\frac{1}{2}$ have one pet.
- $\frac{1}{6}$ have two pets.
- $\frac{1}{10}$ have three pets.
- $\frac{1}{15}$ have four or more pets.

3. **a.** Of the 30 people surveyed, how many have two pets?

   b. Use **Student Activity Sheet 2** to show the results of Jada's survey in a bar chart.

   c. What fraction of the people surveyed have either no pets or one pet?

Jada creates a fraction summary for another pet survey.

- $\frac{1}{3}$ like dogs best.
- $\frac{1}{3}$ like cats best.
- $\frac{1}{5}$ like fish best.
- The rest of the people like some other type of animal best.

The number of people who are involved in a survey is called the **sample size**.

The survey summary above does not give information about the sample size.

4. **a.** How many people do you think were surveyed? Explain your reasoning.

   b. Name some other possible sample sizes for this survey.

   c. Use a bar from **Student Activity Sheet 2** to determine what fraction of the people questioned like some other type of animal.

Airplane Survey

Mike Johnson
Fraction Times **Reporter**

Mike Johnson writes the travel section for *Fraction Times*. He is working on an article about airline passenger satisfaction.

Airlines have cut back on food service. Mike conducts a survey and uncovers some information about what airline passengers think about food service cuts.

- $\frac{1}{3}$ of the passengers miss getting a meal and were happy with the quality of the food before the cutbacks.

- $\frac{1}{4}$ of the passengers miss getting a meal; however, they were not happy with the quality of food before the cutbacks.

- $\frac{1}{6}$ of the passengers are happy that meals are rarely served on airlines anymore.

5. **a.** Summarize the survey information using a bar from **Student Activity Sheet 2**. Hint: Find any possible sample size.

   b. Mike considers the fraction of people who indicated they miss getting meals on airlines. What is this fraction?

Mike finds that $\frac{3}{5}$ of airline passengers are pleased with the way airlines handle baggage and $\frac{1}{4}$ are not pleased.

6. Summarize the baggage information using a bar from **Student Activity Sheet 2**.

Mike wonders if people are nervous flying. Of the people surveyed, half are nervous and $\frac{2}{5}$ are not nervous.

There is an extra category not given in the information: the people surveyed who did not share their opinion on being nervous.

7. **a.** What fraction of the people surveyed did not share an opinion on being nervous? Explain how you know.

   b. Explain how you can find out that there is another category not given in the information.

All of Mike's survey information was presented using fractions. In his feature on Airline Passenger Satisfaction, Mike needs to consider other ways of conveying the survey information.

8. **Reflect** Name other ways to describe the information. Illustrate using examples.

Mike found a survey in which an independent organization had asked people their opinions about the safety of flying. The results were printed in several newspapers. Here are six different headlines about the survey.

a. **Large Majority Consider Planes Safe**

b. **One Out of Every Six Americans Says, "Flying Is Dangerous"**

c. **More Than 15 Percent Indicate That Planes Are Unsafe**

d. **$\frac{3}{4}$ Consider Flying Safe**
By Tom McName
Staff Writer

e. **"No Problem with Flying," Say 80%**

f. **About One-Third Say, "Flying Is Hazardous"**

Do all of these headlines say the same thing?

9. Compare the headlines. Which headlines describe the same message on airline safety? Which are different?

Comparisons

Beatrice Flores
Fraction Times **Reporter**

Beatrice Flores writes the business section for *Fraction Times*. She compares the Computer Division and the Communication Division at Bulk Electronics Company.

Bulk Electronics

A. Research Investment

Computer Division	$\frac{1}{4}$ of its profit
Communications	$\frac{1}{3}$ of its profit

B. Productivity

Computer Division	$\frac{3}{4}$ of the capacity
Communications	$\frac{3}{5}$ of the capacity

C. Market Share

Computer Division	$\frac{1}{2}$ of the market
Communications	$\frac{2}{5}$ of the market

D. Workforce

Computer Division	$\frac{2}{3}$ are male
Communications	$\frac{5}{6}$ are male

10. a. Help Beatrice compare each division by shading the bars on **Student Activity Sheet 4**. You can use what you know about fractions to find out which parts should be colored.

   b. For each category—A, B, C, and D—compare the two fractions and write which one in each pair is larger.

The shaded parts on your first two bars show that the Computer Division profit contribution is less than the Communication Division profit contribution. But drawing bars and shading them is a lot of work.

11. How would you explain that $\frac{1}{4}$ is less than $\frac{1}{3}$ without drawing and shading a bar?

In order to serve healthier drinks, many schools are replacing soda machines with juice machines. Lauren Cook investigates the amount of real fruit in two brands of apple juice.

Burst-o-Apple $\frac{1}{4}$ apple juice

Apple Fizz $\frac{3}{10}$ apple juice

12. Which brand contains more apple juice? How do you know?

Lauren Cook
Fraction Times **Reporter**

In her article, Lauren reports the difference between the apple juice contents of Burst-o-Apple and Apple Fizz.

Lauren uses 40 segments for each bar. She gets tired of marking segments, so she uses bars without segments. She still thinks of the bars as having the same number of segments. She labels each bar with the number of segments that the shaded part represents. Since $\frac{1}{4}$ of 40 segments is 10 segments, she marks one bar like this.

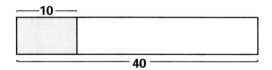

For Apple Fizz, Lauren shades $\frac{3}{10}$ of the 40 segments. Since $\frac{1}{10}$ of 40 segments is four segments, $\frac{3}{10}$ of 40 segments is 12 segments. She marks the second bar like this.

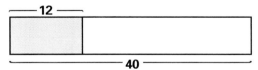

Laura can now see that the difference is two segments, or $\frac{2}{40}$.

	Apples	Oranges	Bananas
Canada	$\frac{1}{4}$	$\frac{1}{3}$	$\frac{1}{6}$
U.S.	$\frac{1}{6}$	$\frac{1}{4}$	$\frac{1}{2}$

Here are the survey results comparing the favorite fruits of Canadian and U.S. middle school students.

13. a. Name three numbers of segments you could use to make bars that represent both $\frac{1}{4}$ and $\frac{1}{6}$.

   b. Choose one of the three numbers and make bars that represent $\frac{1}{4}$ and $\frac{1}{6}$.

   c. What is the difference between the fractions of students in Canada $(\frac{1}{4})$ and in the U.S. $(\frac{1}{6})$ whose favorite fruit is apples?

14. Make similar comparisons for oranges and bananas.

There is one survey category not shown in the table.

15. a. Explain how you know there is a missing category.

   b. Name the missing category and make a similar comparison. Find the difference between the countries' choices.

Compare, Subtract, Add

In this section, you compared fractions with different **denominators** and found the difference. For example, to compare $\frac{3}{4}$ and $\frac{4}{5}$:

$$\frac{3}{4} \xleftrightarrow{\text{different denominators}} \frac{4}{5}$$

You might draw two bars and imagine that each has 20 segments.

16. a. Use the two bars of 20 segments to compare $\frac{3}{4}$ and $\frac{4}{5}$.

   b. Which is more, $\frac{3}{4}$ or $\frac{4}{5}$?

   c. What is the difference between $\frac{3}{4}$ and $\frac{4}{5}$?

   d. How can you know that a bar with 20 segments will allow you to compare $\frac{3}{4}$ and $\frac{4}{5}$? Can you use a different number of segments for the comparison? If so, how many segments?

Part	3	6	9	12	15
Whole	4	8	12	16	20

Part	4	8	12	16
Whole	5	10	15	20

You can also use ratio tables to compare $\frac{3}{4}$ and $\frac{4}{5}$.

17. Use any method to compare these fractions. Show your reasoning.

  a. Which is more, $\frac{3}{4}$ or $\frac{5}{8}$? How much more?

  b. Which is more, $\frac{4}{5}$ or $\frac{1}{2}$? How much more?

  c. Which is more, $\frac{3}{4}$ or $\frac{2}{3}$? How much more?

You have also added fractions with different denominators. For example, you might remember adding $\frac{1}{3}$ and $\frac{1}{4}$ in problem 5b. You used two bars of equal length and the same number of segments.

18. a. How many segments are in each bar?

  b. Copy the bars and use them to represent $\frac{1}{3}$ and $\frac{1}{4}$.

  c. Create another bar of the same length and shade it to represent $\frac{1}{3} + \frac{1}{4}$.

  d. Find the sum of $\frac{1}{3} + \frac{1}{4}$.

Part	1	2	3	4	8
Whole	3	6	9	12	24

Part	1	2	3	4	5	6
Whole	4	8	12	16	20	24

You can use ratio tables to add fractions with different denominators.

19. a. Describe how to set up these ratio tables.

  b. Use the ratio tables to find the sum of $\frac{1}{3} + \frac{1}{4}$.

20. Use any number model to find each sum.

  a. $\frac{1}{2} + \frac{1}{6}$ **b.** $\frac{1}{3} + \frac{2}{5}$

  c. Write your own problem and solve it.

21. Reason whether these number sentences are true or false. Explain your thinking.

  a. $\frac{2}{3} - \frac{1}{3} = \frac{2}{5} - \frac{1}{5}$ **b.** $\frac{4}{5} - \frac{3}{5} = \frac{3}{5} - \frac{2}{5}$

  c. Make up four of your own number sentences—two that are true and two that are false.

Summary

Bars or ratio tables can be helpful when you have to compare, subtract, or add fractions with different denominators.

Example A

If you want to compare $\frac{1}{6}$ and $\frac{4}{5}$, you can draw two bars and imagine that each has 30 segments.

30   30

To show $\frac{1}{6}$, you would color a part to represent five segments.

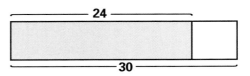

5

30

To show $\frac{4}{5}$, you would color a part to represent 24 segments.

24

30

The two bars show that $\frac{4}{5}$ is larger than $\frac{1}{6}$ by 19 segments out of 30, or $\frac{19}{30}$. Another way to write this is to show the difference $\frac{24}{30} - \frac{5}{30} = \frac{19}{30}$.

You can also use ratio tables to compare $\frac{1}{6}$ and $\frac{4}{5}$.

Part	1	2	3	4	5
Whole	6	12	18	24	30

Part	4	8	16	24
Whole	5	10	20	30

The two ratios tables show that $\frac{4}{5}$ is larger than $\frac{1}{6}$ by 19 parts out of 30, or $\frac{19}{30}$. The difference, $\frac{4}{5} - \frac{1}{6}$, is the same as $\frac{24}{30} - \frac{5}{30}$, which is $\frac{19}{30}$.

Example B

If you want to add $\frac{1}{8}$ and $\frac{2}{3}$, you might draw two bars and imagine that each has 24 segments.

One-eighth of the bar would be three out of 24 segments.

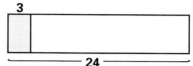

One-third of the bar would be eight out of 24 segments, so $\frac{2}{3}$ would be 16 segments.

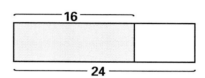

To add $\frac{1}{8}$ and $\frac{2}{3}$, color one part to represent three segments, showing $\frac{1}{8}$, and another part representing 16 segments, or $\frac{2}{3}$. The total is 19 out of 24 segments. Thus, $\frac{1}{8} + \frac{2}{3} = \frac{19}{24}$.

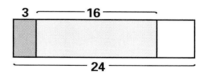

You can also use ratio tables to add $\frac{1}{8}$ and $\frac{2}{3}$.

Part	1	2	3	Part	2	4	8	16
Whole	8	16	24	Whole	3	6	12	24

The two tables show that you can add 3 parts out of 24 and 16 parts out of 24, which is 19 parts out of 24, or $\frac{19}{24}$.

Check Your Work

Enrique has the results of several surveys to use in his column. He wants to make several comparisons and combine some of the results to form new categories. In order to do this, he needs to calculate several comparisons.

Enrique Caston
Fraction Times Reporter

1. Compare $\frac{5}{6}$ and $\frac{2}{3}$. Which one is larger, and by how much?

A survey asked people, "What is your favorite flower?" Here are the results.

$\frac{1}{2}$ like roses best. $\frac{1}{5}$ like tulips best. $\frac{1}{6}$ like lilies best.

The rest had no favorite flower.

2. a. What fraction of the people surveyed had a favorite flower?

   b. What fraction of the people surveyed had no favorite flower?

3. a. Which is more, $\frac{3}{10}$ or $\frac{1}{5}$? How much more? Write your result as a difference

   b. Which is more, $\frac{3}{4}$ or $\frac{5}{6}$? How much more? Write your result as a difference.

4. Calculate each sum.

   a. $\frac{1}{2} + \frac{1}{6}$ **b.** $\frac{2}{3} + \frac{1}{4}$ **c.** $\frac{2}{9} + \frac{1}{6}$

5. Calculate each difference.

   a. $\frac{3}{4} - \frac{2}{3}$ **b.** $\frac{4}{5} - \frac{1}{2}$

For Further Reflection

Your parents ask you what you learned today in math class, specifically how you can compare two fractions that have different denominators. Write what you will tell them.

C

Festival and the Decimal Connection

The Gold Rush

Jada Washington
Fraction Times **Reporter**

Every year, Klondike has a festival. *Fraction Times* covers the festival.

Jada Washington loves the Gold Rush event. During this event, children dig into a huge sand pit for gold cans. Inside each can is money, usually from $1 to $10. One special gold can contains $100!

Many of the older teens team up for the Gold Rush Dig. They promise to share all of the money equally with their teammates.

At the end of the day, Jada overhears one disappointed girl say, "We found only one dollar. When we split it among the four of us, we will get only one quarter each." Jada asks her to explain what she means. The girl explains that she and three friends decided to look for money and share everything they found.

Jada records the following team results from this year's Gold Rush.

Team	Total Money Found	Group Size
Arrows	$5	4
Bears	$3	4
Cougars	$4	5
Diggers	$7	2
Eagles	$6	8
Foxes	$10	8
Giants	$9	5
Heroes	$102	10

1. **a.** Which team most likely found the special gold can?

   b. How much money did each member of the Arrows receive if the money was shared evenly? Use coins to describe the amounts.

   c. Use dollars, quarters, dimes, and nickels to describe the amount each member of the other teams received if the money found was shared evenly.

For problem 2, recall the relationship between benchmark fractions and decimals.

2. Copy and complete the table using your knowledge of benchmark fractions, money, and decimals. The first row is done for you.

Coin	Coin Notation	Fraction of a Dollar
half dollar	$0.50	$\frac{1}{2}$
quarter		
	$0.10	
two dimes		
three quarters		
		$\frac{1}{100}$
	$0.40	

3. **a.** If the fraction of a dollar is not a benchmark fraction, describe how you can use a calculator to change the fraction into a decimal amount.

   b. Write three non-benchmark fractions of a dollar. Use your calculator to change each fraction to a decimal. Write the decimal using money notation.

4. Nehru said, "I won twenty cents." What fraction of a dollar did he win?

5. Find the fraction of a dollar for each of these amounts.
   a. $0.25
   b. $0.10
   c. $0.40
   d. $0.01
   e. $0.17

6. Write a summary of how to convert fractions to decimals and decimals to fractions. Be sure to include all of the strategies that you use successfully; examples would be helpful. Describe any strategies that are confusing to you.

The Treasure Chest

Another favorite activity at the Klondike Festival is the Treasure Chest. People donate items to the Treasure Chest and then shop for interesting items from other people. Willie, who is a retired storekeeper, organizes the Treasure Chest. He records the sales on individual sale sheets.

Here is Willie's record for the Byron's Treasures.

$0.15	$0.15	$0.15	$0.15	$0.15	$0.15				
$0.25	$0.25	$0.25	$0.25	$0.25					
$0.75	$0.75	$0.75	$0.75						
$0.99	$0.99	$0.99	$0.99	$0.99	$0.99	$0.99	$0.99	$0.99	$0.99
$2.05	$2.05	$2.05	$2.05						
$3.33	$3.33	$3.33	$3.33	$3.33					
$4.99	$4.99	$4.99							

Willie could have written the last line as 3 × $4.99.

7. Reflect How can you quickly calculate 3 × $4.99 without the use of a calculator?

8. How can you quickly find the total amount of Byron's Treasure Sheet without using a calculator?

Willie has interesting strategies to make calculations without using a calculator. Instead of 6 × $0.15, he calculates 3 × $0.30, which is $0.90.

If someone asks Willie to explain his strategy, he just puts a number of nickels and dimes on the table, like this.

9. a. How can Willie use these coins to show that 6 × $0.15 is the same as 3 × $0.30?

b. Use Willie's strategy to calculate 4 × $1.35.

c. Make up a similar multiplication problem that can be solved using Willie's strategy.

10. Show a strategy to calculate the total cost of seven items that cost $0.55 each.

Fractions and Decimals

When solving problems, it is helpful if you can easily change back and forth between decimals and fractions. This skill can also be useful in daily life situations.

With this table, you can show most common fractions.

		Numerator								
		1	2	3	4	5	6	7	8	9
Denominator	**2**	$\frac{1}{2} =$ 0.5	$\frac{2}{2} =$ 1							
	3	$\frac{1}{3} =$ $0.3\overline{3}$								
	4									
	5									
	6									
	8									
	10									

11. **a.** Copy the table and color the cells that have a fraction that is greater than 1.

b. Complete the table for fractions less than one. Write both the fraction and the decimal. Three cells are already done for you.

c. Name some equivalent fractions.

Summary

Fractions and decimals are used to describe the same numbers. It is important to be able to change from one form of a number to the other.

To change a fraction to a decimal

- Check for benchmark fractions.

  $$\frac{1}{4} = 0.25$$

- Reason using some familiar benchmark fractions.

  $\frac{3}{5} = ?$ The decimal equivalent is 0.60 since $\frac{1}{5} = 0.20$.

- Think about money notation.

  $\frac{72}{100}$ is 0.72 because $\frac{72}{100}$ of a dollar is 72 cents, or $0.72.

  $\frac{5}{100}$ is 0.05 because $\frac{5}{100}$ of a dollar is 5 cents, which is $0.05.

- Use a calculator to divide the **numerator** by the denominator.

  $\frac{7}{8}$ is $7 \div 8$, which is 0.875.

To change a decimal to a fraction

- Check for benchmarks.

  0.5 is $\frac{1}{2}$.

- Read the decimal using place value knowledge and write the fraction.

  Decimals are read as tenths, hundredths, thousandths, etc.

  0.5 is read as five tenths and written as $\frac{5}{10}$, which is $\frac{1}{2}$.

  0.17 is read as seventeen hundredths and written as $\frac{17}{100}$.

  0.125 is read as one hundred twenty-five thousandths and written as $\frac{125}{1000}$ or $\frac{1}{8}$.

  You can use a ratio table to simplify a fraction.

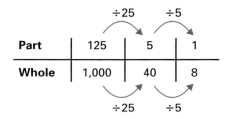

To add or multiply decimal numbers

In this section, you shared and discussed different strategies to add and multiply decimal numbers.

Here is some student work showing how to find
$1.35 + $1.35 + $1.35 + $1.35.

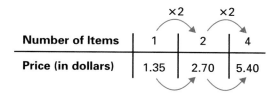

	×2	×2
Number of Items	1	2	4
Price (in dollars)	1.35	2.70	5.40

$1.35 + $1.35 + $1.35 + $1.35 =
4 dollars and 4 quarters and 4 dimes =
$4.00 + $1.00 + $0.40 = $5.40

$1.35 + $1.35 + $1.35 + $1.35 =
4 × $1.35 =
2 × $2.70 = $5.40

Here is an example of how number sense is used to find 5 × $6.49.

5 × $6.49 is 5 pennies less than 5 × $6.50.

5 × $6.50 = $30 + $2.50 = $32.50

Adjusting for the extra 5 pennies:

$32.50 − $0.05 = $32.45

Check Your Work

1. Write each decimal as a fraction.

   a. 0.24

   b. 0.125

   c. 0.375

   d. 0.333

   e. 0.667

2. Find the decimal that is equivalent to each of these fractions.

   a. $\frac{1}{5}$

   b. $\frac{1}{16}$

   c. $\frac{2}{8}$

3. a. Find 8 × $5.26.

   b. List all of the ways you can calculate 4 × $2.49.

4. Write two problems of your own involving decimals and fractions. One should be easy to solve and the other should be challenging. Provide solutions to each problem on a separate piece of paper. Exchange problems with a classmate and solve.

 ## For Further Reflection

Define benchmark fractions in your own words. Give at least two reasons they are easy to use.

Ratios, Fractions, Decimals, and Percents

Friends Come First

Beatrice Flores
Fraction Times **Reporter**

Every Tuesday, *Fraction Times* runs a special section called "Teen Times." Beatrice Flores's assignment is to investigate topics most important to teens.

Beatrice surveys a seventh-grade class and a tenth-grade class.

The survey includes this question.

What is most important to you?
school
health
friends
sports

In the seventh-grade class, 13 out of 20 students selected "friends."

In the tenth-grade class, 16 out of 25 students selected "friends."

To compare the results, you can use two bar models with the same number of segments.

13 out of 20

16 out of 25

1. **a.** How many segments would each bar have?

   b. Use fractions to compare the results.

Beatrice searches for a headline that will attract readers. She thinks percents are better for headlines than fractions.

2. **a.** Use percents to compare the results.

   b. Using percents, write a headline for Beatrice's feature story.

At the end of her article, Beatrice invites teen readers, ages 13 through 18, to visit her webpage and complete the same survey. After one day, she has 400 responses. Here are the results.

What is most important to you? (400)	
school	20
health	80
friends	240
sports	60

Beatrice summarizes the survey on her website. Since she used percents in her headlines, she wants to summarize her survey using percents.

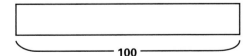

100

3. **a.** Use the bar with 100 segments on **Student Activity Sheet 5**. How many teens represent 1 segment of this bar?

   b. How many segments will you need to color to show that for 20 teens, "school" was most important?

   c. Color the parts of the bar to summarize the survey results. Include a chart key and assign percentages to each category.

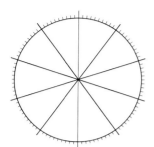

Another tool derived from the 100-segment bar model is the 100-segment circle. One is shown on the left. This tool is great for making pie charts.

Note: Not all 100 lines are drawn to the center of the circle!

4. a. Use the 100-segment circle on **Student Activity Sheet 5** to summarize the web poll results. Include a chart key and assign percentages to each category.

b. What are the advantages and disadvantages of using the 100-segment circle?

c. Create summary statements that Beatrice can post on her website.

Headlines

Mike Johnson
Fraction Times **Reporter**

Mike Johnson lives in Swanborough, close to the airport. In the past ten years, the noise level from the airport has increased dramatically. The residents of Swanborough created a neighborhood watch group, called NMN—No More Noise!

To inform more people about the NMN cause, Mike gathers information for an article in *Fraction Times*.

In a recent survey of 300 Swanborough residents, 216 people said the airport noise is too loud.

Mike's first headline for *Fraction Times* is "216 People Think Airport Noise Too Loud."

He realizes that this is not a good headline and decides against using it.

5. a. Explain why Mike decides not to use the headline.

b. Write a better headline to summarize the situation.

At a staff meeting, Mike shares the data and asks for suggestions for a new headline.

Lauren suggests:

"Two-thirds of the People in Swanborough Complain about Airport Noise."

Enrique thinks that "Three of Every Four People in Swanborough Complain" is a better estimate of the situation.

6. **a.** Describe how Lauren thought of the fraction.

   b. Describe how Enrique thought of his ratio.

   c. Should Mike use either headline? If so, which one, and why?

After the meeting, Jada Washington sends Mike this email.

Mike,

What if you rounded the survey results from *216 out of 300* to *210 out of 300*?

Then you could say, "More than 70% of Swanborough Residents Complain About Airport Noise."

Jada

More than 70% of Swanborough Residents Complain About Airport Noise

7. Explain whether Jada's suggestion is reasonable.

At this point, Mike is confused. He decides to review all of the suggestions again.

- 200 out of 300 is 2 out of 3, which is $\frac{2}{3}$.

- 225 out of 300 is…

- 210 out of 300 is…

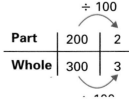

		÷ 100
Part	200	2
Whole	300	3

8. What fractions do you get using the other estimations? Show your work.

9. **Reflect** Which estimate do you think is best? Why?

Mike decides to use a percent in his headline. He asks Jada to explain how she arrived at 70%. She says, "I used 210 out of 300, and that's 7 out of 10. I thought: $\frac{7}{10} = \frac{70}{100}$, which is the same as 70%."

Mike looks confused, so Jada explains a different strategy.

She says, "If I use 210 out of 300 with a ratio table, then I want to find the ratio per 100."

Part	210	...
Whole	300	100

Mike still looks puzzled, so Jada explains a third strategy.

She says, "If I use a 100-segment bar for 300 people, one segment represents 3 people. To represent 210 people, I will need to shade 70 segments (210 ÷ 3); 70 out of 100 is 70%."

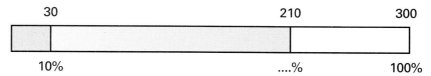

Mike likes the last strategy best. He realizes that this is only an estimate, but he knows he can use it to get an exact answer.

10. **a.** Calculate the exact percent of the 300 people surveyed who are annoyed by the noise and suggest a good headline. They numbered 216.

b. Explain how Mike can use the last strategy to find an exact answer.

11. **a.** Which strategy do you like best?

b. Write a problem and show how it can be solved using your favorite strategy.

Polling for Mayor in Klondike

Four candidates are running for mayor: Lisa Jimenez, Tina Jacobs, Pete Fullhouse, and Dominic Elstein. Three months before the elections, *Fraction Times* conducts a poll of 600 people. The results are shown.

Fraction Times Survey of 600 People		
Candidate	Number of Votes	Percentage
Jimenez	121	20%
Jacobs	149	
Fullhouse	89	
Elstein	182	
Undecided	59	

Beatrice Flores is reporting on the election. She is changing the data into percents. She decides to use the 100-segment bar model and her calculator to see how many bars to shade.

121 out of 600 people for Jimenez;

121 ÷ 600 is 0.20166666, which I round down to 0.20;

0.20 is $\frac{20}{100}$ which is 20%. I shade 20 segments.

Therefore, 20 out of 100 segments, which is 20% of the total, should be colored.

12. a. Use your calculator to help Beatrice find the number of bars to shade for each candidate.

b. Copy the table above and show the results using percents.

In Section A, you compared data from two classes with an unequal number of students. You set up two bars of the same length and with the same number of segments. You summarized each part using fraction numbers. In this section, you used special bars with 100 segments. When you use these bars, it is easy to summarize the results using percentages.

13. a. Summarize the pre-election survey results using fractions.

b. Tina Jacobs and Pete Fullhouse belong to the same political party. What part of the votes did Jacobs and Fullhouse receive together?

One week before the election, *Fraction Times* conducts a second poll of 641 people to determine the candidates' standings.

Fraction Times Survey of 641 People	
Candidate	**Number of Votes**
Jimenez	82
Jacobs	237
Fullhouse	172
Elstein	105
Undecided	45

Beatrice wants to use the 100-segment bar to organize and summarize this new data, just like the previous survey.

14. a. Help Beatrice. Use your calculator to find how many segments need to be shaded for each candidate.

b. Write the percent and fraction for each candidate's result.

c. Write a short news brief comparing the two pre-election surveys. Predict the next mayor of Klondike!

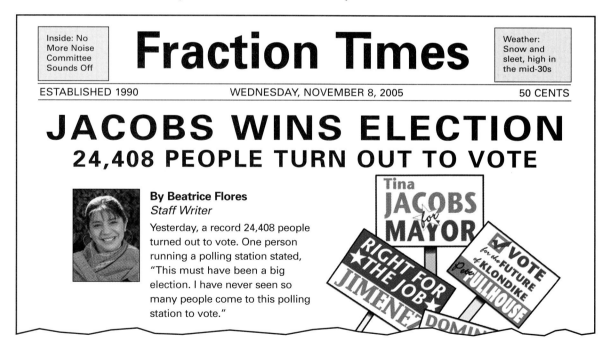

Jacobs won the election with 9,153 votes. Fullhouse came in second with 8,139 votes. Beatrice drafts her final article about the election.

15. Finish her article. You may choose to include fractions, ratios, and charts in your article, and you must include a percent.

D Ratios, Fractions, Decimals, and Percents

Summary ◀◀

Any ratio can be written as a decimal, a fraction, or a percent.

The ratio 247 out of 599
- Written as a fraction: $\frac{247}{599}$.
- Using a calculator to find the decimal:
  $247 \div 599 = 0.41235392321$, which, rounded to the nearest hundredth is the decimal 0.41.
- Changing the decimal 0.41 into a fraction: $\frac{41}{100}$, which, written as a percent, is 41%.

It is very helpful to be able to make estimates of any ratio.

Using the same example, two estimates for 247 out of 599 are:

240 out of 600 (a low estimate) or
250 out of 600 (a high estimate).

Each of these can lead to estimates as a fraction, decimal, and percent.

The ratio 240 out of 600

	÷ 6	÷ 10	÷ 2	
Part	240	40	4	2
Whole	600	100	10	5
	÷ 6	÷ 10	÷ 2	

as a fraction: $\frac{2}{5}$.

as a decimal: 0.40, or 0.4 (second and third columns).

as a percent: 40% (second column).

The ratio 250 out of 600

Part	250	500	5
Whole	600	1200	12

as a fraction: $\frac{5}{12}$.

Use a calculator to find the decimal and the percent:
- As a decimal: calculate $5 \div 12$ is 0.416, which rounds up to 0.42.
- As a percent: $0.42 = \frac{42}{100}$, thus 42%.

In one survey, 250 parents were asked,

"On an average day, how many hours do your children watch TV?"

- 25 out of 250 said more than 3 hours.
- 98 out of 250 said between 1 and 3 hours.

1. a. How many segments of a 100-segment bar would you shade for the group watching more than 3 hours of TV per day?

b. How many segments of a 100-segment bar would you shade for the group watching between 1 and 2 hours? You may use an estimate.

c. What do you know about the group of children that watch less than 1 hour of TV daily?

d. Use the 100-segment circle on a copy of **Student Activity Sheet 5** to make a pie chart of the survey results.

e. Write these survey results as percents and as fractions.

2. a. Use different strategies to show that the ratio 600 out of 800 corresponds to 75%.

b. You might know percents for some familiar fractions. Do you know them all?

Fraction	$\frac{1}{2}$	$\frac{1}{3}$	$\frac{1}{4}$	$\frac{1}{5}$	$\frac{1}{8}$	$\frac{1}{10}$	$\frac{1}{20}$	$\frac{1}{25}$	$\frac{1}{50}$	$\frac{1}{100}$
Percent										

Copy this table in your notebook and write the corresponding percents.

While taking election surveys, interviewers asked each person which party he or she generally supports. The results from 755 individuals are shown here.

Republican	248
Democratic	301
Independent	189
Progressive	17

3. a. Write the fraction and the percent that represent each party. You may estimate.

For an article, Beatrice Flores describes the data with fractions and percents.

b. Write a headline for Beatrice's article. Explain why you used a fraction, percent, or decimal.

 ## For Further Reflection

You must use only one of the following statements to convince your classmate that he or she should read *Tom Sawyer*. Choose the one you think is most persuasive and tell why.

a. Six out of 10 students have read the book.

b. More than half of the students have read the book.

c. About 60% of the students have read the book.

d. Only $\frac{2}{5}$ of the students have not read the book.

Fractional Parts

Recycled Fractions

Enrique Caston is working on an article about recycling bins used at Welcome Woods, a nearby park. So far, he has written this draft.

Welcome Woods Recycles

Last year the Parks and Recreation Department installed recycling bins in Welcome Woods. The bins are for aluminum cans. Park ranger Patricia Selfield stated, "The weight of all of the cans left behind by the park visitors is enormous. We estimate that visitors throw away 250 kilograms of cans per year." Selfield hopes that at least $\frac{4}{5}$ of the used cans will be put into recycling bins. Most of these should make it to the recycling center, since only $\frac{1}{10}$ of the cans from the bins are lost on the way to the recycling center.

250 kilograms (kg) per year

$\frac{4}{5}$

recycle bin

Enrique wants to state the fraction of cans used by park visitors that is expected to be recycled. In order to do this, he has to find which fraction corresponds to $\frac{9}{10}$ of $\frac{4}{5}$.

1. Why does Enrique need to calculate $\frac{9}{10}$ of $\frac{4}{5}$?

Enrique does not know how to calculate $\frac{9}{10}$ of $\frac{4}{5}$. He decides to calculate the quantity that is actually recycled first.

2. a. How many kilograms of aluminum cans are expected to be put into the recycling bins?

   b. How many kilograms of aluminum cans are expected to be recycled?

   c. What is the ratio of the kilograms of aluminum cans that will be recycled to the kilograms of cans used by park visitors each year?

   d. What fraction of the aluminum cans left behind by visitors will probably be recycled?

What Fraction Saved?

Lauren Cook has been assigned to write an article about an oil tanker accident. So far, she has drafted this article.

> **Oil Tanker Stranded**
>
> On Saturday morning, the oil tanker Great Lady hit a reef about 20 miles south of the Bella Coast. Great Lady was carrying 2,000 barrels of oil. The ship lost $\frac{1}{5}$ of its oil while waiting for help. Smith Branch Offshore sent crews to repair the crippled tanker and clean up the oil spill. Although the crew worked tirelessly, the tanker lost $\frac{3}{8}$ of its remaining oil in the 24 hours after the Offshore crews arrived to help.

Lauren decided that the last sentence she wrote is confusing. Instead, she wants to mention the fraction of all of the oil that was lost after the Smith Branch Offshore crews arrived. She decides to find $\frac{3}{8}$ of $\frac{4}{5}$.

3. Why should Lauren calculate $\frac{3}{8}$ of $\frac{4}{5}$?

4. **a.** How many barrels of oil were still in the tanker when the Smith Branch Offshore crews arrived?

   b. How many barrels of oil were lost in the 24 hours after the Smith Branch Offshore crews arrived?

   c. What fraction of the original 2,000 barrels of oil was lost in the 24 hours after the Smith Branch Offshore crews arrived?

Two days after the spill, Great Lady was towed to the port of Bella Harbor. By this time, $\frac{3}{4}$ of the 2,000 barrels of oil had been lost. Experts estimate that 80% of the spilled oil will end up onshore.

5. How much oil will end up onshore?

6. Write a short story to describe the Great Lady oil tanker spill.

Lauren heard of another oil spill. After attempts were made to repair this second tanker, crews realized that only $\frac{1}{3}$ of the remaining $\frac{3}{4}$ of the oil in the damaged tanker had been saved. Lauren was not told the total amount of oil that the tanker originally carried.

7. What amounts could the oil tanker have held? How did you decide?

8. What fraction of the oil was saved?

◆E Fractional Parts

Summary ⮞⮞

It is possible to calculate a fraction of a fraction by using fractions of whole numbers. For example, you can calculate $\frac{3}{4}$ of $\frac{2}{5}$ by making up a new recycling problem. Choose a number of kilograms of cans that can be divided by both denominators—in this case, 4 and 5. Twenty or 40 will work.

Suppose you choose 20 kg of cans. Then $\frac{2}{5}$ of the 20 kg is 8 kg (the amount collected for recycling) and $\frac{3}{4}$ of 8 kg is 6 kg (the amount actually recycled). Thus, $\frac{3}{4}$ of $\frac{2}{5}$ is $\frac{6}{20}$.

Check Your Work ⮞⮞

1. a. In the Summary example, where does $\frac{6}{20}$ come from, and what does it represent?

   b. If 40 kg were chosen instead of 20 kg, how would the final fraction change?

2. a. Find $\frac{1}{2}$ of $\frac{1}{4}$. **b.** Find $\frac{1}{6}$ of $\frac{2}{3}$.

3. Of the 200 students in sixth grade at Franklin Middle School, $\frac{3}{4}$ participate in sports, and $\frac{2}{5}$ of those who are active in sports are on the swim team.

   a. How many sixth graders participate in sports?

   b. How many are on the swim team?

   c. What fraction of sixth graders at Franklin Middle School are on the swim team?

 ## For Further Reflection

"When you multiply two numbers, the product is always larger than either of the factors." Tell if this statement is true or false. Explain your reasoning.

Additional Practice

Ms. Garbett wants to compare the musical tastes of her students to their parents' musical tastes. She conducts a survey in which the students and their parents list their favorite type of music. The table shows the results.

Students (18)	
Rap	5
Classical	1
Jazz	2
Rock	2
Alternative	8

Parents (24)	
Rap	0
Classical	10
Jazz	5
Rock	9
Alternative	0

1. Use a graph to compare the favorite types of music of the students and parents.

Section **B** It Adds Up

Mr. Marcado's 24 students are very interested in music.

$\frac{1}{2}$ of the students play one instrument.

$\frac{1}{4}$ of the students play two instruments.

$\frac{1}{6}$ of the students play three or more instruments.

1. a. Illustrate the information about Mr. Marcado's class on a bar similar to the one shown on the left.

b. What fraction of students play two or more instruments?

c. What fraction of students do not play an instrument?

Mr. Marcado polls two of his classes to find out whether his students like to listen to the piano, guitar, or violin. Each student chooses only one category. The chart shows the results of his poll for the three instruments.

	Class A	Class B
Piano	$\frac{1}{2}$	$\frac{2}{5}$
Guitar	$\frac{1}{10}$	$\frac{1}{4}$
Violin	$\frac{1}{4}$	$\frac{3}{10}$

2. a. Compare the results for two classes.

   b. Which class prefers the violin? Explain your answer using fractions.

   c. What fraction of students in Class A chose something other than the piano, guitar, or violin as their favorite instrument?

While researching his article, Enrique found the results of a different survey on Canadians' favorite fruits.

apples	$\frac{1}{6}$	oranges	$\frac{1}{2}$
pineapples	$\frac{1}{3}$	bananas	$\frac{1}{4}$

He wondered if these data include all of the results of the survey. He finds the sum of the fractions.

3. a. What is the result?

   b. How might you explain this result?

4. Find each sum.

   a. $\frac{5}{6} + \frac{3}{5}$ **b.** $\frac{2}{3} + \frac{1}{2}$ **c.** $\frac{4}{9} + \frac{8}{9}$

Section ◆ Festival and the Decimal Connection

1. How can you use your calculator to change a fraction to a decimal?

2. Rewrite the following fractions as decimals.

   a. $\frac{3}{5}$ **b.** $\frac{1}{8}$ **c.** $\frac{2}{3}$

3. Rewrite the following decimals as fractions. Explain your method.

   a. 0.45

   b. 0.625

   c. 0.80

4. a. What is the price of three items at $1.76 each?

   b. What is the price of four items at $2.31 each?

Section Ⅰ Ratios, Fractions, Decimals, and Percents

Picture This is a company that manufactures television sets. Sandra Lemond bought one of the company's television sets, only to discover that it was defective. After talking to some of her friends, she found that many of them also had trouble with their Picture This televisions. She did a bit of research about the company and found that Picture This sells many defective sets. She became so frustrated that she decided to write a letter to the editorial section of the newspaper.

Picture This? Please Don't!

Dear Editor,

The Picture This television company manufactures and sells defective televisions. Unfortunately, I bought one of these sets two months ago and have had nothing but trouble with it. I have since found out that I am not alone. The company manufactures many defective televisions every month. Last May, $\frac{1}{10}$ of the sets were faulty. In June, 2 out of every 21 failed to work properly. In July, there was something wrong with 2 of every 23 sets. In August, the plant manufactured 56,731 televisions, of which 4,603 were defective. It is time that something be done about the quality of the product produced by this company or close the company forever.

Sincerely,

Sandra Lamond

---

1. **a.** Which month was the worst for the quality of televisions at the Picture This television plant?

   Lauren Cook, Enrique Caston, and Mike Johnson compared the proportions of defective televisions over four months. Lauren wrote each month as a ratio like "two out of .... televisions were defective." Enrique wrote each month as a fraction and as a decimal. Mike calculated the percents.

   b. Show what each person found for each of the months listed in the letter.

The staff at *Fraction Times* is writing an article for this Sunday's paper about the Klondike High School seniors' plans following graduation. The staff surveyed 400 seniors. Here are the results of the survey.

High School Survey (400 Seniors)	
Four-year college	173
Two-year college	98
Job	64
Military	24
Undecided or other	41

2. a. Create a graph to display the results.

b. Write a headline for Sunday's newspaper article based on the survey.

Section **E** Fractional Parts

Of the 180 students in the seventh grade at Franklin, $\frac{2}{3}$ of them are on a sports team, and $\frac{1}{4}$ of those active in sports are on a basketball team.

1. What fraction of seventh graders are on a basketball team?

2. Write as fractions.

a. $\frac{1}{2}$ of $\frac{3}{4}$

b. $\frac{1}{3}$ of $\frac{3}{5}$

c. $\frac{3}{4}$ of $\frac{1}{6}$

Section Ⓐ Survey Results

1. a. Here is a possible solution, where each bar has 60 segments.

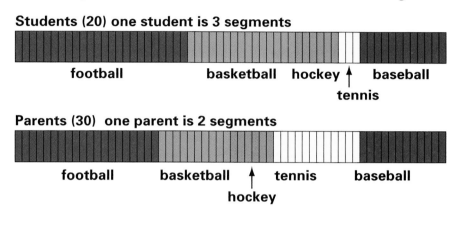

Students (20) one student is 3 segments

football   basketball   hockey ↑   baseball
                                  tennis

Parents (30) one parent is 2 segments

football   basketball   ↑   tennis   baseball
                    hockey

b.   **c.**

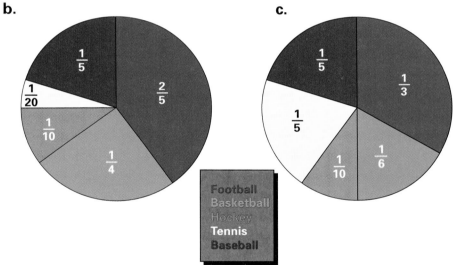

Football
Basketball
Hockey
Tennis
Baseball

d. Basketball is more popular with the parents than with the students even though five people in each group chose basketball.

2. a. Students

Cats	$\frac{8}{22}$ or $\frac{4}{11}$
Dogs	$\frac{10}{22}$ or $\frac{5}{11}$
Rabbits	$\frac{4}{22}$ or $\frac{2}{11}$

Parents

Cats	$\frac{15}{30}$ or $\frac{1}{2}$
Dogs	$\frac{10}{30}$ or $\frac{1}{3}$
Rabbits	$\frac{5}{30}$ or $\frac{1}{6}$

b. Your comparison may be like the sample responses.

In both groups, 10 people said that the dog was their favorite pet. However, since the group of students surveyed was smaller than the group of parents surveyed, the students favored the dog more than the parents did.

Half of the parents chose the cat as their favorite pet, while $\frac{1}{3}$ of the parents chose the dog. About $\frac{1}{3}$ of the students chose the cat, but more students chose the dog.

$\frac{1}{6}$ of the parents chose the rabbit; this was about the same fraction as the students who did.

3. Answers will vary; however, all results should have the same sample size.

The bar chart and the pie chart you create should be similar to what you have created in problems 1 and 3.

Section **B** It Adds Up

1. $\frac{5}{6}$ is larger than $\frac{2}{3}$. The difference is $\frac{1}{6}$. One way to show the difference is to compare the fractions using the bar model.

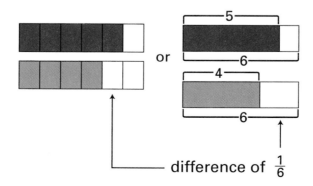

difference of $\frac{1}{6}$

2. a. You can use a ratio table to combine $\frac{1}{5}$ and $\frac{1}{6}$.

Part	1	2	4	6
Whole	5	10	20	30

Part	1	4	5
Whole	6	24	30

So $\frac{1}{5} + \frac{1}{6} = \frac{6}{30} + \frac{5}{30}$. This makes $\frac{11}{30}$.

And $\frac{11}{30} + \frac{1}{2} = \frac{11}{30} + \frac{15}{30} = \frac{26}{30}$.

b. $\frac{4}{30}$ or $\frac{2}{15}$ of the people

3. a. $\frac{3}{10}$ is more. The difference is $\frac{1}{10}$.

You can use a bar to find the answers; for example:

 $\frac{3}{10}$

 $\frac{1}{5}$

b. $\frac{5}{6}$ is more. The difference is $\frac{1}{12}$. One way to compare is to use bars.

4. a. $\frac{4}{6}$ or any equivalent. One strategy is to use bars.

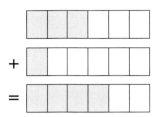

b. $\frac{11}{12}$. One strategy is to use bars.

$$\boxed{} + \boxed{} = \boxed{}$$

c. $\frac{7}{18}$ $\left(\frac{4}{18} + \frac{3}{18}\right)$

5. a. $\frac{1}{12}$ $\left(\frac{9}{12} - \frac{8}{12}\right)$ **b.** $\frac{3}{10}$ $\left(\frac{8}{10} - \frac{5}{10}\right)$

Section **G** Festival and the Decimal Connection

1. Answers will vary. Sample responses:

a. $\frac{24}{100}$ or $\frac{6}{25}$ **d.** $\frac{333}{1000}$ or about $\frac{1}{3}$

b. $\frac{125}{1000}$ or $\frac{1}{8}$ **e.** $\frac{667}{1000}$ or about $\frac{2}{3}$

c. $\frac{375}{1000}$ or $\frac{3}{8}$

2. a. 0.2 or 0.20   **b.** 0.0625   **c.** 0.25

3. a. $42.08. Here is one strategy.
  • 8 × $5.26 is 8 pennies more than $5.25. 8 × $5.25 is $40 + 8 quarters (or $2). The total is $42.

  So 8 × $5.26 = $42 + $0.08 = $42.08.

b. Here are four strategies.
  • Using repeated addition:

$$\begin{array}{r} \$2.49 \\ \$2.49 \\ \$2.49 \\ + \ \$2.49 \\ \hline \$9.96 \end{array}$$

- Using number sense:

  $4 \times \$2.50 = \$10.00$

  $4 \times \$2.49 = \$10.00 - \$0.04 = \$9.96$

- Rewriting $2.49 as $2.00 + $0.40 + $0.09 and multiplying each amount by four (using the **distributive property**):

  $4 \times \$2.00 = \$8.00$

  $4 \times \$0.40 = \$1.60$

  $4 \times \$0.09 = \$0.36$

- Using a ratio table:

Quantity	1	2	4
Cost	$2.49	$4.98	$9.96

4. The problems you created will vary, but be sure to solve and share your answers and strategies with classmates.

Section D Ratios, Fractions, Decimals, and Percents

1. **a.** 10 segments out of 100 should be shaded to represent 25 out of 250. Here are two strategies.

   - Using a ratio table:

Part	25	5	10
Whole	250	50	100

   - Using fractions:

     25 out of 250 can be written as the fraction $\frac{25}{250}$.

     $\frac{25}{250} = \frac{1}{10}$. So you have to color $\frac{1}{10}$ of the 100-segment bar, or 10 segments.

b. The answers 39 and 40 are both acceptable. The answer you get should match your strategy. Here are two strategies.

- Use fractions.

  (0.392): 98 out of 250 can be written as the fraction $\frac{98}{250}$.

  Divide 98 by 250, round the result, and you get 0.39, or $\frac{39}{100}$.

- 98 is about 4 times as much as 25. You colored 10 segments for 25, so for 98, you have to color 4 times as many, which is 40 segments.

c. The number of students is 250 − 25 − 98, which is 127. The segments that are not shaded represent this group. There are 10 + 39 (or 40) segments shaded; thus, for this group, there are 100 − 49 = 51 (or 100 − 50 = 50) segments left.

d.–e.

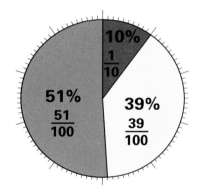

2. a. Examples of different strategies:

- You can make a ratio table and reach 100 by "halving."

Part	600	300	150	75
Whole	800	400	200	100

75 out of 100 is 75%

- Simplify $\frac{600}{800}$ to $\frac{3}{4}$ and use what you know about the relationship between fractions and percents. $\frac{3}{4} = 75\%$.

- You can think of a 100-segment bar. One segment = 8. Then divide 600 by 8 to see how many segments have to be shaded.

  600 ÷ 8 = 75. So 75 out of 100 segments is 75%

- 600 out of 800 is $\frac{600}{800}$. Divide 600 by 800 and you get 0.75, and this can be written as $\frac{75}{100}$, which is 75%.

b.

Fraction	$\frac{1}{2}$	$\frac{1}{3}$	$\frac{1}{4}$	$\frac{1}{5}$	$\frac{1}{8}$	$\frac{1}{10}$	$\frac{1}{20}$	$\frac{1}{25}$	$\frac{1}{50}$	$\frac{1}{100}$
Percent	50	$33\frac{1}{3}$	25	20	12.5	10	5	4	2	1

3. a. Republican: $\frac{248}{755}$ 33%   about $\frac{1}{3}$

      Democratic: $\frac{301}{755}$ 40%   about $\frac{2}{5}$

      Independent: $\frac{189}{755}$ 25%   about $\frac{1}{4}$

      Progressive: $\frac{17}{755}$ 2%   about $\frac{1}{50}$

b. Headlines will vary. You may have used percents or fractions in your headline like the example here.

Forty Percent of People Surveyed Support the Democratic Party

The student who wrote this explained that she finds amounts represented as percents easier to understand, since percents represent part of 100.

Section **E** Fractional Parts

1. a. Six kilograms of the 20 kilograms was recycled.

b. You would get an answer of $\frac{12}{40}$, which is equal to $\frac{6}{20}$, so the final fraction would not change. Strategies will vary. Sample strategy:

$\frac{3}{4}$ of 40 kg is _____ .

$\frac{2}{5}$ of 40 kg is 16 kg.

$\frac{3}{4}$ of 16 kg is 12 kg.

12 kg out of 40 kg is $\frac{12}{40}$, which is the same as $\frac{6}{20}$.

2. a. $\frac{1}{8}$ or any fraction equivalent to $\frac{1}{8}$.

b. $\frac{1}{9}$ or any fraction equivalent to $\frac{1}{9}$.

3. a. 150 students. You may reason that $\frac{1}{4}$ of 200 is 50 (200 ÷ 4 = 50), so $\frac{3}{4}$ of 200 is three times that number, or 150 students.

b. 60 students. You may reason that $\frac{1}{5}$ of 150 is 30 (150 ÷ 5 = 30), so $\frac{2}{5}$ of 150 is two times that number, or 60 students.

c. $\frac{3}{10}$. You may reason that 60 out of 200 is equal to $\frac{60}{200}$, or $\frac{3}{10}$.

Figuring All the Angles

BRITANNICA
Mathematics in Context

Geometry and Measurement

HOLT, RINEHART AND WINSTON

Mathematics in Context is a comprehensive curriculum for the middle grades. It was developed in 1991 through 1997 in collaboration with the Wisconsin Center for Education Research, School of Education, University of Wisconsin-Madison and the Freudenthal Institute at the University of Utrecht, The Netherlands, with the support of the National Science Foundation Grant No. 9054928.

The revision of the curriculum was carried out in 2003 through 2005, with the support of the National Science Foundation Grant No. ESI 0137414.

National Science Foundation
Opinions expressed are those of the authors
and not necessarily those of the Foundation.

deLange, J.,van Reeuwijk, M., Feijs, E., Middleton, J. A., and Pligge, M. A. (2006). *Figuring all the angles*. In Wisconsin Center for Education Research & Freudenthal Institute (Eds.), Mathematics in Context. Chicago: Encyclopædia Britannica, Inc.

ISBN 0-03-039622-0

1 2 3 4 5 6   073   09 08 07 06 05

The *Mathematics in Context* Development Team

Development 1991–1997

The initial version of *Figuring All the Angles* was developed by Jan deLange, Martin van Reeuwijk, and Els Feijs. It was adapted for use in American schools by James A. Middleton, and Margaret A. Pligge.

Wisconsin Center for Education

Research Staff

Thomas A. Romberg
Director

Joan Daniels Pedro
Assistant to the Director

Gail Burrill
Coordinator

Margaret R. Meyer
Coordinator

Project Staff

Jonathan Brendefur	Fae Dremock
Laura Brinker	James A. Middleton
James Browne	Jasmina Milinkovic
Jack Burrill	Margaret A. Pligge
Rose Byrd	Mary C. Shafer
Peter Christiansen	Julia A. Shew
Barbara Clarke	Aaron N. Simon
Doug Clarke	Marvin Smith
Beth R. Cole	Stephanie Z. Smith
Mary Ann Fix	Mary S. Spence
Sherian Foster	

Freudenthal Institute Staff

Jan de Lange
Director

Els Feijs
Coordinator

Martin van Reeuwijk
Coordinator

Mieke Abels	Jansie Niehaus
Nina Boswinkel	Nanda Querelle
Frans van Galen	Anton Roodhardt
Koeno Gravemeijer	Leen Streefland
Marja van den Heuvel-Panhuizen	
Jan Auke de Jong	Adri Treffers
Vincent Jonker	Monica Wijers
Ronald Keijzer	Astrid de Wild
Martin Kindt	

Revision 2003–2005

The revised version of *Figuring All The Angles* was developed by Els Feijs and Jan de Lange. It was adapted for use in American Schools by Margaret A. Pligge.

Wisconsin Center for Education

Research Staff

Thomas A. Romberg
Director

David C. Webb
Coordinator

Gail Burrill
Editorial Coordinator

Margaret A. Pligge
Editorial Coordinator

Project Staff

Sarah Ailts	Margaret R. Meyer
Beth R. Cole	Anne Park
Erin Hazlett	Bryna Rappaport
Teri Hedges	Kathleen A. Steele
Karen Hoiberg	Ana C. Stephens
Carrie Johnson	Candace Ulmer
Jean Krusi	Jill Vettrus
Elaine McGrath	

Freudenthal Institute Staff

Jan de Lange
Director

Truus Dekker
Coordinator

Mieke Abels
Content Coordinator

Monica Wijers
Content Coordinator

Arthur Bakker	Nathalie Kuijpers
Peter Boon	Huub Nilwik
Els Feijs	Sonia Palha
Dédé de Haan	Nanda Querelle
Martin Kindt	Martin van Reeuwijk

Cover photo credits: (left to right) © Comstock Images; © Corbis; © Getty Images

Illustrations
1 James Alexander; **8, 9** Holly Cooper-Olds; **26** Jerry Kraus/© Encyclopædia Britannica, Inc.; **34** © Encyclopædia Britannica, Inc.

Photographs
3 © Corbis; **4** © Charles E. Rotkin/Corbis; **14** © Corbis; **17** © Roger Ressmeyer/Corbis; **21** (top) © Tim Boyle/Newsmaker/Getty Images; (bottom) © PhotoLink/PhotoDisc/Getty Images; **23** ImageGap/Alamy; **26** © Corbis; **28** © PhotoDisc/Getty Images; **30** © Corbis; **42** (top) Historic Urban Plans, Inc.; (bottom) Design Pics; **43** ©PhotoDisc/Getty Images

◆ Contents

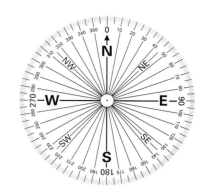

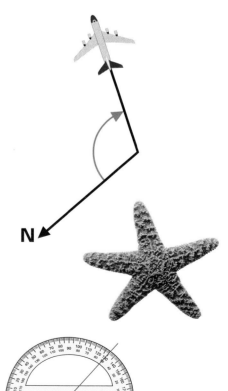

Dear Student,

Welcome to the unit *Figuring All the Angles*.

In this unit, you will learn how planes and boats navigate their way around the globe. You will build upon the cardinal directions of north, east, south, and west to give a better indication of where you want to go.

Along the way, you will pay close attention to the turns made along a route. Turns relate to angles, and you will use these to solve some geometry problems involving shapes.

Sincerely,

The Mathematics in Context Development Team

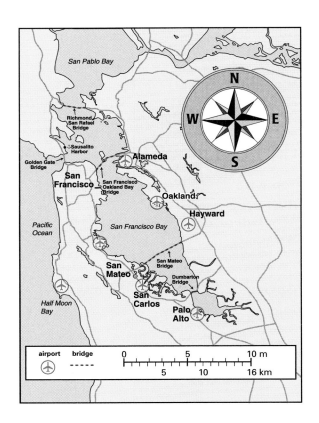

A Sense of Direction

Getting Your Sense of Direction

1. Point toward north. Is everyone in your class pointing in the same **direction**?

2. **a.** Sketch a top view of your classroom. Include the desktops in your sketch. Draw an arrow pointing north on each of the desks.

   b. Do all the arrows point in the same direction?

   c. Will lines from the arrows ever meet?

3. In what direction is south?

4. The position of the sun in the sky is related to the direction south. Record the sun's position in the sky before noon, at noon, and after noon.

5. In which direction from the classroom is your school's playground?

6. Name a town about 50 miles away and point in the direction of that town. Describe this direction.

7. If you traveled north from your school, which towns would you pass through?

Use a compass to answer problems 8 and 9.

8. **a.** Sketch the room where you sleep. Be sure to include windows in your sketch.

   b. Designate where north is in the sketch.

9. Compare the sketches of all the students in your class. Count how many of the windows in the sketches face south.

Here is a partial map of the United States to answer the next questions.

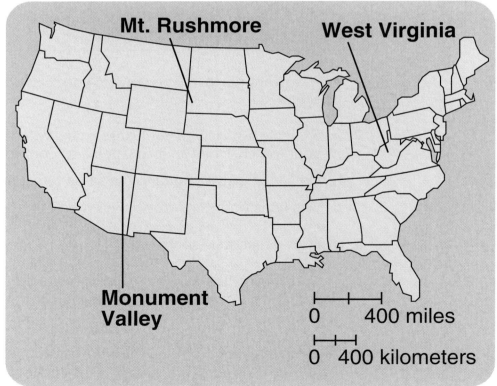

Monument Valley, in Arizona, has many spires and mesas that did not erode as fast as the land around them. You may have seen the picture above in Western movies. Western movies often describe how the West was settled.

10. Why is the West called the West?

On one side of Mount Rushmore, the heads of four United States presidents have been carved out of the mountain. Mount Rushmore is located in South Dakota.

11. Is South Dakota in the South? Why is it called South Dakota?

You have probably read about the North Pole.

12. Explain why the word *North* in North Pole has a different meaning from *West* in West Virginia. (West Virginia is labeled on the partial map of the United States on page 2.)

The state capitol of Wisconsin is located in Madison. The capitol building is unusual because of the four identical wings radiating from the huge central dome.

The four wings of the building point in the four compass directions: north, south, east, and west.

The south wing is indicated in the drawing below.

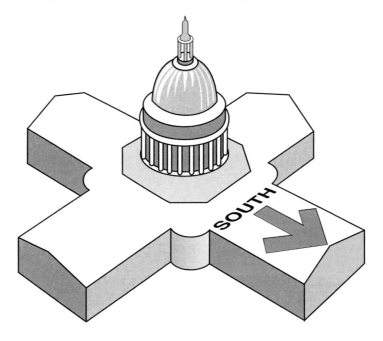

13. Label the directions of the remaining three wings on **Student Activity Sheet 1**.

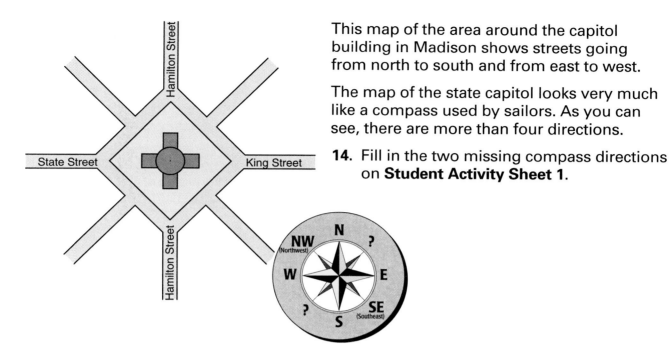

This map of the area around the capitol building in Madison shows streets going from north to south and from east to west.

The map of the state capitol looks very much like a compass used by sailors. As you can see, there are more than four directions.

14. Fill in the two missing compass directions on **Student Activity Sheet 1**.

In Madison, many streets do not run north–south or east–west.

15. Explain why some of the roads in Madison are going southwest–northeast instead of north–south or east–west?

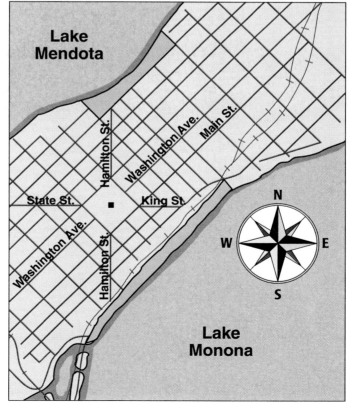

A Sense of Direction

Summary

North, south, east, and west are directions you can use to find places on a map and in the real world. You can combine them to be more specific; for example, you can say northeast, northwest, southeast, and southwest.

Directions are relative. For example, South Dakota is not in the South, but it is south of North Dakota. West Virginia is in the eastern United States, but it is west of Virginia.

Check Your Work

The North Pole is a unique place on earth.

1. Why is it unique? Name another unique place on earth.

2. How would you describe the positions of Hawaii and Alaska relative to the United States mainland?

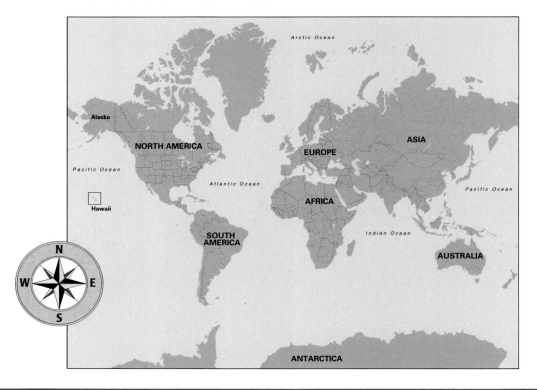

3. How would you describe the position of South America in relation to Europe?

4. Describe the position of South America relative to Australia.

 For Further Reflection

Name at least five more locations—inside or outside the US—with names that relate to compass directions.

Finding Your Way

Sunray (1850)

Small towns often develop along a single road. In Sunray, the first road was called Main Street. Like many towns, Sunray developed in the mid–1800s, when the population of the United States was shifting from the East to the West.

Soon the city expanded and needed more streets. New streets were built either **parallel** or **perpendicular** to Main Street. The roads perpendicular to Main Street were called avenues.

1. Draw a map of Sunray with three streets north of Main Street, two streets south of Main Street, two avenues west of Lincoln Avenue, and three avenues east of Lincoln Avenue.

2. **a.** Why is it convenient to have the avenues run north–south when the streets run east–west?

   b. How are the streets named in the town where you go to school?

Sunray (1900)

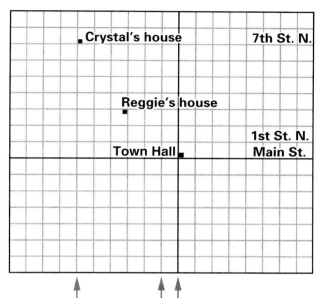

Sunray has grown. It has many streets and avenues. The plan of the city looks like a grid—a combination of horizontal and vertical lines.

Crystal lives at the corner of 7th Street North and 6th Avenue West. Reggie lives at the corner of 3rd Street North and 3rd Avenue West.

Use a copy of this grid on **Student Activity Sheet 2** to help you answer the problems below.

3. Crystal and Reggie are friends. If Crystal wants to visit Reggie at his house, how many blocks will she have to walk?

Crystal and Reggie plan to meet each other for lunch. They like both Tony's Tortellini on the corner of Main Street and 7th Avenue West and Ella's Deli on 5th Street North and Lincoln Avenue.

4. Which restaurant is closer to their homes?

The city will build a theater three blocks south of Main Street. The contractor has a choice of different building sites, all between 3rd Avenue East and 5th Avenue West.

5. a. How far (in number of blocks) from Crystal's house could the theater be built?

 b. Which location would be closest to Crystal's house?

Sunray Today

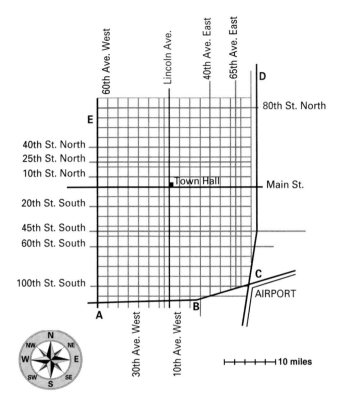

Here is a map of Sunray as it looks now.

You will now use a **scale line** on a map to find a distance. Many maps have scale lines. The scale line on the map of Sun Ray shows 10 miles.

6. On the map's scale, what distance is indicated by each hatch mark?

Use the map on **Student Activity Sheet 3** to solve the following problems. Save this for later use.

The baseball stadium lies exactly 7 miles south of Town Hall.

7. Draw the stadium on the map. Use the scale line and a ruler.

The coliseum is 10 miles northwest of Town Hall. The park is 12 miles southeast of Town Hall. The mall is 3 miles southwest of intersection E. All of these distances are *as the crow flies*.

8. a. What does *as the crow flies* mean?

   b. Mark the positions of the buildings on the map.

When you travel around the city, you follow the roads and do not usually travel as the crow flies. Distances that follow the lines of a map grid or roads are often called **taxicab distances**.

9. Explain why distances on a grid are called taxicab distances.

10. How far do you have to drive to go from the mall to Town Hall?

11. List at least three buildings that you might want to build in Sunray. Locate these buildings on **Student Activity Sheet 3**. Write directions for each of your buildings. Use any information available except street names. Give your directions to a classmate to see if he or she can locate the positions of your buildings on the map.

Downtown Provo, Utah

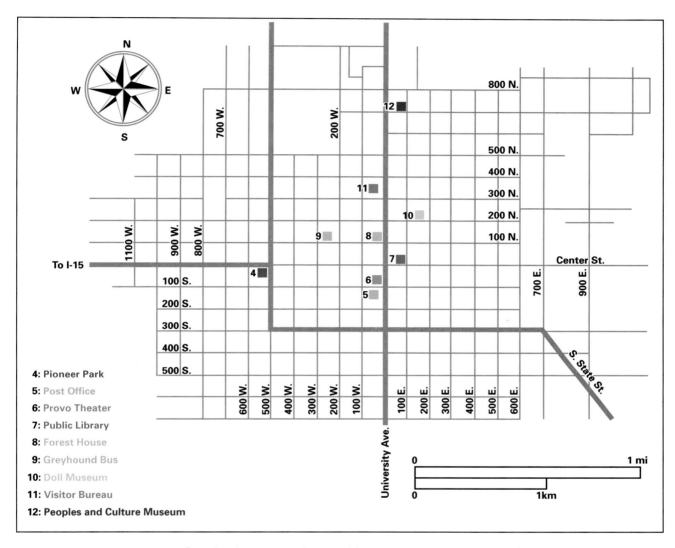

4: Pioneer Park
5: Post Office
6: Provo Theater
7: Public Library
8: Forest House
9: Greyhound Bus
10: Doll Museum
11: Visitor Bureau
12: Peoples and Culture Museum

12. Study the map above. How are the systems of naming streets alike for Sunray and Provo? How are they different?

The Greyhound Bus Station is number 9 on the map. A passenger has just arrived at the bus station. He needs directions to the Visitor Bureau.

13. Give him directions.

At the Peoples and Culture Museum (number 12), someone tells a tourist that Pioneer Park (number 4) is about a half hour's walk directly southwest of the museum.

14. Do you agree? Why or why not?

B   Finding Your Way

Summary ⟫

Sometimes streets and avenues in a city are named so that residents and visitors can find places easily. Some cities have east–west streets and north–south avenues. For example, 5th Avenue West and 3rd Street North identify the exact location on a map or in a city. Distances can be measured as taxicab distances or as the crow flies.

Many maps have scale lines. A scale line tells you how distances are represented on the map.

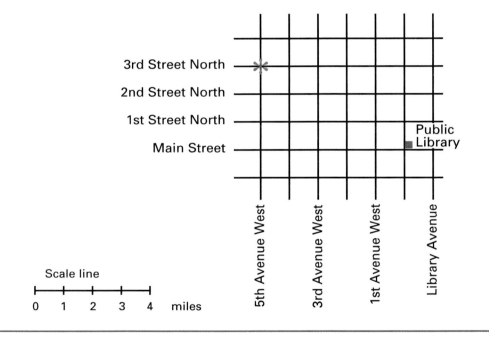

Check Your Work ⟫⟫

1. a. Draw a map of a town that has Town Hall in the center and eight main roads leading from the center in the directions N, S, E, W, NW, NE, SW, and SE.

    b. How is the map of Sunray different from the town you just drew?

2. Would taxicab distances on a street–avenue system be the same as distances measured as the crow flies? Explain.

3. Use **Student Activity Sheet 3** to solve the following problems.

   a. How far is the "as the crow flies" distance from A to E on the map of Sunray?

   b. How far is the "taxicab" distance from A to E on the map of Sunray?

   c. How far is the "as the crow flies" distance from A to D on the map of Sunray?

   d. How far is the "taxicab" distance from A to D on the map of Sunray?

 For Further Reflection

Use a map of the town or city you live in.

Give an example of a place you can go to from your house in which the taxicab distance and the distance as the crow flies are the same.

Give another example in which the taxicab distance is larger.

Estimate the distances using the map's scale.

Directions

San Francisco Bay Area

San Francisco is a city on the west coast of California.

Here is a map of the San Francisco Bay area.

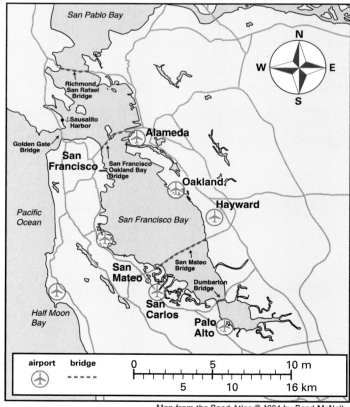

Map from the Road Atlas © 1994 by Rand McNally.

Use **Student Activity Sheet 4** to answer the problems below. Save this activity sheet for later use.

1. A plane starts at San Carlos Airport and flies due west. Over which airport will the plane soon pass?

2. Another plane starts at San Carlos Airport and flies northwest. Over which airport will the plane fly first?

3. In which direction should a pilot fly to go from Hayward to Palo Alto?

The eight main directions, shown in the table below, are not precise enough to describe a flight from San Carlos Airport to Hayward. Your teacher will give you a transparent **compass card**. You will use the compass card to describe the flight using **degrees**.

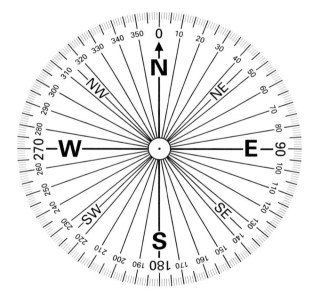

Compass Direction	Course (in degrees)
North	
Northeast	
East	
Southeast	
South	
Southwest	
West	
Northwest	

On the compass card, there are numbers associated with each direction.

- the direction north is the same as zero degrees (0°),
- east is 90°,
- south is 180°,
- and west is 270°.

4. Copy and complete the table above in your notebook.

5. Why would using the compass card with 360° be better for navigation than using just eight directions?

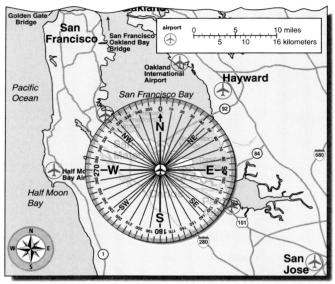

Map from the Road Atlas © 1994 by Rand McNally.

Here is a way to set a **course** from San Carlos Airport to Hayward Airport.

First, put the center of the compass card on San Carlos Airport. Make sure that N is pointing north.

Second, place a ruler from the center of the compass card to Hayward Airport.

Third, read the degree mark at the edge of the compass card. It is about 37°. This is called a **heading**.

6. Use your compass card to determine the heading a pilot would fly to go from Oakland International Airport to Palo Alto.

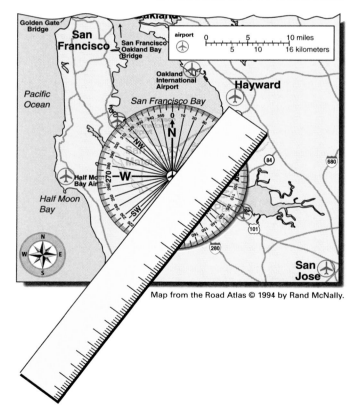

Map from the Road Atlas © 1994 by Rand McNally.

Two pilots planned flights from San Carlos to Oakland. Luiz, the first pilot, said, "It's exactly to the north." Ann, the other pilot, disagreed; she would fly at a heading of 10°.

7. Who is right?

They both arrived at Oakland Airport, but one pilot got there earlier than the other. They had to fly back after a short break. Luiz said, "I don't have to measure the heading back to San Carlos Airport. It is a heading of 190°."

8. Do you agree with Luiz? Explain your reasoning.

Captain Aziz and First Mate Mamphono are boating off the coast of California. They are located south of Half Moon Bay. They want to go to Sausalito Harbor.

9. Use **Student Activity Sheet 4** to draw a route to Sausalito Harbor. Use only straight lines. Give the heading for each leg of the route.

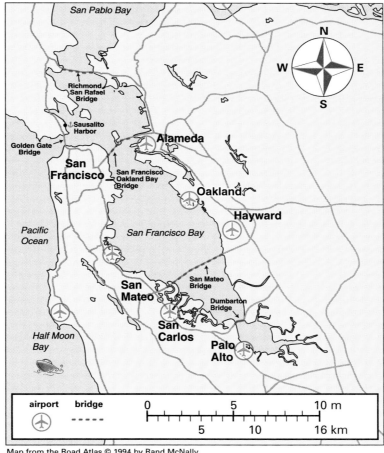

Map from the Road Atlas © 1994 by Rand McNally.

You can sail to Sausalito using many different headings.

After arriving in Sausalito, Captain Aziz says, "I used only three different headings."

10. Is this possible? Explain.

Sun Island

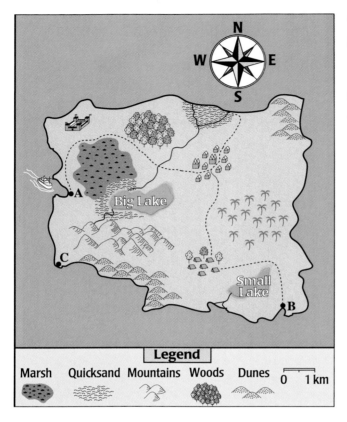

You and your friend are planning to hike on Sun Island. Use your compass card and a ruler to draw the paths described on the left. Use the map on **Student Activity Sheet 5**.

Your Trip

- Dock your boat at Harbor A.

- Walk north 2 km.

- Now walk due east to the closest edge of the woods.

- Now turn to a 160° heading.

- When you get to the river, swim across it.

- At the eastern bank of the river, head 70° for 1.7 km and have a snack.

- Head 210° to get to the mountains.

- At the foot of the first mountain, you can rest. This is the end of your trip.

Your Friends Trip

- Dock your boat at Harbor A.

- Walk south 1 km.

- From there, walk to the coast and travel along the coast to point C.

- Now plot a heading 60° and walk nearly 2.5 km, being careful to avoid the quicksand.

- Turn due east and walk 4 km to your destination.

11. a. How far did you travel?

   b. How far did your friend travel?

When both of you have completed your trips, you decide to visit your friend.

12. Draw the route and estimate the distance you need to travel to reach your friend.

Here are five planes traveling in different directions.

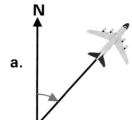

a.

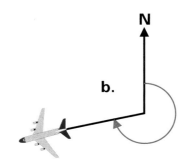

b.

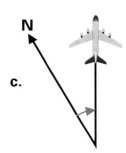

c.

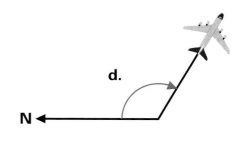

d.

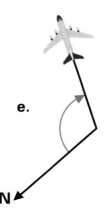

e.

13. Which of these planes has the largest heading?

14. How many degrees apart are the following compass directions?

   a. north and east

   b. west and northeast

   c. south and southwest

   d. east and west

◆G Directions

Summary ✖

Together with distances, you can use headings to plot courses. You measure a heading in degrees to the right from the direction north.

You can use your compass card to plot courses using degrees. North is 0°, east is 90°, south is 180°, and west is 270°.

Directions using degrees can be more accurate than the eight main directions. Degrees divide a circle into 360 parts, while the main directions divide a circle into only eight parts.

Check Your Work ▶▶

1. What heading would you take to fly a plane from San Francisco to Salt Lake City, Utah?

2. Describe the headings pictured below.

 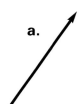 

3. Draw a heading of 215°.

◼ For Further Reflection

Describe how you can find the headings opposite to a heading of 45°, 315°, 120°, and 180°.

Navigation and Orientation

Traffic Control

Some airports are very busy.

At Chicago's O'Hare International Airport, more than one plane lands and takes off every minute! During bad weather, this busy schedule leads to long lines of airplanes waiting for runways and many flight delays.

The traffic control takes place in a tower. Air traffic controllers try to organize traffic so that progress is smooth and travel is safe.

The air traffic controller is at work behind her circular radar screen. The airport tower is at the center of the circle. All the other dots are planes that are leaving or approaching the airport.

The screen looks like your compass card, only it has circles to show how far planes are from the airport.

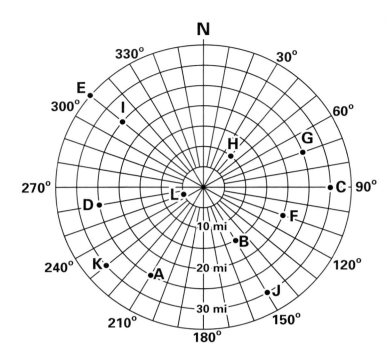

Here is a copy of such a radar screen. This type of grid is called a **circular** or **polar grid**.

On this circular grid, the distance between each circle is 5 miles. Plane G, for instance, is 25 miles from the tower, in the compass direction of 70°.

The notation 70°/25 miles describes the location of plane G on a polar grid.

The information from this radar screen is also on **Student Activity Sheet 6**.

1. Which planes are in the same direction from the airport?

2. Which planes are at the same distance from the airport?

3. In your notebook, make a list of the airplanes and their locations as indicated on the radar screen. Your list should be similar to the list below.

Plane	Monitor
G	70°/25 miles

A little later, the planes are in different locations.

Plane A   moved 10 miles closer to the airport.

Plane B   moved 5 miles farther away from the airport.

Plane C   is the same distance from the airport; but exactly north.

Plane L   landed.

Plane I   was told to go to a position of 270° at 25 miles, but is only halfway there.

Plane G   is at 50°, 35 miles away.

4. Draw new positions for these planes on the radar screen on **Student Activity Sheet 6**.

In Section B you used a coordinate system called the **rectangular grid**.

5. Explain the difference between a circular or polar grid and a rectangular grid. You may give examples.

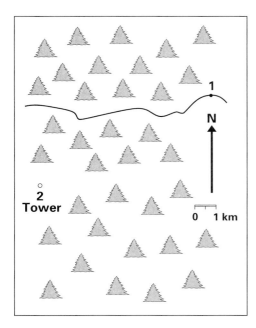

There is a big fire in the Australian capital, Canberra. Chris is at location 1 on the map above. He phones his friend Tarin, who is at location 2. Chris says that he sees smoke in the direction 100°. Tarin says that from her vantage point, the smoke is at 40°.

6. Use **Student Activity Sheet 7** to locate the fire.

A plane has disappeared in a high forest. A ranger, in his jeep on the road at location number 1 says he saw the plane disappear in the direction 200°.

The pilot's last report was that she saw the tower (location 2) in the direction west.

7. Where would you suggest that the rescuers look for the plane? Mark the place on the map on **Student Activity Sheet 7**.

Summary

Air traffic controllers use a polar grid system to identify the locations of planes.

The system consists of two numbers:

- a compass direction expressed in degrees and
- a distance expressed in miles or kilometers.

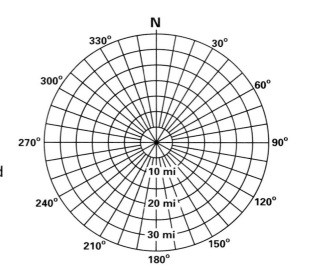

A polar grid is different from a rectangular "city" grid. It has a central point from which the "roads" go in all directions, just like the degree lines on the compass card.

A flight controller describes a plane's location as 90°/15 miles. This means the plane is located directly east of the airport at a distance of 15 miles from the airport.

Check Your Work

One plane is at 90°/15 miles. Another plane is at 90°/35 miles.

1. What is the distance between the planes?

One plane is at 90°/15 miles. Another plane is at 270°/15 miles.

2. What is the distance between the planes?

3. You are a fire fighter who needs to report a forest fire. Name any advantages or disadvantages for each of the following reporting systems.

   a. A compass direction: N, S, E, W, NW, SE, etc.

   b. A compass direction or heading: for example 210°.

   c. A distance and a compass direction or heading: for example 10 miles in direction 130°.

 For Further Reflection

Suppose you have information about two positions on a map (A and B) and their direction to an unknown position. Explain how you can find this position. Make a drawing and add the directions from A and B.

Changing Directions: Turns

Flight Instructions

A pilot uses many instruments to fly a plane safely.

Above is a picture of a heading indicator. It shows the plane heading roughly in a northern direction. The heading indicator looks different from your compass card.

On the heading indicator, the 3 means 30°, the 6 means 60°, and so forth.

1. According to this instrument, at what heading is the plane flying?

A pilot is in radio contact with the control tower. Here is the conversation between the air traffic controller and the pilots.

Conversation	Drawing

Traffic Control:
    Okay. Flight 42.
    What is your heading? Over.
 	
Pilot Flight 42:
    Our heading will be three-five
    degrees. Over.
	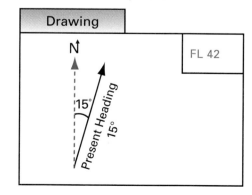

2. What is meant by "one-five" degrees?

Note that the heading is always relative to the north N.

The conversation continues as follows.

Conversation	Drawing

Traffic Control:
    Okay. Flight 42.
    Make your new heading
    three-five degrees. Over.
 	
Pilot Flight 42:
    Our heading will be
    thirty-five degrees. Over.
	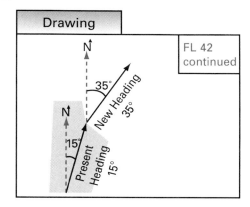

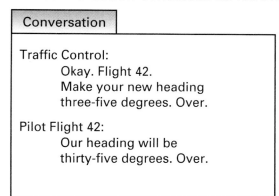

3. Explain how the conversation and the drawing relate to each other.

4. On **Student Activity Sheet 8**, complete the empty boxes with an appropriate drawing or conversation.

a.

Conversation	Drawing

Traffic Control:
    Hello Flight 72.
    What's your present heading.
    Over.
 	
Pilot Flight 72:
    Our heading is seven-five
    degrees. Over.
	FL 72

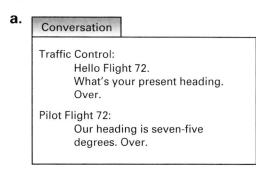 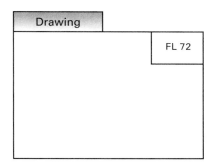

b.

Conversation	Drawing
Traffic Control: Pilot Flight 72:	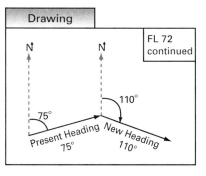

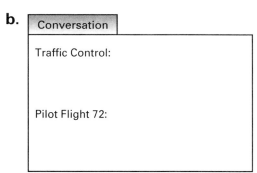

c. Conversation continued with Flight 72 from problem b.

Conversation	Drawing

Traffic Control:
    Okay. Flight 72.
    Make your new heading
    two-five degrees. Over.
 	
Pilot Flight 72:
    Our new heading will be
    two-five degrees. Over.
	FL 72
	continued

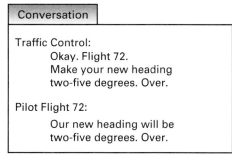 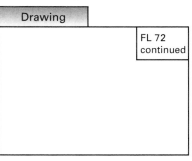

Changing Directions: Turns

The following conversation was taped:

Traffic Control:	Flight 33, what is your present heading?
Pilot FL 33:	Flight 33 heading six-five degrees.
	later...
Traffic Control:	Flight 33, make it three-three-zero.
Pilot FL 33:	Three-three-zero.
	later...
Traffic Control:	Flight 33, make it two-four-zero this time.
Pilot FL 33:	Two-four-zero for Flight 33.

5. Make a drawing of a possible flight path of Flight 33.

In order to change directions the planes have to make a *turn*.

Flight 18 is changing its direction (heading) from 60° to 70°.

Flight 31 is changing its direction (heading) from 45° to 15°.

Flight 73 is changing its direction (heading) from 180° to 210°.

6. Which flight makes the largest turn? And which one makes the smallest turn? How do you know?

The turn is the change between the old and the new heading; turns can go "left" or "right."

Remember that headings are always fixed, relative to the north N (0°).

7. a. Give three examples of turns of 25°.
Be sure to name two headings for each turn.

  b. Give three examples of turns to the right of 40°.

  c. Give three examples of turns to the left of 60°.

You can show turns by comparing the two headings. Consider again Flight 42.

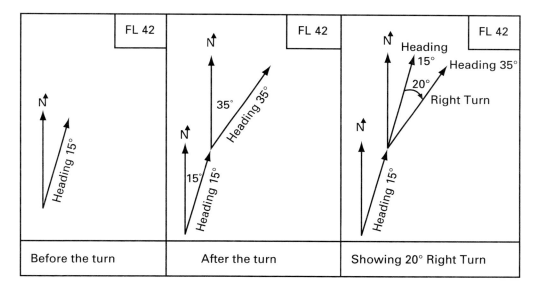

| Before the turn | After the turn | Showing 20° Right Turn |

8. Make a similar drawing showing the first turn for Flight 72. (See problem 4b.)

9. Make a similar drawing showing all the turns for Flight 33. (See problem 5.)

A plane can make left or right turns. It is not always possible to find the total turn by adding up the two individual turns. For example, if a captain first makes a right turn of 45° and then a left turn of 30°, the total turn is only 15° to the right. If he first makes a turn of 45° to the right and then another turn of 30° to the right, the result is a turn of 75° to the right.

A pilot was bothered that the air traffic controller asked her to make so many turns on approach.

"First they made me turn 30° to the right, then 20° to the left, then 15° to the left, then 10° to the right. Finally, I had to make a 5° turn to the left."

10. Explain why the pilot was so irritated.

A pilot made the following turns in this order: 20° right, 40° left, 45° left, 30° right, 10° left, 60° right. The original heading was 330°.

11. What was the heading after all the turns were made?

Plane Landing Activity

Clear an area in your classroom and designate an airport location. Choose three students to act out a scenario. One student acts as the pilot of an airplane, one acts as the flight engineer, and the other is the traffic controller.

The traffic controller gives the pilot a series of headings, one at a time. After each heading is given, the flight engineer tells the pilot how to turn. The pilot follows the directions and simulates the path of the flight by walking on the classroom floor. The rest of the class should use their compass cards to draw the path the plane follows to the airport.

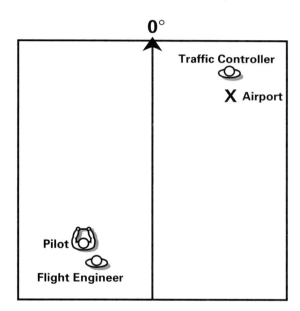

Here is a possible scenario. The pilot reports the plane's heading:

Pilot: Flight 165 heading zero degrees.

The traffic controller requests a new heading:

Traffic Controller: O.K., 165. Make your new heading nine-zero degrees.

The flight engineer directs the plane to make a turn:

Flight Engineer: Turn nine-zero degrees to the right.

The pilot walks three steps in the new direction. The flight engineer should use masking tape to keep a record of the plane's path on the floor.

The goal is to reach the airport, but not necessarily in the most direct way. After the exercise, discuss the flight path, paying attention to the headings and turns. Other members of the class may take over as pilot, flight engineer, or traffic controller and the entire process can begin again.

Changing Directions: Turns

Summary

If you change from one direction or heading to another, you make a turn. Turns can be made to the right or to the left.

For example, if you change from a heading of 30° to a heading of 45°, you make a turn of 15° to the right.

The heading is always relative to North N, or 0°.

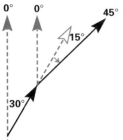

Check Your Work

1. You are traveling at a heading of 200°. Next you turn 40° to the left, and then 20° to the right. What is your new heading?

2. You are traveling at a heading of 100°. Next you turn 45° to the left. Then you make another turn. The result is now a heading of 60°. Describe the second turn.

3. You are flying at a heading of 180°. Next the controller tells you to fly 160° and then finally 180°. Make a drawing representing this part of the flight.

For Further Reflection

In air traffic control and harbor control, the turns to be made are usually relatively small. However, sometimes an air traffic controller will give the following instruction: "Make a (turn of) 360° to the right."

1. What will the new heading be?

2. Why should an air traffic controller make a pilot turn 360°?

From Turns to Angles

Sled Tracks

A sled got lost in the darkness of a polar night. Rescue volunteers received "Mayday" calls throughout the night, but darkness and extreme weather conditions prohibited a search. The next morning, rescue planes searched the area. Here are sled tracks one pilot saw from his plane.

1. Use turns to describe the route of the sled as if you had been on it.

2. If the sled continued in the same way, it might have returned to the starting point. How many turns would the sled have had to make to return to the starting point?

3. How many degrees was the turn each time?

Most of the time in this unit you have been a pilot, a captain, or someone who was in charge of making turns (to change directions).

However, if you are an observer looking at the sled tracks or the path of a plane or boat, you are looking at an angle.

For example:

Turn 30°

The drawing on the left shows the sled tracks after the driver made a 30° right turn in the snow. When the sled is gone, all that remains is the angle. You can identify the angle by marking it.

Angle

or more schematic:

Every time two track sleds intersect, they form an angle. Here is a drawing of an angle formed by two tracks from the lost sled.

You can refer to the angle as "angle A" and write: $\angle A$ (or say, "angle A").

A

In problem 3, you found the turn that was necessary to make the sled tracks. You also know that $\angle A = 150°$.

4. Describe the relation between the sled turn and $\angle A$ that is formed by the sled tracks.

5. a. Draw an angle that measures 120°.

   b. Draw $\angle B$ so that $\angle B = 90°$.

   c. Draw $\angle C$ so that $\angle C = 60°$.

In problem 2, you found out that you have to make 12 turns of 30° to be back in the original direction. The result of all the turning is 360°. (12 × 30° = 360°).

6. Explain this reasoning.

Regular Polygons

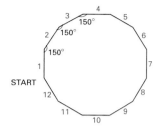

The drawing on the left shows all the sled tracks made when the driver returns to his original starting point. The figure formed is a polygon. Because it has twelve sides, it is called a 12-gon.

There are also 12 angles on the inside, each of them measuring 150°.

Angles inside the polygon are called **interior angles**.

7. What is the sum of all the 12 interior angles of a 12-gon?

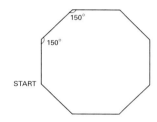

Consider an 8-gon, or octagon, formed by sled tracks made using 8 equal turns.

8. **a.** What is the size (in degrees) of one of the turns the sled driver made?

b. What is the size (in degrees) of one of the interior angles?

c. What is the sum of all 8 interior angles of this octagon?

Here are some regular polygons. All of the sides have the same length.

| 3-gon Triangle | 4-gon Square | 5-gon Pentagon | 6-gon Hexagon | 8-gon Octagon |

9. Copy the following table in your notebook and complete it. You can use the polygons above to help you reason about the size of the angles. If you have trouble, imagine the polygons are sled tracks. How large is each turn? You might want to think about the size of the equal turns.

Name	Triangle	Square				12-gon
Number of Angles	3	4	5			
Measure of One Interior Angle	60°				135°	
Sum of All Interior Angles	180°		540°			1800°

10. What is the sum of the interior angles of a 36-gon? It might help to think of the measurement of the 36 equal turns that are necessary to produce a 36-gon.

From Turns to Angles

Summary

If you are a pilot, captain, or sled driver, you are in charge of setting the course and making turns to change directions (headings).

For example, if your heading is 60° and you make a turn to the left of 20°, your new heading will be 40°.

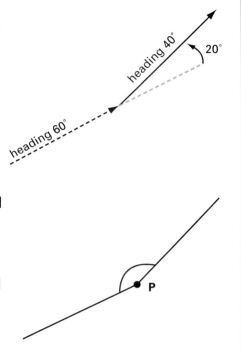

You can also observe the flight path of a plane or boat or sled. The turns are not visible. All that remains are the sled tracks and the angle formed between the two legs of the track.

For example, here is an angle formed by two sled tracks. The angle is marked with the letter P designating the vertex.

You can write: ∠P and say: "angle P."

If you know the measure of the turn, you can figure out the measure of the angle: in this case ∠P 160°.

If you know the measure of the angle, you know the measure of the turn.

Check Your Work

1. **a.** Your present heading is 50°. You make a 90° turn to the right. What is your new heading?

    b. Explain the answer to problem 1a with a drawing of the two headings.

    c. Use your drawing from 1b to find out the measurement of the angle between the two legs of the track.

2. Here is a drawing of ∠Q, which is 130°, showing the final heading of 0°. What was the initial heading?

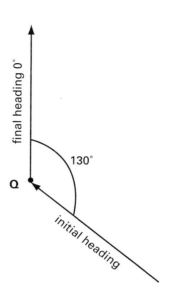

3. With an initial heading of 180°, a sled makes four equal turns. Each turn is 15° to the right.

   a. What is the final heading?

   b. What are the angles formed by the sled tracks?

![For Further Reflection]

For Further Reflection

Suppose you make a sequence of turns of 1° to the right and the legs of the track that is formed are all equally long:

   1. What kind of polygon would you get?

   2. What does the polygon resemble?

Angles and Their Measures

Angles

An angle that is very common is an angle of 90°.

   1. Describe some objects that show 90° angles.

   2. Why do you think 90° angles are so important?

Here are some examples of angles measuring 90° or, as they are called, **right angles**.

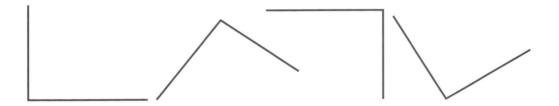

To make sure that we really mean a right angle and not an angle of, say, 89°, we put a special little sign in the corner:

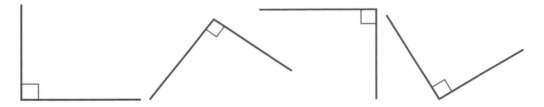

The corner of any angle is called the **vertex**.

The two partial lines or line segments that form the angle are called the **sides** of the angle.

An angle that measures more than 0° and less than 90° is called an **acute angle**. Here are some examples of acute angles.

The mosaic tile below has one right angle and two acute angles.

3. Describe the measures of the acute angles in this tile. It may be helpful to look at the shapes below.

An angle that measures more than 90° but less than 180° is called an **obtuse angle**. Here are some examples of obtuse angles.

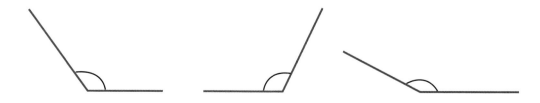

The drawings have a little sign to indicate the angle.

4. For each of the angles below, indicate whether it is right, acute, or obtuse.

a.

b.

c.

d.

e.

f.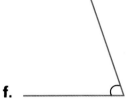

Measures of Angles

The following mosaic tile has three angles of 60°.

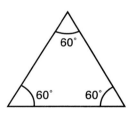

Here is the tile used in problem 3.

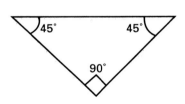

Combining both tiles forms the figure:

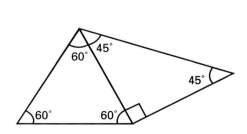

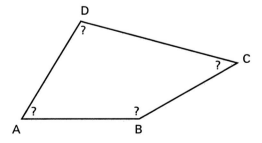

5. **a.** Classify the angles ∠A, ∠B, ∠C, and ∠D according to their size.

   b. Find the measure of each angle.

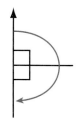

You know there are 360° in one complete turn.

A quarter turn is 90°. There are 90° in a right angle.

Two quarter turns make up a half turn.

A half turn forms an angle of 180°. This angle is a straight angle. It forms a straight line.

To measure angles you can use a compass card or a **protractor**. Here is how you can measure an angle using a protractor.

Place your protractor so that the little hole is on the vertex (or corner) of the angle and the dotted line of your protractor is on one side of the angle.

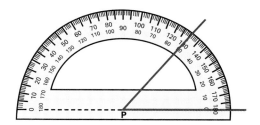

The other side of the angle goes through a number that tells you how many degrees are in the angle.

There are two scales on a protractor. If you align one side of the angle with the 0° and determine whether the angle is acute or obtuse, you won't have a hard time figuring out what is the proper angle measure.

Of the two different angles P and Q shown below, one is clearly is 50°; the other one is 130°.

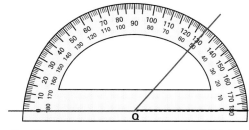

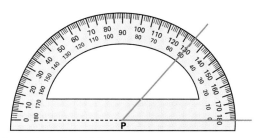

6. Explain which angle is 130° and which is 50°.

Palmanova

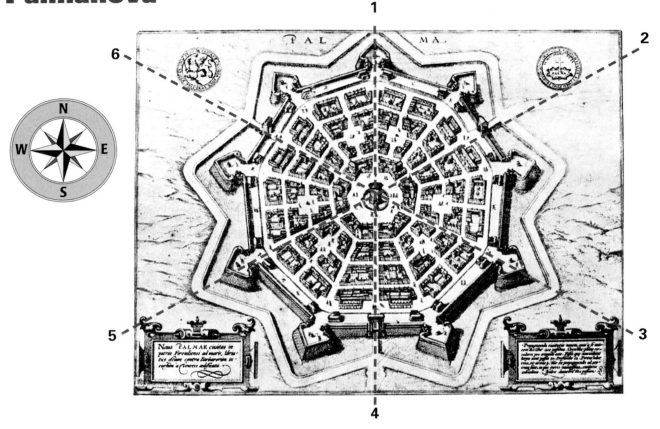

Here is an ancient plan for Palmanova, a 16th-century city in Italy. There are six major roads on the map of Palmanova that extend all the way into the central plaza. These major roads are indicated using numbers 1 through 6.

7. How large is the angle between two adjacent major roads?

There are two smaller roads between two adjacent major roads.

8. How large would the angle between the two smaller roads be?

The city plan of Palmanova has the same structure as a snowflake. The snowflake forms a six-pointed star.

Starfish often form a five-pointed star.

9. About how large is the angle between two adjacent legs of the starfish?

10. Measure each of the following angles.

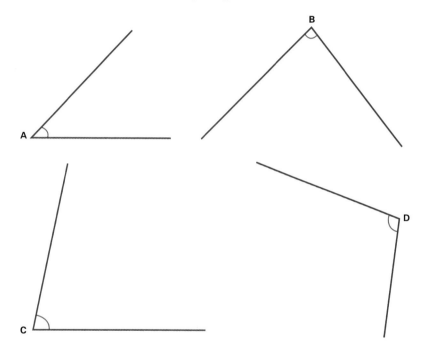

11. a. Measure each of the angles of the following triangles.

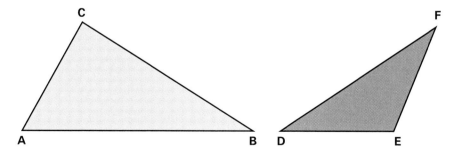

b. For each triangle find the sum of all the angles.

Summary

Angles are formed by two sides and a point where the sides meet: the vertex.

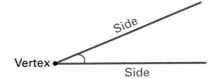

If you give the vertex a name, for example *P*, you call the angle "angle ∠*P*" and write it as ∠*P*.

You can classify angles according to their size:

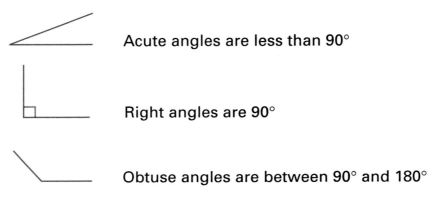

Acute angles are less than 90°

Right angles are 90°

Obtuse angles are between 90° and 180°

A straight angle is 180°

Sometimes you can find the size of an angle by reasoning, sometimes by estimating, and sometimes by measuring. You can measure an angle by using a compass card or a protractor.

1. Measure ∠A, ∠B, and ∠C.

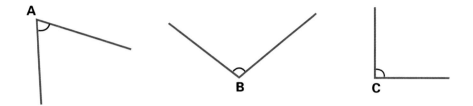

2. **a.** Estimate the size of ∠P, ∠Q, and ∠R.

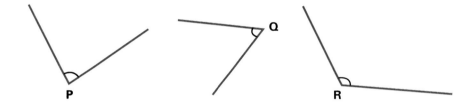

   b. Which angles, if any, are obtuse?

3. Draw an angle of 40° and one of 110°. Label the vertices.

 For Further Reflection

A pilot needs to draw a heading of 330° on her map. She only has a protractor.

1. Explain how she can make this drawing.

2. Describe differences between the compass card and the protractor and the ways you can use them.

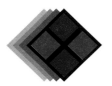
Section Ⓐ A Sense of Direction

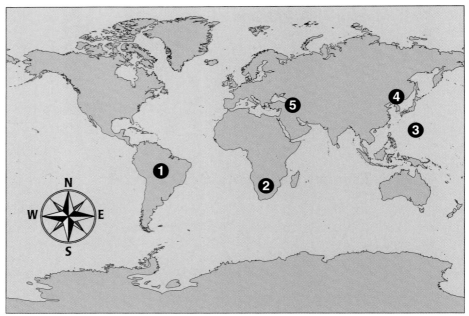

© 1996, Encyclopædia Britannica, Inc.

Use the world map above to answer the following questions.

1. Write the number that corresponds to each of the following places:

> Middle East
>
> South America
>
> South Africa
>
> North Korea
>
> East China Sea

2. How do you think South Africa got its name?

3. In what direction do people from South America have to travel to get to North Korea?

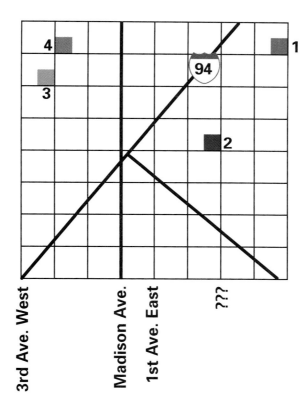

1: Women's Museum
2: Train Station
3: Goldstein Park
4: Water Park

Scale

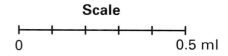

0   0.5 ml

Use the map above to answer the following questions.

1. In what direction does Interstate 94 run?

2. There are question marks by a street name that is missing. Use the given street names to assign an appropriate name for this street. Explain your reasoning.

3. A tourist has arrived at the train station and plans to visit the Women's Museum and Goldstein Park. Give him directions.

4. Use the scale line to find the distance from Women's Museum to Train Station, as the crow flies.

Section G Directions

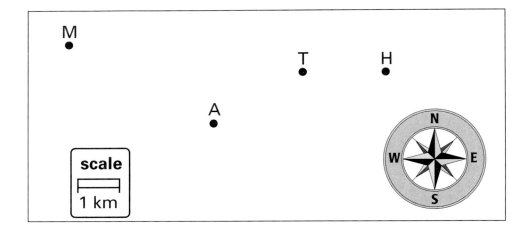

1. Using your compass card and the scale line, write directions to get from point M to point A, to point T, and, finally, to point H. (Directions in degrees, distances in kilometers.)

Section D Navigation and Orientation

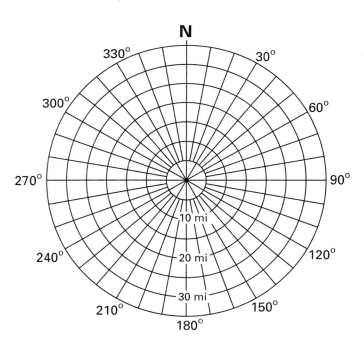

Use the grid to the left to help you answer the following questions.

1. One plane is at 30°/20 miles. Another plane is at 210°/25 miles. What is the distance between the planes?

2. One plane is at 150°/30 miles. Another plane is at 330°/35 miles. What is the distance between the planes?

Section E Changing Directions: Turns

1. Suppose you are traveling at a heading of 126°.

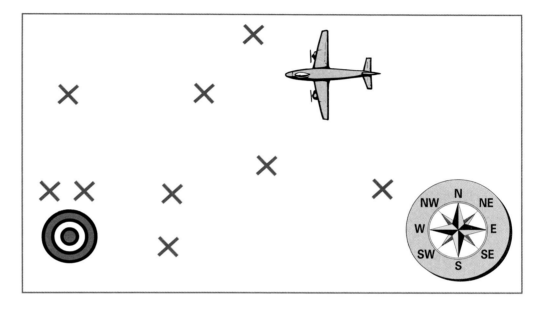

   a. If you turn 98° to the left, what is the new heading?

   b. If you then turn 35° to the right, what is the new heading?

2. Write instructions, using headings or turns, to direct the airplane so that it can drop a parachutist in the target area. Avoid the areas marked with an X; these are dangerous mountains. You do not need to give distances.

Section ◆F◆ From Turns to Angles

1. Here is a top-view drawing of some sled tracks, showing two angles.

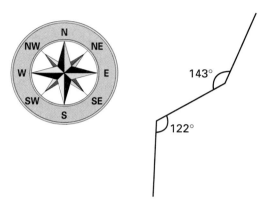

The angles that are known are indicated in the picture.

Which turns did the pilot make (to left or right)?

2. In the star shown below, the heading of leg (1) is 20°. The star is a regular figure. What is the measure of ∠A?

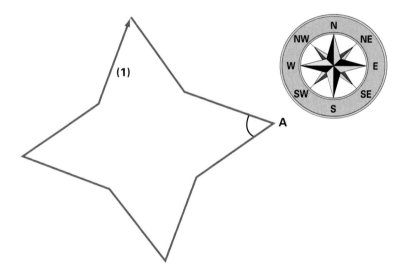

Section G Angles and Their Measures

1. a. How many different right angles are in the picture below?

    b. How many different obtuse angles are in the picture below?

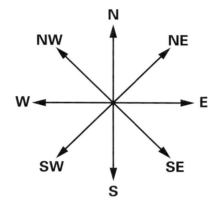

2. Use a protractor to draw an angle of 35°. Properly mark the vertex.

3. Nathalie says, "When it is the same time, the number of degrees between the hands of the clock tower is larger than the number of degrees between the hand on my wristwatch!". Is Nathalie right? Explain your answer.

Here are the mosaic tiles you worked with in Section G on page 40.

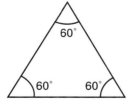

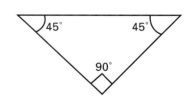

4. Create three new shapes consisting of these two mosaic tiles. Label the size of each angle in your shapes.

Section Ⓐ A Sense of Direction

1. The North Pole is unique because of its fixed position. It is north of every location. Another such unique place is the South Pole.

2. Hawaii is located southwest of the mainland. Alaska is located northwest of the contiguous United States.

3. South America is located southwest of Europe, or Europe is located northeast of South America.

4. South America is located west of Australia, or Australia is located east of South America.

Section Ⓑ Finding Your Way

1. **a.** Here is one possible drawing. Your drawing might be different.

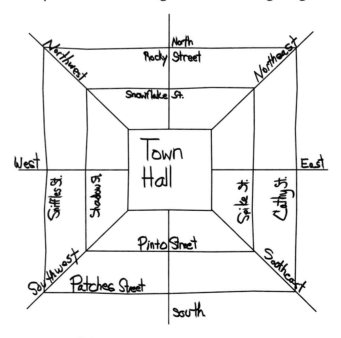

b. Here is one possible response:

In Sunray, all of the blocks are square because there are no streets in the directions NW, NE, SW, SE, and it is easy to find a place if you know its address. In the town I drew, the streets are named after my pets and my friends' pets.

2. Here is one possible response:

Taxicab distances are usually longer than as-the-crow-flies distances. The distances could be the same if you have to go in one direction and a road goes in that direction.

3. a. The distance from A to E "as the crow flies" is about 35 miles.

   b. The "taxicab" distance from A to E is also about 35 miles since you can get there in a straight line, without having to make turns.

   c. The distance from A to D "as the crow flies" is about 55 miles.

   d. The "taxicab" distance from A to D is about 75 miles since you cannot get there in a straight line but will have to make turns.

Section **C** Directions

1. The heading should be about 70°.

2. a. 33°

   b. 110°

3.

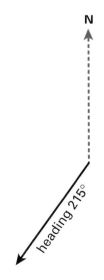

Drawing a dotted line for north may help you make an accurate heading. Don't forget to use your compass card.

Section **D** Navigation and Orientation

1. The distance between the planes is 20 miles.

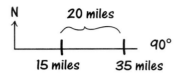

2. The distance between the planes is 30 miles.

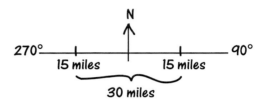

3. The best way to report a fire would be (c); it uses both a heading as well as a distance. There is only one possible location for the fire. Using a compass direction or a heading, (b) is better than (a) because you have at least the exact direction. Both (a) and (b) do not give enough information because you are not given the distance in that direction. You could be wandering in the specified direction for a long time until you found the fire.

Section **E** Changing Directions: Turns

1. The new heading is 180°.

   Here are three solution strategies:

   - Reasoning: left 40°, then right 20° means right 20°. Using a compass card and starting from a 200° heading and turning right 20°, ends up with a 180° heading.

   - Reasoning: 200° minus 40° results in a heading of 160°; then 160° plus 20° results in a heading of 180°.

   - Reasoning by making the drawing shown on the right.

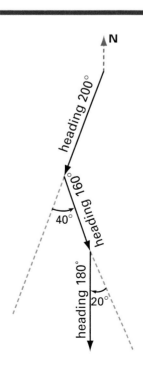

2. The second turn is a turn of 5° to the right.

Here are two solution strategies:

- Reasoning: The first turn results in a new heading of 55°. In order to get a heading of 60°, you have to make a right turn of 5°.

- In a drawing:

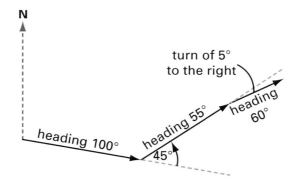

3. Make sure you start your drawing with a line directing north. Use your compass card.

Note that the length of the lines in your drawing may differ from those in the sample drawing. The directions, however, should be the same as in the sample drawing.

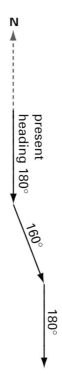

Section **F** From Turns to Angles

1. a. The new heading is 140°.

Here is one solution strategy:

By looking at the compass card, I found that for a right turn I need to add 90° to 50°, which is 140°.

b. Here is the drawing for problem 1a.

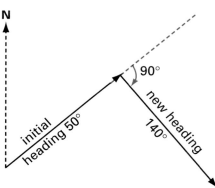

c. The angle between the two legs of the track is 90°.

2. The initial heading was 310°.

Here is one solution strategy:

If ∠*Q* = 130°, then the turn to make a 0° heading has to be 50° to the right.
I used the compass card to see that this would make an initial heading of 310°.

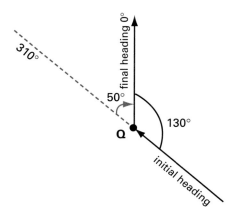

3. **a.** The final heading is 240° (180° + 4 × 15°). This drawing helped me to reason about the four 15° right turns.

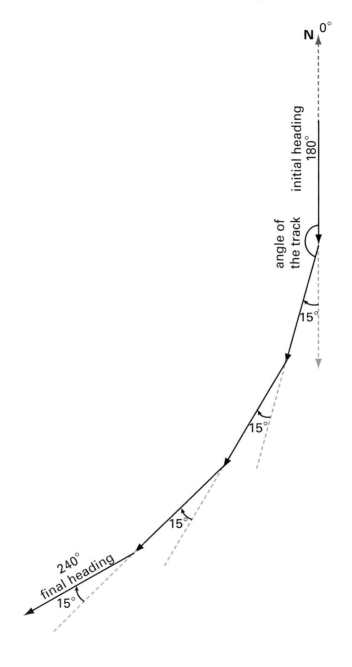

b. The angles formed by the sled are 165° (180° − 15°). Since the turns are equal, the other angles of the track are also 165°.

Section G Angles and Their Measures

1. ∠A is 69°.

   ∠B is 100°.

   ∠C is 90°.

2. **a.** ∠P is less than 90°; it is about 80°.

   ∠Q is between 40° and 90°, so about 60°

   ∠R is between 90° and 180°, so about 120°.

   b. ∠R is an obtuse angle.

3. ∠S = 40°, ∠T = 110°

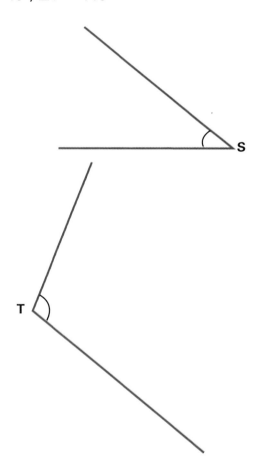

Comparing Quantities

Algebra

BRITANNICA
Mathematics in Context

HOLT, RINEHART AND WINSTON

Mathematics in Context is a comprehensive curriculum for the middle grades.
It was developed in 1991 through 1997 in collaboration with the Wisconsin Center
for Education Research, School of Education, University of Wisconsin-Madison and
the Freudenthal Institute at the University of Utrecht, The Netherlands, with the
support of the National Science Foundation Grant No. 9054928.

The revision of the curriculum was carried out in 2003 through 2005, with the
support of the National Science Foundation Grant No. ESI 0137414.

National Science Foundation
Opinions expressed are those of the authors
and not necessarily those of the Foundation.

Kindt, M., Abels, M., Dekker, T., Meyer, M. R., Pligge M. A., & Burrill, G. (2006).
Comparing Quantities. In Wisconsin Center for Education Research & Freudenthal
Institute (Eds.), Mathematics in Context. Chicago: Encyclopædia Britannica, Inc.

ISBN 0-03039627-1

1 2 3 4 5 6   073   09 08 07 06 05

The *Mathematics in Context* Development Team

Development 1991–1997

The initial version of *Comparing Quantities* was developed by Martin Kindt and Mieke Abels. It was adapted for use in American schools by Margaret R. Meyer, and Margaret A. Pligge.

Wisconsin Center for Education

Research Staff

Thomas A. Romberg
Director

Joan Daniels Pedro
Assistant to the Director

Gail Burrill
Coordinator

Margaret R. Meyer
Coordinator

Project Staff

Jonathan Brendefur
Laura Brinker
James Browne
Jack Burrill
Rose Byrd
Peter Christiansen
Barbara Clarke
Doug Clarke
Beth R. Cole
Fae Dremock
Mary Ann Fix

Sherian Foster
James A, Middleton
Jasmina Milinkovic
Margaret A. Pligge
Mary C. Shafer
Julia A. Shew
Aaron N. Simon
Marvin Smith
Stephanie Z. Smith
Mary S. Spence

Freudenthal Institute Staff

Jan de Lange
Director

Els Feijs
Coordinator

Martin van Reeuwijk
Coordinator

Mieke Abels
Nina Boswinkel
Frans van Galen
Koeno Gravemeijer
Marja van den Heuvel-Panhuizen
Jan Auke de Jong
Vincent Jonker
Ronald Keijzer
Martin Kindt

Jansie Niehaus
Nanda Querelle
Anton Roodhardt
Leen Streefland
Adri Treffers
Monica Wijers
Astrid de Wild

Revision 2003–2005

The revised version of *Comparing Quantities* was developed by Mieke Abels and Truus Dekker. It was adapted for use in American schools by Gail Burrill.

Wisconsin Center for Education

Research Staff

Thomas A. Romberg
Director

David C. Webb
Coordinator

Gail Burrill
Editorial Coordinator

Margaret A. Pligge
Editorial Coordinator

Project Staff

Sarah Ailts
Beth R. Cole
Erin Hazlett
Teri Hedges
Karen Hoiberg
Carrie Johnson
Jean Krusi
Elaine McGrath

Margaret R. Meyer
Anne Park
Bryna Rappaport
Kathleen A. Steele
Ana C. Stephens
Candace Ulmer
Jill Vettrus

Freudenthal Institute Staff

Jan de Lange
Director

Truus Dekker
Coordinator

Mieke Abels
Content Coordinator

Monica Wijers
Content Coordinator

Arthur Bakker
Peter Boon
Els Feijs
Dédé de Haan
Martin Kindt

Nathalie Kuijpers
Huub Nilwik
Sonia Palha
Nanda Querelle
Martin van Reeuwijk

Cover photo credits: (left to right) © PhotoDisc/Getty Images; © Corbis; © Getty Images

Illustrations
1 Holly Cooper-Olds; **2** (top), **3** © Encyclopædia Britannica, Inc.; **23, 29** (left) Holly Cooper-Olds

Photographs
4 (counter clockwise) PhotoDisc/Getty Images; © Stockbyte; © Ingram Publishing; © Corbis; © PhotoDisc/Getty Images; **6, 7** Victoria Smith/HRW; **10** Sam Dudgeon/HRW Photo; **16** © Corbis; **21** © Stockbyte/HRW; **23** PhotoDisc/Getty Images; **25** (left column top to bottom) © Corbis; PhotoDisc/Getty Images; © Corbis; **28** Victoria Smith/HRW; **30** PhotoDisc/Getty Images

◆ Contents

$50.00

ORDER	TACO	SALAD	DRINK	TOTAL
1	1	—	2	¢ 3.00
2	2	1	4	¢ 8.00
3	—	4	4	¢ 11.00
4				
5				
6				
7				

Dear Student,

Welcome to *Comparing Quantities.*

In this unit, you will compare quantities such as prices, weights, and widths.

You will learn about trading and exchanging things in order to develop strategies to solve problems involving combinations of items and prices.

Combination charts and the notebook notation will help you find solutions.

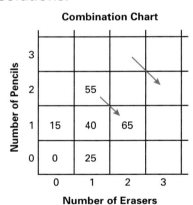

In the end, you will have learned important ideas about algebra and several new ways to solve problems. You will see how pictures can help you think about a problem, how to use number patterns, and will develop some general ways to solve what are called "systems of equations" in math.

Sincerely,

The Mathematics in Context Development Team

Compare and Exchange

Bartering

A long time ago money did not exist. People lived in small communities, grew their own crops, and raised animals such as cattle and sheep. What did they do if they needed something they didn't produce themselves? They traded something they produced for the things their neighbors produced. This method of exchange is called **bartering**.

Paulo lives with his family in a small village. His family needs corn. He is going to the market with two sheep and one goat to barter, or exchange, them for bags of corn.

First he meets Aaron, who says, "I only trade salt for chickens. I will give you one bag of salt for every two chickens."
"But I don't have any chickens," thinks Paulo, "so I can't trade with Aaron."

Later he meets Sarkis, who tells him, "I will give you two bags of corn for three bags of salt."
Paulo thinks, "That doesn't help me either."

Then he meets Ranee. She will trade six chickens for a goat, and she says, "My sister, Nina, is willing to give you six bags of salt for every sheep you have."

Paulo is getting confused. His family wants him to go home with bags of corn, not with goats or sheep or chickens or salt.

1. Show what Paulo can do.

Farmer's Market

2. How many bananas do you need to balance the third scale?
Explain your reasoning.

| 10 bananas | 2 pineapples | 1 pineapple | 2 bananas 1 apple | 1 apple |

3. How many carrots do you need to balance the third scale?
Explain your reasoning.

| 6 carrots | 1 ear of corn 1 pepper | 1 ear of corn | 2 peppers | 1 pepper |

Thirst Quencher

4. How many cups of liquid can you pour from one big bottle? Explain your reasoning.

$6 \times$ $=$

 $=$

$4 \times$ $=$

Tug-of-War

Four oxen are as strong as five horses.

An elephant is as strong as one ox and two horses.

5. Which animals will win the tug-of-war below? Give a reason for your prediction.

A Compare and Exchange

Summary

These problems could be solved using *fair exchange*. In this section, problems were given in words and pictures. You used words, pictures, and symbols to explain your work.

Check Your Work

Delia lives in a community where people trade goods they produce for other things they need. Delia has some fish that she caught, and she wants to trade them for other food. She hears that she can trade fish for melons, but she wants more than just melons. So she decides to see what else is available.

This is what she hears:

- For five fish, you can get two melons.
- For four apples, you can get one loaf of bread.
- For one melon, you can get one ear of corn and two apples.
- For 10 apples, you can get four melons.

1. Rewrite or draw pictures to represent the information so that it is easier to use.

2. Use the information to write two more statements about exchanging apples, melons, corn, fish, and bread.

3. Delia says, "I can trade 10 fish for 10 apples." Is this true? Explain.

4. Can Delia trade three fish for one loaf of bread? Explain why or why not.

5. Explain how Delia can trade her fish for ears of corn.

 For Further Reflection

Explain how to use exchanging to solve a problem.

B ▶ Looking at Combinations

The School Store

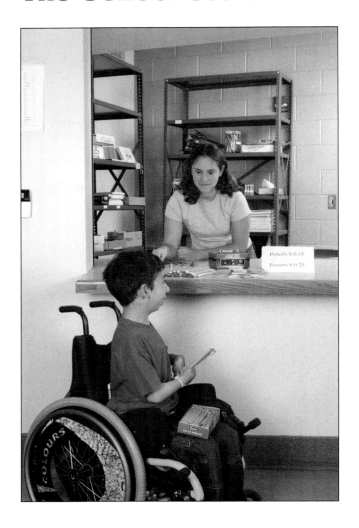

Monica and Martin are responsible for the school store. The store is open all day for students to buy supplies. Unfortunately, Monica and Martin can't be in the store all day to take students' money, so they use an honor system. Pencils and erasers are available for students to purchase on the honor system. Students leave exact change in a small locked box to pay for their purchases. Erasers cost 25¢ each, and pencils cost 15¢ each.

1. One day Monica and Martin find $1.10 in the locked box. How many pencils and how many erasers have been purchased?

2. On another day there is $1.50 in the locked box. Monica and Martin cannot decide what has been purchased. Why?

3. Find another amount of money that would make it impossible to know what has been purchased.

Monica wants to make finding the total price of pencils and erasers easier, so she makes two price lists: one for different numbers of erasers and one for different numbers of pencils.

4. Copy and complete the price lists for the erasers and the pencils.

Erasers	Price
0	$0.00
1	$0.25
2	$0.50
3	$0.75
4	$1.00
5	$1.25
6	
7	

Pencils	Price
0	$0.00
1	$0.15
2	$0.30
3	
4	
5	
6	
7	

One day the box has $1.05 in it.

5. Show how Monica can use her lists to determine how many pencils and erasers have been bought.

Monica and Martin aren't satisfied. Although they now have these two lists, they still have to do many calculations. They are trying to think of a way to get all the prices for all the combinations of pencils and erasers in one chart.

6. Reflect What suggestions can you make for combining the two lists? Discuss your ideas with your class.

Monica and Martin come up with the idea of a combination chart. Here you see part of their chart.

7. **a.** What does the 40 in the chart represent?

   b. How many combinations of erasers and pencils can Monica and Martin show in this chart?

If you extend this chart, as shown below, you can show more combinations.

Combination Chart

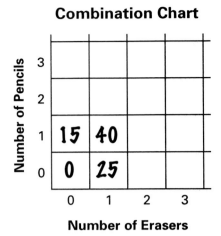

Use the combination chart on **Student Activity Sheet 1** to solve the following problems.

Costs of Combinations (in cents)

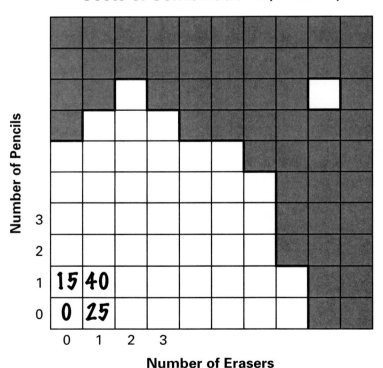

8. Fill in the white squares with the prices of the combinations.

9. Circle the price of two erasers and three pencils.

Use the number **patterns** in your completed **combination chart** on **Student Activity Sheet 1** to answer problems 10–16.

10. a. Where do you find the answer to problem 1 ($1.10) in the chart?

   b. How many erasers and how many pencils can be bought for $1.10?

11. a. Reflect What happens to the numbers in the chart as you move along one of the arrows shown in the diagram?

   b. Reflect Does the answer vary according to which arrow you choose? Explain your reasoning.

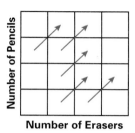

12. What does *moving along an arrow* mean in terms of the numbers of pencils and erasers purchased?

13. a. Mark on your chart a move from one square to another that represents the exchange of one pencil for one eraser.

   b. How much does the price change from one square to another?

14. a. Mark on your chart a move from one square to another that represents the exchange of one eraser for two pencils.

   b. How much does the price change for this move?

15. Describe the move shown in charts **a** and **b** below in terms of the exchange of erasers and pencils.

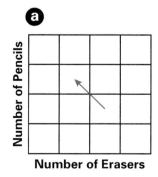

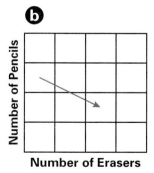

16. There are many other moves and patterns in the chart. Find at least two other patterns. Use different color pencils to mark them on your chart. Describe each pattern you find.

Workroom Cabinets

Anna and Dale are going to remodel a workroom. They want to put new cabinets along one wall of the room. They start by measuring the room and drawing this diagram.

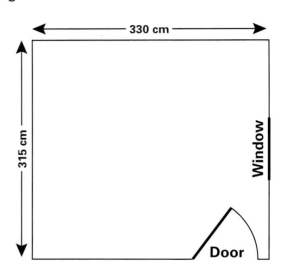

Anna and Dale find out that the cabinets come in two different widths: 45 centimeters (cm) and 60 cm.

17. How many of each cabinet do Anna and Dale need in order for the cabinets to fit exactly along the wall that measures 315 cm? Try to find more than one possibility.

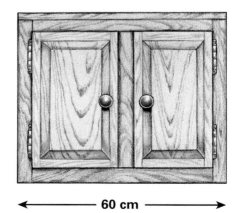

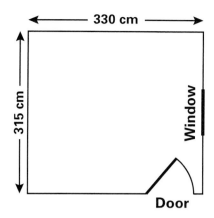

330 cm

315 cm

Window

Door

Anna and Dale wonder how they can design cabinets for the longer wall.

The cabinet store has a convenient chart. The chart makes it easy to find out how many 60-cm and 45-cm cabinets are needed for different wall lengths.

18. Explain how Anna and Dale can use the chart to find the number of cabinets they need for the longer wall in the workroom.

Lengths of Combinations (in cm)

Number of Short Cabinets	0	1	2	3	4	5	6	7	8
11	495	555							
10	450	510	570						
9	405	465	525	585					
8	360	420	480	540					
7	315	375	435	495	555				
6	270	330	390	450	510	570			
5	225	285	345	405	465	525	585		
4	180	240	300	360	420	480	540		
3	135	195	255	315	375	435	495	555	
2	90	150	210	270	330	390	450	510	570
1	45	105	165	225	285	345	405	465	525
0	0	60	120	180	240	300	360	420	480

Number of Long Cabinets

19. Can the cabinet store provide cabinets to fit a wall that is exactly 4 meters (m) long? Explain your answer.

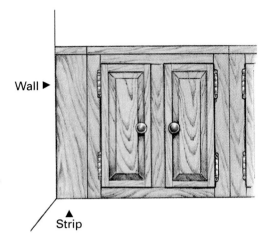

Wall ▶

If cabinets don't fit exactly, the cabinet store sells a strip to fill the gap. Most customers want the strip to be as small as possible.

20. What size strip is necessary for cabinets along a 4-m wall?

▲
Strip

The chart has been completed to only 585 cm because longer rows of cabinets are not purchased often. However, one day an order comes in for cabinets to fit a wall exactly 6 m long. One possible way to fill this order is 10 cabinets of 60 cm each.

21. Reflect What are other possibilities for a cabinet arrangement that will fit a 6-m wall? Note that although you do not see 600 in the chart, you can still use the chart to find the answer. How?

Lengths of Combinations (in cm)

On the left is a part of the cabinet combination chart.

22. What is special about the move shown by the arrow?

23. If you start in another square in this chart and you make the same move, what do you notice? How can you explain this?

7	315	375	435	495	555			
6	270	330	390	450	510	570		
5	225	285	345	405	465	525	585	
4	180	240	300	360	420	480	540	
3	135	195	255	315	375	435	495	555
2	90	150	210	270	330	390	450	510
1	45	105	165	225	285	345	405	465
0	0	60	120	180	240	300	360	420
	0	1	2	3	4	5	6	7

Number of Short Cabinets (vertical axis label)

Number of Long Cabinets

Puzzles

24. Complete the puzzles on **Student Activity Sheet 2**.

ⓐ

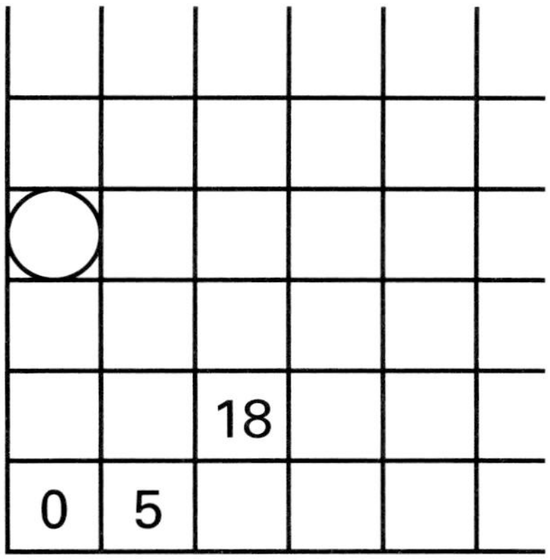

◯					
		18			
0	5				

ⓑ

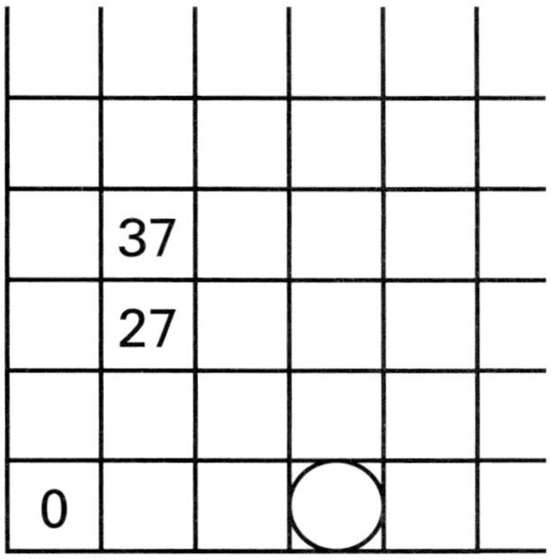

		37			
		27			
0			◯		

ⓒ

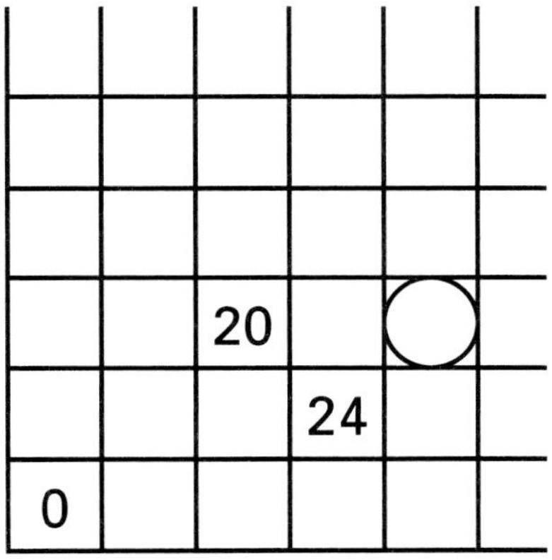

		20		◯	
			24		
0					

ⓓ

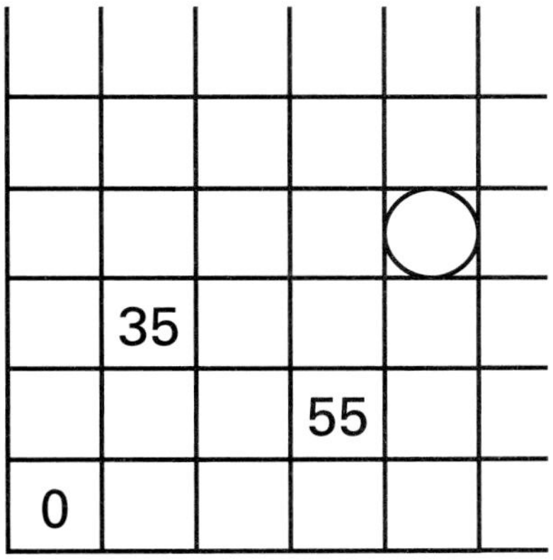

				◯	
		35			
			55		
0					

B Looking at Combinations

Summary ➤➤

A combination chart can help you compare quantities. A combination chart gives a quick view of many combinations.

Discovering patterns within combination charts can make your work easier by allowing you to discover patterns and extend the chart in any direction.

Charts can be used to solve many problems, as you studied in "The School Store" and "Workroom Cabinets." In this chart the arrow represents the exchange of one pencil for one eraser.

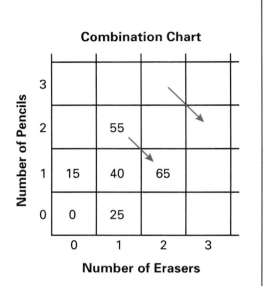

Combination Chart

Check Your Work ➤➤

Numbers of Tickets

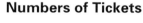
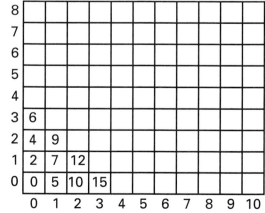

Number of Loop-D-Loop Rides

This year the school fair has two rides. The Loop-D-Loop costs five tickets, and the Whirlybird costs two tickets.

1. In your notebook, copy the combination chart that shows how many tickets are needed for different combinations of these two rides. Complete the chart as necessary to solve the word problems.

2. How many tickets are needed for two rides on the Loop-D-Loop and three rides on the Whirlybird?

3. Janus has 19 tickets. How can she use these tickets for both rides so that she has no leftover tickets?

4. a. On your combination chart, mark a move from one square to another that represents the exchange of one ride on the Whirlybird for two rides on the Loop-D-Loop.

    b. How much does the number of tickets as described in 4a, change as you move from one square to another?

5. Use the combination chart on **Student Activity Sheet 3**.

    a. Write a story problem that uses the combination chart.

    b. Label the bottom and left side of your chart. Give the chart a title and include the units.

    c. What do the circled numbers represent in your story problem?

50	52	54	56	58	60
40	42	44	46	48	50
30	32	34	36	38	40
20	22	24	26	28	30
10	12	14	16	18	20
0	2	4	6	8	10

For Further Reflection

Do you think combination charts will always have a horizontal and vertical pattern? Why or why not? What about a pattern on the diagonal?

C

Finding Prices

Price Combinations

So far you have studied two strategies for solving problems that involve combinations of items. The first strategy, exchanging, applied to the problems about trading food at the beginning of the unit. The second strategy was to make a combination chart and use number patterns found in the chart.

In this section, you will apply the strategy of exchanging to solve problems involving the method of fair exchange.

Use the drawings below to answer problems 1–3.

1. Without knowing the price of a pair of sunglasses or a pair of shorts, can you determine which item is more expensive? Explain.

2. How many pairs of shorts can you buy for $50?

3. What is the price of one pair of sunglasses? Explain your reasoning.

4. What is the price of one umbrella? One cap?

$80.00

$76.00

Sean bought two T-shirts and one sweatshirt for a total of $30. When he got home, he regretted his purchase. He decided to exchange one T-shirt for an additional sweatshirt.

Sean made the exchange, but he had to pay $6 more because the sweatshirt is more expensive than the T-shirt.

5. What is the price of each item? Explain your reasoning.

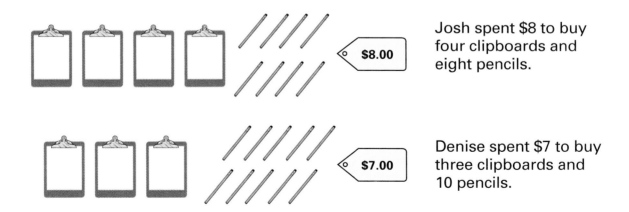

$8.00

Josh spent $8 to buy four clipboards and eight pencils.

$7.00

Denise spent $7 to buy three clipboards and 10 pencils.

Denise wants to trade Josh two pencils for a clipboard.

6. Is the trade a fair exchange? If not, who has to pay the difference, and how much is it?

7. What is the price of a pencil? What is the price of a clipboard? Explain your reasoning.

You can use a chart to solve some of these shopping problems.

This combination chart represents the problem of the caps and the umbrellas (page 17).

8. Complete this chart on **Student Activity Sheet 4**. Then find the prices of one cap and one umbrella. Is this the same answer you found for problem 4 on page 17?

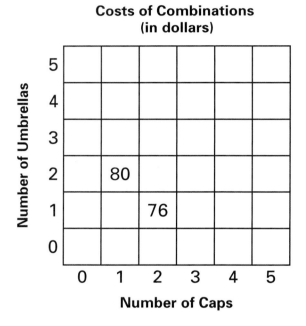

Costs of Combinations (in dollars)

9. Study the two pictures of sunglasses and shorts. Use one of the extra charts on **Student Activity Sheet 4** to make a combination chart for these items. Label your chart. What is the price of one pair of sunglasses? One pair of shorts?

At Doug's Discount Store, all CDs are one price; all DVDs are another price.

David buys three CDs and two DVDs for $67.
Joyce buys two CDs and four DVDs for $90.

10. What is the price of one CD? One DVD? You may use any strategy.

On a visit to Quinn's Quantities, Rashard finds the prices for various combinations of peanuts and raisins.

- A mixture of 3 cups of peanuts and 2 cups of raisins costs $3.30.

- A mixture of 4 cups of peanuts and 3 cups of raisins costs $4.55.

11. What does Rashard pay for a mixture of 5 cups of peanuts and 2 cups of raisins? You may use any strategy.

12. **Reflect** Create your own shopping problem. Solve the problem yourself, and then ask someone else to solve it. Have the person explain to you how he or she found the solution.

In solving shopping problems, you have used exchanging and combination charts. Joe studied the problem below and used a different strategy.

Follow Joe's strategy to see how he found the price of each candle.

13. Explain Joe's reasoning.

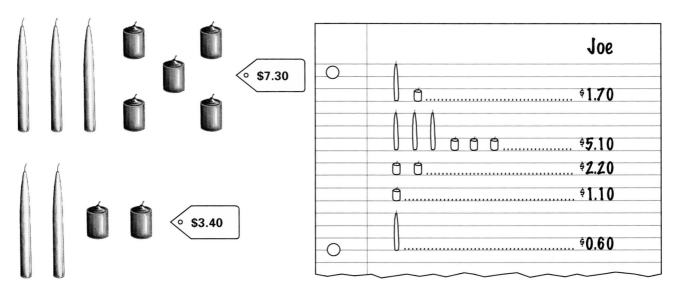

Summary ✕✕

You can use different strategies to solve shopping problems.

If you can find a pattern in a picture, you can use the *fair exchange* method. To do so, continue exchanging until a single item is left so you can find its price. If not, combining information may help you find the price of a single item.

Another strategy is to make a combination chart and look for a pattern in the prices. Use the pattern to find the price of a single item. You may also use the fair exchange method with a combination chart.

Check Your Work ▶▶

1. Felicia and Kenji want to buy candles. The candles are available in different combinations of sizes.

   a. Without calculating prices, determine which is more expensive, the short or the tall candle.

   b. What is the difference in price between one short and one tall candle?

   c. Draw a new picture that shows another combination of short and tall candles. Write the price of the combination.

   d. What is the price of a single short candle?

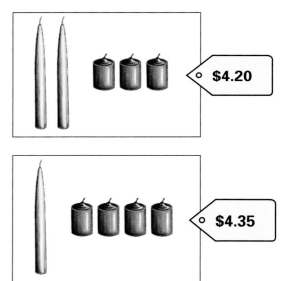

2. Roberto bought two drinks and two bagels for $6.60.

   Anne bought four drinks and three bagels for $11.70.

   Use a combination chart to find the cost of a single drink.

3. The prices of drinks and bagels have changed.

   a. Use any strategy to find the new cost of a drink.

   b. How much is a single bagel now?

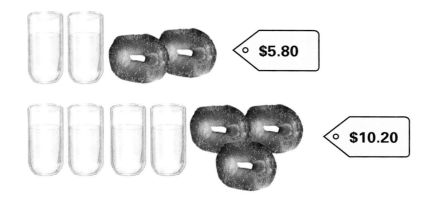

For Further Reflection

Write several sentences describing the differences between using the method of fair exchange and using combination charts to solve problems.

Notebook Notation

Chickens

Three chickens weighed themselves in different combinations.

1. What should the scale read in the fourth picture?

2. Show how to find out how many kilograms (kg) each chicken weighs.

Mario's Restaurant

Mario runs a Mexican restaurant, and he is very busy. He moves from one table to another, writing down all the orders. You can see below how he writes the orders on his order pad.

3. Some of the orders do not have total prices indicated. What are the prices of these orders?

4. Make up two new orders and write them in your notebook. Fill in the prices of these orders.

5. What is the price of each item?

ORDER	TACO	SALAD	DRINK	TOTAL
1	2	4	--	¢10
2	1	2	3	¢8
3	3	--	3	¢9
4	1	2	--	
5	1	--	1	
6	2	2	1	
7	4	2	3	
8				
9				
10				

Chickens Revisited

The way Mario wrote the orders in his notebook gave him a good overview of many combinations. Such notation can also be applied to other problems. If you apply Mario's **notebook notation** to the chicken problems, you might come up with this chart.

Number of Each Size of Chicken

S	M	L	Weight (in kg)
0	1	1	10.6
1	0	1	8.5
1	1	0	6.1

S is the weight of the small chicken.

M is the weight of the medium chicken.

L is the weight of the large chicken.

6. How can you find the total weight of the three chickens by using notebook notation?

7. Make new combinations until you find the weight of each chicken.

Sandwich World

Here are some orders that were served at Sandwich World today. You can write these orders in notebook notation.

Order	Apples	Milk	Sandwich	Total
1	1	0	1	₵3.40
2	0	1	1	₵4.20
3	1	1	0	₵2.80
4				
5				
6				
7				
8				
9				
10				

$3.40

$4.20

$2.80

8. In your own notebook, make new combinations until you can determine the price of each item.

D Notebook Notation

Summary

In this section, you explored notebook notation as a good way to get an overview of the information contained in a problem. You can make new combinations in a notebook by:

- adding rows;
- finding the difference between rows; and
- doubling or halving rows; and so on.

The new combinations you create can help you find solutions to new problems.

Check Your Work

You can write these combinations of fruits in notebook notation.

1. In your own notebook, make new combinations until you find the price of each item.

$1.30

$1.10

$1.20

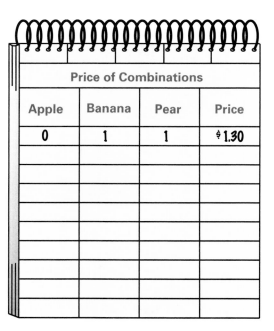

Price of Combinations

Apple	Banana	Pear	Price
0	1	1	$1.30

2. Study the following notebook showing lunch orders at Mario's restaurant.

   a. Find the cost of one salad. Explain how you got your answer.

   b. How can you find the cost of one drink? One taco?

ORDER	TACO	SALAD	DRINK	TOTAL
1	1	—	2	¢ 3.00
2	2	1	4	¢ 8.00
3	—	4	4	¢ 11.00
4				
5				
6				
7				

3. Can you solve problem 2 by using a combination chart? Why or why not?

For Further Reflection

Write a description to tell an adult in your family about all of the ways you have learned so far in this unit to solve problems. Show him or her examples of what you have learned.

Equations

The School Store Revisited

The prices of pencils and erasers have changed, so Martin and Monica have to make a new price chart. **Student Activity Sheet 5** contains a combination chart for you to complete.

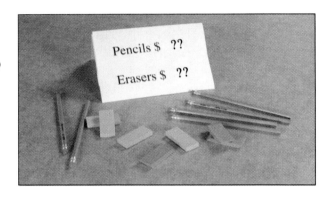

Pencils $??
Erasers $??

Information about the number in the picture above can be expressed in a formula. This formula is also called an **equation**.

$$2E + 3P = 130$$

1. a. What does the letter *E* in this equation represent? What does the letter *P* represent?

   b. Describe in words the meaning of this equation.

Prices of Combinations (in cents)

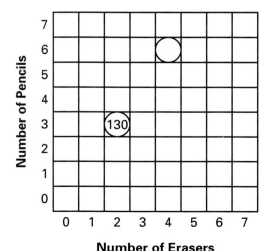

Number of Pencils

Number of Erasers

2. What number belongs in the empty circle? Write an equation representing this situation.

3. Use **Student Activity Sheet 5** to write the information from the two equations in notebook notation.

4. Monica tells you that $1E + 2P = 75$. Express this information in both the combination chart and the notebook notation on **Student Activity Sheet 5**.

5. Find the new price for a single eraser and a single pencil. You may use either notebook notation or the combination chart.

Hats and Sunglasses

6. Each of these pictures can be replaced by an equation. Write the two equations, using the symbol H for the price of a hat and the symbol S for the price of a pair of sunglasses.

7. Write an equation that shows the total price of one hat and four pairs of sunglasses.

8. What is the price of one pair of sunglasses? What is the price of one hat? Show how you found these prices.

Prices of Combinations (in dollars)

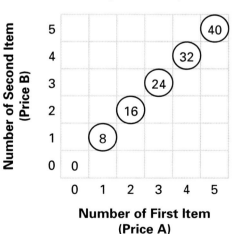

Number of Second Item (Price B)

Number of First Item (Price A)

Here is another chart that represents the prices of combinations of two items.

9. Write an equation in which the price of one item is A and the price of the other item is B for each of the circled numbers. You should have five different equations.

10. Make up a price for each item so that price A is higher than price B. Use your prices to complete the chart in your notebook.

11. **Reflect** Do you think all of the students in your class have the same numbers in their charts? Explain why or why not.

12. Now you can make many equations based on the information in your chart. Write three equations.

Return to Mario's

Some prices in Mario's restaurant have changed. You now have to pay $6.50 if you order one taco, two salads, and one drink. You pay $11.50 for one taco, four salads, and three drinks. For $4.50, you can buy one taco and two drinks.

13. Write an equation that corresponds to each of the orders above.

14. By combining the orders, you can make new equations. What equation do you get when you add the last two orders?

15. Make up two other equations by combining orders.

16. Show how you can combine equations to get the equation $1S + 1D = \$2.50$.

17. Find the new price for each of the three items.

Tickets

This afternoon a new animated movie is playing at the movie theater. Many adults and children are waiting in line to buy their tickets.

18. How much will the ticket seller in the third picture charge?

19. How much will you pay if you go to this theater alone?

E ◆ Equations

Summary ⟫

Many problems compare quantities such as prices, weights, and widths.

One way to describe these problems is by using equations. For example, study the picture of the umbrellas and cap.

If you let U represent the price of one umbrella and C represent the price of one cap, the equation is $2U + 1C = \$80$.

These problems can also be solved with combination charts if there are only two different items. When there are more than two items, you can use notebook notation to find the solution.

Price of Combinations

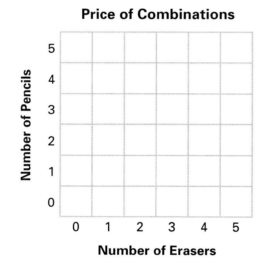

Number of Pencils

Number of Erasers

Notebook Notation

ORDER	TACO	SALAD	DRINK	TOTAL

Check Your Work ⟫

1. At a flower shop Joel paid $10 for three irises and four daisies. Althea paid $9 for two irises and five daisies.

   a. Write equations representing this information.

   b. Write an equation to show the price of one iris and six daisies.

   c. Find the cost of one iris, and the cost of one daisy.

2. At a movie theater, tickets for three adults, two seniors, and two children cost $35. Tickets for one senior and two children cost $12.50. Tickets for one adult, one senior, and two children cost $18.50.

   a. Write three equations representing the ticket information. Use A to represent the price of an adult's ticket, S to represent the price of a senior's ticket, and C to represent the price of a child's ticket.

   b. Write two additional equations by combining your first three equations.

   c. Explain how you can combine equations to get the equation $2A + 1S = \$16.50$.

   d. Explain how you can combine equations to get the equation $A = \$6$.

   e. What is the cost of each ticket?

3. In the following equations, the numbers 96 and 27 can represent lengths, weights, prices, or whatever you wish.

$$4L + 3M = 96$$

$$L + M = 27$$

   a. Write a story to fit these equations.

   b. Find the value of L and the value of M.

4. In the following equations, find the value of C and the value of K. Imagining a story to fit the equations may help you solve for the values.

$$5C + 4K = 50$$

$$4C + 5K = 58$$

 For Further Reflection

Refer back to Quinn's Quantities on page 19. Write an equation that represents the price of the two mixtures. Tell which is easier for you to use, the problem posed in words or represented by equations and explain why.

Additional Practice

Section A Compare and Exchange

Susan and her friends like to collect and trade basketball cards. Today after school, Susan made these trades:

- two Tigers for three Lions
- three Cougars for four Tigers
- one Cougar for one Tiger and two Bears
- four Panthers for two Cougars

1. Use the information to think of two card trades that would be fair.

2. James offers Susan six Lions for three Cougars. Should Susan make this trade? Why or why not?

3. James then offers one Panther for two Tigers. Should Susan make this trade? Why or why not?

4. Susan has five Cougars. How many Bears can she get for her Cougars?

Section B Looking at Combinations

Numbers of People on Canoe Trip

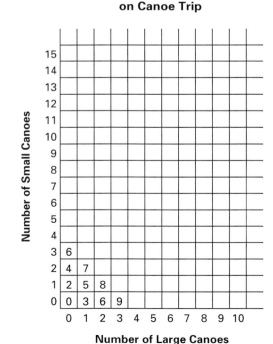

Number of Small Canoes

Number of Large Canoes

A Girl Scout troop wants to rent canoes for a group of 25 people. Both small and large canoes are available. Each small canoe holds two people, and each large canoe carries three people.

Use the combination chart on **Student Activity Sheet 6** to solve the problems. You do not need to complete the entire chart.

1. What combinations of small and large canoes will accommodate exactly 25 people? Find all the possibilities.

2. One person broke her leg a week before the trip and is unable to go on the canoe trip. Name one possibility for a combination of canoes 24 people can rent.

3. Explain why the chart starts with (0, 0) and not with (1, 1).

4. For each of the following puzzles, find the number that goes in the circle and explain your strategy.

a.

◯				
	10	18		
0				

b.

	51			
		◯		
		27		
0				

Section **G** Finding Prices

1. Three T-shirts and four caps are advertised for $96. Two T-shirts and five caps cost $99. How much does a single T-shirt cost? How much does a cap cost? Show your work.

Three tall candles and five short candles cost $7.75. Two tall candles and two short candles cost $3.50.

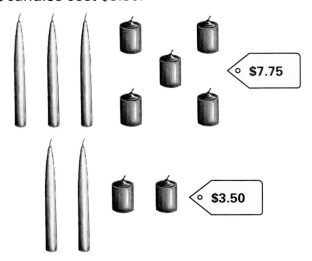

Margarita used a combination chart to find the prices of short and tall candles.

2. **a.** Use Margarita's chart to show how she might solve the problem.

Margarita's Chart

Prices of Combinations (in dollars)

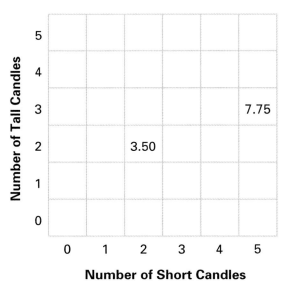

b. Margarita wrote the first combination as $3T + 5S = \$7.75$. What does the letter T represent? The letter S?

c. Write a similar statement for the second combination.

Section D Notebook Notation

Some of today's orders at Fish King are shown in the notebook.

1. **a.** In your own notebook, list at least three new combinations.

   b. What is the price of each item at Fish King?

ORDER	DRINK	FRIES	FISH	TOTAL
1	2	1	2	¢8.80
2	1	—	1	¢3.60
3	3	1	1	¢7.40
4				
5				
6				
7				

For a total cost of $18.40, Gideon went on the Whirling Wheel four times, in the Haunted House two times, and on the Roller Coaster four times.

For a total cost of $18, Louisa went on the Whirling Wheel five times and on the Roller Coaster five times.

Bryce likes only the Roller Coaster, and he rode it 10 times! He spent one dollar less than Louisa.

2. What is the price of each attraction? Solve the problem using notebook notation. Show all of your calculations.

3. Create a problem of your own, using notebook notation. Show a detailed solution to your problem.

Section E Equations

1. Five large rowing boats and two small boats can hold 36 people. Two large rowing boats and one small one can hold 15 people.

   a. Write two equations representing the information. Use the letters L and S.

   b. What do the letters L and S in your equations represent?

   c. How many people can one large boat hold if it is full? Show your work.

2. A mixture of 3 cups of almonds and 2 cups of peanuts costs $9.20. A mixture of 1 cup of almonds and 2 cups of peanuts costs $5.20.

   a. Write two equations representing the information. Use the letters A and P.

   b. What do the letters A and P in your equations represent?

   c. What is the price for a mixture of 2 cups of almonds and 3 cups of peanuts? Show your work.

3. Imagine a story for the system of equations below.

   $2A + 4C = 27$

   $3A + 1C = 23$

   a. What do the letters or variables in this system of equations represent in your story?

   b. Choose any strategy to find the value of A and the value of C.

4. Kevin invented a story that is represented by this system of equations.

   $5P + 3K = 8$

   $10P + 6K = 16$

   Can Kevin find the value for P and the value for K? Explain why or why not.

Section A Compare and Exchange

1. You may sketch pictures, similar to the work below.

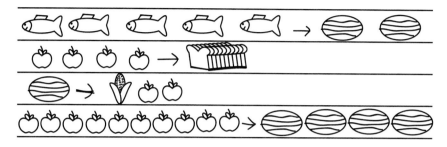

Or you may write words. If so, be sure to check your numbers.

five fish	for two melons
four apples	for one loaf of bread
one melon	for one ear of corn and two apples
10 apples	for four melons

2. You should have two correct statements. If your statement does not appear here, discuss it with a classmate to see if they agree with you.

Sample responses:

eight apples	for two loaves of bread
one melon	for five ears of corn
two melons	for five apples
eight ears of corn	for one loaf of bread
two ears of corn	for one apple
one fish	for one apple
two ears of corn	for one fish
four fish	for one loaf of bread

3. Yes, Delia's statement is true. Remember: you need to provide an explanation!

Sample explanations:

- In problem 2, I found that one fish trades for one apple, so 10 fish trade for 10 apples.

- Since you can trade five fish for two melons, you can trade 10 fish for four melons. You can trade four melons for 10 apples from the original information, so you can trade 10 fish for 10 apples.

4. No, this statement is not true. Remember: you have to give an explanation!

Sample explanations:

- I found in problem 2 that four fish can be traded for one loaf of bread, so three fish are not enough to get one loaf of bread.

- I found in problem 2 that one fish can be traded for one apple, so three fish will be worth only three apples. Because four apples are the same as one loaf of bread, three fish are not enough.

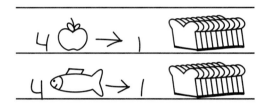

5. You can have several different solutions and still be correct. Check your solution with another student. You may make an assumption about the number of fish Delia has.

Sample responses:

- If she has five fish, she can trade for two melons. Then she can get two ears of corn and four apples, because one melon is worth one ear of corn and two apples. I know from problem 2 that one apple is worth two ears of corn. So if she wants more corn, she can trade four apples for eight ears of corn. Delia will then have traded 10 ears of corn in total for five fish.

  This means that one fish is worth two ears of corn. So for each fish Delia has, she can get two ears of corn.

Section **B** Looking at Combinations

1. You might have filled out the chart in a different way.

Numbers of Tickets

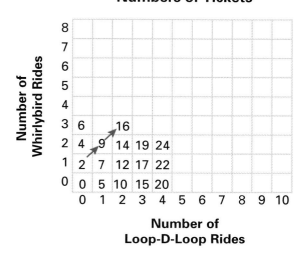

Number of Loop-D-Loop Rides

2. 16 tickets

Different strategies are possible:

- In the chart, you can see that for two Loop-D-Loop rides you need 10 tickets, and for three Whirlybird rides you need six tickets. So altogether you need 16 tickets.

- You can draw arrows that go up one square and to the right one square, like on the chart above. This move adds seven tickets, and 7 + 9 = 16.

3. Janus can go on three Loop-D-Loop rides and two Whirlybird rides or one Loop-D-Loop ride and seven Whirlybird rides.

If you keep filling out the chart, each entry is either greater or less than 19 except for those two combinations. So all of the other combinations are for either too many or too few tickets.

4. **a.** Different charts are possible. You should draw an arrow that goes down one square and to the right two squares, like on the chart below.

b. The number of tickets increases by eight.

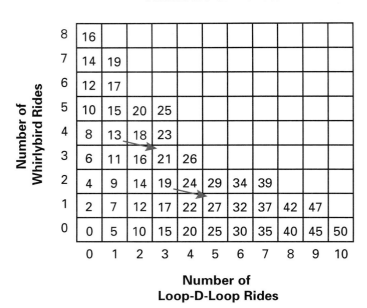

Numbers of Tickets

	0	1	2	3	4	5	6	7	8	9	10
8	16										
7	14	19									
6	12	17									
5	10	15	20	25							
4	8	13	18	23							
3	6	11	16	21	26						
2	4	9	14	19	24	29	34	39			
1	2	7	12	17	22	27	32	37	42	47	
0	0	5	10	15	20	25	30	35	40	45	50

Number of Whirlybird Rides (vertical axis)

Number of Loop-D-Loop Rides

5. Discuss and check your answers to problem 5 with a classmate.

One example of a story:

a. A motorcycle holds two people, and a minibus holds 10 people.

b.

Number of People

	0	1	2	3	4	5
5	50	52	54	56	58	60
4	40	42	44	46	48	50
3	30	32	34	36	38	40
2	20	22	24	26	28	30
1	10	12	14	16	18	20
0	0	2	4	6	8	10

Number of Minibuses (vertical axis)

Number of Motorcycles

c. The circled entry 16 stands for the number of people traveling on three motorcycles and one minibus. The circled entry 40 stands for the number of people traveling in four minibuses.

Section G Finding Prices

1. a. You can have different explanations that are correct. Two examples are:

- In both pictures there are five candles, but the price is higher in the second picture. Since there are more short candles in the picture on the right, they must be more expensive.

- When one tall candle is replaced by one short candle, the price increases $0.15.

The short candles are more expensive than the tall candles.

b. The short candles are $0.15 more expensive than the tall candles.

c. Compare your answer with your classmates. There are several possible combinations. You can add all the candles and prices to get one combination:

Some other examples you get when you exchange candles are below and on the next page.

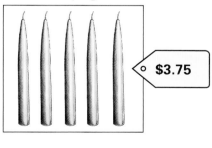

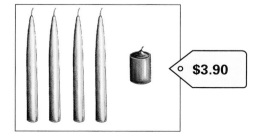

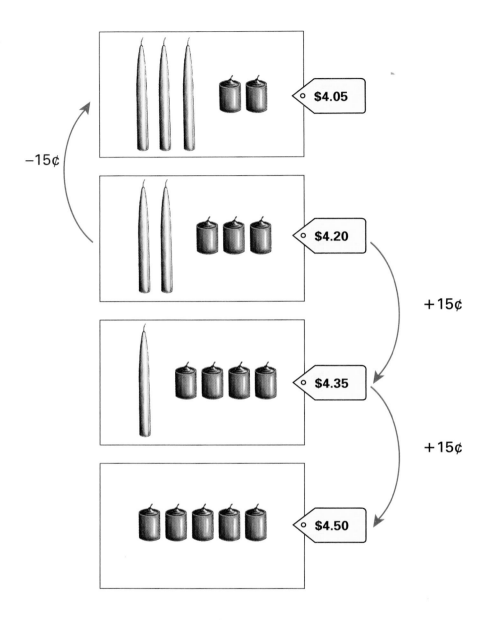

d. One short candle costs $0.90. Different strategies are possible. Discuss your strategy with a classmate.

An example of one strategy follows:

Exchange each tall candle for a short candle. (See pictures in answer **c**.)

When you have five short candles, the total price is $4.50.

$4.50 ÷ 5 = $0.90

**Costs of Combinations
(in dollars)**

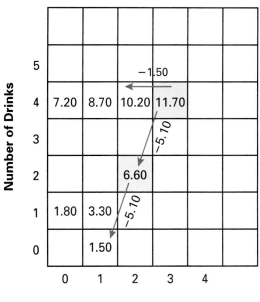

Number of Bagels

2. One strategy is to subtract the price of one bagel and two drinks to find a difference of $5.10 on the diagonal and repeat this to get $1.50 for one bagel. Another strategy is that if the entry for the (2,2) cell is $6.60, then the entry for the (1,1) cell is $3.30. So going up the diagonal by moving over one and up one (an increase of one drink and one bagel), the next diagonal cell would be $9.90 and the next to the right of $11.70 would be $13.20. This makes the cost of one bagel $1.50, which can be used to go back to the cost of 4 drinks and no bagels. Once you know that four drinks cost $7.20, you can divide to find the cost of one drink.

You may have filled out other parts of the chart. You do not need to fill out the whole chart to find the answer.

The cost of a drink is $1.80.

3. **a.** Check your strategy with a classmate.

The cost of a drink is $1.50.

Sample strategy:

Double the first picture:
Four drinks and four bagels cost $11.60.

Compare this with the second picture:

Four drinks and three bagels cost $10.20.
The difference on the left is one bagel.
The difference on the right is $1.40.

So one bagel costs $1.40.

To find the price of a drink, take the first picture:

2 drinks + 2 × $1.40 = $5.80
So two drinks must cost $3.00.
So one drink costs $1.50.

b. The cost of a single bagel is $1.40.

Section **D** Notebook Notation

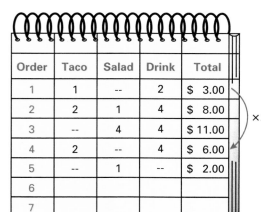

	Apple	Banana	Pear	Price
1	0	1	1	$1.30
2	1	1	0	$1.10
3	1	0	1	$1.20
4	2	2	2	$3.60
5	1	1	1	$1.80
6	1	0	0	$0.50

1. Discuss your solution with a classmate.

    Different strategies are possible. For example:

    Subtract any one of the first three rows from row 4.

    In this example, the price of one apple is found by subtracting row 1 from row 4.

    Answers:
    One apple costs $0.50.
    One banana costs $0.60.
    One pear costs $0.70.

2. **a.** One salad costs $2. You may have doubled the first order and then subtracted this from the second order to find the price of a salad, as shown.

    b. One drink costs $0.75. One taco costs $1.50. Compare your work with a classmate's work.

    Sample strategy:

    From answer **a**, you know that a salad costs $2.00. In order 3, there were four salads: 4 × $2 = $8.00. The price of the order was $11.00, so four drinks cost $11.00 − $8.00 = $3.00. $3.00 ÷ 4 = $0.75 is the price of one drink.

    In order 1:
    1 taco + 2 drinks = $3.00
    1 taco + 2 x $0.75 = $3.00
    1 taco + $1.50 = $3.00
    So one taco costs $1.50.

Order	Taco	Salad	Drink	Total
1	1	--	2	$ 3.00
2	2	1	4	$ 8.00
3	--	4	4	$ 11.00
4	2	--	4	$ 6.00
5	--	1	--	$ 2.00
6				
7				

×2

3. No, a combination chart cannot be used to solve the problem. A combination chart can be used only for a combination of two items.

Section **E** Equations

1. a. $3I + 4D = \$10$

$2I + 5D = \$9$

b. $1I + 6D = \$8$

c. An iris costs $2, and a daisy costs $1. You may have different explanations.

You may continue the pattern by removing one iris and adding one daisy, and then the total cost goes down by one dollar. So $7D = \$7$. One daisy costs $1.
Now, $1I + 6(\$1) = \$8$, so one iris costs $2.

2. a. $3A + 2S + 2C = \$35.00$

$1S + 2C = \$12.50$

$1A + 1S + 2C = \$18.50$

b. Different answers are possible. Sample responses:

$3A + 3S + 4C = \$47.50$

$1A + 2S + 4C = \$31.00$

c. You can subtract the third equation from the first.

$$-\left(\begin{array}{l} 3A + 2C + 2C = \$35.00 \\ \overline{1A + 1S + 2C = \$18.50} \end{array}\right) \text{ subtract}$$

$2A + 1S \qquad = \$16.50$

d. You can subtract the second equation from the third.

$$-\left(\begin{array}{l} 1A + 1S + 2C = \$18.50 \\ \overline{\qquad 1S + 2C = \$12.50} \end{array}\right) \text{ subtract}$$

$1A \qquad\qquad = \$6.00$

e. An adult's ticket costs $6.00.

A senior's ticket costs $4.50, and a child's ticket costs $4.00.

Strategies may vary. Sample strategy:

$2A + 1S = \$16.50$

$2(\$6.00) + 1S = \$16.50$

$1S = \$4.50$

$\$4.50 + 2C = \$12.50$

$2C = \$8.00$

$C = \$4.00$

3. **a.** Different stories are possible. Here is one example of a story.

Ronnie can read four library books and three magazines in 96 hours. He can read one library book and one magazine in 27 hours.

b. $L = 15$, $M = 12$

Discuss your solution with a classmate.
Different strategies are possible.

Sample strategies:

- Notebook notation:

  So $L = 15$, and $L + M = 27$

  $15 + M = 27$

  $M = 12$

- Combination chart:

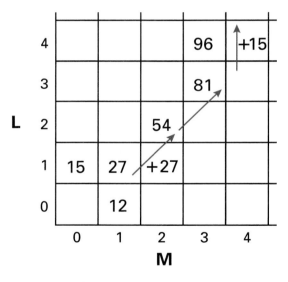

- Equations:

$$\begin{array}{r} 4L + 3M = 96 \\ \times 3 \left(\quad L + M = 27 \right) \text{ subtract} \\ 3L + 3M = 81 \end{array}$$

$$1L = 15$$
$$15 + M = 27$$
$$M = 12$$

4. Discuss your strategy with a classmate.

The combination chart shows one strategy.

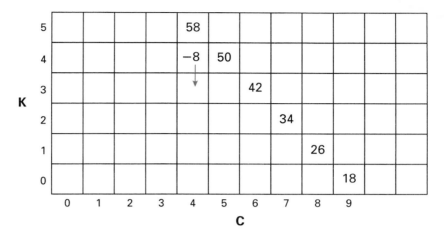

$9\ C = 18$

$C = 2$

Since $C = 2$, then there are several ways of finding K so that: $K = 10$

Reallotment

BRITANNICA
Mathematics in Context

Geometry and Measurement

HOLT, RINEHART AND WINSTON

Mathematics in Context is a comprehensive curriculum for the middle grades.
It was developed in 1991 through 1997 in collaboration with the Wisconsin Center
for Education Research, School of Education, University of Wisconsin-Madison and
the Freudenthal Institute at the University of Utrecht, The Netherlands, with the
support of the National Science Foundation Grant No. 9054928.

The revision of the curriculum was carried out in 2003 through 2005, with the
support of the National Science Foundation Grant No. ESI 0137414.

National Science Foundation
Opinions expressed are those of the authors
and not necessarily those of the Foundation.

Gravemeijer, K., Abels, M., Wijers, M., Pligge, M. A., Clarke, B., and Burrill, G.
(2006). *Reallotment.* In Wisconsin Center for Education Research & Freudenthal
Institute (Eds.), *Mathematics in context.* Chicago: Encyclopædia Britannica.

ISBN 0-03-039614-X

1 2 3 4 5 6   073   09 08 07 06 05

The *Mathematics in Context* Development Team

Development 1991–1997

The initial version of *Reallotment* was developed by Koeno Gravemeijer. It was adapted for use in American schools by Margaret A. Pligge and Barbara Clarke.

Wisconsin Center for Education

Research Staff

Thomas A. Romberg
Director

Joan Daniels Pedro
Assistant to the Director

Gail Burrill
Coordinator

Margaret R. Meyer
Coordinator

Project Staff

Jonathan Brendefur
Laura Brinker
James Browne
Jack Burrill
Rose Byrd
Peter Christiansen
Barbara Clarke
Doug Clarke
Beth R. Cole
Fae Dremock
Mary Ann Fix

Sherian Foster
James A, Middleton
Jasmina Milinkovic
Margaret A. Pligge
Mary C. Shafer
Julia A. Shew
Aaron N. Simon
Marvin Smith
Stephanie Z. Smith
Mary S. Spence

Freudenthal Institute Staff

Jan de Lange
Director

Els Feijs
Coordinator

Martin van Reeuwijk
Coordinator

Mieke Abels
Nina Boswinkel
Frans van Galen
Koeno Gravemeijer
Marja van den Heuvel-Panhuizen
Jan Auke de Jong
Vincent Jonker
Ronald Keijzer
Martin Kindt

Jansie Niehaus
Nanda Querelle
Anton Roodhardt
Leen Streefland

Adri Treffers
Monica Wijers
Astrid de Wild

Revision 2003–2005

The revised version of *Reallotment* was developed by Mieke Abels and Monica Wijers. It was adapted for use in American schools by Gail Burrill.

Wisconsin Center for Education

Research Staff

Thomas A. Romberg
Director

David C. Webb
Coordinator

Gail Burrill
Editorial Coordinator

Margaret A. Pligge
Editorial Coordinator

Project Staff

Sarah Ailts
Beth R. Cole
Erin Hazlett
Teri Hedges
Karen Hoiberg
Carrie Johnson
Jean Krusi
Elaine McGrath

Margaret R. Meyer
Anne Park
Bryna Rappaport
Kathleen A. Steele
Ana C. Stephens
Candace Ulmer
Jill Vettrus

Freudenthal Institute Staff

Jan de Lange
Director

Truus Dekker
Coordinator

Mieke Abels
Content Coordinator

Monica Wijers
Content Coordinator

Arthur Bakker
Peter Boon
Els Feijs
Dédé de Haan
Martin Kindt

Nathalie Kuijpers
Huub Nilwik
Sonia Palha
Nanda Querelle
Martin van Reeuwijk

Cover photo credits: (left to right) © Comstock Images; © Corbis; © Getty Images

Illustrations
1 James Alexander; **39** Holly Cooper-Olds; **49** James Alexander

Photographs
5 M.C. Escher "Symmetry Drawing E21" and "Symmetry Drawing E69" © 2005 The M.C. Escher Company-Holland. All rights reserved. www.mcescher.com; **17** © Age Fotostock/SuperStock; **25** (top) Sam Dudgeon/HRW Photo; (middle) Victoria Smith/HRW; (bottom) EyeWire/PhotoDisc/Getty Images; **30** PhotoDisc/ Getty Images; **32, 40** Victoria Smith/HRW

◆ Contents

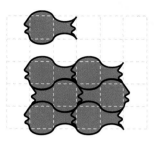

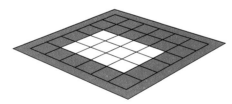

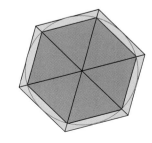

Dear Student,

Welcome to the unit *Reallotment*.

In this unit, you will study different shapes and how to measure certain characteristics of each. You will also study both two- and thee-dimensional shapes.

You will figure out things such as how many people can stand in your classroom. How could you find out without packing people in the entire classroom?

You will also investigate the border or perimeter of a shape, the amount of surface or area a shape covers, and the amount of space or volume inside a three-dimensional figure.

How can you make a shape like the one here that will cover a floor, leaving no open spaces?

In the end, you will have learned some important ideas about algebra, geometry, and arithmetic. We hope you enjoy the unit.

Sincerely,

The Mathematics in Context Development Team

The Size of Shapes

Leaves and Trees

Here is an outline of an elm leaf and an oak leaf. A baker uses these shapes to create cake decorations.

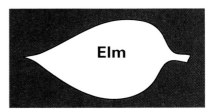

Suppose that one side of each leaf will be frosted with a thin layer of chocolate.

1. Which leaf will have more chocolate? Explain your reasoning.

This map shows two forests separated by a river and a swamp.

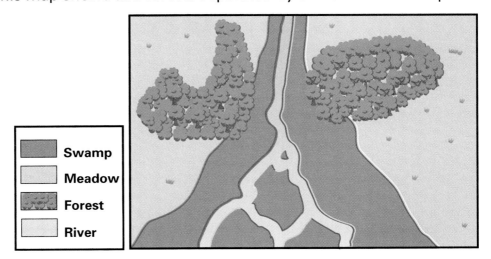

Swamp	
Meadow	
Forest	
River	

2. Which forest is larger? Use the figures below and describe the method you used.

Figure A

Figure B

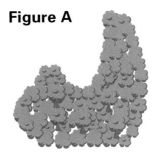

Tulip Fields

Field A **Field B**

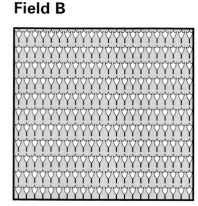

Field C

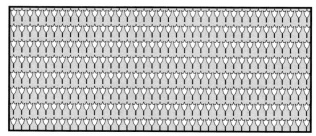

Here are three fields of tulips.

3. Which field has the most tulip plants? Use the tulip fields on **Student Activity Sheet 1** to justify your answer.

Reasonable Prices

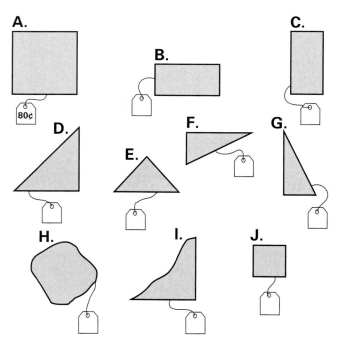

Mary Ann works at a craft store. One of her duties is to price different pieces of cork. She decides that $0.80 is a reasonable price for the big square piece (figure **A**). She has to decide on the prices of the other pieces.

4. Use **Student Activity Sheet 2** to find the prices of the other pieces. Note: All of the pieces have the same thickness.

Here are drawings of tiles with different shapes. Mary Ann decides a reasonable price for the small tile is $5.

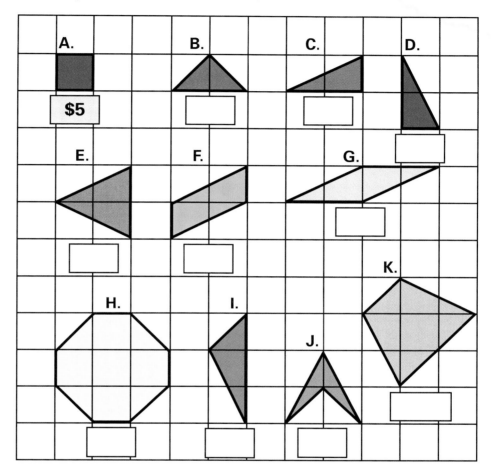

5. a. Use **Student Activity Sheet 3** to find the prices of the other tiles.

   b. **Reflect** Discuss your strategies with some of your classmates. Which tile was most difficult to price? Why?

To figure out prices, you compared the size of the shapes to the $5 square tile. The square was the **measuring unit**. It is helpful to use a measuring unit when comparing sizes.

The number of measuring units needed to cover a shape is called the **area** of the shape.

Tessellations

When you tile a floor, wall, or counter, you want the tiles to fit together without space between them. Patterns without open spaces between the shapes are called **tessellations**.

Sometimes you have to cut tiles to fit together without any gaps. The tiles in the pattern here fit together without any gaps. They form a tessellation.

6. Use the $5 square to estimate the price of each tile.

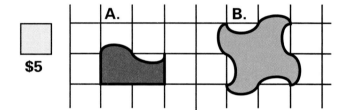

Each of the two tiles in figures **A** and **B** can be used to make a tessellation.

7. **a.** Which of the tiles in problem 5 on page 3 can be used in tessellations? Use **Student Activity Sheet 4** to help you decide.

   b. Choose two of the tiles (from part **a**) and make a tessellation.

Tessellations often produce beautiful patterns. Artists from many cultures have used tessellations in their work. The pictures below are creations from the Dutch artist M. C. Escher.

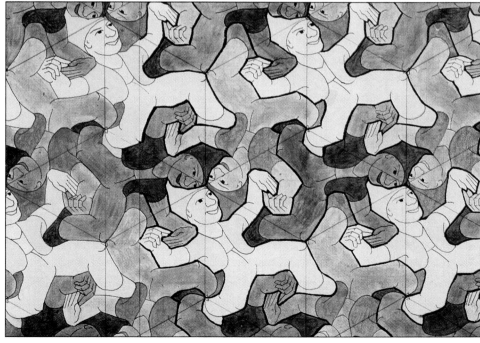

Here is one way to make a tessellation. Start with a rectangular tile and change the shape according to the following rule.

What is changed in one place must be made up for elsewhere.

For example, if you add a shape onto the tile like this,

you have to take away the same shape someplace else. Here are a few possibilities.

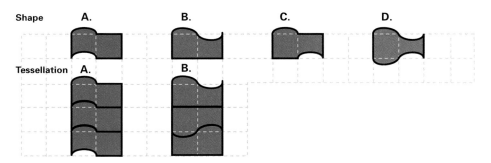

8. How many complete squares make up each of the shapes **A** through **D**?

Shape **D** can be changed into a fish by taking away and adding some more parts. Here is the fish.

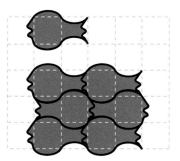

9. **a.** Draw the shape of the fish in your notebook.

b. Show in your drawing how you can change the fish back into a shape that uses only whole squares.

c. How many squares make up one fish?

Another way to ask this last question in part **c** is, "What is the area of one fish measured in squares?" The square is the measuring unit.

Big States, Small States

The shape of a state can often be found on tourism brochures, government stationery, and signs at state borders.

10. **a.** Without looking at a map, draw the shape of the state in which you live.

   b. If you were to list the 50 states from the largest to the smallest in land size, about where would you rank your state?

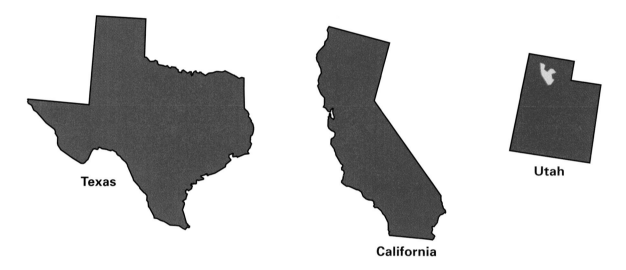

Texas

California

Utah

Three U.S. states, drawn to the same scale, are above.

11. Estimate the answer to the following questions. Explain how you found each estimate.

   a. How many Utahs fit into California?

   b. How many Utahs fit into Texas?

   c. How many Californias fit into Texas?

   d. Compare the areas of these three states.

Forty-eight of the United States are **contiguous**, or physically connected. You will find the drawing of the contiguous states on **Student Activity Sheet 5**.

12. Choose three of the 48 contiguous states and compare the area of your state to the area of each of these three states.

Islands and Shapes

If a shape is drawn on a grid, you can use the squares of the grid to find the area of the shape. Here are two islands: Space Island and Fish Island.

Space Island

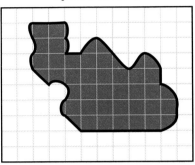

Fish Island

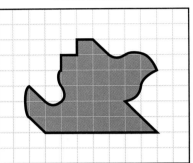

13. a. Which island is bigger? How do you know? Use **Student Activity Sheet 6** to justify your answers.

   b. Estimate the area of each island in square units.

Since the islands have an irregular form, you can only estimate the area for these islands.

You can find the exact area for the number of whole squares, but you have to estimate for the remaining parts. Finding the exact area of a shape is possible if the shape has a more regular form.

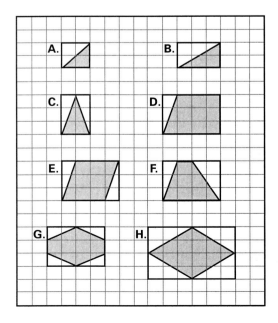

14. What is the area of each of the shaded pieces? Use **Student Activity Sheet 7** to help you. Give your answers in square units. Be prepared to explain your reasoning.

When you know the area of one shape, you can sometimes use that information to help you find the area of another shape. This only works if you can use some relationship between the two shapes.

Here are some shapes that are shaded.

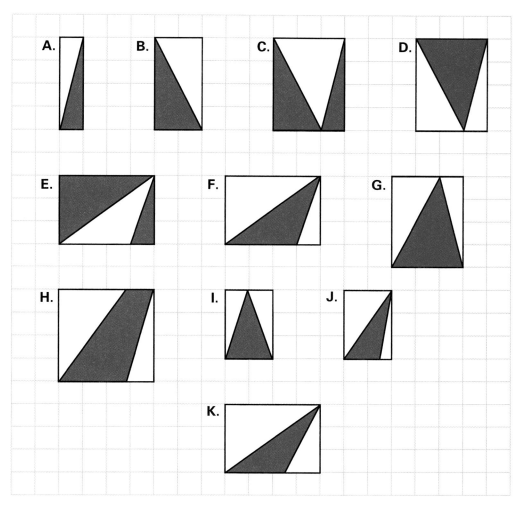

15. a. Choose four blue shapes and describe how you can find the area of each. If possible, use relationships between shapes.

  b. Now find the area (in square units) of each of the blue pieces.

  c. Describe the relationship between the blue area in shapes **C** and **D**.

Summary ❯❯

This section is about areas (sizes) of shapes. You used different methods to compare the areas of two forests, tulip fields, pieces of cork, tiles, and various states and islands. You:

- may have counted tulips;
- compared different-shaped pieces of cork to a larger square piece of cork; and
- divided shapes and put shapes together to make new shapes.

You also actually found the area of shapes by measuring. Area is described by using square units.

You explored several strategies for measuring the areas of various shapes.

- You counted the number of complete squares inside a shape, then reallotted the remaining pieces to make new squares.

  Inside this shape there are   The pieces that remain can be
  four complete squares.   combined into four new squares.

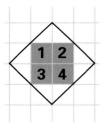   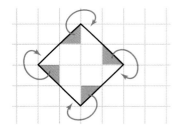

- You may have used relationships between shapes.
  You can see that the shaded piece is half of the rectangle.

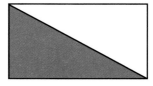

  Or you can see that two shapes together make a third one.

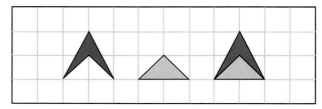

- You may have divided a shape into smaller parts whose area you can find more easily.

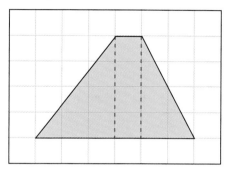

- You may also have enclosed a shape with a rectangle and subtracted the empty areas.

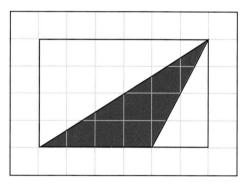

Check Your Work

1. Sue paid $3.60 for a 9 inch (in.)-by-13 in. rectangular piece of board. She cuts the board into three pieces as shown. What is a fair price for each piece?

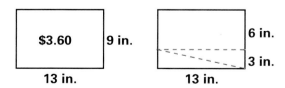

2. Below you see the shapes of two lakes.

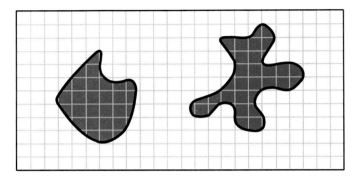

    a. Which lake is bigger? How do you know?

    b. Estimate the area of each lake.

3. Find the area in square units of each of these orange pieces.

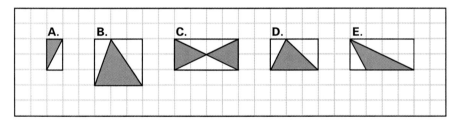

4. Choose two of these shapes and find the area of the green triangles. Explain how you found each area.

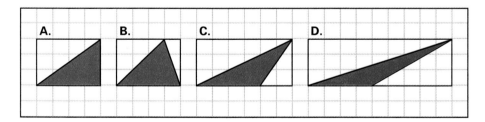

For Further Reflection

Why do you think this unit is called *Reallotment*?

Area Patterns

Rectangles

1. Find the area enclosed by each of the rectangles outlined in the figures below. Explain your methods.

A.
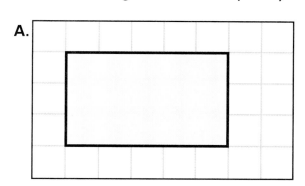

B.
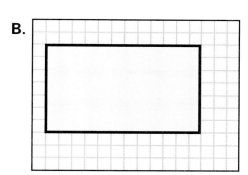

C.
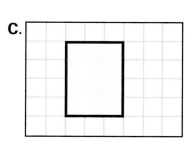

D.
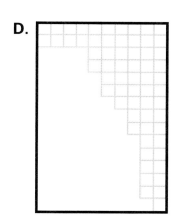

E.
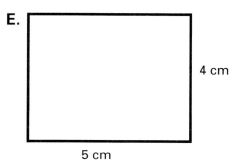

4 cm

5 cm

2. **a.** Describe at least two different methods you can use to find the area enclosed by a rectangle.

   b. **Reflect** Which method do you prefer? Why?

Ms. Petry's class wants to make a wall hanging of geometric shapes. They will use different colors of felt for the geometric shapes. The felt is sold in sheets, 4 feet (ft) by 6 ft. Each sheet costs $12. The store will only charge Ms. Petry's class for the shapes that are cut out.

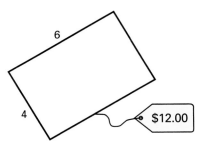

Meggie wants to buy this shaded piece.

3 a. Explain why the piece Meggie wants to buy will cost $6.00.

b. Here are the other shapes they plan to purchase. Use **Student Activity Sheet 8** to calculate the price of the geometric shapes (the shaded pieces).

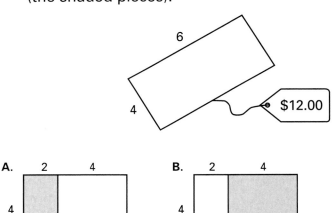

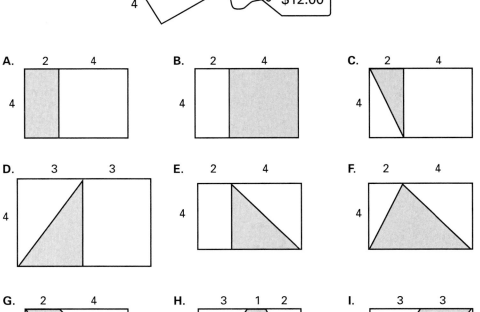

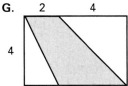

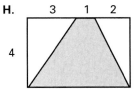

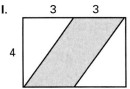

Quadrilateral Patterns

A **quadrilateral** is a four-sided figure.

A **parallelogram** is a special type of quadrilateral.

A parallelogram is a four-sided figure with opposite sides parallel.

4. Is a **rectangle** a parallelogram? Why or why not?

Activity

Looking for Patterns

You can transform a rectangle into many different parallelograms by cutting and pasting a number of times. Try this on graph paper or use a 4 in.-by-6 in. index card.

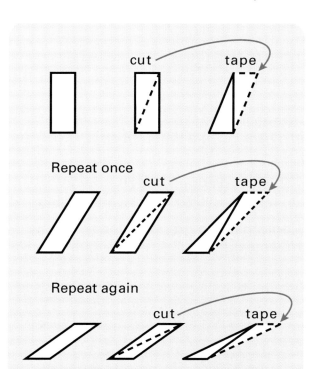

i. Draw a rectangle that is two units wide and three units high or use the index card as the rectangle.

ii. Cut along a **diagonal** and then tape to create a new parallelogram.

iii. Repeat step ii a few more times.

How is the final parallelogram different from the rectangle? How is it the same?

All of the parallelograms below enclose the same area.

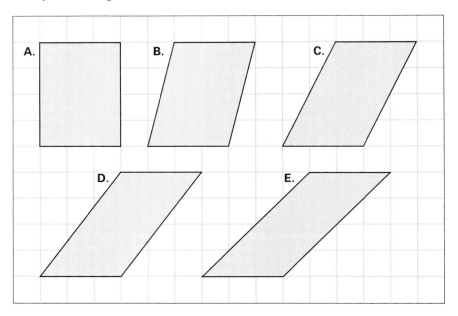

5. a. In addition to having the same area, how are all the parallelograms shown here alike?

b. Describe how each of the parallelograms **B–E** could be transformed into figure **A**.

6. How can your method be used to find the area enclosed by any parallelogram?

In Section A, you learned to **reshape** figures. You cut off a piece of a shape and taped that same piece back on in a different spot. If you do this, the area does not change.

Here are three parallelograms. The first diagram shows how to transform the parallelogram into a rectangle by cutting and taping.

7. Copy the other two parallelograms onto graph paper and show how to transform them into rectangles.

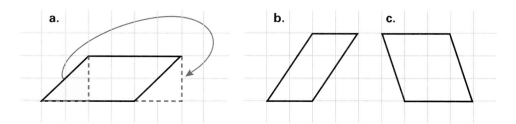

8. Calculate the area of all three parallelograms.

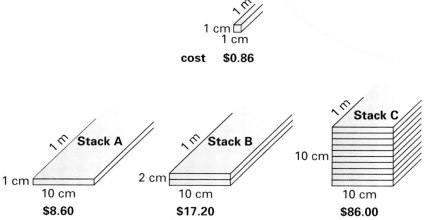

1 cm □ 1 m
1 cm

cost $0.86

Stack A
1 cm
10 cm
$8.60

Stack B
2 cm
10 cm
$17.20

Stack C
10 cm
10 cm
$86.00

Balsa is a lightweight wood used to make model airplanes. For convenience, balsa is sold in standard lengths. This makes it easy to calculate prices. The price of a board that is 1 meter (m) long, 1 centimeter (cm) wide, and 1 centimeter (cm) thick is $0.86. Jim priced each of the three stacks.

9. Explain how Jim could have calculated the price of each stack.

These boards are also 1 m long.

10. a. Estimate the price of the whole stack.

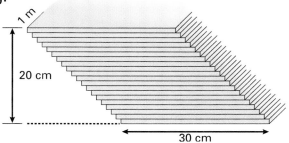

20 cm

30 cm

b. Jim straightened the stack. Now it is much easier to see how to calculate the price. Calculate the price of this stack.

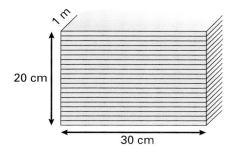

20 cm

30 cm

c. Compare this with your initial estimate.

It is not easy to find the area of some quadrilaterals.

Here are four shaded quadrilaterals that are not parallelograms. Each one is drawn inside a rectangle. Every corner touches one side of the rectangle.

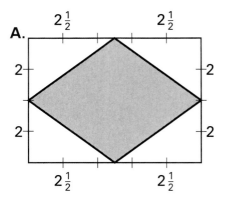

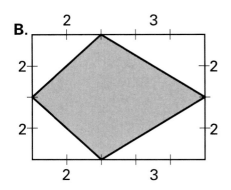

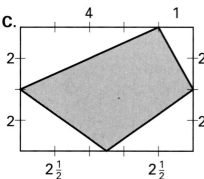

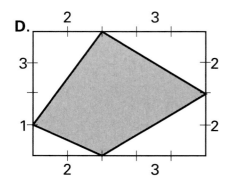

11. a. Use **Student Activity Sheet 9** to calculate the area of each shaded quadrilateral. Show your solution methods; you may describe them with words, calculations, or a drawing. Hint: It may be helpful to draw the gridlines inside the rectangles.

   b. Try to think of a rule for finding the area of a quadrilateral whose corners touch the sides of a rectangle. Explain your rule.

12. a. On graph paper, draw eight different shapes, each with an area of five square units.

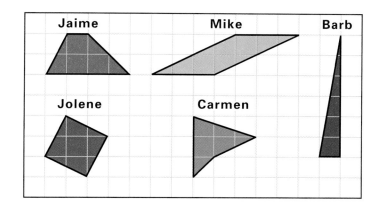

Jaime, Mike, Jolene, Carmen, and Barb drew these shapes.

b. Did they all draw a shape with an area of five square units? Explain why or why not.

c. Draw two triangles that have an area of five square units.

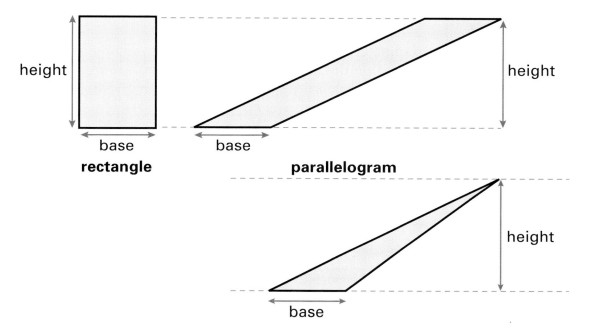

You worked with three shapes in this section. When you describe a rectangle, parallelogram, or triangle, the words **base** and **height** are important. The base describes how wide the figure is. The height describes how tall it is.

13. a. Use the words *base* and *height* to describe ways to find the areas of rectangles, parallelograms, and triangles. Be prepared to explain why your ways work.

b. Check whether your description for finding the area works by finding the area for some of the rectangles, parallelograms, and triangles in problems you did earlier in this section and in Section A.

c. Draw a triangle with base 4 and height 2. Now draw a triangle with base 2 and height 4. What observations can you make?

Strategies and Formulas

The area enclosed by a parallelogram is the same as the area enclosed by a rectangle with the same base and height. You can find the area enclosed by any parallelogram using this formula.

The area (A) is equal to the base (b) times the height (h).

$$A_{\text{rectangle}} = b \times h$$

$$A_{\text{parallelogram}} = b \times h$$

A **triangle** is always half the size of some rectangle or a parallelogram. You can find the area enclosed by a triangle using this formula.

The area (A) is equal to one-half of the base (b) times the height (h).

$$A_{\text{triangle}} = \tfrac{1}{2}b \times h$$

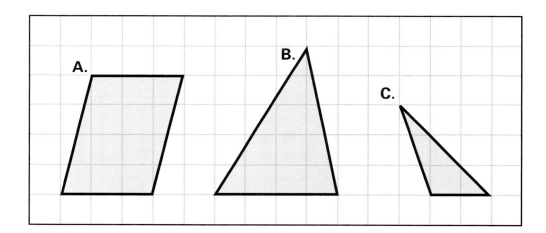

14. Calculate the area enclosed by these shapes.

15. a. On graph paper, draw a parallelogram that encloses an area of 8 square units.

    b. On graph paper, draw a triangle that encloses an area of 8 square units.

For some triangles, the length of the base or height is not easy to establish. This is true for this triangle. Since the triangle is on a "slant," the grid doesn't help you find the length of the base and height.

16. Use a strategy to find the area enclosed by this "slanted" triangle.

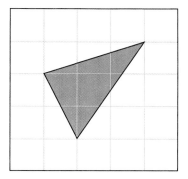

Miguel found the area enclosed by the triangle by drawing a square around it. Then he calculated the area of the three shaded triangles.

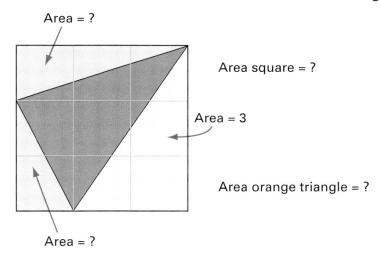

Area = ?

Area square = ?

Area = 3

Area orange triangle = ?

Area = ?

17. Finish Miguel's work. What is the area enclosed by the orange triangle?

18. Copy these images on graph paper and use Miguel's strategy to find the area.

A.
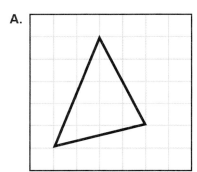

B.
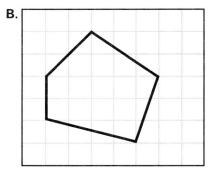

Summary ❯❮

In this section, you learned many ways to calculate the areas enclosed by a variety of shapes.

To find the area enclosed by this shape, you can use any of the following strategies.

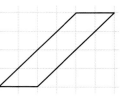

1. Count the squares, cut, and tape partial units.

Count the number of complete squares inside the shape, cut out the remaining pieces, and move them to form new squares.

Step 1

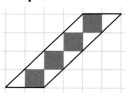

Step 2

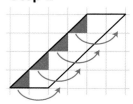

2. Reshape the figure.

Cut off larger parts of the original figure and tape them somewhere else.

Step 1

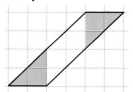

Step 2

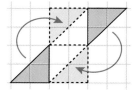

3. Enclose the shape and subtract extras.

Draw a rectangle around the shape in such a way that you can easily subtract the areas that are not part of the shape.

In this case, the area enclosed by the parallelogram is the area enclosed by the rectangle minus the areas of the two triangles.

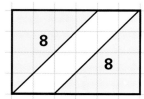

24 − 8 − 8

The area is 8 square units.

4. Double the shape or cut it in half.

The area of the green triangle is half the area enclosed by the corresponding rectangle (square).

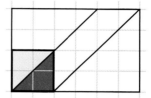

5. Use formulas.

You can use the relationship between a parallelogram and a rectangle.

> The area enclosed by a parallelogram is equal to the area enclosed by a rectangle with the same base and the same height.

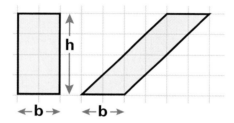

This relationship gives you the formula:

$$A_{\text{parallelogram}} = b \times h$$

For the areas enclosed by a rectangle and a triangle, you can also use formulas.

$$A_{\text{rectangle}} = b \times h$$

$$A_{\text{triangle}} = \tfrac{1}{2} b \times h$$

Check Your Work

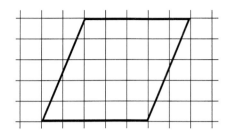

1. **a.** On **Student Activity Sheet 9**, shade a rectangle that encloses the same area as the parallelogram on the left.

   b. Use this parallelogram to shade a triangle on **Student Activity Sheet 9** that encloses an area half the area of the parallelogram.

2. Use **Student Activity Sheet 9** to determine the area of each of these shapes. Use any method.

A. 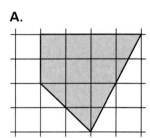 **B.** 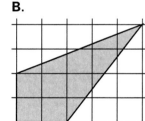 **C.** 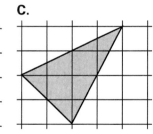 **D.**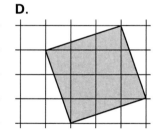

3. For each strategy described in the Summary, find an example of a problem from Section A or B where you used that strategy.

4. On graph paper, draw two different parallelograms and two different triangles each enclosing an area of 12 square units.

 For Further Reflection

Which of the methods described in the Summary for finding the area of a shape do you think will be the most useful? Explain your reasoning.

Measuring Area

Going Metric

Metric units are easy to use because the relationship between units is based on multiples of 10. The United States is one of the few countries that still uses the customary system of measurement.

Today, Americans are buying and selling products from other countries. You might notice that many products in the grocery store, such as bottled water and canned fruits, are measured in metric units. If you run track, you probably measure distance using meters. International games, such as the Olympics, use metric distances. Medicines are weighed in metric units. Food labels usually list fat, protein, and carbohydrates in metric units.

Here are some descriptions to help you understand and remember the sizes of some commonly used metric units for length.

Length

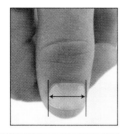

1 centimeter: Your thumbnail is about 1 centimeter wide, which is smaller than one inch.

1 meter: One giant step is about 1 meter long, which is a little more than one yard.

1 kilometer: The length of about ten football fields is about 1 kilometer, which is about 0.6 of a mile.

1. Make a list of things that are approximately the size of:

   a. a centimeter

   b. a meter

   c. a kilometer

You probably worked with the metric system before. See if you can remember the answers to the following problems.

2. a. How many centimeters are in a meter?

   b. How many meters are in a kilometer?

   c. Write two other statements about how metric units relate to each other.

Area

One metric measuring unit for area is the square centimeter. The dimensions of the small square are exactly 1 cm by 1 cm. The area can be written as 1 cm².

$$1 \text{ cm}^2 \quad 1 \text{ cm}$$
$$1 \text{ cm}$$

An example of a customary measuring unit for area is a square inch (in²).

3. a. Draw this measuring unit in your notebook.

   b. About how many square centimeters do you need to cover one square inch?

4. Give an example of something that is about the size of:

   a. a square centimeter

   b. a square inch

   c. a square meter

   d. a square kilometer

You know that a shape that is one square meter in area does not have to be a square. You worked through many examples in Sections A and B where a shape was changed but the area stayed the same. You created a tessellation by cutting and pasting parts in different locations, while keeping the area the same.

Here is a variety of shapes that enclose an area of one square centimeter.

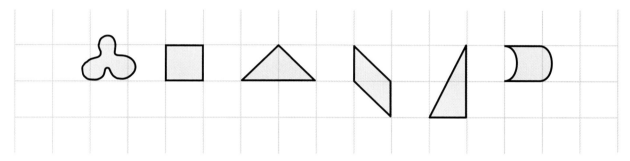

5. On graph paper, draw two different shapes that enclose an area of 1 square centimeter.

Many different types of square units are used to measure area, such as square meters, square centimeters, square yards, or square feet. If you need to measure an area more precisely, you often use smaller square units to measure the same space.

Activity

Draw 1 cm², on a self-stick note.
(Be sure the backside of the square is sticky.)

Cut out your square centimeter.

Have a group of four students use a meter stick and four centimeter squares to mark the four corners of a square whose sides measure 1 m, as in the sketch.

Note that this sketch is not drawn to scale!

6. What is the area of this figure in square meters?

This drawing represents your square figure with side lengths of 1 m.

You can fill the square figure with smaller squares.

In this drawing, the figure is being filled along the bottom row. Each small square represents an area of 1 cm². Note that the squares are very, very small—you can barely see them, but they are there.

7. **a.** How many square centimeters do you need to completely fill the bottom row? (Think about the relationship between meters and centimeters.)

   b. How many rows are needed to fill the whole square?

   c. What is the area of the figure in square centimeters? How did you calculate this?

   d. You found the area of this square using two different units, first using square meters and then using square centimeters.
   If you could choose, which units would you prefer to use for the area of this square? Explain your choice.

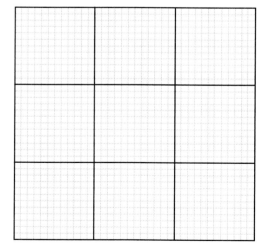

Area can also be measured using the customary measurement system.

A drawing can be used to compare square inches and square yards. Here is a square with side lengths 1 yard long; it is not drawn in its actual size.

8. **a.** What is the area of the figure in square inches?

   b. What is the area of the figure in square yards?

   c. What is the area of the figure in square feet?

A drawing of the larger square unit can help you find the area in a smaller unit of measure. You can imagine filling the larger square with smaller squares. You only need to remember the relationship between units, such as:

1 meter = 100 centimeters   1 kilometer = 1,000 meters

1 yard = 3 feet   1 foot = 12 inches   1 yard = 36 inches

You can use this information to figure out the relationship. If you forget, you can always recreate filling the larger space with smaller squares.

9. Complete the following:

   a. 1 square meter =_____ square centimeters

   b. 1 square yard = _____ square inches

10. **a.** **Reflect** Which units of measure are easier to use, metric units, like the meter and centimeter, or customary units, like the yard and inch? Explain your choice.

    b. What units of measure would you use to find:

       i. the length of a fruit fly?

       ii. the distance a frog hops?

       iii. the area of a soccer field?

       iv. the area of your tabletop?

Floor Covering

Several floors at Hotel Baron will be covered with Italian marble. The marble comes in squares that are exactly 1 m². Leftover pieces will not be wasted; they will be cut to fit spaces where a whole tile will not fit.

Here is one Italian marble tile.

These three floors will be covered with Italian marble.

A.

4 m

3 m

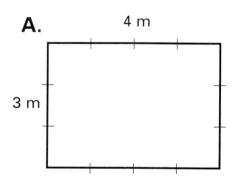

B.

4 m

$2\frac{1}{2}$ m

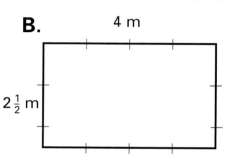

C.

$2\frac{1}{2}$ m

3 m

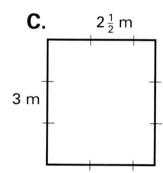

11. How many square meters of marble are needed for each of these floors? Show your calculations.

This floor needs to be covered with marble as well.

$3\frac{1}{2}$ m

$2\frac{1}{2}$ m

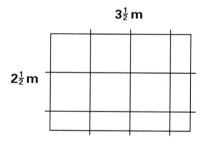

Robert used the formula you learned in the previous section to calculate the area of this floor.

$$A_{rectangle} = base \times height$$

Here is his work:

Area floor $= 3\frac{1}{2} \times 2\frac{1}{2}$ m²

12. How would you calculate $3\frac{1}{2} \times 2\frac{1}{2}$?

Robert didn't remember how to multiply these numbers.

Aisha helps Robert. She marks up the drawing of the floor to explain how to multiply these numbers.

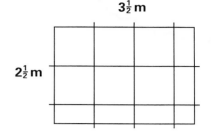

$3\frac{1}{2}$ m

$2\frac{1}{2}$ m

13. How can Aisha's drawing be used to find the answer to $3\frac{1}{2} \times 2\frac{1}{2}$? Show your work.

The hotel has two additional floors to cover with marble.

The hallway floor is $1\frac{1}{2}$ m wide by 8 m long.

The sitting room floor is $3\frac{1}{2}$ m by $5\frac{1}{2}$ m.

14. Calculate the area of both floors. Making a drawing like Aisha's may help you.

Another type of marble tile is available in smaller squares; each edge is 10 cm long.

These smaller tiles come in different colors. Arranging these colored tiles produces different floor patterns.

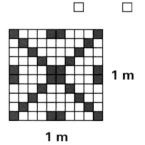

1 m

1 m

15. a. How many small tiles make up this larger square meter?

b. How many small tiles do you need to cover this floor?

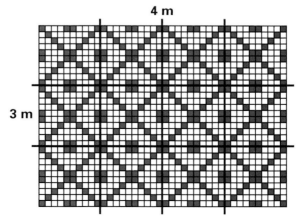

4 m

3 m

c. How many small tiles do you need to cover the floor from problem 11?

Hotel Lobby

14 yd

Floor Lobby

6 yd

The lobby of a new hotel is 14 yards long and 6 yards wide.

The owners are considering three options for covering the floor of the lobby: carpet (which comes in two widths of 3 yards or 4 yards) or vinyl. The current prices of each type of floor covering are shown below. Note that the carpet comes in two widths; 3 yards or 4 yards.

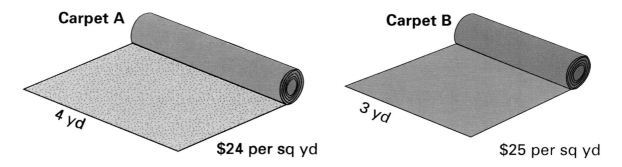

Carpet A
4 yd
$24 per sq yd

Carpet B
3 yd
$25 per sq yd

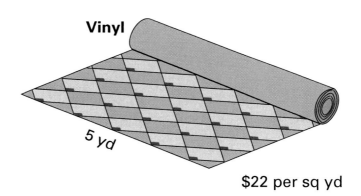

Vinyl
5 yd
$22 per sq yd

You are the salesperson for a floor-covering company. The hotel manager asks you to show with scale drawings how the lobby can be covered with each type of floor covering and to calculate the price for each of the three options for covering the lobby floor. Finally, you are asked to make a purchase recommendation.

16. Use **Student Activity Sheets 10** (with scale drawings of the lobby floor) and **11** to help you write a report that analyzes each floor option. Draw a picture of how each option could be laid out and calculate the price for each example. Don't forget to include a recommendation for the best choice of floor covering and your reasons for making this choice.

Measuring Area

Summary

Two different systems of measurement are the *metric system* and the *customary system*. Each system uses different measuring units for length and area.

	Length	Area
Customary	inches	square inches
	feet	square feet
	yards	square yards
	miles	square miles
Metric	centimeters	square centimeters
	meters	square meters
	kilometers	square kilometers

To become more familiar with these units, it helps to make a list of things that are about the size of the unit. For example, a meter is like a giant step, a little more than a yard. A kilometer is about the distance you walk in ten minutes; to walk a mile takes about 15 minutes.

One square kilometer can be filled with smaller squares, for example, square meters.

Since 1 km = 1,000 m, one row would take up 1,000 m². There would be 1,000 rows, so the entire square kilometer would take one million square meters to completely cover it up (1,000 × 1,000 = 1,000,000).

Finding Area

To calculate or estimate area you can make a drawing, use a formula, or reposition pieces.

Here is one example.

The drawing shows that 12 whole tiles, seven half tiles (or $3\frac{1}{2}$ whole tiles), and $\frac{1}{4}$ of a tile are necessary to cover the floor.

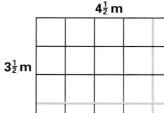

Together $12 + 3\frac{1}{2} + \frac{1}{4} = 15\frac{3}{4}$ tiles, so the area of the floor is $15\frac{3}{4}$ m².

Here is the plan for the main walkway in a new mall. The tiles used to make this floor are in the shape of a hexagon, a six-sided shape.

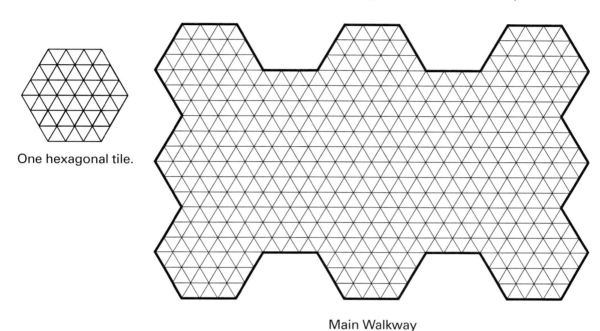

One hexagonal tile.

Main Walkway

1. Use the drawing of the Main Walkway on **Student Activity Sheet 12** to answer the following questions.

   a. How many hexagonal tiles were used to create this walkway?

The hexagonal tiles were made in the factory from small triangular tiles.

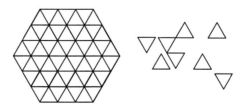

   b. How many of these small triangular tiles are in the floor of the Main Walkway?

Section C: Measuring Area   35

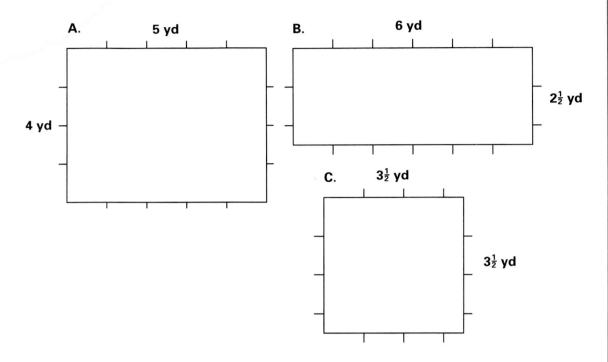

2. Calculate the area (in square yards) of each floor.

3. The floors in problem 2 are covered with colored tiles. Each tile has side lengths of one foot.

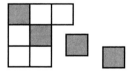

   a. How many tiles do you need to cover each of the floors?

   b. Finish this sentence: 1 square yard = ____ square feet.

4. Name an object and estimate its area using at least two of the measurement units listed in the Summary.

5. Order all the metric and customary units from the Summary in one list from smallest to largest.

 For Further Reflection

Name at least three situations in your house for which it was important to find area.

Perimeter and Area

Perimeter

Danny is a contractor hired to build a bicycle/running trail around each of the lakes pictured below. The owner wants to pay Danny the same amount of money for each trail because the lakes are equal in area. Danny agrees that the lakes are equal in area, but he wants more money for constructing the trail around Lake Marie.

1. Do you agree that Danny should get more money for the Lake Marie trail? Why or why not?

Here are drawings of four gardens the city wants to plant in a downtown park. Along the outside edge of each garden, the city will build an ornamental fence. Each square in the grid represents 10 m by 10 m.

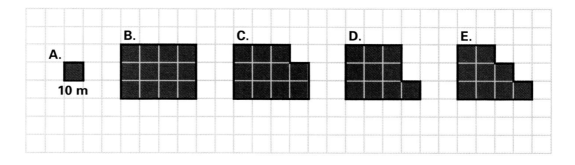

2. How much fencing do you need to fence in each garden?

3. The distance around a shape is called the **perimeter** of the shape.

    a. How is the area of a shape different from its perimeter?

    b. Find the area of each garden.

    c. Compare the area and perimeter of these gardens.

Here is a drawing of a garden with an area of 15 square units.

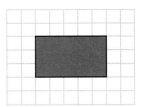

4. Use graph paper to design four other gardens with the same area but with different perimeters. Label the area and perimeter of each garden.

Area and Perimeter Enlarged

Here are three pairs of figures. For each pair, **Figure i** is enlarged to make **Figure ii**. Each pair has the same shape but not the same size.

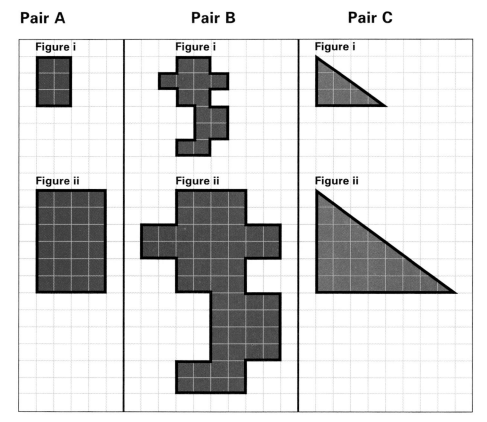

5. For each pair, calculate and compare the area and perimeter of **Figure i** and **Figure ii**. Describe how the area and perimeter are changed it you enlarge a shape by a certain factor.

Here is an original picture of space ships (Picture **A**).

6. Use a centimeter ruler to measure the dimensions of the picture.

This picture can be enlarged. Different enlargements of the same picture have the same shape but not the same dimensions.

Here is an enlargement (Picture **B**) of the original picture. It was enlarged from the original by a factor of two. This means that both the length and width were doubled.

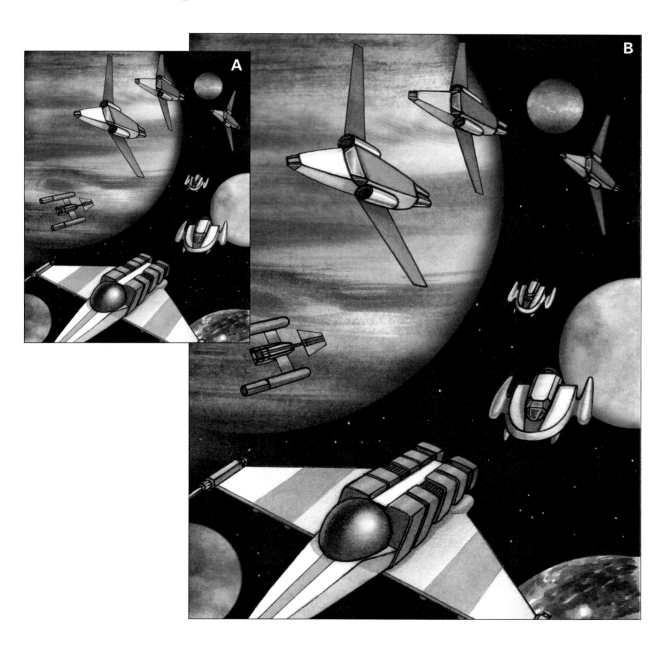

To frame the original picture (A), a piece of glass costs $5, and a wood frame of 28 cm costs $10.

7. a. If the cost is the same per square centimeter of area for the glass, what is the cost to cover the enlargement (picture B) with glass?

   b. If the cost is the same per centimeter of length for the frame, what is the cost of a wood frame for the enlargement?

Suppose the original print was enlarged to 18 cm by 24 cm.

8. a. What is the cost to cover this enlargement with glass?

   b. What is the cost to border this enlargement with a wood frame?

   c. When a figure is enlarged, will the area and perimeter enlarge in the same way? Explain your answer.

Circumference

The perimeter of shapes that have straight sides can be measured or calculated rather easily. Shapes with curved edges make it more challenging to find the perimeter.

Activity

Drawing a Circle

- Take a string of a length between 20 cm and 30 cm.

- Fold it and knot the ends together.

- Hold the knot in one spot on your paper.

- Put a pencil through the loop at the other end.

- Keeping the rope tight, draw a circle.

- Use scissors to cut through the knot.

9. a. What is the special name given to the length of the string?

   b. About how many times does the length of the string fit along the perimeter of the circle?

   c. Compare your answer to part **a** with your classmates'.

Circles

A more precise method to find the perimeter of a circle would be very useful.

First you need an **equilateral triangle**.

Equilateral means that all sides have the same length.

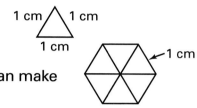

Using six of these regular triangles, you can make a **regular hexagon**.

10. a. What is the perimeter of the regular triangle?

   b. What is the perimeter of the regular hexagon?

Here is an enlargement of this hexagon.

A circle is drawn around the hexagon. The circle passes through all six corners.

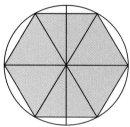

A square is drawn to enclose both the circle and hexagon.

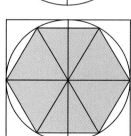

11. Use the drawings to estimate the perimeter of this circle. Show your work.

The perimeter of a circle is usually called the **circumference** of a circle.

The straight line through the center of the circle is called the **diameter** of the circle.

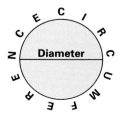

12. What is the length of the diameter of the circle in problem 11?

Here are three new drawings made using different sizes of equilateral triangles. The triangle size is shown in each drawing.

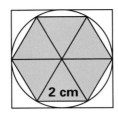

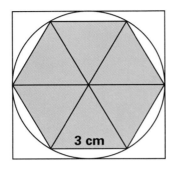

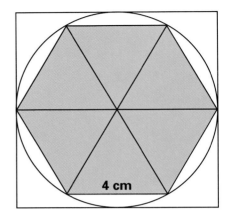

13. Use the figures above to calculate the perimeter of each square and hexagon. Use the diameter of each circle to estimate the circumferences of each circle. Write all the results in the table on **Student Activity Sheet 13**.

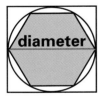

	Estimating the Circumference			
	Using 1-cm Triangles	Using 2-cm Triangles	Using 3-cm Triangles	Using 4-cm Triangles
Diameter of Circle				
Perimeter of Hexagon				
Approximate Circumference of Circle				
Perimeter of Square				

Review the results in your table.

14. a. How is the circumference of each circle related to the perimeter of the hexagon and the square that belongs to it?

b. Describe the relationship between the diameter of a circle and its circumference.

c. Compare this result to your findings from problem 9.

Long ago, people discovered a relationship between the circumference of a circle and the diameter of the circle. They described this relationship like this.

"The circumference of circle is a FIXED NUMBER times the diameter of circle."

15. What is the value of this fixed number based on your findings so far?

The ancient Greeks used a special name for this fixed number. They called it π (a letter in the Greek alphabet, pronounced PYE). Pi is approximately 3.14 or $\frac{22}{7}$.

A rough estimate for the value of pi is the number 3.

The modern formula for the circumference of circle is:

$$circumference\ of\ circle = \pi \times diameter\ of\ circle$$

Using an approximation for π, the formula becomes:

$$circumference\ of\ circle \approx 3.14 \times diameter\ of\ circle$$

Most calculators today have a π button for this special fixed number.

16. a. What value does your calculator display for the number π?

    b. Use one of the formulas above to check your circumference estimates for the circles recorded in your table in problem 13.

Some people prefer to use the **radius** of a circle when they find the circumference of a circle.

The radius of a circle is half the size of the diameter.

17. a. Draw a circle with a diameter of 6 cm in your notebook. Color the radius of the circle and write its length next to the drawing. Find the circumference of the circle.

    b. Use your drawing to explain this formula:

$$circumference\ of\ circle = 2 \times \pi \times radius\ of\ circle$$

Circles and Area

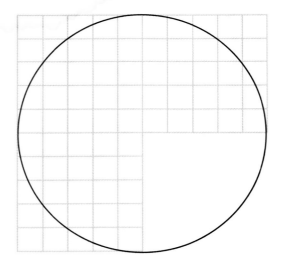

Peter's mother has an L-shaped terrace. She would like to change this L-shaped terrace into a circle shape. Here is a drawing to represent her design.

18. a. How many tiles are in the L-shaped terrace? Use **Student Activity Sheet 14** to help you answer the question. Explain how you found your answer.

   b. Estimate the number of tiles needed to create the circle-shaped terrace.

An ancient formula used to estimate the area enclosed by a circle is: the *area* is about 3 × *radius* × *radius*.

19. a. Use the small drawing above and the drawing for problem 18 on **Student Activity Sheet 15** to explain why this ancient formula is a good estimate for the area enclosed by a circle.

   b. Use this ancient formula to check your answer to problem 18b.

A more precise number you can use instead of 3 is surprisingly the number π!

A modern formula for the area enclosed by a circle is:

area enclosed by a circle = π × *radius* × *radius*

or,   *area* ≈ 3.14 × *radius* × *radius*

The square tiles in problem 18 are 30 cm by 30 cm.

20. a. Calculate the area of the circle-shaped terrace using one of the formulas above.

   b. Compare this result to your estimates for 18b and 19b.

The formulas for area and perimeters related to circles have many practical uses. Here are the designs for two mirrors, one a circle and the other a rectangle with a semicircle on top.

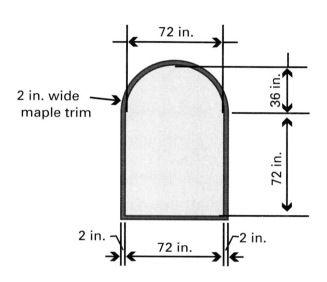

Circular Mirror

Circlehead Mirror

21. Tamae was going to buy the largest mirror she could find.

 a. Which of the two mirrors has the larger viewing area? Explain your reasoning.

 b. Which of the two mirrors has the greater perimeter? How do you know?

 c. Which mirror should Tamae buy? Why?

A pizza that is 10 in. in diameter costs $9.60 while a 12-in. pizza costs $11.80. Joni says, "For 2 in. more, I have to pay an extra $2.20."

Alex states, "But you get a lot more pizza if you by the big one."

22. a. Comment on the statements made by Joni and Alex.

 b. How much more pizza is the big one compared to the small one?

D Perimeter and Area

Summary »

In this section, you studied relationships between perimeter and area. You learned that:

- two shapes with the same perimeter can have different areas, and

- two shapes with the same area can have different perimeters.

You investigated what happens to area and perimeter when a figure is enlarged.

When all the lengths of a shape are doubled, the perimeter of the enlargement doubles, but the area will be enlarged by a factor of 4.

You discovered formulas for circles.

- The perimeter or the distance around the circle is the circumference of the circle (C) and

    is equal to π times the diameter (**d**).

    $$C = \pi \times d$$

If you double the radius, you get the length of the diameter. Another formula is:

    The circumference (C) is equal to two times π times the radius (r).

    $$C = 2 \times \pi \times r$$

π is a fixed number. A good approximation is 3.14 or $\frac{22}{7}$. A rough estimate is 3.

- The **area enclosed by a circle:**

    The area (**A**), enclosed by the circle is equal to π times the radius (r) times the radius (r).

    $$A = \pi \times r \times r \quad \text{or} \quad A = \pi \times r^2$$

1. a. Draw three different rectangles that enclose an area of 16 cm². What is the perimeter of each rectangle?

   b. What is the smallest perimeter you can have for a rectangle that encloses an area of 16 cm²? Explain your answer.

2. a. On graph paper, draw a rectangle that encloses an area of 12 squares. What is its perimeter?

   b. Draw an enlargement of your rectangle by doubling each side.

   c. What is the area enclosed by the enlarged rectangle? What is the perimeter?

   d. In general, if you double all the sides of a rectangle, what happens to the enclosed area? What happens to the perimeter? Explain your answers.

3. Suze wants a clock that is not too large. She is looking at two clocks in the catalog. One has the shape of a circle that is 30 cm in diameter. The other has a rectangular shape (with a clock on it) that is 32 cm by 22 cm.

Compare the area and the perimeter of each clock. Which one should she buy? Support your answer.

4. Mr. Anderson wants to have glass insurance for his house. The premium for this insurance is based on the area of the exterior glass windows.

Most of the exterior windows of Mr. Anderson's house have the shape of rectangles.

   a. Describe how Mr. Anderson can calculate the glass area for these windows.

   b. Three windows have the shape shown in the diagram with a semicircle on the top of a rectangle. Describe how Mr. Anderson can calculate the area of glass in this type of window. Include an example of an area calculation for the window with the dimensions in the drawing.

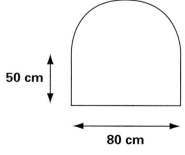

50 cm

80 cm

5. **a.** What happens to the circumference of a circle if you double the length of the diameter? Justify your answer.

   b. What happens to the area enclosed by a circle if you multiply the diameter by 2? Justify your answer.

For Further Reflection

Make a list of all of the terms and formulas in this section. Create a diagram that shows how the terms are related to each other and to the formulas.

Surface Area and Volume

Packages

In Section D you investigated the relationship between perimeter and area.

In a similar way, you can look at the relationship between **surface area** and **volume**. This is like comparing the amount of wrapping paper you need to cover a package with the space inside the package.

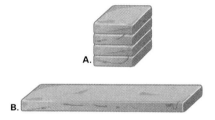

Here are two different packages of modeling clay, drawn to the same scale.

1. **a.** Which package do you think has more clay? Why?

   b. Which package do you think needs more wrapping paper? Why?

The area covered with wrapping paper is the surface area of the package. The top, bottom, and sides are the surfaces or faces.

A packaging machine cuts and folds cardboard packages.

Here is one gift package and the cardboard to make the package. The drawing of the cardboard that can be folded to make the package is called a **net**.

The packages can be filled with cubes.

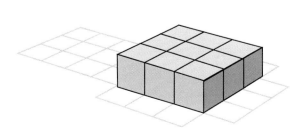

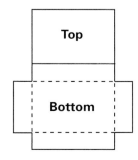

Packages are classified by the maximum number of cubes that each can hold.

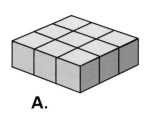

A.

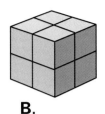

B.

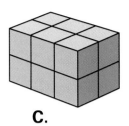

C.

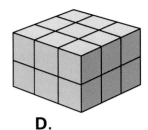

D.

2. a. How many cubes will fit into each package?

   b. On graph paper, draw a net for each package.

   c. Which package requires the least cardboard material to make? Show your work.

The packaging machine makes many different-sized packages.

3. Is it possible to make a package to hold exactly 100 cubes?

If your answer is "yes," give the dimensions of this package.

If your answer is "no," explain why the machine is unable to make this package.

Here is the bottom area for a new package. The package will have a height of 4 cubes.

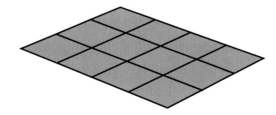

4. How many cubes will fit into this package?

Measuring Inside

You can make a centimeter cube by drawing a figure like this and folding it into a cube. Each edge of the cube must measure exactly 1 cm.

The figure is called the *net* of a cube.

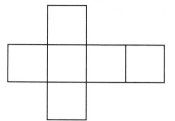

5. a. Use centimeter graph paper to draw a net of a centimeter cube.

Cut it out and fold it to make one cubic centimeter. You don't need to paste it together.

b. Cut the top off a tissue box. How many cubic centimeters are needed to fill it? Explain how you found your answer.

A cube with dimensions 1 cm by 1 cm by 1 cm is said to have a **volume** of 1 cubic centimeter, written as 1 cm^3.

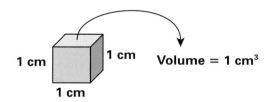

1 cm   1 cm   Volume = 1 cm^3

1 cm

6. What is the surface area of the centimeter cube?

A rectangular package that will hold exactly 24 cubes of 1 cm by 1 cm by 1 cm has a volume of 24 cm^3.

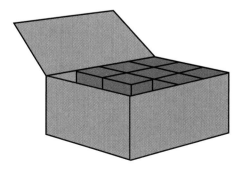

7. a. Use centimeter cubes to find as many different-sized packages as you can that will hold exactly 24 cubes. Use dimensions that are counting numbers.

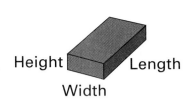

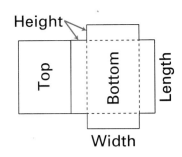

b. Determine how much cardboard is needed to make each package. Do not include cardboard for flaps to paste the edges together. Use a table like the one below to record your results.

Package Dimensions				
Length (in cm)	**Width (in cm)**	**Height (in cm)**	**Volume (in cm³)**	**Surface Area (in cm²)**
			24	
			24	
			24	
			24	
			24	
			24	
			24	

Maria is trying to find the volume of this package. The package has been partially filled with cubes. Maria says, "I can easily find the volume of this package! The bottom of the package measures 8 cm by 7 cm. I can fit 56 cubes on the bottom layer..."

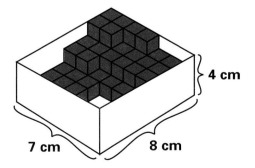

8. a. Explain what else Maria has to do to find the volume of the package.

   b. What is the volume of Maria's package?

Jonathan bought a special vase for his friend Erin who lives in Ireland. He needs to pack the vase very carefully so that he can mail it overseas. His shipping box measures 35 cm by 16 cm and has a height of 10 cm. He bought a sack of packaging material to protect and cushion the vase. The guarantee on the sack claims it "will fill a box as a big as 6,000 cubic centimeters."

9. Will this be enough packaging material to keep the vase safe? Show your work.

To measure the volume of larger packages, you use larger sized cubes. In the metric system, you use cubic decimeters or cubic meters. This drawing represents one cubic decimeter (dm³). Note that one decimeter (dm) = 10 cm.

1 cubic decimeter

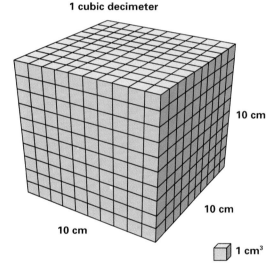

10 cm

10 cm

10 cm

1 cm³

10. a. If everyone in your class made a cubic centimeter, would it be enough to fill 1 dm³?

b. How many cubic centimeters are needed to fill 1 dm³?

11. a. Name some objects whose volume would be measured in cubic decimeters; cubic meters.

b. Write four statements about how cubic centimeters, cubic decimeters, and cubic meters are related.

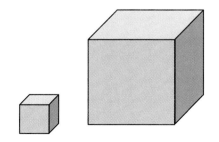

The cubes to the left represent a cubic inch and a cubic foot, two customary units of measure for volume.

12. a. Write a statement about how cubic inches and cubic feet are related.

b. Write two other statements about how cubic feet and cubic yards are related.

Reshaping

These solids are made of cubic centimeter blocks.

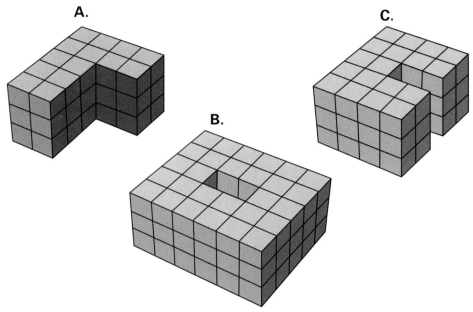

A.

C.

B.

13. Find the volume of each solid and describe your solution strategy.

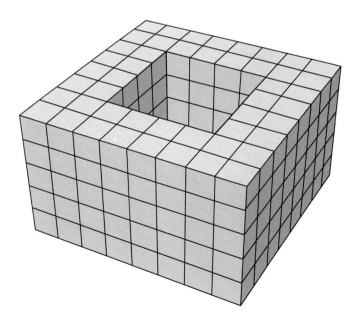

14. a. Describe two different strategies to find the volume of the shape above.

b. Use one of these strategies to find the volume.

A.

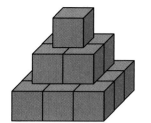

B.

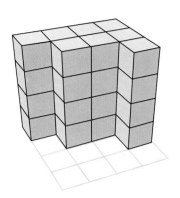

C.

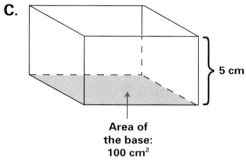

5 cm

**Area of
the base:
100 cm²**

D. Your classroom

E. The stack of boards below.

F. A soda can.

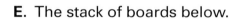
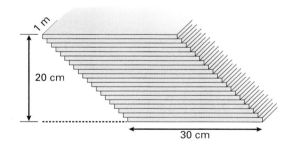

1 m

20 cm

30 cm

G.

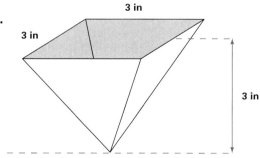

3 in

3 in

3 in

15. Find the volume of each item and describe your strategy.

If an object has a shape that can be cut in **slices** that all have the same size, you can calculate the volume of the object in an easy way, by using the formula:

volume = area of a slice × height

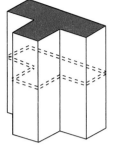 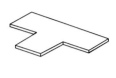

16. a. For which items from problem 15 can you use this volume formula?

  b. For each of the items you chose, describe the shape of the slice. What is the area of each slice for each item you chose?

17. Explain why the formula doesn't work for a cone and a pyramid.

The can has a height of 16 cm, and the diameter of a slice is 6 cm.

18. a. Calculate the area of a slice.

  b. Use your answer from **a** to calculate the volume of the can.

  c. Find a can in the shape of a cylinder with different dimensions that has the same volume.

All slices of this container are rectangles with the same dimensions.

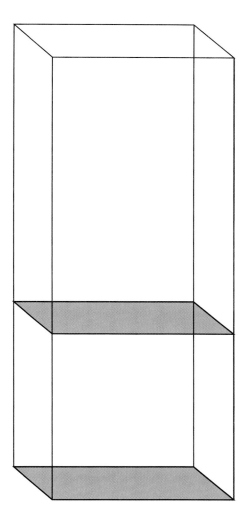

The height is 10 inches.

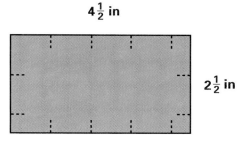

$4\frac{1}{2}$ in

$2\frac{1}{2}$ in

19. a. Name a use for this container.

  b. Calculate the volume of the container. Show your work.

This container is $4\frac{1}{2}$ in. high.
The base of this container is 10 in. by $2\frac{1}{2}$ in.

You can replace the words "area of slice" with the words "area of base."

20. a. Rewrite the volume formula using the word *base*.

   b. Calculate the volume of this container.

   c. Compare your answer to your answer for problem 19.
   What do you notice? Explain.

A container has dimensions of $1\frac{1}{2}$ in. by $2\frac{1}{2}$ in. by 6 in.

21. Calculate the volume of this container.

A gift box has a volume of 240 cm³.

22. a. What dimensions does this gift box have? Find three different
   possibilities. Note: The box does not need to have the shape
   of a block.

   b. Name two objects that have about this same volume.

   c. **Reflect** Does every gift box that has a volume of 240 cm³
   have the same surface area? Explain your thinking. Use
   your examples from part **a** to support your answer with
   calculations.

Math History

History of π

π is one of the most ancient numbers known in history. It represents the most famous ratio in mathematics, the ratio of the circumference of a circle to its diameter.

You can use a calculator to find the value for π. But what did people use in earlier days?

Long ago, people used the number 3. That is not very accurate, but it was easy to use for their calculations.

The Babylonians used a more accurate value: $3 + \frac{1}{8}$.

In the Egyptian Rhind Papyrus, which is dated about 1650 B.C., the value for π was calculated as $4 \times \frac{8}{9} \times \frac{8}{9}$.

About 250 B.C., the famous ancient Greek mathematician and inventor Archimedes used the following strategy.

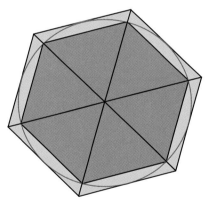

He constructed **polygons** with six sides in and around the circle, like you see here. He knew how to calculate the circumference of both polygons. Then he doubled the number of sides (12), and doubled again and again until he had polygons with 96 sides! He then computed the perimeter of these polygons and found the value of π to lie between $\frac{223}{71}$ and $\frac{22}{7}$.

In the fifth century, the Chinese mathematician Zu Chungzhi found a different value for Archimedes' $\frac{223}{71}$. That more accurate value was $\frac{355}{113}$, and six decimals of π were now known.

This record lasted until 1400, when the Persian mathematician Al-Kashi calculated a value with 16 decimals. He used Archimedes' strategy, but he doubled the number of sides 23 times.

William Jones, an English mathematician, introduced the modern symbol for pi in 1700. The letter π was chosen because π in Greek, pronounced like our letter "p," stands for "perimeter."

As a result of the development of technology, the known decimals for pi have now exceeded 1 trillion.

So the number of times a diameter fits around its circle is

3.1415926535897932384626433832795028841971693993751….

Summary

In this section, you studied packages. Packages have a surface area and a volume.

The surface area is how much covering you need to wrap all the faces of a package. Surface area is measured using square measuring units.

The surface area of this package is 32 square units.

The volume of a package indicates how many cubes totally fill up a package.

To measure the volume of a package, you can count or calculate how many cubic units fit inside the package.

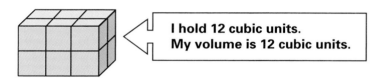

I hold 12 cubic units.
My volume is 12 cubic units.

Volume is measured using cubic measuring units. One common measuring unit for volume is a cubic centimeter (cm^3).

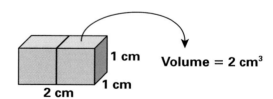

1 cm
2 cm
1 cm
Volume = 2 cm^3

You investigated relationships between surface area and volume. You learned that two objects with the same volume can have different surface areas.

Volume is 4 cm^3.
Surface area is 16 cm^2.

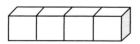

Volume is 4 cm^3.
Surface area is 18 cm^2.

Formula for Volume

If an object has a shape that can be cut in slices that all have the same size, you can calculate its volume with the formula:

volume = area of the slice × height

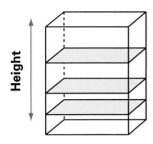 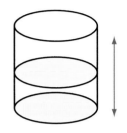

or

volume = area of the base × height

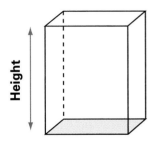 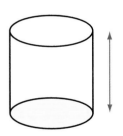

This formula does not work for shapes like cones and pyramids.

Check Your Work

Here are two packages.

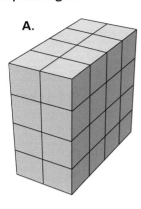

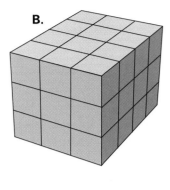

A.

B.

1. **a.** Which package holds more cubes? How many more cubes?

   b. Which package has more surface area? How much more?

2. **a.** Margaret has 4 different packages. Each package can hold exactly 18 one-centimeter cubes. Describe possible dimensions for Margaret's packages.

   b. What is the surface area for each possible package?

You can buy an aquarium in different shapes.

Here is an L-shaped aquarium with its dimensions.

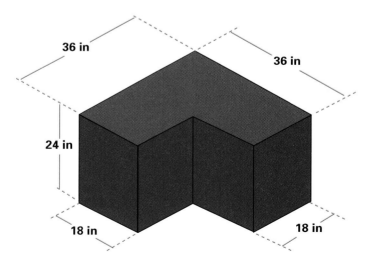

36 in

36 in

24 in

18 in

18 in

3. What is the volume of this aquarium? Show your work.

4. Here are three different trash cans. Which one can hold the most trash? Explain how you know.

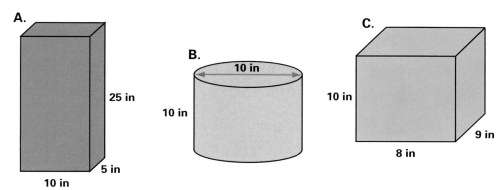

A. 25 in, 10 in, 5 in

B. 10 in, 10 in

C. 10 in, 8 in, 9 in

 For Further Reflection

Write a letter to someone in your family explaining what perimeter, area, surface area, and volume are and how they are used. You can use pictures in your letter if you think they will help explain the ideas. Describe how the reader can avoid mixing up the ideas and formulas.

Additional Practice

Section A The Size of Shapes

1. This square board below costs $20. If it is cut into the pieces shown, how much will each piece cost? Explain your reasoning. What assumptions did you have to make?

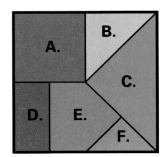

2. What is the area in square units of the shape shown to the right? Show your work.

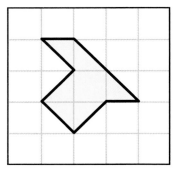

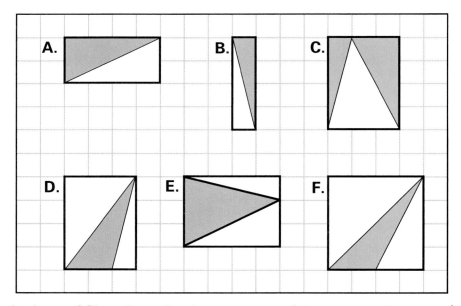

3. A piece of fiberglass that has an area of 4 square units costs $6. How much do the pieces above cost? (The shaded areas represent pieces of fiberglass.)

Section B Area Patterns

1. **a.** On a grid, draw three triangles that have different shapes but the same area and shade them in.

   b. Draw three different parallelograms that all have the same area. Indicate the base and the height measurements for each figure.

2. Find the areas of the following shapes. Use any method.

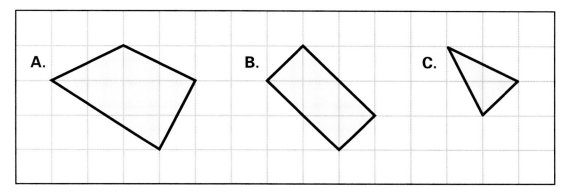

   A.   B.   C.

3. Elroy wants to tile his kitchen floor as shown below. He can use large sections of tile, medium sections, or individual tiles. What combinations of sections and individual tiles can Elroy use to cover his floor? Find two possibilities.

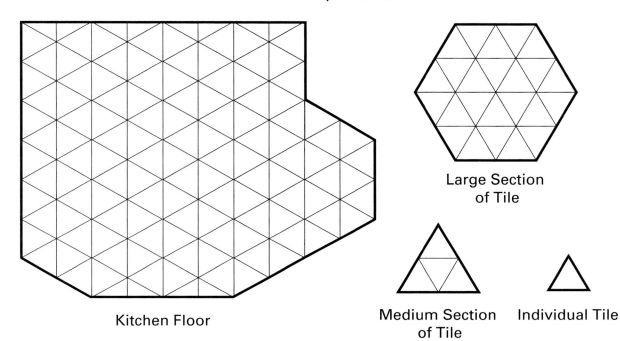

Kitchen Floor

Large Section of Tile

Medium Section of Tile

Individual Tile

Section ◆ **Measuring Area**

1. **a.** Draw a square. Indicate measurements for the sides so the square encloses an area of 9 ft².

   b. What are the measurements for the sides of this figure in yards? What is the area in square yards?

   c. What are the measurements for the sides of this figure in inches? What is the area in square inches?

2. Convert the following area measurements. Make sketches of rectangles to help you.

   a. 5 m² =_____cm²

   b. 3 ft² = ____in²

   c. 18 ft² = __yd²

   d. 50 cm² = ___mm²

3. The principal's new office, which is 4 m by 5.5 m, needs some type of floor covering. She has the following three choices.

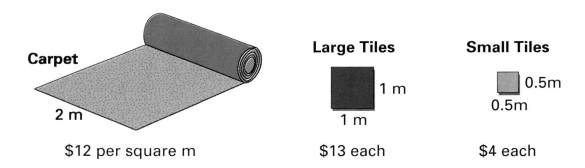

Carpet	Large Tiles	Small Tiles
2 m	1 m / 1 m	0.5m / 0.5m
$12 per square m	$13 each	$4 each

Write a report comparing the three choices. Illustrate your report with sketches of the covered floor for each of the coverings. Be sure to include the cost of each choice. (The carpet and tiles can be cut to fit the shape of the office.)

4. **a.** Assume that 10 people can stand in one square meter. How big an area is needed for all the students in your class?

   b. How big an area is needed for all the students in your school?

   c. Would it be possible for all the people in your city to stand in your classroom? Explain.

Section ❿ Perimeter and Area

1. What are the area and perimeter of each of the following shapes? What do you notice?

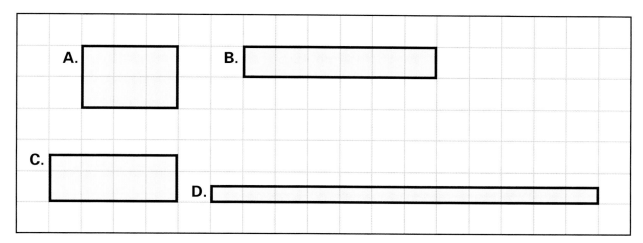

2. **a.** The glass of one of Albert's picture frames is broken. He wants to buy new glass for the picture. The glass must be 12 cm by 15 cm. Glass costs 10 cents per square centimeter. What does Albert have to pay for the glass?

   b. Albert makes an enlargement of the picture: both length and width are now twice as long. How much will the glass for this enlargement cost?

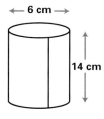

3. Suppose that the container shown above is cut apart into three flat pieces (top, bottom, and side).

   a. Draw the pieces and label their measurements.

   b. What is the area of the top of this container?

   c. What is the circumference of the container?

   d. What is the total surface area of this container? Explain your method.

Section E ▶ Volume and Area

1. Find different-sized boxes using whole numbers as dimensions that will hold exactly 20 one-centimeter cubes. Find as many as you can. Also, find out how much cardboard would be needed to make each box, including the top. Draw a table like the one below for your answers.

Length (in cm)	Width (in cm)	Height (in cm)	Volume (in cm³)	Surface Area (in cm²)
			20	
			20	
			20	
			20	

2. **a.** Name or sketch two objects for which you can use the formula

   volume = area of base × height

   b. Name or sketch two objects for which you cannot use this formula.

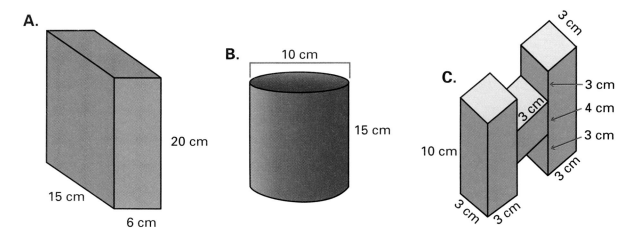

A.

15 cm
6 cm
20 cm

B. 10 cm

15 cm

C.

3 cm
3 cm
3 cm
4 cm
3 cm
3 cm
10 cm
3 cm
3 cm

3. Find the volume of each object above. Describe your method.

   a. A box of 15 cm by 6 cm by 20 cm.

   b. A can with a diameter of 10 cm and a height of 15 cm.

   c. An H-shaped block. Base of all parts 3 cm by 3 cm, the height of the standing parts 11 cm, the length of the connecting part 4 cm.

4. On January 27, 1967, Chicago had a terrible snowstorm that lasted 29 hours. Although January in Chicago is usually cold and snowy, 60 cm of snow from one snowstorm is unusual. For three days, the buses stopped. No trains ran. There was no garbage collection or mail delivery. Few people went to work. Most stores were closed. Chicago looked like a ghost town.

    a. If the snowstorm lasted 29 hours, why was the city affected for three days?

    b. How much is 60 cm of snow?

    c. Use the map below to estimate the volume of snow that buried Chicago on January 27, 1967.

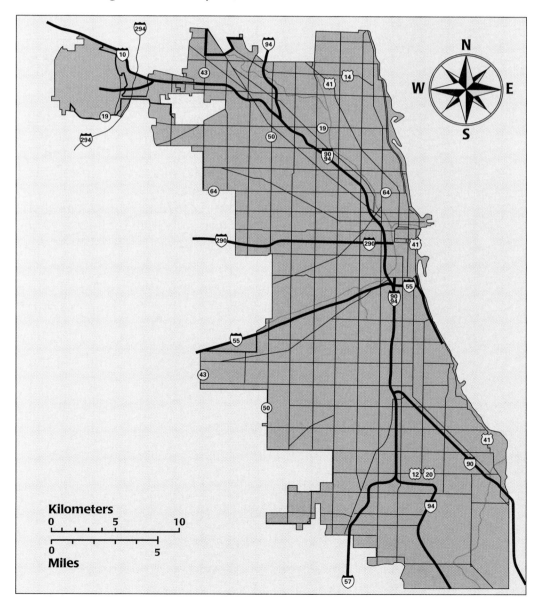

Section Ⓐ The Size of Shapes

1. The biggest rectangular piece of board will cost $2.40, and the two triangular pieces of board will cost $0.60 each.

Sample answer:

The two triangles at the bottom form a 3-by-13-in. piece. I divided the 6-by-13-in. piece in half. Now I have three 3-by-13-in. pieces. Since the whole piece of board costs $3.60, each 3-by–13-in. piece will cost $1.20. So two of the 3-by-13-in. pieces will cost $2.40. A triangular piece is half of a 3-by-13-in. piece, so it costs $0.60.

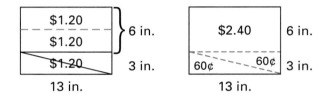

2. a. You might think they are about the same size because if you reshape the right lake into a more compact form, it will be about the same shape and size as the left one. You might also count the number of whole squares in each lake and decide that the lake on the right will be larger because it has more whole squares.

b. You can use different ways to find your answer. One way is to try to make as many whole squares as you can. The left lake is about 23 squares, and the right lake about 28 squares.

3. A. 1 square unit

B. $4\frac{1}{2}$ square units

C. 4 square units

D. 3 square units

E. 6 square units

4. The area enclosed by each triangle is 6 square units. You can find your answer by:

- reallotting portions of the triangle

- subtracting unwanted pieces. For example, to find the area enclosed by triangle **D**, you may use this subtraction strategy as shown below.

Area enclosed by rectangle:
3 × 9 = 27 square units

Area of unwanted sections:

$7\frac{1}{2} + 13\frac{1}{2} = 21$ square units

Area of shaded region =
27 − 21 = 6 square units

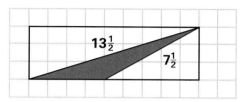

Section **B** Area Patterns

1. a. You can have different drawings. Here is one possible drawing.

Make sure the area enclosed by your rectangle is 25 square units.

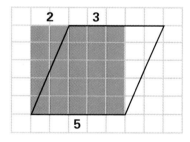

b. You can have different drawings. Here are three possible ones.

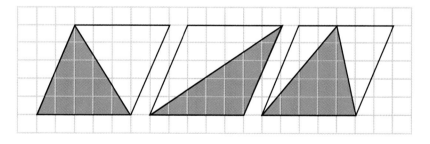

2. A. 10 square units   **B.** 9 square units

     C. 6 square units   **D.** 10 square units

Compare the methods you used with the methods used by one of your classmates.

3. You may have used different strategies than your classmates. Here are some possible answers.

   • Count, cut, tape partial units: Section A, problem 5h.

   • Reshape the figure: Section A, problems 5e, f; Section B, problem 7.

   • Enclose the shape and subtract: Section A, some shapes in problems 14, 15.

   • Double the shape or cut it in half: Section A, problem 4, some shapes in problems 14, 15; Section B, problem 18.

   • Use formulas, Section B, problem 13.

4. You can have different answers. For example, you could have a parallelogram with base 3 and height 4, a parallelogram with base 6 and height 2, a triangle with base 6 and height 4, and one with base 8 and height 3. Have one of your classmates check your drawings by finding the area enclosed by each.

Section ◆C◆ Measuring Area

1. a. You need 13 of these tiles.

   b. For the floor of the main walkway, 702 small tiles are needed. In a hexagonal tile, you can see six triangles, each with 9 small tiles. So a hexagonal tile holds 6 × 9 = 54 small tiles. The whole walkway is 13 × 54 = 702 small tiles.

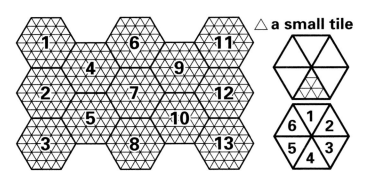

△ a small tile

2. A. The area is 4 × 5 = 20 square yards. You may either use the formula *area* = *b* × *h*, or divide the floor into pieces of 1 yard by 1 yard.

B. The area is $2\frac{1}{2}$ × 6 = 15 square yards. You may either use the formula *area* = *b* × *h*, or divide the floor into pieces like the drawing below and calculate the number of squares.

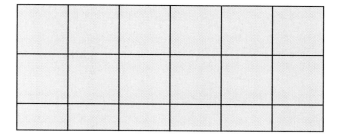

C. The area is $3\frac{1}{2}$ × $3\frac{1}{2}$ = $12\frac{1}{4}$ yd². You may use either one of the strategies used for **B**.

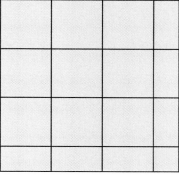

3. a. One yard is 3 feet, so 1 yd² is 9 ft². You may want to make a drawing to see why this is the case.

So floor **A.** needs 20 × 9 = 180 tiles, or you could reason that the dimensions are 15 ft by 12 ft, which would be 15 × 12 = 180 tiles.

Floor **B.** needs 15 × 9 = 135 tiles, or 18 × $7\frac{1}{2}$ = 135 tiles.

Floor **C.** needs $12\frac{1}{4}$ × 9 = $110\frac{1}{4}$ tiles, or $10\frac{1}{2}$ × $10\frac{1}{2}$ = $110\frac{1}{4}$ tiles.

b. 1 yd² = 9 ft²

4. Answers will vary. Some responses you might have are:

- A fingernail is about 1 cm² or about 100 mm².
- A poster is about 1 m² or about 9 ft².
- A seat cushion is about 1 ft² or 144 in².
- Lake Tahoe is about 200 mi² or 100 km².

5. Measures listed in order: 1 cm, 1 in., 1 ft, 1 yd, 1 m, 1 km, 1 mi.

Section ◆D◆ Perimeter and Area

1. a. You can make different drawings. For example:

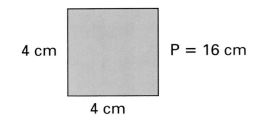

4 cm   P = 16 cm

4 cm

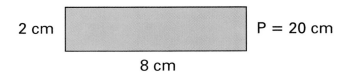

2 cm   P = 20 cm

8 cm

1 cm   P = 34 cm

16 cm

    b. The smallest perimeter you can have is the perimeter of the square, which is 16 cm.

2. a. You may have drawn one of the rectangles below.

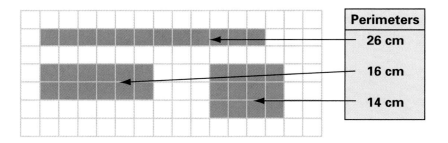

Perimeters
26 cm
16 cm
14 cm

b.

c. The area enclosed by the enlarged rectangle that is 2 by 24 is 48 squares. The perimeter of this rectangle is 52.

The area enclosed by the enlarged rectangle that is 4 by 12 is 48 squares.

The perimeter of this rectangle is 32.

The area enclosed by the enlarged rectangle that is 6 by 8 is 48 squares.

The perimeter of this rectangle is 28.

d. The area is four times as large since the first rectangle encloses an area of 12 squares, and the enlarged rectangle an area of 48 squares. ($4 \times 12 = 48$)

3. The clocks seem to be about the same size. You are asked to compare the area and the perimeter of the clocks.

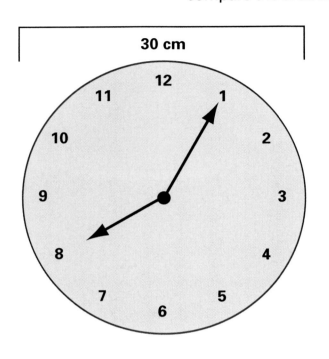

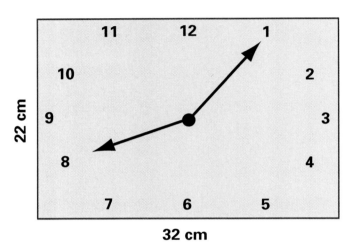

Area of round clock:

The area is $\pi \times r \times r$; the radius r is half of the diameter, so it is 15 cm.

So the area is: $\pi \times 15 \times 15 \approx 707$ cm^2.

Area of rectangular clock is $b \times h$, which is $32 \times 22 = 704$ cm^2.

So the area of the circular clock is slightly larger.

Perimeter of round clock is $2 \times \pi \times 15 \approx 94$ cm.

Perimeter of rectangular clock is $2 \times 32 + 2 \times 22 = 108$ cm.

So the perimeter of the rectangular clock is larger.

Suze will probably use the area to decide which clock is the smallest. The rectangular one will take up slightly less area on the wall. If on the other hand Suze wants to hang the clock on a place that has a maximum height and width of 30 cm, only the round clock will fit.

4. a. Mr. Anderson can calculate the area of glass in the rectangular windows by measuring the height and width of each window, calculating the area by using the rule *area = h × w*, and then adding all the areas.

b. Mr. Anderson can divide the shape of the other window into a rectangular part with half a circle on top.

The area of the rectangular part is *height × width*, which in this case is 50 × 80 = 4,000 cm².

The area of the half circle is 0.5 × π × *r* × *r, which* in this case is 0.5 × π × 40 × 40 ≈ 2,513 cm².

So the glass area of this window is 4,000 + 2,513, or about 6,513 cm².

5. a. The circumference is doubled. You might say:

If you double the diameter, the circumference also doubles. If the diameter is 10cm, then the circumference is 3.14 × 10 cm, or 31.40 cm. If the diameter is 20 cm, then the circumference is 3.14 × 20 cm. or 62.80 cm.

b. The area is four times as big or quadrupled. One explanation you might give is below.

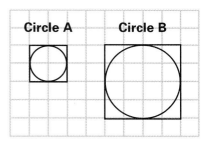

You can draw circles on a grid. Each circle is about $\frac{3}{4}$ of the area enclosed by a square.

The area enclosed by circle A is $\frac{3}{4}$ × 2 × 2 = 3 square units.

The area enclosed by circle B is $\frac{3}{4}$ × 4 × 4 = 12 square units, which is four times as big as 3.

Section ◈ E ▸ Surface Area and Volume

1. a. The left package (A) is made out of four layers of eight cubes, so 4 × 8 = 32 cubes. The package on the right (B) is made out of three layers of 12 cubes, 3 × 12 = 36 cubes. So the package on the right holds more cubes.

b. The surface area of the left package is four faces with 8 squares, 4 × 8 =32.

Two faces with 16 squares: 2 × 16 = 32

Total: 32 + 32 = 64 squares. You can draw a net of the wrapping to find this out.

The surface area of the package on the right is:
4 × 12 + 2 × 9 = 48 + 18 = 66.

So the one on the right has the larger surface area.

2. a. Answers can vary. If you use only whole numbers, possible dimensions of the packages are:

Package A: 3 cm × 3 cm × 2 cm

Package B: 1 cm × 2 cm × 9 cm

Package C: 1 cm × 3 cm × 6 cm

Package D: 1 cm × 1 cm × 18 cm

b. The surface area for the packages from part **a** can be calculated by sketching the net of each package and calculating the area of top and bottom and of the front and back and of the left and right sides.

Package A: $9 \text{ cm}^2 \times 2 + 6 \text{ cm}^2 \times 4 = 18 + 24 = 42 \text{ cm}^2$

Package B: $2 \times 2 \text{ cm}^2 + 2 \times 9 \text{ cm}^2 + 2 \times 18 \text{ cm}^2 = 58 \text{ cm}^2$

Package C: $2 \times 3 \text{ cm}^2 + 2 \times 6 \text{ cm}^2 + 2 \times 18 \text{ cm}^2 = 54 \text{ cm}^2$

Package D: $2 \times 1 \text{cm}^2 + 4 \times 18 \text{ cm}^2 = 74 \text{cm}^2$

3. The volume is 23,328 in³. Sample strategies:

- The L can be reshaped into one rectangular block with a base of 18 in. by (36 + 18) in. and a height of 24 in.

- The L can be split up into a rectangular block with a base of 18 in. by 36 in. and a rectangular block with a base of 18 in. by 18 in. They both have the same height, 24 in.

- The L shape is the difference of a rectangular block with dimensions base: 36 in. by 36 in. and a height 24 inches and a rectangular block with dimensions base 18 in. by 18 in. and height 24 in.

- The L shape can be split into three equal rectangular blocks with a base of 18 in. by 18 in. and a height of 24 in.

4. The container on the left, container **C**, can hold the most trash.

   You can justify your answer by showing your calculations for the volume of each.

   A. *volume*   = *area of base* × *height*

               = (10 × 5) × 25

               = 1,250 in³.

   B. Base is a circle with radius 5 in.

        volume   = *area of base* × *height*

        Surface area of the bottom is:

        π × *radius* × *radius* ≈ 3.14 × 25,

        which is about 78.5 in².

        So *volume* ≈ 78.5 × 10 ≈ 785 in³.

   C. *volume*   = *area of base* x *height*

        volume   = (8 × 9) × 10 = 720 in³.

More or Less

Number

BRITANNICA
Mathematics in Context

HOLT, RINEHART AND WINSTON

Mathematics in Context is a comprehensive curriculum for the middle grades. It was developed in 1991 through 1997 in collaboration with the Wisconsin Center for Education Research, School of Education, University of Wisconsin-Madison and the Freudenthal Institute at the University of Utrecht, The Netherlands, with the support of the National Science Foundation Grant No. 9054928.

The revision of the curriculum was carried out in 2003 through 2005, with the support of the National Science Foundation Grant No. ESI 0137414.

National Science Foundation
Opinions expressed are those of the authors
and not necessarily those of the Foundation.

Keijzer, R., van den Heuvel-Panhuizen, M., Wijers, M., Abels, M., Wijers, M.,Shew, J. A., Brinker, L., Pligge, M. A., Shafer, M., & Brendefur, J. (2006). *More or less*. In Wisconsin Center for Education Research & Freudenthal Institute (Eds.), *Mathematics in context*. Chicago: Encyclopædia Britannica.

ISBN 0-03-039618-2

2 3 4 5 6   073   09 08 07 06 05

The *Mathematics in Context* Development Team

Development 1991–1997

The initial version of *More or Less* was developed by Ronald Keijzer, Marja van den Heuvel-Panhuizen, and Monica Wijers. It was adapted for use in American schools by Julia Shew, Laura Brinker, Margaret A. Pligge, Mary Shafer, and Jonathan Brendefur.

Wisconsin Center for Education

Research Staff

Thomas A. Romberg
Director

Joan Daniels Pedro
Assistant to the Director

Gail Burrill
Coordinator

Margaret R. Meyer
Coordinator

Project Staff

Jonathan Brendefur
Laura Brinker
James Browne
Jack Burrill
Rose Byrd
Peter Christiansen
Barbara Clarke
Doug Clarke
Beth R. Cole
Fae Dremock
Mary Ann Fix

Sherian Foster
James A. Middleton
Jasmina Milinkovic
Margaret A. Pligge
Mary C. Shafer
Julia A. Shew
Aaron N. Simon
Marvin Smith
Stephanie Z. Smith
Mary S. Spence

Freudenthal Institute Staff

Jan de Lange
Director

Els Feijs
Coordinator

Martin van Reeuwijk
Coordinator

Mieke Abels
Nina Boswinkel
Frans van Galen
Koeno Gravemeijer
Marja van den Heuvel-Panhuizen
Jan Auke de Jong
Vincent Jonker
Ronald Keijzer
Martin Kindt

Jansie Niehaus
Nanda Querelle
Anton Roodhardt
Leen Streefland

Adri Treffers
Monica Wijers
Astrid de Wild

Revision 2003–2005

The revised version of *More or Less* was developed Mieke Abels and Monica Wijers.
It was adapted for use in American schools by Margaret A. Pligge.

Wisconsin Center for Education

Research Staff

Thomas A. Romberg
Director

David C. Webb
Coordinator

Gail Burrill
Editorial Coordinator

Margaret A. Pligge
Editorial Coordinator

Freudenthal Institute Staff

Jan de Lange
Director

Truus Dekker
Coordinator

Mieke Abels
Content Coordinator

Monica Wijers
Content Coordinator

Project Staff

Sarah Ailts
Beth R. Cole
Erin Hazlett
Teri Hedges
Karen Hoiberg
Carrie Johnson
Jean Krusi
Elaine McGrath

Margaret R. Meyer
Anne Park
Bryna Rappaport
Kathleen A. Steele
Ana C. Stephens
Candace Ulmer
Jill Vettrus

Arthur Bakker
Peter Boon
Els Feijs
Dédé de Haan
Martin Kindt

Nathalie Kuijpers
Huub Nilwik
Sonia Palha
Nanda Querelle
Martin van Reeuwijk

Cover photo credits: (left to right) © Comstock Images; © Corbis; © Getty Images

Illustrations
5, 18 (left), **19** (top), **20** Christine McCabe/© Encyclopædia Britannica, Inc.; **22** Holly Cooper-Olds; **27** © Encyclopædia Britannica, Inc.; **30** Christine McCabe/© Encyclopædia Britannica, Inc.

Photographs
1–5 Sam Dudgeon/HRW Photo; **6** © PhotoDisc/Getty Images; **12** (left to right) John Langford/HRW; © Ryan McVay/PhotoDisc/Getty Images; Don Couch/HRW Photo; **13** John Langford/HRW; **17** © Ryan McVay/ PhotoDisc/Getty Images; Don Couch/HRW Photo; **19** Sam Dudgeon/ HRW Photo; **26** Comstock Images/Alamy; **28, 29** ©1998 Image Farm Inc

◆ Contents

Dear Student,

This unit is about the ways in which fractions, decimals, and percents are related.

Do you purchase items that need to be weighed? How is the final price determined? Calculating per unit prices and total prices requires multiplication with fraction and decimal numbers.

Do you buy your favorite items on sale? Next time you shop, notice the sale discount. Sale discounts are usually expressed in percents.

In this unit, you will use fractions and percents to find sale prices. You can use models like a double number line, a percent bar, or a ratio table to help you make calculations.

You will investigate the percent by which a photograph increases or decreases in size when you enlarge or reduce it on a photocopier.

You will also use fractions and percents to describe survey results.

While working on this unit, look for ads that list discounts in percents and newspaper articles that give survey results. Share what you find with the class.

All the situations in this unit will help you perfect your operations with fractions, decimals, and percents. Good luck.

Sincerely,

The Mathematics in Context Development Team

Produce Pricing

Scales

Save Supermarket displays fresh fruits and vegetables so customers can select individual pieces and put what they want into bags. When customers check out, cashiers weigh the produce and enter a produce code that calculates the prices.

Many customers want to know the cost of their selections before they check out. Ms. Vander, the produce manager, put a dial scale near the fruit-and-vegetable counter so customers can weigh their own produce. Customers can use the price per weight to **estimate** the costs.

Carol is a customer at Save Supermarket. She wants to buy $1\frac{1}{2}$ kilograms (kg) of Red Delicious apples.

1. What is the cost of $1\frac{1}{2}$ kg of apples if they are priced at $2.40 per kilogram?

Carol places some apples on the scale. A picture of the scale is shown here.

2. Does Carol have the amount of apples she wants? Explain.

Carol decides to buy all of the apples on the scale. She wonders what this will cost.

3. Estimate the total cost of Carol's apple selection. How did you arrive at your estimate?

Carol's friends Pablo, Lia, and Pam are helping Carol estimate the cost of her apples. They are waiting to use the scale after Carol is finished. To help Carol, they make several suggestions to estimate the cost.

Pablo says, "That's almost 2 kilograms of apples."

Lia states, "That's about $1\frac{3}{4}$ kilograms of apples."

Pam suggests, "Use the scale as a double number line."

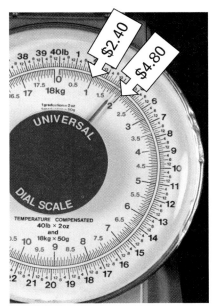

4. **a.** How will Pablo find the answer? What will Pablo estimate?

   b. How will Lia calculate the answer? What will she estimate?

   c. How will Pam use a double number line to estimate the cost of the apples?

You may remember another strategy that can be used to solve this problem: using a **ratio table**.

5. Show how you would use a ratio table to estimate the cost of the apples.

When Carol is finished with the scale, Pam weighs 10 apples she selected. This scale shows the weight of Pam's apples.

6. Estimate what Pam will pay for her apples.

This scale shows the weight of Lia's apples.

7. Estimate what Lia will pay for her apples.

Pablo places his apples on the scale.

8. a. Suppose the weight of his apples is 2.1 kg. Copy the scale's dial and draw the pointer so it represents the weight of Pablo's apples.

   b. What will Pablo pay for 2.1 kg of apples?

Save Supermarket sells several kinds of apples, including Red Delicious and Granny Smith.

Suppose Carol, Pablo, and Pam bought the same weight of Granny Smith apples instead of Red Delicious apples.

9. Using the scale weights from problems 6–8, estimate the price each person will pay for the same weight of Granny Smith apples.

10. Pam wants to buy additional apples. She has $8. Estimate the total weight of Red Delicious apples Pam can buy.

11. Pablo has $2.50 to spend on Granny Smith apples. Estimate the total weight of apples Pablo can buy.

Veggies-R-Us

Veggies-R-Us
Tomatoes

packed on: 05.27.05   sell by:

$/kg   Net weight
3.20   1.250 kg
PRICE
$4.00

0221311 465683

Some supermarkets require customers to use special machines to print the cost of produce before they check out. At Veggies-R-Us, customers place items on the scale, they key in the type of produce, and the machine prints the cost. A sticker for a tomato purchase is shown on the left.

There is something wrong with the machine! Sometimes it gives incorrect prices. The produce manager is checking the receipts to get a sense of how many are wrong.

Veggies-R-Us
Red Delicious Apples

packed on: 05.27.05   sell by:

$/kg   Net weight
2.40   1.330 kg
PRICE
$31.92

0221313 465684

Veggies-R-Us
Peaches

packed on: 05.27.05   sell by:

$/kg   Net weight
0.66   2.500 kg
PRICE
$0.17

0221312 465685

Veggies-R-Us
Grapes

packed on: 05.27.05   sell by:

$/kg   Net weight
2.85   0.750 kg
PRICE
$2.14

0221310 465686

12. Use estimation to determine which receipts are wrong. Decide whether the machine is overcharging or undercharging customers.

The storeowner repaired the machine so that it functions properly.

13. Use **arrow language** to show how the machine calculates the costs of different amounts of Red Delicious apples priced at $2.40 per kilogram.

14. Without using a calculator, describe how to calculate the cost of these amounts of apples at $2.40 per kilogram.

    a. 15 kg   **d.** 0.4 kg   **f.** 7 kg

    b. 1.5 kg   **e.** 0.04 kg   **g.** 0.7 kg

    c. 4 kg

Paul calculated the price for 0.8 kg of Red Delicious apples at Save Supermarket. He used his calculator and made these entries.

0.8 ☒ $2.40 ☰

His calculator displayed 1.92 as the total.

Mary disagrees.

> That can't be right! When you multiply, isn't the answer always larger than the two numbers you started with?

15. Reflect Is Mary right, or is Paul's calculator correct? Defend your position.

16. Describe two ways to use a calculator to determine the cost of $\frac{3}{4}$ kg of walnuts priced at $7.98 per kilogram.

Broken Calculator

Ms. Vander of Save Supermarket likes the calculating scale that customers use at Veggies-R-Us. She decides to keep a calculator next to her dial scale. Customers can calculate the exact cost of their produce before they check out.

Unfortunately, the calculator has been used so much that the **decimal point** key no longer works.

Sean weighs 2.63 kg of strawberries priced at $4.32 per kilogram. He thinks he can use the calculator in spite of the defective decimal point key.

17. a. Make a low estimate and a high estimate of the cost of Sean's strawberries.

   b. Describe how Sean will use the calculator to find the exact cost of his strawberries.

   c. Find the cost of Sean's strawberries.

18. Use your answer to part **c** of problem 17 to determine the prices of these amounts:

   a. 0.263 kg of strawberries

   b. 26.3 kg of strawberries

$4.32 per kg

19. The calculator is still broken. Use the information below to find the actual cost of each strawberry purchase. Describe how you found each answer.

Customer	Weight	Calculator Display
Sally	3.98 kg	*171936*
Devin	1.72 kg	*74304*
Niya	0.39 kg	*16848*

A ▸ Produce Pricing

Summary ✖

There are many ways to **estimate** or find the cost of produce.

You may use number tools such as a double number line, a ratio table, or a calculator.

For example, there are several strategies to find the cost of 1.8 kg of Golden Delicious apples priced at $1.60 per kilogram.

- **Estimate by rounding decimals to whole numbers.**

You might reason like this.

> 1.8 is almost 2, so 1.8 × $1.60 is a little less than 2 × $1.60.

$$2 \times \$1.60 = \$1.60 + \$1.60$$
$$= \$1.50 + \$0.10 + \$1.50 + \$0.10$$
$$= \$1.50 + \$1.50 + \$0.10 + \$0.10 = \$3.20$$

$3.20 is a high estimate.

- **Estimate by using simple fractions like halves or quarters.**

You might reason like this.

> 1.8 × $1.60 is a little more than 1.75 × $1.60, which is the same as $1\frac{3}{4}$ of $1.60.

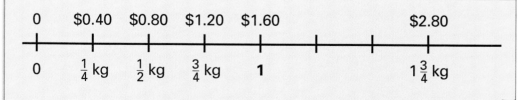

0	$0.40	$0.80	$1.20	$1.60			$2.80
0	$\frac{1}{4}$ kg	$\frac{1}{2}$ kg	$\frac{3}{4}$ kg	1			$1\frac{3}{4}$ kg

$2.80 is a low estimate.

- Use an exact calculation by changing the decimals into fractions.

You might reason like this.

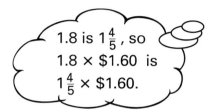

1.8 is $1\frac{4}{5}$, so
1.8 × $1.60 is
$1\frac{4}{5}$ × $1.60.

Price	$1.60	$0.32	$1.28	$2.88
Weight (kg)	1	$\frac{1}{5}$	$\frac{4}{5}$	$1\frac{4}{5}$

$2.88 is the exact price.

- When the numbers are not easy to calculate mentally, use a calculator.

> **Remember: Multiplying can produce results smaller than what you start with!**

Whichever method you choose, it is wise to estimate the answer before calculating. You never know when you might make an entry error or your calculator might not be working properly. It is smart to compare a reasonable estimate to your final price.

Check Your Work

At Puno's Produce, Gala apples are priced at $2.10 per kilogram.

1. Estimate the cost of each of these amounts.

a.

b.

Paul has $7 to spend on apples.

2. How many kilograms of Gala apples can he buy?

The price of Golden Delicious apples is $3.60 per kilogram.

3. Describe how you would calculate the cost of each of these amounts of apples without using a calculator.

    a. 3 kg   **b.** 0.3 kg   **c.** 2.3 kg

4. a. Describe how to determine $\frac{1}{2}$ × $47.00 without using a calculator.

   b. Describe how to determine $1\frac{1}{4}$ × $8.20 without using a calculator.

Kenji used his calculator at home to calculate 12.54 × 0.39. He wrote the answer 48906 in his notebook. It wasn't until he was at school that he discovered he had forgotten to write the decimal point in his answer. He found where the decimal point should be by estimating the answer.

5. Explain what Kenji did. Place the decimal point in his answer.

 For Further Reflection

Here is a multiplication problem and the correct answer, without the decimal point:

$$568 \times 356 = 202208$$

Put a decimal point in either 568, 356, or both numbers so that you will get a new multiplication problem. Be sure that your answer for the new problem is correct!

Create at least four more problems using this method.

Discounts

Surveys

Ms.Vander of Save Supermarket replaced the old dial scales in the produce section with digital scales.

She wanted to know how the customers felt about the new scales, so she surveyed 650 customers.

The first survey question asked, "Do you like the new scales?"

Here are the results from the first survey question.

Customer Opinion of New Scales	
Number of Customers	**Customer's Opinion**
320	very pleased with the new scales
220	somewhat pleased with the new scales
65	not pleased with the new scales
The rest of the customers surveyed said they did not notice the difference.	

1. Do the customers think the new scales are a good idea? Use the survey results to explain your answer.

Ms. Vander made a pie chart to help her interpret the survey results.

2. **a.** Display the results using the segmented bar and pie chart on **Student Activity Sheet 1**.

   b. Describe the results of the survey using fractions.

   c. Describe the results of the survey using **percents**.

The second survey question asked, "Do the new scales help you estimate the cost of your selection?"

Ms. Vander was amazed at the results of the second survey question. She decided to show her staff members the results on a bar chart. Here are some of their reactions.

I noticed that 25% of the customers say that the new scales don't help them estimate the costs.

Bert Loggen
Produce Manager

But half of the customers say they can estimate the costs more easily with the new scales.

Janice Vander
Store Manager

A tenth of the customers don't even want to estimate the costs. For the remaining customers surveyed, neither scale makes a difference.

Juan Sanchez
Produce Buyer

3. **a.** Draw a bar chart that Ms. Vander could have shown her staff.

   b. Describe the part of the chart that represents the number of customers who say it doesn't make any difference which scale is used.

4. **a.** Which type of graph, the pie chart or the bar chart, makes it easier to see the parts that are larger as compared to the parts that are smaller? Explain.

   b. **Reflect** How can these charts help you figure out the percents for the parts?

   c. Can the charts help you find the fractions that describe the parts? Explain your answer.

Percents and Fractions

Some store managers do not make pie charts or bar charts to show the results of customer surveys. They use only percents. Some percents, like 50% and 25%, are as easy to write as fractions. Check that you know the fraction equivalents of 50% and 25%.

$33\frac{1}{3}$ % of 180 is 60.

Ms. Vander told Mr. Loggen that $33\frac{1}{3}$% of 180 customers wish Save Supermarket would carry a wider variety of apples. Without a calculator, Mr. Loggen quickly figured out that $33\frac{1}{3}$% of 180 customers is 60 customers.

5. What strategy do you think Mr. Loggen used to find the answer?

6. List percents that are easy to rewrite as fractions. Include the corresponding fractions.

Fractions like $\frac{1}{2}$ and $\frac{1}{4}$ and $\frac{1}{10}$ are often called **benchmark fractions**.

7. Show how you can use benchmark fractions to calculate each of these percent problems.

   a. 25% of 364   **d.** 5% of 364   **g.** 20% of 364
   b. 75% of 364   **e.** 30% of 364   **h.** 80% of 364
   c. 10% of 364   **f.** 35% of 364

Dale's Department Store is having a sale. Dale wants all his employees to be able to do mental calculations quickly and easily in case customers have questions about the sale **discounts**.

8. Complete these mental calculations. You do not have to answer them in any particular order. You may want to start with those you find the easiest. Write your answers in your notebook.

   a. $\frac{15}{100}$ of $360 is ____.   **h.** 0.333 × $360 is ____.
   b. 35% of $360 is ____.   **i.** $\frac{1}{5}$ of $250 is ____.
   c. 20% of $250 is ____.   **j.** 1% of $250 is ____.
   d. $33\frac{1}{3}$% of $120 is ____.   **k.** $\frac{1}{3}$ of $360 is ____.
   e. 0.25 × $360 is ____.   **l.** 40% of $250 is ____.
   f. $\frac{1}{4}$ of $360 is ____.   **m.** $\frac{3}{4}$ of $360 is ____.
   g. 25% × $360 is ____.   **n.** 15% of $360 is ____.

9. Choose three of your mental calculations and describe your solution strategy for each one.

10. Which of the mental calculations you used in problem 8 are related? Explain how they are related.

■ 11. **Reflect** Which of the calculations you used in problem 8 are the easiest for you to compute mentally? Which of the calculations would you rather do using a calculator?

Percents or Cents?

During a sale, Dale offers two types of discounts. Sometimes he gives a cash discount and other times he gives a percent off the regular price.

12. **a.** On **Student Activity Sheet 2**, you will find a copy of the table below. For each item in the table, determine whether the percent discount or cash discount gives the lower sale price. Mark your choice on the activity sheet and give an explanation for it.

   b. Add two of your own items to the table on the activity sheet. Include the regular prices, two types of discounts, your choice, and an explanation.

Item	Regular Price	Sale Price	Explanation
In-line Skates	$55.00	• 30% off • $10.00 off	
Jeans	$23.75	• 20% off • $5.00 off	
Cell Phone	$75.00	• 25% off • $17.50 off	
Baseball Cap	$19.95	• 15% off • $3.50 off	
Sneakers	$45.95	• 20% off • $9.00 off	
Earrings	$9.95	• 40% off • $3.50 off	

Reasonable Discounts

13. Dale's Department Store is having a 24-hour sale. For each of the items below, the regular price is given along with the wholesale price (the price Dale's Department Store paid for the item). In each case, decide whether a discount of 10%, 25%, or 40% is reasonable. Reasonable, in this case, means a discount will provide savings for the customer but will also give the store some profit. Mark the **sale price** for each item in your notebook and defend your decision.

a. Wholesale Price: $42.50
Regular Price: $59.95

Sale Price

b. Wholesale Price: $129.95
Regular Price: $149.95

Sale Price

c. Wholesale Price: $18.00
Regular Price: $25.95

Sale Price

d. Wholesale Price: $70.00
Regular Price: $109.99

Sale Price

e. Wholesale Price: $40.00
Regular Price: $45.00

Sale Price

B Discounts

Summary

- Results of a survey can be displayed in a bar chart or a pie chart. These charts help you compare the parts using **percents** or fractions.

- **Discounts** are often expressed in percents. The strategy you use when finding discounts depends on the percent and the price given.

  Some percents, like 10%, 25%, and 75%, can easily be written as fractions. These fractions can then be used to make the calculations. For example:

  25% of 488 is $\frac{1}{4}$ of 488, which is 122.

  75% of 488 is $\frac{3}{4}$ of 488, which is 366.

Fractions that are easy to work with are called **benchmark fractions**. You can calculate with these fractions mentally.

For discounts that are not easy to compute, you can separate the percentage into the sum of several percents that are easier to calculate, such as 10% or 1%. The use of a percent bar, a double number line, or a ratio table can be helpful.

For example, to calculate 35% of $250, you can use 10% + 10% + 10% + 5% (half of 10%), or 3 × 10% + 5% (half of 10%).

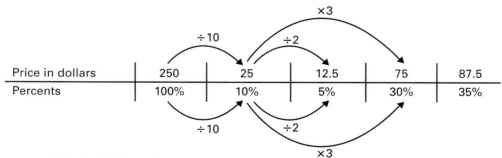

35% is 30% + 5%

3 × 10% + half of 10%

Since 10% of $250 is $25 and half of $25 is $12.50,

35% of $250 is 3 × $25 + $12.50 or

$75 + $12.50 or $87.50.

Dale is having a sale on small fans that regularly cost $5.98 each. Customers can choose from these three discounts.

Discount 1: 5% off   Discount 2: $0.50 off

Discount 3: $\frac{1}{5}$ off

1. Which discount gives the lowest sale price? Explain your reasoning.

Dale is selling all the air conditioners in his store to make room for other merchandise. He gives his customers a huge discount of 60%.

2. Explain how you would find the discount for an air conditioner that costs $240.

Dale has three other air conditioners to sell for $280, $200, and $275.

3. How much will each one cost after the 60% discount?

I know 10% is $\frac{1}{10}$.

I know 50% of 800 is half of it.

Ms. Vander and Mr. Sanchez are studying a survey of 800 customers. The survey shows that 45% of the customers gave the same response. Ms. Vander and Mr. Sanchez want to know how many customers that is. They begin by using percents they can easily write as fractions.

4. How do you think Ms. Vander and Mr. Sanchez will continue? Complete their calculations.

5. Write at least two ways to calculate 25% of 900.

 For Further Reflection

Look for at least three different sale items listed in a newspaper or magazine. Calculate the discount and the sale price. Rewrite the percent discount as a fraction.

Many Changes

Design a Sign

Save Supermarket is planning a super sale. They want to design a sale sign showing the produce prices. Ms. Vander gives these discounts.

Grapes
Were $3.20/kg
Now 25% off

Granny Smith Apples
Were $2.89/kg
Now 20% off

Red Delicious Apples
Were $2.40/kg
Now 15% off

1. Are these good sales for customers?

The employees brainstorm about what to write on the sale signs.

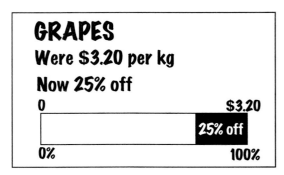

Bert sketched this sign for grapes. He used a percent discount and a **percent bar** to visually show the relationship between the original price and the discount price.

2. Sketch signs for Granny Smith and Red Delicious apples using Bert's suggestions.

Janice proposes that they include fractions instead of percents. She believes customers can estimate the discounts more easily if they use fractions.

3. a. Reflect Do you agree with Janice? Defend your position.

   b. Draw one sign using Janice's suggestion.

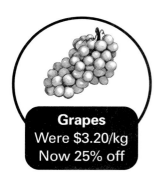

Grapes
Were $3.20/kg
Now 25% off

Granny Smith Apples
Were $2.89/kg
Now 20% off

Red Delicious Apples
Were $2.40/kg
Now 15% off

Ms. Vander is in favor of displaying the discount in dollars.

Pedro thinks it will be easier for customers if only the new price appears on the signs.

4. What kind of sign do you prefer? Why?

The employees decide to combine ideas. They will use a percent bar, the percent discount, and both the original price and the sale price on each sign.

5. Use their ideas to design new signs for each of the items on the left.

Pedro studies the new grapes sign and says, "This is great! You can tell just by looking at the sign what fraction or percent the customers will have to pay. You can check the sale price by doing one simple multiplication."

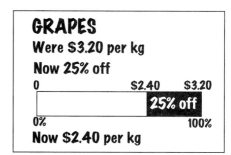

GRAPES
Were $3.20 per kg
Now 25% off

0       $2.40 $3.20

25% off

0%   100%

Now $2.40 per kg

6. a. What fraction and percent of the original price do customers have to pay for grapes?

   b. What multiplication can customers use to check the sale price for grapes?

   c. Compute the new prices for the Granny Smith and Red Delicious apples using only one multiplication for each.

Profit Fractions

The owner of Save Supermarket, Ms. Jao, compared this year's **profits** to last year's profits. This is what she found.

Department	Change in Profit
Health and Beauty	One-quarter less
Dairy	One-fifth less
Produce	One-and-one-half times as much
Bakery	Three-tenths less
Meat	One-quarter more
Deli	Two-thirds more

To help her visualize the changes in profits, Ms. Jao used bars to represent last year's profits.

7. a. Which departments increased profit from last year to this year?

b. Use the bars on **Student Activity Sheet 3** to indicate the change in profit for each department. Label the bars.

This year's Health and Beauty profit can be described as three-fourths times ($\frac{3}{4}$ ×) last year's profit.

8. Describe the change in profit for the other departments in fractions.

The table below shows last year's profit for each department of Ms. Jao's store.

Department	Last Year's Profit
Health and Beauty	$46,800
Dairy	$35,600
Produce	$22,500
Bakery	$55,900
Meat	$60,200
Deli	$47,100

9. For each department, use last year's profit and the change in profit to find this year's profit.

In problem 9, Ms. Jao calculated this year's profit for the bakery like this.

$$\frac{7}{10} \times 55{,}900 = 0.7 \times 55{,}900$$

She then used her calculator.

10. a. Compare Ms. Jao's calculation to the bakery profit calculation you made in problem 9. What is the same and what is different?

   b. How would Ms. Jao calculate this year's profit for the Health and Beauty department, using multiplication with decimals?

Fractions can be written as decimals.

11. On **Student Activity Sheet 4**, connect the fraction and decimal that express the same number.

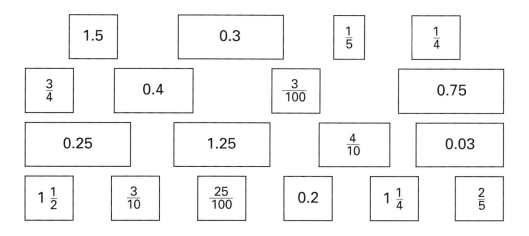

| 1.5 | 0.3 | $\frac{1}{5}$ | $\frac{1}{4}$ |

| $\frac{3}{4}$ | 0.4 | $\frac{3}{100}$ | 0.75 |

| 0.25 | 1.25 | $\frac{4}{10}$ | 0.03 |

| $1\frac{1}{2}$ | $\frac{3}{10}$ | $\frac{25}{100}$ | 0.2 | $1\frac{1}{4}$ | $\frac{2}{5}$ |

12. Describe how you can find the answer to these multiplication problems on a calculator that does not allow you to enter fractions.

   a. $\frac{3}{4} \times 1{,}257$

   b. $1\frac{1}{4} \times 1{,}257$

   c. $\frac{17}{100} \times 1{,}257$

Ms. Jao decided to use percents to change the prices of some items in her store. She made this table.

Product	Old Price	Change	New Price	New Price as Percentage of Old Price
Whole Milk	$2.10	−10%		90%
Frozen Dinner	$4.68	−25%		
Roasted Turkey	$13.25	+25%		
6 Cans of Juice	$2.98	−5%		
Canned Salmon	$3.60	+15%		

13. Use **Student Activity Sheet 5** to fill in the columns labeled "New Price" and "New Price as Percentage of Old Price."

14. Describe and compare two ways of finding the sale price of cookies that normally sell for $4.98 but are now 15% off.

While Ms. Jao was working in her office, her two children, Jim and Michelle, came by to visit. She decided to take a break and have a glass of lemonade with them.

The children discussed the amount of lemonade in their glasses.

15. a. Reflect Do you agree with Jim or Michelle? Defend your position.

   b. Can the other person also be right? Why?

After they finished their lemonade, Jim and Michelle went to Dale's Department Store to buy a birthday present for their friend Puno. Jim and Michelle agreed on a gift and took it to the cashier to make their purchase. The cashier made a mistake and gave them a 20% discount. When she caught her mistake, she decided to just add 20% of the total back on.

16. a. Do you think adding 20% of the total price corrects the mistake?

   b. Copy and fill in the receipt.

Dale's Department Store

Nontaxable
Merchandise $23.70

−20% .... $_____

TOTAL .... $_____

+20% .... $_____

TOTAL .... $_____

---

17. Explain the effect of subtracting 20% of the price and then adding 20% of that total price back.

Dale reminded his employees to check the sale prices, using the percent discount and the sale price.

18. Find the original price of a T-shirt with a 20% discount and a sale price of $15.

Summary

To calculate the sale price of an item with a discount given as a percent or fraction, you can do it with one multiplication calculation.

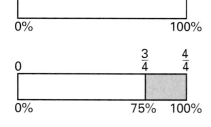

For example, suppose an item is discounted by 25%.

The discount is 25%, or $\frac{1}{4}$.

The new price is 75%, or, $\frac{3}{4}$, of the old price, so multiply $\frac{3}{4}$ times the original price.

Increasing a price by a percent is the same as taking 100% plus the percent increase of the price.

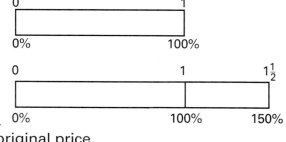

For example, increasing a price by 50% is the same as finding 150% of the price, or multiplying $1\frac{1}{2}$ times the original price.

In other words, increasing by 50% is the same as multiplying the original price by $1\frac{1}{2}$ or 1.5.

Check Your Work

Save Supermarket orders fresh fruit each day. Tim records changes in weight on a chart. The manager compared today's weight to yesterday's weight on a chart.

Fruit Order	Change in Weight
Apples	One-quarter more
Pears	One-third less
Oranges	Two-fifths less
Bananas	Three-tenths more

1. Use bars to indicate the change in weight for each type of fruit Save Supermarket orders. Label the bars.

The table below shows the weight of yesterday's fruit order.

Fruit Order	Weight Yesterday
Apples	80 kg
Pears	45 kg
Oranges	100 kg
Bananas	120 kg

2. Use the information in both charts to find the weight of today's fruit order. Show your calculations.

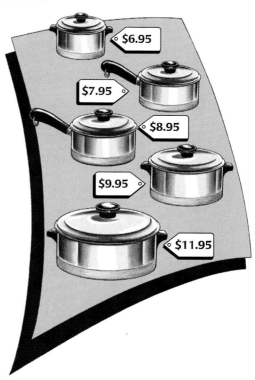

3. Tim buys an entire set of pots and pans at Dale's Department Store. Which discount saves him more money, $1.50 off each item or 15% off each item?

4. An item is discounted 20%. What fraction of the original price do you pay?

5. Describe how you can find the original price if you know the sale price is $42 and the original price was discounted 25%.

 For Further Reflection

Consider an item that had an original price of $75.00. It was discounted 25%. Then it was discounted a second time, at 15% off the sale price. Is this the same as an original discount of 40%? Explain and show the calculations.

D More or Less

Enlarge or Reduce

Maritza, Laura, and Jamel are opening a new store called Roll On. To advertise the grand opening, Maritza and Jamel designed a flyer with a picture of an in-line skater.

Here is the picture that Maritza and Jamel want to use for the flyer.

They realized that the picture had to be reduced to fit on the flyer. Laura suggested that they use a photocopier to see what the reduced picture would look like. Jamel and Maritza agreed. They found a photocopier that could reduce originals to 25 percent and enlarge originals to 400 percent.

1. **Reflect** What does it mean to reduce to 25 percent and enlarge to 400 percent? Give examples to illustrate your explanation.

2. **a.** Suppose they reduce the picture to 50%. What will the new width and length be? Show your calculations.

   b. Complete the arrow string to describe a reduction to 50%.

original length $\xrightarrow{\ \times\cdots\ }$ reduced length

The result of this reduction is still too large to fit on the flyer.

Maritza suggests, "Just take the reduced copy and reduce it again to 50%. Then we will see if that fits."

3. **a.** What are the width and length after two successive reductions to 50%?

   b. Describe the calculation to make two reductions of 50%.

   c. How can they get the same result, starting with the original and using just one reduction?

The group has gone to a lot of trouble to find the effect of a reduction. It would be a lot easier if the print shop had a chart that shows the measurements of an object after it is reduced.

4. Copy and fill in the table below for making a reduction to 30%.

Original Length (in cm)	10	15	20	1	2	3	4	5
Length Reduced to 30%								

5. **a.** How can you use a calculator to find the effect of a reduction to 30%?

   b. Use arrow language to describe this calculation.

The group wants to make a poster using the original picture. This time the picture has to be enlarged.

6. Find the dimensions of a picture 10 centimeters (cm) by 15 cm enlarged to 200%. Show your calculations.

The result is too small for the poster, so they decide to enlarge the original picture to 250%.

7. a. Find the dimensions of the picture (10 cm by 15 cm) enlarged to 250%. Show your calculations.

   b. Use arrow language to describe this calculation.

Suppose you want to make an enlargement to 200%. The photocopier you are using enlarges to only 150%.

8. a. Will two enlargements to 150% give the desired result? Explain.

   b. Find two enlargements that can be used with this photocopier to produce a final enlargement as close as possible to 200%. Copy the arrow string to describe your result.

original length $\xrightarrow{\times\cdots}$ .... $\xrightarrow{\times\cdots}$ enlarged length

Discount

$12.80

discount 25%

Maritza and Jamel went to the Office Supply Store to buy a frame for the poster. There were several frames for sale. Maritza liked the one shown on the left.

9. a. What is the discount in dollars?

   b. Maritza calculated the discount with one multiplication: 0.25 × $12.80.

Explain why this is correct. The percent bar can be helpful for finding an explanation.

$0 $12.80

	discount 25%

0%   100%

   c. Calculate the sale price for this frame.

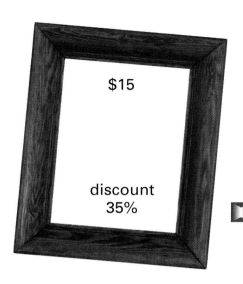

$15

discount
35%

10. a. Explain one multiplication that can be used to calculate the discount of this frame.

b. Find the sale price of this frame.

Maritza and Jamel decided to buy this frame. When they checked out, they saw the cashier use a calculator to calculate the sale price.

15 ☒ 0.65 ☰

11. Reflect Explain why this method works for calculating the sale price.

Sales Tax

Maritza and Jamel paid more than $9.75 for the frame. When they looked at the bill, they noticed a **sales tax** added to their purchase. Sales taxes help pay for local community services.

In many cities, the sales tax is 8%. So for an item priced at $20, you pay $20 plus 8% of $20.

Here are three ways to calculate the sales tax (8%) for a $20 purchase.

• One method uses a **ratio table**.

12. a. Copy the ratio table and fill in the dollar amounts for an 8% tax.

Price (in dollars)	$100	$10	$1	$0.10	
8% Tax (in dollars)					

b. Use this ratio table to find the sales tax (8%) for a $20 purchase.

• Another method uses a **percent bar**.

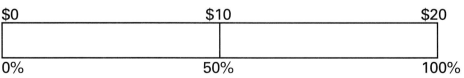

13. Copy this percent bar in your notebook and use it to find the sales tax (8%) for a $20 purchase.

- A third method uses **arrow language**.

Price   ——×···——→   Tax amount

It helps to remember the benchmark relationships for 1%, which are $\frac{1}{100}$ and 0.01.

14. a. What fraction corresponds to 8%?

b. What decimal corresponds to 8%?

c. Use arrow language (and a calculator) to show how to find the sales tax (8%) for a $20 purchase.

15. Copy the chart and fill in the last two rows. Use a sales tax of 19%.

Price in Dollars	$100.00	$10.00	$1.00
Tax in Dollars			
Total Cost with Tax			

Laura wants to compute the final cost of an item with a 19% sales tax, using one multiplication calculation. She uses arrow language to show what to multiply.

Price   ——× 1.19——→   Total cost with tax

16. a. Explain why this arrow language is correct.

b. Write the arrow string for calculating the total cost with an 8% sales tax.

$0.88 PAPER TOWELS
DISH SOAP $2.33
$1.90 PEANUTS
APPLES $0.92
WHOLE CHICKEN $4.98

As Maritza and Jamel left Save Supermarket, Jamel bought the items on the left.

17. Find Jamel's total bill, with a sales tax of 8% included.

Maritza paid $12.63 at Save Supermarket. She wonders how much of the dollar amount is tax. The sales tax is 8%.

18. a. How can Maritza find out using arrow language?

b. Calculate the tax Maritza paid.

Growing Interest

Laura visited the local bank to open business accounts for their new store, Roll On. She spoke with Leticia Beligrado. When she finished setting up the accounts, she asked Ms. Beligrado to make a donation for the grand opening. Ms. Beligrado was willing to donate a $250 savings account as a grand opening prize, but she wanted to make the prize more attractive by specifying that the money must stay in the bank for three years. The savings account earns 2% **interest** every year.

19. Reflect Research the savings plans available at your local bank. Write a paragraph describing the options.

If you win the grand opening prize, you would begin with $250 in the savings account. With a 2% annual interest rate, the bank would add 2% of $250 by the end of the first year. As a result, you would have 102% of the original prize.

0%   100% 102%

20. a. How much money would you have after one year?

   b. The savings account would earn an additional 2% of the new balance by the end of the next year. How much money would be in your account at the end of the second year?

   c. At the end of the third year?

The money in the account grows quite nicely in just a few years.

21. Reflect Explain why the total interest earned grows larger each year.

◆D◆ More or Less

Summary ⬥⬥

In this section, you studied **percent increase** and **decrease** and applied it to resizing pictures and calculating **sales tax** and **interest**.

There are many tools you can use to calculate a percent increase or decrease.

- Use a **ratio table**.

For a percent increase, to find the tax and total cost using a sales tax of 8%:

Price in Dollars	$100	$10	$1	$12	
Tax in Dollars	$8	$0.80	$0.08	$0.96	

Total Cost		$108	$10.80	$1.08	$12.96	

- Use a **percent bar**.

For a percent decrease, to find the sale price of a $12.80 item with a 25% discount:

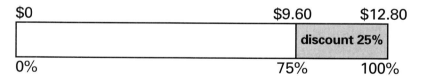

For a percent increase, to find this year's profit increased 25% from last year's profit of $12,800:

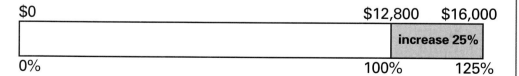

- Use a **double number line**.

For a percent decrease, to find the length of a 20-cm photo reduced to 80%:

0 cm   4 cm   **16 cm**   20 cm

0%   20%   80%   100%

- Use **arrow language**.

For a percent increase, to find the total cost of an item with a 19% sales tax included:

Price $\xrightarrow{\times 1.19}$ Total, tax included

Check Your Work

Brenda and Kim are writing an article for the school newspaper. They need to reduce a photo with dimensions 12 cm by 18 cm.

1. a. What are the new dimensions of the picture if it is reduced to 50%?

    b. If the original picture is reduced to 75%?

Afterward, the layout editor informs them that she allotted a blank space of 5 cm by 10 cm for their photo.

2. What reduction can Brenda and Kim use to fit their photo in the allotted blank space?

Ron and Ben are designing a poster for the school band concert. They have a picture they want to make 5 times as long and wide as it is now.

3. a. What enlargement would they have to make to have all measurements 5 times as big?

The copier they are using enlarges to only 200%. They will need to make several enlargements.

b. How can they do this? Use arrow language to describe the enlargements they might use.

4. Which multiplication calculation can you use to find the total cost of an item that has a 12% sales tax?

Salali buys the following items. (Prices do not include tax.)

Envelopes	$2.05
A set of 12 pens	$5.99
A birthday card	$1.80
A magazine	$3.95

5. Find Salali's total bill including 12% tax.

For Further Reflection

You have used percent bars, double number lines, arrow language, and multiplications to describe increases and decreases. Which one do you prefer? Why?

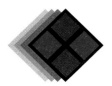

Additional Practice

Red Delicious apples are priced at $2.40 per kilogram.

1. Estimate the cost of the apples.

  a.   **b.**

Paul has $7 to spend on apples.

2. How many kilograms of Red Delicious apples can he buy?

3. Describe how to calculate the cost of the following amounts of apples, priced at $3.60 per kilogram, using a ratio table.

   a. 8 kg   **b.** $2\frac{1}{4}$ kg   **c.** 1.6 kg

At Veggies-R-Us, customers use a special scale to find the cost of produce. It prints these receipts.

  a.   **b.**   **c.**   **d.**

Pears	Cucumbers	Red Peppers	Potatoes
$2.75/kg	$2.19/kg	$4.25/kg	$0.99/kg
1.35 kg	2.86 kg	3.87 kg	0.63 kg
Total: $37125	Total: $62634	Total: $16448	Total: $62370

Unfortunately, the scale is not printing the decimal point for the total price.

4. Use estimation to determine what the total price should be on each of the receipts.

Section B Discounts

1. Rewrite the percents as fractions.

    a. 75%
    b. 10%

    c. $33\frac{1}{3}$%
    d. 50%

    e. $66\frac{2}{3}$%
    f. 25%

2. Rewrite the fractions as percents.

    a. $\frac{3}{10}$
    b. $\frac{1}{2}$

    c. $\frac{1}{5}$
    d. $\frac{3}{4}$

    e. $\frac{8}{10}$
    f. $\frac{1}{3}$

3. Describe a logical way you can solve each of the problems.
   Then write your answers

    a. 50% of 280
    b. 10% of 165

    c. 20% of 500
    d. 51% of 210

    e. 60% of 240
    f. 14% of 70

4. Seymour Sporting Goods and Sport-O-Rama are having sales.
   Which store has the better sale price for each item listed?
   Explain your choices.

Item	Seymour Sporting Goods		Sport-O-Rama	
Football	$20.00	25% off	$19.00	$4.00 off
Golf Glove	$8.40	20% off	$8.65	$1.75 off
Bowling Ball Bag	$24.95	25% off	$26.49	$8.00 off
Swimming Goggles	$5.14	30% off	$5.20	$1.50 off
Softball	$16.89	40% off	$17.00	$6.75 off
Soccer Shoes	$52.90	15% off	$50.95	$6.00 off

Section C Many Changes

Samantha's recipe for Key lime pie was selected for a Healthy Makeover. Here is the nutritional information for both recipes.

KEY LIME PIE SERVING SIZE: ONE SLICE		NUTRITION FACTS
Nutritional Category	**Original Recipe**	**Healthful Changes**
Calories	450	One-third fewer
Fat	18 grams	Two-thirds less
Cholesterol	150 milligrams	Three-fifths less
Sodium	300 milligrams	One-quarter less
Carbohydrates	50 grams	Three-tenths more

1. Use a bar to illustrate the healthful changes in each of the five categories. Label each bar clearly.

One way to find the number of calories in one slice of the healthy recipe for Key lime pie is to multiply 450 by $\frac{2}{3}$.

2. a. What fraction can you use to calculate the new amount of fat? Amount of cholesterol? Amount of sodium? Number of grams of carbohydrates?

   b. Find the amount of each nutritional category for the healthy recipe. Explain your reasoning.

Section D More or Less

Darnel must make a poster for a presentation in his history class. He plans to enlarge a small drawing that is 28 cm by 40 cm.

1. a. How big is the poster if Darnel enlarges the drawing to 115%? 125%?

   b. Darnel enlarges the drawing to 150%. It is too small. He decides he would like to enlarge it another 150%. How large is the resulting poster?

During his presentation, Darnel plans to hand out two pictures. The pictures are both 21 cm by 27 cm. The photocopier can reduce pictures only to 75%, 70%, or 60%.

2. Explain what Darnel can do to reduce his two pictures so they both fit onto one sheet of paper that is 21.5 cm by 28 cm and the pictures are as large as possible.

Laura's grandparents started a college fund for her on her twelfth birthday. They put $500 in a savings account that earns 4% interest every year.

3. a. How much is in the account after one year? What percent of the original amount is this?

   b. When Laura enters college in six years, how much money will she have in her account?

Section Ⓐ Produce Pricing

1. a. There are different strategies to solve this problem, and there are different good solutions. However, if your answer is not between $4.20 (= 2 × $2.10) and $6.30 (= 3 × $2.10), then you should redo the problem or ask help from a classmate or your teacher.

Sample good solutions:
- $5.20, because that is about halfway between $4.20 and $6.30.
- $4.62, because 2 kg of apples cost $4.20.
  0.1 kg of apples cost $0.21, so 0.2 kg cost $0.42.
  2.2 kg of apples cost $4.20 + $0.42 = $4.62.

b. There are different strategies to solve this problem, and there are different good solutions. However, if your answer is not between $1.05 (= $\frac{1}{2}$ × $2.10) and $2.10, then you should redo the problem or ask help from a classmate or your teacher.

Sample good solutions:
- $1.50, because that is about halfway between $1.05 and $2.10.
- $1.68, because 1 kg of apples cost $2.10.
  0.1 kg of apples cost $0.21, so 0.2 kg cost $0.42.
  0.8 kg of apples cost $2.10 − $0.42 = $1.68.

2. Your answer should be a little more than 3 kg.

Sample strategy:

Three kg of apples cost $6.30, so Paul has $0.70 left ($7 − $6.30 = $0.70).

From here, there are different strategies to continue.
- $0.70 is about $1, and 1 kg costs about $2.
  $1 out of $2 is $\frac{1}{2}$, so he can buy $1 + \frac{1}{2} = 1\frac{1}{2}$ kg of apples.
- One kg of apples costs $2.10
  $0.70 out of $2.10 is $\frac{70}{210}$ is $\frac{1}{3}$, so he can buy $3\frac{1}{3}$ kg of apples.

The price of Golden Delicious is $3.60 per kg.

3. **a.** There are different strategies to find the price without the use of a calculator. You may have described one of the following strategies.

- Calculate the price for 3 kg using a ratio table.

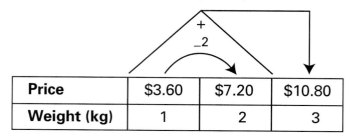

Price	$3.60	$7.20	$10.80
Weight (kg)	1	2	3

- Calculate 3 × $3.60 mentally.

  3 × $3 + 3 × $0.60 = $9 + $1.80 = $10.80

b. There are different strategies to find the price without using a calculator. You may have described the following strategy.

- In part **a**, I calculated the price for 3 kg. Since 0.3 kg is one tenth of 3 kg, I can calculate one tenth of $10.80, which is $1.08.

c. There are different strategies to find the price without using a calculator. You may have described the following strategy.

- In part **b**, I calculated the price for 0.3 kg ($1.08), so I only have to add the price of two kg ($7.20). The answer is $1.08 + $7.20 = $8.28.

4. **a.** $\frac{1}{2}$ × $47.00 = $23.50. Many strategies are possible. Here are some.

- Separating $47.00 as $46.00 + $1.00:

  $\frac{1}{2}$ of $47.00 = $\frac{1}{2}$ of ($46.00 + $1.00)

  $\qquad\qquad = \frac{1}{2}$ of $46.00 + $\frac{1}{2}$ of $1.00

  $\qquad\qquad = \qquad$ $23.00 + $0.50

  $\qquad\qquad = \qquad\qquad$ $23.50

- Separating $47.00 as $40.00 + $7.00:

  $47.00 is equal to $40.00 + $7.00.

  $\frac{1}{2}$ of $40.00 is $20.00 and $\frac{1}{2}$ of $7.00 is $3.50

  So $\frac{1}{2}$ × $47.00

  = $20.00 + $3.50 = $23.50.

- Thinking of $47.00 as $50.00 − $3.00:

$$\frac{1}{2} \text{ of } \$47.00 = \frac{1}{2} \text{ of } (\$50.00 - \$3.00)$$
$$= \frac{1}{2} \text{ of } \$50.00 - \frac{1}{2} \text{ of } \$3.00$$
$$= \quad \$25.00 - \$1.50$$
$$= \quad\quad \$23.50$$

b. $1\frac{1}{4} \times \$8.20 = \$10.25$. Strategies will vary.

- $\frac{1}{2}$ of $8.20 = $4.10, so

$\frac{1}{4}$ of $8.20 = $2.05.

So $1\frac{1}{4} \times \$8.20$

$= \$8.20 + \$2.05 = \$10.25$.

- Using a ratio table:

Price	$8.20	$4.10	$2.05	$10.25
Weight (kg)	1	$\frac{1}{2}$	$\frac{1}{4}$	$1\frac{1}{4}$

5. Kenji might have thought:

- 12.54 is more than 12 and 0.39 is more than $\frac{1}{3}$. So the answer will be more than $\frac{1}{3}$ of 12, which is 4. Checking 4.8096 is more than 4.

- 12.54 is close to 12 and 0.39 is close to 0.5. So that would be like taking $\frac{1}{2}$ of 12, which is 6. Checking 4.8906 is reasonable.

Section **B** Discounts

1. Discount 3 gives the best sale price. You may have used one of the following strategies:

- Calculate and compare the discount prices.

  Discount 1: 10% of $5.98 is about $0.60. So 5% of $5.98 is about $0.30.
  The sale price is $5.98 − $0.30 = $5.68.

  Discount 2: The discount is $0.50 off. So the sale price is $5.98 − $0.50 = $5.48.

  Discount 3: One-fifth of $5.98 is about $1.20. So the sale price is $5.98 − $1.20 = $4.78.

  So Discount 3 gives the best sale price (largest discount).

- Calculate and compare the discount fractions.
  Discount 1: 5% off is $\frac{1}{20}$ off.

  Discount 2: $0.50 off of $6.00 is
  $\frac{50}{600} = \frac{5}{60} = \frac{1}{12}$.

  Discount 3: $\frac{1}{5}$ off
  $\frac{1}{5}$ is greater than $\frac{1}{20}$ and $\frac{1}{12}$.
  So Discount 3 gives the best sale price.

- Use percents to compare the discounts:
  Discount 1: 5%

  Discount 2: $0.50 is a bit less than 10% of $5.98.
  Discount 3: $\frac{1}{5}$ is 20%.

  So Discount 3 gives the best sale price.

2. The discount is $144. You may have used one of the following strategies.

   - Thinking of 60% as 50% + 10%:
     Use a percent bar.

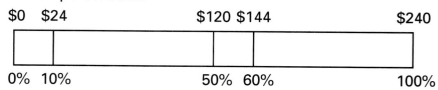

     Since 60% can be written as 50% + 10%, find 50% of $240, which is equal to $120.
     Then find 10% of $240, which is equal to $24.
     So 60% of $240 = $120 + $24 = $144.

   - Thinking of 60% as six 10%s:
     Since 60% can be written as six 10%s, find 10% of $240, which is equal to 24.
     Then multiply 24 by 6, which is equal to 144.
     So 60% of $240 = $144.
   - Using a calculator:
     Enter: 0.60 × 240 = 144.

3. The $280 air conditioner will cost $112; the $200 air conditioner will cost $80; the $275 air conditioner will cost $110. You may have used the following strategy.

$280 air conditioner:
60% of $280 = $168.
The sale price is $280 − $168 = $112.

$200 air conditioner:
60% of $200 = $120.
The sale price is $200 − $120 = $80.

$275 air conditioner:
60% of $275 = $165.
The sale price is $275 − $165 = $110.

4. a. There are different ways to finish their calculations. You may have used one of these strategies.

- Ms. Vander uses $\frac{1}{10}$ of 800 = 80:
  $\frac{1}{10}$ of 800 = 80, and
  4 × 80 = 40% of 800 = 320. Also,
  since 10% of 800 = 80, 5% is equal to
  one-half of 80, which is 40.
  So 45% of 800 = 320 + 40 = 360.

- Ms. Vander could have also used a 10% strategy:
  10% of 800 is 80, so 40% is 320 (4 × 80).
  5% is half of 10%, so 5% is 40 ($\frac{1}{2}$ × 80).
  So 45% is 360 (320 + 4).

- Mr. Sanchez uses a 45% is 50% − 5% strategy:
  50% is 400 ($\frac{1}{2}$ of 800). I need to take off 5%.
  5% is 40 ($\frac{1}{10}$ of 50%).
  45% is 360 (400 − 40).

  Or using a ratio table:

Number of Customers	800	400	40	360
Percent	100%	50%	5%	45%

5. Answers will vary. Sample responses:

- Half of 50% is 25%.
  50% of 900 is 450 ($\frac{1}{2}$ of 900).
  Half of 50% is 225.
  25% is $\frac{1}{4}$ of the whole. I can find
  $\frac{1}{4}$ of 900 by dividing 900 by four; $900 \div 4 = 225$.

Section ◆C◆ Many Changes

1. Answers will vary. Sample answers are shown.

Apples

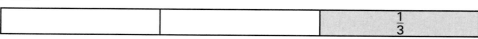

Pears

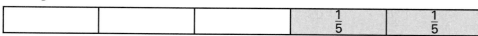

Oranges

Bananas

2. You may have used strategies like these.

Apples: $\frac{1}{4}$ more is 100 kg; $\frac{1}{4}$ of 80 kg is 20 kg; $\frac{1}{4}$ more is 100 kg (80 + 20).

Pears: $\frac{1}{3}$ less leaves 30 kg. $\frac{1}{3}$ of 45 is 15, and 45 − 15 is 30 kg.

Oranges: $\frac{2}{5}$ less is 60 kg. $\frac{1}{5}$ of 100 is 20 kg, so $\frac{3}{5}$ of 100 is 3 × 20 = 60 kg.

Bananas: $\frac{3}{10}$ more is 156 kg. $\frac{1}{10}$ of 120 kg is 12 kg, so $\frac{3}{10}$ of 120 is 3 × 12 = 36; 36 + 120 = 156 kg.

3. Tim saves more money with a discount of $1.50 for each item, which is a discount of $7.50 (5 × $1.50). You may have used one of these strategies.

- Calculating 15% of the total:

  15% of ($11.95 + $9.95 + $8.95 + 7.95 + 6.95) 15% of $45.75 is a little more than $6.86, which is not as good as a $7.50 discount.

- Calculating 15% off each item using a calculator:

  0.15 × $11.95 + 0.15 x $9.95 + 0.15 × $8.95 + 0.15 × $7.95 + 0.15 × $6.95 = 6.8625 about $6.86, which is not as good as a $7.50 discount.

- Estimating 15% of total:

  Estimate of total is $46 ($7 + $8 +$9 +$10 +$12).

  15% of $46, which is 10% + 5% of $46, which is $4.60 + $2.30 = $6.90, and this is less than the discount of $7.50.

  If you make a more accurate estimate, you might get:

  The total is $7 + $8 + $9 + $10 + $12 – 5 × $0.05 = $45.75.

  15% of $45.75 is about $6.86, which is less than $7.50.

4. You have to pay $\frac{4}{5}$ of the old price.

Sample strategy, using a percent bar:

				80%		100%
				discount		

$\frac{4}{5}$ $-\frac{1}{5}$

5. The original price is $56.

Note that the original price wasn't given here!

There are several ways to solve this problem.

- Using a percent bar:

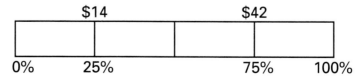

Since $42 is the sale price after a 25% discount, 75% or $\frac{3}{4}$ of the bar represents $42. So 25% of the bar is $14 and the whole bar has to be 4 of these, or $56.

• Using a double number line with fractions and decimals:

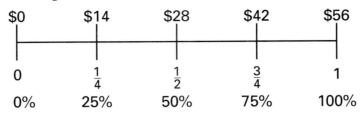

• Using a ratio table:

Price	$42	$14	$56
Percent	75%	25%	100%

Section Ⓓ More or Less

1. **a.** The new measurements are 6 cm by 9 cm.
   Sample calculations:
   50% of 12 cm is $\frac{1}{2}$ of 12 cm or 6 cm.
   50% of 18 cm is half of 18 cm or 9 cm.

   b. The new measurements are 9 cm by 13.5 cm.
   Sample calculations:
   Reduced to 75%, new measurements are $\frac{3}{4}$ of old measurements.
   $\frac{1}{4}$ of 12 cm is 3 cm, and $\frac{3}{4}$ is 3 times as much, so
   3 × 3 cm = 9 cm.
   $\frac{1}{4}$ of 18 cm is 18 ÷ 4 = 4.5 cm, and $\frac{3}{4}$ is 3 times as much, so
   3 × 4.5 cm = 13.5 cm.

2. Reductions must be close to and a little less than reducing to 42%. Here is one strategy.

   Using **1a**, reducing the picture to 50% is too wide, but not too long. Reducing to 40%, I need to check only the width.

   40% of 12 cm:
   10% of 12 cm is 1.2 cm, so 40% is 4.8 cm (4 × 1.2 cm).

   So the width (4.8 cm) is less than 5 cm, so reducing to 40% will fit.

3. a. 5 times as big is an enlargement to 500%.

  b. measurement $\xrightarrow{\times 2}$ .... $\xrightarrow{\times 2}$ .... $\xrightarrow{\times 1.25}$ new measurement

There are different ways to solve this problem. One way is the following.

They need to make several enlargements. Start with 200% or × 2. Then use this 200% or × 2 enlargement again. This means the result is now 400%, or × 4. This is still too small. An enlargement of the enlarged picture to 125% will result in an enlargement of the original picture to 500%.

Another way to solve this problem is to choose a measurement (for example, 100 cm) and then use the arrows to find the final amount.

$$100 \xrightarrow{\times 2} 200 \xrightarrow{\times 2} 400 \xrightarrow{\times ?} 500$$

To get from 400 to 500, you need to multiply by 1.25.

$$400 + 100 = 400 \times (1 + \tfrac{1}{4})$$
$$= 400 \times (1.25)$$

4. Multiply by 1.12.

5. Total including tax is $15.44. You can calculate the tax on each item and find the price and add all prices, but it is easier to add the prices first and calculate the tax for the total.

Total without tax is $13.79.

Including tax:

$13.79 $\xrightarrow{\times\ 1.12}$ $15.44

CAMBRIDGE
UNIVERSITY PRESS

Travel and Tourism

for Cambridge IGCSE™ and O Level

COURSEBOOK

Stephen Rickerby, John Smith & Ruth Figg

Shaftesbury Road, Cambridge CB2 8EA, United Kingdom

One Liberty Plaza, 20th Floor, New York, NY 10006, USA

477 Williamstown Road, Port Melbourne, VIC 3207, Australia

314–321, 3rd Floor, Plot 3, Splendor Forum, Jasola District Centre, New Delhi – 110025, India

103 Penang Road, #05–06/07, Visioncrest Commercial, Singapore 238467

Cambridge University Press is part of the University of Cambridge.

It furthers the University's mission by disseminating knowledge in the pursuit of education, learning and research at the highest international levels of excellence.

www.cambridge.org
Information on this title: www.cambridge.org/9781009064682

© Cambridge University Press & Assessment 2022

First published 2012

20 19 18 17 16 15 14 13 12 11 10 9 8 7 6 5 4 3

Printed in Poland by Opolgraf

A catalogue record for this publication is available from the British Library

ISBN 9781009064682 Paperback with Digital Access (2 Years)
ISBN 9781009073578 Digital Coursebook (2 Years)
ISBN 9781009073608 eBook

Cambridge University Press has no responsibility for the persistence or accuracy of URLs for external or third-party internet websites referred to in this publication, and does not guarantee that any content on such websites is, or will remain, accurate or appropriate. Information regarding prices, travel timetables, and other factual information given in this work is correct at the time of first printing but Cambridge University Press does not guarantee the accuracy of such information thereafter.

Cambridge International copyright material in this publication is reproduced under licence and remains the intellectual property of Cambridge Assessment International Education.

Exam-style questions and sample answers have been written by the authors. In examinations, the way marks are awarded may be different. References to assessment and/or assessment preparation are the publisher's interpretation of the curriculum framework requirements and may not fully reflect the approach of Cambridge Assessment International Education.

Third-party websites and resources referred to in this publication have not been endorsed by Cambridge Assessment International Education.

....

DEDICATED TEACHER AWARDS

Teachers play an important part in shaping futures. Our Dedicated Teacher Awards recognise the hard work that teachers put in every day.

Thank you to everyone who nominated this year; we have been inspired and moved by all of your stories. Well done to all of our nominees for your dedication to learning and for inspiring the next generation of thinkers, leaders and innovators.

Congratulations to our incredible winners!

WINNER

Regional Winner	Regional Winner	Regional Winner	Regional Winner	Regional Winner	Regional Winner
Middle East & North Africa	Europe	North & South America	Central & Southern Africa	Australia, New Zealand & South-East Asia	East & South Asia
Annamma Lucy	**Anna Murray**	**Melissa Crosby**	**Nonhlanhla Masina**	**Peggy Pesik**	**Raminder Kaur Mac**
GEMS Our Own English High School, Sharjah - Boys' Branch, UAE	British Council, France	Frankfort High School, USA	African School for Excellence, South Africa	Sekolah Buin Batu, Indonesia	Choithram School, India

For more information about our dedicated teachers and their stories, go to
dedicatedteacher.cambridge.org

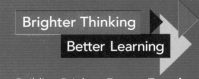

> Contents

> How to use this series

This suite of resources supports learners and teachers following the Cambridge IGCSE™ and O Level Travel & Tourism syllabuses (0471/7096). The components in the series are designed to work together and help learners develop the necessary knowledge and skills for this subject. With clear language and style, they are designed for international learners.

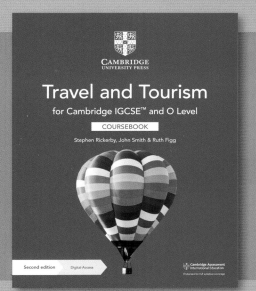

The Coursebook is designed for learners to use in class with guidance from the teacher. It offers complete coverage of the Cambridge IGCSE™ and O Level Travel and Tourism syllabuses. Each unit contains in-depth explanation of Travel and Tourism concepts, definitions of key words, and a variety of activities, case studies and images to engage learners, help them make real-world connections and develop their critical thinking skills.

The Teacher's Resource is the foundation of this series because it offers inspiring ideas about how to teach this course. It contains teaching guidance, learning plans, suggestions for differentiation, assessment and language support, answers and extra materials including downloadable language worksheets.

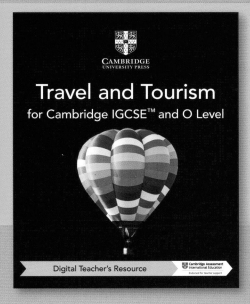

> How to use this book

Throughout this book, you will notice lots of different features that will help your learning. These are explained below.

LEARNING INTENTIONS

These set the scene for each sub-unit, help with navigation through the coursebook and indicate the important concepts in each topic.

TRAVEL AND TOURISM IN CONTEXT

This feature presents real-world examples and applications of the content in a sub-unit, encouraging you to look further into topics. There are discussion questions at the end which look at some of the benefits and problems of these applications.

KEY WORDS

Key vocabulary is highlighted in the text when it is first introduced, and definitions are given in boxes near the vocabulary. You will also find definitions of these words in the Glossary at the back of this book.

CASE STUDIES

These are up-to-date and real-life case studies, taken from different destinations around the world. The case studies and the accompanying questions allow you to actively explore real global travel and tourism. You are provided with opportunities to produce your own work, either as an individual, in pairs or in groups.

COMMAND WORDS

Command words that appear in the syllabus and might be used in exams are highlighted in the exam-style questions when they are first introduced. You will also find these definitions in the Introduction to command words section with some further explanation on their meanings.

ACTIVITIES

Activities give you an opportunity to check your understanding throughout the text in a more active way, for example, by creating presentations, posters or role plays.

REFLECTION

These activities ask you to think about the approach that you take to your work, and how you might improve this in the future.

EXAM-STYLE QUESTIONS

Questions at the end of each sub-unit provide more demanding exam-style questions, some of which may require the use of knowledge from previous sub-units. The answers to these questions can be found in the digital version of the coursebook.

SELF-EVALUATION CHECKLIST

The summary checklists provide you with a series of statements at the end of each unit outlining the content you should now understand. You will be asked to rate your confidence for each of these statements when revising. You should revisit any topics that you rated 'Needs more work' or 'Almost there'.

I am now able to:	Needs more work	Almost there	Ready to move on

> Introduction

Who is this book for?

This edition of the coursebook comprehensively supports the syllabus content for Cambridge IGCSE™ and O Level Travel & Tourism syllabuses (0471/7096). As a Travel and Tourism learner following this syllabus, or a teacher guiding learners through it, you can be confident that the book fully covers this content to the appropriate level.

Other learners of this subject who are using different GCSE or equivalent courses should also be able to benefit from the subject content, activities and features, such as the exam-style questions that this book contains.

What makes this book different?

The key distinctive features of this book are its:

- active learning approach
- focus on sustainability.

Firmly driven by its **active learning** approach, this book enables you to achieve your travel and tourism learning objectives through:

- scaffolded **activities** that offer opportunities for group work and project work, such as research and student-led presentations, supporting the development of critical thinking skills for every topic
- visual means, including **figures** such as **tables** and diagrams
- carefully researched and composed **case studies** and accompanying **questions**
- **key words** and **key concept links** – features that explain travel and tourism words and reveal links to important travel and tourism concepts
- **reflection** on your travel and tourism learning process
- a **self-evaluation checklist** allowing you to rate yourself on how confident you are to move on to the next topic.

The book contains many up-to-date and real-life case studies taken from different destinations around the world. The case studies and the accompanying questions allow you to actively explore real global travel and tourism. This book engagingly and fully reflects worldwide sustainable travel and tourism with its wide-ranging international examples and destination case studies.

Without any doubt, the most important new element of this course is the focus on sustainability. This is a central theme of the book: it is interwoven throughout. The questions and activities in every unit give you opportunities to learn actively and to investigate, understand, discuss and explain the nature, impacts and sustainable management of travel and tourism. You will build your awareness of the importance of the customer and of marketing in the travel and tourism industry, and you will evaluate and communicate different values and attitudes relating to travel and tourism.

There are a lot of questions, activities and exam-style questions throughout this book that will enable you to:

- gain confidence in understanding, communicating and explaining the nature, sustainability, management and marketing of travel and tourism

- take responsibility for yourself in being responsive to and respectful of others, through becoming aware of the importance of sustainability and of your own responsibility to the environment and to the future of destination communities

- be reflective as a learner, by considering your approach to assessing the customer appeal, growth, management, impacts and sustainability of travel and tourism

- be innovative by applying your travel and tourism learning to unfamiliar contexts, locally and in the wider world.

You will become engaged in exploring travel and tourism issues of today, as well as being ready to make a difference by developing your own personal interests and opinions.

It is not intended that even the keenest learner will read this coursebook from cover to cover like a novel! Instead, the authors' intention is to make sure that you use this coursebook as a support and guide for each section of the syllabus as you progress through your course.

We hope you will enjoy your study of Travel and Tourism and that you will find this book an invaluable resource, guide and support towards achieving success in your course.

Stephen Rickerby

⟩ Introduction to command words

The command words and definitions in the following table are taken from the Cambridge IGCSE™ and O Level Travel & Tourism syllabuses (0471/7096) for examination from 2024. You should always refer to the appropriate syllabus document for the year of your examination to confirm the details and for more information. The syllabus document is available on the Cambridge International website at www.cambridgeinternational.org.

Some questions in the exam will start with a command word. The command word will help you to understand how you need to answer the question. The definition for the command words is taken verbatim from the syllabus. The content in the 'Guidance' and 'How to approach these questions' are suggestions from the author.

These command words are used in the exam-style questions and some of the activities in this book.

When you first read a question in a practice activity, it can be helpful to underline or highlight the command word. This will help to focus your attention on the skills you need to demonstrate to answer the question.

Command word	Definition	Guidance	How to approach these questions
Assess	Make an informed judgement about something.	Give a number of points and weigh up/analyse their relative significance or importance. It is not necessary to explain key term/s used in the question.	It is important to only raise points that are applied to the context of the question. Once you have raised the point, you need to go on to analyse its importance. For example, what difference does it make? What are the advantages or disadvantages? Finally, you need to end with a supported conclusion.
Define	Give the precise meaning of a term.	Use your knowledge and understanding to give the meaning of the term.	Ensure that the answer explains the term clearly. Try to avoid using the words in the key term itself. For example, when defining *business tourists*, do not use the word 'business'; instead, replace it with a similar word, such as 'work'.
Describe	Give the characteristics and main features of something.	Use your knowledge and understanding to give a characteristic and follow on with its main features.	Ensure that you extend what you are saying about the characteristic by giving the features of the characteristic raised, rather than simply giving another characteristic.

Command word	Definition	Guidance	How to approach these questions
Discuss	Write about issue(s) or topic(s) in depth and in a structured way.	Analyse the issues relevant to the question. Consider both sides of an argument or make a comparison. For example, consider advantages and disadvantages, or reasons for and reasons against.	It is important to write only about issues that are applied to the context of the question. It can be helpful to use connectives to analyse. For example, 'because', 'leading to', 'therefore' and 'however'. After analysing and considering both sides of the argument, finish with a reasoned conclusion.
Evaluate	Judge or calculate the quality, importance, amount or value of something.	Make a decision or give your opinion regarding which of the points you raise are the most important or significant in the context given.	Raise points that are within the context of the question. Analyse their significance and finish your answer with a conclusion. Your conclusion should be your opinion on which one of the points raised is more significant, and why.
Explain	Set out purposes or reasons/make the relationships between things clear/say why and/or how and support with relevant evidence.	Give details about what happens because of the point you have raised.	First, you need to show your knowledge by giving a relevant point. This should be followed by giving the reasons for what happens as a result of the point raised. Always make sure the point you raise is in the context of the question. An explanation is more than just giving an example of something.
Give	Produce an answer from a given source or from memory.	Use your knowledge and understanding to recall and state a relevant point.	Simply state what has been asked.
Identify	Name/select/recognise.	You should locate and state the relevant point. This will be located in the stimulus material (insert).	Make sure that you state the term correctly. For example, if it is a percentage amount or amount of money, make sure you include the relevant sign (%/$).
State	Express in clear terms.	You only need to state the information required. It does not have to be in a sentence or be detailed.	You need to recall from memory the information required. Remember to be accurate!
Suggest	Apply knowledge and understanding to situations where there is a range of valid responses in order to make proposals/put forward considerations.	Use your knowledge and understanding to give a relevant point.	State your selected point.

Key concepts of travel and tourism

LEARNING INTENTIONS

In this unit you will learn how to:

- identify and describe the main types of tourism

- explain the main reasons why people travel and analyse the importance of the different reasons

- understand and explain the importance of sustainability in travel and tourism

- identify the different characteristics of travel and tourism, explain how they are related and analyse the associated difficulties

- identify and describe the different types of tourists

- identify and describe the different types of destinations.

TRAVEL AND TOURISM IN CONTEXT

A global phenomenon!

For as long as humans have been on the earth, they have travelled. In early times, they travelled to find food, trade, explore new territories or visit neighbouring communities.

Today, the world is more connected than ever. It is now easier and cheaper than ever to travel to other countries and experience different cultures. Compared with our ancestors, we travel for longer and farther. We travel within our own country or region and much farther, sometimes to the other side of the world.

Developments in technology have made us more aware of other countries, destinations, cultures and events. Technology such as the internet and mobile phones means we can easily research other countries. We watch international programmes, listen to global news and easily communicate with people from all over the world from our home or even whilst we are out. All of this stimulates a desire to go and experience the wonders we see and learn about.

There is no doubt that travel and tourism is a global phenomenon. It is one of the world's largest and fastest growing industries, generating over US$8.9 trillion and supporting 330 million jobs. This means that, around the world, on average, one in every ten jobs is in the travel and tourism industry. The industry is resilient: it has experienced continued growth, which is expected to keep going long into the future, despite local, national or global 'shocks', such as the COVID-19 pandemic.

The United Nations World Tourism Organization (UNWTO) states:

Tourism can be a force for good in our world, playing a part in protecting our planet and its biodiversity, and celebrating what makes us human: from discovering new places and cultures to connecting with new people and experiences.

Figure 1.1: Moraine Lake, Banff, Canada

Questions

1   Make a list of the reasons why people travel.

2   Discuss the factors that have enabled us to travel farther distances and for longer.

3   Discuss whether you agree with the statement from the UNWTO. Are there any reasons why tourism is not always a good thing?

KEY WORDS

destination: the place a tourist visits

resilient: able to continue after a bad event. For example, a resilient destination will soon recover from an extreme weather event such as a severe storm, or from a natural disaster such as flooding

1.1 Main types of tourism

Introduction

Tourism is the business of providing services such as transport, places to stay or entertainment for people who temporarily leave the place where they normally live, work or study. It includes how they move around and what they do when they get there. Tourism is a valuable industry that is worth a lot of money to many countries around the world. Tourists travel from place to place using the services and facilities provided by the tourism organisations and industry.

> **KEY WORDS**
>
> **tourism:** the business of providing services such as transport, places to stay and entertainment for people who temporarily leave the place where they normally live, work or study
>
> **tourist:** a person who travels temporarily from one place to another

> **TIP**
>
> In statistics and research into tourism, tourists are sometimes also called 'visitors'.

Domestic tourism

Domestic tourism is when a tourist travels within their own country.

> **KEY WORD**
>
> **domestic tourism:** a type of tourism where tourists travel within their country of residence (where they live)

Domestic tourism has advantages for tourists. These are:

- There are no language barriers. This allows the tourist to travel around easily.

- The currency is the same, therefore the tourist does not have to pay currency exchange costs.

- The culture is similar, which ensures the tourist does not experience culture shock.

- Travel documentation (for example, a passport or a visa) is not required. These can cost money and take time to acquire.

- Tourists may be able to use their own transport (for example, cars). This can reduce costs and increase the convenience for the tourist.

Because of these advantages, domestic tourists can prepare their trip and depart very quickly. For example, they can decide to leave and be ready to depart the next day. This helps to increase the demand for domestic tourism. The UNWTO reports that worldwide, domestic tourism is over six times bigger than international tourism. Countries such as China, India and the United States of America have a larger percentage of domestic tourism due to the geographical size of the country.

In addition to the benefits to tourists, domestic tourism has other advantages, for example:

- The environmental impacts of domestic tourism are often less. There are more opportunities for tourists to avoid flying, travel shorter distances and use public transport.

- Domestic tourism is less affected by global shocks as tourists will often feel safer from any threats or a lack of certainty when travelling in their own country.

- Domestic tourism can increase the understanding of national culture and heritage.

> **CASE STUDY**
>
> **'We Travel Together'**
>
>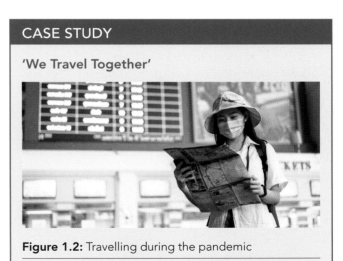
>
> **Figure 1.2:** Travelling during the pandemic

During the COVID-19 pandemic, the government of Thailand provided Thai nationals over the age of 18 with an opportunity to take part in domestic tourism at a reduced cost. The domestic tourism campaign, known as 'We Travel Together', encouraged Thai nationals to travel within their own country. Tourists could stay in hotels, take domestic flights and use other tourism services such as food and attractions at a reduced price, with the government paying up to 40% of the costs.

Questions

Discuss in pairs or groups:

1   Explain the likely reasons why the Government of Thailand introduced the 'We Travel Together' campaign.

2   What are the benefits of this campaign for Thai nationals?

3   What are the benefits of this campaign for the tourism industry in Thailand?

Inbound tourism

Inbound tourism is when a tourist from one country travels to another that is not their normal country of residence. They are known as inbound tourists. For example, if a tourist travelled from China to Malaysia, they would be an inbound tourist to Malaysia.

The tourism industry in a country will closely monitor which countries their inbound tourists are from; they are known as the country's source market for tourism. The government or ministry responsible for tourism in a country will create detailed tourism statistics of tourist numbers and trends.

TIP

In tourism statistics, inbound tourists are often referred to as tourist arrivals. They are the tourists arriving in that country.

Outbound tourism

Outbound tourism is when a tourist leaves the country where they normally live and travel to another country. For example, a tourist who travels from China to Malaysia would be considered an outbound tourist as they are travelling out of China.

KEY WORDS

inbound tourism: a type of tourism where tourists travel to a country

source market: the country that inbound tourists to a destination have travelled from (their country of residence)

touristor arrivals: the number of international tourists/visitors who travel to a country during a given time. The term is used in tourism statistics

outbound tourism: a type of tourism where tourists travel out of their country of residence

Project: In small groups, research the rates of tourism in your country and produce a report on what you have found. Tourism statistics are usually published online by the Ministry of Tourism or similar government departments. Other useful sources of information are the UNWTO Tourism Data Dashboard and the World Travel and Tourism Council (WTTC) Economic Impact Reports.

1   Research the rates of domestic, inbound and outbound tourism over the past five to ten years.

2   What trends do you notice in the data? Have the different types of tourism increased or decreased?

3   Suggest reasons for the trends you have identified.

4   Identify the main source markets for inbound tourism to your country and suggest reasons why.

5   Identify the countries most visited for outbound tourism from your country and suggest reasons why.

6   Considering all the information you have researched, make predictions for future trends in tourism in your country. Provide reasons for your predictions.

REFLECTION

What did you learn from this activity about the size and importance of tourism in your country? How do you think you could apply your findings from this activity?

International tourism

Tourists travelling internationally, inbound or outbound, is called international tourism.

International tourism takes more preparation and planning than domestic tourism. This depends on where tourists travel from and how far they travel. Preparation may include:

- currency exchange

- transport e.g. flights need to be booked before travel can take place

- passports documents need to be up to date

- visas must be obtained for entry into the country

- preparing for experiencing a different language and culture.

Day trip

Not all forms of tourism require the tourist to stay overnight in another place. A **day trip** is a form of tourism where the tourist returns home the same day; they travel for less than 24 hours, therefore there is no overnight stay. There are many reasons why people take day trips. Reasons include pleasure (e.g. travelling to the beach or a city); work (e.g. attending a meeting in another city or country); or visiting friends and relatives.

Often people do not realise they are a tourist when taking a day trip. It is useful to think back to the explanation of what tourism is. If the person is travelling away from the place where they normally live, work or study, they are a tourist.

KEY WORD

day trip: when a tourist travels for less than 24 hours

TIP

Tourists taking a day trip are sometimes referred to as day trippers or day visitors.

Short break

Figure 1.3: A short break in Barcelona

A **short break** is a type of tourism. This is when a tourist stays away from their home for four nights or less. This could be a weekend trip or a mid-week trip.

Short breaks are popular as second holidays or for people who cannot stay away from home for longer periods of time because of work, health or other commitments.

Short breaks have increased in popularity because of several factors; these include:

- more and easier access to different transport methods

- increased wealth in some countries

- increasing demand for tourism.

When thinking about the different types of tourism, it is important to consider where the tourist's home is, where they are normally resident. There are so many variables, for example, some countries are large, and travel can take a long time; in Russia or the United States of America, for example, domestic tourism can require a **long-haul flight**. Other countries are small, or the tourist may live close to an international border and can travel internationally as a day trip.

KEY WORDS

short break: a trip lasting four nights or less

long-haul flight: a flight lasting longer than six hours

ACTIVITY 1.2

Which of the following statements about types of tourism are *True* and which are *False*?

1   Domestic tourists can also be called international tourists.

2   Inbound tourists travel to another country.

3   Outbound tourists stay within their own country of residence.

4   A short break is five nights or less.

5   A person who travels for less than 24 hours is not a tourist.

1.2 Main reasons why people travel

Introduction

The reasons why people travel are categorised based on the tourist's main motivation for travel.

There are three main reasons why people travel. These are:

- leisure

- business

- visiting friends and family (VFR).

Leisure travel

Leisure travel is when tourists travel for the purpose of leisure, enjoyment or recreation, widely known as a holiday or vacation. These travellers are known as **leisure tourists**.

KEY WORDS

leisure travel: travel for the purpose of leisure, enjoyment or recreation

leisure tourists: people who travel for the purpose of leisure, enjoyment or recreation

KEY CONCEPT LINK

The different characteristics, wants and needs of leisure tourists and business tourists are explained in *1.5 Types of tourists*.

The most common type of holidays are sun, sea and sand holidays; however, there are many other types of holidays, for example, sightseeing, shopping and pilgrimages.

Leisure tourists are only able to travel for the time they have available away from commitments such as work, school or family responsibilities. When they are away, their main focus is enjoyment. Leisure travel varies in length from short breaks of up to four nights or longer, or for one or two weeks. The distance travelled has a significant influence on leisure holidays. Few leisure tourists are willing to travel long distances for a short break lasting three or four days as the journey itself can take a day of their available time.

CASE STUDY

Slow travel

Slow travel is a form of sustainable tourism. Slow travel means tourists travel to a place and make the journey to that place part of the holiday experience. Generally, tourists will choose the fastest transport method available to them, usually flying, so they can spend as much time as possible at the destination they are travelling to. Slow travel tourists choose not to fly, and instead use other methods of transport, for example, trains or boats.

Figure 1.4: Glacier express train, Swiss Alps

The result is that the travel experience is slowed down and becomes more enjoyable, allowing the tourist to appreciate the journey, too. Slow travel tourists also try to make their experiences and purchases throughout their journey locally, by choosing local transport methods whenever possible. This allows the tourists to experience local cultures, eat local food and have a more authentic (real) experience as they travel. This improves the whole experience.

Slow travel does not necessarily require more time away from home. It is a change of focus from the destination being the main emphasis of the holiday to the whole journey becoming the holiday.

CONTINUED

Questions

1 List the ways tourists can travel other than flying.

2 Analyse the benefits of slow travel for leisure tourists.

3 Discuss in groups the likely benefits of slow travel to destinations.

Business travel

Business travel is when tourists travel for the purpose of work – they are known as business tourists. Business tourists travel alone or with other work colleagues.

KEY WORDS

business travel: travel for the purpose of work to attend a meeting, take an incentive trip, attend a conference or an exhibition

business tourist: a person who travels for the purpose of work to attend a meeting, take an incentive trip, attend a conference or an exhibition

Business travel is paid for by the company the tourist works for. In most cases the company will choose and organise the transport for the business tourist. The business also choose and organise a place for the tourist to stay. However, in some cases, business tourists will be given a budget and the freedom to choose a place to stay within that particular budget.

Business tourists travel throughout the year, and travel is not influenced by as many factors as leisure travel, such as the weather or school holidays. Business tourists have to travel when their company tells them to, or when there is a work-related need to go. Equally, they need to return once the work is complete, so they rarely have time to enjoy sightseeing in the destination they are visiting.

The different types of business travel are known by the acronym MICE. Each type of business travel has a set of typical characteristics as seen in **Table 1.1** and **Figure 1.5**.

Meetings	Business tourists meet for the purpose of exchanging information and making sales or future plans. • Typically, they involve a small number of people. • They can be hosted within the company's own offices. • The length of time depends on what needs to be achieved in the meeting and can vary from one hour to several days.
Incentives	A trip given to an employee as a reward for good work. Business tourists may be required to work while taking the incentive, for example, teamwork days or learning about a place or product. • They can be for an individual or for a small number of people. • Incentives can be hosted anywhere and for any length of time. These are decided by the company giving the incentive and are heavily influenced by the cost.
Conferences	Business tourists attend for the purpose of learning about and discussing a topic of common interest with guest speakers. • Large numbers of people attend. • They require a large space and specialist equipment so are typically hosted in specialist venues. • Conferences will have a set agenda (timetable of events) and usually take place over several days e.g. 3–5 days.
Exhibitions	Business tourists attend to network (meet other people in their industry) and to stay up to date on the latest developments in their industry. Products are displayed and business tourists walk around meeting and talking to people from other companies. • Exhibitions vary in size, typically medium to large. • They are usually hosted over 3–5 days. • They require a large space and are often held in specialist venues.

Table 1.1: The characteristics of different types of business travel

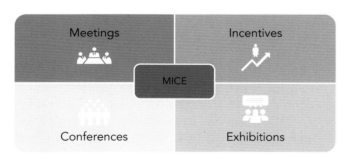

Figure 1.5: MICE tourism

Advances in technology and changing global situations, such as the COVID-19 pandemic, along with an increased knowledge and understanding of the environmental impact of travel, have changed the way businesses communicate. More meetings are held virtually, guests can join a conference remotely or follow industry developments online, resulting in less need for business travel. Business travel is likely to change further in the future as society and technology changes even more.

Visiting friends and relatives

Visiting friends and relatives (VFR), is when tourists travel for the primary purpose of visiting other people, such as friends or family, to spend time with them. They are known as VFR tourists; this includes weddings and funerals.

KEY WORDS

companies: business organisations. Hotel providers are examples of travel and tourism companies

visiting friends and relatives (VFR): travel for the purpose of visiting people, such as friends/family

Most VFR tourists will stay with their friends or family. This makes it cheaper for the tourist. However, this is less beneficial for the travel and tourism industry because the tourists are not spending money on hotels or other forms of accommodation, which contributes to the local economy. VFR tourists usually have days out or meals in restaurants with their friends or family, go shopping and spend money on other goods or services within the area they are visiting.

Increased global migration and opportunities to work or study abroad have resulted in more VFR travel and tourism as people visit their friends and family a round the world.

ACTIVITY 1.3

Copy and complete the grid below, thinking about the different reasons for travel. For each one, provide a brief explanation.

	Leisure	Business	VFR
What is the main purpose of the travel?			
Who pays for the travel?			
What is the average length of a trip?			
Who decides where the tourist travels to?			
Who travels?			

Special interest travel

The reasons why we travel are complex. There are reasons for travel that are hard to place into one of the three main categories of leisure, business or VFR. Tourists may travel for a special purpose or a special interest which is not travel for business or for VFR. However, it may also not be simply for pleasure and enjoyment as with leisure travel. A good example of this is travel for medical reasons.

Travel for medical reasons is when a tourist travels for an essential or non-essential procedure, such as surgery. This may be because the procedure is not available in

their home country or because it is cheaper in another country. This includes travel for cosmetic (when people want to change their appearance) or dental procedures.

Other types of special interest travel include:

- religious reasons – travel for religious journeys or **pilgrimages** to special places, for example, to Jerusalem or Mecca

KEY WORD

pilgrimage: a religious or spiritual journey

- adventure – travel aimed at taking part in adventurous activities or travel with a degree of risk, for example, trekking, climbing or kayaking
- cultural reasons – travel to learn or experience other cultures
- sports – travel to watch a sports team or to take part in sports, for example, competing in a marathon in another city or country
- health and well-being – travel to improve happiness, health and wellness. An example of this is spa tourism.

These categories of special interest travel are forever changing as global situations, fashions and trends change.

REFLECTION

What strategies have you found the most useful for remembering the different reasons why people travel? Share your strategies with another learner.

1.3 Sustainability in travel and tourism

Introduction

Our actions today can affect the future. For example, travelling to a tourist destination can cause pollution. Aircraft, ships, boats, cars, trains and buses can cause air pollution. Tourism developments such as built attractions affect the natural environment. Building airports can mean clearing forests. Clean sea water can be polluted by waste water from hotels. Animal habitats (homes) can be damaged.

Tourism developments can affect the people who live in these destinations. Traditional ways of life can be lost. For example, developing a tourism resort beside the sea may stop local people from fishing. Some local people's way of making a living could be lost.

Sustainability

Sustainability is about trying to protect the future environment and people's way of life from harm. Sustainable tourism today protects the future environment and people's way of life into the future. Tourists and tourism providers can behave in sustainable ways by reducing, reusing and recycling **resources**. In **Figure 1.6**, Rose explains how tourism can reduce, reuse and recycle. Reduce, reuse and recycle are the 3Rs of sustainability.

> **KEY WORDS**
>
> **sustainability:** our ability to sustain or conserve the environment and peoples' way of life into the future
>
> **resources:** things that are useful to people, for example, water, wood, oil and equipment

Sustainable travel and tourism

Sustainable travel and tourism is:

- travelling to destinations in ways that are sustainable, for example, travelling by train instead of by air

- staying in and visiting destinations in ways that are sustainable, for example, staying in **eco-friendly** accommodation.

> **KEY WORDS**
>
> **sustainable travel and tourism:** going to visit places in ways that help sustain or conserve the environment and how people live
>
> **eco-friendly:** describes products and behaviours that do little or no harm to the natural environment

Ecotourism and responsible tourism

Ecotourism and **responsible tourism** are two types of sustainable tourism. **Figure 1.7** shows how they relate to each other. Ecotourism is tourism for visitors who want to visit the natural environment. A tourist staying overnight on an organic farm in France could be an example of an ecotourist. The farm might provide eco-friendly accommodation if, for example:

- meals are made from organic food produced on the farm

- waste is recycled

- electricity is generated on the farm using wind or solar power.

Ecotourism is responsible tourism because responsible tourism involves behaving respectfully towards the environment and local people. Tourism to any destination can be responsible if visitors behave respectfully towards the environment and the local

I have been thinking about food and sustainable tourism.

A restaurant chef can reuse surplus food that has not been used. They can reuse the surplus food for another meal and can recycle food waste. The 3Rs can also be followed for water, soap, paper . . . anything really.

Tourists can eat organic food produced where they are staying to reduce pollution from chemical pesticides and from transporting bought-in food.

Figure 1.6: Rose talks about the 3Rs

Figure 1.7: Types of sustainable tourism

people. Tourists to a city destination can be responsible tourists if, for example, the tourists:

- do not litter in the streets or make too much noise
- hire a local **tour guide**
- spend money in locally owned shops and restaurants.

> ### KEY WORDS
>
> **ecotourism:** visiting a destination to enjoy the natural environment without causing any damage
>
> **responsible tourism:** behaving respectfully towards the environment and local people
>
> **tour guide:** a person who shows tourists around a destination

CASE STUDY

Tourism today helps save tomorrow

De ferme en ferme (From farm to farm) is a weekend tourism event that happens in France every year. Tourists and local people visit farms that practise sustainable farming. Visitors drive or cycle a few kilometres from farm to farm to discover the traditional ways of life of farming families. They explore the environmentally friendly methods the farmers use to produce organic food.

Many of the farmers who take part in the event sell the food they grow in their own farm shops and at local markets. Farm shops, local markets and the *De ferme en ferme* event are very popular with tourists who visit the French countryside. This event helps farmers to promote their businesses to tourists and gain more income. The money that the farmers make means they can continue living on their own land in the countryside and have no need to move to towns to find jobs.

Questions

1   Who do you think would enjoy the *De ferme en ferme* tourism event? Would you enjoy it? Why?

Figure 1.8: Sustainable farming in France

2   In pairs, discuss how the *De ferme en ferme* tourism event can help save tomorrow.

3   As a group, debate how well the *De ferme en ferme* tourism event shows sustainable travel and tourism. Think about:

   a   ways the event helps sustainability

   b   ways the event may not help sustainability.

TIPS

- Remember that sustainability is about what we do today to save and protect the environment and people's lives in the future.

- Ecotourism is about only visiting the natural environment, but responsible tourism can be about visiting any type of destination.

KEY CONCEPT LINK

Key concepts of travel and tourism are sustainability and responsibility. To help ensure sustainability in travel and tourism, tourists can behave responsibly, and travel and tourism can be responsibly managed. Ecotourism is a type of responsible tourism. Ecotourists visit the natural environment in destinations that are usually rural. Ecotourism is managed so that visits to the natural environment do not damage it.

ACTIVITY 1.4

1   As a **project**, design a poster or **flyer** that a local **tourist information centre** could use to promote the *De ferme en ferme* tourism event.

2   Make a chart with the title **De ferme en ferme – an example of sustainability in travel and tourism**.

   Your chart should include:

   - the meanings of sustainability, ecotourism and responsible tourism

   - ways the *De ferme en ferme* tourism event helps sustainability

   - ways the *De ferme en ferme* tourism event may not be helping sustainability.

   Present your chart to the rest of the class.

3   In pairs, research sustainable tourism, responsible tourism and ecotourism. What are the relationships between sustainable tourism, responsible tourism and ecotourism?

CONTINUED

Choose one natural environment destination and one city destination. Work with a partner to find out about one holiday to each destination. Produce a report to:

a   explain how the holiday to the natural destination could be ecotourism

b   explain how tourists to the urban destination can be responsible tourists

c   assess how sustainable both holidays are.

Include a conclusion that clearly summarises the relationships between sustainable tourism, responsible tourism and ecotourism.

Prepare to be interviewed about your report's findings by your teacher or another class member.

KEY WORDS

flyer: a one-page piece of promotional material that can be used to market a tourism event

tourist information centre (TIC): an office where useful information is made available to tourists

REFLECTION

Think about the research you and your partner did for your report on the relationships between sustainable tourism, responsible tourism and ecotourism. With your partner, discuss what you both have learnt:

- What were your conclusions?

- Do you think your conclusions would be different if you had researched different holidays to different destinations?

- What do you think was good about the way you did your research?

- What could you change in terms of how you did your research?

- How would your change have improved your report?

1.4 Characteristics of travel and tourism

Introduction

The travel and tourism industry has specific characteristics that make it different from any other industry. Understanding these characteristics is critical to understanding travel and tourism.

Products

There are two different types of travel and tourism **products**. These are: **goods** and **services**. Goods are physical products, items that are tangible and that you can touch and store, for example, a suitcase or a travel guidebook. A service is **intangible**: you cannot touch it as it is an action done on your behalf, for example, a taxi ride from the airport to a hotel.

Figure 1.9: Staten Island Ferry, New York

> ### KEY WORDS
>
> **products:** goods or services that are sold or made available to tourists
>
> **goods:** tangible objects that you can touch and store
>
> **service:** an action done on your behalf; it is someone doing something for you. Services are intangible
>
> **intangible:** describes something that you cannot touch; it has no physical presence

Intangible

Travel and tourism services are intangible. This makes it very difficult for organisations to represent their service before a tourist buys it. For example, a tourist cannot test or sample the ferry journey before purchasing a ticket; all they can do is read the information provided about the journey and trust that it will meet their needs and wants as stated in the marketing materials.

Travel and tourism services are experiences. These organisations sell a promise: a promise of an enjoyable time, of good customer service and having all needs and wants met. This can cause problems as different tourists will have different needs and wants. One tourist may want the ferry journey to be fast and efficient so they can get to their next destination quickly. Another tourist may want the journey to be relaxing – an opportunity to view the scenery. Despite potential differences, there are some wants and needs that are similar, for example, both of these tourists need the journey to be safe and comfortable.

Services

Travel and tourism is a service. It involves people doing things for the tourist. For example, when a tourist buys a ferry ticket, they are paying to ride the ferry at the stated time and experience the services provided on that trip. The captain will steer the ferry on the tourists' behalf so they can experience the journey.

Travel and tourism organisations provide a wide variety of services, for example, transport, accommodation, guided tours, entertainment, visitor attractions, food and beverage and currency exchange.

> ### KEY CONCEPT LINK
>
> Because services are intangible, they can be difficult to market. Tourists cannot test the service before purchasing the experience; instead, promotion has to represent it and inform customers of what is included and how their needs and wants are going to be met.

Perishable

Travel and tourism services are perishable. This means they cannot be stored for use or sale at another time. If a ferry has a maximum of 200 tickets available for each specific journey and they only sell 150 tickets for that particular trip, they cannot store the extra 50 tickets and sell them with their next journey – the tickets have perished and can no longer be used. This results in the ferry operator missing out on sales and money.

> ### KEY WORD
>
> perishable: describes something that cannot be stored; if the service is not sold, it expires

Products: goods and services

Although travel and tourism is a service, many organisations will also sell goods, for example, a museum may sell or provide guidebooks to increase tourists' enjoyment and understanding when at the museum, or a visitor attraction may sell souvenirs so tourists can remember their time at the attraction.

> ### KEY CONCEPT LINK
>
> It is important to remember that it is only services that are perishable and intangible. Travel and tourism goods can be stored and are tangible.

Sometimes it can be difficult to determine whether the product can be termed a good or a service. For example, think about a meal in a restaurant: the food provided is tangible, therefore it is considered to be a good. However, the meal will have been cooked and prepared by a chef, which is an intangible service. Therefore, the meal in the restaurant can be regarded as both a good and a service. It can be helpful to think about travel and tourism products as being on a continuum, as seen in **Figure 1.10**. A meal in a restaurant would be in the middle of this continuum.

Service	Good
Intangible	Tangible
Perishable	Can be stored
An action done on your behalf	Physical objects

Figure 1.10: Goods and services continuum

All travel and tourism products are provided for tourists' enjoyment, regardless of being a good or a service. The products are there to meet the needs and wants of the tourist, and to ensure they have a safe and enjoyable experience.

> ### ACTIVITY 1.5
>
> Select one travel and tourism organisation you know. Research or use your existing knowledge to:
>
> - list the products
> - classify these products into goods or services.
>
> How many products did you identify that had elements of both goods and services?

> ### REFLECTION
>
> Thinking about Activity 1.5, consider the following questions:
>
> - Which elements of the product did you think about when deciding if the products are goods or services?
> - How does your list and classifications compare to other learners?
> - Can you explain to another learner how you classified the products?
> - How can you improve your understanding of tourism products?

Seasonality

Travel and tourism is seasonal. The demand for products will vary throughout the year; this is known as seasonality. At certain times of the year, destinations or tourism organisations may receive high numbers of tourists; at other times, the number of tourists may be low. Travel and tourism organisations also experience changes in demand over a week. For example, an attraction may be very busy at the weekend and less busy in the week.

There are several factors that cause seasonality:

- weather and climate
- religion
- school and national holidays
- special events or festivals.

Travel and tourism organisations and destinations will split the year into different seasons so they can understand and manage their seasonality. The most common split is **peak season** and **off-peak season**.

KEY WORDS

seasonality: the way in which tourism demand fluctuates throughout a year

peak season: the time when travel and tourism products have the greatest demand

off-peak season: the time when travel and tourism products have the least demand

TIPS

- It is important to remember that seasonality is not just the weather or climate. They are just one factor of seasonality.

- Peak season may also be called *high season* and off-peak season can be called *low season*.

KEY CONCEPT LINKS

- Perishability becomes more of a problem in off-peak seasons. Hotels that do not sell many rooms/nights cannot store them for later in the season when demand may increase.

- Goods are affected less by seasonality as they are not perishable, for example, a guidebook can be stored for use or sale next season.

ACTIVITY 1.6

1 Research each of the factors that cause seasonality in your own country.

For each factor:

a list the factors that cause changes in tourism demand

b state the time(s) of year each factor is evident

c state the effect the factor has on tourism demand.

CONTINUED

2 Produce a timeline for a year in tourism in your country. Using the months of the year, identify when the factors are evident and when the peak and off-peak seasons are.

3 Think back to the organisation you considered in Activity 1.5. Identify the times in the week you think the organisation would have higher demand, and explain why.

Overcoming seasonality can be a difficult challenge. Travel and tourism organisations and destinations need to attract tourists in the months when demand is low, or lower than peak season. This can be done by:

- reducing the price of the services to encourage tourists

- providing different facilities or activities for different weather conditions

- providing all-weather facilities

- hosting events and festivals

- attracting other types of tourists who are able and willing to travel in the off-peak season.

CASE STUDY

The role of domestic tourism in managing seasonality

Domestic tourism is an important form of tourism for countries around the world. It is estimated that tourists make on average over nine billion domestic tourism trips a year – many more than international trips.

Domestic tourism plays a vital role in managing the impacts of seasonality. Often, domestic tourists will visit areas and destinations that are less popular with international visitors, helping to spread the demand for tourism throughout the country. This is helpful for travel and tourism organisations during peak season when demand is at its highest. Domestic tourists often take more trips per year and at different times of the year to international tourists. This helps to spread the demand for tourism throughout the year, helping tourism organisations and destinations to manage the problem of over-demand in the peak season.

CONTINUED

In addition to helping destinations to overcome seasonality, domestic tourism can help destinations to manage other changes in demand, for example, from local or global 'shocks'. This was evident during the COVID-19 pandemic when many countries closed borders and restricted international travel. Destinations saw their demand disappear in both peak season and off-peak season. However, in some countries tourists were allowed to travel within their own country or area. Domestic tourists created some demand for tourism products.

Questions

1 Identify the reasons why domestic tourists may:

   a travel to different areas within a destination

   b travel at different times of the year

   c take more trips per year.

2 Analyse the importance of managing seasonality.

Dynamic

Travel and tourism products are **dynamic**. They are always changing and evolving as the industry develops to meet changing customer needs and wants, external influences and developments in technology. Travel and tourism organisations have to adapt and change their products to meet changing customer demands. Increasingly, tourists want products they can adapt or personalise to their own specific needs and wants. This is evident in air travel: tourists can now book specific aircraft seats, meals and airport lounge experiences on the airline's website.

KEY WORD

dynamic: constantly changing

KEY CONCEPT LINK

Dynamic packages are a good example of how tour operators have adapted to changing customer needs and wants. There is more information on dynamic packages in *3.1 The role of tourism organisations*.

Increasingly sustainable

Tourists increasingly want travel and tourism products to be sustainable. They are more aware of the impact travel has on the environment, economies and people. As a result, tourism organisations are now making products more sustainable. For example, many visitor attractions work with local schools to provide educational experiences. This benefits both the visitor attraction and the local community.

Resilient

The travel and tourism industry is resilient. It can survive and recover after difficult situations or conditions. Difficult situations, often called 'shocks', can be on a global scale, for example, the COVID-19 pandemic. They can be on a national scale, for example, terrorist attacks; or local, for example, natural disasters like floods or hurricanes. These 'shocks' disrupt our ability and willingness to travel and take part in tourism. However, because the industry is so dynamic, it is able to quickly adapt, change and survive. This has been proven time and time again.

Resilience and the other characteristics make travel and tourism a very special and unique industry.

1.5 Types of tourists

Introduction

There are many different types of tourists, all of which have their own set of characteristics. These characteristics will affect the decisions tourists make when travelling and using different travel and tourism products.

Different types of tourists can be classified according to their:

- *reason* for travel (e.g. leisure, business, special interest)

- *preferences* when choosing or using travel and tourism products (e.g. the preferences of independent tourists, responsible tourists or ecotourists)

- *needs* when travelling and using tourism products (e.g. the needs of families, individuals, couples, groups, or tourists with specific needs).

Some travel and tourism products will be suitable for all types of tourists. For example, a **hotel** or a journey on an aeroplane could be used by any type of tourist. Other products are specifically for different tourist types, for example, a conference room is provided for business tourists to host a conference or to attend an exhibition.

> **KEY WORD**
>
> **hotel:** a place where tourists can pay to stay. A hotel provides meals, room-cleaning and other services

An outline of the reasons for travel is provided in *1.2 Main reasons why people travel.* Looking at the characteristics of these tourists gives a greater understanding of them.

Leisure tourists

Figure 1.11: Leisure tourists in Japan

Leisure tourists are usually concerned about price and will have a budgeted amount of money available for the holiday/trip; therefore, they are **price sensitive**. They use their free time to travel; enjoyment and value for money are their main aims. Many leisure tourists are time-constrained and can only travel when they have time available away from work or education. Therefore, leisure tourists are one of the main reasons for seasonal demand in the industry.

The products tourists use depend on their reason for travel. On the one hand, a leisure tourist on a sun, sea and sand holiday may want an affordable hotel located close to the beach. On the other hand, a leisure tourist taking a day trip to a domestic city may want to visit a **museum** or use local transport providers.

> **KEY WORDS**
>
> **price sensitive:** describes someone whose decisions are greatly influenced by price. A price-sensitive tourist is unlikely to buy a product if they think it is too expensive
>
> **museum:** a place that holds historical, cultural, artistic or other artefacts. Museums are popular tourist attractions

Business tourists

Business tourists travel for specific work tasks and, as a result, they have little or no time to enjoy the destination they are visiting. They travel to a destination to complete a work task, and then travel back as soon as the task is complete. Therefore they are **time sensitive**.

Business tourists have a specific set of characteristics:

- They have little or no choice regarding when or where they travel. This is decided by the business task to be completed.

- Travel is often arranged at short notice.

- Location is essential. They will want to be located close to amenities such as transport and restaurants, for their convenience.

- They require products that fit around their work commitments, for example, early breakfast.

> **KEY WORD**
>
> **time sensitive:** describes someone whose decisions are greatly influenced by time. A time-sensitive tourist needs the product to be delivered at an exact time, often as quickly as possible

- Travel expenses are paid for by the business. As a result, they generally spend more than leisure tourists.

- They travel all year round, often out of peak season. This helps to solve the problem of seasonality for some travel and tourism organisations.

- They typically travel alone or sometimes with other colleagues.

ACTIVITY 1.7

Research online **two** different large international airlines to identify what they specifically provide for business tourists.

Special interest tourists

Tourists may travel for a special purpose or interest. Examples of these are discussed in *1.2 Main reasons why people travel*. These tourists will have specific requirements depending on the reason they are travelling. For example, a special interest tourist who is travelling for cultural reasons may want products which allow them to experience and learn about the local culture of the place they are visiting. This could be a local event or festival, a museum, local cuisine, local music or dance. In contrast, a special interest tourist who is travelling for adventure tourism will want physically challenging activities that are exciting and safe. This may come in the form of an instructor as part of a holiday package or simply any necessary equipment the tourist hires.

When thinking about special interest tourists, it is important to consider exactly what their special interest is. This will influence the products they are interested in, their needs and their requirements. There are a lot of different travel and tourism products available for special interest tourists. This is because of the increasing variety of options for special interest travel.

ACTIVITY 1.8

Select a type of special interest tourism using the list from *1.2 Main reasons why people travel*. Alternatively, select a special interest you are interested in or a new emerging type.

CONTINUED

For your selected special interest:

- make a list of travel and tourism products and services relevant for your chosen special interest tourism

- explain what you think tourists will need from each of the products you have identified

- share your findings with other learners by presenting your ideas to your class.

REFLECTION

- How easy was it to think about the needs of the special interest tourism you chose?

- Did you understand the tourism type well enough to be able to complete the task?

- How did you improve your understanding of special interest tourists?

- Are there other ways you could improve your understanding?

- Can you use your learning for this task to aid your understanding of other areas of the syllabus?

Some tourists have specific preferences when choosing or using travel and tourism products.

Independent tourists

Independent tourists book their travel and holiday experiences themselves. They are focused on having the freedom to choose. They will put together a travel itinerary or holiday experience according to their own preferences. They will book transport and activities separately, allowing them to have greater flexibility and independence.

The number of independent tourists is increasing. More and more people are preferring greater flexibility and variety in their travel and tourism experiences.

Responsible tourists

Figure 1.12: A boat trip in Peru

Responsible tourists focus on behaving respectfully towards the environment and local people when travelling. Their requirements when travelling can vary according to their personal preferences. A common preference for all responsible tourists is focusing on travelling in a responsible way that minimises any negative impacts – this is responsible tourism.

Ecotourists

Figure 1.13: A family watching elephants in Namibia

Ecotourists travel to experience the natural environment, making as little impact on the environment as possible. They are focused on nature and the natural elements of the place they are visiting,

and will seek to experience that as responsibly as possible. Ecotourism is their entire focus throughout the whole experience. Therefore, they will only be interested in travel and tourism products that are environmentally friendly and responsible. This might include locally sourced food, environmentally friendly transport methods, or nature-based activities such as trekking or wildlife watching.

Characteristics of ecotourists include the following:

* They travel to experience specific natural elements of the place they are visiting.

* They want to minimise any negative impacts, environmental or other wise.

* They seek education and want to raise environmental awareness.

* They want to provide financial benefits for the environment and local area. This can be done by purchasing food and activities locally.

* They respect the local culture.

Some tourists will have specific needs when travelling and using travel and tourism products. Their needs and wants, and the ways in which travel and tourism organisations provide for them, is considered in *2.2 The features and appeal of destinations.*

Families

Figure 1.14: A family enjoying a beach holiday

Families come in many different forms and will usually include people from different age groups.

There are many variations of family groups. Some common types are:

- parent(s) with babies and/or young children
- parent(s) with teenage children
- parent(s) with young children and teenagers
- grandparents, parents and children
- grandparents and grandchildren
- adults and senior/older relatives.

Families may travel for leisure, special interest or VFR. This category of tourist does not include business tourists.

Family tourists prefer products that are suitable for all members of the family, regardless of the combination of their family group. For example, a family taking a short break to a city and visiting a museum may want children's activities, detailed information on the exhibits for the adults, and a café or restaurant for them all to have refreshments together.

Individuals

Figure 1.15: Individual tourist in Luxor, Egypt

Individual tourists travel alone. They can be of any age, and their reason for travel could be leisure, business, VFR or special interest. Individuals may look for travel and tourism products that allow them to join in with other people, for example, joining a guided tour or a group-based activity. Alternatively, they may prefer their own company and seek solitude in their tourism activities and products.

Couples

Figure 1.16: A couple on holiday in Brazil

A couple is two adults travelling together. Couples will be focused on spending time together; as with individuals, this may be with other tourists or on their own. There are many travel and tourism products designed for couples, from romantic hotels and restaurant tables set apart from others to a well-being spa holiday for two.

Groups

Figure 1.17: A group of holidaymakers in the UK

Tourists may travel as part of a group. There are a variety of different groups, which may include:

- education groups
- sports or hobby groups
- groups of young people
- groups of senior or retired tourists.

Groups can include people of different ages. Each person in the group will have their own individual needs and preferences as well as the needs of a group of tourists. A group may require a large table in the restaurant where they can all eat together, or rooms in a hotel located close to each other.

Specific needs

Some tourists will have specific needs when travelling. Tourists may have:

- mobility disabilities: these can range from being a wheelchair user to being unable to walk or stand for a long time

- sensory disabilities, such as hearing and **visual impairments**

- a medical condition

- dietary requirements – this could be due to allergies or religious beliefs

- language, religious or cultural differences.

Each person will have their own specific requirements and needs when using travel and tourism products. These requirements will vary according to the specific need, but the common requirement of all these tourists is to have equal access to products.

KEY CONCEPT LINK

Although the different tourist types can be classified, as discussed, it is important to remember that these classifications are not exclusive. For example, an ecotourist could be a family who have booked their holiday independently, making them an independent tourist as well.

KEY WORD

visual impairment: some loss of the ability to see. For example, some tourists have difficulty seeing. Tourists who have this difficulty tend to have trouble reading signage and finding their way, for example, in an unfamiliar place such as an airport.

CASE STUDY

Undersea restaurant

Figure 1.18: The Ithaa Undersea Restaurant

The Conrad Maldives Rangali Island resort, situated on Rangali Island, Maldives, offers tourists a luxurious product – an undersea restaurant. The island is located a 30-minute seaplane ride from Male, the capital of the Maldives.

The Ithaa Undersea Restaurant, the first in the world, is located five metres under the Indian Ocean. Tourists enjoy a panoramic view of the ocean, fishes and coral gardens while eating high-quality, contemporary Maldivian cuisine.

The resort and restaurant are committed to operating in an environmentally friendly way. They have removed all single-use plastic, such as plastic bottles, and replaced them with bottles made from glass or other reusable materials. Guests staying at the resort also have the option of being involved in eco-activities, such as beach clean-ups and coral regeneration projects.

The restaurant is open to guests of the resort and other tourists. Ithaa can also be booked for private dining or special occasions, for example, a wedding. Children are welcome at the restaurant for lunch, but in the evening it is exclusively for adults.

CONTINUED

Questions

1 Explain which tourists are most likely to be interested in the Ithaa restaurant.

2 Analyse the ways in which the Conrad Maldives Rangali Island resort is likely to appeal to ecotourists.

3 Evaluate the reasons why the Conrad Maldives Rangali Island resort is committed to operating in an environmentally friendly way.

Figure 1.19: Grand Baie

1.6 Types of destinations

Introduction

Destinations are places that tourists visit. There are different types of destinations. These include:

- beach and coastal destinations
- rural or countryside destinations
- urban, town or city destinations
- island destinations
- resorts.

Figure 1.20: Port Louis

Beach and coastal destinations

Beach and coastal destinations are places tourists visit near the sea. Grand Baie is an example of a beach destination in Mauritius (see **Figure 1.19**). Port Louis is a coastal destination in the same country (see **Figure 1.20**). Coastal destinations are not always beach destinations. For example, some coastal destinations are port towns or cities. Port Louis is a port town and city destination in Mauritius.

KEY WORD

beach and coastal destination: a destination that has a beach and is on a coastline. Some coastal destinations are urban destinations. Some beach destinations are countryside or lake destinations

Rural or countryside destinations

Black River Gorges National Park (see **Figure 1.21**) is an example of a rural destination in Mauritius. Rural (or countryside) destinations include lake and mountain destinations, such as Breckenridge in Colorado, USA (see **Figure 1.23**). Breckenridge is an example of a mountain destination that is also a ski resort.

Figure 1.21: Black River Gorges National Park

Resorts

Resorts are places tourists visit for fun, for holidays, to relax and to enjoy tourism activities. For example, tourists enjoy skiing at ski resorts. Purpose-built resorts such as theme parks have been deliberately built to be places tourists visit for fun. Some resorts are destinations in and of themselves. For example, beach destinations that are towns are sometimes called seaside resorts. Some destinations have integrated resort complexes that include hotel accommodation and facilities such as restaurants and entertainment venues at a single site. Eco-resorts are environmentally friendly resorts.

KEY WORDS

resort: a place visited by leisure tourists for holidays (vacations), relaxation or activities. For example, a ski resort is a place leisure tourists go to ski

purpose-built resort: a resort that is planned and built especially for tourism

theme park: a large tourist attraction with amusements and rides. Theme parks often have accommodation such as hotels and restaurants. Theme parks such as Tokyo Disneyland in Japan, Kingdom of Dreams in India and Universal Studios Hollywood in the USA have clear identities

eco-resort: an environmentally sustainable, ecotourism resort

KEY WORD

integrated resort: a single-site complex of hotel accommodation and facilities such as restaurants, entertainment venues, casinos and conference facilities. The term *integrated resort* is often used in Singapore. The Government of Mauritius has an Integrated Resort Scheme (IRS), which has a different meaning. The IRS scheme allows people who are not from Mauritius to buy and live in luxury properties in Mauritius

Urban destinations

Urban, town or city destinations are towns and cities that tourists visit. Port Louis (**Figure 1.20**) in Mauritius is:

- a port town
- the biggest city in Mauritius
- an urban destination.

Island destinations

Island destinations are islands that tourists visit. Mauritius is an example of an island destination. Some destinations, for example, the island destination of Mauritius, can be more than one destination type. Grand Baie is a beach and coastal destination on the island of Mauritius. There are different scales of destinations. Some smaller destinations are within larger destinations. For example, Black River Gorges National Park and Seven Coloured Earth Geopark (**Figure 1.22**) are rural destinations within the island destination of Mauritius.

Figure 1.22: Seven Coloured Earth Geopark

CASE STUDY

Breckenridge green destination

Green destinations are sustainable destinations. Breckenridge has been listed as one of the world's top sustainable destinations. Breckenridge is a mountain and ski resort destination in Colorado. Colorado is a state in the United States of America (USA). The USA is a large country in North America.

Breckenridge is a historic, former gold-mining town in the Rocky Mountains. The destination's tourists can enjoy different outdoor and adventure tourism activities.

Tourist activities in the Rocky Mountains destination of Breckenridge include:

- hiking

- mountain biking

- trout fishing.

Breckenridge is a year-round destination. There are ski slopes on five nearby mountains. The ski season starts after snow has fallen in November and continues until April. The destination is busy with many tourists during the winter. By April it is spring. Breckenridge still has sufficient snow for skiing, but the destination is quieter. Other tourist activities begin to become more popular.

Spectacular mountains surround Breckenridge. The destination's tourists can:

- mountain bike on winding roads and trails or along the family-friendly Blue River Recreational Path

- hike through the impressive mountain scenery

- fish for trout in the Blue River

- paddleboard, go white-water rafting, play golf or try zip-lining

- photograph the beautiful scenery.

Breckenridge is a historic town. Tourists walking along Main Street can admire the 19th century

Figure 1.23: Breckenridge on the day of a cycle race

architecture. There are old buildins like those featured in many movies. Restaurants offer different foods from around the world, including American, Thai and Mediterranean-style options. Artists and performers can be seen in the Arts District. There are art galleries, performance spaces, creative workshops and cafés.

Questions

1   Describe the range of outdoor tourist activities available at Breckenridge green destination:

    a   in winter

    b   from spring to fall (autumn).

2   Suggest which of Breckenridge's green destination activities are suitable for each of these tourist groups:

    a   a family with teenaged children

    b   a grey market couple.

Explain your suggestions.

3   Make a leaflet to promote adventure tourism for thrill seekers in Breckenridge.

4   Discuss why you think Breckenridge has green destination status.

5   *Extension:* Evaluate the extent to which the destination of Breckenridge exemplifies sustainable tourism development.

KEY WORDS

zip-lining: the adventure tourism activity of swinging through the air hanging from a suspended cable

performance space: a place where tourists can see live shows

creative workshop: a tourist attraction where tourists can see or share in activities such as pottery, painting or weaving

grey market: the category of travel and tourism for customers who are older: senior citizens or retired people

adventure tourism: visiting a destination for excitement

thrill seeker: someone who enjoys exciting or adventurous activities

appeal to: be attractive to

TIPS

- A destination can be any place that tourists visit. Destinations can be any scale. A destination can, for example, be:
    - a village or a town such as Breckenridge
    - a region such as the Rocky Mountains
    - a country such as the USA.
- Some destinations can be within larger destinations. For example, the Black River Gorges rural destination is within the island destination of Mauritius.

KEY CONCEPT LINKS

- Different types of destinations can **appeal to** different types of tourists. For example, a purpose-built resort such as a theme park and a rural destination such as a national park may appeal to different tourist types. However, some tourists may enjoy both a theme park and a national park.
- A place tourists visit can be more than one type of destination. Mauritius is an island destination including beach, coastal, urban and rural destinations. Breckenridge is a rural mountain destination with some urban destination appeal.

ACTIVITY 1.9

1   Identify and give examples of any five destination types.

2   Outline the difference in meaning between:

   a   a beach destination and a coastal destination

   b   a countryside destination and an island destination.

3   Name a destination you would like to visit.

   Explain:

   - your destination's type
   - why the destination appeals to you
   - why it might not appeal to some types of tourists.

4   Choose a destination with smaller destinations within it. Your chosen destination could, for example, be an island such as Mauritius or a rural area such as the Rocky Mountains.

   Evaluate:

   a   the range of types of destinations in your chosen area

   b   the range of tourist types who would find the destination appealing.

EXAM-STYLE QUESTIONS

1 Refer to **Figure 1**, information about tourism in the Andalucía region of Spain.

Last year Andalucía received 12.1 million international tourists, 3.4% up on the previous year. There has been consistent growth in visitor numbers in recent years. These figures would place Andalucía (if it were a country) about 25th in the world for the number of foreign tourist arrivals.

The total an international tourist spends on an average holiday in Andalucía is US$1067.00. With an average stay of 11 nights, the tourist spends US$97.00 daily.

A minority of foreign tourists now arrive as part of a package holiday as 80% travel independently.

The peak season in Andalucía is July to September. During this time, 3.2 million or 37% of tourists visit the region.

The main reasons why people travel to Andalucía are:

- climate 26%
- beach 15%
- culture 17%
- monuments 11%
- visit family 8%

- price 5%
- nature 5%
- golf 3%
- skiing 1%
- other reasons 10%

Source: Adapted from www.andalucia.com

Figure 1: Tourism in the Andalucía region of Spain

CONTINUED

a **Identify** the following:

- the percentage of visitors who travel for sport

- the percentage of visitors who could be classified as VFR. [2]

b A total of 80% of visitors to Andalucía travel independently. **Describe** the main characteristics of an independent traveller. [2]

c Hotel accommodation is an example of an intangible product and cannot easily be experienced by customers in advance of purchase. **Explain** how **each** of the following can help to overcome the problem of intangibility:

- printed material

- website. [4]

d Many destinations have recorded an increase in the number of tourists travelling to visit friends and relatives. **Discuss two** factors that are likely to account for this recent growth. [6]

e Leisure tourism in many destinations is highly seasonal. **Assess** how the creation of new products and the offering of new services might allow large hotels in such destinations to extend their season. [6]

[Total 20 marks]

2 Refer to **Figure 2**, a news item about a travel agency.

Toucan Travel, an independent travel agency established in 1982, held their annual travel show at a local hotel on 21 January. Potential customers were invited to come along to the free travel show and meet a dedicated team of staff who would introduce them to a selection of tour operators showcasing a series of their fabulous destinations.

Visitors also had the chance to pre-register for one of the following informative travel talks:

10:30 am – 'NEW ZEALAND' by Anzcro

11:30 am – 'CANADA/ROCKIES' by Travelpack

12:30 pm – 'VIETNAM/CAMBODIA' by Wendy Wu

1:30 pm – 'CRUISING/MUSIC CRUISES' by Cruisco

Refreshments were available throughout the day, and visitors had the chance to win a US$500 holiday voucher.

Figure 2: Toucan Travel hosts a travel show at a local hotel

a Which of the tour operators listed in **Figure 2** is most likely to have offered **each** of the following holiday packages:

- a six-night twin-centre trip to Toronto and Niagara Falls

- a 'Back to the 80s Experience', calling at the port cities of Bilbao, Vigo and Lisbon. [2]

b Most travel products are perishable, which means they cannot be stored for sale at a later date. Toucan Travel's window display area is full of adverts for a variety of 'special offers'. Describe the likely appeal of a 'No single person supplement' offer to Toucan Travel's customers. [2]

CONTINUED

c Many of Toucan Travel's customers will travel because they have a special interest. For example, some customers interested in sports tourism will book a trip to go to the Swiss Alps to go skiing on the slopes around St. Moritz.

For **each** of the following types of special interest tourism, **state** an activity that is carried out and name a destination where it takes place:

- religious tourism
- adventure tourism. [4]

d Discuss **two** ways in which the travel show described in **Figure 2** can be classified as being an example of a business travel event. [6]

e Toucan Travel offers its customers a range of leisure travel products including day trips, short breaks, short-haul holidays and packages to long-haul destinations.

Evaluate the differences and similarities between a short break and a package to a long-haul destination. [6]

[Total 20 marks]

3 Refer to **Figure 3**, which gives information about the L'Heure Bleue eco-resort in Nosy Be, Madagascar.

The L'Heure Bleue eco-resort in Nosy Be, Madagascar, has been created as a model for sustainable tourism. Everything has been designed in a spirit of respect for the environment and sustainable development, in harmony with local people. The property offers true luxury and high-quality services, and promotes concern for the environment.

A dedicated eco-team monitors the measures taken by the resort and assesses the extent to which L'Heure Bleue is meets its environmental goals. The resort is equipped with solar power – the first in Madagascar. Water supply comes from the surrounding hills; it is drawn through pumps and stored in a 10,000-litre-capacity tank. Waste water is collected and processed through filters made of coconut and dead coral, feeding and watering the garden. Waste treatment is optimised at the property: food waste is used to make compost, and a comprehensive recycling system is in place.

Source: Adapted from www.heurebleue.com

Figure 3: An eco-resort designed with respect for the environment

a Identify **two** ways in which the L'Heure Bleue resort has been made **eco-friendly**. [2]

b The L'Heure Bleue resort has been created as a model for sustainable tourism. **Define** the term 'sustainable tourism' and state the principles on which it is based. [2]

c Some guests travelling to L'Heure Bleue will be cultural tourists. Explain **two** ways in which resorts such as L'Heure Bleue can allow guests to experience the local culture during their stay. [4]

CONTINUED

d Many international resorts will accommodate guests who have special needs. Discuss **two** ways in which customers with mobility difficulties can be catered for at such properties. [6]

e Responsible tourism can be regarded as being a type of behaviour. It represents an approach to engaging with the destination and its host community so that the overall tourism experience should become 'better' as a result of a responsible tourist's actions.

Evaluate the ways in which the responsible behaviour of an individual international traveller is likely to differ from that of a family with young children. [6]

[Total 20 marks]

SELF-EVALUATION CHECKLIST

After studying this unit, copy and complete this table:

I am now able to:	Needs more work	Almost there	Ready to move on
identify and describe the main types of tourism.			
explain the main reasons why people travel and analyse the importance of the different reasons.			
understand and explain the importance of sustainability in travel and tourism.			
identify the different characteristics of travel and tourism, explain how they are related and analyse the associated difficulties.			
identify and describe the different types of tourists.			
identify and describe the different types of destinations.			

Unit 2
Global tourism

LEARNING INTENTIONS

In this unit you will learn how to:

- understand factors affecting the scale of global tourism demand

- explain reasons for the growth of sustainable tourism

- understand features of destinations and their appeal to different types of tourists

- explain the role of organisations involved in the development and management of destinations

- understand factors affecting tourism development and management

- evaluate the economic, environmental and sociocultural impacts of travel and tourism

- discuss sustainable practices in destinations.

TRAVEL AND TOURISM IN CONTEXT

Islands saved!

People and tourist destinations can be affected by travel and tourism. The impacts of travel and tourism can be good or bad – positive or negative.

The two tiny islands of Madivaru and Madivaru Finolhu in the Maldives are now a protected area. Tourists and local people will continue to be able to enjoy the islands in the future.

The Maldives is a country in the Indian Ocean, made up of almost 1,200 islands. More than 150 islands in the Maldives have tourist resorts. Tourism is very important to the economy of the Maldives. In 2019, 1.7 million tourists visited the Maldives destination and 32.5 % of the country's GDP (gross domestic product) came from tourism, which was the second highest percentage in the world.

Rasdhoo is a small island in the Maldives. There are 16 guesthouses on the island, as well as gift shops and restaurants. Tourists enjoy scuba-diving on the island's coral reef. Madivaru and Madivaru Finolhu are two even smaller islands less than 1 km from Rasdhoo. Local people call Madivaru and Madivaru Finolhu the 'picnic islands'. Tourists sunbathe, snorkel and admire spectacular sunsets from the sandy beaches on Madivaru and Madivaru Finolhu. The beach on Rasdhoo island is rocky and not very good for snorkelling.

In 2015, Madivaru and Madivaru Finolhu islands were bought by a developer who wanted to build a luxury resort. Some local people objected to the idea of building a new resort on Madivaru because of the likely negative impacts. Local people from Rasdhoo would no longer be allowed to visit Madivaru for picnics and would also lose income from tourism and fishing. People from Rasdhoo have always used the flowers and sap of the coconut palm trees on Madivaru to make *toddy* drinks and *coconut honey* to sell. The people also sell mats made from coconut palm materials.

Building a new resort on Madivaru would also have negative environmental impacts. Damage to the coral reef would have affected the biodiversity of the ecosystem, as well as reducing protection from storm waves.

Local people from Rasdhoo used social media to campaign against the Madivaru resort development.

Figure 2.1: An island in the Maldives

The campaign helped inform other people about the impacts of a new resort on Madivaru island. The government decided that the new resort should not be built, and instead made Rasdhoo-Madivaru a protected area.

Questions

1   Why do you think many people want to travel to island destinations like the Maldives?

2   Suggest why some local people did not object to building a new resort on Madivaru.

3   To help sustainability in travel and tourism, tourists can behave responsibly, and travel and tourism can be responsibly managed. Is that what has happened in the case of Madivaru?

4   Hold a debate on whether the new resort on Madivaru island should or should not have been allowed.

KEY WORDS

protected area: a place conserved by a set of rules

GDP (gross domestic product): the total value of all goods and services produced in a country in a year

negative impacts: bad effects that travel and tourism has on a place and/or local people

biodiversity: the degree of variation in living things

ecosytem: the network of links between living things and the environment

2.1 The scale of travel and tourism demand

Introduction

Travel and tourism has grown, and has kept growing, for many years. More tourists have wanted to travel to more destinations and demand for tourism has increased. Growth in travel and tourism has had economic, environmental and sociocultural impacts on a wide scale.

KEY WORDS

economic impact: the effects that travel and tourism has on money and jobs

environmental impact: the effects that travel and tourism has on the environment. Impacts can be positive (good) or negative (bad)

sociocultural impact: the effects that travel and tourism has on people and their way of life

---

Factors affecting tourism demand and how they are managed

Economic

Economic factors also affect tourism demand. Factors that affect tourism demand are managed. For example, national governments of countries manage the factors that affect demand for tourism in their countries.

Economic factors include:

- the disposable income people have to spend on travel

- the amount of money governments invest in tourism.

KEY WORDS

economic factors: to do with money

tourism demand: how much desire there is to travel to destinations

disposable income: the remaining part of income after paying tax and buying necessities

---

National governments invest in travel and tourism by using money for development. For example, a country's government can use money to improve transport facilities such as airports, roads and railways. A government could also invest in tourism by paying for the marketing of its country as a destination.

Social

Social factors affect tourism demand.

- Demographics include the number, age and level of disposable income of the population of locations. Demographics affect the numbers of outbound tourists from a country. For example, some countries have increasing numbers of retired people who have increased disposable income and leisure time to travel, go on holiday or visit friends and relatives.

- Health awareness has increased globally. Consumers are more aware of the importance of diet, exercise and fresh air for good health. Health awareness has increased the demand for active, outdoor holidays. This awareness has increased the availability of health, fitness and spa products and services, which many large hotels now provide to satisfy consumers' demands.

- Social consciousness has increased. Media and social media have increased consumer awareness of other people and the difficulties others face in life. The demand for socially sustainable tourism has increased. More consumers want to buy travel and tourism products and services that bring positive social impacts to destinations.

- Fashion and trends affect the demand for tourism products and services. Destinations can become more

---

KEY WORDS

social factors: to do with people and communities

demographics: facts about population, including number, age and disposable income

social consciousness: an awareness of other people and the difficulties they face in life

socially sustainable tourism: minimises the negative sociocultural impacts of travel and tourism on destinations. Socially sustainable tourism maximises the positive sociocultural impacts of travel and tourism on destinations

---

or less fashionable. A trend is the general direction of change. One trend is for more sustainable tourism. This means that eco-friendly destinations are becoming more fashionable. More people are also becoming aware of the importance of looking after their health. Increased health awareness is a trend that has affected tourism demand for some types of destinations.

Technological

Technological factors affecting tourism demand include:

- transport developments, for example, more airports, bigger aircraft and faster trains

---

KEY WORDS

technological factors: to do with practical science applications and engineering

online booking: use of the internet to reserve, for example, accommodation and transport

social media: ways of sharing information using the internet

political factors: to do with how countries are governed and what can happen as a result

---

- developments in information technology (IT), for example, **online booking** and the growth of **social media**.

Political

Political factors affect tourism demand.

- Terrorism can deter tourists when attacks take place in a destination.

- War reduces the number of tourists who want to travel to an affected country.

- Political stability is a factor affecting tourism demand. Political instability in a destination can include riots and demonstrations, which may be seen in the media. Tourism becomes reduced in a destination where there is political instability.

- Safety and security concerns are caused by terrorist attacks, war and political instability. These concerns reduce the demand for travel and tourism to affected destinations.

- Imposed limitations on travel affect tourism demand. National governments can decide to limit tourism. For example, the COVID-19 pandemic caused governments to impose limits on travel within and between countries.

In **Figure 2.2**, Rose explains the political factors that can affect tourism demand.

War and terrorism both reduce demand for tourism. Tourists may be frightened to visit a destination where there have been a war or terrorist attacks. Tourists may prefer a peaceful destination with little risk of terrorism.

Political stability can help tourism. For example, tourists may feel safe visiting destinations with few workers' strikes or street protests. Riots in a destination may scare tourists away.

Tourists may feel secure in a low crime destination. Tourists may feel safe where, for example, fire regulations help hotels to be safe. A safe destination may be a destination where there is little risk of a natural disaster such as an earthquake.

Governments can impose limits on tourism. During the COVID-19 pandemic, many national governments strictly limited international and domestic tourism. Reducing tourist numbers was a way to reduce the spread of the disease

Figure 2.2: Rose explains how political factors can affect tourism demand

Environmental

Environmental factors that can reduce tourism demand include:

- extreme weather, such as storms, hurricanes and typhoons

- natural disasters, such as earthquakes, tsunamis and volcanic eruptions.

More people are now concerned about the environment. Increased consumer concern about the environment is a trend. This concern about the environment affects the ways people travel and the destinations they choose to visit. Sustainability in travel and tourism has increased as consumers demand more sustainable transport and more sustainable products and services in destinations.

Health

Health factors affect the level of tourism demand. In 2020, the world began to be badly affected by a pandemic, which was caused by the COVID-19 virus. The disease spread around the world and affected tourism demand. The risk of disease reduces tourism demand. Pandemics reduce tourism demand greatly, as shown by the case study *Pandemic and tourism: what next?*

KEY WORDS

factors: reasons that affect how things are and how things change. Factors can include:

environmental factors: to do with nature and climate

health factors: to do with people's health and with disease

CASE STUDY

Pandemic and tourism: what next?

In 2020, the world began to be badly affected by a pandemic caused by the COVID-19 virus. The disease affected tourism demand.

The graph in **Figure 2.3** shows the number of international tourist arrivals in the world between 2000 and 2020.

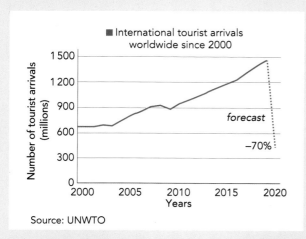

Source: UNWTO

Figure 2.3: Worldwide international tourist arrivals, 2000–2020

Questions

1 Describe how the number of international tourist arrivals changed between 2000 and 2020.

2 Suggest how economic factors could have affected worldwide international tourist arrivals between 2000 and 2020.

3 Explain why worldwide international tourist arrivals fell in 2020.

4 Discuss as a class:

   a what happened to worldwide international tourist arrivals after 2020

   b what you think will happen to worldwide international tourist arrivals in the future.

5 *Extension:* Evaluate the impact of the pandemic of the early 2020s on international tourism.

- Factors help to explain things. Factors are the factual parts used to build an explanation. For example, there is no single reason that explains why tourism demand has changed. Several factors explain why tourism demand has changed.

- Tourist security and tourist safety are different. Security is protecting tourists from the risk of crime or terrorism. Safety is tourists not being in physical danger, for example, from fire, accident or earthquake.

KEY CONCEPT LINKS

- Travel and tourism is global and has been growing. The COVID-19 pandemic was a big change. Before the pandemic it was assumed that worldwide travel and tourism demand would keep growing. The pandemic ended the assumption that the number of tourist arrivals around the world would continue to increase.

- Travel and tourism changes because of factors in the wider world. Disease is one factor that affects tourism demand. The trend towards increased sustainability is a factor that affects the type of destination and type of holiday that tourists demand.

ACTIVITY 2.1

1 Make a chart to show the factors that can affect the scale of tourism demand.

2 Suggest how the risk of disease in a destination can affect tourism demand. Is the risk of disease in a destination likely to increase or reduce demand? Why?

3 In **Figure 2.2**, Rose explains how political factors can affect tourism demand. Explain how one other set of factors can affect tourism demand.

4 Work on this *project* in small groups. Discuss other factors not mentioned in **3** above that can affect tourism demand.

CONTINUED

Each group can choose a different set of factors, for example, environmental factors or social factors.

Groups can either make presentations and report back to the rest of the class, or listen to other groups' presentations and make a note of what they say.

You can then work together to compile a classroom display showing how different factors affect the scale of tourism demand in the world.

REFLECTION

Think about the group discussion activity you have done. What do you think you learnt from the discussion? What process did your group follow to reach your conclusions? What problems did you need to overcome?

Reasons for the growth of sustainable tourism

Sustainable tourism is tourism that seeks to conserve the natural environment and people's way of life into the future. Sustainable tourism seeks to avoid pollution and waste that damage the environment. For example, air travel and hotels cause pollution and waste. Sustainable travel and sustainable hotels seek to reduce pollution and waste.

Tourism provides jobs. Sustainable tourism provides jobs that will continue into the future. People working in sustainable tourism can have a sustainable economic future. Sustainable tourism seeks to conserve people's culture. Sometimes the local culture of people living in destinations can be affected by tourism. For example, some local people may copy the behaviour of inbound tourists and local culture could be lost. Sustainable tourism seeks to conserve local ways of life.

The growth of sustainable tourism is a trend in travel and tourism. There are four main reasons for the growth of sustainable tourism.

Changing consumer attitudes

Tourists are consumers of travel and tourism products and services. Consumers are customers, who are becoming more concerned about the impacts of tourism. More tourists would now like the environment and local people's way of life to be conserved into the future. Consumers want tourism to be more sustainable. They want to feel that travel and holidays does not damage the environment or harm the ways of life of people who live in destinations.

Media

Media such as television, radio, newspapers and magazines have influenced consumers' attitudes about the sustainability of tourism. Social media has also influenced consumers' attitudes. Consumers and influencers share information using social media. Information about **green tourism** is spread by media such as magazines, radio and television. Social media platforms enable people to share information about sustainable tourism and influence people's attitudes. The attitude of consumers is more favourable towards sustainable tourism because of the influence of the media and social media.

Availability and promotion of sustainable tourism products and services

Changed consumer attitudes have increased global demand for sustainable tourism. Travel and tourism providers want to sell travel and tourism products and services to tourist customers. An increased demand causes increased supply. Travel and tourism providers make sustainable tourism products and services more available for consumers to buy. Providers promote tourism products and services to attract customers. Changed consumer attitudes have caused providers to promote sustainability. Promoting sustainability helps travel and tourism providers to sell more products and services.

Government policies

National governments want tourism to grow because tourism brings money and jobs to countries. An increased demand for sustainable tourism has

encouraged national governments to develop sustainable tourism, which protects the environment and local people's way of life. These governments want to protect the environment and the ways of life of local people in countries' destinations. For example, the Government of Mauritius encourages sustainable tourism to the country as shown by the case study *Sustainable Mauritius*.

Reasons for the growth of sustainable tourism are shown in **Figure 2.4.**

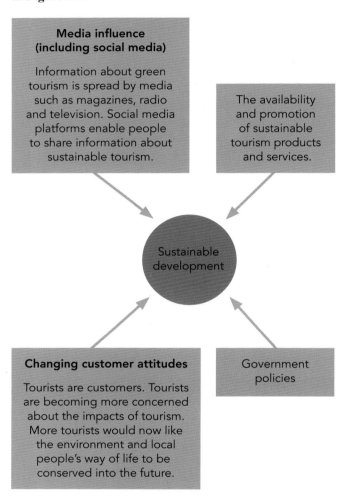

Figure 2.4: Reasons for the growth of sustainable tourism

CASE STUDY

Sustainable Mauritius

Mauritius is a country of islands in the Indian Ocean. Mauritius itself is the biggest island in the country, while Rodrigues is the second largest. There are several other smaller, outer islands.

Tourism is very important to Mauritius. In 2019, 1.38 million tourists arrived in Mauritius. Income from travel and tourism is an important part of the country's GDP. Tens of thousands of people are directly employed in travel and tourism in Mauritius.

The Government of Mauritius has a policy of promoting the growth of sustainable tourism. The Mauritius Tourism Development Plan aims for Mauritius to reach 'Green Destination' status by 2030. **Figure 2.5** shows the front of a leaflet, 'Sustainable Island Mauritius', published by the Mauritius Government's Mauritius Tourism Authority (MTA).

Sustainable Island Mauritius promotes the growth of sustainable tourism by showing local tourism organisations how greening available products

and services can help their businesses to succeed. Tour operators are one type of organisation along the travel and tourism value chain. **Figure 2.6** shows the products and services of the travel and tourism value chain.

Questions

1   What has happened to the number of tourist arrivals in Mauritius since 2020?

2   Identify **two** reasons for the growth of sustainable tourism in Mauritius.

3   Suggest how the travel and tourism value chain shown in **Figure 2.6** helps to create income for the destination of Mauritius.

4   Discuss how greening products and services can help tourism organisations to succeed as businesses.

5   *Extension:* Assess the extent to which tourism in Mauritius is sustainable.

KEY WORDS

directly employed: in travel and tourism, this means having a job in a travel and tourism organisation

Green Destination: a status awarded by the Green Destinations Foundation

greening: making something environmentally sustainable

value chain: the set of linked products and services on which tourists spend money to create income for a destination

Figure 2.5: 'Sustainable Island Mauritius'

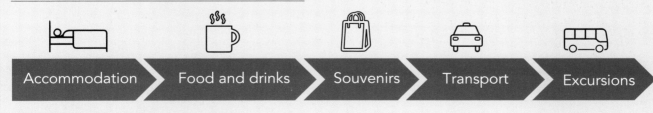

Figure 2.6: Travel and tourism value chain

KEY CONCEPT LINKS

- Sustainable tourism has become very important in travel and tourism. Tourists, travel and tourism organisations and governments want to conserve the environment and people's way of life into the future.

- Governments of countries such as Mauritius promote the growth of sustainable tourism to:

    - help conserve the environment and people's way of life

    - bring more tourism income into the country.

ACTIVITY 2.2

1 Outline **two** reasons for the growth of sustainable tourism.

2 Explain how government policies can help to grow sustainable tourism.

3 Suggest how the availability and promotion of sustainable products and services can help to grow sustainable tourism.

4 Make a presentation to show travel and tourism organisations how greening can help to ensure business success.

2.2 The features and appeal of destinations

Introduction

Different people find different destinations appealing or interesting. This may be related to how reachable the destination is in terms of topographical features, infrastructure and location. In this section, you will discover information on how features of destinations appeal to different types of tourists.

Features affecting the appeal of destinations

Features affecting the appeal of destinations are:

- **Location**: some destinations are either easier to travel to for tourists around the world (for example, Paris in France), or more appealing because of where they are located (for example, the Maldives). Paris is the capital of France, and will be the Olympic Games host city in 2024. It has a good location for transport links. International airports for Paris are Charles de Gaulle, Orly and, for budget flights, Beauvais. Major road and rail links connect Paris to the rest of France and much of Western Europe. High-speed trains link Paris to other capital cities in Europe and to most other big cities in France.

- **Weather and seasonal characteristics**: certain destinations are appealing because tourists can rely on them for the weather. For example, they can expect sunshine in Santa Barbara, California, on the West Coast of the USA, for a summer beach holiday, or snow for a winter sports holiday in a mountain resort such as Breckenridge, Colorado, USA. Breckenridge has ski slopes on five nearby mountains. The ski season starts after snow has fallen in November and continues until April.

- **Topographical features**: mountains, rivers and lakes can add to a destination's appeal for adventure and sightseeing tourists, for example, spectacular mountains surround Breckenridge. In the winter, Breckenridge is a ski resort. From spring to autumn (fall), tourists can mountain bike, hike through the impressive mountain scenery, fish for trout, paddleboard, go white-water rafting, play golf or photograph the beautiful scenery.

- Accessibility: some destinations are easier to reach than others because of transport links, for example, Orlando, Florida, USA, or because of provision for tourists with specific needs, such as at Copenhagen Airport, Denmark. Orlando has two main international airports. Orlando International Airport is used by many long-haul flights. Sanford International Airport has more low-cost (budget) and charter flights. Accessibility services provided for tourists at Copenhagen Airport in Denmark include sustainable electric vehicles used to transport tourists with specific mobility needs through the airport.

- **Travel and transport** gateways and hubs help to make some destinations such as Orlando more accessible than others. Orlando International Airport is a gateway airport and a hub airport. Some tourists arrive at the airport on inbound flights and transfer to domestic flights, for example, to other airports in Florida, such as Fort Lauderdale and Key West.

- Infrastructure, including public transport, roads, airports and ports, can make some destinations more accessible than others, for example, the Olympic city of Paris in France. International airports for Paris are Charles de Gaulle, Orly and Beauvais. Major motorways (freeways) and high-speed rail links connect Paris to the rest of France and to other large cities in Europe, including London, via the Channel Tunnel.

KEY WORDS

location: where a destination is

topographical features: surface features of the landscape such as mountains, lakes, rivers and valleys

accessibility: how easy a destination is to reach

gateways: an entry point to a destination. Examples of gateways include airports, railway stations and arrival towns

hubs: places where tourists change from one type of transport to another

infrastructure: the transport framework of a destination, including public transport, roads, airport and port

- Built and natural attractions add to the appeal of destinations to leisure tourists, for example, Ha Long in Vietnam. The beautiful natural attractions of Ha Long Bay appeal to many domestic and inbound tourists. Boat tours allow tourists to admire the impressive scenery. Thousands of limestone islands rise from the clear, emerald-green water. On top of the island cliffs are rainforests. Tourists can scuba-dive, rock-climb and hike in the surrounding mountains. The built environment of the old port area of Hoi An town appeals to tourists. Some of the well-preserved architecture of the port dates from the 15th century. Buildings are in a mix of Vietnamese and foreign styles that many tourists like to photograph. The old Japanese Bridge is a very popular built attraction.

- Culture, including traditions, language, arts and music, adds to the appeal of destinations such as Marrakesh to cultural tourists. Marrakesh in Morocco, North Africa, is a historic city. The centre of the old city (the Medina) is Jemaa el-Fna. Jemaa el-Fna is a large open space. The Jemaa el-Fna square appeals to cultural tourists, with traders selling local orange juice, traditional leather bags and brass cups. The many Moroccan food stalls in Jemaa el-Fna attract crowds of tourists and local people. Cultural tourists enjoy watching performers in Jemaa el-Fna, which include groups of traditional musicians and dancers, storytellers, magicians and circus acts. Alongside the Jemaa el-Fna square is a traditional market. This lively market has many small shops and stalls selling a great variety of traditional local goods, including traditional rugs and Moroccan lamps, leather bags, bright fabrics, embroidered slippers, silver jewellery and spices.

- Expected behaviours, for example, respecting local customs, rules and regulations, can affect the appeal of some destinations such as Marrakesh and New Zealand's Bay of Plenty to some inbound tourists. In Marrakesh, tourists are often expected to dress modestly and to behave soberly and respectfully in public. Tourists visiting New Zealand's Bay of Plenty, meanwhile, are encouraged to behave responsibly and sustainably in order to respect the local Maori people's culture.

- Tourism organisations and providers affect the appeal of destinations because of the products and services made available and promoted to customers. For example, in Australia, tour operators organise package tours that include accommodation, visits to natural and built attraction, and ancillary services, such as travel insurance and the provision of trained tour guides.

- Sustainable provisions, for example, ecotourism products and services in New Zealand's Bay of Plenty destination, appeal to responsible tourists. The local tourism authority educates tourists on responsible tourism. Tourists are told how to care for the environment and people. Responsible tourism advice is also made available online to tourists.

The *Marrakesh* case study shows how different factors can affect the appeal of a destination.

CASE STUDY

Does Marrakesh appeal to you?

Marrakesh is an inland city destination in Morocco, a country in north-west Africa.

Marrakesh is a historic city. Traditionally, the oldest part of Marrakesh (called the Medina) has been an important meeting place and market. The centre of the Medina is Jemaa el-Fna, a large open space in the centre of the Medina and in the centre of Marrakesh.

Figure 2.7: Jemaa el-Fna

The square of Jemaa el-Fna appeals to many tourists. Traders sell local orange juice, traditional leather bags and brass cups. Summers are hot and sunny, but the evenings are cooler. The many Moroccan food stalls attract crowds of tourists and local people to Jemaa el-Fna. Tourists and locals enjoy watching performers, including groups of traditional musicians and dancers, storytellers, magicians and circus acts.

Next to the square is a traditional market – a *souk*. The souk is a very lively place. Narrow passages are lined by many small shops and stalls. On sale is a great variety of local goods, including traditional rugs and Moroccan lamps, leather bags, bright fabrics, embroidered slippers, silver jewellery, olives, orange juice and spices.

There are hotels near Jemaa el-Fna, as well as gardens and café terraces. Old, narrow streets and alleys lead into the rest of the historic Medina. Marrakesh's built attractions include the ruins of the El Badi Palace, the carved Saadian Tombs and the tall tower of the Koutoubia Minaret (see photo).

Jemaa el-Fna is very important to the tourism economy of Marrakesh. The square has been closed to motor traffic since the early 2000s and police patrols ensure tourists' safety and security.

Questions

1   Identify the features of Marrakesh that appeal to tourists.

2   Discuss with a partner:

   a   Does Marrakesh appeal to you?

   b   Which types of tourists would find Marrakesh appealing? Why?

3   Analyse the appeal of Marrakesh by using **Table 2.1** to help complete this chart:

Feature	Link to the appeal of Marrakesh
Weather	
Built attractions	
Culture	
Tourism providers	

4   Evaluate the appeal of Marrakesh to a range of tourist types.

Links between destination features and appeal are shown in **Table 2.1**:

Feature	Link to appeal
Location	Where a destination is. For example, a destination may be beside the sea or in the mountains.
Weather and seasonal characteristics	What the weather is like at different times of the year. For example, seasons may be hot, sunny and dry or have rain or snow or wind.
Topographical features	The surface geographical features of a destination, including mountains, lakes, rivers and valleys.
Accessibility	How easy it is to reach a destination. Good transport links by air, water or land make most destinations easily accessible.
Travel and transport gateways and hubs	Destination arrival points and transport interchanges. A tourist arriving at a destination's airport *(gateway)* might then change to a train at the airport's railway station *(hub)*. Ports, airports and railway stations are important examples of transport gateways and hubs.
Infrastructure, including public transport, roads, airports and ports	The transport framework of a destination. Bus and rail routes, the road network, a nearby airport and port or harbour facilities can be part of a destination's infrastructure.
Built and natural attractions	Visitor attractions for tourists. Some tourist attractions are part of the natural environment, for example, waterfalls, beaches and mountains. Other tourist attractions have been built by people. Built attractions include museums, aquariums, theme parks, forts and castles.
Culture, including traditions, language, arts and music	People's way of living, including traditional lifestyles and local art, can appeal to tourists. Language can affect tourism appeal. Sometimes a local language and the tourists' language is the same; however, some tourists like to experience a different language.
Expected behaviours, for example, respecting local customs, rules and regulations	Some destinations have local codes for how people should dress and behave. Tourists are expected to respect local customs, rules and regulations. Expected behaviours can affect the appeal of a destination.
Tourism organisations and providers	Tour operators and accommodation and transport providers are examples of tourism organisations. Products and services provided by tourism organisations help to make a destination appealing.
Sustainable provisions	A destination with sustainable products and services may have a greater appeal to some tourists.

Table 2.1: Links between destination features and appeal

Destination features may appeal differently to different types of tourists. For example, beaches may appeal to some leisure tourists, whereas conference rooms could appeal to some business tourists.

TIPS

- Some destinations appeal to you more than others. When explaining appeal, remember that this is the same for other people: the destinations that appeal to others may not appeal to you.

- When discussing appeal, remember that the same destination may have a different appeal to different types of tourists.

KEY CONCEPT LINKS

- The appeal of a destination is what attracts its tourists.

- Different destinations appeal to different types of tourists. Different types of tourists include:

  - leisure tourists and business tourists

  - families, individuals and couples

  - tourist groups and independent travellers

  - responsible tourists and ecotourists

  - tourists with special interests and tourists with specific needs.

ACTIVITY 2.3

I would prefer a more natural destination. I like outdoor activities.

My friends find different destinations appealing. We did a class survey. Beach destinations were most popular.

Figure 2.8: Rose talks about destinations

1   Identify destinations that might appeal to:
    - Rose
    - Rose's friends.

2   Explain why you think the destinations you identified in **1** would appeal to Rose and her friends.

3   Discuss the differing appeal of one destination to different types of tourists.

4   Survey other people's destination likes and dislikes. Which destination features appeal to them most?

CONTINUED

5   Interview people to find out why some destination features are important to them.

    a   Present and analyse your findings. What is your conclusion?

    b   Research and recommend a destination that would appeal to one of the people you interviewed.

REFLECTION

Think about the survey you have done.

- Why did you choose this method?

- What did you learn from the interviews?

2.3 Destination development and management organisations

Introduction

Destinations within countries are developed and managed by different organisations. Destination development and management organisations may be national, regional or local.

National, regional and local destination development and management organisations:

- are responsible for management activities such as planning tourism development and encouraging sustainable tourism

- provide services, including promoting the destination and providing tourist information.

National, regional and local organisations

National, regional and local organisations are involved in the development and management of destinations. Organisations develop destinations by making changes that attract more tourism. These organisations make sure that tourism continues. The *Heartbeat Jamaica* case study gives information about destination management organisations in Jamaica. Organisations that develop and manage destinations are:

- governments, including tourism ministries such as in Jamaica (see case study) and local tourism authorities such as local councils (see *Who comes to Cambridge* case study **5.5**)

- national tourism organisations (NTOs) such as the Jamaica Tourist Board

- destination management companies (DMCs), for example, *Glamour DMC* in Montego Bay, Jamaica

- non-government organisations (NGOs) such as *The Jamaican Hotel and Tourist Association*

- tourist information centres (TICs), including *Negril TIC* in Jamaica.

Management activities

The management activities of organisations involved in the development and management of Jamaica and other destinations are:

- encouraging sustainable tourism

- ensuring resilience and managing risks, such as the risk of disease during the COVID-19 pandemic

- managing tourism demand to encourage tourists to visit without causing negative impacts through overtourism

- making tourism policies to attract and manage inbound and domestic tourism

- planning the development of tourism in destinations such as Jamaica.

Services provided

Different organisations in Jamaica and other destinations provide a range of destination development and management services:

- marketing strategies, including developing a destination's brand, image and reputation

- promoting the destination

- developing tourism products and services

- researching and funding destination developments, including infrastructure developments

- providing information to tourists and to travel and tourism providers

- advising tourists and providing consultation support for tourism providers

- maintaining standards and quality to help build the reputation and encourage repeat visits.

KEY WORDS

marketing strategies: plans that aim to market destinations. Marketing destinations involves making destinations attractive to tourism customers

consultation support: advice provided to help tourism organisations

The *Heartbeat Jamaica* case study gives information about destination development and management organisations, including information about:

- the management activities of destination development and management organisations

- services that destination development and management organisations provide.

CASE STUDY

Heartbeat Jamaica

Jamaica is a country and island destination in the Caribbean Sea. Many of the destinations in Jamaica are coastal destinations. **Figure 2.9** is a map showing the location of some destinations in Jamaica.

The national government decides Jamaica's tourism policy. The government wants tourism to help develop Jamaica's economy for the benefit of Jamaicans.

The Ministry of Tourism is part of the national government, while the Jamaican Ministry of Tourism is responsible for the management and promotion of Jamaica's tourism product. The Ministry of Tourism (MOT) wants tourism to bring economic benefits to Jamaica. The MOT also wants to develop tourism in Jamaica in ways that follow trends in global tourism demand. For example, there is a growth in demand for more sustainable tourism.

One department of Jamaica's MOT is the Jamaica Tourist Board (JTB). This board is a national tourism organisation (NTO). The JTB's job is to develop and market Jamaica's tourism industry. NTOs develop destination brands to market tourism to countries. In 2020, the JTB developed a new destination brand for Jamaica: *Jamaica, Heartbeat of the World*.

Destination brands help to market destinations. The destination brand *Jamaica, Heartbeat of the World* tries to give a clear image of Jamaica that will appeal to tourists. The JTB chose the *Jamaica, Heartbeat of the World* brand to build Jamaica's reputation as an exciting and friendly destination. Tourists remember destination brands and *Jamaica, Heartbeat of the World* is therefore a destination brand chosen to attract tourists to Jamaica.

Glamour DMC is a destination management company (DMC) based in Montego Bay.

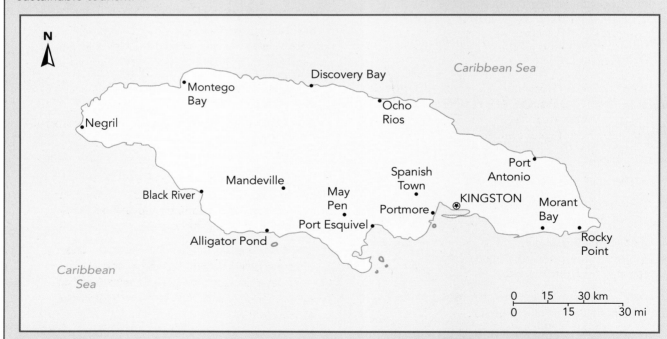

Figure 2.9: Some destinations in Jamaica

CONTINUED

DMCs such as *Glamour* employ staff who know the destination well. The company organises hotel accommodation, business tourism (MICE) facilities and sports facilities, transport and leisure visits to tourist attractions. DMCs provide advice and consultancy services for tourism business customers. Sustainable tourism includes conserving the way of life of local communities. *Glamour DMC* is a commercial business trying to make a profit. It also aims to be sustainable by being socially responsible. *Glamour DMC* helps local community organisations, including schools and places of worship in Jamaica.

The Jamaican Hotel and Tourist Association (JHTA) is a tourism industry **non-government organisation** (NGO) in Jamaica. The JHTA:

- is a group that Jamaican hotels and tourism providers can join

- speaks for Jamaica's hotel and tourism businesses at JTB meetings

- helps the JTB to promote tourism to Jamaica in ways that benefit the country's hotels and tourism providers.

The Negril Tourist Information Centre (TIC) provides information for tourists to Negril, which is a coastal destination in the west of Jamaica. The TICs provide information about local tourist attractions, places to stay, restaurants, transport and excursions.

Questions

1   Identify Jamaican examples of each of the following:

   a   an NTO

   b   a DMC

   c   a TIC.

2   Describe examples of how organisations in Jamaica:

   a   market a destination

   b   provide information and advice to tourists

   c   provide consultation services to tourism providers.

3   Explain why the Ministry of Tourism supports development of:

   a   destination branding

   b   tourism products and services.

4   Discuss how Jamaican destination development and marketing organisations can:

   a   promote awareness of sustainable tourism in Jamaica

   b   research and fund destination developments

   c   maintain standards and quality.

KEY WORDS

national tourism organisation (NTO): a government agency that promotes and markets the tourism product of a country

destination management company (DMC): a tourism business with local knowledge of a destination. A DMC provides customers with events, activities, tours, transport and other services in the destination

non-government organisation (NGO): a not-for-profit organisation of people who want to promote a product, service or cause, such as sustainable tourism. NGOs are independent of government

CONTINUED

4   How do destination development and management organisations in your chosen destination compare with destination development and management organisations in Jamaica? Discuss with a partner.

TIPS

- Be aware that NGOs may be business associations such as the Jamaica Hotel and Tourist Association. Other NGOs include the Green Destinations Foundation, which promotes sustainable tourism.

- Remember that Tourist Information Centres may be:

    - not-for-profit and organised by governments or by volunteers

    - commercial businesses, such as the Negril Tourist Information Centre.

KEY CONCEPT LINKS

- Travel and tourism benefits destinations. Governments want to develop and promote tourism to destinations, but tourism can have negative impacts on destinations. Some NGOs want to promote sustainable tourism to destinations.

- Governments want tourists to visit destinations. Government Ministries of Tourism and NTOs organise destination development and marketing.

- Other destination development and marketing organisations are DMCs, NGOs and TICs.

ACTIVITY 2.4

1   Choose a destination other than Jamaica.

　a　Identify, using a map, destinations found within your chosen destination.

　b　Describe the appeal of your chosen destination.

2　a　Outline the brand of a destination other than Jamaica.

　b　Make a display of destination brands.

3   Investigate destination development and management organisations in your chosen destination.

2.4 Factors affecting tourism development and management

Introduction

Tourism development and management is affected by different factors. The *Sustainable Vietnam* case study gives information about factors affecting tourism development and management in Vietnam.

Factors affecting tourism development and management are:

- opportunities and constraints of the natural and built environment

- sustainability

- risks and resilience

- carrying capacity and overtourism

- seasonality

- government objectives.

Opportunities and constraints of the natural and built environment

The natural and built environment creates opportunities for tourism development in destinations, but also limits what development is possible. For example, the beautiful natural environment of Ha Long Bay and historic built environment of Hoi An attract tourists and create economic opportunities for travel and tourism organisations. Conserving the natural and built environment is important to maintain appeal. Conservation can limit or constrain travel and tourism providers. For example, a food and drink provider in Hoi An's historic old town may be constrained by the need to maintain an old building's tourist appeal.

Sustainability

National governments such as the Government of Vietnam wants to encourage more sustainable tourism. For example, reducing, reusing and recycling waste and resources helps the environment and the economy of the country because it reduces the need for food and energy imports.

Risks and resilience

Risks to tourism development and management in destinations include natural disasters and extreme weather events such as volcanic eruptions, earthquakes and severe storms. Natural disasters and exteme weather events damage travel and tourism infrastructure, including hotels, visitor attractions and transport facilites such as ports, airports and road and rail links. Repairing and replacing damaged infrastructure is very expensive for travel and tourism organisations and for national governments.

Resilience is being able to continue after bad events. For example, a resilient destination will soon recover from an extreme weather event such as a severe storm or from a natural disaster such as flooding. National governments try to make destinations resilient. For example, governments may have reserves of money to help with rebuilding programmes and to pay for damage-prevention measures such as flood barriers.

Carrying capacity and overtourism

The need to manage the number of tourists visiting a destination or attraction is a factor in managing tourism development. Destination management organisations try to ensure that visitor numbers are within the destination's carrying capacity. These organisations want to encourage tourism development without causing environmental damage or spoiling visitors' tourism experience. Managing visitor numbers to within a destination's carrying capacity is a way to ensure overtourism does not spoil the destination.

KEY WORDS

carrying capacity: the maximum number of visitors a destination or attraction can welcome without causing environmental damage or spoiling the tourism experience

overtourism: when there are too many tourists in a destination. Overtourism harms the destination environment and causes difficulties for local people. Tourists do not enjoy the destination as much

---

Seasonality

Seasonality can affect tourism development. Destinations may have a high season, when visitor numbers are high; and a low season, when visitor numbers are lower. For example, seasonality affects the management of tourism in Vietnam. Fewer tourists travel to Vietnam during the rainy season when the weather can be very wet, especially in northern Vietnam. The rainy season is usually from May to October. The rainy season is therefore the low season. Tourism activities may not be possible in the low season, when the weather is very wet.

Destination management organisations and governments may try to overcome the constraint of seasonality. For example, in beach destinations such as Negril in Jamaica (see **2.6**), destination management organisations try to develop tourism products and services to attract tourists during the low season. The development of business tourism MICE (Meetings, Incentives, Conferences Exhibitions) venues (see **5.4**) is often a good way to attract more tourists in the low season.

Government objectives

Government objectives are what governments want tourism to achieve for their country. National government objectives for tourism development and management are shown in **Table 2.2.**

The *Sustainable Vietnam* case study gives information about factors affecting tourism development and management in Vietnam.

Economic objectives	Political objectives	Environmental objectives	Sociocultural objectives
• Bring more money into the country • Create more jobs.	• Improve the image and reputation of the country.	• Conserve the natural environment • Rejuvenate (give new life to) the built environment.	• Preserve and protect people's traditional culture • Create positive relationships between tourists and the host community.

Table 2.2: Government objectives for tourism

KEY WORD

host community: a destination's local people

CASE STUDY

Sustainable Vietnam

Vietnam is a country in Southeast Asia. The natural and built environments of Vietnam appeal to tourists. The Vietnam Government wants tourism to develop sustainably. Tourism helps government achieve its objectives (**Table 2.2**).

The government's Vietnam National Administration of Tourism (VNAT) and the Vietnam Tourism Advisory Board (VTAB) work together. The VNAT and VTAB created the Vietnam national tourism website to market Vietnam as a sustainable tourism destination. The website encourages tourists to visit the country. *Sustainable Vietnam* became part of the Vietnam national tourism website in 2020. *Sustainable Vietnam* promotes sustainable tourism products and services in Vietnam.

Ha Long Bay is a destination in north-east Vietnam. The beautiful natural environment of Ha Long Bay appeals to tourists. Its natural environment has created opportunities for tourism to develop. Boat tours allow tourists to admire the impressive scenery as thousands of limestone islands rise from the clear, emerald-green water. On top of the island cliffs are rainforests.

Ha Long Bay's natural environment has created opportunities to develop tourism activities. Tourists can scuba-dive, rock-climb and hike in the surrounding mountains. Sustainable boat-cruise operators cause little water pollution. Customer meals feature local, sustainably produced food. Regular bay clean-up days are organised. Excursions to local fishing villages educate tourists about the lives of Ha Long Bay's people.

Figure 2.10: Ha Long Bay

Seasonality affects the management of tourism in Vietnam. The weather can be very wet during the rainy season, especially in northern Vietnam. The rainy season is usually from May to October and fewer tourists travel to Vietnam during this time. Some tourist activities are not available when the weather is very wet.

Ha Long Bay is one of Vietnam's World Heritage Sites (WHSs). Hoi An is an urban destination in central Vietnam and is also a World Heritage Site. The built environment of the old part of Hoi An town appeals to tourists. Some of the well-preserved architecture of the port dates back to the 15th century. Buildings are a mix of Vietnamese and foreign styles that many tourists like to photograph. The old Japanese Bridge is a very popular attraction.

CONTINUED

Figure 2.11: The old bridge, Hoi An

Figure 2.12: In a Mekong Delta market

The Mekong Delta is a rural destination in southern Vietnam. **Homestay holidays** in the Mekong Delta allow tourists to stay in the homes of local people. Hosts cook local food for visitors using fresh fruit and fish sourced locally. Tourists can ride in traditional wooden sampan boats, cycle, visit local floating markets and take part in cooking classes. Eco-tours are organised that visit local craft workshops to learn more about the Delta people's way of life.

Questions

1   Describe the tourism developments in Vietnam that are because of:

   a   the natural environment

   b   the built environment.

2   With a partner, discuss how you think tourism can be structured in Vietnam to avoid overtourism.

3   Explain how:

   a   the natural environment limits tourism development in Vietnam

   b   tourism in Vietnam can rejuvenate the built environment.

4   Discuss how tourism development in Vietnam has been affected by government objectives.

5   *Extension:* Assess the range of factors affecting sustainable tourism development and management in Vietnam.

KEY WORDS

World Heritage Sites (WHSs): destinations and attractions that have been identified as especially important part of the natural or built environment by UNESCO (United Nations Educational, Scientific and Cultural Organisation). WHSs should be conserved for the future. They appeal to tourists.

homestay holidays: holidays involving tourists staying in local people's houses

TIPS

Be clear that:

*   tourism development is change that increases or improves tourism to a destination

*   managing tourism means organising tourism to maintain its success

*   sustainable tourism products and services are developed to encourage tourism. Managing tourism sustainably keeps tourists visiting.

KEY CONCEPT LINKS

- Tourism development means change that encourages tourism. Governments want tourism because of its benefits, while tourism benefits meet government objectives. Government objectives are an important factor affecting tourism development and management.

- The environment is an important factor affecting tourism development and management. The natural and built environments appeal to tourists. These environments create opportunities for tourism development.

- Managing tourism to avoid overtourism protects, conserves and rejuvenates destination environments.

ACTIVITY 2.5

1   Identify the benefits that tourism brings to destination countries.

2   Describe the differences between:

   a   the natural environment and built environment

   b   tourism development and tourism management.

   Create illustrations to show the differences you have described.

3   Discuss seasonality with a partner.

   a   What is seasonality?

   b   How can seasonality affect tourism development?

   c   How do you think seasonality can be managed?

   Make a display to summarise your discussion.

4   **Project**: Think of a destination.

   Either on your own or with a partner, investigate how factors affect tourism development in your chosen destination. With the aid of a diagram or chart, create a poster and present your findings to the rest of the class.

REFLECTION

- How easy or difficult did you find the topic of tourism development and management?

- Why did you find the topic of tourism development and management easy or difficult?

2.5 Managing destinations sustainably

Introduction

Destinations are managed sustainably in order to:

- protect the natural and built environment of destinations

- **combat climate change** through encouraging and enabling responsible tourism

- empower local and **indigenous communities**

- support **social enterprise** development.

KEY WORDS

combat climate change: to take action against changes in the earth's climate. Actions such as producing less pollution are aimed at reducing climate change

indigenous communities: communities of the original inhabitants of a place

social enterprises: organisations that try to be profitable whilst also supporting local and indigenous communities. Community tourism organisations are social enterprises. Examples of community tourism organisations are guest houses, cafés and restaurants owned by local people

The *New Zealand 100%* case study gives information about how the Bay of Plenty destination is managed sustainably.

Protect the natural and built environment of destinations

The sustainable management of destinations aims to protect the natural and built environment of destinations by:

- maintaining the biodiversity of destinations such as New Zealand's Bay of Plenty

- preserving, conserving and regenerating the natural and built environment (see **Figure 2.13**)

- controlling visitor numbers and managing visitor behaviour to limit tourism's negative impacts (see **2.6**)

- sustainably using and reusing resources such as water and limiting air, water and land pollution, for example, in the Okavango Delta, Botswana (see **2.6**).

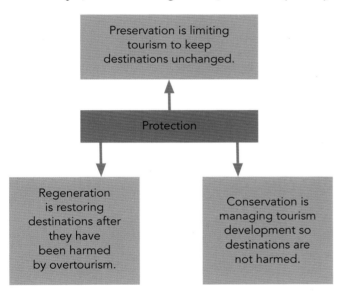

Figure 2.13: Ways to protect the environment of destinations

Combat climate change through encouraging and enabling responsible tourism

As shown in the *New Zealand 100%* case study, destinations are sustainably managed to combat climate change by:

- organising education programmes for local people and visitors so that responsible tourism behaviour reduces pollution

- having recycling and reuse schemes, for example, for plastic water bottles

- reducing over-consumption and waste, for example, of food, energy and water in hotels.

Empower local and indigenous communities

The sustainable management of destinations empowers local and indigenous communities, such as Maori people in New Zealand's Bay of Plenty, by:

- enabling the people who live in destinations to protect local cultures and preserve traditional local customs

- involving local communities in managing tourism in their own community and being involved in decision-making that affects the destination management of tourism where they live

- training travel and tourism staff in sustainable tourism behaviours to limit pollution and educating tourists about responsible tourism behaviours.

Support social enterprise development

Managing destinations such as New Zealand's Bay of Plenty sustainably supports social enterprise development through:

- supporting local economies, local wealth creation and **sustainable infrastructural development**, for example, by developing pollution-free destination transport systems and developing tourism facilities sustainably

- **community tourism**, where local and indigenous communities invite tourists to visit and stay in local people's homes

- creating jobs for local people to increase the economic and social sustainability of destinations.

KEY WORDS

customs: long-established ways of behaving. Local and indigenous destination communities may have traditional customs or ways of living

sustainable infrastructural development: improving destination transport systems and tourism facilities sustainably

community tourism: local and indigenous communities invite tourists to visit and stay in their homes

CASE STUDY

New Zealand 100%

New Zealand (NZ) is a destination in the south-west Pacific Ocean. The country's tourism businesses work together as *Tourism Industry Aotearoa* (TIA). (*Aotearoa* is the Maori name for New Zealand. The Maori are the indigenous people of New Zealand.) The TIA wants every tourism business in New Zealand to practise sustainable tourism. The organisation is 100% 'Committed to Sustainable Tourism' and is determined that all NZ tourism businesses will practise sustainable tourism.

The Coastal Bay of Plenty shows TIA's commitment to sustainable tourism. This location is a destination within New Zealand. The Coastal Bay of Plenty (*Te Moananui a Toi* in the Maori language) was chosen by the Green Destinations Foundation to be one of the world's Sustainable Top 100 Destinations in 2020. The Bay of Plenty won the Sustainable Top 100 Destinations listing because of the appeal of the natural environment.

The natural attractions of the Coastal Bay of Plenty's 125 kilometres of coastline include land and marine (sea) nature reserves, scenic islands, forests, rivers, waterfalls and some of New Zealand's most popular beaches, such as at Mount Maunganui and Tauranga.

Figure 2.14: Mount Maunganui beach

Many tourist activities are linked to the natural environment. Adventure activities in the Bay of Plenty destination include surfing, deep-water fishing, swimming with dolphins, river kayaking, white-water rafting and mountain biking. Places for sightseeing

include waterfalls: Kaiate Falls and McLaren Falls are both in protected Bay of Plenty nature reserves. Nature reserves help to protect the biodiversity of the Bay of Plenty.

Kiwi fruit are native New Zealand fruit. Tourists can choose to visit a kiwi orchard: a scenic 16 km path starts and finishes in the small town of Whakatane. Walkers enjoy views of sea cliffs and remote bays, ancient *pa* (traditional Maori village) sites, bird colonies and *pohutukawa* evergreen forest.

The Bay of Plenty is not only a rural destination. Both Tauranga and Mount Maunganui also have urban attractions. Tourists enjoy visiting shops, the fish market, art galleries, restaurants and cafés.

Local people and tourists want to protect the natural environment of the Bay of Plenty. *Tourism New Zealand* is the national tourism organisation (NTO) for New Zealand. *Tourism New Zealand* has promised *Tiaki*, a Maori word meaning 'to care for people and place'. *Tourism Bay of Plenty* is a regional tourism organisation (RTO) and destination management company (DMC). *Tourism Bay of Plenty* promotes sustainable tourism in the Bay of Plenty destination because sustainable tourism cares for people and places. The increasing global tourism demand for sustainable tourism has helped the development of the Bay of Plenty in ways that protect the environment, the traditional Maori culture and the way of life of local people. Tourism development in the Bay of Plenty also has a positive economic impact. Tourism development in the area creates wealth in the destination, and wealth creation is part of economic sustainability.

Some places are affected by overtourism. Omanawa Falls, for example, has been closed to tourists to avoid harming the biodiversity. *Tourism Bay of Plenty* educates tourists about responsible tourism. Visitors are told how to care for the environment and people. Websites are one way to educate tourists: **Table 2.3** shows responsible tourism advice that is available online for tourists. Community tourism in the Bay of Plenty is a way of educating tourists that:

- empowers local Maori communities

- supports the development of social enterprises.

CONTINUED

Be a *kaitiaki* (guardian or carer)	
beaches • keep to marked paths • take rubbish away • use litter bins • take part in clean-ups • go to quiet spots; avoid overcrowding	**birds and wildlife** • give animals space • keep your distance and avoid disturbing wildlife • keep out of closed areas such as birds' nesting sites
forests and land • keep to paths and tracks • clean shoes to avoid spreading tree disease • use the toilets and restrooms provided • avoid overcrowded and closed areas • recycle waste	**local ways of life** • reuse cups in cafés • be polite and respect other people; drive carefully • check the weather forecast and tell people what you are doing if it is dangerous, to avoid having to use rescue teams

Table 2.3: Responsible tourism advice given to tourists

Community tourism in the Bay of Plenty includes cultural homestays. For example, tourists can stay in a beach cottage in the village of Ohope that is managed by local Maori people. Homestay customers staying in one of these cottages can learn about the indigenous Maori culture. Customers can also enjoy the beach, fishing trips with local people, cycling or canoeing.

KEY WORDS

nature reserves: places where the natural environment and biodiversity are protected

regional tourism organisation (RTO): an organisation that promotes and markets the tourism product of a part (region) of a country. RTOs are part of national tourism organisations (NTOs)

clean-ups: tourist activities involving visitors helping locals to tidy the environment by removing rubbish

cultural homestay: a type of community tourism. Tourist customers stay in the homes of local people and experience indigenous culture

Questions

1   Describe the appeal of the Coastal Bay of Plenty to different types of tourists.

2   There is some Maori language used in this case study:

   a   Identify the Maori words used in the *New Zealand 100%* case study.

   b   Suggest why using words from the language of indigenous people helps tourism sustainability.

3   Explain the roles of organisations in developing and managing the Coastal Bay of Plenty destination.

4   Discuss:

   a   how the Coastal Bay of Plenty tourism is being made more sustainable

   b   why the Coastal Bay of Plenty tourism is being made more sustainable

   c   different ways that can be used to educate tourists about responsible tourism.

5   *Extension:* Evaluate the extent to which New Zealand's Bay of Plenty has avoided overtourism.

2.6 Economic, environmental and sociocultural impacts of travel and tourism

Introduction

Travel and tourism impacts are the effects that it has on places and people. Some effects are good (positive impacts) and some are bad (negative impacts). The impacts of travel and tourism are:

- economic – affecting money and jobs

- environmental – affecting the environment

- sociocultural – affecting people and their way of life.

Positive economic impacts

The economic impacts of travel and tourism are the effects has on money and jobs. These economic impacts can be positive or negative – good or bad.

The positive economic impacts can benefit local people, for example, tourism brings jobs and money.

Tourists spend money in destinations. Tourists are customers of local travel and tourism organisations. For example, tourists spend money in attractions, in cafés and restaurants, on entertainment, in hotels and on local transport. Travel and tourism organisations employ people, so large numbers of jobs are created in destinations. This is a positive economic impact of tourism on the local, host community, shown in the *Jesse in Jamaica* case study.

The money tourists spend helps travel and tourism organisations to make a profit. Money spent by visitors allows travel and tourism organisations and other businesses to invest profits. Investing profits then helps travel and tourism organisations and other businesses to grow bigger. Organisations need to employ more staff and create more jobs. Employees are paid and some of the money employees earn is spent at other businesses in the destination, such as local shops and services. Other businesses in the destination make more money and employ more staff, who also spend money. The economy of the whole destination benefits through the **multiplier effect** (**Figure 2.15**).

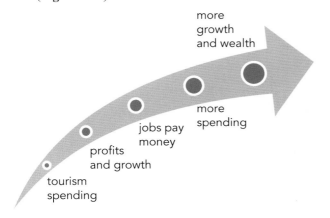

Figure 2.15: The multiplier effect

Money from travel and tourism is multiplied and helps to create wealth and increase the standard of living in destinations.

All destinations in a country benefit from the positive economic impact of the multiplier effect. The total money a country makes is the country's GDP. Money from travel and tourism is an important part of the GDP of countries such as Jamaica and Mauritius.

Profitable travel and tourism organisations and other businesses in destinations pay taxes to the government. Governments can use taxes to develop infrastructure. Funds can be used, for example, to build new roads, enlarge airports and provide health care, social care and education for local people.

Negative economic impacts

Travel and tourism can also have negative economic impacts. These include:

- **inflation**: this happens when shop prices and the cost of living for local people in destinations increase. Tourists sometimes have more money than local people and spend more money in destination shops. The demand for goods sold by shops, such as food and clothing, increases. As demand increases, so do prices. This is inflation.

- **economic leakage**: this is when money from travel and tourism that has come into a country then leaves (or leaks from) the country again. There can be **import leakage** and **export leakage**:

  - Import leakage happens when travel and tourism providers spend money on goods

---

KEY WORDS

multiplier effect: how wealth is created from tourist spending

inflation: when prices and the cost of living increase

economic leakage: when money from travel and tourism leaves (or leaks from) a country

import leakage: when tourists are supplied with goods, such as food and drink, that have to be imported. Imports cost money that is lost, or leaked, from the country's economy

export leakage: when destination organisations such as hotels are foreign-owned. Profits are exported from the destination country

---

imported from abroad instead of buying goods locally. For example, some hotels import expensive food and drink from abroad.

- Export leakage can happen if hotels in a destination are owned by travel and tourism organisations that are based in other countries. Profits made by some destination hotels go to foreign-owned businesses. Profits leak abroad. by leaving the country.

- Seasonal employment is a problem because some travel and tourism staff do not have jobs in the low season. During the high season, demand is high.

> ### KEY WORDS
>
> opportunity costs: when choices are made. The opportunity cost is the loss of the chance to do something because something else has been chosen instead. For example, the opportunity to expand an airport can be lost if the government decides to spend the money on new roads instead
>
> over-dependence: when a destination depends too much on travel and tourism

High demand creates jobs in destinations. There are more high-season jobs in travel and tourism businesses and more jobs in other businesses, such as local shops. For example, hotels, restaurants and visitor attractions employ more staff during the high season. People lose their jobs during the low season.

- Opportunity costs happen when management decisons are made in destinations. An opportunity cost is the loss of the chance to do something because of deciding to do something else instead. For example, the opportunity to build new schools for local people can be lost if the government decides to spend the money on expanding the international airport instead.

- Over-dependence happens when a destination relies too much on travel and tourism. The destination economy depends too much on income from travel and tourism. Jobs and money will be lost from the destination if fewer tourists visit and the standard of living of local people may decrease. Fewer tourists may decide to visit a destination after a natural disaster such as a volcanic eruption.

Rose explains the negative economic impacts of travel and tourism in **Figure 2.16**.

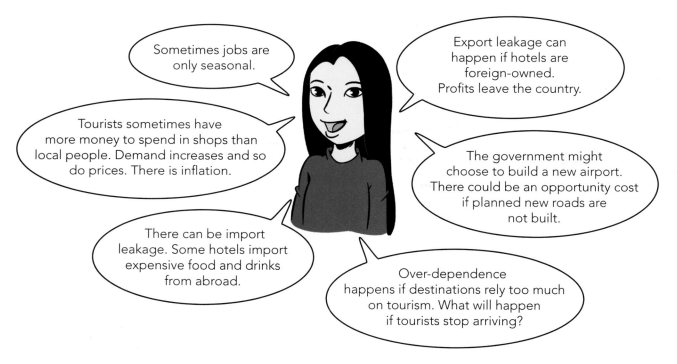

Figure 2.16: Rose explains the negative economic impacts of travel and tourism

CASE STUDY

Figure 2.17: Beach vendors in Negril

Jesse in Jamaica

Jesse and his family visit Jamaica on holiday every two or three years. Jesse's family like to stay in Negril. Negril is a coastal destination in the west of Jamaica. Jesse's family stay in an **all-inclusive** resort hotel. The hotel is owned by a foreign company, although most of the staff are Jamaican.

Jesse's mother is originally from Jamaica and likes to visit her sister (Jesse's aunt), who still lives on the island. Jesse and his family try to be responsible tourists and try to make a positive economic impact. The family enjoy visiting local restaurants. Jesse's family like to buy souvenirs from beach vendors (see **Figure 2.17**).

Questions

1   Identify two reasons for Jesse's family visits to Jamaica.

2   Describe ways in which Jesse's family behave as responsible tourists.

3   Explain the positive economic impacts of Jesse's family visits to Jamaica.

4   Discuss the possible negative economic impacts of Jesse's family visits to Jamaica.

5   *Extension:* Evaluate the extent to which Jesse's family's visit to Jamaica shows an overall positive impact of tourism.

KEY WORD

all-inclusive: resorts or hotels provide a wide range of products and services on one site. Customers often make just one advance payment

TIPS

- To explain tourism's positive economic impacts, think beyond just jobs and money. Think about the multiplier effect, infrastructure development, GDP and wealth creation.

- The economic impacts of travel and tourism on one destination are partly positive and partly negative. Remember that impacts can be both positive and negative.

KEY CONCEPT LINKS

- Travel and tourism has economic impacts on destinations. Economic impacts can be positive and negative. Tourism is sustainable when impacts on destinations and people are positive. Positive impacts protect the environment and ways of life of people into the future.

- Responsible tourists behave in ways that bring positive economic impacts to destinations and local people.

ACTIVITY 2.7

1 Identify the positive economic impacts of travel and tourism on destinations.

2 Explain the negative impacts of travel and tourism on destinations.

3 Research an example of an all-inclusive resort hotel holiday.

Describe the products and services that are charged within the inclusive price.

Outline any examples of other charges customers may pay for optional extra products and services.

4 As a class, discuss the positive and negative economic impacts of all-inclusive resorts on destinations.

Create a display to show the results of your class discussion.

REFLECTION

What methods could you use to research and analyse different views about all-inclusive hotels? Why?

Positive environmental impacts

Travel and tourism has positive environmental impacts and negative environmental impacts. The Okavango Delta case study *(Delta tourism – threat or protector?)* is about the environmental impacts of travel and tourism.

Rose thinks that travel and tourism can be good for the environment. She outlines some positive impacts of travel and tourism in **Figure 2.18**.

The positive environmental impacts of travel and tourism include investment in the environment. Money is invested by travel and tourism organisations and by destination management organisations to protect and improve the natural and built environment. Money for investment in the environment is from the profits of travel and tourism organisations and from the tax income of government destination management organisations. Investment in the environment is used for:

Figure 2.18: Rose identifies positive environmental impacts of travel and tourism

- the conservation and regeneration of natural and built environment **assets**, such as:
  - wildlife, natural landscape features (for example, beaches, waterfalls, rivers and lakes) and biodiversity in destinations such as wetlands and coral reefs
  - historic buildings, monuments and destinations of special architectural or cultural interest.
- responsible tourism education and increased environmental awareness programmes for tourists and for travel and tourism organisation staff.

KEY WORD

assets: valued things. Assets of the natural environment include wildlife, landscape features such as waterfalls and the biodiversity of places like wetlands and coral reefs. Built assets include monuments, interesting buildings and historic architecture. Natural and built assets can add to the appeal of destinations

The work of tourism organisations in destinations, including destination management organisations, includes visitor management. Tourism organisations try to ensure that the numbers of visitors to destinations and attractions is within the carrying capacity. For example, limiting visitor numbers to destinations where the natural and built environment is fragile can help regeneration investment to succeed.

Negative environmental impacts

Negative environmental impacts of travel and tourism are shown in **Figure 2.19**. Air, water and noise pollution are negative effects of travel and tourism on the natural and built environment. Air, land and sea transport – including aircraft, motor vehicles and ships – pollute the atmosphere, rives, seas and lakes. Transport for travel also causes noise. Tourism traffic creates congestion in destinations, which spoils the environmental appeal of destinations for tourists.

Tourism facilities, including hotels, produce waste, and the disposal of waste uses pollution. Tourism facilities such as hotels use resources like food, energy and water. Overtourism can cause a depletion or shortage of resources

such as water. Litter is a negative impact of overtourism, spoiling the appeal of destinations and causing harm to flora and fauna. Wildlife may be disturbed by tourism as natural habitats can be damaged or lost from destinations where natural attraction visitor numbers are too high.

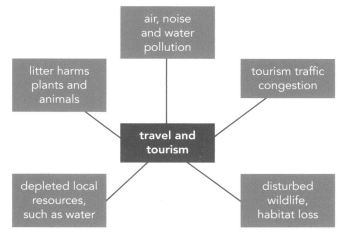

Figure 2.19: Negative environmental impacts of travel and tourism

CASE STUDY

Delta tourism: threat or protector?

Does tourism to the Okavango Delta threaten or protect the environment?

The Okavango Delta is an inland wetlands destination in Botswana, a country in southern Africa. Tourist accommodation in the Okavango Delta includes lodges such as the one in the photograph.

Tourist activities in the Okavango Delta include game drives, safari walks, traditional *mokoro* canoe cruises and horse riding. Wildlife species in the Okavango Delta include elephant, giraffe, zebra, hippopotamus, crocodile, rhinoceros, leopard and antelope. There is also a wide variety of fish and birds.

Many tourists travel to the Okavango Delta by air. There are international flights from Johannesburg in South Africa to Maun, which is the gateway town to the Okavango Delta area.

Figure 2.20: A tourist lodge in the Okavango Delta

Tourism brings threats and protections to the Okavango Delta environment. One of the main threats is pollution. For example, the disposal of waste water from tourist lodges, hotels and camps could damage the wetlands ecosystem.

CONTINUED

Botswana Tourism is the national tourism organisation (NTO) for Botswana. Botswana Tourism's Ecotourism Certification Programme sets standards for ecotourism accommodation in the Okavango Delta. Eco-friendly features of tourist accommodation in the Okavango Delta are as follows:

- Developments are small to help protect the assets of the natural environment.

- Local sustainable building materials include wood from surrounding trees and grass for thatched roofs.

- Trees used for wood are replaced.

- Drinking water is filtered from channels in the Delta.

- Solar panels are used to generate electricity and to heat water in an environmentally clean and quiet way.

- Waste is separated:

  - Organic waste is buried to keep it away from local fauna (animals)

  - Plastic, glass, metal and paper waste is sent to Maun for recycling.

- Locally grown organic food reduces the carbon footprint.

- Online ecotourism education and training for staff raises environmental awareness.

Questions

1 Explain why some tourists choose to visit the Okavango Delta.

2 Suggest **two** negative environmental impacts of travel and tourism to the Okavango Delta.

3 Discuss how the eco-friendly features of accommodation in the Okavango Delta reduce the negative environmental impacts of travel and tourism.

4 Make a poster to show how eco-friendly features of tourist developments can bring positive impacts to the environment.

KEY WORDS

game drive: a drive in an open 4 x 4 vehicle to view wildlife in its natural habitat

safari walks: an overland journey to view wildlife in its natural habitat

carbon footprint: the amount of carbon dioxide pollution produced by the activities of a person or organisation

TIPS

- Remember that travel and tourism's environmental impacts can be positive as well as negative.

- People have different views and attitudes about the impacts of travel and tourism. You need to understand the differing views even if you do not agree with them.

KEY CONCEPT LINKS

- Travel and tourism has been growing for many years. More tourists have been travelling more often and greater distances to more destinations.

- Travel and tourism affects the environment. As travel and tourism has grown, impacts on the environment have also increased. Some travel and tourism environmental impacts are positive, whereas others are negative.

- Travel and tourism organisations try to maximise positive environmental impacts and minimise negative environmental impacts.

Visitor management in some destinations includes using tourist quotas to limit the number of visitors. Venice is a city destination in Italy with many built assets. Quotas have been used in Venice to protect precious historic buildings. Other destinations where quotas have been used or considered include the Galapagos Islands, Barcelona and Bhutan.

1   Work as a pair to research **two** of these destinations:

   a   Where are they?

   b   What are they like?

   c   Why might they have quotas?

Discuss with your partner whether or not your two destinations should have quotas, and why.

2   Compile a report to show your research and discussion results.

   Remember to include the sources you used to collect your information.

3   *Project:* Choose a destination. Work with a partner to investigate the positive and negative impacts of travel and tourism in your chosen destination. Make a presentation showing:

   •   the positive and negative impacts of travel and tourism on the destination you have chosen

   •   your conclusion to the question, 'Is it true that travel and tourism has equally positive and negative impacts on destinations?'

Give your presentation to an audience, such as the rest of the class.

Be an active audience participant for another group's or class member's project presentation.

KEY WORD

quota: a limit to the number of visitors allowed in a destination or attraction

REFLECTION

Think about your investigation into the positive and negative impacts of the destination you chose

Discuss what you have learnt:

•   What do you think was good about the way you did your investigation?

•   What could you do to improve the way in which you did your investigation?

•   Do you think it likely that your investigation's conclusion would be true for all destinations? Explain your answer.

Positive sociocultural impacts

The sociocultural impacts of travel and tourism are the effects that it has on people and their way of life. *The towers of Kaiping* case study shows both positive and negative impacts of travel and tourism.

Positive sociocultural impacts of travel and tourism include the following:

•   Tourism helps to preserve the traditional arts and crafts of destinations such as Kaiping.

•   Money from tourism can be invested to provide community facilities for local people in destinations.

•   Tourists and local people are educated about the natural and built environment of destinations.

•   There is increased cultural understanding as tourists and people from local and indigenous communities meet each other.

•   Local people feel greater cultural pride in their destination and their way of life.

Negative sociocultural impacts

Travel and tourism can have negative sociocultural impacts. These include:

•   changes in the traditional way of life of local and indigenous people in destinations, such as:

   •   changes in family structure, for example, in island destinations, some young people move away from traditional inland homes to live and work in tourism in beach destinations

- loss of traditional employment in jobs such as fishing, forestry and farming

- social change, for example, destination populations become increasingly young and culturally diverse as young people seek jobs in travel and tourism, and retired people are attracted to live in tourist destinations.

- loss of national identity as local traditions and cultures are lost to more globalised identities

- the demonstration effect, which occurs when local people in a destination copy the dress and behaviour of visiting tourists, causing national identity loss when the dress and behaviour of inbound tourists is copied

- an increase in criminal activity as tourists are targeted by thieves and other criminals

- culture clashes, when the dress and behaviour of tourists conflicts with that of local people

- commodification in travel and tourism is when local culture is treated as a product or commodity to be sold to tourists. Traditional performances of dance and music by local people may be packaged for tourist consumption. For example, a dance that may traditionally have been performed only for special occasions may be presented as a spectacle of evening entertainment at an all-inclusive resort hotel. The dancers may earn some money and tourists may enjoy the show. However, there is a negative impact if the importance of traditions has been debased. Long-term local culture may be damaged or devalued.

KEY WORDS

demonstration effect: when the people living in a destination copy the behaviour of visiting tourists

culture clash: conflict between people because of differences in values, beliefs or ways of life

commodification: in travel and tourism, when local culture is treated as a product or commodity to be sold to tourists

CASE STUDY

The Towers of Kaiping

Kaiping is a destination in Guandong Province in south-east China. China is a large country in Asia. Kaiping is a rural area with villages and more than 1,000 unusual towers called *diaolou* (see photo). The Kaiping *diaolou* are a World Heritage Site (WHS) and appeal to tourists.

Kaiping's towers were built in the early 20th century. The owners were Chinese people who had worked abroad and come back to China to live in the towers they built. The towers have different designs: some towers copy Islamic architecture; some have European designs. All the towers were homes with several stories (levels). The tower shape was chosen because the area around Kaiping can be flooded by water from the Pearl River. The *diaolou* also protected people from attack, as the early 20th century was a period of political instability and war in China.

The Kaiping *diaolou* and villages became a World Heritage Site in 2007. Tourism to the destination of Kaiping increased after this.

Figure 2.21: A *diaolou* tower

Cultural tourists are attracted by the unusual history and architecture of the *diaolou*. The lives of the local village people were changed by the sociocultural impacts of tourism. Until 2007, local people farmed the land around the villages, but nowadays young people often move away to work in towns.

CONTINUED

Tourists buy tickets to visit the *diaolou*, with villagers receiving a share of the ticket money. Some local people have started businesses selling food and souvenirs to tourists. Some of the sociocultural impacts of tourism on the people who live in Kaiping's villages are shown in **Table 2.4**.

Positive impacts	Negative impacts
Jobs for local people, such as in tourism businesses, in security and in cleaning, and help young people to continue living locally. Local people opening businesses such as restaurants, food stalls, guiding and souvenir-selling helps to preserve traditional arts and crafts and increases cultural pride. Road and house improvements and providing local community facilities help to reduce social change. More leisure time for local people helps young people to remain living locally and reduces social change.	Some villagers have abandoned farmland, so fewer crops are grown and a traditional way of life is lost. Some young people's career opportunities are reduced. Young people sometimes have the chance of promotion when they move to towns for jobs. Crime rates are at risk of rising. The demonstration effect: some local people have copied some tourists' bad behaviour and foreign clothes so there is a degree of loss of national identity.

Table 2.4: Sociocultural impacts of tourism in Kaiping

KEY WORD

cultural pride: when local people are proud of the destination where they live, and proud of their local heritage, traditions and culture

Local people have different views about the sociocultural impacts of tourism. Opinions differ. Some views are positive and some are negative, while others have mixed views (see **Figure 2.22**).

Questions

1 a Describe the appeal of Kaiping as a destination.

 b Make a poster or flyer to promote Kaiping's *diaolou* as a tourist attraction.

2 a Suggest some types of tourists who are likely to be attracted to Kaiping.

 b Explain your suggestions.

3 Work with a partner to:

 a explain the positive and negative sociocultural impacts of tourism on people in Kaiping.

 b discuss why young people from Kaiping may have different views about the sociocultural impacts of tourism.

4 As a class, debate one of the following:

 whether the growth of tourism in Kaiping has been good or bad for local people, **or** whether or not becoming part of a WHS has been good for the people of Kaiping's villages.

We have more money now. We no longer think about money first. We argue less and care more about each other and the community. Profits leave the country.

Some people have made money and are less willing to work hard. Others have not made much money and feel unhappy.

We have lost some of our own **cultural identity**, but we understand people from different cultures better.

Figure 2.22: Local views about tourism's sociocultural impacts

KEY WORD

cultural identity: the sense of belonging that people have. People like to feel that they belong to a group of people like them

TIPS

- Remember, people feel that identities are important. Think about how identities can be linked to people's nationality, to ethnicity, to religion, to social class, to generation or to locality.

- Understand that conflicts caused by culture clashes may not be violent. People may peacefully dislike or peacefully disagree with how some tourists dress and behave.

KEY CONCEPT LINKS

- The impacts of travel and tourism can be positive and negative. These impacts can be sociocultural, environmental or economic. Socially sustainable tourism tries to manage the sociocultural impacts of travel and tourism to protect the future of people and their communities.

- People have different views and attitudes about increased tourism. Some people view increased tourism as being good for destination communities. Others have a negative attitude about the sociocultural effects of travel and tourism. People's opinions on the sociocultural impacts of travel and tourism can also be mixed.

ACTIVITY 2.9

1 Identify positive and negative sociocultural impacts of travel and tourism. Some of these impacts are shown in **Table 2.4**.

2 In a group, discuss how you think tourism can have these impacts:

   a Preserving a destination's traditional arts and crafts

   b Providing local community facilities for people, such as libraries, sports facilities and social centres

   c Educating local people and tourists

   d Changing the level of crime in a destination.

   Present the results of your discussion to the rest of the class.

   Listen to or read the presentations of other groups. Take notes and ask questions.

3 *Project:* Investigate the demonstration effect further.

   As a class, choose a range of destinations. Evaluate how much of a problem the demonstration effect might be in your chosen destinations.

   Report your findings.

EXAM-STYLE QUESTIONS

1 Refer to **Figure 4**, which gives information about Trinidad and Tobago's Revised National Tourism Policy.

The Ministry of Tourism wants to hear from you! We have been revising the National Tourism Policy (2010) and the first draft of the revised policy (2020–2030) is now ready for public comment.

Recognising the resilience and dynamic nature of the tourism industry, Trinidad and Tobago must now reposition itself to recover and advance its tourism sector to support national recovery and a post-COVID-19 growth agenda. In this way, through the multiplier effect, the country will gain benefits such as:

- job creation and employment

- foreign exchange earnings

- tax and other income generation

- foreign investment

- cultural preservation

- preservation of natural assets, demand for local agriculture

- manufactured goods, art and entertainment products

- creating opportunities for innovation in art, business and science.

In a post-COVID-19 world, tourism will continue to play a significant role; however, as with all other sectors, aspects of the business operations will have to be altered. Travel, tourism and hospitality services will rebound, as they did post 9/11 and after the 2008–2009 global economic crisis.

Figure 4: Revised National Tourism Policy, Trinidad and Tobago

a **Identify two** positive economic impacts which the Ministry of Tourism hopes will result from the repositioning of Trinidad and Tobago's tourism sector.   **[2]**

b **Describe** how the outbreak of a disease such as COVID-19 causes a major reduction in tourism demand.   **[2]**

c The Government of Trinidad and Tobago hopes that the Ministry of Tourism's Revised National Tourism Policy will create a multiplier effect on the nation's economy.

Explain how producers of **each** of the following might receive economic benefits from the growth of tourism:

- local agriculture

- locally manufactured goods.   **[4]**

CONTINUED

d Many destinations, such as Trinidad and Tobago, want to preserve their natural assets. **Discuss two** ways in which the creation and operation of national parks will be likely to help secure the protection of the natural environment. [6]

e The development and expansion of tourism can have significant negative economic impacts on particular destinations. **Evaluate** the roles played by leakages and opportunity costs in generating negative economic impacts. [6]

[Total 20 marks]

2 Refer to **Figure 5**, which gives information about the Grand Canyon National Park in Arizona, USA.

Welcome to Grand Canyon National Park!

For many, a visit to Grand Canyon is a once-in-a-lifetime opportunity, and we hope you find the following pages useful for trip planning. Whether this is your first visit or your tenth, this planner can help you to design the trip of your dreams.

As we welcome over six million visitors a year to Grand Canyon, your safety is of the utmost importance to us. We want you to have an enjoyable and memorable visit, but most importantly we want you to have a safe visit.

Our knowledgeable rangers can help to perfect any itinerary you put together, and ensure that you leave with happy memories. Exploring any park, Grand Canyon included, can have some dangers. Be sure you are drinking enough water if hiking. Look down to see where your feet are; we know the views are breathtaking, but don't forget to keep a safe distance from the rim of the Canyon.

The highest point in Grand Canyon National Park, at 8,803 feet (2,683 m), Point Imperial is also the most northern boundary of the park. From here, visitors have views of the Painted Desert and the eastern end of Grand Canyon. It is from this area that the canyon transforms from the narrow walls of Marble Canyon, visible only as a winding gash, to a more open and dramatic 'grand' canyon.

Park entrance fees

Fees collected support projects in the park. Admission to the park is $35 per private vehicle; $30 per motorcycle; and $20 per person entering the park via Grand Canyon Railway, park shuttle bus, private rafting trip, walking, or riding a bicycle. The pass can be used for seven days and includes both rims. Pay fees at park entrance stations or at some businesses outside the park.

Source: Adapted from www.nps.gov/grca

Figure 5: Information for visitors to the Grand Canyon National Park

a Identify the **two** prominent landscape features which can be seen from Point Imperial. [2]

b With reference to **Figure 5**, describe **two** threats to visitor safety when visiting the Grand Canyon National Park. [2]

c **Figure 6** is a photograph of a signpost to Cameron Trading Post, one of the businesses located just outside the Grand Canyon National Park.

CONTINUED

Explain **two** ways in which the Cameron Trading Post is likely to appeal to tourists visiting the Grand Canyon National Park. [4]

d The Grand Canyon National Park attracts over six million visitors and some locations such as the Point Imperial viewpoint are at risk from overtourism. Discuss **two** negative environmental impacts associated with over tourism at such sites. [6]

e Evaluate the extent to which a culture clash and loss of cultural identity are, in some destinations, significant negative sociocultural impacts resulting from tourism. [6]

Figure 6: Signpost to Cameron Trading Post business

[Total 20 marks]

3 Refer to **Figure 7**, information about tourism in Barcelona, Spain.

Barcelona is the capital of the Catalonia region in Spain and one of Europe's most popular city destinations for international tourism. This is reflected in the relatively high occupancy rates of the city's hotels, which cater for some nine million visitors to the destination. Passenger numbers passing through Barcelona's airport have more than doubled since 2000 and cruise ships now bring over three million additional tourists to this important port of call.

Although most visitors travel for leisure purposes, about one fifth of all arrivals are business travellers. The city is very popular with younger adults. Surveys show that 25–34-year-olds are the main market demographic. Barcelona's appeal as a travel destination is based on its Mediterranean climate, sandy beaches, interesting cultural sites, famous architecture, restaurants and varied nightlife. The city's proximity to other Mediterranean coastal resorts therefore makes a visit to Barcelona an ideal excursion for summer tourists in Spain.

Figure 7: Information about tourism in Barcelona

CONTINUED

a   Identify the following:

   • Barcelona's main market demographic

   • The number of visitors to Barcelona Zoo.   [2]

b   Barcelona, with its sandy beaches and Mediterranean climate, attracts leisure tourists interested
   in outdoor recreational activities. **State one** such outdoor recreational activity and describe how it is
   influenced by the weather conditions.   [2]

c   **Figure 7** indicates that Barcelona appeals to different types of tourists. Photographs A, B, C and
   D were taken by different types of visitor to the city.

   Identify the photograph most likely to have been taken by **each** of the following named visitor types:

   • a family on an excursion to Barcelona from a nearby resort looking for a fun day out

   • a young person in Barcelona attending a festival

   • a business tourist looking at possible conference locations

   • cultural tourists visiting the city's historic landmarks.   [4]

Photograph A

Photograph B

Photograph C

Photograph D

CONTINUED

d The central areas of cities – which are important tourist destinations – can suffer from congestion during the high season. Discuss **two** effective ways in which central city areas can be managed in order to reduce congestion. [6]

e Many international tourists staying in destinations such as Barcelona will visit a tourist information centre during their stay. Evaluate the types of information and advice which these centres are able to provide. [6]

[**Total 20 marks**]

4 Refer to **Figure 8**, a review of Cape Town's V&A Waterfront project.

In November 1988, the Victoria and Alfred Waterfront (Pty) Ltd was established as a wholly owned subsidiary by Transnet Ltd. Its aim was to redevelop the historic docklands around the Victoria and Alfred Basins as a mixed-use area with a focus on retail, tourism and residential development and a working harbour at its centre.

The V&A Waterfront project has been very successful in transforming the underutilised historic part of the Port of Cape Town. There has been a sustained growth in visitor numbers over the years, and the V&A Waterfront has now become one of Africa's most visited destinations, with an average of over of 20 million people each year since 1997. Today, the V&A Waterfront is a 123-hectare mixed-use development, which caters for both local and international visitors, offering everything from residential and commercial property, hotels and retail districts to extensive dining, leisure, recreational open spaces and entertainment facilities.

With regard to retaining the area's unique working waterfront character, the authenticity of the working harbour and historic nature of the V&A Waterfront have been key factors in avoiding a 'theme park' development: Cape Town's Waterfront is a real place. The project was environmentally and culturally sensitive by the adaptive reuse of historic old dock buildings, thus creating a special character and ambience for the destination. For example, the Victorian gothic-style Clock Tower, an icon of the old Cape Town Harbour, is now a small retail centre.

What was a loss-making asset for the landowner of the Port of Cape Town in 1988 has, under the stewardship of the Victoria and Albert Waterfront (Pty) Ltd, become a vibrant and profitable property development project that enjoys a high international profile. The organisation has been responsible for the planning, development and management of the V&A Waterfront project in Cape Town since its inception.

Figure 8: Cape Town's V&A Waterfront project

a With reference to **Figure 8** describe why the V&A Waterfront development can be referred to as being 'a mixed-use area'. [2]

b The V&A Waterfront project is an example of the ways in which a destination can sustainably develop and grow. Describe **one** way in which the project has supported social enterprise development. [2]

c With reference to Photograph E, explain **two** ways in which the Waterfront development has been made visitor-friendly. [4]

CONTINUED

d The Victoria and Alfred Waterfront (Pty) Ltd is the organisation involved in the development and management of the project. Discuss **two** ways in which the project has had a positive environmental impact on Cape Town's waterfront. [6]

e Visitors to Cape Town's V&A Waterfront will have the opportunity to go on a 'marine eco tour'. Evaluate how going on such a tour is likely to increase both visitors' awareness and concern for the environment and of the need for its conservation and protection. [6]

Photograph E

[Total 20 marks]

5 Refer to **Figure 9**, a press release about the Ninki Nanka Trail in The Gambia.

The Republic of The Gambia, commonly referred to as 'the smiling coast of Africa', is situated in the western region of Africa. It has a land area of 11,295 sq. km with an estimated population of two million. The agriculturally fertile country, dominated by farming, fishing and tourism, has its capital in Banjul.

The Gambia Tourism Board, in collaboration with the Institute of Travel and Tourism of The Gambia and the Youth Empowerment Project, have launched the much-awaited Ninki Nanka Trail. This product is in marked contrast to 'sun, sand and sea' packaged tourism, and builds on the untapped potential of the River Gambia.

It is aimed largely at the adventure traveller and other special interest groups, such as cultural tourists and ecotourists. The trail provides a well-rounded visitor experience through a combination of river-based and overland excursions. Furthermore, the trail offers visitors a meaningful interaction with local people through this community-based tourism initiative. It will also enable visitors to discover the variety of Gambian natural and cultural heritage whilst experiencing the important oral legend of the Ninki Nanka dragon. According to tradition, the Ninki Nanka lives in the swamps along the banks of the River Gambia. The animal is said to be extremely large and very dangerous. It is said that when children disobey their parents and go to the swamps, they will be taken by the Ninki Nanka.

The trail is a responsible product which aims to spread the economic benefits of tourism to inland rural areas and to create opportunities for tourist activities to continue outside of the traditional high season. In addition, the product takes an innovative approach by engaging with private sector tour operators in tourism development. This will lead to poverty reduction in accordance with the concepts of shared values and the principles of responsible tourism. Such an approach will help in creating better places to live and therefore better places to visit.

CONTINUED

The Gambia Tourism Board, in partnership with the International Trade Centre through the EU-funded Youth Empowerment Project, has provided support in terms of product development, marketing and skills training in hospitality. This type of responsible tourism and community-based tourism will improve local ownership, sustainability, quality, safety and management.

Source: Adapted from www.voicegambia.com

Figure 9: A press release about the Ninki Nanka Trail in The Gambia

a   Identify **two** types of special interest tourist the Ninki Nanka Trail is intended to attract. [2]

b   The Gambia Tourism Board is one of the organisations involved in the development of the Ninki Nanka Trail. With reference to **Figure 9**, describe its role in the project. [2]

c   Many destinations, such as The Gambia in West Africa, face a variety of threats to their tourism industry. State **two** such threats and in **each** case explain why it is associated with a drop in tourism demand. [4]

d   Discuss **two** of the ways in which host communities along the River Gambia might benefit from the Ninki Nanka Trail. [6]

e   Tour operators will offer Ninki Nanka Trail excursions to their clients. Evaluate the ways in which tour operators, such as those working in partnership with The Gambia Tourism Board, can provide education about and promote an awareness of sustainable tourism to visiting tourists. [6]

[Total 20 marks]

6   Refer to **Figure 10**, a sample visitor 'Code of Conduct' produced by the Tanzania Ministry of Natural Resources and Tourism.

Welcome to _____.

Please remember that you are a welcome guest. Please enjoy our natural environment, culture, and warm hospitality.

To make your visit more pleasurable, make sure you do the following:

- Do ask us if we would like to have our pictures taken, and remember to send us a copy.

- Do buy our goods and handicrafts and remember to bargain with a smile.

- Do help us to preserve our natural environment, by:

  - putting trash into proper bins

  - looking at our beautiful plants and flowers without taking them

  - enjoying our wildlife without feeding them

  - enjoying our coral reefs and marine life without touching or taking anything.

CONTINUED

- Do help us to preserve our historical and cultural heritage by:
  - resisting the temptation to remove objects or to alter monuments or ruins
  - refusing to buy historical artefacts, such as coins and pottery.
- Do bask in the sun on our beautiful beaches, and remember to cover up when venturing into the village or town.
- Do ask us if you may enter our homes or gardens.
- Do resist giving money or gifts to individuals, unless it is a tip for excellent service.
- Do contribute. If you desire, to our Community Development Fund. Boxes for contributions can be found at _____.
- Do feel safe when walking around, but remember to leave your valuables at the hotel or guest house.
- Do ask to see our schools and dispensary, and give us advice on how to improve them.
- Do sign our guestbook and make suggestions on how we can be better hosts.
- And one thing you must never do: **don't forget** to tell your family and friends about your wonderful visit to _____!

Figure 10: A code of conduct for visitors to Tanzania

a   Identify **two** negative environmental impacts caused by visitors to Tanzania. [2]

b   With reference to **Figure 10**, describe how visitors could help Tanzania to reduce the social problems of crime and begging. [2]

c   In many destinations there are historic sites and attractions such as museums which will have important artefacts on display. Explain **two** ways in which such locations can prevent visitors causing damage to the items on display. [4]

d   Many types of visitor attractions are able to earn additional revenue from business tourism customers. Discuss **two** ways in which some visitor attractions are likely to provide services to meet the needs of business customers. [6]

e   A variety of negative impacts can result when large 'all-inclusive' resorts are established in the coastal areas of less economically developed destinations. Evaluate how both the local economy and the local environment may suffer negative impacts. [6]

[Total 20 marks]

SELF-EVALUATION CHECKLIST

After studying this unit, copy and complete this table.

I am now able to:	Needs more work	Almost there	Ready to move on
understand factors affecting the scale of global tourism demand.			
explain reasons for the growth of sustainable tourism.			
understand features of destinations and their appeal to different types of tourists.			
explain the role of organisations involved in the development and management of destinations.			
understand factors affecting tourism development and management.			
evaluate the economic, environmental and sociocultural impacts of travel and tourism.			
discuss sustainable practices in destinations.			

> Unit 3
Travel and tourism organisations

LEARNING INTENTIONS

In this unit you will learn how to:

- discuss tourism organisations, their sustainable practices, the products and services they provide and their appeal

- understand ways travel and tourism organisations work together

- explain the appeal of different types of transport

- explain sustainable developments in travel and transport

- evaluate domestic and international travel and transport infrastructure.

TRAVEL AND TOURISM IN CONTEXT

Olympic city

The Olympic Games is a major international sporting event, which take place every four years. **Figure 3.1** shows some early 21st century summer Olympic Games host cities. The summer Olympic Games are the main Olympic Games. There are also Winter Olympic Games and the Youth Olympic Games.

People travel from all around the world to see the Olympic Games. Many Olympic Games spectators are tourists. These visitors travel to the Olympic host city and use local transport to travel around the host city area.

Figure 3.2 shows sustainable travel and transport provided for the 2024 Olympic Games in Paris, which is the biggest city destination in France.

Tourists from around the world travel to be spectators at major international sporting events such as the Olympic Games. Many tourists use air transport. International airports are often located several kilometres away from city centres. International airports for Paris are Charles de Gaulle, Orly and, for budget flights, Beauvais. Transport links between international airports and host cities are important for spectator tourists. Most 2024 Olympic Games events will be in the host city. Spectator tourists need to transfer (travel) to the city to see events and also need to reach their accommodation.

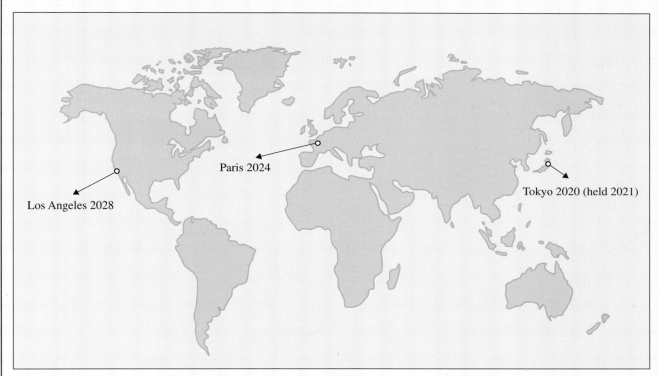

Figure 3.1: Summer Olympic Games host cities in the early 21st century

KEY WORDS

host city: a city where a major event is happening

spectators: people who watch an event

international airports: airports with flights to and from other countries

CONTINUED

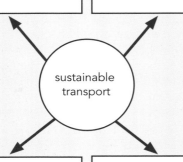

| 100% of spectators travelling to events by **public transport**, by cycle or by walking | free public transport (including buses, trams and trains) for Olympic Games ticket-holders |
| high-speed trains linking Paris to other capital cities in Europe and to most other big cities in France | zero-emission buses |

sustainable transport

Figure 3.2: Sustainable transport for the 2024 Paris Olympics.

Tourism organisations provide products and services for tourists visiting Olympic host cities. For example:

- Spectators stay in accommodation provided by travel and tourism organisations, often in hotels.

- Restaurants provide spectator tourists with food and drink.

- Some tourism organisations provide **ancillary services**, such as tour guiding, cycle hire and **currency exchange**.

Host cities have visitor attractions that appeal to tourists, who will usually visit attractions in the host city. Visitor attractions are provided by tourism organisations; in the Paris area these include the Eiffel Tower (see photo), the Louvre Museum and the Disneyland Paris theme park.

Tourists visiting destinations for major events such as the 2024 Paris Olympics may choose to buy a tour package from a travel agent. Travel agents sell packages provided by tour operators – travel

and tourism organisations that provide packages. Packages include holiday or tour **components**, such as transport and accommodation within one product. A typical tour package to a major event such as the 2024 Paris Olympics includes flights, transfers, event tickets, hotel accommodation and visits to attractions.

Figure 3.3: Olympic rings and the Eiffel Tower, Paris

KEY WORDS

budget flights: sometimes called no-frills flights, these are cheaper, **low-cost** flights. Budget flight ticket prices do not include certain services such as **in-flight** food and drink

low-cost flights: budget flights. Low-cost flights do not include additional passenger services (frills) in the ticket price

in-flight: describes passenger services provided by airlines during aircraft flights. In-flight services include food and drink and entertainment such as movies

transfer: travel between a transport hub or gateway, such as an airport, and a destination

public transport: transport available for anyone to use. Buses, trams and trains are examples of public transport

CONTINUED

KEY WORDS

ancillary services: extra support services. Travel and tourism ancillary services include tour guiding, car and cycle hire and currency exchange

components: parts of a package holiday or package tour. Examples of package components are travel and accommodation

currency exchange: changing the cash used in one country into the cash used in another. For example, an American tourist visiting Paris may change US dollars into euros

Questions

1   Identify **six** types of tourism organisations providing products and services to tourists visiting the 2024 Paris Olympics.

2   Outline different types of sustainable transport tourists could use for airport transfers.

3   Explain why event spectators may also choose to visit attractions in the host city.

4   Research some visitor attractions in Paris. Make a poster or flyer to promote them to event spectators.

5   **a**   Find out the next host city for a major international sporting event, such as:

     i   Winter Olympic Games

     ii   Olympic Games (after Paris 2024)

     iii   FIFA World Cup and FIFA Women's World Cup

     iv   Women's Cricket World Cup and Men's Cricket World Cup.

   b   Choose one major international sporting event other than the 2024 Paris Olympics. Discuss the tourism organisations that could be involved in planning a visit to the event from your home country or another country.

6   ***Extension:*** Assess how hosting the Olympic Games can help the development of sustainable tourism in host cities such as Paris.

3.1 The role of tourism organisations

Introduction

The travel and tourism industry includes organisations that are:

- travel organisations, such as airlines, train companies and cruise operators

- tourism organisations, including travel agents, tour operators, accommodation providers, food and drink providers, visitor attractions and ancillary service providers.

Table 3.1 summarises the various types of tourism organisations. These organisations are described in more detail after **Table 3.1**.

Figure 3.4: A travel agent is an example of a tourism organisation

Types of tourism organisations	Products and services
Travel agents	Travel agents sell the products and services that other tourism organisations provide, including ancillary services. Travel agents can be: • retail shops • online businesses, using websites or social media • specialists in one type of tourism, such as business tourism or independent travel.
Tour operators	Tour operators organise travel and tourism packages. Package holidays are made up of components (parts), which are the products and services included in the package. Packages can be sold: • directly by a tour operator • indirectly through a travel agent. **Figure 3.5** shows examples of types of package holidays.
Accommodation providers	Accommodation is where tourists stay overnight. Examples are: • hotels • guest houses, including B&Bs • hostels • homestays • camping • serviced apartments. **Figure 3.6** gives more details about classes of accommodation.
Food and drink providers	Examples of food and drink providers are: • restaurants • cafés • street food vendors (sellers) • takeaways (takeouts).
Visitor attractions	Visitor attractions appeal to tourists. Visitor attractions can be: • natural, such as beaches and waterfalls • built, such as museums and theme parks • events, such as sports competitions and arts festivals.
Ancillary service providers	Examples of ancillary services are: • guided tours • currency exchange • car hire and bike (bicycle) hire.

Table 3.1: Types of tourism organisation

guest house: accommodation on a small-scale, such as in a house

B&B (bed and breakfast): sleeping accommodation (room with bed) and breakfast

hostel: a basic type of accommodation. Hostels often have shared sleeping accommodation such as dormitories.

serviced apartment: a type of self-catering accommodation. Services such as cleaning are provided in serviced apartments.

Types of tourism organisation are as follows:

Travel agents

Travel agents sell products and services that other travel and tourism organisations provide. Products sold by travel agents include air, ferry and rail tickets. Travel agents also sell package holidays, cruises and travel insurance. Travel insurance is an example of an ancillary service provided by travel agents. Customers of travel agents include individual tourists and businesses who offer MICE (Meetings, Incentives, Conferences, Exhibitions) business tourism.

KEY WORD

package holiday: a holiday made up of components put together and sold as one product. Typical package holiday components include travel and accommodation.

Types of travel agents include:

- retail shops, often found in shopping districts and shopping centres (malls)

- online travel agents, which use websites and social media to sell products and services to customers

- travel agents that are specialists in one type of tourism, such as in business tourism or in independent travel.

Independent tours/packages

Travel agents sell products for independent tours as well as package products. Independent travellers organise independent tours on their own. Travel agents reserve accommodation and sell travel tickets and travel insurance to independent travellers. For example, an independent traveller can use social media to reserve accommodation and buy travel tickets from an online travel agent's website.

Ancillary services

Travel agents sell ancillary services, which are extra products and services that tourist customers buy. Examples of ancillary services sold by travel agents include travel insurance, car and bicycle hire in destinations and tickets for visitor attractions and events. Currency exchange is another ancillary service provided by travel agents.

Tour operators

Tour operators organise travel and tourism packages for outbound and inbound tourism customers. Packages are made up of travel and tourism components, which are put together and sold as one product. Typical components of outbound package holidays include travel and accommodation. Packages can be sold:

- directly by a tour operator

- indirectly through a travel agent.

Tour operators provide products and services for inbound tourism customers in destinations. For example, a tour operator in Australia may organise tours for inbound tourists who are staying in Australia.

Types of package holidays

There are different types of package holidays.

- All-inclusive packages are holidays that include travel, accommodation and all meals sold as one product. All-inclusive packages are often mass market packages.

KEY WORD

mass market: relating to the total market of all customer types

- Mass market package holidays are sold to all types of customers. Tour operators provide mass market holiday packages to be sold to many customers. Examples of these packages include holidays to beach and island destinations such as Mauritius and to theme park destinations such as Orlando in Florida, USA.

- Tour operators provide specialist packages to be sold to special interest tourists. For example, a specialist tour operator may organise a luxury rail journey tour package for customers interested in trains or a specialist watersports package for sports tourism customers.

- Dynamic packages are packages organised by tour operators from components that are chosen by customers. For example, an inbound tour operator in Australia may organise a package tour for a customer who has chosen destinations to visit in Australia.

Figure 3.5 shows types of package holidays.

KEY WORD

dynamic packages: holiday packages made up of components chosen by the customer

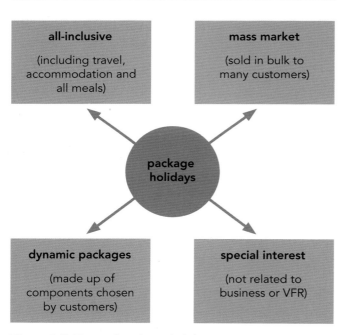

Figure 3.5: Types of package holidays

Components of different holiday packages

Tour operators make holiday packages from component parts, such as travel and accommodation. Different holiday packages are made up of different components. For example, an all-inclusive package holiday to a luxury beach hotel in Mauritius would include components that are different from a domestic tourism package for a weekend break in a city destination apartment. All-inclusive package holidays often include air travel, whereas a weekend city break may include rail travel.

Accommodation providers

Accommodation is where tourists stay overnight. Accommodation providers are tourism organisations that provide overnight-stay products and services for tourists.

Types of accommodation providers

There are many different types of accommodation provided for tourists:

- Hotels provide rooms that tourists can pay to stay in. Hotels often have restaurants to provide food and drink services to customers.

- Guest houses provide accommodation on a small scale, such as in a house. Guest houses are usually smaller buildings than hotels.

- B&Bs (bed and breakfasts) are small-scale organisations. They provide sleeping accommodation (room with bed) and breakfast.

- Hostels are a basic type of accommodation. They often have shared sleeping accommodation, such as dormitories.

- Homestay is a type of destination holiday accommodation. Homestay tourists stay in the homes of local people.

- Camping is a style of accommodation that appeals to some tourists. These visitors stay in tents or caravans. Campsites are travel and tourism organisations that provide camping accommodation and have large open spaces. Campsites often provide services such as swimming pools, sports facilities (such as tennis courts), cafés and restaurants, and toilets and showers for customers.

- Serviced apartments are a type of serviced self-catering accommodation provided in destinations. Services such as cleaning are provided in serviced apartments.

KEY WORD

self-catering: a style of accommodation. Self-catering customers provide and cook food themselves.

Accommodation types can be described as:

- luxury: more expensive, luxurious accommodation with many services, such as restaurants serving high-quality meals

- budget: cheaper, more basic accommodation

- eco-friendly: environmentally sustainable accommodation.

Figure 3.6 gives more information about styles of accommodation.

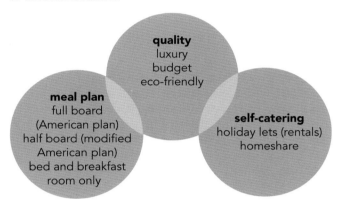

Figure 3.6: Styles of accommodation

Luxury accommodation is usually more expensive than budget accommodation. Examples of luxury accommodation include luxury hotels, luxury trains and cruise ships. Budget accommodation examples include cheaper, more basic hotels, guest houses, B&Bs, hostels and campsites. However, any accommodation type can be provided at a luxury standard. Luxury guest houses and B&Bs, for example, have higher standards of comfort and service.

Eco-friendly accommodation can be accommodation of any type. Eco-friendly accommodation is environmentally sustainable accommodation. Eco-lodges are small-scale hotels that are environmentally sustainable, often found in rural (countryside) destinations.

Serviced accommodation

Serviced accommodation is where tourists can overnight and be provided with services such as food and drink, cleaning and housekeeping. Hotels are an example of serviced accommodation. Hotels and other types of serviced accommodation often provide meals for customers. Full board, half board, bed and breakfast and room only are examples of **meal plans**. A meal plan is a way of serving meals in accommodation establishments.

Meal plans that are international are provided in destinations around the world. Bed and breakfast is an example of an international meal plan. International plans for providing meals range from no meals being provided (room only) to all meals being provided (American plan or full board). A meal plan of breakfast and one meal per day is described as half board or modified American plan. Some accommodation providers provide alternative meal plans – a meal plan that differs from international meal plans. For example, a hotel providing two meals a day but not breakfast would be providing an alternative meal plan.

Self-catering accommodation

Self-catering is a style of accommodation. Self-catering customers provide and cook food for themselves. Examples of self-catering accommodation include :

- homesharing: tourists share the home of local people

- holiday lets (rentals): tourists rent a house or apartment.

Occupancy rates

The **occupancy rate** is the percentage of accommodation space or rooms in use. For example, a hotel with an occupancy rate of 50% is half full. Accommodation providers try to have high occupancy rates. High occupancy rates mean the business is more profitable. Low occupancy rates often happen in the low season. Accommodation providers may reduce prices when occupancy rates are low as this attracts more customers.

Food and drink providers

Food and drink providers are travel and tourism organisations that provide food and/or drinks for sale.

Types of food and drink providers

Examples of types of food and drink providers are:

- restaurants, which serve meals to customers who sit down to eat

- cafés, which provide drinks, snacks and sometimes meals to customers who may sit or stand

- local street food vendors, who have stalls or carts in the street and sell snacks that are typical of the local food of a destination

- takeaways (takeouts), which are travel and tourism businesses that sell food for customers to take away to eat elsewhere, for example, in tourists' self-catering accommodation.

Visitor attractions

Visitor attractions are places and events that appeal to tourists. Visitor attractions can be:

- natural attractions, for example, beaches and waterfalls

- built attractions, for example, museums and theme parks

- events such as sports competitions and arts festivals, which also attract tourists.

Natural attractions

Natural attractions are places that appeal to tourists because of the environment. Natural attractions include spectacular scenery for sightseeing. Waterfalls, volcanoes, mountains, valleys, beautiful lakes and cliff coastlines are examples of natural attractions that appeal to tourists because of the scenery. Beaches can be scenically beautiful and also attract tourists who want to sunbathe, picnic, swim or enjoy watersports. The nature and wildlife of rural areas and the marine life of coral reefs are also examples of how natural attractions appeal to tourists.

Built attractions

Built attractions are buildings and monuments that appeal to visitors. Museums, art galleries and historical monuments attract cultural tourists. Historic and beautiful buildings and ruins such as castles, fortresses and religious buildings also attract tourists. Travel and tourism organisations manage built attractions and often sell tickets to tourists, as well as providing guided tours, gift shops and cafés.

Events

Events are time-limited happenings that appeal to tourists. Sports competitions such as the Olympic Games, arts festivals and religious celebrations are examples of events that appeal to tourists. Events in destinations attract visitors and help to increase low-season occupancy rates at hotels.

Ancillary service providers

Ancillary service providers are travel and tourism organisations that provide services to tourists other than travel, accommodation, food and drink and visitor attractions. Ancillary services are extra or additonal services that are not usually included in package holidays.

Tour agents/guided tours

Tour agents in destinations are tour operators that provide guided tours as a tourism service. For example, tourists visiting a historic city destination may choose to hire a local guide to show them the local built attractions. Tourists visiting a rural (countryside) destination may hire a local guide to explain the local scenery and wildlife.

Currency exchange

International tourists may need to exchange the currency of their home country for the currency of the destination country. For example, inbound tourists to countries in Europe may need euros (the local currency of many European countries), tourists to the USA need US (American) dollars and visitors to India need rupees. Travel and tourism organisations including travel agents and some larger hotels provide currency exchange as an additinal, ancillary service for customers.

Car hire/bike hire

Car hire and bicycle hire are examples of local transport rental services in destinations. Tourists visiting a destination may choose to rent a car or a bicycle to move around more easily. Travel agents may provide car and bicycle hire as ancillary services. Customers buying a package holiday from a travel agent could choose to pay for car or bicycle hire as an optional extra. Large hotels in destinations sometimes allow car and bicycle hire providers to operate desks in the hotel. Car and bicycle hire desks in an all-inclusive hotel may be provided as an extra, ancillary service for customers.

CASE STUDY

Australian adventures

Australia is a large country and destination between the Indian Ocean and the Pacific Ocean. Tour operators provide package holidays for tourists to explore some of the many destinations in Australia. Two examples of Australian adventure package tours are shown in **Table 3.2**. Some visitor attractions included in the two tours in **Table 3.2** are shown in **Figure 3.7**.

Uluru is a natural attraction. Uluru is a 348 m-high rock that appears to change colour during the day. Uluru is a World Heritage Site and is sacred to local indigenous people.

Sydney Opera House and Sydney Harbour Bridge are built attractions. Sydney is Australia's largest city destination.

Figure 3.7: Uluru and Sydney

CONTINUED

| Package tour | Products and services components | | |
	Accommodation	Attraction visits	Ancillary services
A **A 17-day overland tour from Melbourne to Darwin**	camping (9 nights) budget self-catering (7 nights)	Includes: wildlife, such as koalas scenery, including Uluru (see **Figure 3.7)** and MacKenzie Falls waterfall visits to mines, see art by indigenous Aborigine people and the world's largest cattle ranch	travel insurance trained tour guide
B **A 15-day East Coast fly-drive tour from Sydney to Brisbane**	hotels room only (3 nights) bed and breakfast (6 nights) luxury hotel resort (2 nights) All-inclusive resort (all meals included, full board, 3 nights)	beaches coral reef famous sights such as Sydney Opera House and Sydney Harbour Bridge (see **Figure 3.7)** scenic coastal walks and cruises mountain scenery art gallery visit	car hire

Table 3.2: Two package tours in Australia

Questions

Table 3.2 shows two examples of Australian adventure package tours.

1 Copy and complete:

Package tour	Number of days	Number of nights
A		16
B	15	

2 Suggest:

  a why the numbers of days and nights in a package holiday tour are different

  b what is meant by fly-drive

  c how the tours can be sold:

   • directly

   • indirectly.

3 Compare the range of products and services provided on package tours A and B.

4 Explain:

  a the differences between the products and services provided on package tour A and those provided on package tour B.

  b why neither tour includes both Sydney and Uluru.

5 Discuss with a partner:

  a which tourist types packages A and B would appeal to

  b the range of food and drink providers you would expect in Sydney, a large city destination

  c the likely sustainable practices of tourism organisations involved in tour A and in tour B.

6 *Extension:* Evaluate the relative sustainability of packages A and B.

CONTINUED

KEY WORDS

coral reef: an underwater ecosystem that appeals to tourists. Tourists dive and snorkel to see coral reefs' biodiversity. A coral reef is a coastal natural attraction

sustainable practices: the ways in which travel and tourism organisations ensure sustainability

TIPS

- Remember that different types of tourist customers are likely to prefer different products and services. Different package tours, for example, are likely to appeal to different tourist types.

- Understand that destination size (scale) varies. Destinations such as Australia are big because of their physical size. Australia is almost 2,500 miles (about 4,000 km) wide. Destinations such as Orlando are big for their type. Orlando is a city destination with many theme parks, which are often several kilometres (miles) apart. Big destinations can be too extensive for one tourist to visit all the attractions in one visit.

KEY CONCEPT LINKS

- Travel and tourism products and services are provided by different travel and tourism industry components. A single tour such as a holiday, a business (MICE) trip or a visit to friends and relatives (VFR) includes different components. A package holiday, for example, may include components such as travel, accommodation, meals, attraction visits and ancillary services.

- The demand for sustainable products and services has increased and many tourism organisations have sustainable practices. Tour operators, for example, educate customers in responsible tourism. Accommodation providers follow the 3Rs of sustainability (reduce, reuse and recycle).

ACTIVITY 3.1

1   You may find it helpful to refer to **Figure 3.5**, which summarises different types of tourism organisations.

    a   Identify four types of package holidays.

    b   Outline what is meant by:

        i   dynamic packaging

        ii   all-inclusive

        iii mass market.

    c   Suggest **three** examples of specialist package holidays.

2   Describe:

    a   the range of international meal plans available in different types of accommodation

    b   the differences between luxury and budget accommodation.

3   With a partner, discuss what is meant by:

    a   eco-friendly accommodation

    b   holiday lets (rentals)

    c   homeshare

4   *Project:* Work in groups. Make a class display showing the products and services provided by different tourism organisations. Include the following detail:

    a   the sustainable practices of different tourism organisations

    b   the appeal of different types of travel agents and accommodation providers to different types of tourists.

3.2 Ways travel and tourism organisations work together

Introduction

Travel and tourism organisations do not work in isolation; they need to work together and rely on each other for success.

Interdependencies

An interdependency is where two or more travel and tourism organisations rely on each other to provide their products and services. For example, an airline cannot operate without airports to land at, and a travel agent needs tour operators to create package holidays for them to sell. It is common for travel and tourism organisations to have more than one interdependency, as seen in **Figure 3.8**.

An interdependency means that the organisations are mutually dependent on each other; they rely on each other and could not provide their products without the other.

Interrelationships

An interrelationship is when travel and tourism organisations choose to work together. The interrelationship benefits both organisations. However, unlike interdependencies, the organisations can exist without the interrelationship. For example, a hostel that does not provide food and drink might form an interrelationship with a local restaurant. The restaurant may offer a discount to tourists staying at the hostel. Both the hostel and the restaurant benefit from this arrangement. The hostel provides good customer service to tourists by making recommendations and providing access to services they do not have, and the restaurant benefits from having more customers.

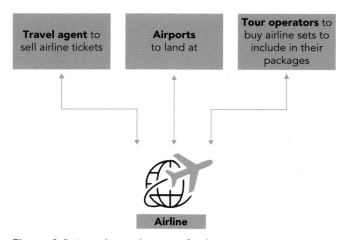

Figure 3.8: Interdependencies of airlines

CASE STUDY

Figure 3.9: Horse riding in the sea in Jamaica

Nature-based adventure park

Located on the northern coast of Jamaica, this visitor attraction is built on a former historic sugar plantation. The nature adventure park was built in a sustainable way. It has protected the natural environment, and preserved cultural and historical features, while introducing new and exciting nature-based adventure facilities to the area.

The nature adventure park has something for everyone. Tourists can enjoy seaside activities, take a boat tour, go on a sand-dune safari, go snorkelling, go horse riding in the sea, follow walking routes or simply relax on the golden Caribbean sands. The park also includes two restaurants, changing facilities and the historic ruins of the sugar plantation.

The nature adventure park works closely with the Jamaican Tourist Board and the Tourism Product Development Company, a destination management company (DMC) in Jamaica. They sell tickets to local hotels, local tour companies and cruise ships visiting the area.

The owners of the nature adventure park are committed to creating a positive sociocultural impact in the Caribbean. They employ over 700 people and provide opportunities for education and skills development for local people working at the park.

ACTIVITY 3.3

1   State which tourist types are likely to be attracted to the nature adventure park.

2   For **two** of the tourist types identified, explain why they would be attracted to the nature adventure park.

3   Identify and explain the likely interdependencies of the nature adventure park.

4   Explain the likely reasons why the nature adventure park has an interrelationship with the Tourism Product Development Company.

5   Create a visual representation of the interrelationships and interdependencies of the nature adventure park. This could be a diagram, a collection of photos with connecting lines or a drawing. Include a written explanation in your image of the benefits to each organisation in the interrelationships and interdependencies.

REFLECTION

- How confident do you feel about your understanding of the difference between interrelationships and interdependencies?

- What could you do to increase your confidence in this topic?

- Share your visual representation of the interrelationships and interdependencies with another learner. Explain your diagram to them and listen to their explanation of their diagram. Does this help your understanding?

3.3 Different types of transport and their appeal

Introduction

Travel and tourism organisations provide different types of transport.

Air transport

Air transport is used by domestic and international tourists. Travel by air is often quicker than travel by water, rail or road. Flying appeals to all types of tourists who want to travel long distances between countries, for example, on long-haul flights of over six hours. International tourists often choose air travel because it is fast. However, air travel can be expensive, although budget airlines have made some flights cheaper. Cheaper budget flights have increased the number of tourists choosing to fly. Budget flights are often short-haul flights of less than a few (between three and six) hours.

KEY WORD

short-haul flight: a flight lasting less than a few (between three and six) hours

Air travel can pollute the atmosphere. More sustainable air travel has been made possible using newer, bigger aircraft with more modern engines that cause less pollution. However, some countries have recently decided to limit domestic travel by air to reduce pollution.

The time it takes to pass through airports has increased because of increased security checks in the 21st century. Domestic and short-haul journey times have increased. Air travel appeals to business tourists for speed. However, longer journey times and sustainability concerns have decreased the appeal of air travel to some MICE tourists.

Water transport

Tourists use water transport for cruise holidays. A cruise around the Caribbean Sea is one example of water transport use. Cruises also take place along rivers and across lakes. Ferries provide water transport. These are boats or ships that link places. Ferries carry tourists and vehicles such as cars and buses between destinations or between different places within a destination.

Ferries often appeal to families who want to travel to a holiday destination in their own car and are a quick and easy way for tourists to cross harbours and rivers within destinations. Ferries provide timetabled water transport services between destinations or across water within destinations. Water taxis are small boats that tourists can hire to travel from one part of a destination to another. Gondolas are a special type of water transport. These are traditional boats used by tourists in the city destination of Venice in Italy.

KEY WORDS

cruise: a leisure journey, usually on water

water taxi: a type of urban public transport. Water taxis are small boats that tourists can hire to travel between places within a destination. Timetabled boat services between destinations or across water are ferry services

gondola: a traditional boat used by tourists in the city destination of Venice in Italy

Rail transport

- Trains provide rail transport between and within urban (city) destinations. Trains appeal to tourists who want to travel between cities within a country or between cities in neighbouring countries. Long-distance journeys, however, are usually quicker by air.

- Luxury train services are a leisure tourism product. Some special interest tourists enjoy travelling in a luxurious train, sometimes through spectacular scenery. The Blue Train in South Africa is an example of a luxury train service.

- Trams, **mass rapid transit (MRT)** and underground railway services appeal to tourists visiting urban (city) destinations.

KEY WORD

mass rapid transit (MRT): a type of rail transport used in some city destinations. MRT trains transport large numbers of people quickly and often cheaply. Many tourists use MRT trains to move around city destinations easily.

Road transport

Tourists use road transport to travel to destinations and within destinations. Car travel between destinations appeals to some tourist types, for example, families. Cars are convenient for door-to-door travel between home and accommodation.

Luxury coach travel appeals to some tourist types including older people and budget travellers. Luxury coach holidays are a tourism product that appeals to older couples. Inter-city coaches appeal to independent travellers who want to travel cheaply between city destinations.

Car hire, taxis and buses, including shuttle buses, are examples of types of road transport that tourists can use within destinations. Shuttle buses appeal to independent travellers for travel within destinations, for example, for travel between airport and hotel.

Air transport		scheduled and charter flights
		low-cost (budget) flights
		long-haul and short-haul flights
Water transport		ferry services
		cruises
		water taxis
		gondolas
		barges
		canoes
Rail transport		trains, including luxury train services
		trams
		mass rapid transit (MRT) and underground railways
Road transport		car hire
		taxis
		luxury coaches
		buses, including shuttle buses

Table 3.3: Different types of transport

KEY WORDS

scheduled flight: an air flight that is timetabled

charter flight: an air flight that is specially organised. Charter flights are not part of an airline's timetable or schedule

Tourists use transport to travel to destinations and within destinations. Different types of transport can appeal to different types of tourists.

Factors that affect the appeal of different types of transport include:

- cost: some transport is cheaper to use
- time: some transport is quicker
- sustainability: some transport is more eco-friendly
- comfort and enjoyment.

In **Figure 3.10**, Rose and her friends explain the appeal of different types of transport.

To travel to a destination, I prefer the train. Sometimes the train can be cheaper than flying. I can see the scenery along the way.

I like to be eco-friendly and I need to save money, so I cycle when I can. Cycling is slow.

To travel quickly around a destination, I use public transport – bus, MRT or tram.

Figure 3.10: Rose and her friends explain the appeal of different types of transport

CASE STUDY

Figure 3.11: Singapore's mass rapid transit (MRT) train

Destination Singapore

Singapore is a country and a city destination in Southeast Asia. Tourists can travel to Singapore using different types of transport.

Tourists can travel to Singapore by air: Changi Airport is Singapore's international airport. More than 100 airlines provide flights to Singapore from about 400 cities around the world. The City Shuttle bus service takes tourists to hotels in the city centre. Buses run every 30 minutes and travellers pay only a few dollars for the 25-minute journey.

Some tourists travel to Singapore using water transport. Cruise ships bring tourists to Singapore's two cruise terminals: Singapore Cruise Centre and Marina Bay Cruise Centre. The largest cruise ships use Marina Bay Cruise Centre.

Tourists can also travel to Singapore using road transport. Some drive into Singapore from the neighbouring country of Malaysia. Singapore's land border checkpoints are at Tuas and Woodlands. The governments of Malaysia and Singapore planned a high-speed rail link between Malaysia's capital city of Kuala Lumpur and Singapore. However, in 2021, the Kuala Lumpur–Singapore High Speed Rail Project was cancelled.

Tourists can use different types of transport within Singapore. They often use public transport to move around within destinations. Tourists can travel around Singapore by rail using Singapore's mass rapid transit (MRT) system.

CONTINUED

For many tourists, the MRT is the fastest way to move around Singapore city. Many tourist attractions are only a short walk from an MRT station. For example, tourists using the East–West MRT line can visit Pasir Ris Park and its beach, enjoy traditional food at Geylang Serai food market and shop in Queenstown at the Queensway Shopping Centre.

Singapore has a large network of bus routes. Buses allow tourists to travel to most places in the city. Buses are popular with VFR tourists as buses are an economical type of transport for tourists. Singapore's air-conditioned buses allow tourists to see the attractive architecture and green scenery of the destination in comfort. Singapore is a green city destination and has been described as 'a city in a garden'. Taxis are another way for tourists to travel around the 'city in a garden'. Taxis are usually more expensive than buses, but they are sometimes more comfortable and can reach places that are not accessible by bus or MRT.

Cycling is a healthy and sustainable type of transport. Some tourists hire bicycles. Tourists can use Singapore's network of cycle routes to enjoy the city's green spaces. Cycle routes make cycling safer and separate cyclists from other traffic. Separating cyclists from other traffic also protects cyclists from pollution. Tourists who have foldable bicycles can take them onto trains and buses in Singapore.

Questions

1   Identify **three** different types of public transport that tourists can use in Singapore.

2   Describe the appeal of rail travel to a tourist visiting Singapore.

3   Explain the advantages and disadvantages of **two** transport types for tourists visiting Singapore.

4   With a partner, discuss why you think the high-speed Kuala Lumpur to Singapore rail project was cancelled in 2021.

5   *Extension:* Evaluate the range of transport choices available to tourists in Singapore.

TIPS

- Be aware that different transport types appeal to different people for different trips for different reasons. The same person may prefer to fly sometimes but take the train at other times.

- Remember that tourists travel for different reasons, including leisure, business (MICE) and visiting friends and relatives (VFR). The reason for travelling can affect the appeal of different types of transport.

KEY CONCEPT LINKS

- Tourists use different types of transport to travel to destinations. They then use different types of transport to travel within destinations. Different types of transport appeal to different types of tourists for different reasons.

- Factors affecting the appeal of different types of transport include:

  - cost: some transport is cheaper to use

  - time: some transport is quicker

  - sustainability: some transport is more eco-friendly

  - comfort and enjoyment.

ACTIVITY 3.4

1   Think about tourist travel to and around a destination. Work with a partner to:

   a   identify the different types of transport tourists can use

   b   suggest the types of transport that would appeal to different types of tourists visiting your destination

   c   explain which types of transport you and your partner would choose.

2   Use examples to describe the difference between:

   a   charter flights and scheduled flights

   b   long-haul flights and short-haul flights

   c   water taxis and ferry services.

3   Explain factors that, according to Rose, contribute to the appeal of:

   a   rail travel

   b   cycling.

4   Read this text:

   'Tourists can use canoes for slow travel. Canoe travel is eco-friendly. Tourists feel close to the environment. Canoe travel can be cheap and is a sustainable way to reach some eco-resorts.'

   a   Suggest **two** types of tourists who would find canoe travel appealing.

   b   Explain why.

5   *Project:* Do some research on the types of tourist transport (i–vi) listed below.

   i   barge

   ii   water taxi

   iii   tram

   iv   underground railway

   v   luxury train and luxury coach

   vi   car hire.

   a   Describe, with the aid of diagrams, examples of each transport type.

   b   Suggest why each type of transport might appeal to some tourists.

   c   Show and explain your findings to the rest of the class.

3.4 Sustainable developments in travel and transport

Introduction

Tourists use transport to travel. Transport types include air, water, rail and road transport. Sustainable travel and sustainable transport have become important, with tourists and tourism providers becoming more aware of the need to protect the future from harm.

Reduced or low emissions

Sustainable developments in the travel and transport industry reduce emissions of polluting gases such as carbon dioxide, which is a gas emitted by transport exhaust – from aircraft, ships, trains, buses and cars, for example. Carbon dioxide harms the environment and pollutes the atmosphere. Low-emission transport reduces the amount of air pollution. Low-emission aircraft and low-emission cruise ships are examples of reduced-emission transport used by tourists.

KEY WORDS

emissions: gases that come out of the exhausts of engines. Engines that use carbon-based fuels such as diesel and petrol emit carbon dioxide

low-emission: describes transport that causes reduced air pollution. Emissions of polluting exhaust gases such as carbon dioxide are low

Lately, larger aircraft and cruise ships that can carry more passengers have been built; these transport types emit less pollution per passenger.

Sustainable travel choices

As global demand for sustainable tourism has increased, some tourists have made sustainable travel choices. Tourists can reduce pollution by choosing a sustainable method of transport, such as cycling. Tourists can also choose domestic tourism instead of an international holiday.

Alternative energy sources

Alternative energy sources make transport more sustainable. Some types of more sustainable transport use carbon replacement to reduce emissions. For example, some buses use hydrogen fuel instead of carbon-based diesel fuel or are hybrid diesel-electric buses. Hybrid vehicles such as buses use a mix of fuels, and electric cars and solar-powered buses use alternative energy sources. Solar-powered and other electric cars and buses use batteries and reduce carbon emissions. Examples of sustainable developments in travel and transport are shown by the *Fortaleza* case study.

CASE STUDY

Fortaleza: a sustainable travel winner

Fortaleza is a coastal beach and city destination in north-east Brazil, the largest country in South America. Fortaleza was the world Sustainable Travel Award (STA) winner in 2019.

Figure 3.12: Fortaleza cycles for hire

Tourists visiting Fortaleza want to travel around the destination. Public transport in Fortaleza is

sustainable. Public transport is more sustainable than private transport because a single bus or train journey carries many more people than a single car journey. Public transport journeys are less polluting; in Fortaleza this includes hybrid buses and bicycles for hire, and is an integrated transport system. For example, bicycle racks are located at bus stations and near bus stops. Fortaleza has more than 100 km of bus lanes, which are reserved for public transport use. Bus lanes make bus journeys quicker. Bus travel in Fortaleza is less polluting because bus lanes help to reduce congestion.

Fortaleza has more than 200 km of cycle routes. Tourists can hire bicycles. The *Bicicletar* bike share scheme attracts tourist families. Mini-bikes are available for children. Alongside the main *Praia de Meireles* beach is a flat, 6 km-long, paved route that cyclists can use.

KEY WORD

integrated transport: linked transport. Integrated transport makes it easy to change from one transport type to another. For example, it is easy to change from tram/bus to bicycle at a tram/bus stop with a cycle rack

Questions

1   Identify **four** sustainable transport developments in Fortaleza.

2   Describe how integrated transport, bus lanes and hybrid buses help sustainability.

CONTINUED

3 Explain why sustainable transport in Fortaleza appeals to tourists who are:

a families

b business (MICE) tourists.

4 The Sustainable Travel Award (STA) is awarded annually. In 2019, Fortaleza was the winner. In 2021, the STA winner was Jakarta. Jakarta is the biggest city in Indonesia, a country in Southeast Asia. Discuss with a partner:

a why STA winners are usually cities

b whether all cities are tourist destinations

c further sustainable travel developments that Fortaleza could introduce.

5 **Extension:** Evaluate the extent to which Fortaleza has developed sustainable transport in comparison with a destination of your choice.

Figure 3.13: A cycle rack at a tram stop

TIPS

- Remember that sustainability is about reducing harm to protect the future. Sustainable transport reduces environmental pollution, but may still cause some.

- Be aware that new and improved types of sustainable transport are being developed. Solar-powered cars are an example.

KEY CONCEPT LINKS

- Global demand for sustainable travel and tourism is increasing. Tourists want to travel sustainably. Destinations are developing sustainable transport that tourists can use. Destinations encourage tourists to use public transport as one way of developing more sustainable transport. Shared transport is also sustainable transport. Many destinations have shared bicycle hire racks.

- Low-emission vehicles and integrated transport systems help to develop sustainable travel and transport to destinations and within destinations. Examples of reduced-emission vehicles include low-emission aircraft, low-emission cruise ships, trains, buses and taxis.

ACTIVITY 3.5

1 Identify a range of different types of sustainable transport. Make an illustrated poster to illustrate the types of sustainable transport you have identified.

2 Describe ways of reducing transport emissions.

3 Explain why sustainable travel and sustainable transport have become important.

4 Work with a partner to investigate sustainable travel to a destination other than Fortaleza. Find out:

a what sustainable travel choices tourists can make

b how sustainable those travel choices are.

Present your findings to another pair in your class.

REFLECTION

Write down an explanation of the method you and your partner used to investigate sustainable travel to a destination. Share this with another pair of class members.

Did the other pair use the same method? Can you think of a better one?

3.5 Domestic and international travel and transport infrastructure

Introduction

Travel within a country is domestic travel. International travel is between countries. Transport infrastructure includes:

- airports
- sea and river ports
- roads and railways, bus stations and railway stations
- canals
- bicycle and electric scooter rental schemes.

> **KEY WORD**
>
> **electric scooter:** a personal-use scooter. Electric scooters are a sustainable type of mass personal-use transport. Electric scooters are available for public use in many destinations.

Interdependency of transport methods

Domestic and international transport types are interdependent because domestic and international transport depend on each other. For example, local buses, trains and taxis from an airport depend on international travel to the airport. International flights from an airport depend on tourists being able to use local transport to get to the airport.

> **KEY WORD**
>
> **interdependent transport:** transport that depends on another linked type of transport. For example, express link trains from an airport depend on aircraft flights to the airport.

Local public transport provision

Tourists arrive at destination gateways. International tourists may arrive at an airport gateway, a cruise terminal gateway or an international railway station gateway. Visitors use local domestic transport to transfer (transit) from the gateway to their accommodation. Buses, trains, taxis and mass rapid transit (MRT) systems are examples of local domestic transport in destinations.

Improving accessibility

Transport infrastructure developments that improve accessibility include:

- **express links:** these are fast transfer (transit) transport services connecting, for example, airports and destination city centres (downtown areas). For example, express link rail services are planned to operate from Orlando International Airport in the USA.

- **integrated rapid transit systems:** these are transport systems in destinations that make it easy for people to change from one type of transport to another, for example, the MRT system in Singapore.

- **contactless payments:** these are made without physical contact between a payment card and a payment device. Paying contactlessly improves accessibility because it is quicker.

- apps: these are a way for tourists to pay contactlessly. Tourists can use a smartphone app to make payments. Visitors also use apps to find out about transport choices, buy e-tickets and make online reservations.

- **hub airports:** these are airports with flights and transport to other places. Tourists arriving at a

> **KEY WORDS**
>
> **express link:** a fast transfer (transit) transport service connecting, for example, an airport and a destination city centre (downtown area)
>
> **integrated rapid transit system:** a transport system in a destination that makes it easy for people to change from one type of transport to another
>
> **contactless payment:** a payment made without physical contact between a payment card and a payment device. Apps are one way of paying contactlessly.
>
> **hub airport:** an airport with flights and transport to other places. Tourists arriving at a hub airport can travel to other cities or countries.

hub airport can travel to other cities or countries. Examples of hub ariports include Orlando International Airport in the USA and Copenhagen Airport in Denmark, Europe.

- Transfers (transits) in destinations improve accessibility. For example, in Orlando, shuttle buses are operated by theme park and hotel providers. Some tourists use shuttle buses to transit (transfer) from Orlando International Airport to hotels and theme parks in Orlando.

Increased sustainability

Transport infrastructure developments can increase sustainability. Ways in which transport infrastructure developments increase sustainability include public transport and **urban transit** systems (such as MRTs, as in Singapore). Dedicated cycle and bus lanes/routes also improve both sustainability and accessibility. The *Fortaleza* case study (*Fortaleza: a sustainable travel winner?*) gives examples of transport infrastructure developments that increase sustainability.

KEY WORD

urban transit: travel within a city destination, for example, transfer between airport and hotel.

Alternative transport options

Alternative transport options differ from traditional transport choices such as buses, cars or privately owned bicycles. Alternative transport options are sustainable. Rental schemes for publicly shared bicycles and electric scooters are examples of alternative transport options. Shared bicycle and electric scooter rental schemes are common in city destinations around the world, for example, in Fortaleza in Brazil.

Information about domestic and international travel and transport infrastructure in a destination is given in the *Orlando: theme park city* case study.

CASE STUDY

Orlando: theme park city

Orlando is a destination in Florida, a state in the south-east of the USA. Orlando's theme parks appeal to both domestic and international tourists.

Figure 3.14: A theme park in Orlando

Examples of theme parks in and near Orlando include Walt Disney World, Universal Resort Orlando, SeaWorld and Discovery Cove. Walt Disney World and Universal Orlando are large resorts. Theme parks at Walt Disney World include: Magic Kingdom, Animal Kingdom, Epcot and Hollywood Studios. Universal Orlando Resort theme parks include Universal Studios and Islands of Adventure.

Some tourists to the Orlando area also visit:

- Legoland – a theme park about 75 km (45 miles) from Orlando

- Busch Gardens in Tampa. Tampa is a coastal destination about 140 km (85 miles) from Orlando.

Orlando has two main airports: Orlando International Airport is closer to the theme parks and has more flights than Sanford International Airport. Sanford has more low-cost (budget) and charter flights. Orlando International Airport is also a hub airport. Some tourists arrive in Orlando on international flights and transfer to domestic flights, for example, to other airports in Florida such as Fort Lauderdale and Key West.

Sanford International Airport and Orlando International Airport are important tourist gateways to the theme park destination of Orlando. **Figure 3.15** shows the locations of theme parks and airports in Orlando.

CONTINUED

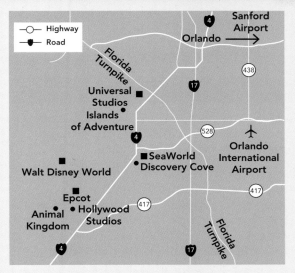

Figure 3.15: Some theme park locations in Orlando

Orlando's theme parks, attractions and hotels are spread over a large area and visitors need transport to move around the destination. Tourists arriving at one of the gateway airports can hire a car or choose local public transport.

Many tourists use road transport, such as a cars, buses and taxis, to get around Orlando. Major roads such as International Drive connect the airports, downtown (town centre) Orlando, theme parks,

hotels, restaurants and other tourist attractions such as shopping malls and the Orange County Convention Center. International Drive (I-Drive) is about 18 km (11 miles) long. The SeaWorld and Discovery Cove theme parks are close to International Drive. I-Drive has a public bus service (the I-Ride Trolley) that tourists can use.

Local public transport choices at Orlando International Airport are shown in **Figure 3.16**.

Shuttle buses are operated by theme park and hotel providers. Some tourists use shuttle buses to transit (transfer) from Orlando International Airport to hotels and theme park resorts such as Universal Orlando. Car-share (carpool) and shuttle van (minibus) providers offer **ride sharing** as a cheap and more sustainable choice.

The City of Orlando local government wants to increase sustainable transport in the destination of Orlando. The City Council would like most travel

KEY WORD

ride sharing: sharing transport with other people. Ride sharing is in a vehicle that is often used for only one customer. Ride shares are in small vehicles such as a car or a taxi.

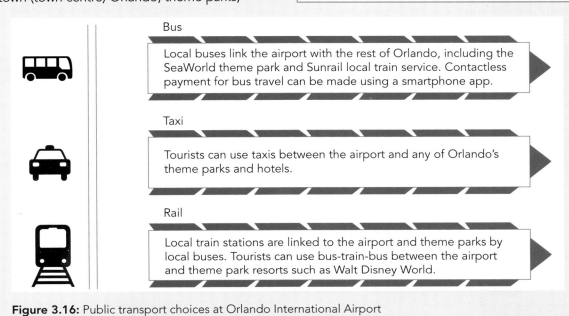

Figure 3.16: Public transport choices at Orlando International Airport

Bus

Local buses link the airport with the rest of Orlando, including the SeaWorld theme park and Sunrail local train service. Contactless payment for bus travel can be made using a smartphone app.

Taxi

Tourists can use taxis between the airport and any of Orlando's theme parks and hotels.

Rail

Local train stations are linked to the airport and theme parks by local buses. Tourists can use bus-train-bus between the airport and theme park resorts such as Walt Disney World.

CONTINUED

within Orlando to be sustainable by 2040. **Complete streets** are an example of infrastructure development that could help to make travel in Orlando more sustainable. Electric scooters are a type of sustainable transport. Electric scooter rental is an example of an **alternative transport** option. Bicycle rental is another. Scooter rental was introduced in downtown Orlando in 2020.

Carbon-neutral express link rail services are planned from Orlando International Airport to Miami (a coastal and city destination in southern Florida) and to Tampa on Florida's west coast, with a station for Walt Disney World.

Questions

1 Identify some types of domestic transport that international tourists can use in Orlando.

2 Choose a theme park in Orlando. Describe the travel choices to your chosen theme park for a tourist arriving at Orlando International Airport.

3 Explain the advantages and disadvantages of local transport types for different tourist types.

4 In a group, discuss sustainable transport in Orlando:

   a how useful sustainable transport in Orlando is

   b how sustainable transport in Orlando is

   c what else could be done to increase the sustainability of transport in Orlando.

KEY WORDS

complete streets: sustainable streets that are easy and safe for everyone. Complete streets often have bus lanes and cycle lanes

alternative transport: sustainable transport. Alternative transport options are transport choices that are different from traditional options such as buses or privately owned cars and bicycles. Rental schemes for publicly shared bicycles and electric scooters are examples of alternative transport options. Shared bicycle and electric scooter rental schemes are common in city destinations

carbon neutral: describes a vehicle or an activity that reduces carbon emissions either by reducing them to zero or by balancing them to make zero. For example, planting trees can absorb the same amount of carbon that is emitted

TIPS

- Revise your learning on domestic and international transport by using what you've learnt from other destination case studies. For example, use your Fortaleza learning to help revise sustainable domestic transport.

- Help your revision by applying your learning about sustainable transport in Orlando to other destinations you have studied, for example, Singapore.

KEY CONCEPT LINKS

- Travel and tourism organisations are interrelated. Transport providers are interdependent. International and domestic transport organisations depend on each other. International airlines flying into Orlando International Airport are linked to domestic airlines and to local public transport providers. Linked travel and transport organisations depend on each other. The tourist customers of interdependent transport providers are the same people.

- Increasing demand for sustainable tourism affects interdependent travel and tourism organisations. For example, tourists choosing an airline because of its low-emission aircraft expect to be able to choose sustainable domestic transport to travel within a destination.

ACTIVITY 3.6

1   Outline what is meant by:

- hub airport

- gateway airport

- express link

- alternative transport.

2   Design a poster or leaflet to promote local public transport in Orlando.

Think about sustainability, ease of use, special needs, cost and speed.

3   Read this:

'Integrated rapid transit systems allow tourists to travel quickly within destinations. Singapore's MRT system is an urban transit system that is integrated with other transport types. For example, some MRT stations and bus stations are the same. Tourists can easily change between MRT and bus transport.'

Debate as a class:

- if urban transit in Orlando can be described as an integrated rapid transit system

- whether it is important for Orlando to develop an integrated rapid transit system.

4   Work with a partner to plan a trip to an Orlando or Tampa theme park for a responsible tourist.

Your plan should include sustainable international and domestic travel.

REFLECTION

How do you think you could use your learning about Orlando's travel and transport infrastructure to help develop your understanding of other destinations?

EXAM-STYLE QUESTIONS

1 Refer to **Figure 11**, which gives information about Dubai International Airport (DXB).

Dubai International Airport (DXB) is the principal airport of the United Arab Emirates and is the third busiest airport in the world in terms of passenger traffic. It is a major international hub, the home base for Emirates airline; it is also a significant contributor to Dubai's economy, and sees the largest amount of traffic from Airbus A380 and Boeing 777 aircraft of any airport in the world.

DXB has been declared the world's leading hub for international passenger traffic for the sixth consecutive year, welcoming 86.4 million passengers. DXB marked several important milestones, confirming its status as one of the world's most efficient and passenger-friendly airports. The installation of new technologies aiding passenger flows – including additional smart gates – saw waiting times fall by 15 per cent year on year, even during the months of July and August, when passenger numbers exceeded eight million. The airport also set a new benchmark for baggage volumes, delivering 73.1 million bags at a record delivery success rate of 99.96 per cent.

India was once again the most popular destination for passengers flying from DXB, with traffic reaching 11.9 million, followed by Saudi Arabia with 6.3 million and the UK with 6.2 million. Other popular destinations included China (3.6 million) and the USA (3.2 million). The top three city destinations were London (3.6 million), Mumbai (2.3 million) and Riyadh (2.2 million).

Figure 11: Dubai International Airport in the United Arab Emirates

a **Identify** the following:

   i   The number of passengers handled by Dubai International Airport (DXB)

   ii The number of passengers flying from DXB to India.   [2]

b With reference to **Figure 11**, **describe two** ways in which DXB is a passenger-friendly
   international airport.   [2]

c Emirates airline operates scheduled flights. Describe the characteristic features of long-haul
   scheduled flights.   [4]

d **Discuss two** advantages of using taxis for airport transfers for passengers flying from
   major international airports.   [6]

e **Evaluate** the relative advantages for a leisure traveller of booking online or visiting a retail
   travel agent when making their travel arrangements.   [6]

[Total 20 marks]

CONTINUED

2 Refer to **Figure 12**, a review of developments in Hong Kong's public transport.

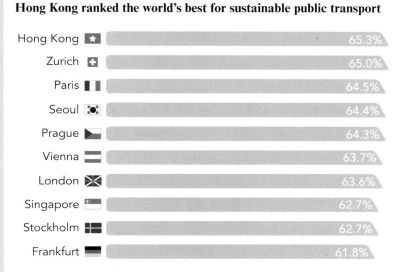

Hong Kong ranked the world's best for sustainable public transport

Hong Kong	65.3%
Zurich	65.0%
Paris	64.5%
Seoul	64.4%
Prague	64.3%
Vienna	63.7%
London	63.6%
Singapore	62.7%
Stockholm	62.7%
Frankfurt	61.8%

As one of the world's most densely populated cities, Hong Kong faced unique challenges in providing a safe, efficient and reliable transport system to meet the economic, social and recreational needs of the community in an environmentally acceptable manner.

Hong Kong is a highly mobile city that depends on an efficient and affordable public transport system. Each day, some 11 million passenger journeys are made on its network of trains, buses, minibuses, taxis, trams and ferries. However, the system needed to be upgraded by rationlising and improving coordination of public transport services to better match demand, minimising wasteful competition and duplication of effort and reducing, in some cases, low-demand services.

Convenient and comfortable interchange facilities at transport hubs, especially railway stations, were included in plans for new and major land-use or transport developments. Existing interchange facilities were upgraded.

Railways are environmentally friendly and efficient mass carriers. Locating future strategic developments along rail alignments would reduce reliance on road-based transport, enhance the efficiency of the rail network and ensure affordable fare levels. Railway 'trunk lines' were supplemented by 'feeder' services using other public transport modes. Park-and-ride facilities were developed.

Source: Adapted from www.thb.gov.hk

Figure 12: Public transport in Hong Kong

a Identify the following:

   i The number of methods of public transport available in Hong Kong

   ii The number of passenger journeys made each day on Hong Kong's public transport. [2]

b Describe the characteristics of a public transport interchange. [2]

c With reference to **Figure 12**, **explain two** ways in which the railway system has helped to make public transport in Hong Kong sustainable. [4]

CONTINUED

> **d** Ferries form part of the public transport system of many waterside cities, such as Hong Kong, New York and Dubai. These ferries are frequently used by visiting tourists. Discuss **two** ways in which these ferry services are likely to appeal to visiting tourists. [6]
>
> **e** Destinations such as Hong Kong act as ports of call for visiting cruise liners. Larger modern cruise ships attract a variety of different types of passenger.
>
> Evaluate the range of accommodation and the facilities available on board these modern cruise ships as factors that attract a variety of passenger types. [6]
>
> [Total 20 marks]

3 Refer to **Figure 13**, which gives details about Peterson Travel's Culinary Tour in Malaysia.

Peterson Travel is a one-stop Malaysia travel agency offering a wide variety of tour packages in Peninsular Malaysia and Borneo. From excursions into the lush forests to get close to native wildlife, to stays in which visitors experience the cultural aspects of Malaysia, you can find it here at Peterson Travel, Malaysia's leading tour operator.

Join us for a typical culinary tour in Malaysia, visiting Malacca, Kuala Lumpur and Penang, where you can enjoy traditional-style cooking classes featuring local favourites like laksa, curry, nasi lemak and lots more. Explore the night markets whilst you are happily travelling around Malaysia. There is a whole range of restaurants in the cities. You can find anything you want. For the real experience, explore the hawker food scene at stalls set up by the roadside, in hawker centres or in street-side coffee shops.

The local cuisine has great variety, with predominantly Chinese, Indian and Malay flavours. Malaysian food culture has the best blend of Malay, Chinese and Indian flavours and ingredients. The combination of Chinese and Malay gives rise to the delectable Peranakan cuisine. The Peranakans are descendants of early Chinese migrants who settled in Penang, Malacca and Singapore, inter-marrying with local Malays.

Then you will find Indian Muslim (known as Mamak) dishes infused with local Malay flavours. Today, Mamak food stalls are found across Malaysia, particularly in the capital Kuala Lumpur. Often open around the clock, these no-frills eateries offer a range of quick, affordable meals.

All this has continued to evolve through the years since the turn of the 19th century. With such a diversity of food styles and cultures, Malaysia is a great place to experience a feasting vacation trip.

Figure 13: Information about a culinary tour in Malaysia

CONTINUED

a **Give** the name of **two** destinations included in Peterson Travel's Culinary Tour itinerary. [2]

b Describe the range of food providers tourists can experience whilst they are taking part in the culinary tour. [2]

c Peterson Travel is Malaysia's leading tour operator. Describe the role of a tour operator. [4]

d Tourists visiting city destinations will often take an open-top bus sightseeing tour. Discuss **two** features of these tours that make them popular with visiting tourists. [6]

e The Eastern & Oriental Express is one example of a luxury train service popular with international tourists. It carries passengers between Singapore and Bangkok, and calls at various destinations in Malaysia.

Evaluate the tourist appeal of a luxury train service in terms of the on-board facilities and the itineraries that are followed. [6]

[Total 20 marks]

SELF-EVALUATION CHECKLIST

After studying this unit, complete this table:

I am now able to:	Needs more work	Almost there	Ready to move on
understand interrelationships between travel and tourism organisations.			
explain: • the appeal of different types of transport • sustainable developments in travel and transport.			
evaluate domestic and international travel and transport options.			
discuss tourism organisations, their sustainable practices, the products and services they provide and their appeal.			

Customer service in travel and tourism

TRAVEL AND TOURISM IN CONTEXT

All-in in Costa Rica

Costa Rica is a country located in Central America. The country appeals to tourists as a destination because of its warm tropical climate and many natural attractions, including beaches, forests and volcanoes.

All-inclusive resort hotels appeal to tourists because almost everything is included in one price. Customers pay a fee, usually in advance. The price includes accommodation, meals, most drinks and some activities. For example, some watersports such as windsurfing and snorkelling may be included, but others such as jet-skiing or scuba diving may not.

The photo shows The Westin Golf Resort & Spa, one of Costa Rica's all-inclusive hotels.

Figure 4.1: An all-inclusive resort hotel in Costa Rica

The resort hotel provides customer service for different types of tourists, including families and adult couples.

The resort has several restaurants, which provide either buffets or à la carte table service. Customers can choose from local Costa Rican dishes, Italian foods including pizza, Mexican and Asian cuisines. Restaurant-based customer service staff meet the special dietary requirements of some customers. For example, gluten-free foods are available.

To meet the needs of families, the resort hotel arranges family activities such as forest walks, has a babysitting service, and provides a Kids' Club

for children up to 12 years old. The Kids' Club has playgrounds, games and classes for children.

Leisure activities provided for the resort hotel's customers include watersports, aerobics, yoga and beach volleyball, as well as group walks and bike rides to explore the surrounding natural environment.

Staff deliver customer service at different locations within the resort (see **Figure 4.2**). For example, customer service is delivered at the front desk (location A) and in the spa (location H).

KEY WORDS

resort hotel: a type of hotel. Resort hotels provide a wide range of services and activities, as well as accommodation and meals. Resort hotels are often spread across a large site. Many resort hotels provide all-inclusive packages

customer service: helping customers by providing them with products and services

buffet: a way of serving food. Customers serve themselves from food presented as a display

à la carte: a way in which customers choose food in a restaurant. Customers order items separately from a menu

table service: a way of serving food in a restaurant. Customers are seated at a table and are served food by staff

special dietary requirements: particular food needs. For example, a customer may require gluten-free food

gluten-free foods: food items not containing gluten. Gluten is a protein found in cereals such as wheat

staff: people employed to work in a travel and tourism organisation. Customer service staff deliver customer service to tourists by providing them with products and services

CONTINUED

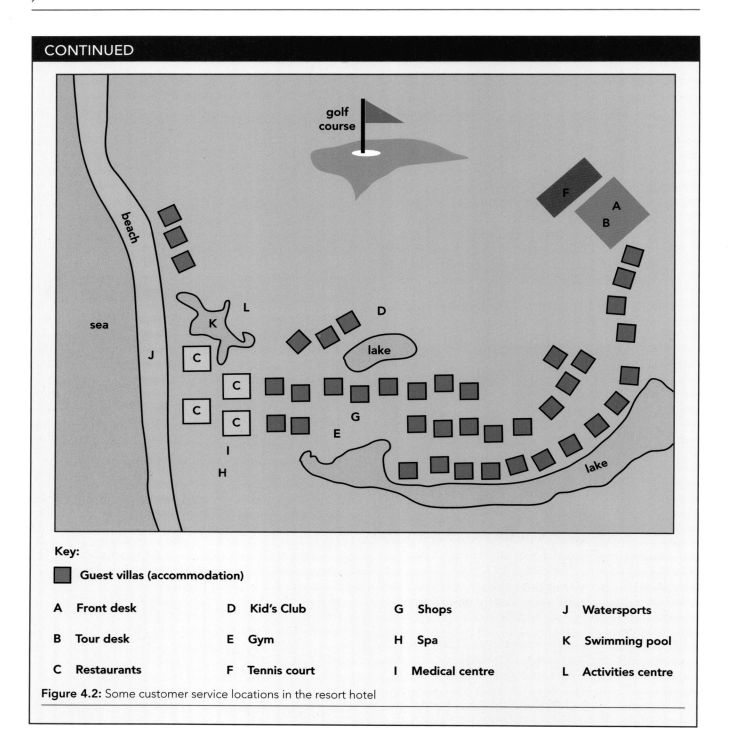

Key:

■ **Guest villas (accommodation)**

A Front desk	**D** Kid's Club	**G** Shops	**J** Watersports
B Tour desk	**E** Gym	**H** Spa	**K** Swimming pool
C Restaurants	**F** Tennis court	**I** Medical centre	**L** Activities centre

Figure 4.2: Some customer service locations in the resort hotel

CONTINUED

Tourists want to enjoy their holiday. Staff in an all-inclusive resort know they are delivering good customer service when tourists are relaxed and having fun. Good customer service delivery is very important to travel and tourism organisations. Happy and satisfied customers may:

- return to the hotel, bringing repeat business

- tell people about a good customer experience

- write online or social media reviews

- make hotel staff happy, too.

Staff working in the travel and tourism industry need customer service skills. Some of these skills needed by staff working at the resort hotel are:

- personal skills, such as communicating clearly and being able to use ICT (information and communication technology)

- interpersonal skills, such as:

  - listening patiently to other people

  - being welcoming and flexible

  - working well in a team.

The ability to speak other languages is a useful customer service skill for hotel staff. Many tourists to Costa Rica are from different parts of the world, particularly North America and Europe, as well as countries such as India, China and Japan. The language of Costa Rica is Spanish, but English is spoken by many hotel staff members. Some employees are able to speak some phrases of other langages, such as French and German.

Costa Rica has a reputation for ecotourism. The resort hotel in **Figure 4.1** encourages environmentally sustainable tourism. The Costa Rica Tourism Board has awarded the hotel a Level 5 Certificate of Sustainable Tourism (CST). Level 5 is the highest CST level. Resort staff are able to address (meet) the needs of responsible tourists. Some tourist customers want to explore Costa Rica's natural environment, visiting forests and viewing wildlife, including monkeys, iguana lizards and colourful tropical birds.

Environmentally sustainable practices at the resort hotel are shown in **Figure 4.3.** Staff are trained to help provide customer service to sustainable customer service standards.

KEY WORDS

repeat business: when customers return to a travel and tourism organisation where they previously had a good customer experience

customer experience: how a customer feels about the customer service they receive. For example, a restaurant customer may feel that receiving good, well-served food is a good customer experience

customer service skills: abilities that enable staff to provide good customer service

personal skills: personal abilities that enable a member of staff to provide good customer service

ICT (information and communication technology): the range of computer and other electronic devices, such as smartphones, used to store and send information

interpersonal skills: abilities that enable staff members to work together to provide good customer service

reputation: a general opinion that people have about how good or bad someone or something is. A hotel delivering good customer service is likely to have a good reputation

sustainable customer service standards: levels of customer service that encourage sustainable practices

CONTINUED

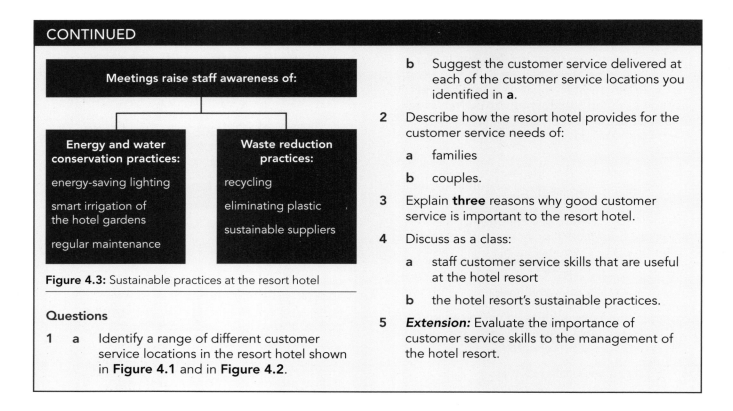

Figure 4.3: Sustainable practices at the resort hotel

Questions

1   a   Identify a range of different customer service locations in the resort hotel shown in **Figure 4.1** and in **Figure 4.2**.

b   Suggest the customer service delivered at each of the customer service locations you identified in **a**.

2   Describe how the resort hotel provides for the customer service needs of:

a   families

b   couples.

3   Explain **three** reasons why good customer service is important to the resort hotel.

4   Discuss as a class:

a   staff customer service skills that are useful at the hotel resort

b   the hotel resort's sustainable practices.

5   *Extension:* Evaluate the importance of customer service skills to the management of the hotel resort.

4.1 The importance of customer service

Introduction

Customer service is very important to travel and tourism organisations. All travel and tourism organisations deliver customer service. These organisations deliver customer service to different customer types. For example, the resort hotel in Costa Rica that featured in the case study *All-in in Costa Rica* delivers customer service to families and couples.

Different customer types have different wants and needs. Travel and tourism organisations try to deliver good customer service that satisfies the wants and needs of different customer types.

Service delivery in different travel and tourism organisations

Destination management companies (DMCs) are a type of tourism organisation. DMCs deliver customer service to customers who are inbound tourists. Inbound tourists include:

- all types of leisure tourists

- business (MICE) tourists.

CASE STUDY

Aurore on holiday in Mauritius

Aurore and William are inbound tourists in Mauritius. Mauritius is a destination in the Indian Ocean and is a country of islands. *Sustainable Mauritius* is a case study in Unit 2 of this book.

Aurore is a potential customer for destination management companies (DMCs) in Mauritius. Destination management companies in Mauritius are tourism businesses with local knowledge of Mauritius as a destination. Mauritian DMCs include inbound tour operators, which provide customers with tours, transport, event and attraction tickets and activities in Mauritius.

The DMCs in Mauritius can be members of an organisation called the Association of Inbound Operators of Mauritius (AIOM). AIOM members provide tours and packages for inbound tourists in Mauritius.

Packages can be customised to meet customers' needs. DMCs in Mauritius work with local providers of transport, visitor attractions and activities, including watersports such as windsurfing, kite surfing, diving, snorkelling and sport fishing.

Aurore contacted AIOM member DMCs with the request shown in **Figure 4.5**.

AIOM members want Mauritius to gain a good reputation as a destination. High customer service standards can give a destination a good reputation. Mauritian DMCs want to provide a good standard of customer service, including sustainable standards. Global demand for sustainable tourism has increased. Good customer service for Mauritian DMCs includes providing customers with sustainable packages. Mauritian DMCs accept paperless payments and train staff in sustainable tourism practices. Tour guides trained in sustainable practices can:

- educate tourists about responsible tourism

- encourage other tourism organisations to be eco-friendly.

Figure 4.4: Watersports at a beach in Mauritius

KEY WORDS

potential customer: someone who might become an actual customer of a travel and tourism organisation. For example, tourists visiting a destination are potential customers of local tourism organisations such as DMCs, restaurants and visitor attractions

inbound operator: a tour operator who provides tours and packages for inbound tourists to a destination. Inbound tour operators are also known as destination management companies (DMCs)

customised package: a package tour organised by a tour operator to provide for a particular customer's identified needs. For example, a customised package for an inbound tourist might include airport transfer, hotel, restaurant booking and visitor attraction ticket. Each part of a customised package is chosen by the tour operator to meet a particular customer's needs. Customised packages can also be called tailor-made packages or bespoke packages

customer service standards: levels of customer service quality. Tourism organisations try to deliver customer service at high standards. Customer service standards include sustainability standards. A high standard of DMC sustainable customer service could include paperless transactions, recommending sustainable local providers and sustainable activity options

paperless payment: electronic payment. Contactless payment is an example of paperless payment. Paperless payments are sustainable and help to reduce the paper that tourism organisations use

CONTINUED

Contact us	
We:	

- are your local tourism experts
- are here to help you create your Mauritian dream holiday
- provide you with 24-hour customer support
- provide quick email confirmation of your online paperless payment.

Please let us know how we can help you.

Your name*	Your email*
Aurore Beaucet	abwi@ecambridge.au

Your request*

My partner William and I are on holiday in Mauritius next month. It's his birthday. I want to make it a special day. William loves snorkelling, windsurfing and all eco-friendly watersports.
Please can you recommend some local providers?

I'd like to book a restaurant too – somewhere that serves good local food. Thank you.

Send

Figure 4.5: Aurore's request

Figure 4.6: Rose explains the impacts of good and bad customer service

CONTINUED

Mauritian DMCs deliver customer service to leisure tourists and to business tourist customers.

Business (MICE) tourism customers include organisations that want to arrange events for their customers or their staff. AIOM DMC members provide packages including:

- accommodation
- meeting and conference venues
- transport
- social activities and entertainment.

Providing good customer service is very important to AIOM members. Rose explains the impacts of good and bad customer service in **Figure 4.6**.

Questions

1 Outline how DMCs in Mauritius can provide a good standard of sustainable customer service.

2 Suggest how DMC responses to Aurore's request can deliver good customer service.

3 Explain the impacts of bad customer service.

4 Discuss:

- how DMCs in Mauritius can deliver good customer service to business tourists
- why delivering good customer service to business tourists is important to Mauritian DMCs.

5 *Extension:* Assess the importance of DMCs to the sustainable development of destinations such as Mauritius.

TIPS

- To help with your revision, think about links between Aurore's holiday to Mauritius and:
  - Mauritius as a sustainable destination (see 2.1)
  - DMCs as tourism organisations (see 2.5).

- To help think about links between Aurore's holiday to Mauritius and DMCs, remember that Aurore is a potential customer for a DMC. It is DMCs that provide packages for inbound tourists. The AIOM does not provide packages. The AIOM is an association of DMCs in Mauritius.

- To help understand good customer service, remember to consider:
  - different types of travel and tourism organisations
  - different types of tourists.

KEY CONCEPT LINKS

- Customer service is very important in travel and tourism. Travel and tourism organisations are businesses with tourist customers. These organisations depend on tourist customers choosing their products and services. Money spent by customers helps travel and tourism businesses to grow.

- The impacts of good and bad customer service are very important to travel and tourism organisations. Good customer service brings more customers and more income to travel and tourism organisations. Good customer service helps tourism businesses to grow. Bad customer service, however, can cause difficulties for tourism businesses. Difficulties can include fewer customers and a poor reputation. It is very important for travel and tourism organisations to avoid the difficulties caused by poor customer service. Tourism businesses in difficulty may have to reduce staff numbers, may lose money, and may even close.

ACTIVITY 4.1

1 a Identify a range of different types of leisure tourists.

   b Outline what is meant by a business (MICE) tourism customer.

   c Describe the importance of customer service in travel and tourism.

2 Explain how customer service can help to meet the increasing demand for sustainable tourism.

3 As a class, discuss examples of good and bad customer service you have experienced.

4 *Project:* Choose a destination and a type of customer.

   Recommend a customised package for the customer you have chosen in the destination you have chosen that:

   • uses local providers in your chosen destination

   • includes sustainable options.

   Justify your recommendation.

   Explain how your recommendation delivers good customer service.

REFLECTION

How did you come to your recommendation for a customised package for a chosen customer?

How could you improve the method you used?

4.2 Delivery of customer service

Introduction

All travel and tourism organisations deliver customer service. Customer service involves helping customers by providing them with products and services.

Customer care policies

Travel and tourism organisations have customer care policies. The *Customer care in a Colaba café* case study gives information that shows how customer care policies help staff to deliver good customer service. A travel and tourism organisation's customer care policy may include how to:

• answer customer enquiries

• make reservations

• take payments

• handle complaints.

KEY WORD

customer care policy: a plan relating to how staff should deliver customer service. Travel and tourism organisations decide how staff should serve customers

Teamwork is very important in the delivery of good customer service in travel and tourism. Customer care policies help staff to work well as a team. Different members of staff:

• work together to serve customers

• serve customers in the same way

• serve customers to the same standard.

Travel and tourism customer care policies may set standards for staff. An example of a customer care standard is that staff members should politely greet every customer.

Product knowledge

Product knowledge is very important in delivering good customer service. Travel and tourism organisation staff need to have a good knowledge of the products and services provided by the organisation. Good product knowledge helps staff to deliver good customer service. Staff who have good product knowledge can better explain products and services to customers. Customers are more likely to buy products and services that have been well explained.

KEY WORD

product knowledge: the knowledge that travel and tourism organisation staff have of the products and services provided by the organisation. Good product knowledge enables staff to deliver good customer service. Staff with good product knowledge are better able to explain products and services to customers

Delivery of customer service

The *Customer care in a Colaba café* case study gives information about the delivery of customer service, including:

- handling customer enquiries
- procedures for handling complaints
- making reservations and taking orders
- having good product knowledge.

CASE STUDY

Customer care in a Colaba café

Colaba is part of the Indian city of Mumbai, which is a city destination on the west coast of India. India is the largest country in southern Asia. Mumbai is a very big city. More than 18 million people live in Mumbai.

Colaba is popular with inbound tourists to Mumbai. Cultural tourists enjoy sightseeing in Colaba. Built attractions include the Gateway of India monument and the historic Taj Mahal Palace Hotel.

Figure 4.7: The Gateway of India monument

Tourists visiting Colaba are customers of food and drink providers. Food and drink providers include restaurants, cafés, local street food vendors and takeaways (takeouts). **Figure 4.8** shows customer service in a restaurant in Colaba.

Figure 4.8: Customer service in a restaurant dining room in Colaba

Staff in the restaurant work together in teams. Kitchen staff include the chef's team. The chef's team prepare the food together. Dining room staff work as a team to:

- take reservations
- welcome customers and show them to a table
- take meal orders
- serve food to customers
- check that the customer is happy with the food served
- take payments and handle complaints.

Stages in the dining room team's customer service delivery are shown in **Figure 4.9**.

CONTINUED

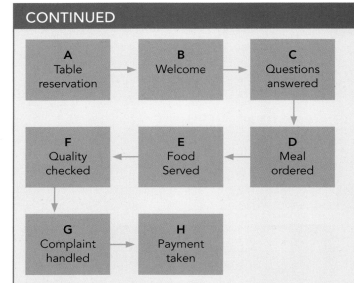

Figure 4.9: Stages in delivering customer service in a restaurant dining room

Sometimes, customers have complaints. Restaurant customer care policies include how staff should handle a customer complaint (see **Figure 4.10**). A dining room team member such as a server (waitron) handles some complaints personally. For example, a customer may complain that the food is not hot. The server should listen carefully and acknowledge the complaint. The server should then take the food back to the kitchen to be reheated or replaced. Sometimes, staff members such as servers refer complaints to senior colleagues.

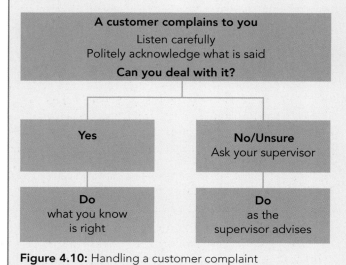

Figure 4.10: Handling a customer complaint

Questions

1   Refer to **Figure 4.9**. Identify stages in restaurant dining room customer service for each of the following:

   a   *Is everything OK with your meal?*

   b   *How many people will the table be for, Madam?*

   c   *Hello. My name is Sai, I'm your server today.*

   d   *I'm sorry to hear that, Sir. I'll find the manager for you.*

For example, the answer to question a, *Is everything OK with your meal?* happens at stage **F** Quality checked.

2   **Figure 4.8** shows customer service in a restaurant dining room in Colaba.

   Suggest **two** reasons why the chef might speak with a customer in the dining room.

3   Explain how customer complaints are handled in a restaurant.

4   In a group, discuss the customer care policies you would recommend to the restaurant for:

   •   welcoming customers

   •   taking a meal order

   •   checking food quality with customers.

5   *Extension:* Evaluate the importance of team work in a restaurant.

KEY WORDS

acknowledge the complaint: part of handling a complaint. Staff politely let the customer know that the complaint is heard and understood.

refer complaints: part of handling complaints. Staff members tell a senior colleague about a serious complaint. The senior colleague handles the complaint.

senior colleagues: staff members who have more responsibility. Senior colleagues in travel and tourism organisations include supervisors and managers.

- Understand the difference between customer care and customer service. Customer care is how customers should be served. Travel and tourism organisations decide on customer care policies. These policies state how customers will be served. Customer service is actually serving customers.

- Be aware that:

  - different travel and tourism organisations have different customer care policies

  - the customer care policies of different organisations have similarities.

KEY CONCEPT LINKS

- The delivery of customer service is very important to travel and tourism organisations. These organisations have customer care policies which state how customer service should be delivered. Good customer service benefits travel and tourism organisations.

- Customers complain. Customer care policies include how staff should handle customer complaints. Staff members such as restaurant servers (waitrons) handle simple complaints. Staff understand that serious complaints should be handled by senior colleagues.

ACTIVITY 4.2

1 Types of travel and tourism organisations include:

- travel agents
- tour operators
- accommodation providers
- food and drink providers
- visitor attractions
- ancillary service providers.

CONTINUED

a Identify types of travel and tourism organisations that handle customer enquiries by:

   i giving directions

   ii preparing itineraries

   iii providing information

   iv making recommendations to tourists.

b Describe ways in which travel and tourism organisations handle customer enquiries.

2 Explain:

a the difference between customer care and customer service

b why the customer care policies of different organisations have similarities

c how customer care policies help staff to work together as a team.

3 Explain how good customer service benefits travel and tourism organisations.

4 Work with a partner to role-play each of the following customer service delivery situations:

a a restaurant customer ordering a meal

b a tour guide welcoming a customer

c a hotel front-desk team member handling a customer complaint.

5 Discuss with a partner:

a your feelings when handling a complaint

b how you would approach handling a complaint in a real customer service delivery situation.

KEY WORD

itinerary: a tour plan or programme. Itineraries give details of routes, directions, times and places. For example, a business tourism (MICE) itinerary might include air flight details, hotel and transfer details, and event venues and times.

4.3 The provision of customer service for different types of tourists

Introduction

Travel and tourism organisations provide customer service for different types of tourists. Different types of tourists include:

- leisure tourists

- business tourists

- families with children

- tourists of different age groups, including older people

- tourists with specific needs, such as **mobility**, **visual**, hearing, language and cultural needs.

Rose explains some specific needs in **Figure 4.11**.

The *Access for all* case study shows how a travel and tourism organisation (Copenhagen Airport) provides customer service for different types of tourists, including:

- **access**

- information

- assisting tourists with specific needs

- **facilities**, including sustainably managed facilities

- ancillary services.

Figure 4.11: Rose explains some specific needs

CASE STUDY

Access for all: Copenhagen Airport

Copenhagen is the biggest city in Denmark, a country in north-west Europe. Different types of tourists are customers of Copenhagen Airport (CPH). Inbound tourists visit Copenhagen and the rest of Denmark, while outbound tourists travel to other destinations around the world.

Figure 4.12: Copenhagen Airport

Copenhagen Airport provides customer services to improve accessibility for persons with reduced mobility (PRMs). In fact, the airport won the 2020 Accessible Airport Award.

Figure 4.13: Inside Copenhagen Airport

Accessibility services provided for tourists at Copenhagen Airport include the PRM-friendly accessibility services shown in **Figure 4.14**.

CPH smartphone app	e-gates and online check-in
public transport close to the airport entrance	website and online customer service

Figure 4.14: PRM-friendly accessibility services at Copenhagen Airport

The interactive CPH smartphone app provides customers with information to help guide them through the airport. The CPH app is available in different languages. CPH app languages are English and Danish (the language spoken in Denmark). The CPH app includes:

- flight departure and arrival times, departure gate numbers and alerts of any changes

- reservations and payments for car parking at Copenhagen Airport

KEY WORDS

e-gates: automatic electronic gates. E-gates are used in airports for passport and border controls. Tourists go through e-gates to board aircraft

online check-in: using the internet to register people and their baggage (luggage) for an air flight

accessibility: the ease of reaching or entering places. For example, is it easy to reach the airport? Facilities that are easy for everyone to enter are easily accessible to all

PRMs (persons with reduced mobility): tourists who are less able to move around freely. Tourists with physical or hidden disability, tourists with visual impairment, older tourists and tourists with sports injuries are examples of PRMs

PRM-friendly: describes a facility that PRMs can use easily

CONTINUED

- a map of the airport

- information about shops, banks, passenger lounges, restaurants and cafés

- ordering and payment for food to take onto aircraft and to avoid queues (lines)

- online shopping.

Some PRM tourists need staff assistance to move around the airport. CPH has meeting points with push-button and telephone links so PRM tourists can ask for a staff member to come and help. A visual message is provided for people who have hearing difficulties. PRM tourists can use the CPH smartphone app, an SMS text or the website's online customer service link to ask for staff assistance. PRM assistance is managed from the CPH Assistance Centre.

Tourists with hidden disabilities can wear a special CPH badge, bearing a picture of a sunflower. The sunflower badge shows airport staff that the tourist is a PRM with a hidden disability. Staff at Copenhagen Airport receive training in PRM accessiblity. PRM accessibility training is for all staff working at CPH, including ancillary services staff, sales staff in airport shops and security staff.

Sustainably managed facilities at CPH include e-mobility facilities. Electric vehicles are used to transport PRMs through the airport. Charging points for electric cars are provided in the car parks.

Questions

1 Outline the customer services at Copenhagen Airport that:

- improve access

- provide information

- are sustainably managed facilities

- involve ancillary services.

2 Suggest how signage helps to provide good customer service in Copenhagen Airport.

3 Explain how customer services provided at Copenhagen Airport help PRMs.

4 In a group, discuss how airports such as Copenhagen Airport can provide services for customers with the following specific needs:

a language

b dietary

c cultural.

5 *Extension:* Evaluate the extent to which Copenhagen Airport provides for the specific needs of customers.

KEY WORDS

hidden disability: reduced mobility for reasons that other people may not see immediately. Hidden disabilities include learning difficulties, mental health problems and speech, visual or hearing impairments

e-mobility: moving using electric vehicles. For example, electric vehicles are often used in airports to transport people with mobility difficulties

signage: a set of signs and direction indicators used to guide tourists. For example, an airport has signs indicating directions to facilities such as toilets (restrooms), departure gates and taxis

Figure 4.15: E-gates in an airport

TIPS

- Understand that accessibility includes access for all people with reduced mobility (PRMs) and that PRMs include people with all disabilities that affect mobility. People with physical disabilities and people with hidden disabilities are PRMs. PRMs include people with visual, hearing, speech and learning difficulties.

- Be aware that PRM-friendly facilities benefit customers who are not PRMs as well as customers who are PRMs. For example, e-gates are quicker to use for all customers, not just PRM customers.

- Remember that ancillary services are travel and tourism services that are additional to tours, accommodation, food and drink, and visitor attraction services. Examples of ancillary services include car hire, currency exchange, information and travel insurance services.

KEY CONCEPT LINKS

- Providing good service to all customers is very important to travel and tourism organisations. Providing good customer service to all types of tourists brings more repeat business to travel and tourism organisations.

- Reputation is very important to travel and tourism organisations. Providing good customer service to customers with specific needs improves the reputation of travel and tourism organisations.

ACTIVITY 4.3

1   Some tourists have specific needs:

    a   Identify **three** specific needs of some tourists.

    b   Describe **three** customer services provided by travel and tourism organisations for tourists with specific needs.

2   a   Outline **three** PRM-friendly customer services provided by travel and tourism organisations

    b   Explain how all types of tourists can benefit from PRM-friendly customer services.

3   *Project:* Work with a partner to:

- investigate PRM-friendly customer service provision at a travel and tourism organisation other than Copenhagen Airport.

- present the findings of your investigation to the rest of the class.

4   Evaluate the extent to which different travel and tourism organisations provide good customer service to customers with specific mobility needs.

REFLECTION

How confident do you feel in your understanding of the provision of customer service for different types of tourists?

What can you do in order to increase your level of confidence?

4.4 Skills required when working in the travel and tourism industry

Introduction

Important skills for staff working in travel and tourism organisations include:

- personal skills such as personal presentation and body language, communication, clear speech, numeracy, literacy, ICT and problem-solving

- interpersonal skills such as listening, patience, being welcoming, being flexible, working in a team and some ability to speak more than one language.

Personal skills

Personal skills such as personal presentation and body language create a good first impression. Personal skills such as communication, clear speech, numeracy, literacy, ICT and problem-solving help staff to deliver good customer service. A good first impression and good customer service makes customers more likely to spend money and more likely to give positive customer feedback.

Interpersonal skills

Interpersonal skills such as listening, patience, being welcoming, being flexible, working in a team and having some ability to speak in more than one language are important in travel and tourism. All interpersonal skills help staff to deliver good customer service. Good customer service makes customers more likely to spend money and more likely to give positive customer feedback.

Importance of training and types of training

Skills enable staff to provide good customer service to tourists, including responsible tourists. Staff learn and improve skills by practise and through training.

Training is very important in travel and tourism. Trained staff deliver better customer service.

Some important types of staff training in travel and tourism, including in sustainable tourism practices, are:

- on-the-job training, including:
  - work shadowing
  - job rotation
  - mentoring.
- formal learning, including:
  - classroom-based training
  - online learning.

The *Check in to world hotel training* case study gives information about important skills and types of training in travel and tourism organisations.

KEY WORDS

personal presentation: how staff present themselves to customers. Personal presentation includes how staff look, what they say and what they do. Dress, grooming, speech and behaviour are all part of personal presentation

body language: communication without words. Facial expressions, gestures and body posture are parts of body language communication

on-the-job training: learning skills whilst working

work shadowing: a form of training. The trainee observes an experienced staff member at work. The trainee learns skills by observing a senior colleague

job rotation: a way in which staff and trainees can experience different jobs in an organisation. Staff and trainees change jobs for a temporary period. For example, a restaurant server (waitron) may work for a short time as a member of the front desk staff

mentoring: a form of training. Senior colleagues show staff and trainees how to do tasks. For example, an experienced member of a hotel's food and beverage staff may train an apprentice on how to deliver good customer service

---

CASE STUDY

Check in to world hotel training

Travel and tourism organisations include global hotel chains, such as the Marriott, Hilton, Wyndham, Accor, Shangri-La, IHG and NH hotels. Hotel chains often use different brand names. For example, Sofitel is an Accor brand name; Holiday Inn and Crowne Plaza are IHG hotel brand names. Companies such as Accor and IHG operate hotels around the world. World hotel companies provide training to improve staff skills.

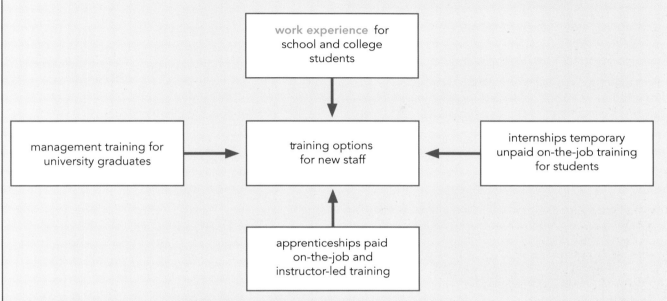

Figure 4.16: Training options provided by a world hotel chain for new staff

KEY WORD

work experience: working unpaid in an organisation for a short time. Work experience students learn about working in an organisation. Work experience students learn skills through observing and helping staff. Work experience placements are often for one or two weeks. Some short work experience placements are for one day

CONTINUED

Young people hoping to work in a hotel receive training provided by the company. **Figure 4.16** shows in-house training options provided by a world (global) hotel chain for new staff.

> **KEY WORD**
>
> in-house training: staff training provided in an organisation

In-house training helps new staff to learn skills needed to work in a hotel. **Figure 4.17** shows how much new staff learn from different forms of training provided by a global hotel chain.

Learning comes from

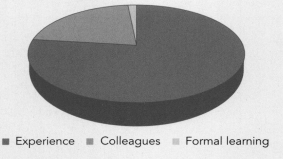

■ Experience ■ Colleagues ■ Formal learning

Figure 4.17: New staff learning from different forms of training provided by a global hotel chain

Staff in a large hotel work in different departments. **Figure 4.18** shows some hotel departments. Different hotel operating companies may have different department names.

Training for new hotel staff often begins with orientation. Orientation is learning about working in the hotel. Orientation helps new staff to understand the quality of customer service expected. During orientation, staff receive a copy of the hotel's staff handbook. Staff handbooks are usually e-documents that staff access via an app. The staff handbook provides practical information about working in the hotel. For example, the handbook has names and contact details for some senior colleagues at the hotel. These senior colleagues can provide new staff with advice and support. New staff receive training in using the hotel's ICT equipment and in how to use the hotel's computer software.

Work shadowing is an important part of training new hotel staff. New staff shadow senior colleagues to learn how to serve customers in ways that the company expects. Managers may act as coaches, observing staff performance and providing feedback and guidance. Manager coaching helps new staff to learn how to do their job well. Training courses may be available for new staff. The staff handbook and senior colleagues make staff aware of training opportunities that are available.

Front office	Housekeeping (room cleaning and bedmaking)	Kitchen	Sales and marketing	Spa and recreation
Food and beverage (drink)	Human resources (staff)	Finance	Building and maintenance	Event management

Figure 4.18: Some hotel departments

CONTINUED

Hotel staff learn a lot by doing their job. It is important that new staff are able to quickly access support from the handbook app and from senior colleagues. Support helps staff to serve customers well.

José is a new member of staff in a large hotel. Ling is a more experienced member of staff in the same hotel. José and Ling share their stories in a staff group discussion in **Figure 4.19**.

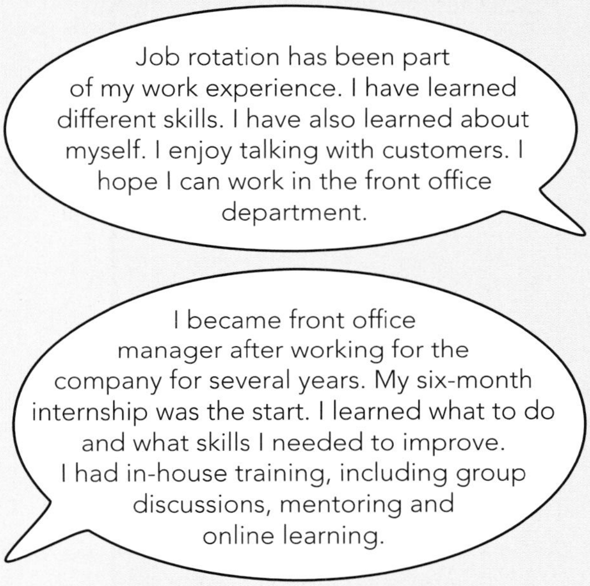

> Job rotation has been part of my work experience. I have learned different skills. I have also learned about myself. I enjoy talking with customers. I hope I can work in the front office department.

> I became front office manager after working for the company for several years. My six-month internship was the start. I learned what to do and what skills I needed to improve. I had in-house training, including group discussions, mentoring and online learning.

Figure 4.19: José and Ling talk about training

Questions

1 Customer service skills are important.

    a Identify **three** hotel departments where customer service skills are important.

    b Explain how customer service skills are important in the departments you have identified.

2 Do this question as a project. Choose a hotel chain that you are familiar with, or do your resarch first.

    a Outline **four** training options provided for new staff by the global hotel chain.

    b Suggest training options for each of the following people:

        i   a school or college student

        ii a university graduate.

    c Give reasons for your suggested training options.

3 This question refers to **Figure 4.19**.

    Discuss the importance of José sharing stories with Ling in a group discussion.

4 Evaluate the importance of on-the-job training for hotel staff.

TIPS

- Observe people's personal and interpersonal skills. People show personal and interpersonal skills in many situations you may experience. For example, people working in shops, in markets, on transport or in a school or college display skills that are transferable to the travel and tourism industry.

- Develop your self-awareness of your own future. Compare what you know about yourself with different ways to begin job training. For example, would you benefit from work experience, an internship, an apprenticeship or from management training for university graduates?

KEY WORD

transferable skills: skills that people can use in different jobs and in different situations. For example, good customer service skills are transferable from a job in a visitor attraction to working in a restaurant.

KEY CONCEPT LINKS

- Good customer service is very important in travel and tourism. Skills are needed to deliver good customer service. Training helps travel and tourism staff to improve their customer service skills.

- Travel and tourism staff work at different levels of seniority. Senior staff include managers. Senior colleagues including managers help to train other staff members. For example, in a hotel kitchen, the head chef may mentor an apprentice.

ACTIVITY 4.4

1 Personal and interpersonal skills are important attributes.

   a Describe **two** personal and **two** interpersonal skills that are useful in travel and tourism.

   b Outline the difference between *personal skills* and *interpersonal skills*.

2 Suggest how body language and personal presentation help staff to deliver good customer service.

3 Training is a requirement in the hospitality industry.

   a Explain the usefulness of different types of on-the-job training and formal training in travel and tourism.

   b Suggest how training in sustainable practices can help staff to deliver good customer service.

4 With a partner, discuss examples of good customer service you have observed. How did personal and interpersonal skills help staff to deliver good customer service in the examples you observed?

REFLECTION

How do you think you could apply your learning about the skills required when working in the travel and tourism industry?

1   Refer to **Figure 14**, a copy of the customer feedback form completed by an international traveller after their recent experience at a visitor attraction.

How did we do today?

	Excellent	Good	Satisfactory	Poor	Very poor
Welcome				X	
Value for money		X			
Activities offered	X				
Quality of products		X			
Food and drink selection	X				
Speed of service			X		
Friendliness of staff		X			
Cleanliness	X				
Overall visitor experience		X			

Figure 14: A completed customer feedback form

a   **Identify** the following:

  • The customer's least satisfactory part of their visit

  • The customer's rating of the attraction's cleanliness.   [2]

b   Name **two** aspects of the questionnaire which will help the visitor attraction to make an assessment of the ways in which the staff interact with customers.   [2]

c   **Describe** how poor customer service will have a negative effect on a tourism business.   [4]

d   **Discuss two** ways in which visitor attractions could cater for international customers who are not fluent speakers of a foreign language.   [6]

e   **Evaluate** the likely need for staff at the attraction's ticket office to have good communication and numeracy skills.   [6]

[Total 20 marks]

CONTINUED

2 Refer to **Figure 15**, part of a resort hotel's training manual for its hospitality staff.

Restaurant host/hostess customer service standards

It is important that you should:

- always acknowledge guests
- always walk guests at a comfortable pace
- assist guests as much as possible
- always keep guests fully informed e.g. about delays
- always smile and show enthusiasm
- always acknowledge guests as they leave
- never leave a table before guests are completely seated
- never leave the host stand unattended
- never argue with a guest
- always sell the outlet and its products and act as a source of information
- never chew gum, eat or drink on the job.

When bidding farewell to guests, you should:

- say, 'Have a good day' or 'Good night' to all departing guests. Be polite, warm and courteous. Treat guests as you would a guest leaving your own home.
- check on how everything went during their visit. Ask, 'How was everything?' If there were any problems, try to convince the guests not to leave whilst you get the manager.
- say, 'Thank you for coming. We hope to see you soon.' Use their name whenever possible.
- invite the guest back
- be able to assist them with further information, if required
- give guests a smile as they leave. Smiles are contagious – when guests that are leaving are smiling, incoming guests will notice.

Figure 15: Guidance for hospitality staff at a resort hotel

a   With reference to **Figure 15**, describe how the host/hostess is expected to greet arriving and departing restaurant guests. [2]

b   Some of the guests will have special needs. **State one** type of special dietary need and describe how the restaurant is likely to respond in order to achieve guest satisfaction. [2]

c   The host/hostess will sometimes receive a complaint from a restaurant guest. **Suggest** the ways in which the staff member should deal with customer complaints. [4]

d   Discuss **two** ways in which the host/hostess is likely to use their teamwork skills to help ensure the smooth running of the restaurant. [6]

e   Evaluate the ways in which front line staff's body language and personal presentation contribute to the organisation's delivery of excellent customer service. [6]

[Total 20 marks]

3 Refer to **Figure 16**, which gives details about Emirates Service Reviews.

TRIPADVISOR REVIEWS

Emirates Service Reviews

Were we helpful, friendly and attentive? Find out from customers who have flown with us in these Emirates service reviews.

Emirates service   ⊙⊙ tripadvisor

⦿⦿⦿⦿◖ 40,924 reviews

Excellent	24,265
Very Good	8,782
Average	3,238
Poor	1,824
Terrible	2,815

Your opinion matters.

Write a review on TripAdvisor to share your experience about Emirates

Write a review ☐

Your comfort and most importantly your safety are our top priorities at Emirates. We hope you find our world-class service friendly, helpful, attentive and reassuring along your whole journey. You can read through these Emirates service reviews on TripAdvisor to find out what our customers think of their experience of our teams at check-in, in the departure lounge, boarding gate and then through to our cabin crew on board.

Our teams have extensive training in safety, security and service to make your flight safe, comfortable and memorable all the way. Read through Emirates airport service reviews to see how our ground teams help you to enjoy a smooth journey through to your flight. And if you need special assistance, you can check out the Emirates wheelchair assistance reviews to see how we support you at the airport and on board.

If you're curious about our meal service, drinks service and general comfort, read through these Emirates in-flight service reviews and Emirates cabin crew service reviews. And if you've flown with us before, share your own experience in your Emirates customer service review on TripAdvisor.

Figure 16: Information about Emirates customer reviews

CONTINUED

a Identify the following:

- The number of reviews that rated the services offered by Emirates as being 'poor'

- The passenger special needs that Emirates makes provision to meet. **[2]**

b With reference to **Figure 16**, name **two** aspects of the Emirates in-flight experience that passengers can read about on TripAdvisor reviews. **[2]**

c Describe how passengers will experience Emirates' customer service before they take their seats on board the aircraft. **[4]**

d Discuss **two** ways in which long-haul international airlines such as Emirates attempt to meet the needs of families travelling with young children. **[6]**

e All airline cabin crew will have received appropriate training. They will also be encouraged to develop their own personal skills. Evaluate the likely importance of clear speech and problem-solving in helping members of the cabin crew to deliver an excellent standard of customer service to passengers. **[6]**

[Total 20 marks]

SELF-EVALUATION CHECKLIST

After studying this unit, copy and complete this table:

I am now able to:	Needs more work	Almost there	Ready to move on
understand the importance of customer service in travel and tourism.			
explain the delivery of customer service in travel and tourism.			
discuss the provision of customer service for different types of tourists.			
evaluate the skills required when working in the travel and tourism industry.			

Destination marketing

TRAVEL AND TOURISM IN CONTEXT

Marketing Fred's coffee stall

Local street food vendors provide tourists and local people with food and drinks. The vendors serve customers on streets, in markets and at events. Fred sells a variety of coffee, tea and chocolate drinks to local people and tourists in street markets, which appeals to many tourists.

Figure 5.1: Fred's coffee stall

Fred sells coffee and other hot drinks to go (to take away). He also has cookies and small bottles of water for customers to buy. He provides tables and chairs for customers, who can relax whilst enjoying their coffee and the sights and sounds of the market around them. Fred plays recorded music for them.

When he was younger, Fred worked in a café. This experience helped him to understand the importance of **marketing** and promotion. In **Figure 5.2**, Fred explains why marketing and promotion are important to his coffee stall business.

Fred has thought about factors affecting the marketing of his coffee. He needs to:

- meet the needs of target **market segments** – local people and tourists

- plan for appropriate opening times – opening the stall when people want to buy coffee

KEY WORDS

marketing: ensuring products and services are attractive to customers

market segments: the elements of a destination's market

business cards: small cards giving details of a business. Business cards are often 8.5cm long and 5.5cm wide. Details on business cards often include the name of the business, the service it offers, when it is open and how to make contact

> To make money, I need to attract people to my stall.

> I promote the stall with music and by using signs. One sign says, "Smile, there's coffee". People do smile when they see the sign. I need people to say, "Let's buy coffee from that stall".

> Tourists like to be responsible. I sell organic coffee. I use recyclable cups. I have bins. say, "Let's buy coffee from that stall".

> People enjoy my coffee. I like to talk to the tourists. Customers come back and tell other people about me. I have **business cards** to give customers.

Figure 5.2: Fred explains the importance of marketing

CONTINUED

- consider costs such as rent, ingredients, water, electricity, cups and fuel

- have a strong and sustainable brand image that attracts customers

- monitor the business: is the stall busy? Is the stall making money?

Figure 5.3 shows the marketing mix of Fred's coffee stall. The marketing mix is the combination of product, promotion, price and place used to market products and services.

Fred has a marketing mix that succeeds in attracting customers to his coffee stall because he has a good combination of product, promotion, price and place:

- product is what Fred sells

- promotion is how Fred informs customers about his coffee stall

- price is how much money Fred charges

- place is where Fred markets his coffee stall business.

Travel and tourism organisations do market research. Analysing market research helps travel and tourism businesses to develop their product/service mix. The product/service mix targets different market segments.

Travel and tourism students interviewed Fred about his market research. The students asked Fred about the product/service mix of his coffee stall. **Figure 5.4** shows some of the interview.

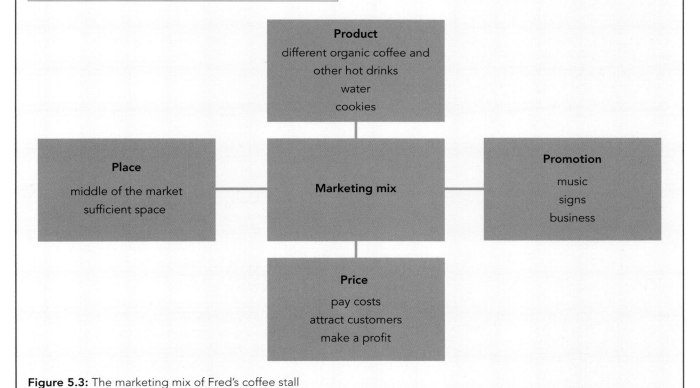

Figure 5.3: The marketing mix of Fred's coffee stall

CONTINUED

What market research did you do?

How did market research help you develop your product/service mix?

I talked to people in the café where worked. I observed what customers bought at what price. I visited the markets before I began the stall. I saw who was in the market at different times. I asked tourists about coffee. I asked tourists about organic ingredients. Tourists spoke to me in different languages. Tourists wanted somewhere to sit down to relax.

Market research gave me useful information. Tourists come to the market in couples and groups. Tourist groups are often families. Most tourists like coffee but some prefer tea or chocolate drinks. Some tourists wanted cookies or bottles of water. Tourists liked to be able to sit down or stand and talk to me. Music attracts tourists to the stall.

Figure 5.4: Interviewing Fred

The travel and tourism students thought about Fred's stall using **market analysis tools**:

- SWOT analysis
- PESTLE analysis

SWOT analysis identifies strengths, weaknesses, opportunities and threats. PESTLE analysis considers external factors that affect a travel and tourism business. External factors are factors from outside the business. For example, a travel and tourism business must obey the law (legal factors). External factors that affect businesses are shown in **Figure 5.6. Figure 5.5** and **Figure 5.6** show the students' SWOT and PESTLE analyses of Fred's coffee stall business.

Travel and tourism providers use SWOT and PESTLE analysis to help plan the future of their business. For example, a street food vendor such as Fred might wonder if he should change his product/service mix. Should he provide cakes, for example? Should he sell ice cream?

KEY WORDS

market analysis tool: something you use to investigate the market for travel and tourism products and services

SWOT analysis: a market analysis tool. SWOT analysis identifies the strengths and weaknesses of a travel and tourism business as well as the opportunities and threats that exist for the business.

PESTLE analysis: a market analysis tool. PESTLE analysis considers factors that affect a travel and tourism business. Factors that affect a travel and tourism business are political (government-related), economic (money-related), sociological (society-related), technological, legal and environmental factors.

CONTINUED

Marketing travel and tourism businesses is an ongoing activity. Fred needs to think about marketing on an ongoing basis. Large travel and tourism organisations have managers who think about marketing. Marketing attracts customers. Customers spend money. Money makes travel and tourism businesses profitable. Profits help travel and tourism businesses grow.

Strengths
friendly and efficient good coffee to take away seating and music several languages spoken

Weaknesses
not much space limited seating lines (queues) in high season cookies are the only food sold

Opportunities
the only coffee stall in the market could widen food range could find a bigger site

Threats
possible future competition bad weather decline in tourism less demand

Figure 5.5: A SWOT analysis of Fred's coffee stall business

P Political	E Economic	S Sociological	T Technological	L Legal	E Environmental
local government permit to operate and maybe grow	cost of ingredients such as coffee beans cost of water and electricity the price customers will pay	age of potential customers social class volume and type of tourism	coffee machine electronic payment methods such as contactless payment	food safety laws customer safety laws	responsible practices organic ingredients locally sourced ingredients recyclable cups bins

Figure 5.6: A PESTLE analysis of Fred's coffee stall business

Questions

1 a What is meant by product/service mix?

   b Outline the product/service mix of Fred's coffee stall.

2 Describe:
   - how Fred attracts tourists to the stall
   - the four parts of the marketing mix of Fred's coffee stall.

3 Explain **three** factors that affect the marketing of Fred's coffee stall.

4 Discuss with a partner
   - how market research helped Fred develop his stall's product/service mix
   - the students' PESTLE analysis shown in **Figure 5.6**.

5 *Extension:* Assess the importance of the marketing mix to Fred's coffee stall.

5.1 The importance of marketing to travel and tourism organisations

Introduction

Marketing makes travel and tourism organisations attractive to customers. Customers are attracted by the four **P**s of the marketing mix. Successful travel and tourism organisations market attractive **p**roducts, at attractive **p**rices, in **p**laces customers find attractive. Successful marketing includes successful **p**romotion, which is part of marketing. Promotion is how travel and tourism organisations tell customers about their products and services.

The importance of marketing to travel and tourism organisations is shown by the case study *South Africa's luxury train-hotels*. Marketing is important to travel and tourism organisations for the following reasons.

More customers

Marketing and promotion bring more customers to travel and tourism organisations. More customers using services increases the sales of travel and tourism organisations. These organisations can become more profitable because of marketing and promotion. More profit helps travel and tourism businesses to pay for more marketing and promotion, and more marketing and promotion increases the market share and widens the customer base.

> **KEY WORDS**
>
> **market share:** the proportion of potential customers who use or buy an organisation's products and services. For example, if one tenth of tourists visiting a destination stay at one hotel, the hotel's market share is one tenth (10%).
>
> **customer base:** the set of people who use or buy the products of a travel and tourism organisation. The customer base of a travel and tourism organisation are types of tourist.

Competitive advantage

Marketing helps travel and tourism organisations to have a competitive advantage because marketing and promotion help to make travel and tourism organisations more attractive than competitor organisations. The competitive advantage example of Rovos Rail, a South African luxury train operator, is given in the case study *South Africa's luxury train-hotels*.

> **KEY WORD**
>
> **competitive advantage:** makes a travel and tourism organisation more attractive than competitor organisations

Positive image and reputation for sustainable practices

Marketing promotes what is good about a travel and tourism organisation's product, price and place. Promotional materials create a positive image of a travel and tourism organisation in the minds of potential customers. Positive images of organisations and of products help to attract customers. More customers brings more sales and more profitabilty. The circle of links between marketing and promotion, customers and profits is shown in **Figure 5.7**.

Good customer feedback helps travel and tourism organisations to build good reputations. Marketing uses a good reputation to attract customers. The good reputation of an organisation can be promoted to help increase sales. A reputation for good sustainable practices can be promoted to help attract more customers.

Figure 5.7: The circle of marketing, customers and profits

Greater customer satisfaction

Greater customer satisfaction encourages **brand loyalty** and repeat business. The choice of customers to continue buying the same product from the same organisation brings more profitability. More profitability enables more marketing and promotion. More marketing and promotion can attract more customers. More customers increase profitability (see **Figure 5.7**).

KEY WORD

brand loyalty: the choice of customers to continue buying the same product from the same organisation

CASE STUDY

South Africa's luxury train-hotels

South Africa is a country and destination in southern Africa. Travel and tourism organisations in South Africa provide three luxury **train-hotel** services:

- the Blue Train
- Rovos Rail
- the Shongololo Express.

The luxury train-hotel routes are long-distance routes, for example, between Cape Town and Pretoria (about 1,500 km, over 900 miles). Journeys are overnight travel experiences. The Blue Train travel experience packages usually include two nights spent on the train. Some train-hotel journey experiences last several days or longer. Sleeping accommodation is in private luxury cabins. Customers are attracted by the idea of viewing spectacular scenery from a luxury train whilst enjoying a high-quality on-board restaurant and room service.

Figure 5.8 shows a private cabin where passengers sleep. **Figure 5.9** shows the interior of one of the train-hotel dining (restaurant) cars. All three luxury train-hotel services in South Africa have similar historic, wood-lined luxury interiors.

Figure 5.8: A private cabin where passengers sleep

Figure 5.9: The interior of a luxury train-hotel dining car

South Africa's luxury train-hotels are operated by two different travel and tourism organisations. Rovos operates both Rovos Rail and the Shongololo Express. The Blue Train is owned by a different organisation, called Transnet. The train-hotel providers market products and services to attract customers. The Blue Train and the Rovos train-hotels are in **competition** for market share.

South Africa's train-hotel providers aim to widen their customer base by seeking a competitive advantage. Rovos Rail, for example, operates traditional steam locomotives (engines). Traditional steam locomotives appeal to tourists with a special interest in railways.

KEY WORDS

train-hotel: a train with hotel services on board. Hotel services on a train-hotel include sleeping accommodation and restaurant services

competition: trying to be better than others. Travel and tourism organisations try to be better than each other at attracting customers

CONTINUED

South Africa's luxury train-hotel providers use similar promotional techniques. The internet and social media are important ways to contact potential and existing customers. Rovos and the Blue Train use their own websites to promote products and services. Tour operator websites promote Blue Train and Rovos packages. Some packages include:

- overnight accommodation in a hotel before or after the train journey

- visits to attractions along the route.

Figure 5.10 shows an example of a South African train-hotel package.

On the train:
- En-suite luxury sleeping accommodation in cabins
- All meals served in the dining car
- 24-hour room service
- Limited laundry service.

Before and after:
- One night's hotel accommodation before departure or after arrival
- Shuttle transfer (transit) between hotel and railway station.

Also included:
- Guided attraction visit
- Government tax.

Figure 5.10: A South African train-hotel package

Questions

1   Using the information you have read:

   a   describe a South African train-hotel package.

   b   outline why the Blue Train, Rovos Rail and Shongololo Express trains are also luxury hotels.

2   Competition has been defined as a key word.

   a   Define *competitive advantage*.

   b   Identify how one South African train-hotel provider seeks competitive advantage.

   c   Suggest other ways South Africa's train-hotel providers could gain a competitive advantage.

3   Assess the importance of marketing and promotion for South Africa's train-hotel providers.

4   a   Discuss how South African train-hotel providers can develop brand loyalty.

   b   *Project:* Make a piece of promotional material to promote a South African train-hotel experience to existing customers.

5   *Extension:* Assess the importance of marketing and promotion to South Africa's train-hotel providers.

KEY WORDS

existing customers: tourists who already use or buy the products and services of a travel and tourism organisation

promotional material: something used to promote a product or service. Examples of travel and tourism promotional materials include posters, flyers, leaflets, brochures, websites, video clips and social media posts

TIPS

- Understand that marketing is everything an organisation does. Travel and tourism products, prices, promotion and places are all parts of the marketing mix. Train-hotel journey experiences, for example, are products. Products are designed to appeal to customers. Attracting customers is marketing.

- Remember that promotion is a very important part of marketing. Promotion is contacting customers. Customer spending makes travel and tourism organisations profitable. Travel and tourism organisations use promotion to raise customer awareness and interest customers in products.

KEY CONCEPT LINKS

- Travel and tourism organisations need customers. Marketing and promotion are very important to travel and tourism organisations and destinations. Marketing attracts customers. Promotion is part of marketing. Promotion tells customers what products are available and interests customers in using and buying products.

- Travel and tourism organisations compete. These organisations promote products at prices and in places that appeal to tourist customers. Travel and tourism organisations use promotion to suggest that their products, prices and places are better than the products, prices and places of competitors.

ACTIVITY 5.1

1 You can work in pairs, or as individuals and share your answers. Think about the 4Ps of the marketing mix.

   a Identify the 4Ps of the marketing mix.

   b Describe the difference in meaning between *marketing* and *promotion*.

   c Make a chart to show the meanings of the 4Ps.

CONTINUED

2 Describe how travel and tourism organisations can increase sales and profitability.

3 Work with a partner to:

   a explain why customer satisfaction is important to travel and tourism organisations.

   b suggest how travel and tourism organisations can use marketing and promotion to help satisfy customers.

4 As a class, discuss the importance of marketing and promotion in creating a positive image and reputation for sustainable practices.

   Use your learning to include appropriate examples of travel and tourism organisations and destinations in your discussion.

REFLECTION

How confident do you feel in your understanding of the importance of marketing and promotion in travel and tourism?

What can you do to increase your level of confidence?

5.2 Factors affecting marketing

Introduction

Travel and tourism organisations attract customers by marketing products and services. Factors affecting marketing in travel and tourism are shown in **Figure 5.11**.

Figure 5.11: Factors affecting marketing

Travel and tourism organisations consider the factors shown in **Figure 5.11**. The factors shown in this figure affect how travel and tourism organisations market their products and services. The factors affecting marketing are:

- **target market** – the type of customer a travel and tourism organisation tries to attract, for example, families with children

- appropriate **timing** is planning when to market products and services, considering the most suitable time to attract customers

- costs always need to be considered, for example, the costs of promotion and place

- an organisation's reputation, for example, any industry awards that can be featured in a promotion

- **brand image** – the impression potential customers have of an organisation

- **monitoring** – checking the organisation's performance, for example, sales, usage, profitability and quality.

Holiday lets (vacation rentals) are a type of self-catering accommodation in travel and tourism destinations. Owners of properties in tourism destinations use the **internet and social media platforms** to market holiday apartments and villas (houses) to tourists. Specialist

holiday let platforms include Airbnb, Vrbo, Flipkey and Turnkey (rentals).

Internet and social media platforms are online services that allow customers and travel and tourism providers to exchange information. Internet platforms allow customers to research and reserve holiday apartments online. Some internet booking platforms provide an **online chat**. Customers can use this facility to discuss accommodation with a travel agent in real time. Customers type questions and the agent immediately answers. The customer and the agent are therefore in an online conservation by text.

Social media platforms allow customers and providers to share information in ways that are open to other people. For example, customers share reviews of accommodation with providers and with other customers. Potential customers use social media reviews to help choose accommodation. Providers monitor social media reviews. Sometimes providers reply to customer reviews posted on the platform.

CASE STUDY

Mary and Oliver's condo

Mary and Oliver own a **condominium (condo) apartment** in Santa Barbara. Santa Barbara is a coastal destination in California, which is a state on the west coast of the USA.

Figure 5.12: Santa Barbara, California

Santa Barbara appeals to leisure tourists because of its warm climate and sandy beaches. Sightseeing in Santa Barbara includes natural and built attractions. Old Spanish-style buildings attract cultural tourists. There are museums, botanic gardens and a zoo. Adventure tourists can enjoy sea-cave kayaking.

Mary and Oliver have decided to market their condo in Santa Barbara as a holiday let. Mary and Oliver explain factors affecting the marketing of the condo in **Figure 5.13**.

KEY WORD

condominium (condo) apartment: an apartment that is privately owned. Some condo owners rent the apartment to tourists for holidays (vacations).

> Our condo is upstairs and has two bedrooms. We aim for adult couples. Sometimes we have two couples of friends. Sometimes two generations of the same family stay. Some customers are single people and some stay as one couple.

> We thought about costs when we chose our price. We have to pay for cleaning and housekeeping. Promotion on the platform is free. We pay the platform provider a 3% fee for each booking.

> We keep records to monitor our profitability and read the reviews customers post on social media.

> We accept bookings up to six months in advance on the platform. Summer is our busiest season. The condo is soon booked in summer. Some repeat business customers book with us directly. Repeat business customers book up to one year ahead.

> Our brand image is our good reputation. Customer reviews posted on the platform are very important. We try to have a sustainable tourism image. We recommend local organic food shops and restaurants to customers. We suggest customers cycle to the beach.

Figure 5.13: Mary and Oliver explain the factors affecting the marketing of their condo

CONTINUED

Questions

1 Outline **two** target markets for Mary and Oliver's condo apartment.

2 Suggest why Mary and Oliver:

   a use an internet platform to market the condo

   b accept bookings on the platform up to six months in advance.

3 Explain **two** monitoring methods Mary and Oliver use.

4 Complete the table to assess the effect of different factors on marketing the condo:

5 **Extension:** Evaluate the importance of different factors in the marketing of Mary and Oliver's condo.

Factor	Effect
Target market	Customers are mostly couples. Sometimes there are two couples at once (friends or people from the same family). Some single people also stay. Repeat business is because the customer needs and wants of our target market have been met.
Appropriate timing	
Consideration of costs	
A strong, sustainable brand image	
Monitoring methods	

TIPS

- Be aware that all types of tourists can be customers for a travel and tourism provider. Travel and tourism providers choose target market segments on which to focus their marketing. Some customers may still be from other market segments. For example, a visitor attraction such as a theme park may target families with children, but older people may still become customers.

- Understand that marketing costs are not only promotion costs. The marketing mix includes the Ps of product, price and place as well as promotion. The consideration of the costs of all 4Ps affects marketing. For example, the costs of cleaning and housekeeping for a condo holiday let are product costs that affect the marketing of the condo.

KEY CONCEPT LINKS

- All travel and tourism providers need marketing. Marketing is everything that attracts customers. Marketing is done by both small-scale independent travel and tourism providers and by large travel and tourism organisations. The factors of target market segments, timing, costs, brand image and monitoring affect the marketing of all travel and tourism providers.

- Reputation and image are very important in all travel and tourism marketing. Travel and tourism providers depend on customers. Customers are attracted by a good image and a good reputation. Good customer reviews are very important to travel and tourism providers. Travel and tourism providers will post good customer reviews on the internet and social media platforms. Good customer reviews posted on the internet and social media platforms are part of promoting travel and tourism providers.

ACTIVITY 5.2

1   Outline what is meant by:

   a   target market segments

   b   brand image.

2   Describe how travel and tourism providers can use the internet and social media platforms to monitor progress.

3   Assess the advantages and disadvantages of online platforms to travel and tourism providers.

4   Explain how travel and tourism marketing is affected by:

   a   appropriate timing

   b   consideration of costs.

5   *Project:* Work as a group.

   Choose a travel and tourism product or provider.

   a   Discuss your chosen product or provider's:

   - brand image

   - target market segments.

   b   Suggest how costs and timing might affect your chosen product or provider's marketing.

REFLECTION

How do you think you could apply your learning about the factors that affect marketing in travel and tourism?

5.3 The marketing mix

Introduction

Travel and tourism organisations market products and services to attract customers.

The 4Ps

The marketing mix includes the 4Ps of product, promotion, price and place. Product includes products and services. Sustainable products and services are part of the product of the marketing mix. Promotion, price and place are also parts of the marketing mix. **Figure 5.14** shows the marketing mix in more detail.

Product	Promotion
Products and services, including sustainable products and services	marketing campaigns • web-based internet and social media platforms, blogs and podcasts • destination branding • direct marketing
	• television, radio, newspaper and magazine advertising sales promotions public relations • e-brochures and leaflets trade promotions
Price	Place

• market penetration
• market skimming
• pricing strategies
   • discount pricing
   • variable pricing
   • loss leader pricing
   • promotional pricing
   • premium pricing
• price bundling
	• distribution channels
	   • wholesalers and retailers
	   • online marketing
	   • direct selling
	• physical location

Figure 5.14: The marketing mix in detail

KEY WORDS

marketing campaigns: are projects involving product promotion that are time-limited. For example, a tour operator may have a six-week marketing campaign of placing television, radio, newspaper and magazine advertisements or commercials to attract customers

sales promotions: temporary offers to attract customers. For example, a tour operator may offer discounted prices for educational groups during the low season

public relations: involves managing contacts between providers and customers. Providers make contact with potential customers to market products. For example, guided tour operators can be present in hotel lobbies to promote products to potential customers

trade promotions: when tourism organisations advertise at travel and tourism industry events. For example, travel and tourism providers meet at travel markets such as the World Travel Market. A travel and tourism organisation can be a customer of another travel and tourism organisation. Accommodation providers can promote products to tour operators at travel markets

market penetration: part of price in the marketing mix. A provider such as a tour operator charges a low price for a newly marketed product. The low price attracts customers. The price is later increased as demand also increases

market skimming: part of price in the marketing mix. A provider such as a tour operator charges a high price for a newly marketed product. The tour operator may be the only provider of the new product. Customers accept the higher price. Competition causes the price to decrease later

wholesalers and retailers: part of place in the marketing mix. Wholesalers buy products from providers. Wholesalers sell products to retailers. Retailers sell products to customers. Tour operators are wholesalers. Travel agents are retailers

KEY WORDS

price bundling: part of price in the marketing mix. Providers such as tour operators price packages or bundles of products. For example, a bundle of two walking tours and one tour including travel might be priced more cheaply than the total price of the individual tours

Place

Place in the marketing mix includes distribution channels and physical location. Distribution channels are ways in which products reach customers. Physical location is the actual place where a travel and tourism business is located. Physical location includes:

- the cost, character and features of the local area surrounding the business

- adjacent (nearby) facilities such as toilets, car park or other businesses that may help to attract customers

- the availability of a suitable site or premises

- the availability of staff, for example, staff who live nearby

- access and transport links, so that customers can easily reach the business.

Product life cycle

The product life cycle (see **Figure 5.15**) is the stages in the marketing existence of a product. The four product life cycle stages are:

- introduction: a new product starts to be sold

- growth: sales increase

- maturity: the period of maximum sales

- decline: sales reduce.

KEY WORDS

distribution channels: the ways in which products reach customers. For example, a tour guide's guided tour product may reach customers via a tour operator's website

product life cycle: the stages in the marketing existence of a product. The product life cycle stages are introduction, growth, maturity and decline

For example, a walking tour product may sell slowly when first introduced by a tour operator. Later there is a growth in sales, which reach their maximum during the maturity stage. Afterwards, sales decline. A new walking tour is then introduced to restart the cycle of product life.

When the tour is introduced, few customers know about it and so sales are low. The tour becomes well known after there has been some promotion and positive customer reviews. More customers become attracted and so there is sales growth. More people become aware of the tour and sales increase until a maximum number is reached. Sales reach maximum during the stage of maturity. Potential customers may begin to find newer, cheaper or better competing tours and so sales start to

decline. The tour operator may then decide to market a new tour. The product life cycle begins again.

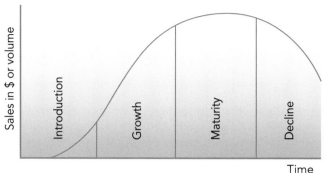

Figure 5.15: The product life cycle

CASE STUDY

Quito and the Middle of the World

Quito is the largest city in Ecuador, a country in South America. Ecuador is named after the equator, which is the line of latitude 0° around the world. The equator is midway between the North Pole and the South Pole and passes through Ecuador. The Middle of the World visitor attraction is near the historic city destination of Quito and includes the Monument to the Equator (see photo).

Quito appeals to tourists because of the culture of the area's indigenous people and because of the Spanish colonial history of the city. Walking tours of Quito include visits to local markets, which appeal to inbound tourists. Tourists like to buy clothes, food, and art and crafts made by indigenous people. Street performances by indigenous musicians and dancers also appeal to tourists. The colonial architecture of Quito appeals to cultural tourists (see photo).

Figure 5.16: The Monument to the Equator

Figure 5.17: Colonial architecture in central Quito

CONTINUED

Tour guides and tour operators market guided tours in Quito. Different tours marketed in the city include walking tours of the historic centre of Quito and visits to nearby attractions, such as the Middle of the World attraction.

Individual guides and tour operators use different marketing channels to make guided tour products available to tourists. Some marketing channels used to market guided tour products in Quito are shown in **Figure 5.18**.

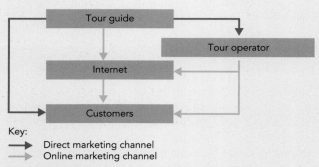

Key:
→ Direct marketing channel
→ Online marketing channel

Figure 5.18: Marketing channels for guided tours in Quito

The direct marketing channel is face-to-face selling. Tour guides in Quito use face-to-face selling to sell guided walk products directly to customers.

KEY WORDS

marketing channels: the ways products are made attractive to customers. For example, a tour guide's guided tour product may attract customers via a tour operator's website

direct marketing: providers making products directly attractive to customers. For example, a tour guide may market tours to customers face to face. Direct marketing may also include marketing tours using the tour guide's own website or social media page

face-to-face selling: part of place in the marketing mix. The customer and provider are physically in the same place. For example, travel agents sell products and services to customers face to face. A travel agent is an example of a place where marketing happens

Online marketing channels include internet sites such as tour operator websites. Tour operator websites are used to make guided tour products attractive to customers in Quito.

Tour operators use online marketing to promote walking tours in the historic centre of Quito and tours to the Middle of the World attraction. Target market customers for Middle of the World tours are groups of independent travellers who are visiting Quito.

Tour operator websites are linked to social media platforms. Tour operators and customers share information on web-based social media platforms. Customers who have used tour operator products post reviews on social media. Reviews influence potential customers. Sometimes tour operators reply to customer reviews posted on social media platforms. Some tourists write blogs on internet websites and social media. Blogs include reviews. Some travel and tourism providers post blogs on the web to promote their products and services.

Supply chains are made of the linked places where guided tours are supplied to customers in Quito. For example, some guided walk products provided by guides in the historic centre of Quito are sold to customers at the front desk of accommodation providers such as hostels.

Distribution channels are used in the marketing of guided tour products. Distribution channels are the ways that products reach customers. Distribution channels of guided tours in **Figure 5.18** include one way that is direct. The direct channel is from the tour guide direct to customers. Distribution channels link

KEY WORDS

blogs: series of internet posts. For example, some tourists post travel diaries on social media

supply chains: part of place in the marketing mix. Supply chains are the sets of linked places where travel and tourism products and services are marketed. For example, a guided walking tour can be marketed directly or by an accommodation provider or tour operator

CONTINUED

places where products are available for sale. One distribution channel shown in **Figure 5.18** is via a tour operator and the internet. Places where Middle of the World guided tour products are available for sale in Quito include tour operator websites and the front desks of accommodation providers.

Tour operators use different pricing strategies to market walking tours in the historic centre of Quito and visits to the Middle of the World attraction. **Figure 5.19** shows different pricing strategies.

Some tour guides and tour operators use promotional pricing to market 'free' guided walking tours in the historic centre of Quito. There is no fixed price for a 'free' tour but the tour is usually not actually free. At the end of the tour, customers decide what the tour was worth. Customers who enjoyed the tour pay the guide.

Customers are often in groups. Customers pay guides between US $10 and US $50 per person. Guides make a living from tourist groups. Discount pricing can be used to encourage bigger groups.

Examples include discounts for groups of a certain size, for educational groups or for older people.

Variable pricing is a pricing strategy that tour operators in Quito can use. Tour operators vary prices among tours and between seasons. Tour operators set prices for some special interest tours. Food tours visiting cafés and restaurants in Quito are examples of special interest tours. Prices vary because cafés and restaurants that customers want to visit vary. Premium pricing is a pricing strategy that may be used for visits to some specialist organic food cafés and restaurants.

Prices may vary among tours because of travel costs. Tours to the the Middle of the World attraction include some travel. Transfer (transit) costs are therefore included in the price.

KEY WORDS

pricing strategies: methods used to attract customers by managing the price

premium pricing: a pricing strategy. Premium prices are higher prices. Travel and tourism organisations sometimes choose to charge higher prices than competitors. Charging a higher price creates the impression that a product is special and worth more money.

Higher prices due to demand for sustainable products		Discount pricing reducing some prices
	Loss leader pricing a low price for a promoted product	
Pricing strategies that attract customers		
Promotional pricing temporary low prices		Variable pricing different prices for one product

Figure 5.19: Pricing strategies

Questions

1   Work in pairs.

   a   Outline the appeal of guided tour products to cultural tourists visiting Quito.

   b   Suggest how social media platforms can help to promote guided tours in Quito.

2   Describe different pricing strategies used in the marketing of guided tours in Quito.

3   Using your own words:

   a   describe marketing and distribution channels used for guided tour products in Quito.

   b   explain how 'place' is used in the marketing of guided tours in Quito.

CONTINUED

4   Discuss how tour operators marketing guided tours in Quito could make use of:

   a   loss leader pricing

   b   market penetration

   c   market skimming

   d   price bundling.

5   *Extension:* Evaluate the importance of different elements of the marketing mix to tour operators in destinations such as Quito.

TIPS

- Remember that marketing is making products and services attractive to customers. Think about place. Place is one of the 4Ps of the marketing mix. Understand that place is where marketing happens. Marketing may happen online. Websites are internet places where marketing happens.

- Think carefully about marketing channels and distribution channels. Marketing channels link places where marketing happens. Distribution channels link places where products and services are supplied to customers.

KEY CONCEPT LINKS

- Marketing is making products and services attractive to customers. The marketing mix is the mix of ways used to make products and services attractive to customers. Travel and tourism organisations need to attract customers. Marketing and the marketing mix are very important to travel and tourism organisations.

- Travel and tourism organisations use the marketing mix to make **p**roducts attractive to customers. Travel and tourism organisations:

    - **p**romote products to attract customers

    - set **p**rices to make products attractive to customers

    - use different **p**laces to market products.

    All four marketing **P**s are mixed together to attract customers to travel and tourism organisations.

ACTIVITY 5.3

1   Pricing strategies are methods used to attract customers by managing price.

   a   Use the terms listed below to complete this table of definitions:

      i   loss leader pricing

      ii   variable pricing

      iii   premium pricing

      iv   discount pricing

      v   promotional pricing.

Pricing strategy term	Definition
	attracts customers by reducing some prices, such as for groups of more than six tourists
	is charging different prices for the same product, for example, reducing prices in low season
	attracts customers by setting a temporary low price for a promoted product, for example, a new tour on e-scooters
	is setting a low price for one product to raise customer interest in other products, for example, a free introductory tour to promote other available tours
	setting higher prices to make products seem special to create demand, for example, for luxury eco-friendly accommodation

CONTINUED

b   Describe the difference between *market penetration* and *market skimming*.

2   Suggest how a travel and tourism organisation can be a trade customer of another travel and tourism organisation.

3   Choose a travel and tourism destination other than Quito.

     a   Recommend ways to promote guided tours in your chosen destination.

     b   Explain your recommendations.

4   Investigate the marketing mix of a travel and tourism product. Make a chart to show the 4Ps of your chosen product.

REFLECTION

What methods will you use to help you to remember the meanings of marketing terms?

5.4 Market research and analysis

Introduction

Travel and tourism organisations research the market for travel and tourism products and services. These organisations do different types of market research.

Types of market research

Primary research

Primary research is direct research. For example, travel and tourism organisations use **questionnaires**, **surveys**, **interviews** and **focus groups** to talk directly to customers to research customers' needs and wants.

KEY WORDS

primary research: direct research. For example, asking customers questions about the products and services provided by a travel and tourism organisation is a type of primary market research

questionnaires: sets of questions. For example, a market researcher may ask business tourism customers a set of questions about the products and services provided by a travel and tourism organisation

surveys: a way of researching people's opinions. Surveys can be carried out using questionnaires or interviews to collect quantative data about travel and tourism markets. Quantitative data may be analysed to investigate travel and tourism market trends

interviews: question-and-answer conversations. Interviews are a way to do primary market research. For example, a market researcher may ask a customer some questions about the products and services provided by a travel and tourism organisation

focus groups: small discussion groups. Small groups of customers discuss products and services provided by a travel and tourism organisation. Focus groups are a type of primary market research. Focus groups are an example of qualitative market research

secondary research: research using documents. For example, a MICE venue provider may use government reports and NTO statistics to investigate the market for MICE products and services

Secondary research

Secondary research is using sources of information that already exist. For example, travel and tourism organisations do secondary research using existing sources, such as government reports and statistics from national tourism organisations (NTOs).

Qualitative and quantitative methods

Travel and tourism organisations use qualitative methods and quantitative methods to research markets. Examples of qualitative market research methods include observation, informal conversations and interviews. Travel and tourism organisations can observe customer behaviour, talk to customers informally or interview customers to find out about their needs and wants.

KEY WORDS

qualitative methods: a type of market research method. Examples of qualitative market research methods are observation, informal conversations and interviews.

quantitative methods: a type of market research method. Quantitative methods collect data in the form of numbers. Customer surveys are an example of a quantitative market research method.

Quantitative methods collect data in the form of numbers. Customer surveys are an example of a quantitative market research method where customers answer survey questions. How many customers answer in a certain way is counted, often as a percentage.

Market research tools

Market research provides information for travel and tourism organisations to analyse. These organisations use tools to analyse travel and tourism markets. Market analysis tools include:

- SWOT analysis
- PESTLE analysis.

Examples of a SWOT analysis and PESTLE analysis are explained in the Travel and tourism in context case study *Marketing Fred's coffee stall* in this unit.

Travel and tourism organisations use market research findings to help their identify strengths, weaknesses, opportunities and threats (SWOT analysis). A PESTLE analysis considers external factors that affect travel and tourism organisations. External factors are factors outside the organisation. External factors that affect businesses are: **p**olitical factors, **e**conomic factors, **s**ociological factors, **t**echnological factors, **l**egal factors and **e**nvironmental factors (see **Figure 5.6**).

Reasons for market research

Travel and tourism organisations use market research to find out what attracts customers. These organisations research the market to understand the organisation's position in the market and identify the needs and wants of customers and potential customers. This research is done by analysing their market competitors. Travel and tourism organisations conclude market research by creating marketing plans.

Understand the organisation's position in the market

Travel and tourism businesses understand the organisation's position in the market by asking key questions:

- Does the organisation have a strong position in the market?
- Is the organisation the market leader?
- Are competitors overtaking the organisation's position in the market?

KEY WORD

market leader: the organisation with the strongest market position. The market leader sells more products and services than competing travel and tourism organisations.

Identify the needs and wants of customers and potential customers

To identify the needs and wants of customers and potential customers, travel and tourism organisations research:

- what products customers want
- the prices customers will pay
- the marketing places that customers find attractive.

Analyse competitors

An analysis of competitors is part of the market research carried out by travel and tourism organisations. Travel and tourism organisations ask the following questions:

- Are other organisations out-competing or overtaking the organisation in the market?
- Is the marketing mix of competitors stronger?
- What can be learned from the marketing mix of the organisation's competitors?

Create marketing plans

Travel and tourism organisations reflect on market research findings to create marketing plans. These organisations ask the following questions:

- What has the organisation learned from the market research?

- How will the organisation market its products and services now and in the future?

CASE STUDY

MICE future

Travel and tourism organisations provide MICE products and services in MICE venues. MICE (Meetings, Incentives, Conferences and Exhibitions) tourism is business tourism. MICE venues are places where MICE products and services are provided. Hotels and specialist MICE providers such as conference venues and conference (convention) centres provide MICE products and services.

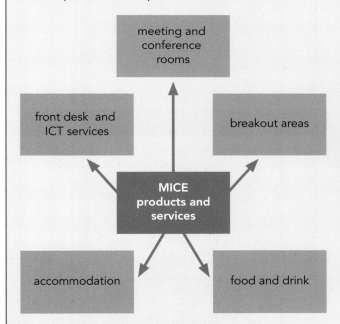

Figure 5.20: MICE products and services

MICE products and services are often sold as packages. Business tourism customers use meeting rooms for group discussions and presentations. Conference rooms are larger and may have space for hundreds of customers.

Breakout areas are spaces where business tourists can take breaks from meetings. Breakout areas provide refreshments and comfortable seating so business tourist customers can talk informally. Breakout areas may be indoor or outdoor spaces.

Outdoor spaces such as patios, terraces and gardens provide human–nature connections. Human–nature connection spaces are relaxing and healthy for business tourists. Human–nature connection spaces such as gardens are sustainable spaces.

Food and drink is often provided in breakout areas and in on-site cafés and restaurants. Some on-site cafés and restaurants have outdoor spaces. Some MICE venues also provide hotel-syle sleeping accommodation for business travellers.

Figure 5.21 shows a MICE market meeting room.

Figure 5.21: A MICE market meeting room

KEY WORDS

breakout areas: spaces provided in MICE venues. Breakout areas are used by business tourists to take a break from a meeting

human–nature connections: links between people and the environment. MICE venues increasingly provide human–nature connections. Good human–nature connections provided by MICE venues include planted outdoor spaces, natural light and fresh air. Good human–nature connections are part of good customer service

CONTINUED

IACC is a global organisation of MICE providers and is an international association. MICE providers can become members of IACC. In 2020 IACC published the *Meeting Room of the Future* report.

Figure 5.22 shows some features of the future MICE meeting room.

1 Open
2 Flexible
3 Bright
4 Fun
5 Well-equipped
   with technology

Figure 5.22: Future MICE meeting room features

The *Meeting Room of the Future* report was based on market research. IACC wanted to investigate the future of the MICE market. IACC wanted to help MICE providers:

- understand the MICE provider's position in the market

- identify customers' needs and wants

- analyse competitors

- create marketing plans.

IACC used primary quantitative market research to find out about trends in the MICE market. **Figure 5.23** shows the research findings from a survey on some products and services at MICE venues.

Market research question	Yes (%)
Will responsible business tourism become more important in the future?	74
Do MICE venues already provide human–nature connections?	73
Will flexible meeting rooms become more important in the future?	72
Has there been internet provision development in MICE venues in the last two years?	73
Do you think there will be more internet provision development in MICE venues next year?	44
Will the quality of food and drink customer service in MICE venues become more important in the future?	72

Figure 5.23: Research findings on products and services at MICE venues

KEY WORD

flexible meeting rooms: meeting rooms that can easily be adapted to customers' needs. For example, furniture can easily be moved in flexible meeting rooms. Moving the furniture may adapt a meeting room to customers' needs. For example, the number of chairs and the arrangement of tables and chairs can be changed

CONTINUED

Market research findings
Food and drink in MICE venues

Food labelling

Is food labelling with dietary needs information provided at every MICE venue meal?

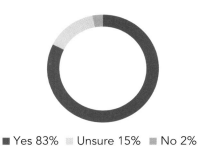

■ Yes 83%   ■ Unsure 15%   ■ No 2%

Dietary need requests

Are customers making more dietary needs requests in MICE venues?

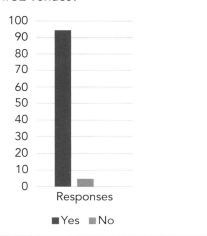

■ Yes   ■ No

Dietary needs training

Are MICE venue food preparation and food service staff trained about customer dietary needs?

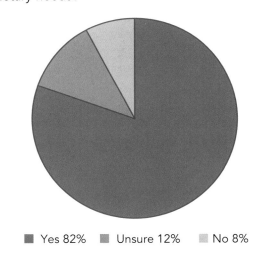

■ Yes 82%   ■ Unsure 12%   ■ No 8%

Local food

Do MICE venues use locally sourced food and drink products whenever possible?

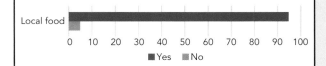

■ Yes   ■ No

Figure 5.24: Research findings on food and drink in MICE venues

CONTINUED

Figure 5.23 shows that 72% of respondents thought that the quality of food and drink customer service in MICE venues is a customer need or want and will become more important to business tourism customers in the future. The graphs in **Figure 5.24** show the MICE quantitative market research findings on the quality of food and drink customer service in MICE venues.

The qualitative market research findings on the MICE market showed IACC that ICT is likely to become even more important in business meetings in the future. Stronger internet security in meeting rooms is likely to continue to become more and more important to business tourism customers.

Market research for the *Meeting Room of the Future* report also showed IACC that:

- many young people work in MICE venues, but few are managers

- younger staff often have better ICT, internet and social media skills than senior colleagues

- smaller and more local meetings, conferences and events are more likely in the future

- MICE venues may need to make costly changes in the future.

Questions

1 Outline what is meant by a MICE business tourism venue.

2 Identify:

   a **four** quantitative market research findings on food and drink in MICE venues

   b **two** qualitative market research findings on future MICE venues.

3 Describe the features of the MICE market meeting room shown in **Figure 5.21**.

4 Assess how closely the features of the meeting room shown in **Figure 5.21** match the features of the future MICE meeting room shown in **Figure 5.22**.

5 Refer to the market research findings shown in **Figures 5.23** and **5.24**. Market research found that many young people work in MICE venues, but few are managers. Do you think this is:

   a a strength or a weakness

   b an opportunity or a threat?

   Discuss with a partner.

6 Analyse the strengths, weaknesses, opportunities and threats of MICE venues shown in **Figures 5.23** and **5.24**.

7 Discuss how external factors are likely to affect MICE tourism venues in the future.

8 *Extension:* Evaluate the future importance of market research and analysis to MICE meeting room providers.

TIPS

- Understand that primary research can be what you learn yourself and that secondary research is what you look up in books, documents and on the internet.

- Realise that quantitative data is numbers and that qualitative data is what people see, think or say.

KEY CONCEPT LINKS

- Some tourists travel for the purpose of work. Tourists who travel for work are business tourists. Business travel and tourism is MICE (Meetings, Incentives, Conferences and Exhibitions) tourism. Meetings, incentives, conferences and exhibitions are the reasons that business tourists travel. Travel and tourism organisations provide products and services for the business tourism market. Business tourism providers research the business tourism market.

- Market research helps travel and tourism organisations to understand the market better. Understanding the market better helps travel and tourism businesses to better understand business tourist customers. Understanding business tourist customers better helps MICE providers to deliver better customer service.

ACTIVITY 5.4

1   In this activity:

   a   Identify different types of primary research.

   b   Outline the differences between:

      i   primary research and secondary research

      ii   qualitative methods and quantitative methods.

2   Work with a partner.

   Suggest why good human–nature connections are important to travel and tourism organisations.

3   Explain the following acronyms to another learner:

   a   **SWOT** analysis

   b   the external factors in a **PESTLE** analysis.

4   Discuss how disease pandemics such as **COVID-19** affect global tourism.

5   Make a **PESTLE** analysis chart to show the ways a pandemic can affect travel and tourism organisations.

REFLECTION

What strategies do you find most useful for revising? How will you revise the travel and tourism marketing topics? Share your strategies with a partner.

5.5 Market segmentation and targeting

Introduction

The markets of travel and tourism organisations are divided into different parts, called segments. Travel and tourism organisations develop the product/service mix to target different market segments.

Different market segments

Markets for travel and tourism products and services have different parts or elements. The different elements of travel and tourism markets are market segments. **Figure 5.25** shows travel and tourism market segments:

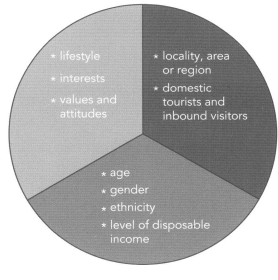

- ■ Geographic segmentation
- ■ Demographic segmentation
- ▩ Psychographic segmentation

Figure 5.25: Travel and tourism market segments

KEY WORDS

demographic segmentation: dividing a market into types of people, such as customers of different ages, genders, ethnicities or levels of disposable income

psychographic segmentation: dividing a market by customer lifestyle, such as customers with different interests or customers with different values and attitudes

The development of product/service mix to target different market segments

Travel and tourism organisations develop their **product/service mix** to target different market segments.

Market segmentation is the dividing of markets into segments. For example, the geographic segments of a destination's market can be made by dividing the market into:

1   the different localities, areas or regions that customers are from, or

2   customers who are domestic tourists and customers who are inbound tourists.

Travel and tourism organisations develop their product/service mix by evaluating their products, services and facilities. These organisations evaluate the relationship between their product/service mix and market segments. Travel and tourism organisations evaluate:

- types of customer targeted

- quality, economy and value for money of products and services

- accessibility of facilities

- sustainability.

KEY WORD

product/service mix: the blend of travel and tourism products and services developed by travel and tourism organisations in a destination. The product/service mix is developed in order to target different market segments

market segmentation: dividing of markets into segments

CASE STUDY

Who comes to Cambridge?

Tourists come to Cambridge, which is a university town in eastern England. England is part of the United Kingdom (UK), a country in north-west Europe. Tourists visiting Cambridge include:

- leisure tourists, business (MICE) tourists and VFR tourists

- domestic tourists and inbound tourists from around the world.

Inbound tourists include tourists who stay in Cambridge for at least one night and tourists visiting Cambridge on a day trip. Inbound tourists who visit Cambridge for a day usually stay in accommodation in another destination. London is not far from Cambridge. London is the biggest city destination in the UK. Cambridge is about 50 miles (80 km) from London. Train journeys from London to Cambridge can take less than 50 minutes.

Visit Cambridge is the official destination management organisation for Cambridge. *Visit Cambridge* is managed by the Cambridge City Council and NGOs including Fitzwilliam Museum Enterprises.

Leisure tourists visit Cambridge for sightseeing. Historic university buildings such as King's College appeal to many cultural tourists. Cultural tourists enjoy guided tours of Cambridge University colleges and the famous views of Cambridge (see **Figure 5.26**).

CONTINUED

Figure 5.26: King's College and punting on the River Cam, from the Backs

The River Cam flows through Cambridge. The green spaces on either side of the river are called *the Backs*. *The Backs* provide scenic views over the backs of the old colleges of Cambridge University. Many leisure tourists enjoy taking photographs of *the Backs*. Punting on the River Cam is an activity enjoyed by many leisure tourist visitors to Cambridge. Punts are narrow, flat-bottomed boats pushed along by a pole (see photo).

Tourist attractions in Cambridge include the Cambridge University Botanic Garden and museums such as the Fitzwilliam Musuem. The Fitzwilliam is an arts and antiquities museum. The Centre for Computing History, meanwhile, is a museum about the history of computing, with hands-on ICT and computer activities that appeal to younger visitors. Shopping in the old narrow streets of Cambridge's historic town centre is a popular tourist activity.

Business (MICE) tourists visit Cambridge. Cambridge Science Park has more than 130 technology and science businesses, which employ over 7,000 people. Business tourists visit Cambridge for meetings, conferences and events. Cambridge Science Park businesses organise meetings, conferences and events attended by business tourists. Some business tourists visit Cambridge to attend MICE events at

Cambridge University. Incentive visits to Cambridge University colleges are a form of business tourism to the destination.

Students come to Cambridge. Cambridge University is one of the oldest and most famous universities in the world. Students studying here are not tourists. Friends and relatives who visit students in Cambridge, however, are VFR tourists.

Travel and tourism organisations provide products and services for tourists who come to Cambridge. Punting on the River Cam is a popular tourist activity and travel and tourism organisations provide punts for hire. Punt providers market sightseeing tours by punt. Travel and tourism organisations marketing punting in Cambridge develop their product/service mix by evaluating their products, services and facilities (see **Figure 5.27**).

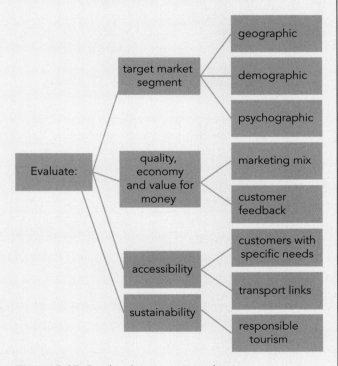

Figure 5.27: Product/service mix evaluation

CONTINUED

Questions

1 Outline the different types of tourists who visit Cambridge.

2 You can work in pairs:

   a Suggest activities for a family from London visiting Cambridge on a VFR day trip.

   b Describe the appeal of Cambridge as an incentive tourism destination.

3 Explain **three** target market segments for travel and tourism providers in Cambridge.

4 Refer to **Figure 5.27**. Analyse how punting providers in Cambridge evaluate their product/service mix.

5 **Extension:** Assess the importance of marketing segmentation and targeting to travel and tourism providers in Cambridge.

TIPS

- Realise that market segments include types of tourist and where they come from. Travel and tourism organisations market products and services to target market segments.

- Think about the 4Ps of the marketing mix to help evaluate the product/service mix of travel and tourism organisations. How well does the organisation use product, price, promotion and place? How well do the 4Ps target the organisation's market?

- Do not try to completely separate products from services. Products are not entirely separate from services – there is a product–service continuum. A travel and tourism organisation markets a product/service mix.

KEY CONCEPT LINKS

- Market segments are part of the travel and tourism market. Travel and tourism organisations target market segments to attract customers. Travel and tourism organisations evaluate their product/service mix. Travel and tourism organisations evaluate their product/service mix to better meet the needs of target market segments.

- Travel and tourism organisations develop their product/service mix. Travel and tourism organisations want to have the correct mix of products and services. The correct mix of products and services attracts more

CONTINUED

- customers. Travel and tourism organisations evaluate their product/service mix to help develop their mix of products and services.

ACTIVITY 5.5

1 Identify ways of segmenting markets:

   a demographically

   b psychographically.

2 Choose a travel and tourism destination. Describe the target market segments of your chosen destination.

3 Travel and tourism organisations evaluate the relationship between their product/service mix and market segments. Explain:

   a why

   b how.

4 Choose a travel and tourism organisation. Evaluate the product/service mix of your chosen organisation.

REFLECTION

What do you need to do to improve your understanding of market segmentation and targeting?

EXAM-STYLE QUESTIONS

1   Refer to **Figure 17**, information about the 'Taken by Albania' promotional campaign.

The new promotional initiative 'Taken by Albania' was launched during a large public relations event held at Tirana's international airport. Created and produced with support from the Swiss Entrepreneurship Programme, it will run throughout the year in traditional and social media.

'Let us be taken by Albania. I am taken by its friendly people, its beautiful landscapes, its impressive history. This country is safe, welcoming, and interesting,' said the Swiss Ambassador in Albania, Adrian Maître.

'In order to achieve our target for 10 million tourists annually, and I know seasonality is a problem, we need tourism for all 12 months of the year by combining culture, nature and human heritage,' said Minister of Tourism and Environment Blendi Klosi.

The EU Head of Delegation Luigi Soreca said: 'I have been "Taken by Albania" for some time now. By its natural beauties, rich cultural heritage, delicious food and warm-hearted people! Often good news doesn't make the news. You might want to know the real Albania, beyond prejudices.'

'I know that if there is any sure way for Albania to develop, this is sustainable tourism,' said Blerina Ago, the campaign founder. 'I have seen the joy and hope that tourism brings in the most isolated areas of Albania and the transformation power of this industry in changing the lives of inhabitants, opening new jobs,' added Ms. Ago.

The campaign 'Taken by Albania' addresses the negative stereotypes prevalent in some Western movies and media which have given the world the impression that Albania is a haven for organised crime and kidnappers. The campaign tries to show that the reality is in fact the opposite. It takes its premise from the movie *Taken* starring Liam Neeson and invites him and others to come and see for themselves the beauty, hospitality and uniqueness of Albania. 'Taken by Albania' will run throughout the year and will gather individual videos captured by both visitors and locals in various spots in the country under the hashtag #takenbyalbania. The videos will then be promoted online by the campaign organisers.

Figure 17: Details of an initiative to increase tourism to Albania

a   From **Figure 17**, **identify three** strengths of Albania as a tourist destination. [3]

b   With reference to **Figure 17**, **explain two** likely threats to Albania being able to achieve its target of 10 million visitors a year. [4]

c   Explain **two** ways in which the campaign will help to present a positive image of Albania. [4]

d   **Evaluate** the importance of traditional and social media as methods of promotion for the 'Taken by Albania' campaign. [9]

[Total 20 marks]

CONTINUED

2   Refer to **Figure 18**, a table showing the stages of the product life cycle as experienced by a themed restaurant opened in the central area of an expanding tourist destination.

Stage A	Stage B	Stage C 'maturity'	Stage D
Few customers	Substantial increase in customers	Customer numbers level off, with no business growth	Severe drop in customer numbers
New equipment and facilities			High employee turnover
Modern technology	Equipment and facilities experience high levels of use	Fabric in need of refurbishment	
Team is new and motivated	Team working well	Employees become stagnant and bored	Aggressive discounting and promotion
Few competitors	Some competitors	Lots more competition	Product defects
Spending on advertising and PR to create awareness	Advertising changes from promotion to being more broad	More promotions and special offers to attract customers	No capital investment
	Few discounts		

Figure 18: Product life cycle experienced by restaurant in a tourist destination

a   From **Figure 18**, identify Stages A, B and D according to the product life cycle. [3]

b   **Describe** how a customer's restaurant dining experience contains **both** tangible and intangible elements. [4]

c   Name a pricing policy which the restaurant might introduce at the following **Figure 18** stages and briefly explain why **each** would be used:

   • Stage A

   • Stage B [4]

d   Evaluate the importance of the availability of suitable premises and adjacent facilities when opening a new themed restaurant. [9]

[Total 20 marks]

CONTINUED

3   Refer to **Figure 19**, a summary of a PESTLE analysis for Singapore.

FACTOR	KEY FEATURES
Political	Political stability
	Free Trade Agreements
	Level of corruption is low
	Overall political risk is low
Economic	Resilient economy
	GDP expected to grow 2%
	Inflation low (less than 3%)
	Corporate taxation less than 20%
	High per capita income
	Asian culture
	Literacy levels high
	Educated labour force
	Many white-collar employees
Technological	Technological readiness is strong
	Infrastructure has grown
	Strong e-governance
	Freedom of speech
	Laws are strict
	Implementation rigid
	Risks of oil spillage high
	Secure waste treatment and disposal
	Threat from rising sea levels

Figure 19: Singapore PESTLE Analysis

a   Name the **three** PESTLE factors that are missing from **Figure 19**.   [3]

b   Describe the circumstances in which a tourism organisation would wish to carry out a
    PESTLE analysis.   [4]

c   Explain **two** advantages for the tourism organisation of using wholesalers as a distribution channel
    for its product.   [4]

d Tourism organisations will usually undertake market research prior to the launch of a new product. Evaluate the usefulness of questionnaires and focus groups as methods of primary market research. **[9]**

[Total 20 marks]

4 Refer to **Figures 20** and **21**, information about tourist activities in Costa Rica.

Meetings and incentive trips
Families
Rural tourism
Adventure
Culture
Cruises
Sun and beaches
Ecotourism
Honeymoon and weddings
Wellness
Birdwatching
Great wildlife spectacles

Figure 20: Things to do in Costa Rica

Adventure tourism activities

Activities on offer include:

- swinging through the canopy of the rainforest on zip lines

- other canopy adventures, where participants swing through the trees using ropes, harnesses and treetop platforms

- horse riding

- Central America's longest water slide (measuring 450 metres) near the Rincon de la Vieja National Park

- rafting or kayaking down some of the world's best white-water rivers, with grades of rapids from easy to the extremely tough grade six

- mountain biking, either cross-country or downhill

- hiking trips through the rainforests and/or up the mountains (e.g. a four-day ascent of Chirripo, the country's highest peak at 3,820 metres).

Figure 21: Adventure tourism activities in Costa Rica

CONTINUED

a Costa Rica is aiming to attract a variety of market segments. Identify **three** market segments which are not primarily interested in the country's natural environment.   **[3]**

b Describe **two** ways in which Costa Rica's rainforests have provided an opportunity for tourism development.   **[4]**

c A variety of operators offer water-based adventure tourism activities in Costa Rica. Explain **two** ways in which a particular water-based organisation might differentiate their operation from that of their competitors.   **[4]**

d With reference to **Figures 20** and **21**, evaluate Costa Rica's ability to appeal to different demographic and psychographic (lifestyle) market segments.   **[9]**

[Total 20 marks]

5 Refer to **Figure 22**, a message with text and images sent by a tourist who was visiting Barcelona's Camp Nou stadium.

The stadium is home to the Barcelona Football Club; its museum attracts some 1.9 million visitors a year and is the city's third most visited tourist attraction. Barcelona's home games regularly have crowds in excess of 90,000, particularly when playing Champions League opponents.

Figure 22: Text and photos from a tourist in Barcelona

CONTINUED

a   Identify **three** elements of Camp Nou's product/service mix.   [3]

b   Describe **two** features of the Barcelona FC brand image.   [4]

c   Until recently, Qatar Airways was the official sponsor of Barcelona FC. Explain **two** ways in which Qatar Airways was likely to benefit from this sponsorship deal.   [4]

d   Evaluate the use of face-to-face surveys versus reading web-based comments such as TripAdvisor reviews as methods of monitoring customer satisfaction at the Barcelona FC museum.   [9]

[Total 20 marks]

SELF-EVALUATION CHECKLIST

After studying this unit, copy and complete this table:

I am now able to:	Needs more work	Almost there	Ready to move on
explain the importance of marketing and promotion in travel and tourism.			
understand the factors affecting marketing.			
discuss the marketing mix.			
understand different types of market research.			
analyse travel and tourism markets using market analysis tools.			
understand different market segments.			
evaluate the development of the product/service mix to target different market segments.			

> Preparing for assessment

In this section you will learn how to:

- approach the two Cambridge IGCSE Travel and Tourism assessments

- understand the key skills such as application, analysis and evaluation

- revise more effectively.

The guidance in this sub-unit has been written by the author. References to assessment and/or assessment preparation are the publisher's interpretation of the syllabus requirements and may not fully reflect the approach of Cambridge Assessment International Education.

You should always refer to the appropriate syllabus document for the year of your examination to confirm the details and for more information. The syllabus document is available on the Cambridge International website at www.cambridgeinternational.org.

Introduction

As you prepare for your assessment, you may find it helpful to follow some important guidelines. By preparing yourself thoroughly, you can look forward to this important stage of your course with a degree of confidence. A thorough programme of revision is, of course, one of the keys to success. To begin with, you are strongly advised to familiarise yourself with the Specimen Question Paper and its associated Mark Scheme. From 2024 there will also be past papers to look at.

Each question will usually be based on at least one piece of stimulus material, derived mainly from travel and tourism industry sources. These will have been selected solely on the basis of their ability to illustrate key aspects of the syllabus content. These pieces of stimulus material may involve text, images and/or tourism facts and figures displayed in graphs and data tables.

However, there is more to exam preparation and revision than just attempting to learn various facts and figures.

It is very important to recall the skills you have learned to use throughout your course and to think about how you will use these skills in your examinations and future studies.

Syllabus coverage

During the course of your studies following the IGCSE Travel and Tourism syllabus, you will have had the opportunity to develop:

- an understanding of the nature of travel and tourism, globally, nationally and locally

- an understanding of the positive and negative impacts of travel and tourism, and how these can be managed

- an understanding of the importance of sustainability and resilience in travel and tourism

- an awareness of the importance of the customer in the travel and tourism industry

- an understanding of the importance of marketing in travel and tourism

- communication skills and an awareness of different values and attitudes in relation to travel and tourism.

The assessment objectives (AOs) are taken from the Cambridge IGCSE Travel and Tourism syllabus. The content in How to use the key skills and the sample questions/answers are suggestions from the author.

The four assessment objectives (AOs) of the Cambridge IGCSE Travel and Tourism syllabus are:

- **AO1 Knowledge and understanding**

  Demonstrate knowledge and understanding of facts, terms and concepts of travel and tourism.

- **AO2 Application**

  Apply knowledge and understanding of facts, terms and concepts to familiar and unfamiliar contexts in travel and tourism.

- **AO3 Analysis**

  Analyse travel and tourism issues and show an understanding of the possible impacts of those issues on travel and tourism.

- **AO4 Evaluation**

  Evaluate information to develop arguments, understand implications, draw inferences and make judgements, recommendations and decisions.

How to use the key skills
Knowledge and understanding

The skill of demonstrating knowledge and understanding should be your only focus when you are asked to *identify*, *name*, *state*, *define* or *describe* something. Here are a couple of examples to help make things clear.

What do the British do in Dubai?

- 42% of British business travellers are in Dubai as incentive travellers.

- 44% of leisure travellers are in Dubai for rest and recreation: 16% are visiting friends and relatives and 14% are cruise passengers.

- For all visitors, shopping (77%), sightseeing (69%), visiting heritage sites (48%), taking guided trips (45%) and going to the beach (41%) are the most popular activities.

- Tourists generally shop in shopping malls (84%), the Gold Souq (42%) and other souqs (41%), where they usually buy clothing (58%), souvenirs (33%) and gold or jewellery (32%).

- They typically eat in restaurants (65%) and shopping mall food courts (35%).

- Tourists normally use taxis (82%) and hotel transport services (17%) to get around Dubai.

- Dubai's particular attraction is recommendation (25%), as well as the pull of friends and relatives who live there (18%) and the weather (18%).

Sample question

Refer to the above extract from a Dubai visitor survey.

a   Identify the following:

  - The most popular activity for British visitors in Dubai

  - The percentage of British visitors who eat in mall food courts.

Sample answer

Shopping is the most popular activity and 35% of tourists eat in food courts.

Comment

Both answers are correct, clear and to the point, with no unasked - for detail.

Sample question

b   Incentive travel is one of the components of the MICE business tourism market. Name the other **three** components.

Sample answer

Meetings, conferences and exhibitions.

Comment

All three responses are correct. No further explanation is required and no application is necessary.

It is important that you always demonstrate knowledge and understanding. When the command words *explain*, *discuss* or *evaluate* are used, it is still important to demonstrate relevant subject knowledge and your understanding of that knowledge. For example, if you are asked to 'discuss two benefits for Dubai visitors of using taxis', you should show your knowledge by stating two benefits of travelling by taxi, such as comfort and door-to-door service. These two points then become the basis on which you build the rest of your answer, which should also demonstrate the skills of application and analysis.

Application

Applying Travel and Tourism subject knowledge and understanding is an important skill. The ability to apply knowledge and understanding to different tourism situations can be shown in the following ways:

When questions are based on details provided in the stimulus material, the skill of application can be shown by making direct and relevant reference to the text information, the data provided or the issues that have been highlighted. This is particularly significant when you take both Papers 1 and 2, as the syllabus points out the 'need to answer questions using relevant and appropriate information from the stimulus and applying your own knowledge to the context of the destination detailed to support your answers'.

You should always make reference to your own personal experiences if these are relevant to a particular question. For example, have you:

- participated in any educational visits to tourism providers as part of your course?

- had any tourism-related work experience or done any customer service role-plays?

- completed any tourism fieldwork exercises?

- acquired any particular knowledge of a destination from holiday travels?

Providing appropriate details of any of these aspects would be evidence of your ability to 'apply knowledge and understanding of facts, terms and concepts to familiar and unfamiliar contexts in travel and tourism'.

Sample question

c   Explain **two** advantages for the Dubai Ministry of Tourism (DTCM) of collecting visitor statistics on a regular basis.

Sample answer

Many destinations undertake surveys, and official statistics record a visitor's origin (international or domestic) so that potential target markets can be identified. This information can then be broken down country by country and region by region. Also, it is important to understand which tourism market segments the destination wishes to attract and serve as tourists fall into a very diverse set of categories with quite distinct needs and wants. For example, those on business, leisure or VFR are clearly tied to particular resources, businesses and facilities within a particular destination. However, many locations widen their appeal to particular niche markets, and recording the purpose of visits provides information about this. The Ministry can then monitor the development of such things as medical, religious and sports tourism. Furthermore, in deciding the relative importance of these different segments, planners need to assess both their ability to provide the required services (do you have enough rooms?) and the demand for different types of trips relative to the supply and the competition elsewhere.

Comment

This is a very good answer with two advantages being explained in some detail. There is clear evidence of application in terms of statistics being used for particular purposes.

Analysis

The skill of analysis is important in your responses to questions that use the command words *discuss, assess* and *evaluate*.

Sample question

d Discuss **two** ways in which national tourist boards promote visitor arrivals.

Sample answer

National Tourist Boards such as the DTCM in Dubai use a variety of marketing and promotion methods. They have an extensive website which makes destination information available to the world, thus maximising market potential. Overseas offices make promotional material available to key target markets: they will often run publicity campaigns to promote events and attend travel fairs to showcase the destination's tourist facilities. However, the fact that most boards such as the DTCM host familiarisation visits suggests that these are a very significant part of any marketing and promotion strategy. Such visits will mean that overseas agents will have first-hand experience of the destination and it is they who will advise potential visitors about the destination and influence their choice.

Comment

This is a clearly written answer that contains some very good analytical comment. In particular, there is an analysis of three promotional methods (website, overseas offices and familiarisation visits), which are fully relevant to the promotion of visitor arrivals. Furthermore, there is even an evaluative comment about visits being a significant part of the overall marketing and promotion strategy.

Evaluation

It is important to show the skill of evaluation in your responses to questions that use the command words *discuss, assess* and *evaluate*.

Sample question

e Evaluate the product/service mix as factors in the visitor appeal of cultural attractions.

Sample answer 1

A visit to the Dubai Museum is a must for leisure tourists staying in the destination. Housed within the beautifully restored Al Fahidi Fort, which was erected in around 1787 to defend the city against invasion, the museum's diverse collection of exhibits offers fascinating insights into the destination's rich history and cultural heritage. Renovated in 1971 for use as a museum, its colourful, life-size displays depict everyday life in the days before the discovery of oil. Galleries re-create scenes from Dubai Creek, traditional Arab houses, mosques, the souk, date farms and desert and marine life. One of the more spectacular exhibits portrays pearl diving, including sets of pearl merchants' weights and scales. Also on display are artefacts from several excavations in the Emirate, recovered from graves that date back to the third millennium BC.

Sample answer 2

One of Europe's leading cultural attractions, the Louvre in Paris has many types of visitors, including people (individuals and groups) on educational trips, leisure tourists on holiday excursions and those attending an event or other specialised activity. Made up of eight departments, the Louvre now displays 35,000 works in 60,000 square metres of exhibition space. The Louvre provides a wide range of aids and amenities to ensure any given visit is fruitful: floor plans enabling visitors to locate items of interest, audio guides providing extra information and programme listings highlighting forthcoming attractions. Visitors' needs are further met with a café for light refreshment, media centres and a bookstore for publications and souvenirs. The Louvre's libraries and multimedia centres enable visitors to learn about the collections in greater depth. In addition to these, the museum's various curatorial departments have research centres and libraries that contain a wealth of material for use by researchers, students and other interested parties.

The Musée du Louvre and the Musée Delacroix can provide a prestigious setting for private receptions, gala evenings, prize-giving ceremonies, product launches, concerts and film premieres with dinners, cocktails and breakfasts. Open to all since 1793, the Louvre has embodied the concept of a truly 'universal' institution. Universal in the scope of its collections, it is also universal in its appeal to some six million business and leisure visitors every year.

Comment(s)

Both answers are clear and well-written, displaying a very good command of written English. However, in response (1), the appeal of each aspect is not stated or even considered. Furthermore, there is little, if any, analytical comment and there is no evaluation whatsoever. In contrast, response (2) clearly considers both products and services with an appropriate analysis of the features that have been identified. Furthermore, it clearly attempts to be evaluative, thus answering the question in a much more thorough fashion. The issue is therefore to decide the extent to which the question has been fully answered. To help decide this, the following checklist can be applied:

- An evaluation of more than one feature – expressing a point of view

- An evaluation/judgement without an overall conclusion/prioritisation

- The above with an overall supporting conclusion.

The answer offers a point of view and the 'universal' comments related to a mix of visitors warrants the award of a high mark.

IGCSE Travel and Tourism Papers 1 and 2

Paper 1

Written paper, 1 hour 30 minutes, 80 marks

Paper 1 contains **four** compulsory questions of 20 marks each.

It tests learners' understanding of the terms and concepts central to travel and tourism. Questions are set in context with a short piece of stimulus material, but learners will be required to draw on their own knowledge and understanding to answer questions.

Each question includes a stimulus text that contains information in written, numerical and/or diagrammatic form. Learners are required to write short answers, up to a few sentences or a paragraph. Learners need to answer questions using relevant and appropriate information from both their own knowledge and from the stimulus to support their answers. Each question is divided into sub-questions.

Learners answer all questions.

Learners should be aware of the number of marks available for each part-question. These are printed on the question paper. Learners should use these as a guide for the amount of detail and length of response expected, and to help them to manage their time effectively.

Learners write their answers on the question paper.

The paper assesses content drawn from the entire syllabus.

Paper 2

Written paper, 2 hours, 80 marks

Paper 2 contains **four** compulsory questions of 20 marks each.

It tests learners' understanding of the way that destinations are managed and marketed. A piece of stimulus material giving details of a destination or organisation will be provided for each question. Learners need to use their knowledge and understanding of destination management and marketing strategies and apply these to the context of the set of questions.

Each question includes a stimulus text that contains information in written, numerical and/or diagrammatic form. Learners are required to write short answers containing a couple of sentences or extended answers of a few paragraphs. Learners need to answer questions using relevant and appropriate information from the stimulus, applying their own knowledge to the context of the destination detailed to support their answers. Each question is divided into sub-questions.

Learners answer all questions.

Learners should be aware of the marks for each part-question. These are printed on the question paper. Learners should use them as a guide for the amount of detail and length of response expected, and to help them to manage their time effectively.

Learners write their answers on the question paper.

The paper assesses content drawn from the entire syllabus.

Preparing for revision

For your revision to be effective, you will need, in addition to this coursebook, the following:

- a revision timetable to help allocate enough time to each topic

- well laid-out subject notes that you took during your course

- responses to activities and exam-style questions that you have attempted

- a copy of the syllabus – you can use this to check that you have revised all of the content in this course.

Revision techniques

1   Make revision a routine and avoid simply re-reading notes:

- Study a section of your notes and memorise the essential points.

- Hide your notes and try to write down everything you can remember.

- Check what you've written against your notes.

- Note what you got wrong, or forgot, and learn them.

- Summarise the essential points on flash cards and make a different one for each topic.

2   Pace yourself:

- Use your time effectively.

- Remove all distractions and structure your day.

- Give yourself regular breaks to help with concentration and productivity, avoiding procrastination.

- Be active during your breaks to rest your mind and get your body moving.

In the assessment room

Read each question carefully and make sure you understand what you have been asked to do before you start writing.

Remember that the number of marks per sub-question gives you an indication of how much you are expected to write.

For the *discuss* and *evaluate* questions, you should spend a few moments writing a brief plan or list of key points that you intend to include in your response.

Your course is now complete and the assessments lie ahead. Take care in your final preparation. We hope that the outcome will meet your highest expectations.

Good luck and do your best!

> Glossary

access: how people can reach or enter a place. For example, access to an airport is how to reach the airport, and access in an airport is about entering facilities such as toilets (restrooms) and cafés in the airport

accessibility: how easy a destination is to reach

acknowledge the complaint: part of handling a complaint. Staff politely let the customer know that the complaint has been heard and understood

adventure tourism: visiting a destination for excitement

à la carte: a way in which customers choose food in a restaurant. Customers order items separately from a menu

all-inclusive: resorts or hotels providing a wide range of products and services at one site. Customers often make just one advance payment

alternative transport: sustainable transport. Alternative transport options are transport choices that are different from traditional options such as buses or privately owned cars and bicycles. Rental schemes for publicly shared bicycles and electric scooters are examples of alternative transport options. Shared bicycle and electric scooter rental schemes are common in city destinations

ancillary services: extra support services. Travel and tourism ancillary services include tour guiding, car and bicycle hire and currency exchange

appeal to: be attractive to

apprenticeships: paid jobs. Young people learn skills on-the-job whilst also receiving training and a qualification

assets: valued things. Assets of the natural environment include wildlife, landscape features such as waterfalls and the biodiversity of places like wetlands and coral reefs. Built assets include monuments, interesting buildings and historic architecture. Natural and built assets can add to the appeal of destinations

B&B (bed and breakfast): sleeping accommodation (room with bed) and breakfast

beach and coastal destination: a destination that has a beach and is on a coastline. Some coastal destinations are urban destinations. Some beach destinations are countryside or lake destinations

biodiversity: the degree of variation in living things

blogs: series of internet posts. For example, some tourists post travel diaries on social media

body language: communication without words. Facial expressions, gestures and body posture are parts of body language communication

Braille: a system of raised or embossed text. Braille enables reading by touch instead of reading using sight

brand image: the impression potential customers have of a product or organisation

brand loyalty: the choice of customers to continue buying the same product from the same organisation

breakout areas: spaces provided in MICE venues. Breakout areas are used by business tourists to take a break from a meeting

budget flights: sometimes called no-frills flights; cheaper, low-cost flights. Budget flight ticket prices do not include some services such as in-flight food and drink

buffet: a way of serving food. Customers serve themselves from food presented as a display

business cards: small cards giving details of a business. Business cards are often 8.5 cm long and 5.5 cm wide. Details on business cards include the name of the business, the service it offers, when it is open and how to make contact

business tourist: a person who travels for the purpose of work to attend a meeting, take an incentive trip, attend a conference or an exhibition

business travel: travel for the purpose of work to attend a meeting, take an incentive trip, attend a conference or an exhibition

carbon footprint: the amount of carbon dioxide pollution produced by the activities of a person or organisation.

carbon neutral: describes a vehicle or an activity that reduces carbon emissions either by reducing them to zero or by balancing them to make zero. For example, planting trees can absorb the same amount of carbon that is emitted

carrying capacity: the maximum number of visitors a destination or attraction can welcome without causing environmental damage or spoiling the tourism experience

charter flight: an air flight that is specially organised. Charter flights are not part of an airline's timetable or schedule

chef: the leader of a restaurant kitchen's food preparation and cooking team. In a large kitchen, the head chef works with a team of assistant chefs

clean-ups: tourist activities involving visitors helping locals to tidy the environment by removing rubbish

combat climate change: to take action against changes in the earth's climate. Actions such as producing less pollution are aimed at reducing climate change

commodification: in travel and tourism, when local culture is treated as a product or commodity to be sold to tourists

community tourism: local and indigenous communities invite tourists to visit and stay in their homes

companies: business organisations. Hotel providers are examples of travel and tourism companies

competition: trying to be better than others. Travel and tourism organisations try to be better than each other at attracting customers

competitive advantage: makes a travel and tourism organisation more attractive than competitor organisations

complete streets: sustainable streets that are easy and safe for everyone. Complete streets often have bus lanes and cycle lanes

components: parts of a package holiday or package tour. Examples of package components are travel and accommodation

condominium (condo) apartment: an apartment that is privately owned. Some condo owners rent the apartment to tourists for holidays (vacations)

consultation support: advice provided to help tourism organisations

contactless payment: a payment made without physical contact between a payment card and a payment device. Apps are one way to pay contactlessly

coral reef: an underwater ecosystem that appeals to tourists. Tourists dive and snorkel to see coral reefs' biodiversity. A coral reef is a coastal natural attraction

creative workshops: tourist attractions where tourists can see or share in activities such as pottery, painting or weaving

cruise: a leisure journey, usually on water

cultural homestay: a type of community tourism. Tourist customers stay in the homes of local people and experience indigenous culture

cultural identity: the sense of belonging that people have. People like to feel they belong to a group of people like them

cultural pride: when local people are proud of the destination where they live, and proud of their local heritage, traditions and culture

culture clash: conflict between people because of differences in values, beliefs or way of life

currency exchange: changing the cash used in one country into the cash used in another. For example, an American tourist visiting Paris may change US dollars into euros

customer base: the set of people who use or buy the products of a travel and tourism organisation. The customer base of a travel and tourism organisation are types of tourists

customer care policy: a plan or set of ideas relating to how staff should deliver customer service. Travel and tourism organisations decide how staff should serve customers

customer experience: how a customer feels about the customer service they receive. For example, a restaurant customer may feel that receiving good, well-served food is a good customer experience

customer service: helping customers by providing them with products and services

customer service skills: abilities that enable staff to provide good customer service

customer service standards: levels of customer service quality. Tourism organisations try to deliver customer service at high standards. Customer service standards include sustainability standards. A high standard of DMC sustainable customer service could include paperless transactions, recommending sustainable local providers and sustainable activity options

customised package: a package tour organised by a tour operator to provide for a particular customer's identified needs. For example, a customised package for an inbound tourist might include airport transfer, hotel, restaurant booking and visitor attraction ticket. Each part of a customised package is chosen by the tour operator to meet a particular customer's needs. Customised packages can also be called tailor-made packages or bespoke packages

customs: long-established ways of behaving. Local and indigenous destination communities may have traditional customs or ways of living

day trip: when a tourist travels for less than 24 hours

demographics: facts about population, including number, age and disposable income

demographic segmentation: dividing a market into types of people, such as customers of different ages, genders, ethnicities or levels of disposable income

demonstration effect: when the people living in a destination copy the behaviour of visiting tourists

destination: the place a tourist visits

destination management company (DMC): a tourism business with local knowledge of a destination. A DMC provides customers with events, activities, tours, transport and other services in the destination

directly employed: in travel and tourism, this means having a job in a travel and tourism organisation

direct marketing: providers making products directly attractive to customers. For example, a tour guide may market tours to customers face to face. Direct marketing may also include marketing tours using the tour guide's own website or social media page

disposable income: the remaining part of income after paying tax and buying necessities

distribution channels: the ways in which products reach customers. For example, a tour guide's guided tour product may reach customers via a tour operator's website

domestic tourism: a type of tourism where tourists travel within their country of residence (where they live)

dynamic: constantly changing

dynamic packages: holiday packages made up of components chosen by the customer

eco-friendly: describes products and behaviours that do little or no harm to the natural environment

eco-resorts: environmentally sustainable, ecotourism resorts

economic impact: the effect that travel and tourism has on money and jobs

economic leakage: when money from travel and tourism leaves (or leaks from) a country

ecosytem: the network of links between living things and the environment

ecotourism: visiting a destination to enjoy the natural environment without causing damage

e-gates: automatic electronic gates. E-gates are used in airports for passport and border control. Tourists go through e-gates to board aircraft

electric scooter: a personal-use scooter. Electric scooters are a sustainable type of mass personal-use transport. Electric scooters are available for public use in many destinations

emissions: gases that come out of the exhausts of engines. Engines that use carbon-based fuels such as diesel and petrol emit carbon dioxide

e-mobility: moving using electric vehicles. For example, electric vehicles are often used in airports to transport people with mobility difficulties

environmental impact: the effects that travel and tourism has on the environment. Impacts can be positive (good) or negative (bad)

existing customers: tourists who already use or buy the products and services of a travel and tourism organisation

export leakage: when destination organisations such as hotels are foreign-owned. Profits are exported from the destination country

express link: a fast transfer (transit) transport service connecting, for example, an airport and a destination city centre (downtown area)

face-to-face selling: part of place in the marketing mix. The customer and provider are physically in the same place. For example, travel agents sell products and services to customers face-to-face. A travel agent is an example of a place where marketing happens

facilities: provisions for the benefit of tourists. Departure lounges, toilets (restrooms) and prayer rooms are examples of airport facilities

factors: reasons that affect how things are and how things change. Factors can include:

- **economic factors:** to do with money
- **environmental factors:** to do with nature and climate
- **health factors:** to do with people's health and with disease
- **political factors:** to do with how countries are governed and what can happen as a result
- **social factors:** to do with people and communities
- **technological factors:** to do with practical science applications and engineering

flexible meeting rooms: meeting rooms that can easily be adapted to customers' needs. For example, furniture can easily be moved in flexible meeting rooms. Moving the furniture may adapt a meeting room to customers' needs. For example, the number of chairs and the arrangement of tables and chairs can be changed

flyer: a one-page piece of promotional material that can be used to market a tourism event

focus groups: small discussion groups. Small groups of customers discuss products and services provided by a travel and tourism organisation. Focus groups are a type of primary market research. Focus groups are an example of qualitative market research

game drive: a drive in an open 4x4 vehicle to view wildlife in its natural habitat

gateway: an entry point to a destination. Examples of gateways include airports, railway stations and arrival towns

GDP (gross domestic product): the total value of all goods and services produced in a country in a year

gluten-free foods: food items not containing gluten. Gluten is a protein found in cereals such as wheat

gondola: a traditional boat used by tourists in the city destination of Venice in Italy

goods: tangible objects that you can touch and store

Green Destination: a status awarded by the Green Destinations Foundation. A *Green Destination* is:

- **G** enuine in supporting local culture and tradition
- **R** esponsible and respectful towards other people
- **E** conomically sustainable
- **E** co-friendly
- **N** ature-friendly by conserving scenery, animal habitats and wildlife

greening: making something environmentally sustainable

grey market: the set of travel and tourism customers who are older, senior citizens or retired people

guest house: accommodation on a small-scale, such as in a house

handle complaints: respond to complaints. Travel and tourism staff respond to customer complaints

hearing loop: a wireless sound system used to help people who have a hearing aid. Hearing loops help people who have a hearing aid to hear announcements more clearly

hidden disability: reduced mobility for reasons that other people may not see immediately. Hidden disabilities include learning difficulties, mental health problems and speech, visual or hearing impairments

homestay holidays: holidays involving tourists staying in local people's houses

host city: a city where a major event is happening

host community: a destination's local people

hostel: a basic type of accommodation. Hostels often have shared sleeping accommodation such as dormitories

hotel: a place where tourists can pay to stay. A hotel will provide meals, room cleaning and other services

hub airport: an airport with flights and transport to other places. Tourists arriving at a hub airport can travel to other cities or countries

hubs: places where tourists change from one type of transport to another

human–nature connections: links between people and the environment. MICE venues increasingly provide human–nature connections. These connections provided by MICE venues include planted outdoor spaces, natural light and fresh air. Good human–nature connections are part of good customer service

ICT (information and communication technology): the range of computer and other electronic devices, such as smartphones, used to store and send information

import leakage: when tourists are supplied with goods, such as food and drink, that have to be imported. Imports cost money that is lost, or leaked, from the country's economy

inbound operator: a tour operator who provides tours and packages for inbound tourists to a destination. Inbound tour operators are also known as destination management companies (DMCs)

inbound tourism: a type of tourism where tourists travel into a country

indigenous communities: communities of the original inhabitants of a place

in-flight: passenger services provided by airlines during aircraft flights. In-flight services include food and drink and entertainment such as movies

inflation: when prices and the cost of living increase

infrastructure: the transport framework of a destination, including public transport, roads, airport and port

in-house training: staff training provided within an organisation

intangible: describes something that you cannot touch; it has no physical presence. Services are intangible

integrated rapid transit system: a transport system in a destination that makes it easy for people to change from one type of transport to another

integrated resorts: single-site complexes of hotel accommodation and facilities such as restaurants, entertainment venues, casinos and conference facilities. The term *integrated resort* is often used in Singapore. The Government of Mauritius has an Integrated Resort Scheme (IRS). The IRS scheme has a different meaning and allows people who are not from Mauritius to buy and live in luxury properties in Mauritius

integrated transport: linked transport. Integrated transport makes it easy to change from one transport type to another. For example, it makes it easy to change from tram/bus to bicycle at a tram/bus stop with a cycle rack

interdependencies: two or more travel and tourism organisations that are dependent on each other

interdependent transport: transport that depends on another linked type of transport. For example, express link trains from an airport depend on aircraft flights to the airport

international airports: airports with flights to and from other countries

internet and social media platforms: online services. Online platforms allow customers and travel and tourism providers to exchange or share information

internships: may not be paid. Students work temporarily in an organisation. Internships vary. Some internships may be for two weeks, others for 12 months. Interns learn skills on the job and also receive training. Successful interns may be offered a permanent job

interpersonal skills: abilities that enable staff members to work together to provide good customer service

interrelationship: when travel and tourism organisations choose to work together

interviews: question-and-answer conversations. Interviews are a way to do primary market research. For example, a market researcher may ask a customer some questions about the products and services provided by a travel and tourism organisation

itinerary: a tour plan or programme. Itineraries give details of routes, directions, times and places. For example, a business tourism (MICE) itinerary might include air flight details, hotel and transfer information, and event venues and times

job rotation: a way in which staff and trainees can experience different jobs in an organisation. Staff and trainees change jobs for a temporary period. For example, a restaurant server (waitron) may work for a short time as a member of the front desk staff

leisure tourists: people who travel for the purpose of leisure, enjoyment or recreation

leisure travel: travel for the purpose of leisure, enjoyment or recreation

location: where a destination is

long-haul flight: a flight lasting longer than six hours

low-cost flights: budget flights. Low-cost flights do not include additional passenger services (frills) in the ticket price

low-emission: describes transport that causes reduced air pollution. Emissions of polluting exhaust gases such as carbon dioxide are low

market analysis tool: something you use to investigate the market for travel and tourism products and services

market leader: the organisation with the strongest market position. The market leader sells more products and services than competing travel and tourism organisations

market penetration: part of price in the marketing mix. A provider such as a tour operator charges a low price for a newly marketed product. The low price attracts customers. The price is later increased as demand also increases

market research: investigating the types of customers that make up the target market

market segmentation: the dividing of markets into segments

market segments: the elements of a destination's market

market share: the proportion of potential customers who use or buy an organisation's products and services. For example, if one tenth of tourists visiting a destination stay at one hotel, the hotel's market share is one tenth (10%)

market skimming: part of price in the marketing mix. A provider such as a tour operator charges a high price for a newly marketed product. The tour operator may be the only provider of the new product. Customers accept the higher price. Competition causes the price to decrease later

marketing: ensuring products and services are attractive to customers

marketing campaigns: part of promotion in the marketing mix. Marketing campaigns are product promotion projects that are time-limited. For example, a tour operator may have a six-week marketing campaign of placing television, radio, newspaper and magazine advertisements or commercials to attract customers

marketing channels: the ways products are made attractive to customers. For example, a tour guide's guided tour product may attract customers via a tour operator's website

marketing mix: the combination of product, promotion, price and place used to market products and services

marketing strategies: plans that aim to market destinations. Marketing destinations involves making destinations attractive to tourism customers

mass market: relating to the total market of all customer types

mass rapid transit (MRT): a type of rail transport used in some city destinations. MRT trains transport large numbers of people quickly and often cheaply. Many tourists use MRT trains to move around city destinations easily

meal plan: a way of serving meals in accommodation establishment. Bed and breakfast is one international plan. International plans for providing meals range from no meals being provided (room only) to all meals being provided (American plan or full board). A meal plan of breakfast and one meal per day is described as half board (modified American plan)

mentoring: a form of training. Senior colleagues show staff and trainees how to do tasks. For example, an experienced member of a hotel's food and beverage staff may train an apprentice on how to deliver good customer service

mobility: the ability to move freely. Some tourists are PRMs (persons with reduced mobility)

monitoring: checking or observing progress. For example, travel and tourism providers monitor sales, usage, profitability and quality

multiplier effect: how wealth is created from tourist spending

museum: a place that holds historical, cultural, artistic or other artefacts. Museums are popular tourist attractions

national tourism organisation (NTO): a government agency that promotes and markets the tourism product of a country

nature reserves: places where the natural environment and biodiversity are protected

negative impacts: bad effects that travel and tourism has on a place and/or local people

non-government organisation (NGO): a not-for-profit organisation of people who want to promote a product, service or cause, such as sustainable tourism. NGOs are independent of government

occupancy rate: the percentage of accommodation space or rooms in use. For example, a hotel with an occupancy rate of 50% is half full

off-peak season: the time when travel and tourism products have the least demand

online booking: use of the internet to reserve, for example, accommodation and transport

online chat: a real-time discussion via the internet. For example, a customer can type questions about travel to a travel agent who can immediately type a reply. An online conversation occurs

online check-in: using the internet to register people and their baggage (luggage) for an air flight

on-the-job training: learning skills whilst working

opportunity costs: when choices are made. The opportunity cost is the loss of the chance to do something because something else has been chosen instead. For example, the opportunity to expand an airport can be lost if the government decides to spend the money on new roads instead

outbound tourism: a type of tourism where tourists travel out of their country of residence

over-dependence: when a destination depends too much on travel and tourism

overtourism: too many tourists in a destination. Overtourism harms the destination environment and causes difficulties for local people. Tourists do not enjoy the destination as much

package holiday: a holiday made of components put together and sold as one product. Typical package holiday components include travel and accommodation

paperless payment: electronic payment. Contactless payment is an example of paperless payment. Paperless payments are sustainable and help to reduce the paper that tourism organisations use

peak season: the time when travel and tourism products have the greatest demand

performance spaces: places where tourists can see live shows

perishable: describes something that cannot be stored; if the service is not sold it expires

personal presentation: how staff present themselves to customers. Personal presentation includes how staff look, what they say and what they do. Dress, grooming, speech and behaviour are all part of personal presentation

personal skills: personal abilities that enable a member of staff to provide good customer service

PESTLE analysis: a market analysis tool. A PESTLE analysis considers the factors that affect a travel and tourism business. Factors that affect a travel and tourism business are political (government-related), economic (money-related), sociological (society-related), technological, legal and environmental

pilgrimage: a religious or spiritual journey

potential customer: someone who might become an actual customer of a travel and tourism organisation. For example, tourists visiting a destination are potential customers of local tourism organisations such as DMCs, restaurants and visitor attractions

premium pricing: a pricing strategy. Premium prices are higher prices. Travel and tourism organisations sometimes choose to charge higher prices than competitors. Charging a higher price creates the impression that a product is special and worth more money

price bundling: part of price in the marketing mix. Providers such as tour operators price packages or bundles of products. For example, a bundle of two walking tours and one tour including travel might be priced more cheaply than the total price of the individual tours

price sensitive: describes someone whose decisions are greatly influenced by price. A price-sensitive tourist is unlikely to buy a product if they think it is too expensive

pricing strategies: methods used to attract customers by managing price

primary research: direct research. For example, asking customers questions about the products and services provided by a travel and tourism organisation is a type of primary market research

PRMs (persons with reduced mobility): includes tourists who are less able to move around freely. Tourists with physical or hidden disability, tourists with visual impairment, older tourists and tourists with sports injuries are examples of PRMs

PRM-friendly: describes a facility that PRMs can use easily

product knowledge: the knowledge that travel and tourism organisation staff have of the products and services provided by the organisation. Good product knowledge enables staff to deliver good customer service. Staff with good product knowledge are better able to explain products and services to customers

product life cycle: the stages in the marketing existence of a product. The product life cycle stages are introduction, growth, maturity and decline

products: either goods or a service, they are sold or made available to tourists

product/service mix: the blend of travel and tourism products and services developed by travel and tourism organisations in a destination. The product/service mix is developed to target different market segments

promotional material: something used to promote a product or service. Examples of travel and tourism promotional materials include posters, flyers, leaflets, brochures, websites, video clips and social media posts

protected area: a place conserved by a set of rules

psychographic segmentation: dividing a market by customer lifestyle, such as customers with different interests or customers with different values and attitudes

public relations: part of promotion in the marketing mix. Public relations involves managing contacts between providers and customers. Providers make contact with potential customers to market products. For example, guided tour operators can be present in hotel lobbies to promote products to potential customers

public transport: transport available for anyone to use. Buses, trams and trains are examples of public transport

purpose-built resort: a resort that is planned and built especially for tourism

qualitative methods: a type of market research method. Examples of qualitative market research methods are observation, informal conversations and interviews

quantitative methods: a type of market research method. Quantitative methods collect data in the form of numbers. Customer surveys are an example of a quantitative market research method

questionnaires: sets of questions. For example, a market researcher may ask business tourism customers a set of questions about the products and services provided by a travel and tourism organisation

quota: a limit to the number of visitors allowed in a destination or attraction

refer complaints: part of handling complaints. Staff members tell a senior colleague about a serious complaint. The senior colleague handles the complaint

regional tourism organisation (RTO): an organisation that promotes and markets the tourism product of a part (region) of a country. RTOs are part of national tourism organisations (NTOs)

repeat business: when customers return to a travel and tourism organisation where they previously had a good customer experience

reputation: a general opinion that people have about how good or bad someone or something is. A hotel delivering good customer service tends to have a good reputation

resilient: able to continue after a bad event. For example, a resilient destination will soon recover from an extreme weather event such as a severe storm, or from a natural disaster such as flooding

resort hotel: a type of hotel. Resort hotels provide a wide range of services and activities, as well as accommodation and meals. Resort hotels are often spread across a large site. Many resort hotels provide all-inclusive packages

resorts: places visited by leisure tourists for holidays (vacations), relaxation or activities. For example, a ski resort is a place leisure tourists go to ski

resources: things that are useful to people, for example, water, wood, oil or equipment

responsible tourism: behaving respectfully towards the environment and local people

ride sharing: sharing transport with other people. Ride sharing is in a vehicle that is often used for only one customer. Ride shares are in smaller vehicles such as a car or taxi

safari: an overland journey to view wildlife in its natural habitat

sales promotions: temporary offers to attract customers. For example, a tour operator may offer discounted prices for educational groups during the low season

scheduled flight: an air flight that is timetabled

seasonality: the way in which tourism demand fluctuates throughout a year

secondary research: research using documents. For example, a MICE venue provider may use government reports and NTO statistics to investigate the market for MICE products and services

self-catering: a style of accommodation. Self-catering customers provide and cook food themselves

senior colleagues: staff members who have more responsibility. Senior colleagues in travel and tourism organisations include supervisors and managers

service: an action done on your behalf; it is someone doing something for you. Services are intangible

serviced apartment: a type of self-catering accommodation. Services such as cleaning are provided in serviced apartments

short break: a trip lasting four nights or less

short-haul flight: a flight lasting less than a few (between three and six) hours

signage: a set of signs and direction indicators used to guide tourists. For example, an airport has signs indicating directions to facilities such as toilets (restrooms), departure gates and taxis

social consciousness: awareness of other people and the difficulties they face in life

social enterprises: organisations that try to be profitable whilst also supporting local and indigenous communities. Community tourism organisations are social enterprises. Examples of community tourism organisations are guest houses, cafés and restaurants owned by local people

social media: ways of sharing information using the internet

socially sustainable tourism: minimises the negative sociocultural impacts of travel and tourism on destinations. Socially sustainable tourism maximises the positive sociocultural impacts of travel and tourism on destinations

sociocultural impact: the effects that travel and tourism has on people and on their way of life

source market: the country that inbound tourists to a destination have travelled from (their country of residence)

special dietary requirements: particular food needs. For example, a customer may require gluten-free food

spectators: people who watch an event

staff: people employed to work in a travel and tourism organisation. Customer service staff deliver customer service to tourists by providing them with products and services

supply chains: part of place in the marketing mix. Supply chains are the sets of linked places where travel and tourism products and services are marketed. For example, a guided walking tour can be marketed directly or by an accommodation provider or tour operator

surveys: a way of researching people's opinions. Surveys can be carried out using questionnaires or interviews to collect quantative data about travel and tourism markets. Quantitative data may be analysed to investigate travel and tourism market trends

sustainability: our ability to sustain or conserve the environment and peoples' way of life into the future

sustainable customer service standards: levels of customer service that encourage sustainable practices

sustainable infrastructural development: improving destination transport systems and tourism facilities sustainably

sustainable practices: the ways in which travel and tourism organisations ensure sustainability

sustainable travel and tourism: going to visit places in ways that help to sustain or conserve the environment and how people live

SWOT analysis: a market analysis tool. A SWOT analysis identifies the strengths and weaknesses of a travel and tourism business as well as the opportunities and threats that exist

table service: a way of serving food in a restaurant. Customers are seated at a table and served food by staff

target market: the type of customers a travel and tourism organisation tries to attract

theme parks: large tourist attractions with amusements and rides. Theme parks often have accommodation such as hotels and restaurants. Theme parks such as Tokyo Disneyland in Japan, Kingdom of Dreams in India and Universal Studios Hollywood in the USA have clear identities

thrill seekers: people who enjoy exciting or adventurous activities

time sensitive: decisions are greatly influenced by time. A time-sensitive tourist needs the product to be delivered at an exact time, often as quickly as possible

timing: planning when something should happen. For example, travel and tourism providers plan when to market products and services

topographical features: surface features of the landscape such as mountains, lakes, rivers and valleys

tour guide: a person who shows tourists around a destination

tourism: the business of providing services such as transport, places to stay or entertainment for people who temporarily leave the place where they normally live, work or study

tourism demand: how much desire there is to travel to destinations

tourist: a person who travels temporarily from one place to another

tourist information centre (TIC): an office where useful information is made available to tourists

touristor arrivals: the number of international tourists/visitors who travel to a country during a given time. The term is used in tourism statistics

trade promotions: when tourism organisations advertise at travel and tourism industry events. For example, travel and tourism providers meet at travel markets such as the World Travel Market. A travel and tourism organisation can be a customer of another travel and tourism organisation. Accommodation providers can promote products to tour operators at travel markets

train-hotel: a train with hotel services on board. Hotel services on a train-hotel include sleeping accommodation and restaurant services

transfer: travel between a transport hub or gateway, such as an airport, and a destination

transferable skills: skills that people can use in different jobs and in different situations. For example, good customer service skills are transferable from a job in a visitor attraction to working in a restaurant

urban transit: travel within a city destination, for example, transfer between airport and hotel

value chain: is the set of linked products and services on which tourists spend money to create income for a destination

visiting friends and relatives (VFR): travel for the purpose of visiting other people, such as friends or family

visual: to do with seeing or sight

visual impairment: some loss of the ability to see. For example, some tourists have difficulty seeing. Tourists who have this difficulty tend to have trouble reading signage and finding their way, for example, in an unfamiliar place such as an airport

water taxis: a type of urban public transport. Water taxis are small boats that tourists can pay to use between places within a destination. Timetabled boat services between destinations or across water are ferry services

wholesalers and retailers: part of place in the marketing mix. Wholesalers buy products from providers. Wholesalers sell products to retailers. Retailers sell products to customers. Tour operators are wholesalers. Travel agents are retailers

work experience: working unpaid in an organisation for a short time. Work experience students learn about working in an organisation. Work experience students learn skills through observing and helping staff. Work experience placements are often for one or two weeks. Some short work experience placements are for one day

work shadowing: a form of training. The trainee observes an experienced staff member at work. The trainee learns skills by observing a senior colleague

World Heritage Sites (WHSs): destinations and attractions that have been identified as especially important parts of the natural or built environment by UNESCO (United Nations Educational, Scientific and Cultural Organization). These sites should be conserved for the future. They appeal to tourists

zip-lining: the adventure tourism activity of swinging through the air, hanging from a suspended cable.

> Acknowledgements

The authors and publishers acknowledge the following sources of copyright material and are grateful for the permissions granted. While every effort has been made, it has not always been possible to identify the sources of all the material used, or to trace all copyright holders. If any omissions are brought to our notice, we will be happy to include the appropriate acknowledgements on reprinting.

Unit 1: Text used from UNWTO statement on Tourism; Adapted data from UNWTO research; Adapted 'Definition of Tourism' from Cambridge dictionary; Factual data from UNWTO on Tourism; Adapted texts from Hilton Honors websites; Adapted text from 'Statistics on Tourism' in Andalucia website; Adapted text from L'Heure Bleue website; **Unit 2:** Adapted graph from UNWTO on 'Worldwide international tourist arrivals since 2000'; Adapted diagram and brochure from Tourism Authority. Used with the permission of Tourism Authority; Text from Trinidad and Tobago on 'Coat of arms of Trinidad and Tobago'; Adapted text from Trinidad and Tobago on 'Information about Trinidad and Tobago's Revised Tourism Policy'; Adapted text from 'Information about the Grand Canyon National Park in USA'; Graph showing number of visitors to major attractions in Barcelona from StatInvestor; Adapted text from Waterfront on 'The Information on Cape Town's V&A Waterfront project'; Abridged text and artworks from Voice Gambia website; Text from 'Guidelines for Coatal Tourism Development in Tanzania'. Used with the permission of Coastal Resources Center; **Unit 3:** Adapted Map from Maps of World on 'Summer Olympic host cities in the 21st century'; Adapted text from the Information on Dubai International Airport; Graph from Statista on 'The World's Top Cities For Sustainable Public Transport'; Adapted extract from 'Transport and Housing Bureau' publications. Used with the permission of Transport and Housing Bureau; Adapted extract from 'Peterson Travel' website. Used with the permission of Peterson Travel; **Unit 4:** Adapted extract and photo from 'Marriot' website; **Unit 5:** A Trip Advisor review of Emirates service. Used with the permission of Emirates Group and Trip Advisor; Adapted extracts from IACC. Used with the permission of IACC, a global collection of meetings and conference focused venues; Adapted extract from 'Taken by Albania' website. Used with the permission of Blerina Ago, Founder of Active Albania (www.activealbania.com)

Thanks to the following for permission to reproduce images:

Unit 1: Matteo Colombo/GI; Seksan Mongkhonkhamsao/GI; Albertc111/GI; Bruce Yuanyue Bi/GI; Fred Tanneau/GI; Frankvandenbergh/GI; Ippei Naoi/GI; Matthew Williams-Ellis/GI; Jeff Overs/BBC News & Current Affairs via Getty Images; Buena Vista Images/GI; Pankaj & Insy Shah/GI; Oleh_Slobodeniuk/GI; Nickylloyd/GI; Solstock/GI; Imaginechina Limited/Alamy Stock Photo; Anthony Asael/GI; Majority World/GI; Wolfgang Kaehler/GI; Anton Petrus/GI; Tim De Waele/GI; Pierre-Yves Babelon/GI; Denny Allen/GI; **Unit 2:** Vold77GI; Yuriko Nakao/GI; VW Pics/GI; Ullstein Bild/GI; VW Pics/GI; Tim Clayton - Corbis/GI; Ralf Liebhold/GI; Martin Harvey/GI; Barcroft Media/GI; Hermsdorf/GI; Magnez2/GI; Chris Pancewicz/Alamy Stock Photo; Jordi Vidal/GI; Wolfgang Kaehler/GI; Wolfgang Kaehler/GI; Bart Brouwer/GI; **Unit 3:** Melissa Kopka/GI; SOPA Images/GI; South_Agency/GI; Simonbradfield/GI; Dea/C.Dani I. Jeske/GI; Holger Leue/GI; Undefined/GI; Mondadori Portfolio/GI; Photononstop/Alamy Stock Photo; Pauws99/GI; Roberto Machado Noa/GI; Walter Bibikow/GI; Lanolan/GI; Inigoarza/GI; **Unit 4:** Xavier Rossi/GI; The India Today Group/GI; Frank Bienewald/GI; Miles_Around/GI; Matthew Micah Wright/GI; Horacio Villalobos/GI; Ute Grabowsky/GI; View Pictures/GI; Artur Debat/GI; **Unit 5:** Ryanjlane/GI; David Lefranc/GI(X2); Education Images/GI; George Rose/GI; John Elk III/GI; Avalon/GI; View Pictures/GI; Geography Photos/GI; Didier Marti/GI; Jim Zuckerman/GI; Manuel Blondeau-Corbis/GI.

Key: GI= Getty Images

> Index